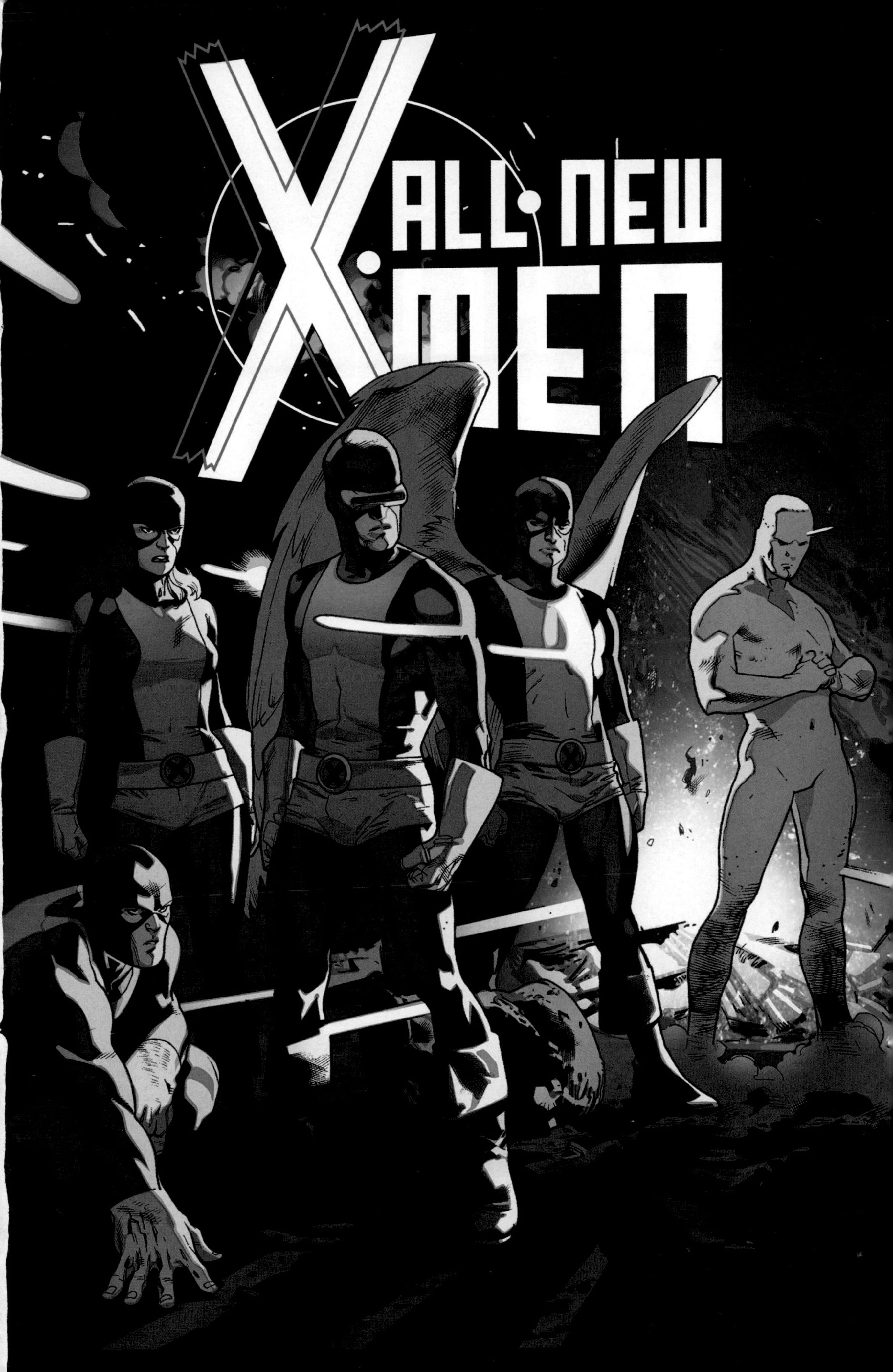
X ALL-NEW
MEN

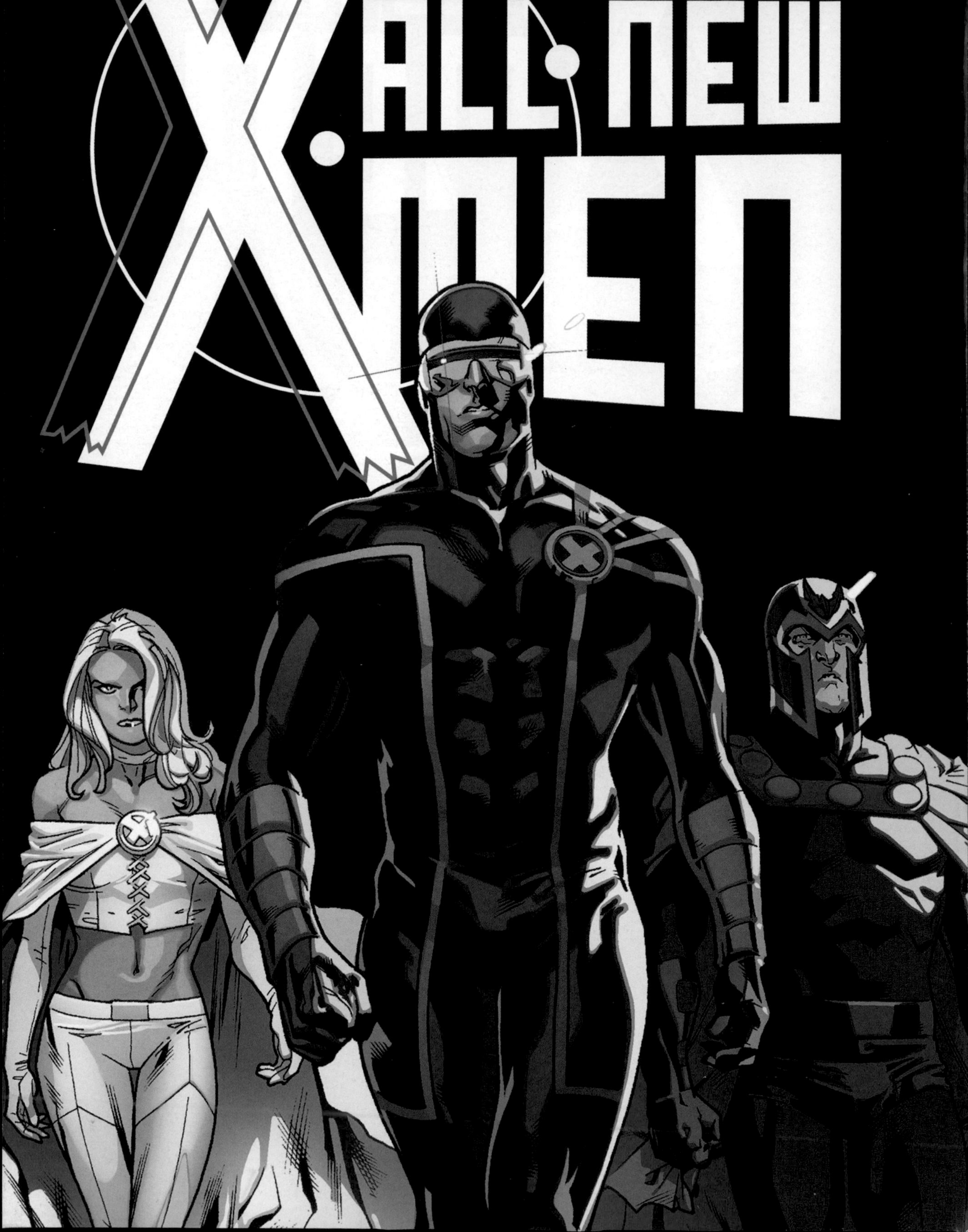
ALL·NEW
X·MEN

BEAST
HANK McCOY

MARVEL GIRL
JEAN GREY

CYCLOPS
SCOTT SUMMERS

ANGEL
WARREN WORTHINGTON III

ICEMAN
BOBBY DRAKE

....

Born with genetic mutations that give them abilities beyond those of normal humans, mutants are the next stage in evolution. As such, they are feared and hated by humanity. But a group of mutants known as the X-Men fight for peaceful coexistence between mutants and humankind.

This fight seemed lost when the Scarlet Witch depowered 99% of mutants, leaving X-Men leader Cyclops and his species on the brink of extinction. But when the Phoenix, a cosmic force of both destruction and creation, returned to Earth, Cyclops saw it as a sign of hope for the future of the mutants. In the end, Cyclops, possessed and corrupted by the Phoenix Force, struck down Professor Xavier, and it took the combined might of the Avengers and X-Men to defeat him. Just when all seemed lost, the power of the Phoenix Force was dispersed, sparking the rebirth of mutantkind.

As the rest of the X-Men settle back into life at the Jean Grey School for Higher Learning, Cyclops finds himself a fugitive and outcast with few allies.

....

BRIAN MICHAEL
BENDIS
WRITER

STUART
IMMONEN
PENCILER, #1-5 & #9-10

WADE VON
GRAWBADGER
INKER, #1-5 & #9-10

DAVID
MARQUEZ
ARTIST, #6-8

MARTE
GRACIA
WITH RAIN BEREDO (#9-10)
COLORISTS

VC'S CORY
PETIT
LETTERER

JORDAN D.
WHITE
ASSISTANT EDITOR

NICK
LOWE
EDITOR

COVER ART: **STUART IMMONEN, WADE VON GRAWBADGER & MARTE GRACIA**

COLLECTION EDITOR: **JENNIFER GRÜNWALD**
ASSISTANT EDITOR: **SARAH BRUNSTAD**
ASSOCIATE MANAGING EDITOR: **ALEX STARBUCK**
EDITOR, SPECIAL PROJECTS: **MARK D. BEAZLEY**
SENIOR EDITOR, SPECIAL PROJECTS: **JEFF YOUNGQUIST**
SVP PRINT, SALES & MARKETING: **DAVID GABRIEL**

EDITOR IN CHIEF: **AXEL ALONSO**
CHIEF CREATIVE OFFICER: **JOE QUESADA**
PUBLISHER: **DAN BUCKLEY**
EXECUTIVE PRODUCER: **ALAN FINE**

ALL-NEW X-MEN VOL. 1. Contains material originally published in magazine form as ALL-NEW X-MEN #1-10. First printing 2014. ISBN# 978-0-7851-9115-5. Published by MARVEL WORLDWIDE, INC., a subsidiary of MARVEL ENTERTAINMENT, LLC. OFFICE OF PUBLICATION: 135 West 50th Street, New York, NY 10020. Copyright © 2012, 2013 and 2014 Marvel Characters, Inc. All rights reserved. All characters featured in this issue and the distinctive names and likenesses thereof, and all related indicia are trademarks of Marvel Characters, Inc. No similarity between any of the names, characters, persons, and/or institutions in this magazine with those of any living or dead person or institution is intended, and any such similarity which may exist is purely coincidental. **Printed in China.** ALAN FINE, EVP - Office of the President, Marvel Worldwide, Inc. and EVP & CMO Marvel Characters B.V.; DAN BUCKLEY, Publisher & President - Print, Animation & Digital Divisions; JOE QUESADA, Chief Creative Officer; TOM BREVOORT, SVP of Publishing; DAVID BOGART, SVP of Operations & Procurement, Publishing; C.B. CEBULSKI, SVP of Creator & Content Development; DAVID GABRIEL, SVP Print, Sales & Marketing; JIM O'KEEFE, VP of Operations & Logistics; DAN CARR, Executive Director of Publishing Technology; SUSAN CRESPI, Editorial Operations Manager; ALEX MORALES, Publishing Operations Manager; STAN LEE, Chairman Emeritus. For information regarding advertising in Marvel Comics or on Marvel.com, please contact Niza Disla, Director of Marvel Partnerships, at ndisla@marvel.com. For Marvel subscription inquiries, please call 800-217-9158. **Manufactured between 5/16/2014 and 7/14/2014 by R.R. DONNELLEY ASIA PRINTING SOLUTIONS, CHINA.**

10 9 8 7 6 5 4 3 2 1

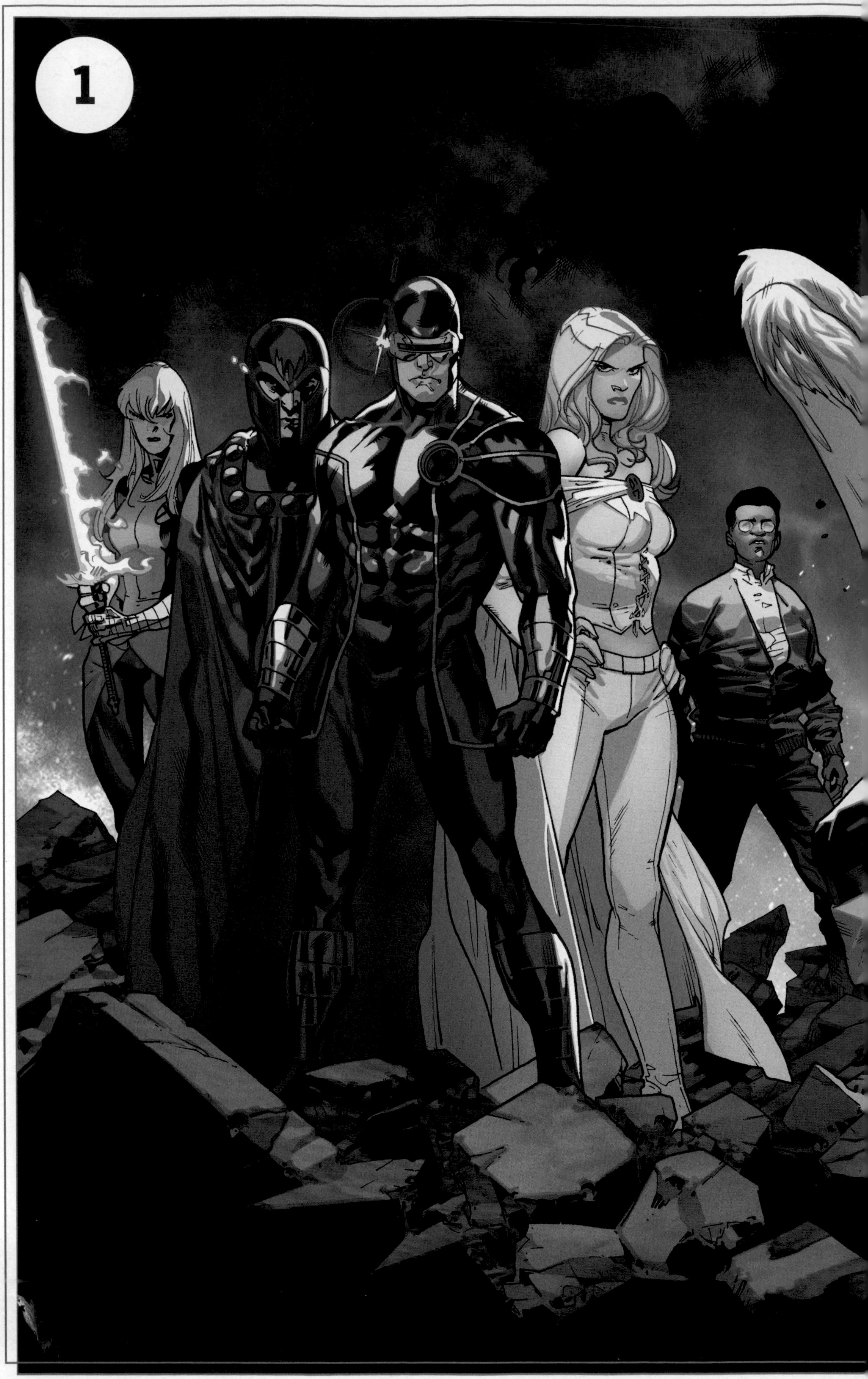
1

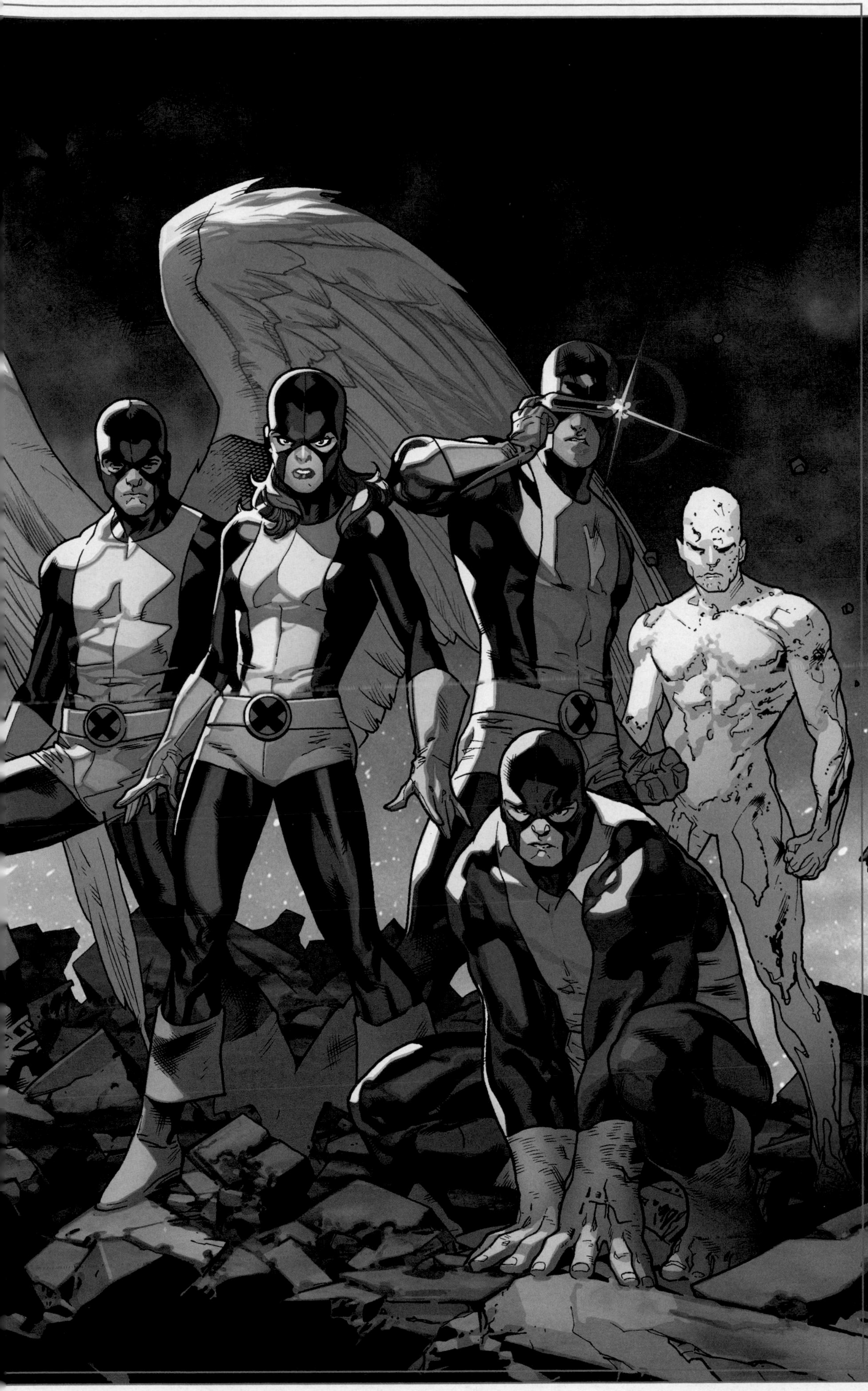

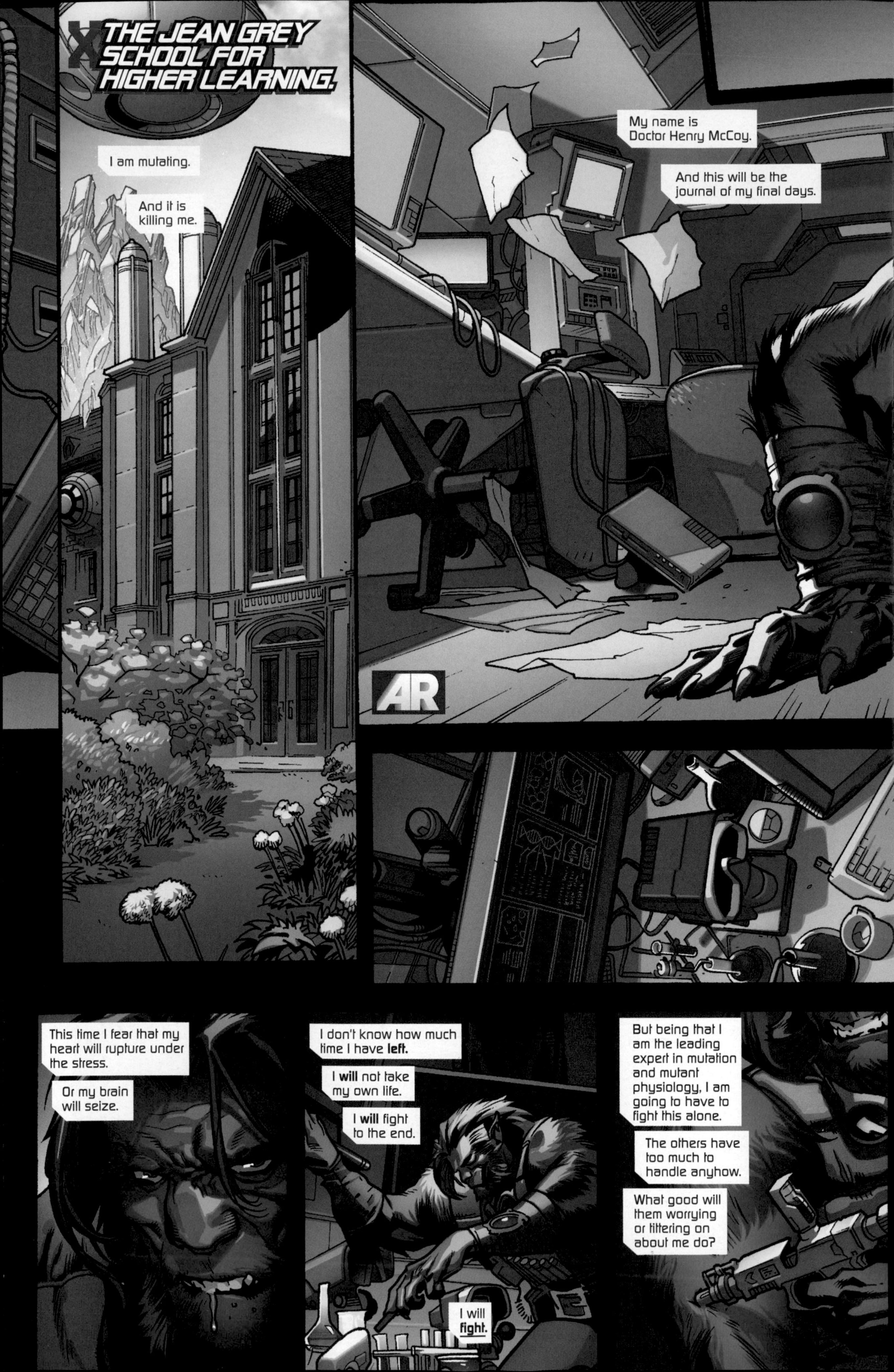
THE JEAN GREY SCHOOL FOR HIGHER LEARNING.
I am mutating.
And it is killing me.
My name is Doctor Henry McCoy.
And this will be the journal of my final days.
AR
This time I fear that my heart will rupture under the stress.
Or my brain will seize.
I don't know how much time I have **left.**
I **will** not take my own life.
I **will** fight to the end.
I will **fight.**
But being that I am the leading expert in mutation and mutant physiology, I am going to have to fight this alone.
The others have too much to handle anyhow.
What good will them worrying or tittering on about me do?

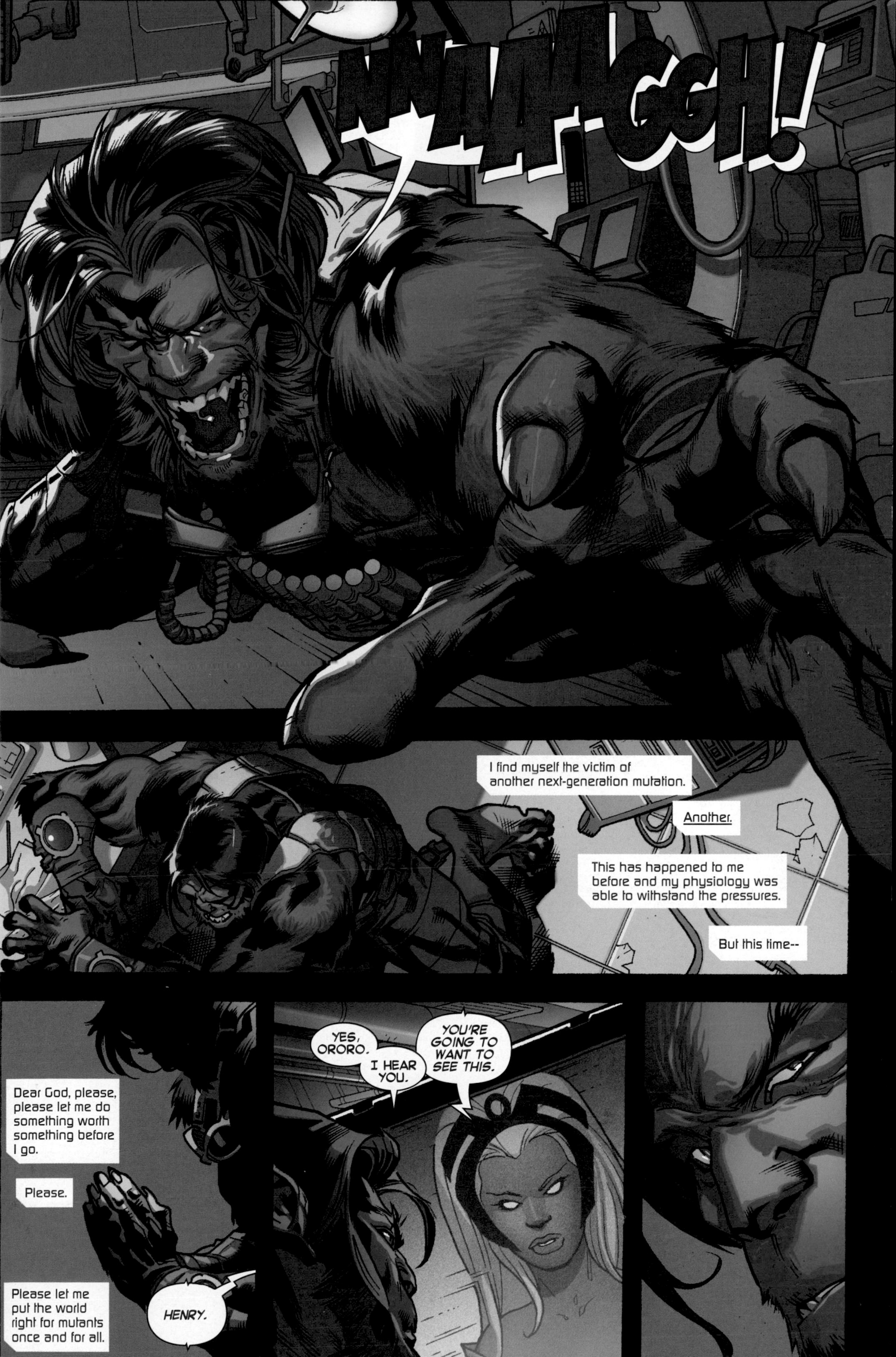
NNAAAGGH!
I find myself the victim of another next-generation mutation.
Another.
This has happened to me before and my physiology was able to withstand the pressures.
But this time--
Dear God, please, please let me do something worth something before I go.
Please.
Please let me put the world right for mutants once and for all.
HENRY.
YES, ORORO.
I HEAR YOU.
YOU'RE GOING TO WANT TO SEE THIS.

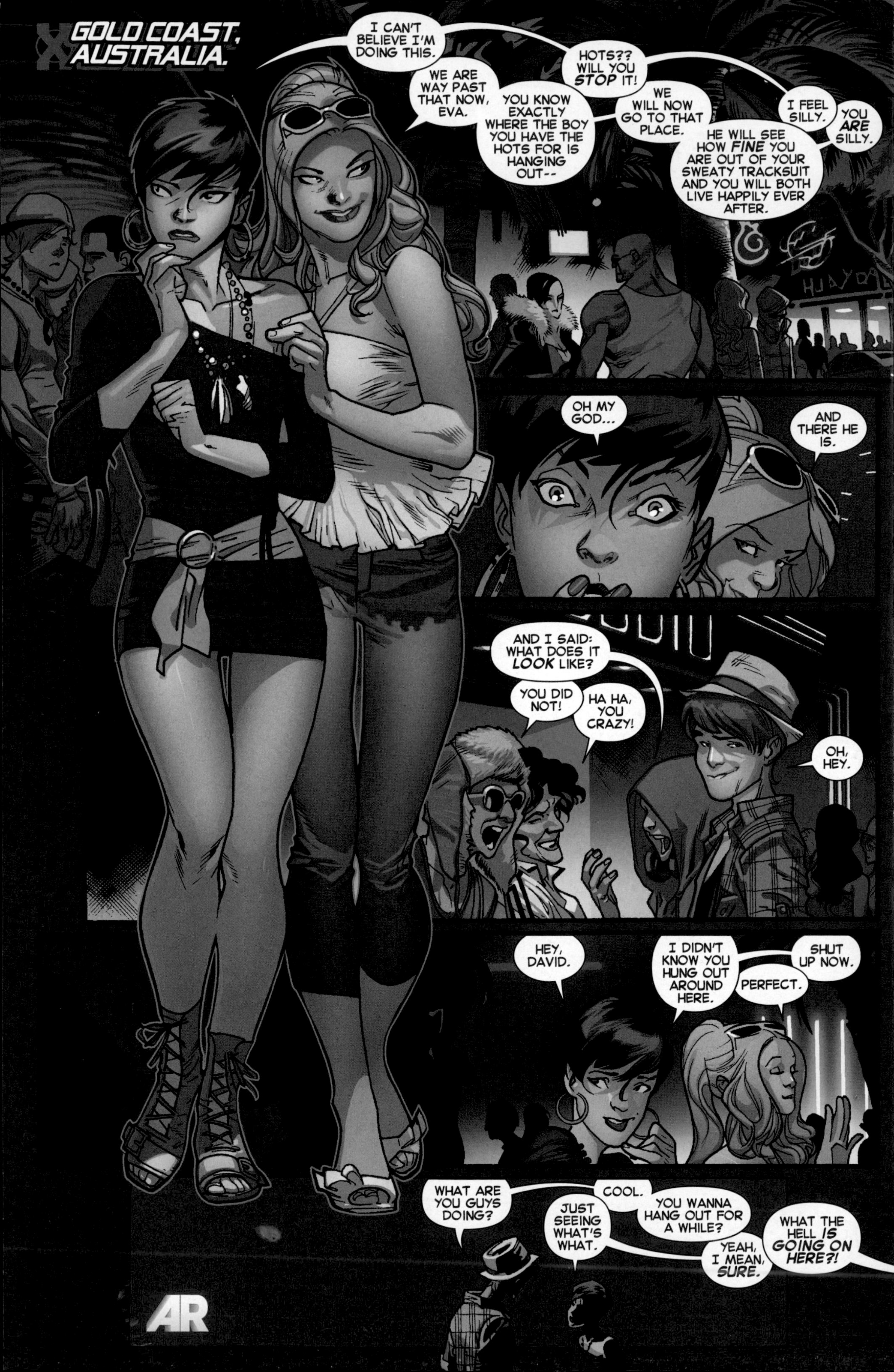
GOLD COAST, AUSTRALIA.
I CAN'T BELIEVE I'M DOING THIS.
WE ARE WAY PAST THAT NOW, EVA.
YOU KNOW EXACTLY WHERE THE BOY YOU HAVE THE HOTS FOR IS HANGING OUT--
HOTS?? WILL YOU STOP IT!
WE WILL NOW GO TO THAT PLACE.
HE WILL SEE HOW FINE YOU ARE OUT OF YOUR SWEATY TRACKSUIT AND YOU WILL BOTH LIVE HAPPILY EVER AFTER.
I FEEL SILLY.
YOU ARE SILLY.
OH MY GOD...
AND THERE HE IS.
AND I SAID: WHAT DOES IT LOOK LIKE?
YOU DID NOT!
HA HA, YOU CRAZY!
OH, HEY.
HEY, DAVID.
I DIDN'T KNOW YOU HUNG OUT AROUND HERE.
SHUT UP NOW.
PERFECT.
WHAT ARE YOU GUYS DOING?
JUST SEEING WHAT'S WHAT.
COOL.
YOU WANNA HANG OUT FOR A WHILE?
YEAH, I MEAN, SURE.
WHAT THE HELL IS GOING ON HERE?!
AR

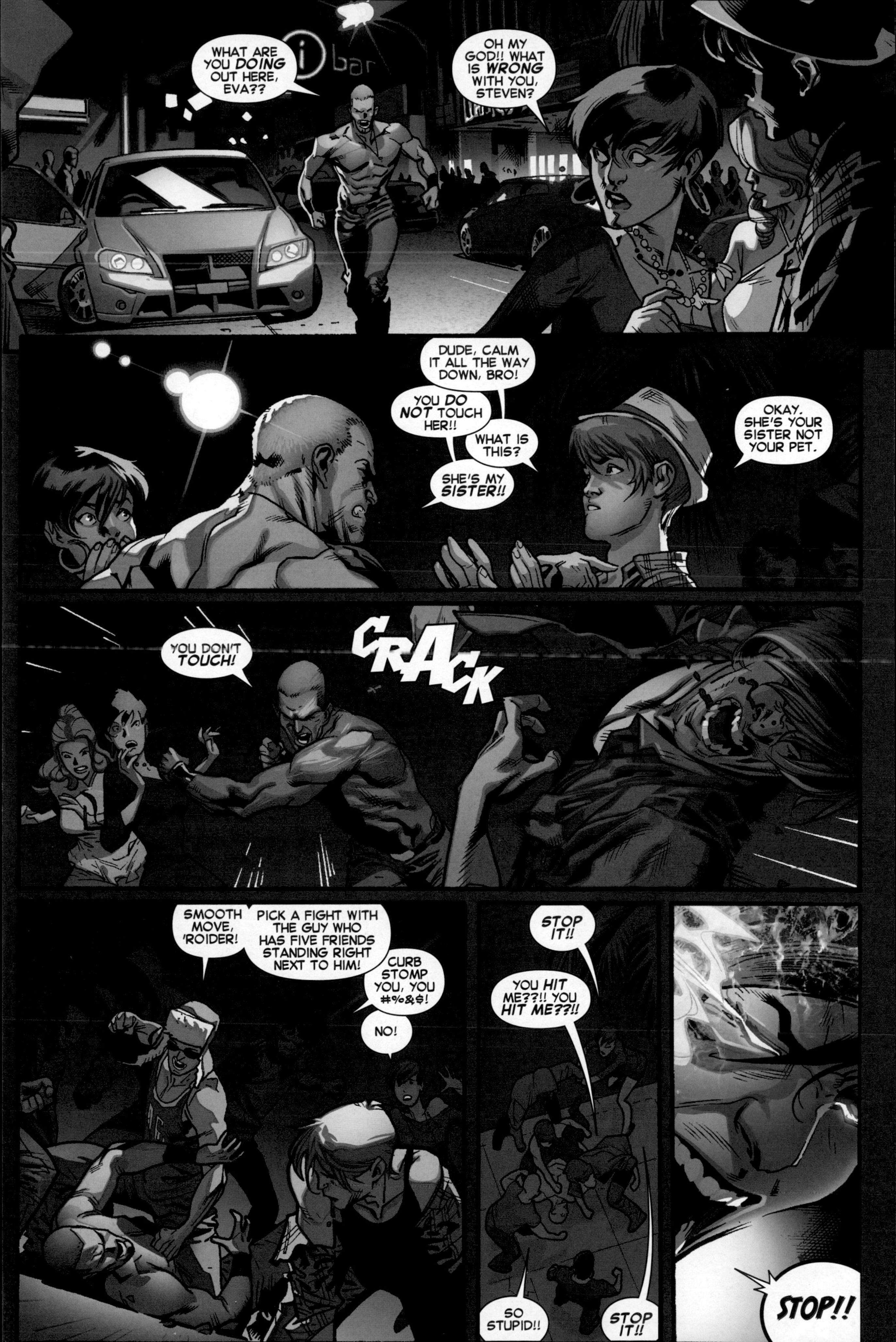
WHAT ARE YOU DOING OUT HERE, EVA??
OH MY GOD!! WHAT IS WRONG WITH YOU, STEVEN?
DUDE, CALM IT ALL THE WAY DOWN, BRO!
YOU DO NOT TOUCH HER!!
WHAT IS THIS?
SHE'S MY SISTER!!
OKAY. SHE'S YOUR SISTER NOT YOUR PET.
YOU DON'T TOUCH!
CRACK
SMOOTH MOVE, 'ROIDER!
PICK A FIGHT WITH THE GUY WHO HAS FIVE FRIENDS STANDING RIGHT NEXT TO HIM!
CURB STOMP YOU, YOU #%&$!
NO!
STOP IT!!
YOU HIT ME??!! YOU HIT ME??!!
SO STUPID!!
STOP IT!!
STOP!!

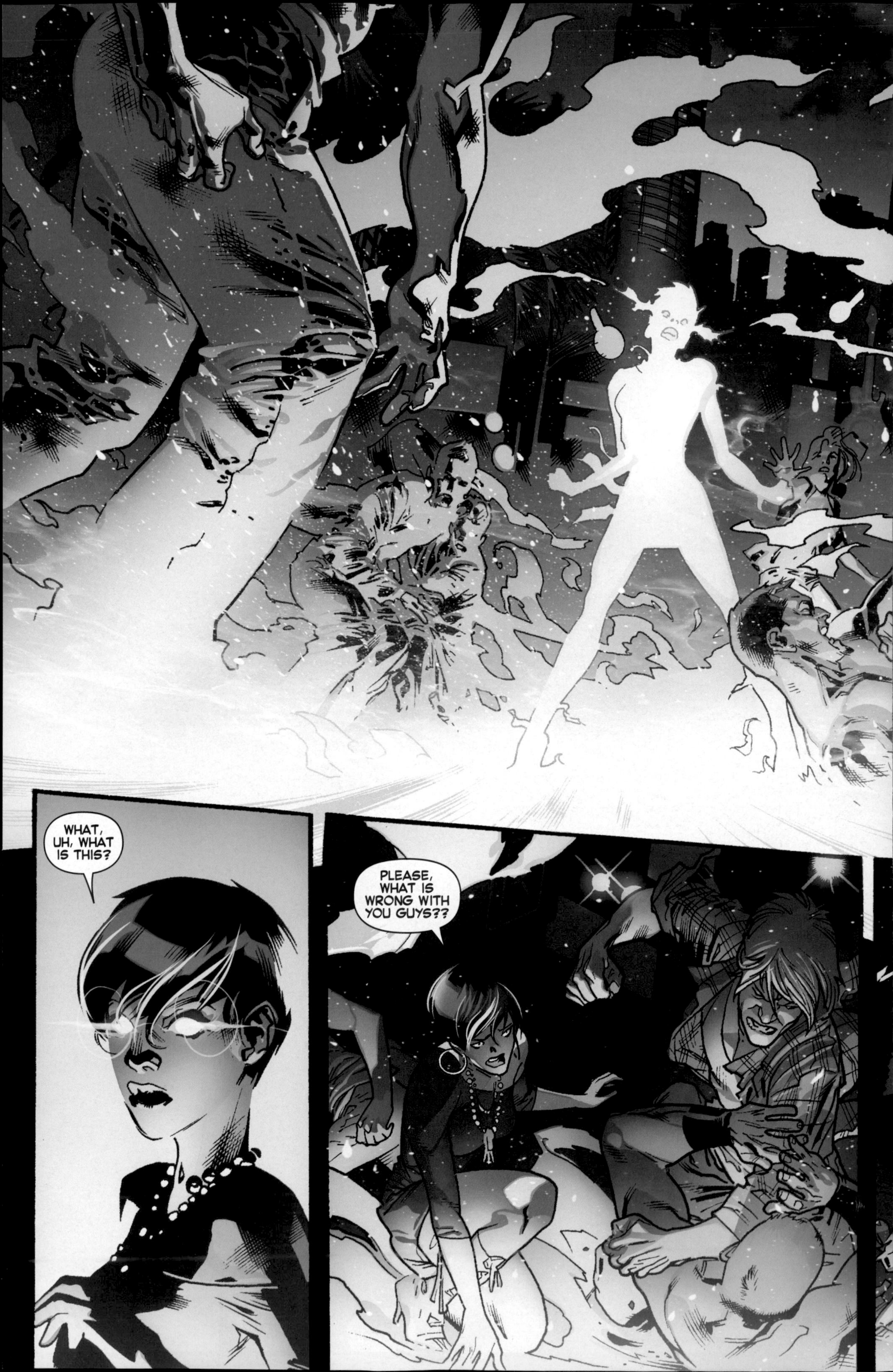
WHAT, UH, WHAT IS THIS?
PLEASE, WHAT IS WRONG WITH YOU GUYS??

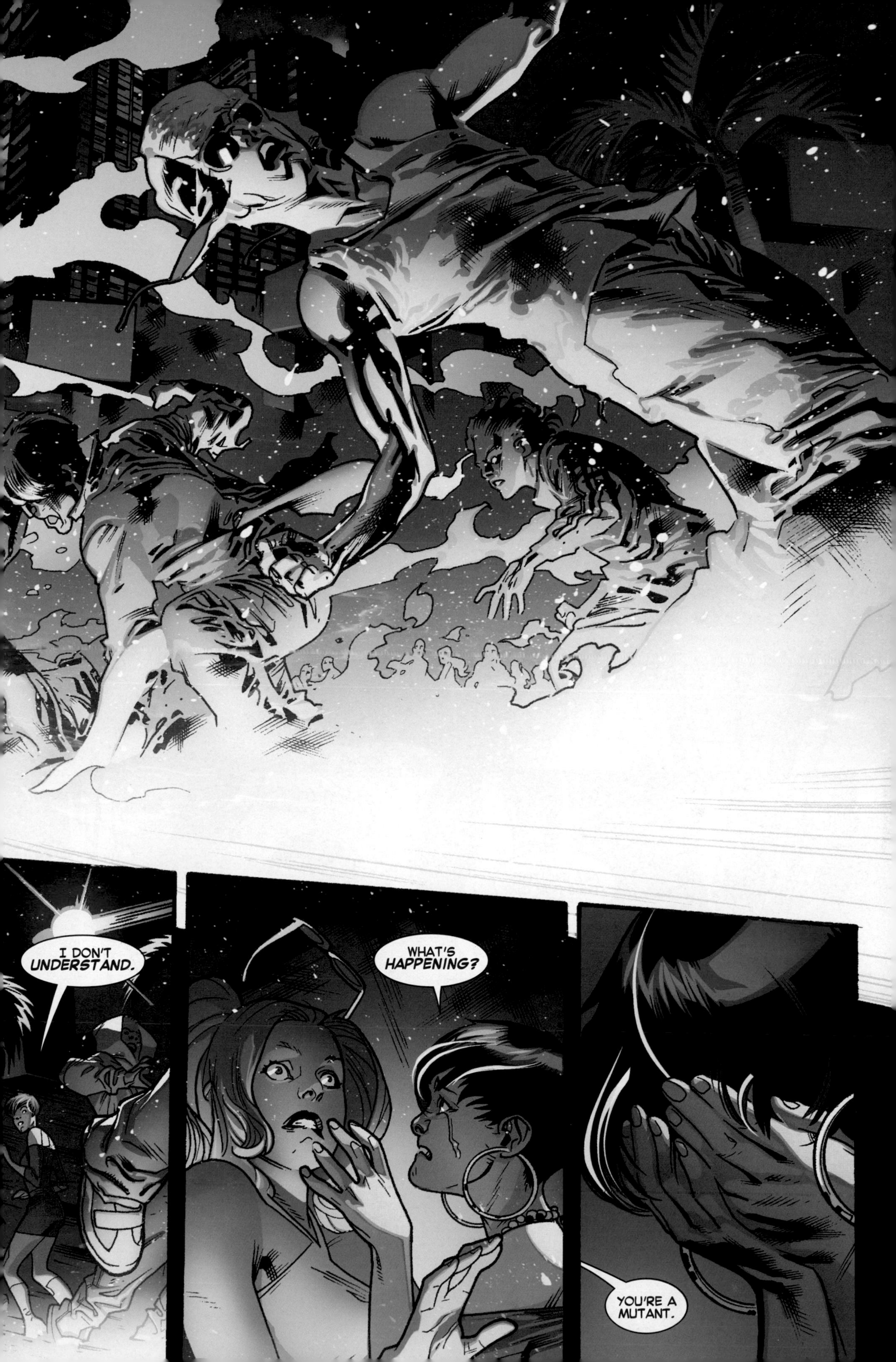
I DON'T UNDERSTAND.
WHAT'S HAPPENING?
YOU'RE A MUTANT.

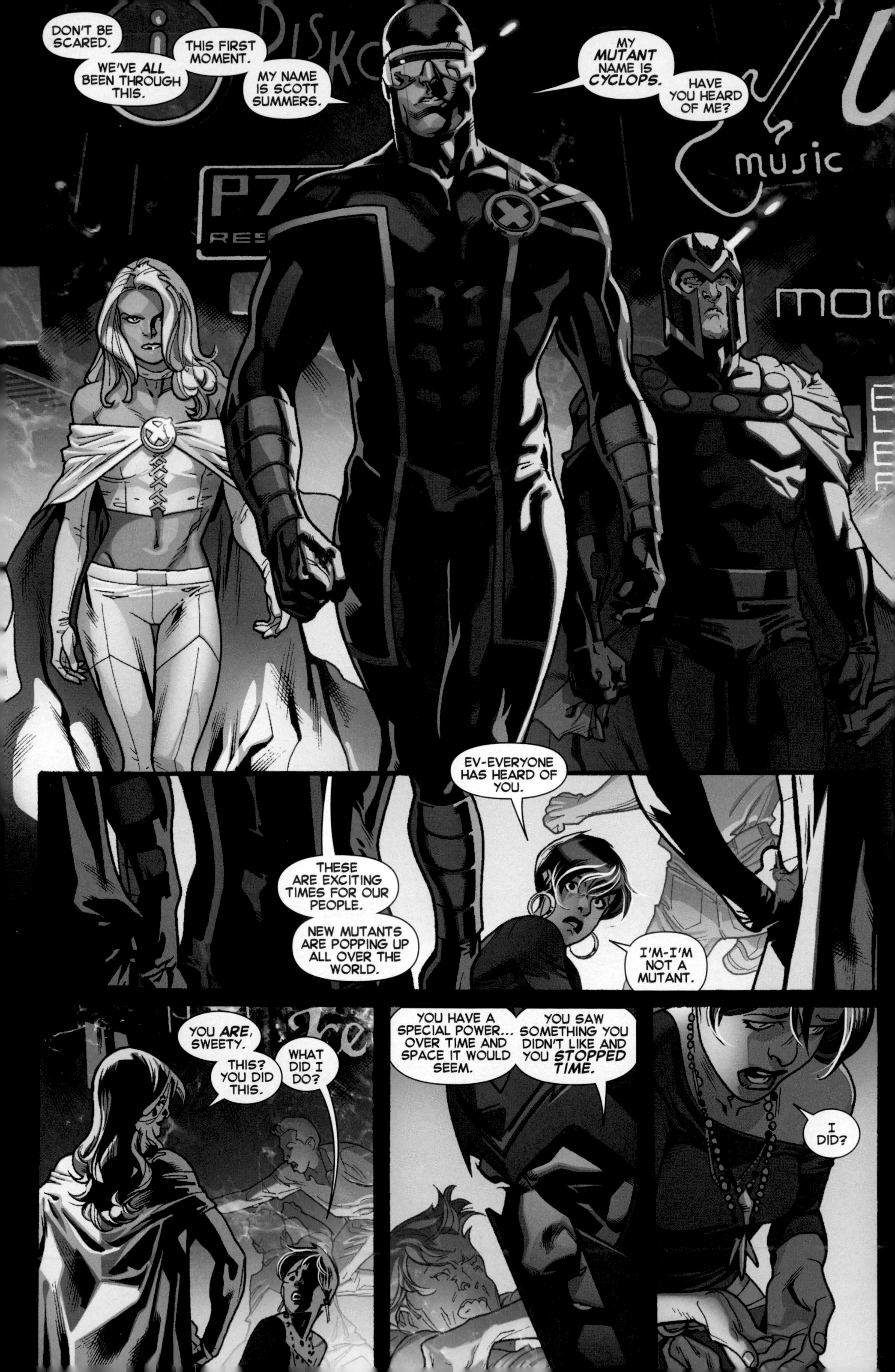
DISKO
DON'T BE SCARED.
WE'VE ALL BEEN THROUGH THIS.
THIS FIRST MOMENT.
MY NAME IS SCOTT SUMMERS.
MY MUTANT NAME IS CYCLOPS.
HAVE YOU HEARD OF ME?
music
EV-EVERYONE HAS HEARD OF YOU.
THESE ARE EXCITING TIMES FOR OUR PEOPLE.
NEW MUTANTS ARE POPPING UP ALL OVER THE WORLD.
I'M-I'M NOT A MUTANT.
YOU ARE, SWEETY.
THIS? YOU DID THIS.
WHAT DID I DO?
YOU HAVE A SPECIAL POWER... OVER TIME AND SPACE IT WOULD SEEM.
YOU SAW SOMETHING YOU DIDN'T LIKE AND YOU STOPPED TIME.
I DID?

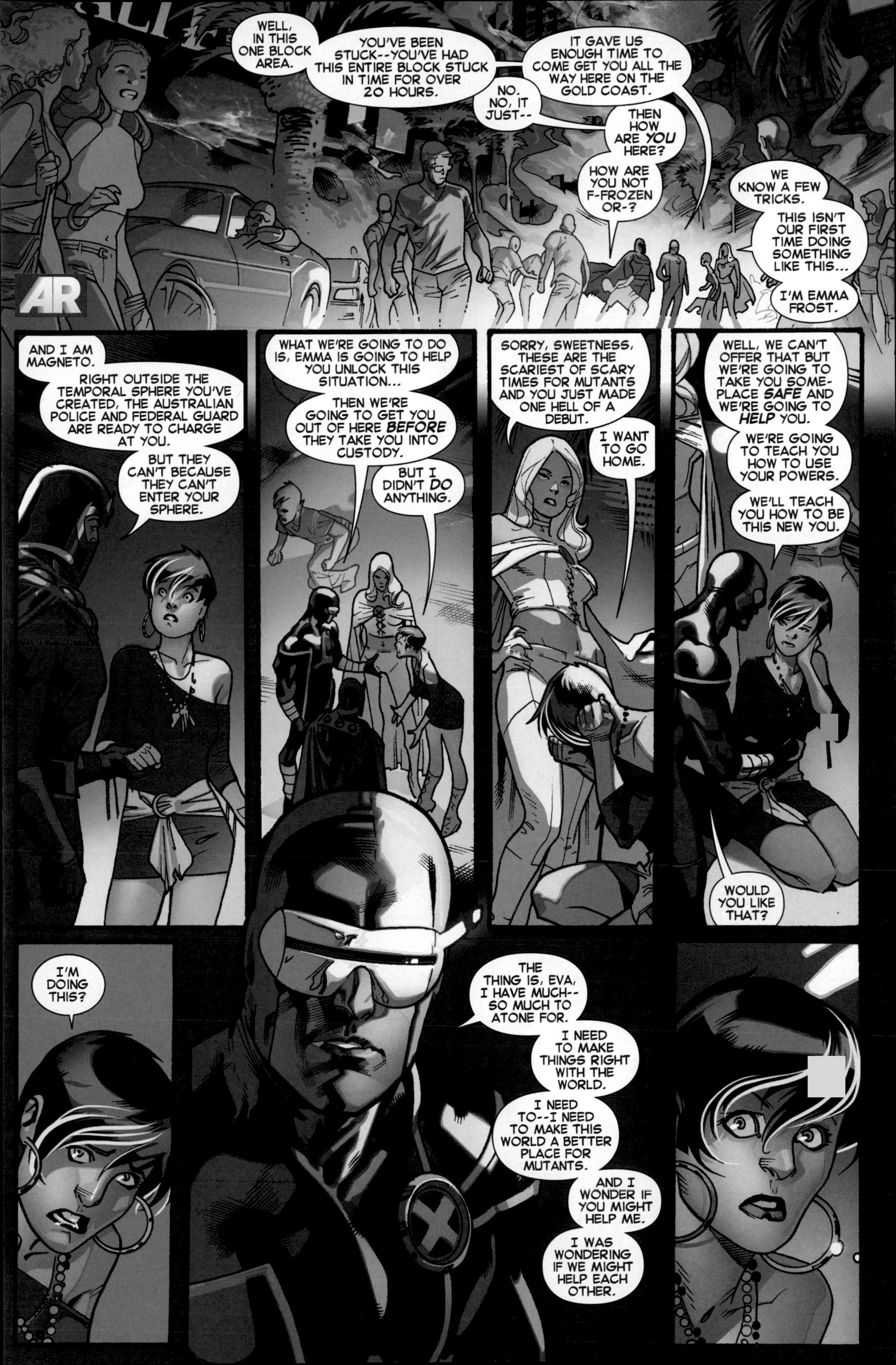

WELL, IN THIS ONE BLOCK AREA.
YOU'VE BEEN STUCK--YOU'VE HAD THIS ENTIRE BLOCK STUCK IN TIME FOR OVER 20 HOURS.
NO. NO, IT JUST--
IT GAVE US ENOUGH TIME TO COME GET YOU ALL THE WAY HERE ON THE GOLD COAST.
THEN HOW ARE YOU HERE?
HOW ARE YOU NOT F-FROZEN OR-?
WE KNOW A FEW TRICKS.
THIS ISN'T OUR FIRST TIME DOING SOMETHING LIKE THIS...
I'M EMMA FROST.
AR
AND I AM MAGNETO.
RIGHT OUTSIDE THE TEMPORAL SPHERE YOU'VE CREATED, THE AUSTRALIAN POLICE AND FEDERAL GUARD ARE READY TO CHARGE AT YOU.
BUT THEY CAN'T BECAUSE THEY CAN'T ENTER YOUR SPHERE.
WHAT WE'RE GOING TO DO IS, EMMA IS GOING TO HELP YOU UNLOCK THIS SITUATION...
THEN WE'RE GOING TO GET YOU OUT OF HERE BEFORE THEY TAKE YOU INTO CUSTODY.
BUT I DIDN'T DO ANYTHING.
SORRY, SWEETNESS, THESE ARE THE SCARIEST OF SCARY TIMES FOR MUTANTS AND YOU JUST MADE ONE HELL OF A DEBUT.
I WANT TO GO HOME.
WELL, WE CAN'T OFFER THAT BUT WE'RE GOING TO TAKE YOU SOME-PLACE SAFE AND WE'RE GOING TO HELP YOU.
WE'RE GOING TO TEACH YOU HOW TO USE YOUR POWERS.
WE'LL TEACH YOU HOW TO BE THIS NEW YOU.
WOULD YOU LIKE THAT?
I'M DOING THIS?
THE THING IS, EVA, I HAVE MUCH--SO MUCH TO ATONE FOR.
I NEED TO MAKE THINGS RIGHT WITH THE WORLD.
I NEED TO--I NEED TO MAKE THIS WORLD A BETTER PLACE FOR MUTANTS.
AND I WONDER IF YOU MIGHT HELP ME.
I WAS WONDERING IF WE MIGHT HELP EACH OTHER.

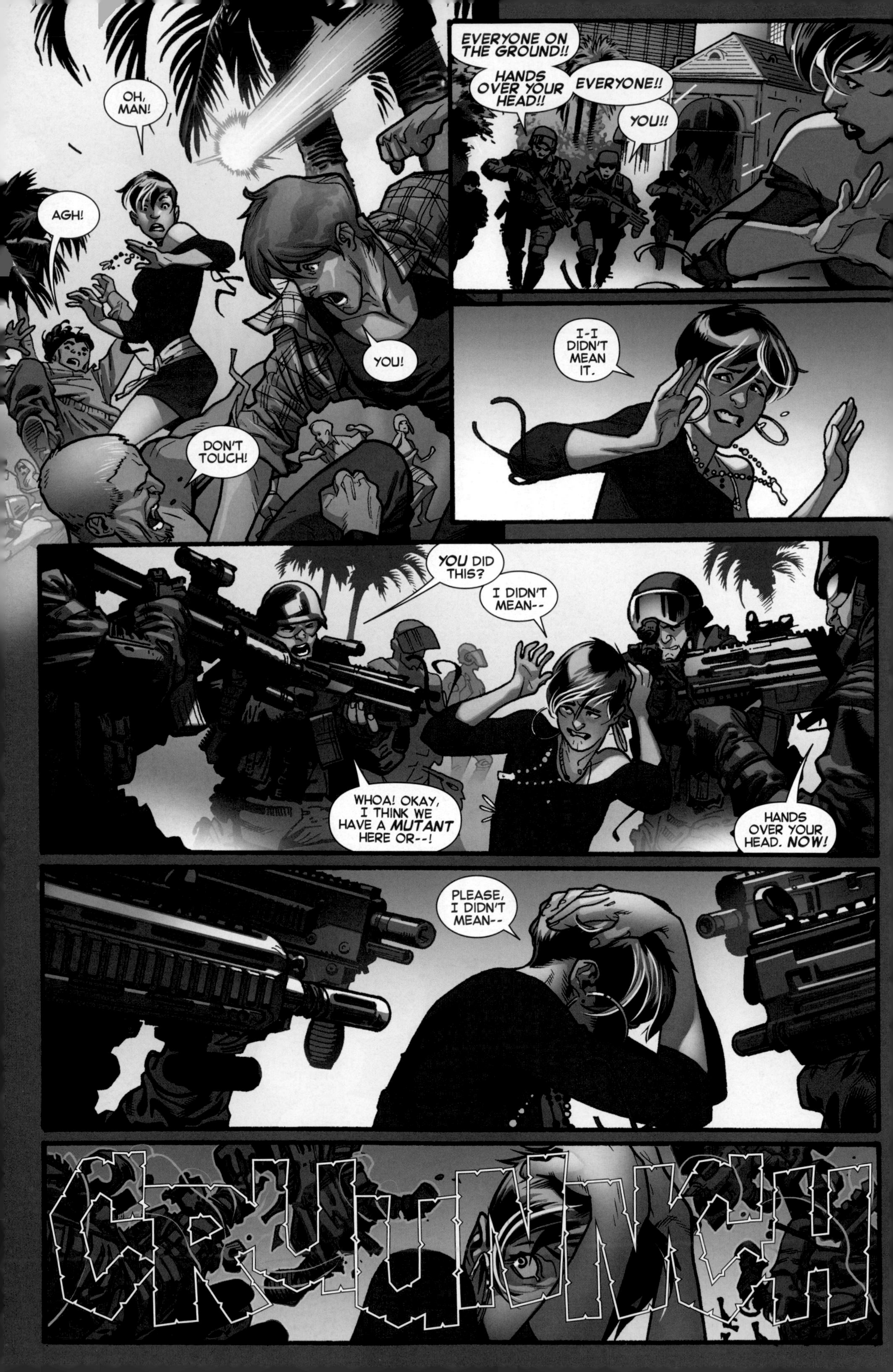
OH, MAN!
AGH!
YOU!
DON'T TOUCH!
EVERYONE ON THE GROUND!!
HANDS OVER YOUR HEAD!!
EVERYONE!!
YOU!!
I-I DIDN'T MEAN IT.
YOU DID THIS?
I DIDN'T MEAN--
WHOA! OKAY, I THINK WE HAVE A MUTANT HERE OR--!
HANDS OVER YOUR HEAD. NOW!
PLEASE, I DIDN'T MEAN--
CRUUNNCH

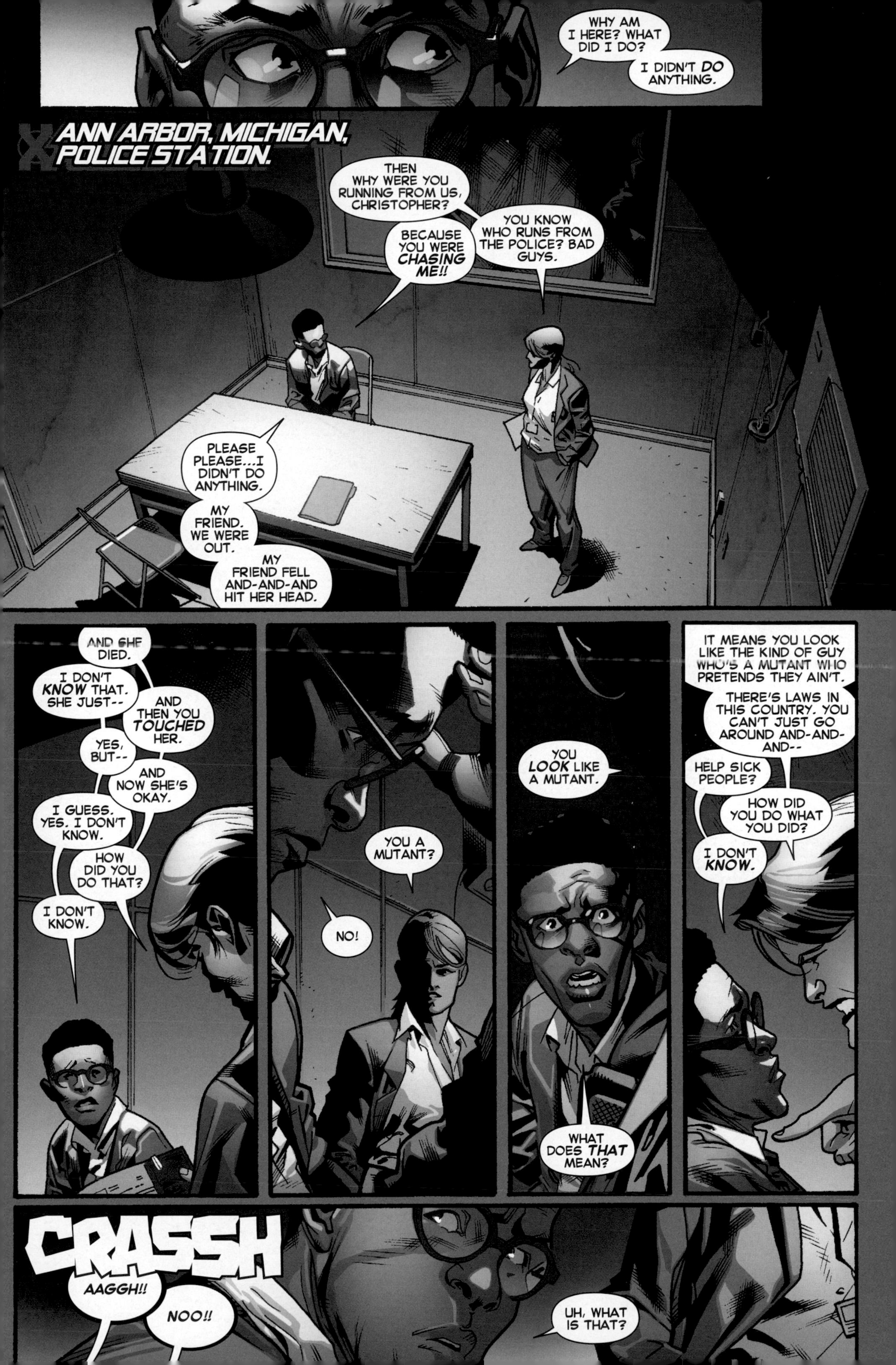
WHY AM I HERE? WHAT DID I DO?
I DIDN'T DO ANYTHING.
ANN ARBOR, MICHIGAN, POLICE STATION.
THEN WHY WERE YOU RUNNING FROM US, CHRISTOPHER?
BECAUSE YOU WERE CHASING ME!!
YOU KNOW WHO RUNS FROM THE POLICE? BAD GUYS.
PLEASE PLEASE...I DIDN'T DO ANYTHING.
MY FRIEND. WE WERE OUT.
MY FRIEND FELL AND-AND-AND HIT HER HEAD.
AND SHE DIED.
I DON'T KNOW THAT. SHE JUST--
AND THEN YOU TOUCHED HER.
YES, BUT--
AND NOW SHE'S OKAY.
I GUESS. YES. I DON'T KNOW.
HOW DID YOU DO THAT?
I DON'T KNOW.
YOU A MUTANT?
NO!
YOU LOOK LIKE A MUTANT.
WHAT DOES THAT MEAN?
IT MEANS YOU LOOK LIKE THE KIND OF GUY WHO'S A MUTANT WHO PRETENDS THEY AIN'T.
THERE'S LAWS IN THIS COUNTRY. YOU CAN'T JUST GO AROUND AND-AND-AND--
HELP SICK PEOPLE?
HOW DID YOU DO WHAT YOU DID?
I DON'T KNOW.
CRASSH
AAGGH!!
NOO!!
UH, WHAT IS THAT?

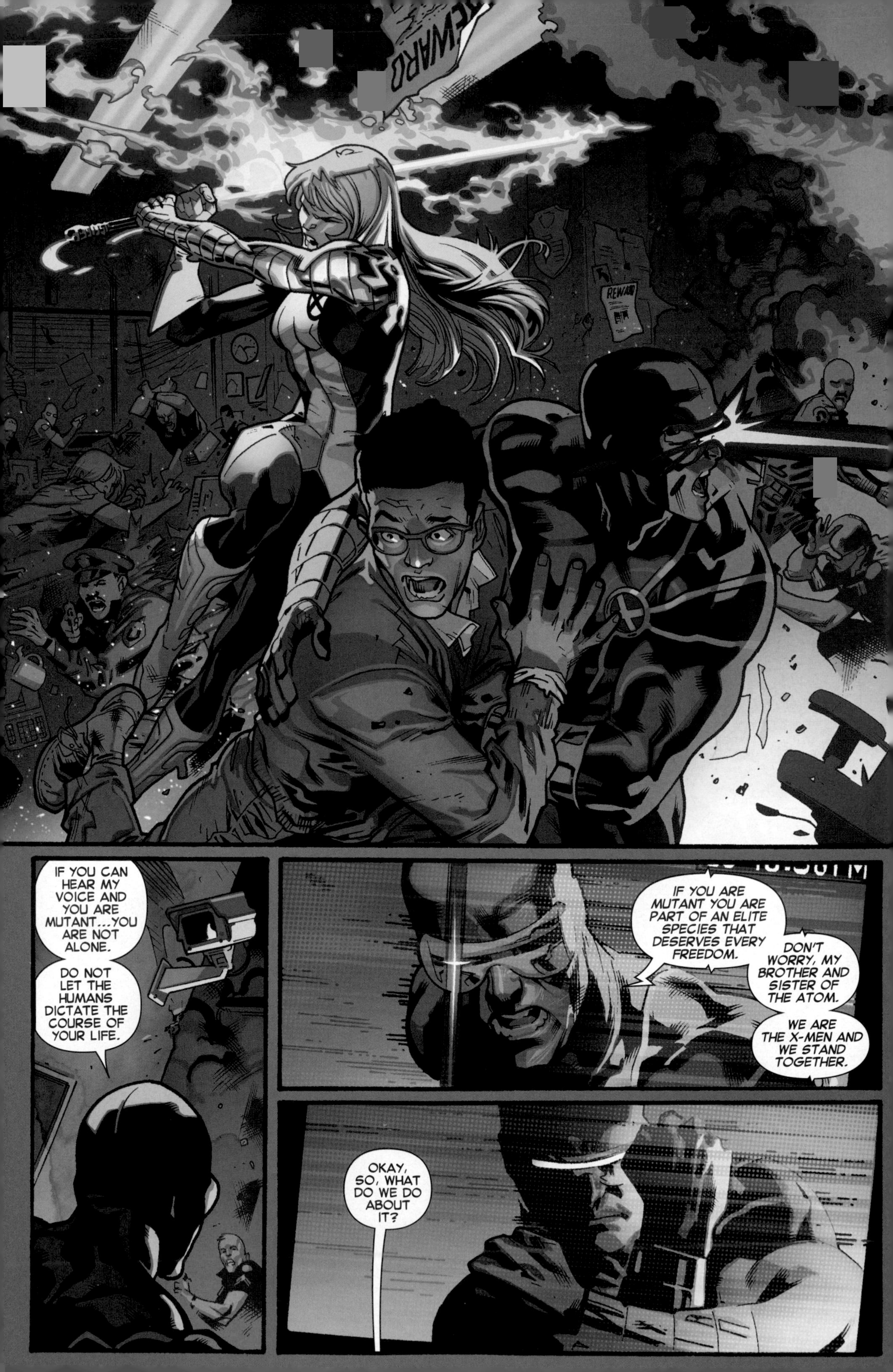
REWARD
IF YOU CAN HEAR MY VOICE AND YOU ARE MUTANT...YOU ARE NOT ALONE.
DO NOT LET THE HUMANS DICTATE THE COURSE OF YOUR LIFE.
IF YOU ARE MUTANT YOU ARE PART OF AN ELITE SPECIES THAT DESERVES EVERY FREEDOM.
DON'T WORRY, MY BROTHER AND SISTER OF THE ATOM.
WE ARE THE X-MEN AND WE STAND TOGETHER.
OKAY, SO, WHAT DO WE DO ABOUT IT?

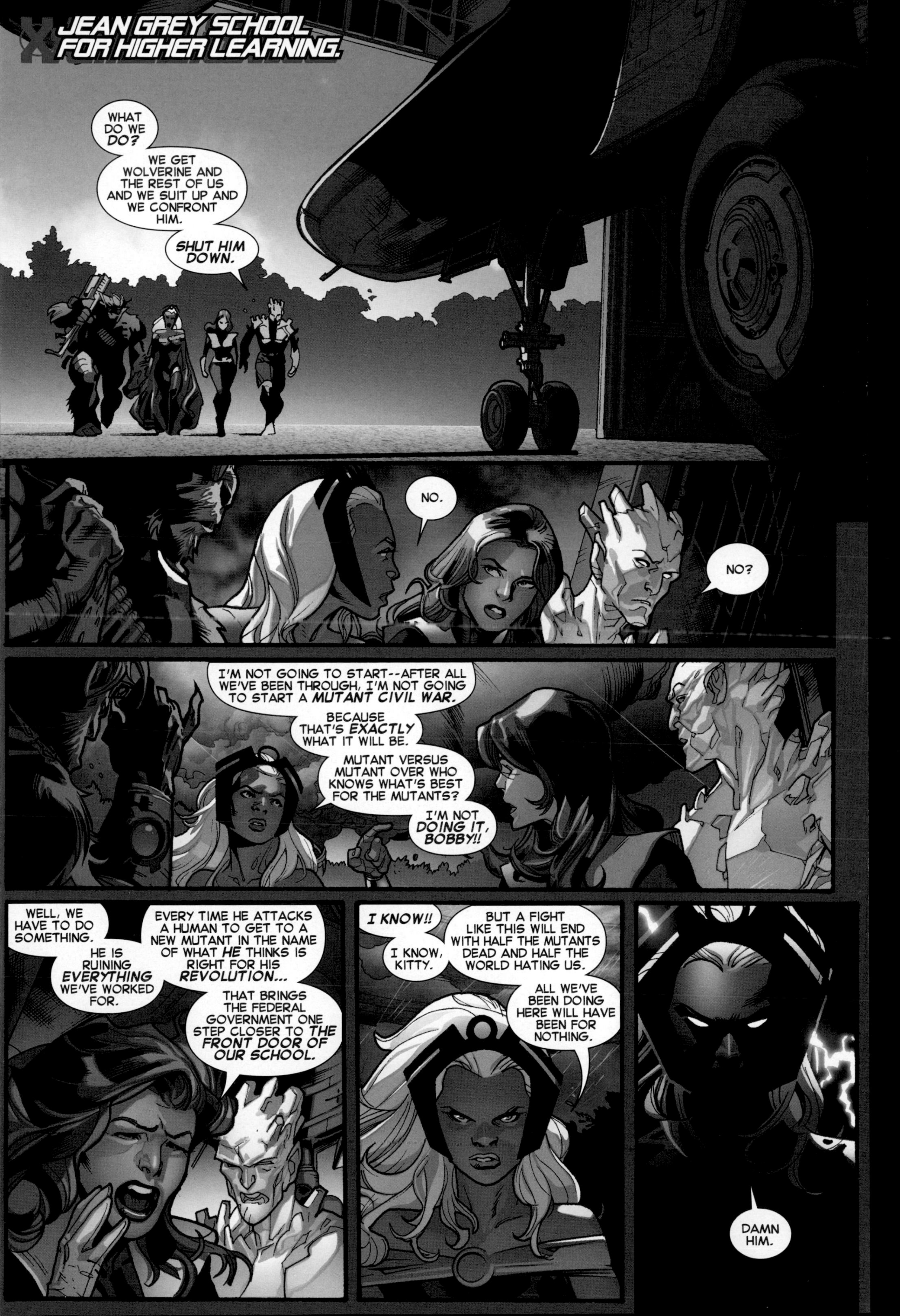
JEAN GREY SCHOOL FOR HIGHER LEARNING.
WHAT DO WE DO?
WE GET WOLVERINE AND THE REST OF US AND WE SUIT UP AND WE CONFRONT HIM.
SHUT HIM DOWN.
NO.
NO?
I'M NOT GOING TO START--AFTER ALL WE'VE BEEN THROUGH, I'M NOT GOING TO START A MUTANT CIVIL WAR.
BECAUSE THAT'S EXACTLY WHAT IT WILL BE.
MUTANT VERSUS MUTANT OVER WHO KNOWS WHAT'S BEST FOR THE MUTANTS?
I'M NOT DOING IT, BOBBY!!
WELL, WE HAVE TO DO SOMETHING.
HE IS RUINING EVERYTHING WE'VE WORKED FOR.
EVERY TIME HE ATTACKS A HUMAN TO GET TO A NEW MUTANT IN THE NAME OF WHAT HE THINKS IS RIGHT FOR HIS REVOLUTION...
THAT BRINGS THE FEDERAL GOVERNMENT ONE STEP CLOSER TO THE FRONT DOOR OF OUR SCHOOL.
I KNOW!!
I KNOW, KITTY.
BUT A FIGHT LIKE THIS WILL END WITH HALF THE MUTANTS DEAD AND HALF THE WORLD HATING US.
ALL WE'VE BEEN DOING HERE WILL HAVE BEEN FOR NOTHING.
DAMN HIM.

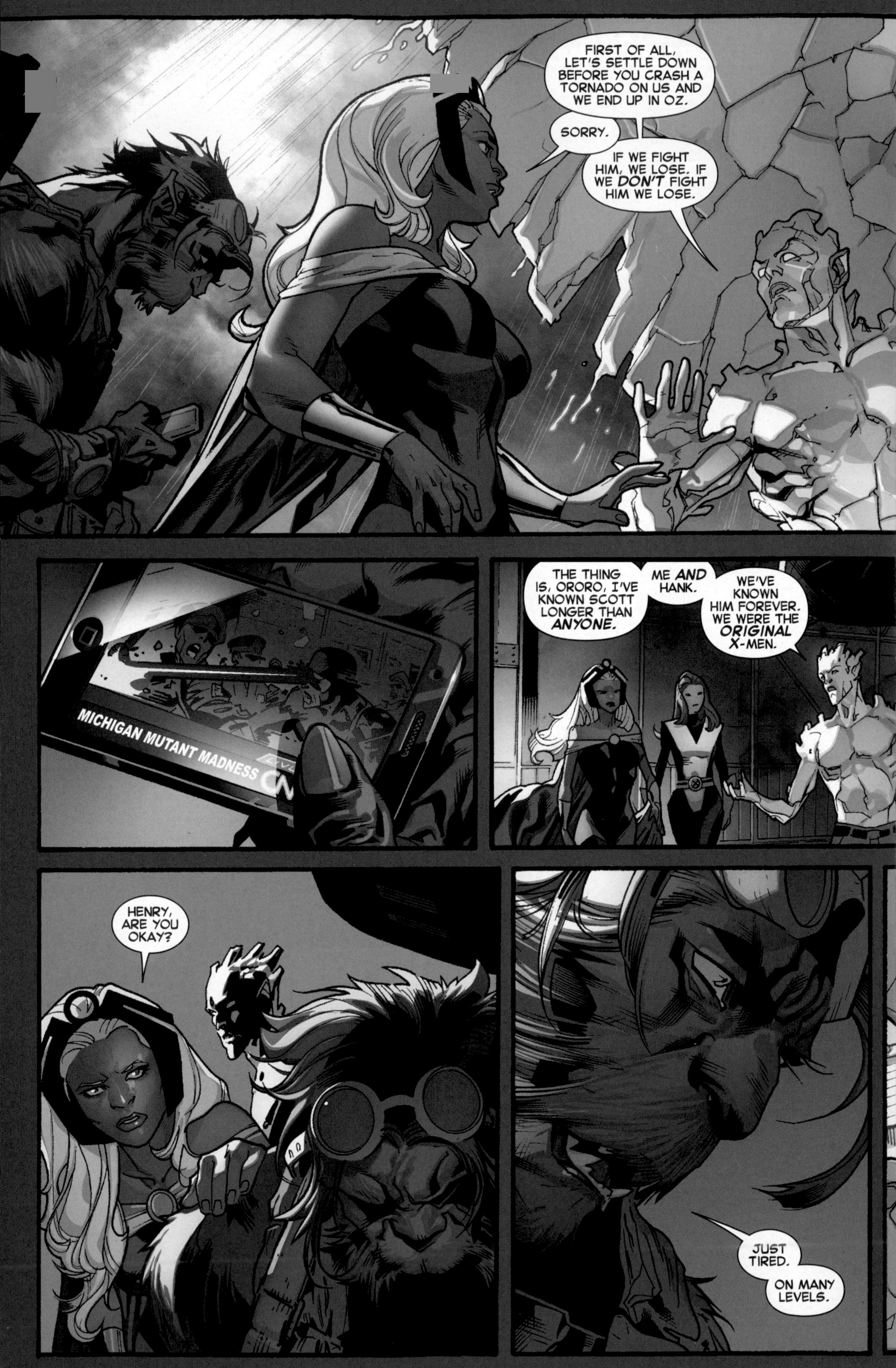
FIRST OF ALL, LET'S SETTLE DOWN BEFORE YOU CRASH A TORNADO ON US AND WE END UP IN OZ.
SORRY.
IF WE FIGHT HIM, WE LOSE. IF WE *DON'T* FIGHT HIM WE LOSE.
MICHIGAN MUTANT MADNESS
THE THING IS, ORORO, I'VE KNOWN SCOTT LONGER THAN *ANYONE.*
ME *AND* HANK.
WE'VE KNOWN HIM FOREVER. WE WERE THE *ORIGINAL* X-MEN.
HENRY, ARE YOU OKAY?
JUST TIRED.
ON MANY LEVELS.

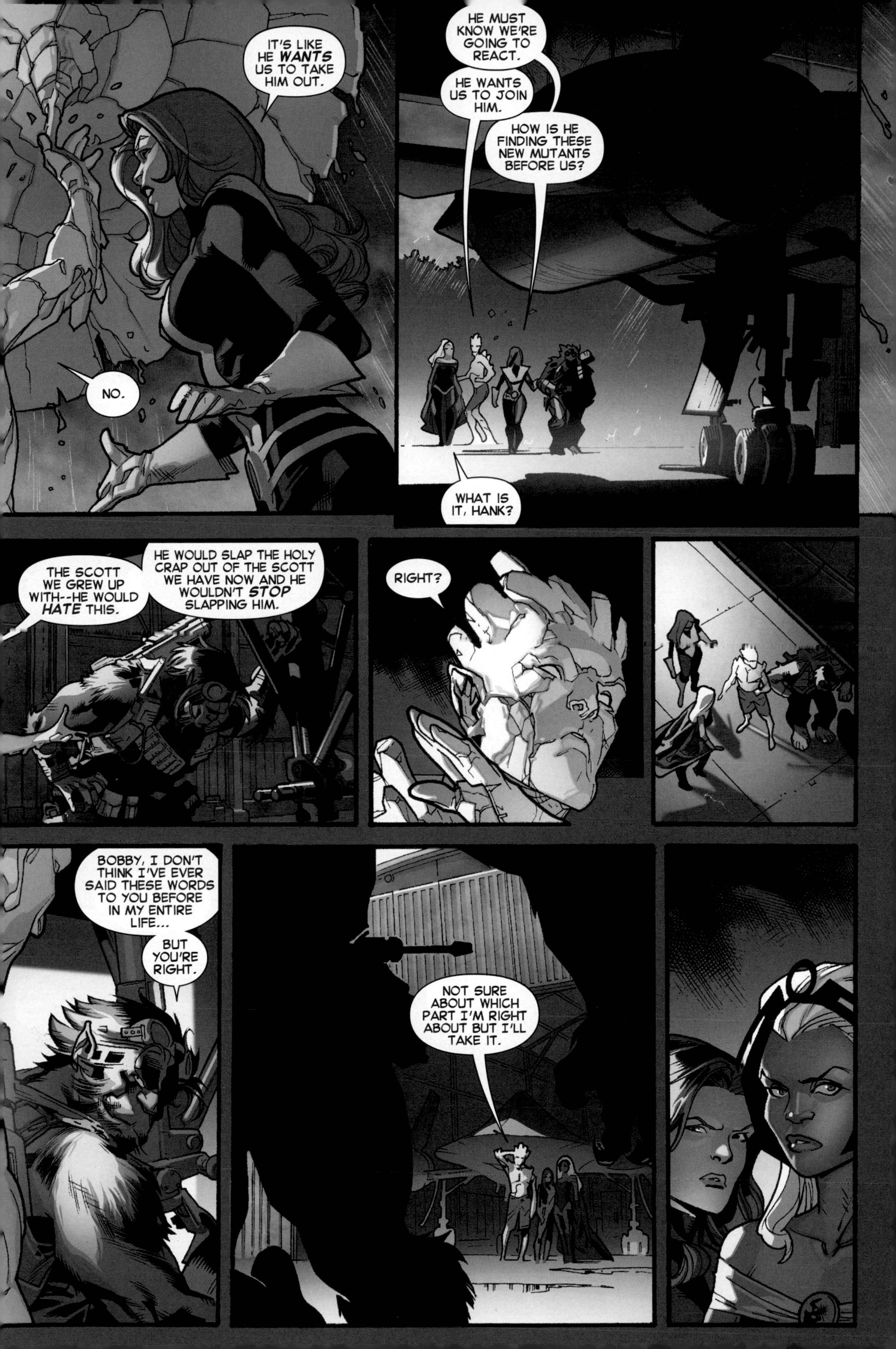
IT'S LIKE HE **WANTS** US TO TAKE HIM OUT.
NO.
HE MUST KNOW WE'RE GOING TO REACT.
HE WANTS US TO JOIN HIM.
HOW IS HE FINDING THESE NEW MUTANTS BEFORE US?
WHAT IS IT, HANK?
THE SCOTT WE GREW UP WITH--HE WOULD **HATE** THIS.
HE WOULD SLAP THE HOLY CRAP OUT OF THE SCOTT WE HAVE NOW AND HE WOULDN'T **STOP** SLAPPING HIM.
RIGHT?
BOBBY, I DON'T THINK I'VE EVER SAID THESE WORDS TO YOU BEFORE IN MY ENTIRE LIFE...
BUT YOU'RE RIGHT.
NOT SURE ABOUT WHICH PART I'M RIGHT ABOUT BUT I'LL TAKE IT.

Dear Jean
Please don't be
alarmed by this
letter. I have been
thinking of all the
ways I wanted to
tell you this and
all of the missed
opportunities we had

I'M THROUGH, SCOTT! I'VE **HAD** IT!!

WHOA! HANK, BOBBY, WHAT HAPPENED?!

A MOB OF **WHAT**?

A MOB. AN HONEST-TO-GOODNESS MOB!!

OF ANGRY **HUMANS**!!

AND THEY ALMOST GOT THEIR PAWS ON US.

AR

I CANNOT TELL YOU HOW COMPLETELY DONE I AM WITH RISKING MY LIFE FOR THE HUMANS!

THE SAME DAMN HUMANS THAT COMPLETELY AND TOTALLY HATE US? YES! I'M DONE.

HANK!

YOU'RE UPSET, I GET IT!

UPSET?! I'M **MORE** THAN UPSET, SCOTT.

I'M **DONE!**

DAYS LIKE THIS-- I SEE WHY MAGNETO AND HIS EVIL MUTANTS DO WHAT THEY DO.

HOMO SAPIENS JUST AREN'T WORTH IT--

THEY **MIGHT** BE RIGHT.

OH, HANK, COME ON.

I MEAN IT.

YOU CAN'T POSSIBLY MEAN WHAT YOU'RE SAYING...

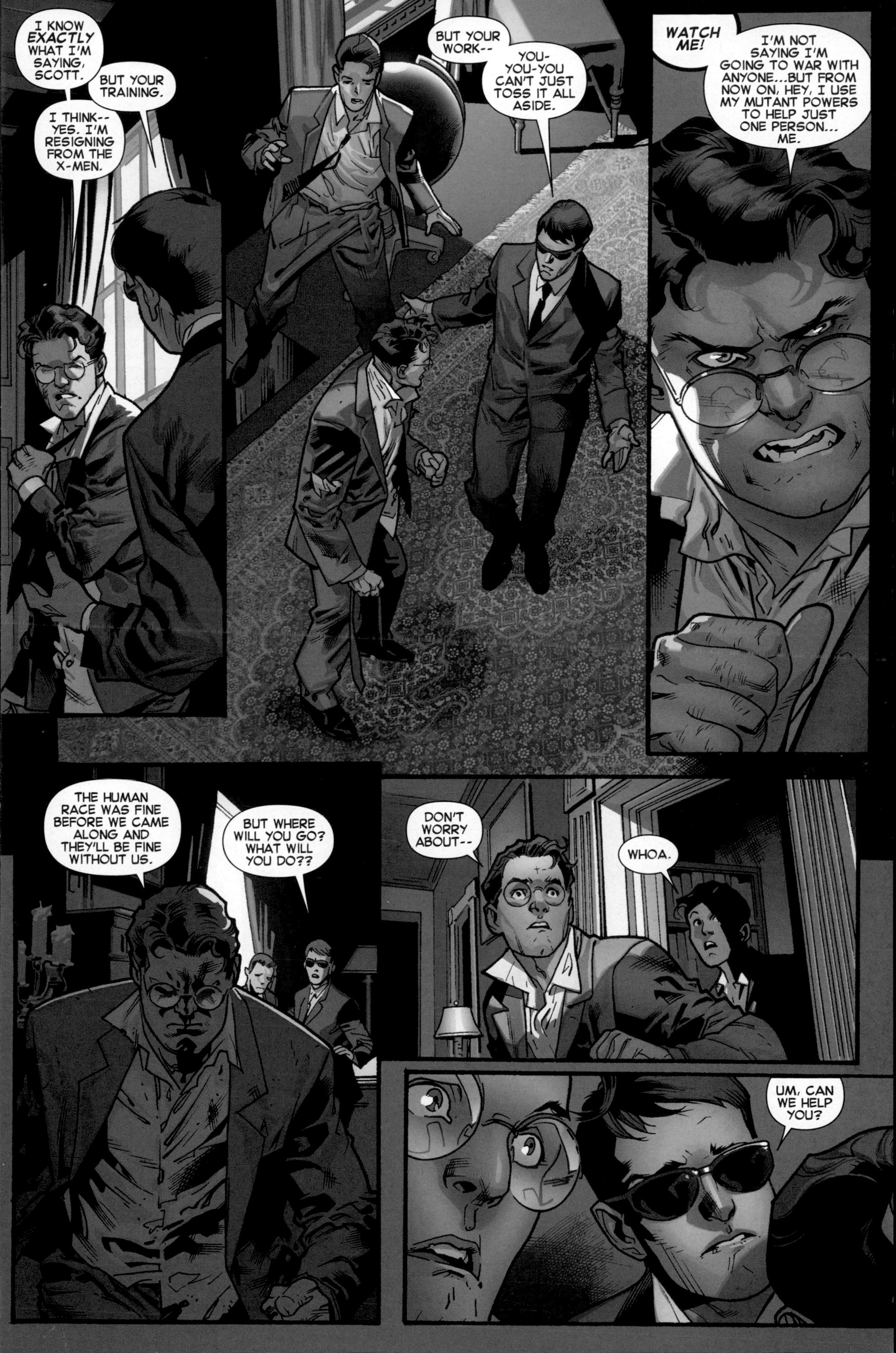
I KNOW EXACTLY WHAT I'M SAYING, SCOTT.
BUT YOUR TRAINING.
I THINK-- YES. I'M RESIGNING FROM THE X-MEN.
BUT YOUR WORK--
YOU- YOU-YOU CAN'T JUST TOSS IT ALL ASIDE.
WATCH ME!
I'M NOT SAYING I'M GOING TO WAR WITH ANYONE...BUT FROM NOW ON, HEY, I USE MY MUTANT POWERS TO HELP JUST ONE PERSON... ME.
THE HUMAN RACE WAS FINE BEFORE WE CAME ALONG AND THEY'LL BE FINE WITHOUT US.
BUT WHERE WILL YOU GO? WHAT WILL YOU DO??
DON'T WORRY ABOUT--
WHOA.
UM, CAN WE HELP YOU?

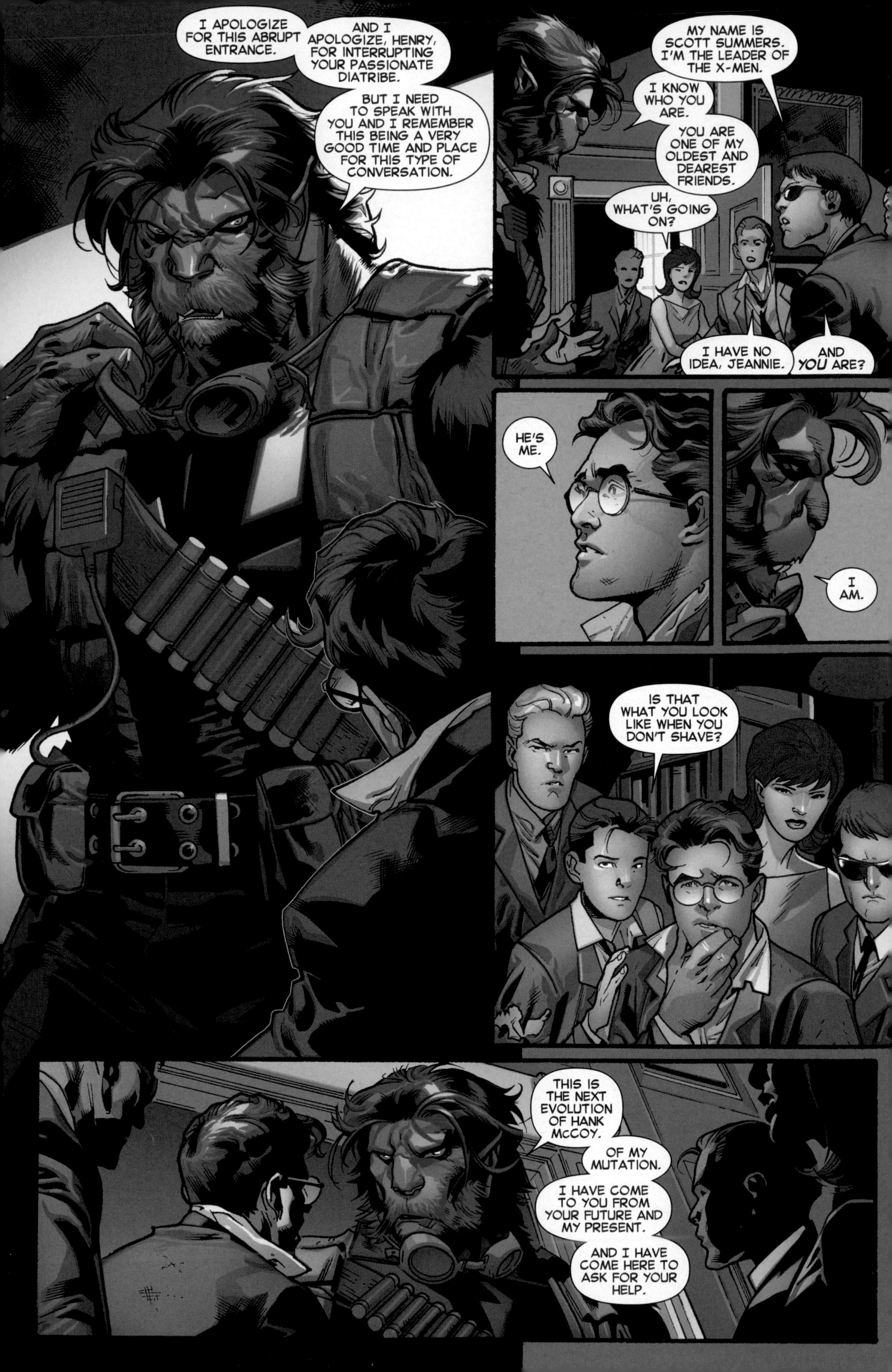
I APOLOGIZE FOR THIS ABRUPT ENTRANCE.
AND I APOLOGIZE, HENRY, FOR INTERRUPTING YOUR PASSIONATE DIATRIBE.
BUT I NEED TO SPEAK WITH YOU AND I REMEMBER THIS BEING A VERY GOOD TIME AND PLACE FOR THIS TYPE OF CONVERSATION.
MY NAME IS SCOTT SUMMERS. I'M THE LEADER OF THE X-MEN.
I KNOW WHO YOU ARE.
YOU ARE ONE OF MY OLDEST AND DEAREST FRIENDS.
UH, WHAT'S GOING ON?
I HAVE NO IDEA, JEANNIE.
AND YOU ARE?
HE'S ME.
I AM.
IS THAT WHAT YOU LOOK LIKE WHEN YOU DON'T SHAVE?
THIS IS THE NEXT EVOLUTION OF HANK McCOY.
OF MY MUTATION.
I HAVE COME TO YOU FROM YOUR FUTURE AND MY PRESENT.
AND I HAVE COME HERE TO ASK FOR YOUR HELP.

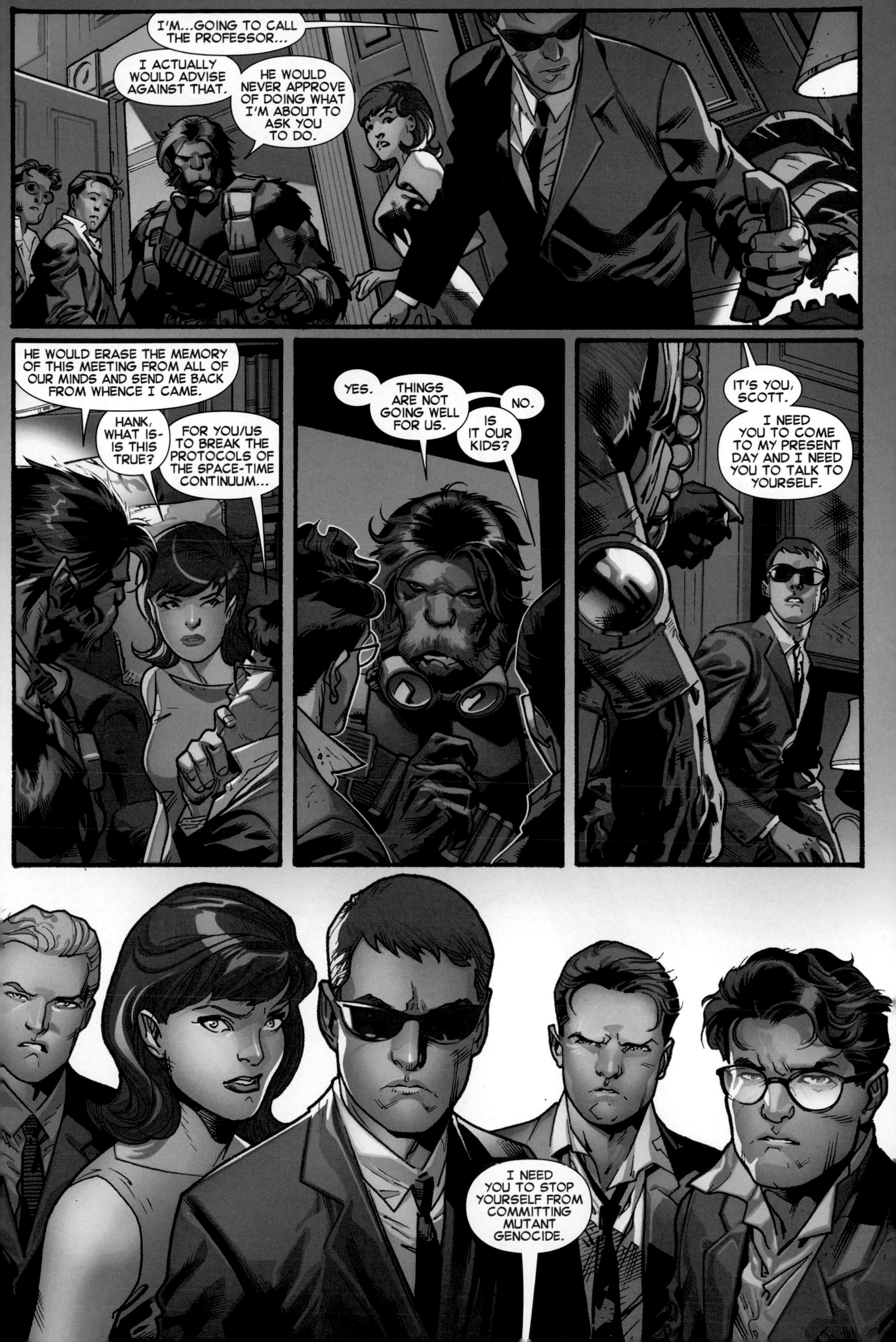

I'M...GOING TO CALL THE PROFESSOR...
I ACTUALLY WOULD ADVISE AGAINST THAT.
HE WOULD NEVER APPROVE OF DOING WHAT I'M ABOUT TO ASK YOU TO DO.
HE WOULD ERASE THE MEMORY OF THIS MEETING FROM ALL OF OUR MINDS AND SEND ME BACK FROM WHENCE I CAME.
HANK, WHAT IS- IS THIS TRUE?
FOR YOU/US TO BREAK THE PROTOCOLS OF THE SPACE-TIME CONTINUUM...
YES.
THINGS ARE NOT GOING WELL FOR US.
NO.
IS IT OUR KIDS?
IT'S YOU, SCOTT.
I NEED YOU TO COME TO MY PRESENT DAY AND I NEED YOU TO TALK TO YOURSELF.
I NEED YOU TO STOP YOURSELF FROM COMMITTING MUTANT GENOCIDE.

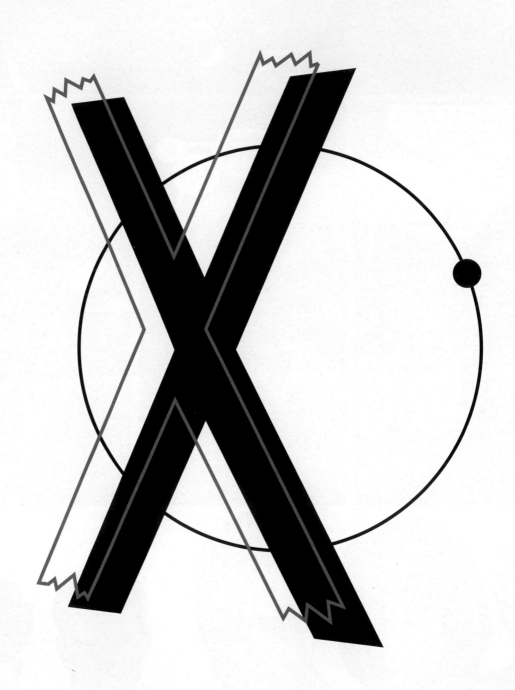

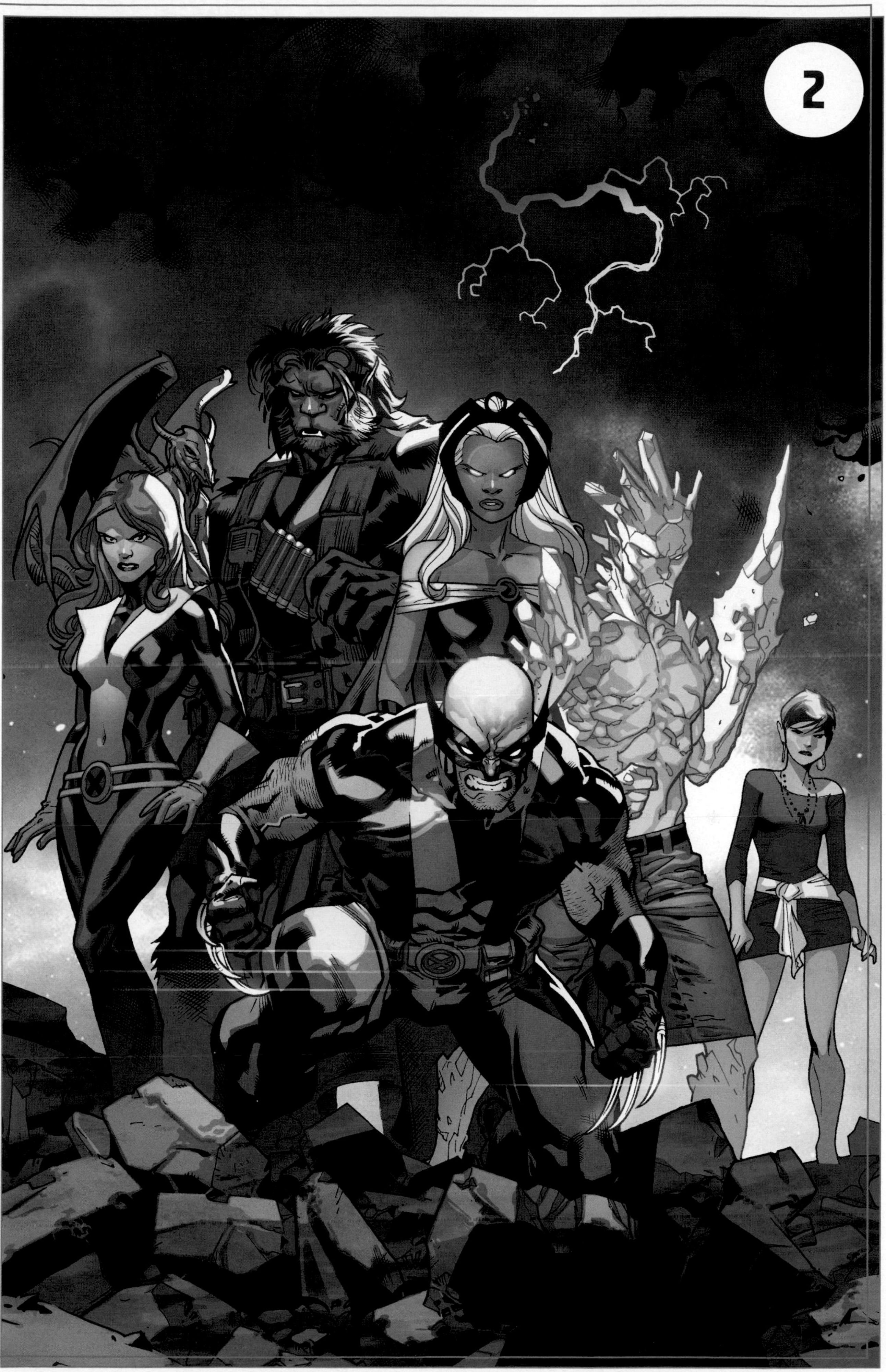
2

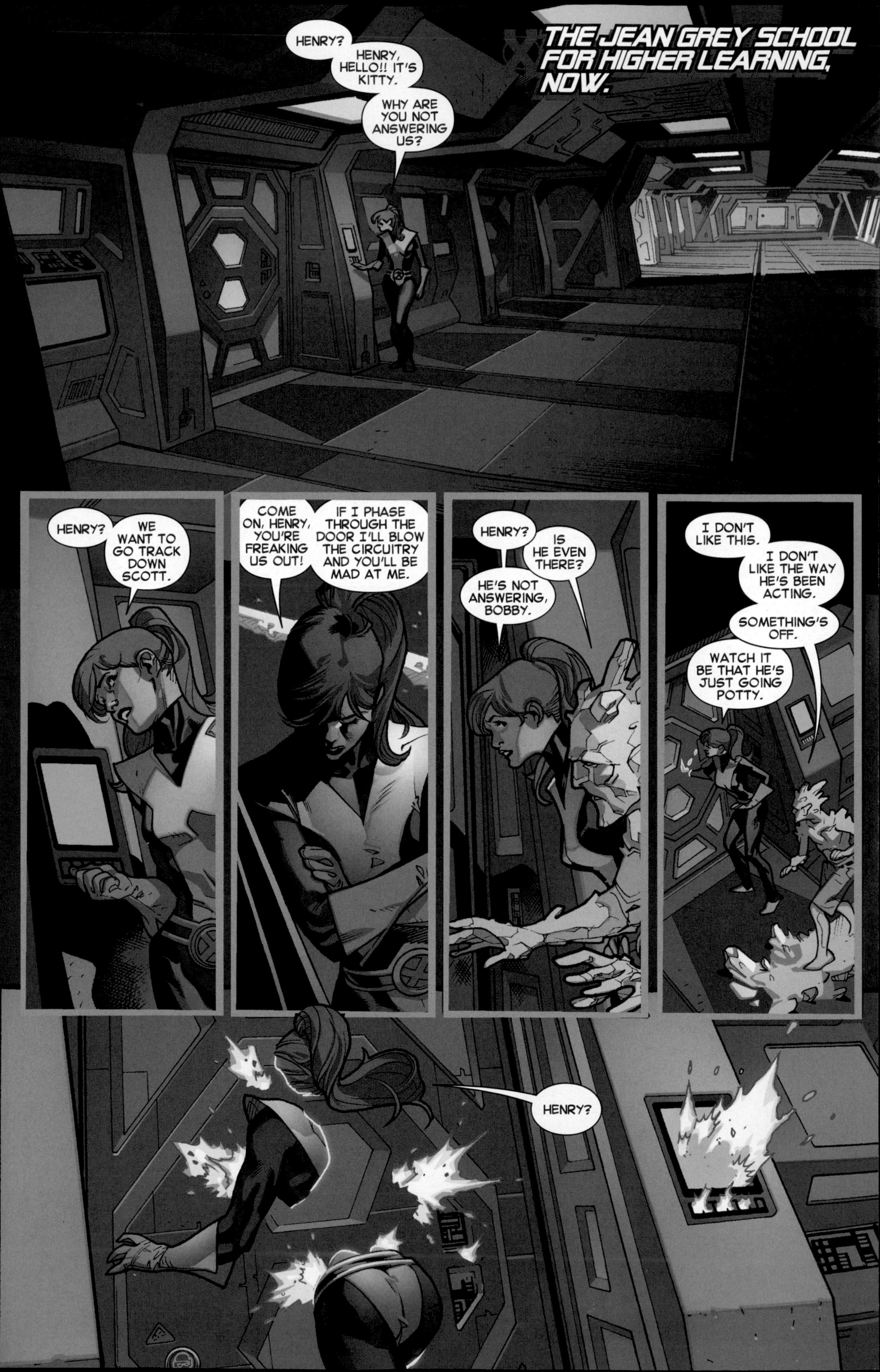
THE JEAN GREY SCHOOL FOR HIGHER LEARNING, NOW.
HENRY?
HENRY, HELLO!! IT'S KITTY.
WHY ARE YOU NOT ANSWERING US?
HENRY?
WE WANT TO GO TRACK DOWN SCOTT.
COME ON, HENRY, YOU'RE FREAKING US OUT!
IF I PHASE THROUGH THE DOOR I'LL BLOW THE CIRCUITRY AND YOU'LL BE MAD AT ME.
HENRY?
HE'S NOT ANSWERING, BOBBY.
IS HE EVEN THERE?
I DON'T LIKE THIS.
I DON'T LIKE THE WAY HE'S BEEN ACTING.
SOMETHING'S OFF.
WATCH IT BE THAT HE'S JUST GOING POTTY.
HENRY?

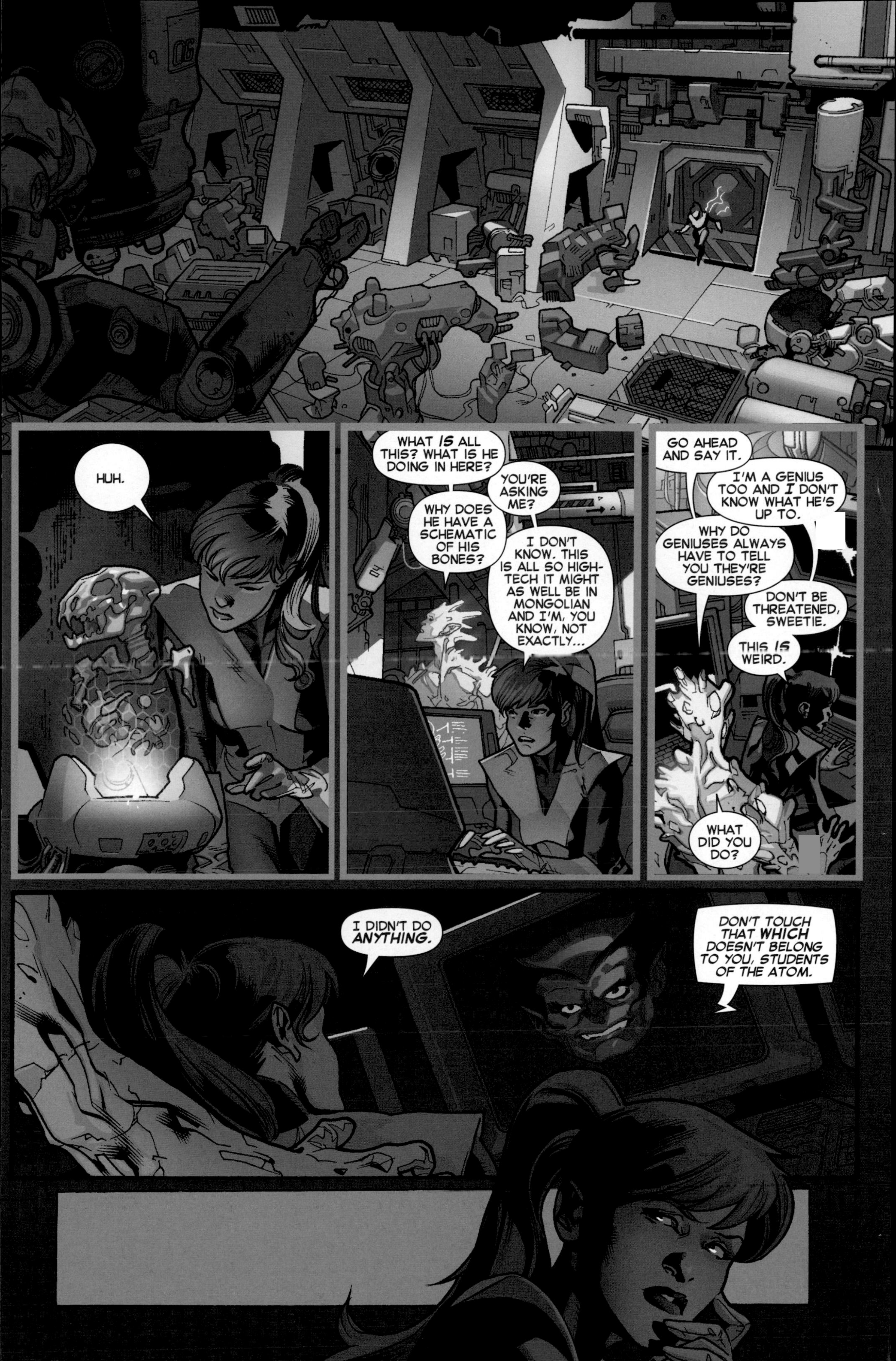
HUH.
WHAT *IS* ALL THIS? WHAT IS HE DOING IN HERE?
WHY DOES HE HAVE A SCHEMATIC OF HIS BONES?
YOU'RE ASKING ME?
I DON'T KNOW. THIS IS ALL SO HIGH-TECH IT MIGHT AS WELL BE IN MONGOLIAN AND I'M, YOU KNOW, NOT EXACTLY...
GO AHEAD AND SAY IT.
I'M A GENIUS TOO AND *I* DON'T KNOW WHAT HE'S UP TO.
WHY DO GENIUSES ALWAYS HAVE TO TELL YOU THEY'RE GENIUSES?
DON'T BE THREATENED, SWEETIE.
THIS *IS* WEIRD.
WHAT DID YOU DO?
I DIDN'T DO **ANYTHING.**
DON'T TOUCH THAT **WHICH** *DOESN'T BELONG TO YOU, STUDENTS OF THE ATOM.*

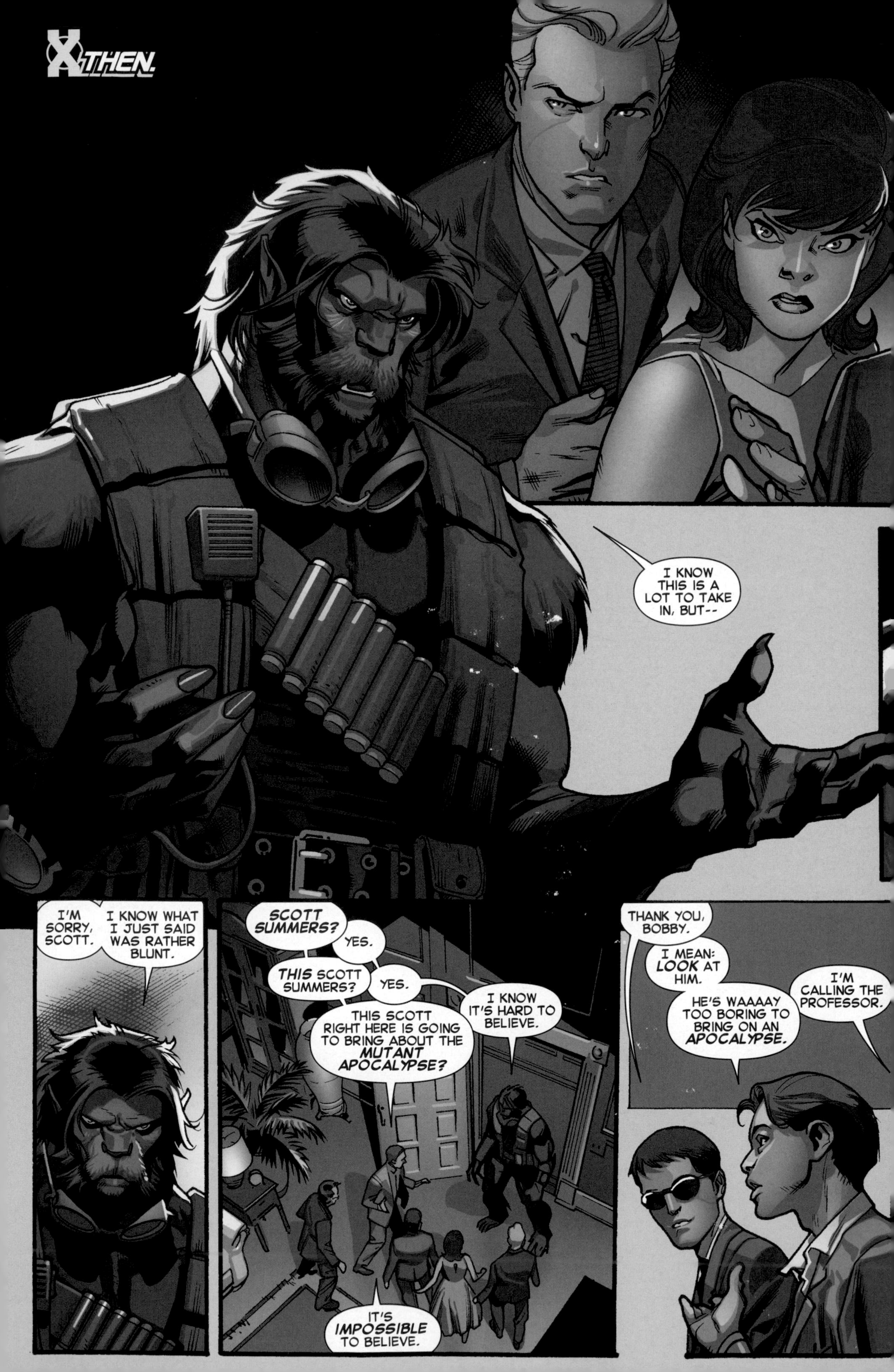
X THEN.
I KNOW THIS IS A LOT TO TAKE IN, BUT--
I'M SORRY, SCOTT.
I KNOW WHAT I JUST SAID WAS RATHER BLUNT.
SCOTT SUMMERS?
YES.
THIS SCOTT SUMMERS?
YES.
THIS SCOTT RIGHT HERE IS GOING TO BRING ABOUT THE MUTANT APOCALYPSE?
I KNOW IT'S HARD TO BELIEVE.
IT'S IMPOSSIBLE TO BELIEVE.
THANK YOU, BOBBY.
I MEAN: LOOK AT HIM.
HE'S WAAAAY TOO BORING TO BRING ON AN APOCALYPSE.
I'M CALLING THE PROFESSOR.

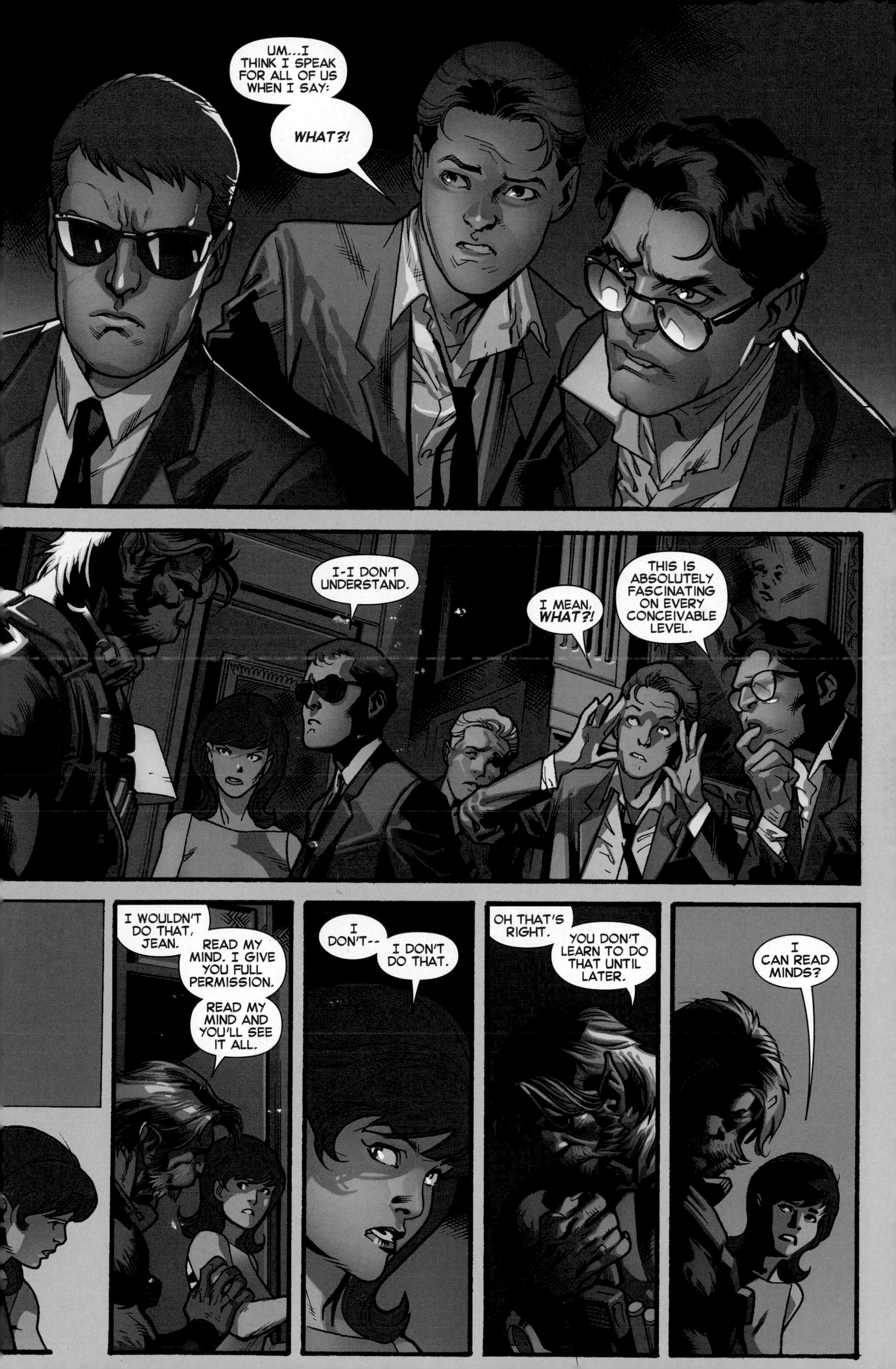
UM...I THINK I SPEAK FOR ALL OF US WHEN I SAY:
WHAT?!
I-I DON'T UNDERSTAND.
I MEAN, WHAT?!
THIS IS ABSOLUTELY FASCINATING ON EVERY CONCEIVABLE LEVEL.
I WOULDN'T DO THAT, JEAN.
READ MY MIND. I GIVE YOU FULL PERMISSION.
READ MY MIND AND YOU'LL SEE IT ALL.
I DON'T--
I DON'T DO THAT.
OH THAT'S RIGHT.
YOU DON'T LEARN TO DO THAT UNTIL LATER.
I CAN READ MINDS?

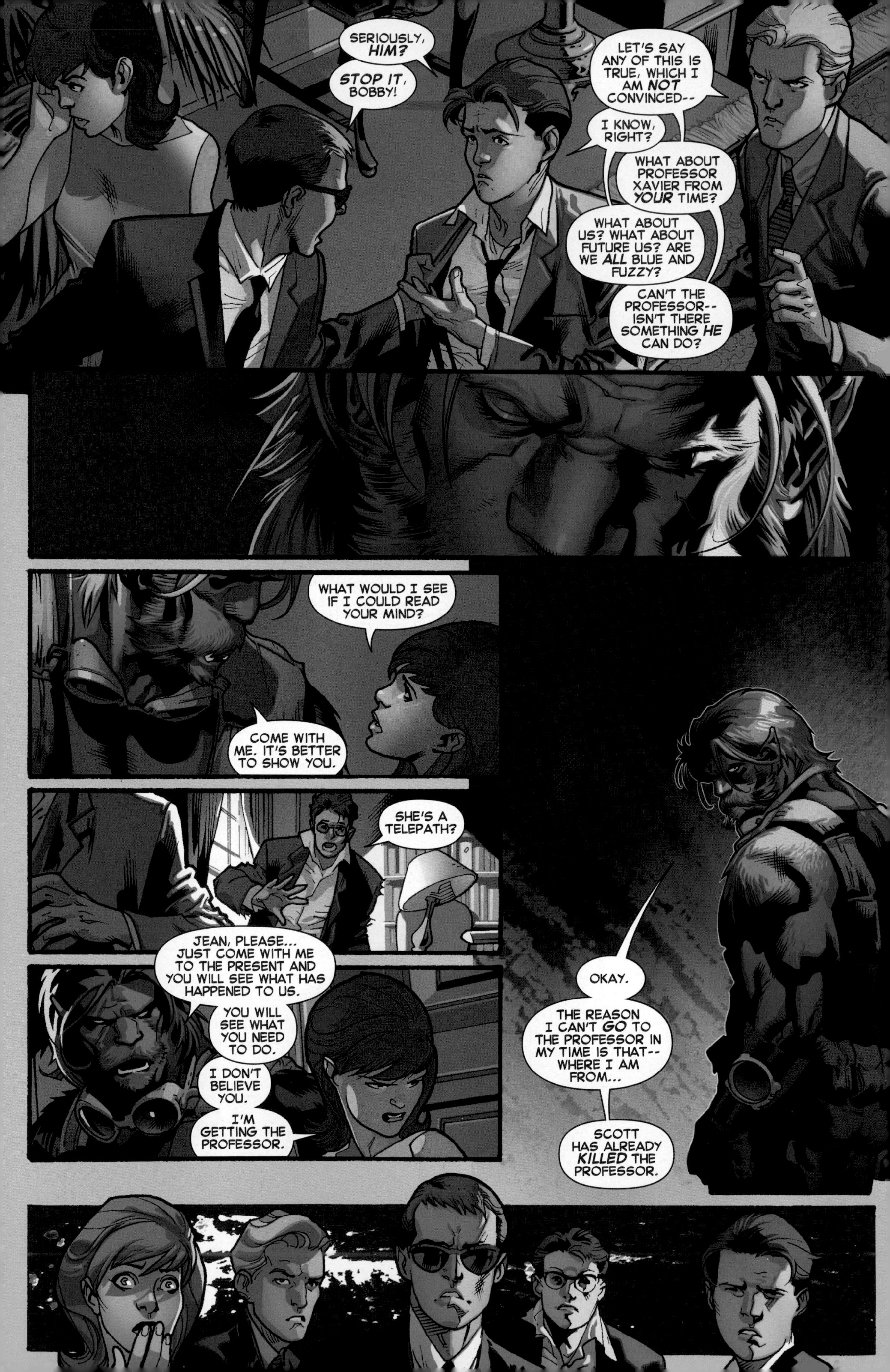
SERIOUSLY, HIM?
STOP IT, BOBBY!
LET'S SAY ANY OF THIS IS TRUE, WHICH I AM NOT CONVINCED--
I KNOW, RIGHT?
WHAT ABOUT PROFESSOR XAVIER FROM YOUR TIME?
WHAT ABOUT US? WHAT ABOUT FUTURE US? ARE WE ALL BLUE AND FUZZY?
CAN'T THE PROFESSOR-- ISN'T THERE SOMETHING HE CAN DO?
WHAT WOULD I SEE IF I COULD READ YOUR MIND?
COME WITH ME. IT'S BETTER TO SHOW YOU.
SHE'S A TELEPATH?
JEAN, PLEASE... JUST COME WITH ME TO THE PRESENT AND YOU WILL SEE WHAT HAS HAPPENED TO US.
YOU WILL SEE WHAT YOU NEED TO DO.
I DON'T BELIEVE YOU.
I'M GETTING THE PROFESSOR.
OKAY.
THE REASON I CAN'T GO TO THE PROFESSOR IN MY TIME IS THAT-- WHERE I AM FROM...
SCOTT HAS ALREADY KILLED THE PROFESSOR.

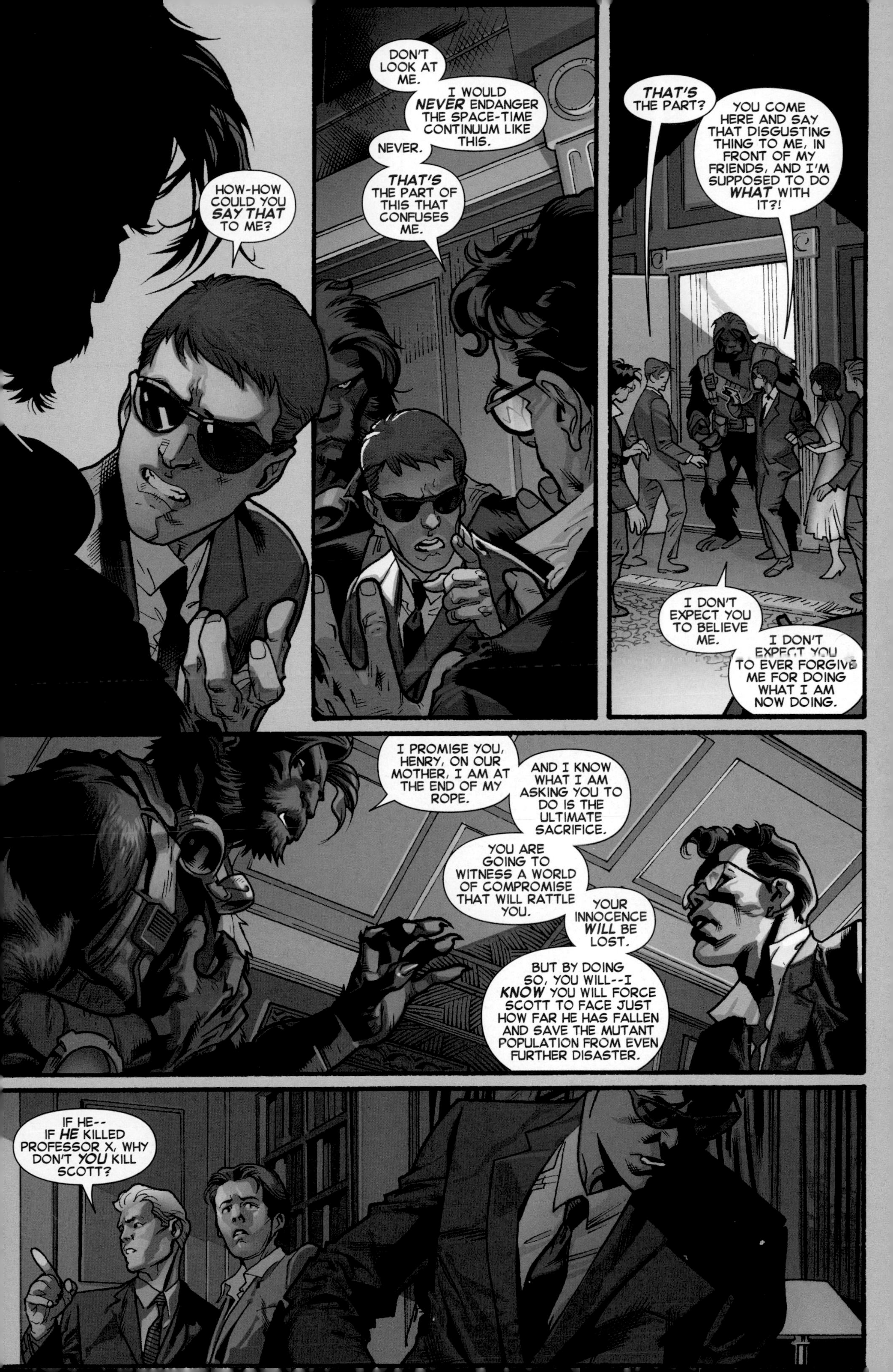
HOW-HOW COULD YOU SAY THAT TO ME?
DON'T LOOK AT ME.
I WOULD NEVER ENDANGER THE SPACE-TIME CONTINUUM LIKE THIS.
NEVER.
THAT'S THE PART OF THIS THAT CONFUSES ME.
THAT'S THE PART?
YOU COME HERE AND SAY THAT DISGUSTING THING TO ME, IN FRONT OF MY FRIENDS, AND I'M SUPPOSED TO DO WHAT WITH IT?!
I DON'T EXPECT YOU TO BELIEVE ME.
I DON'T EXPECT YOU TO EVER FORGIVE ME FOR DOING WHAT I AM NOW DOING.
I PROMISE YOU, HENRY, ON OUR MOTHER, I AM AT THE END OF MY ROPE.
AND I KNOW WHAT I AM ASKING YOU TO DO IS THE ULTIMATE SACRIFICE.
YOU ARE GOING TO WITNESS A WORLD OF COMPROMISE THAT WILL RATTLE YOU.
YOUR INNOCENCE WILL BE LOST.
BUT BY DOING SO, YOU WILL--I KNOW YOU WILL FORCE SCOTT TO FACE JUST HOW FAR HE HAS FALLEN AND SAVE THE MUTANT POPULATION FROM EVEN FURTHER DISASTER.
IF HE-- IF HE KILLED PROFESSOR X, WHY DON'T YOU KILL SCOTT?

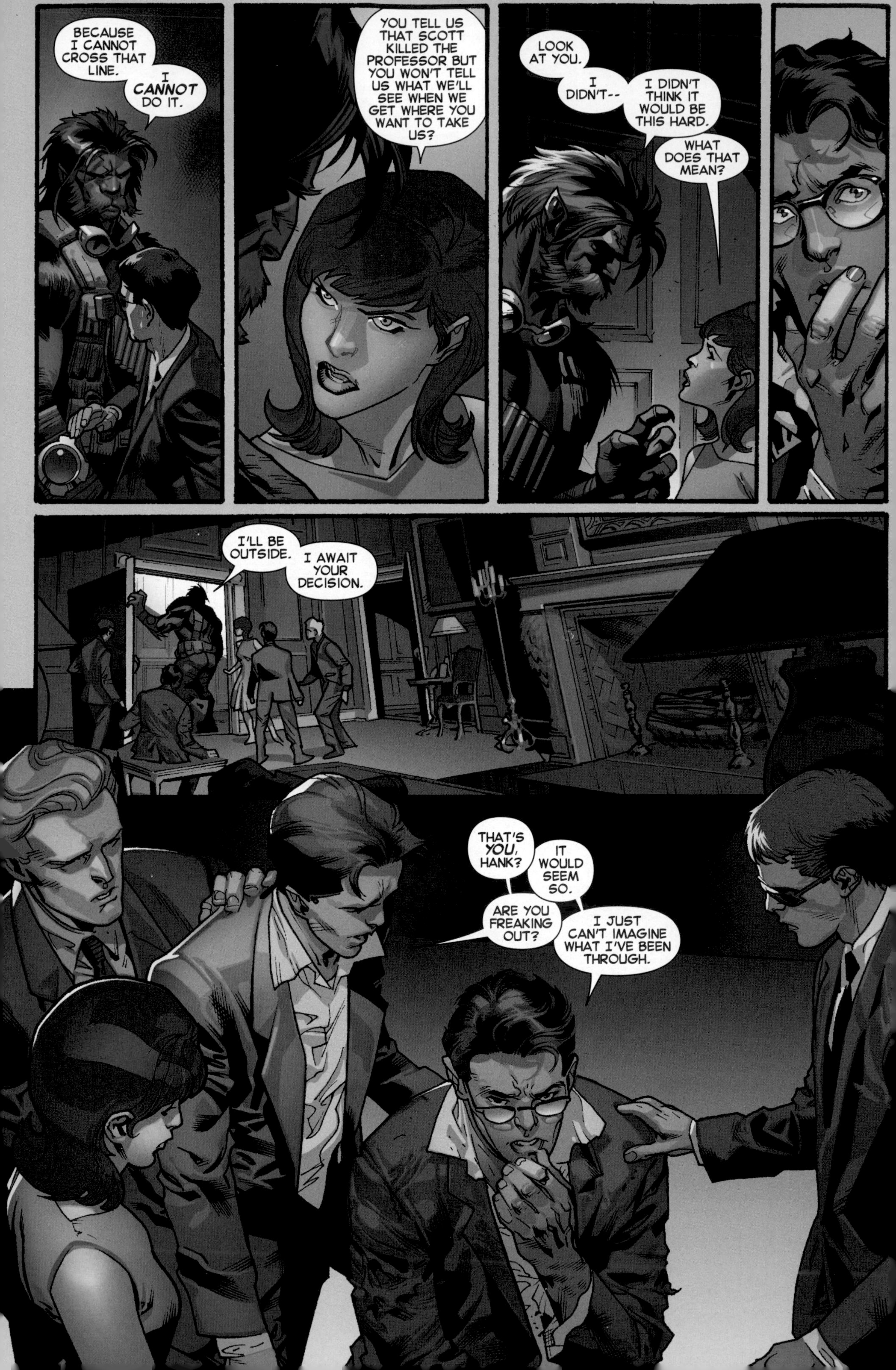
BECAUSE I CANNOT CROSS THAT LINE.
I CANNOT DO IT.
YOU TELL US THAT SCOTT KILLED THE PROFESSOR BUT YOU WON'T TELL US WHAT WE'LL SEE WHEN WE GET WHERE YOU WANT TO TAKE US?
LOOK AT YOU.
I DIDN'T--
I DIDN'T THINK IT WOULD BE THIS HARD.
WHAT DOES THAT MEAN?
I'LL BE OUTSIDE.
I AWAIT YOUR DECISION.
THAT'S YOU, HANK?
IT WOULD SEEM SO.
ARE YOU FREAKING OUT?
I JUST CAN'T IMAGINE WHAT I'VE BEEN THROUGH.

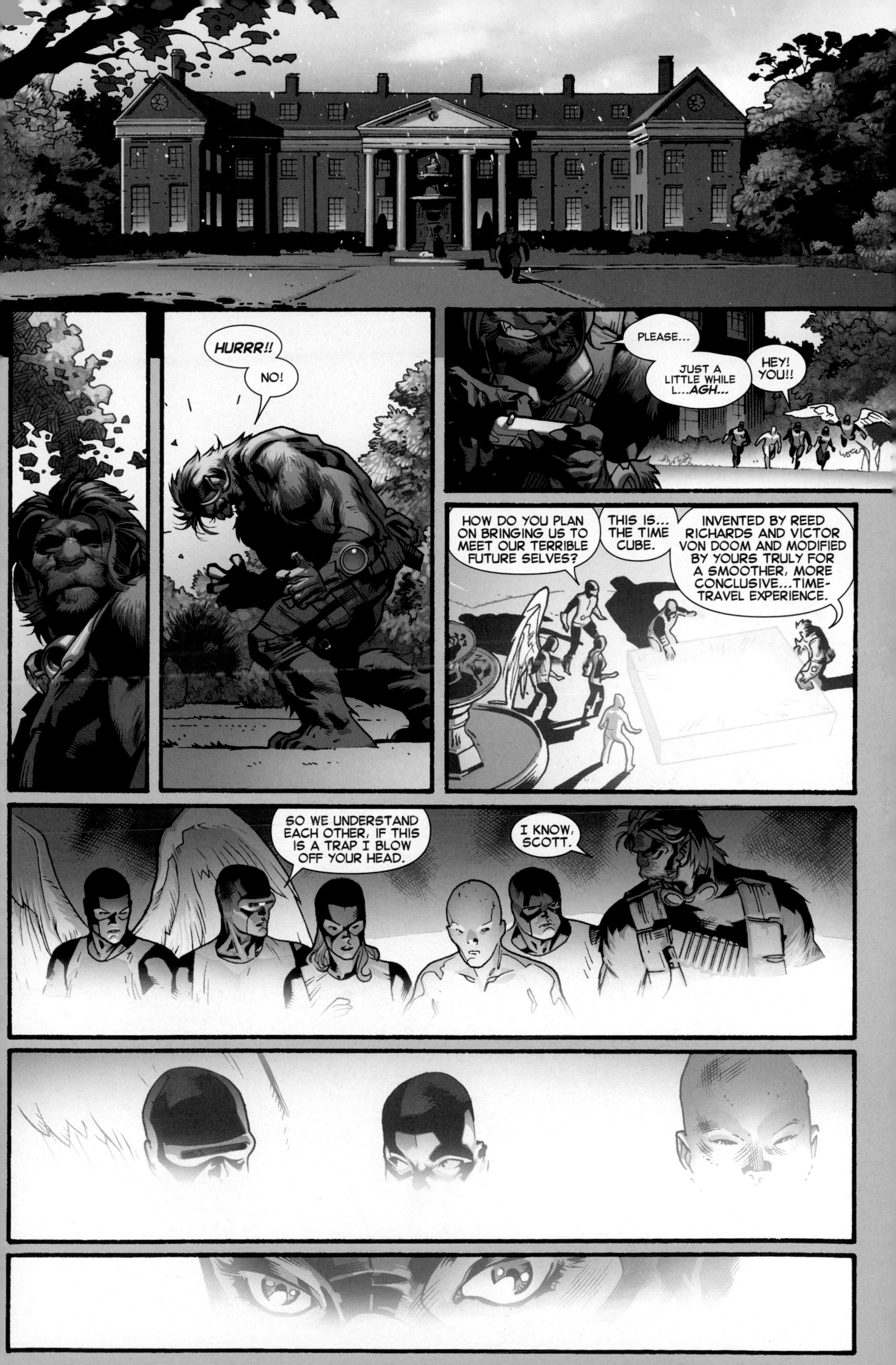
HURRR!!
NO!
PLEASE...
JUST A LITTLE WHILE L...AGH...
HEY! YOU!!
HOW DO YOU PLAN ON BRINGING US TO MEET OUR TERRIBLE FUTURE SELVES?
THIS IS... THE TIME CUBE.
INVENTED BY REED RICHARDS AND VICTOR VON DOOM AND MODIFIED BY YOURS TRULY FOR A SMOOTHER, MORE CONCLUSIVE...TIME-TRAVEL EXPERIENCE.
SO WE UNDERSTAND EACH OTHER, IF THIS IS A TRAP I BLOW OFF YOUR HEAD.
I KNOW, SCOTT.

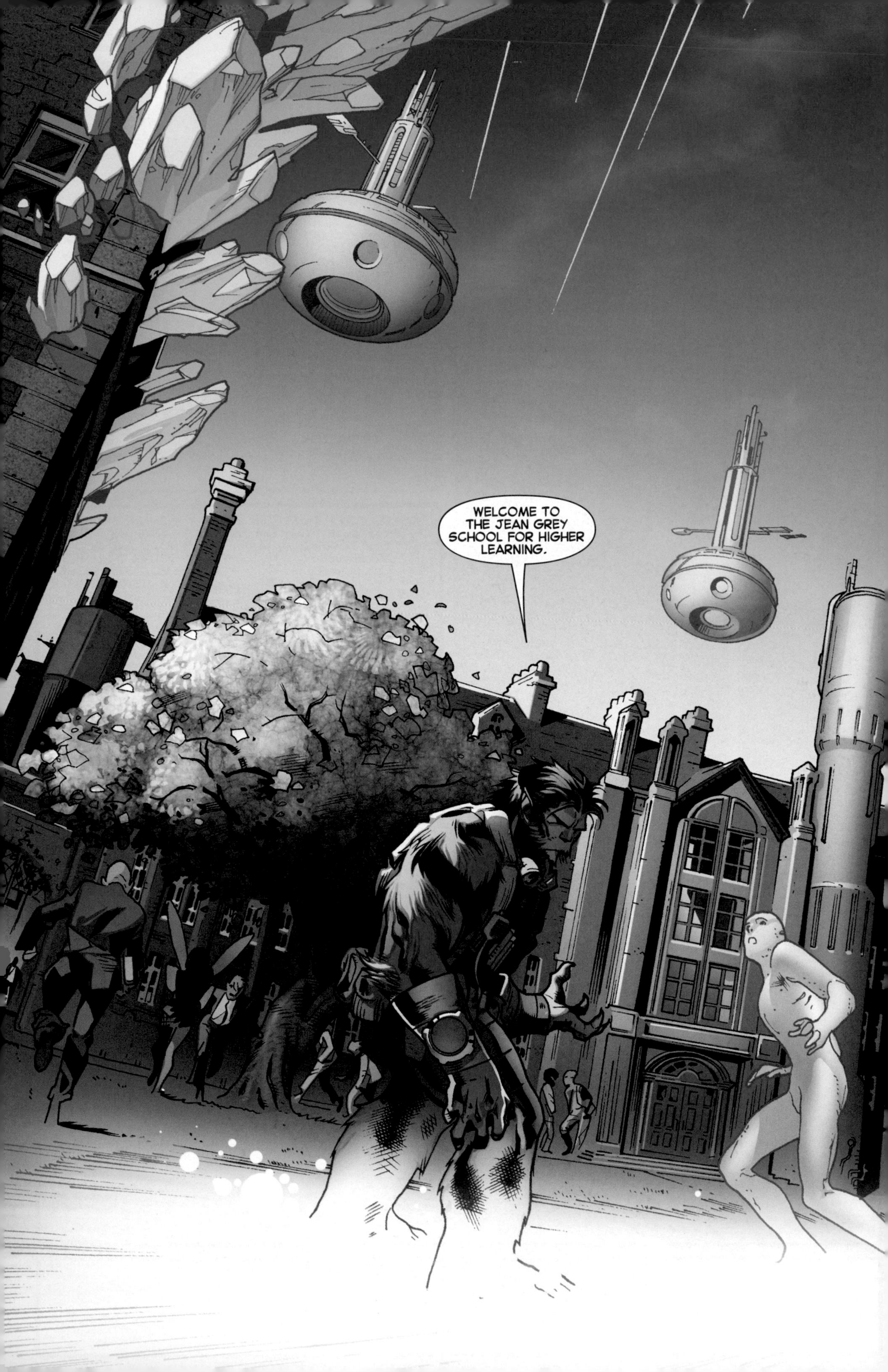
WELCOME TO THE JEAN GREY SCHOOL FOR HIGHER LEARNING.

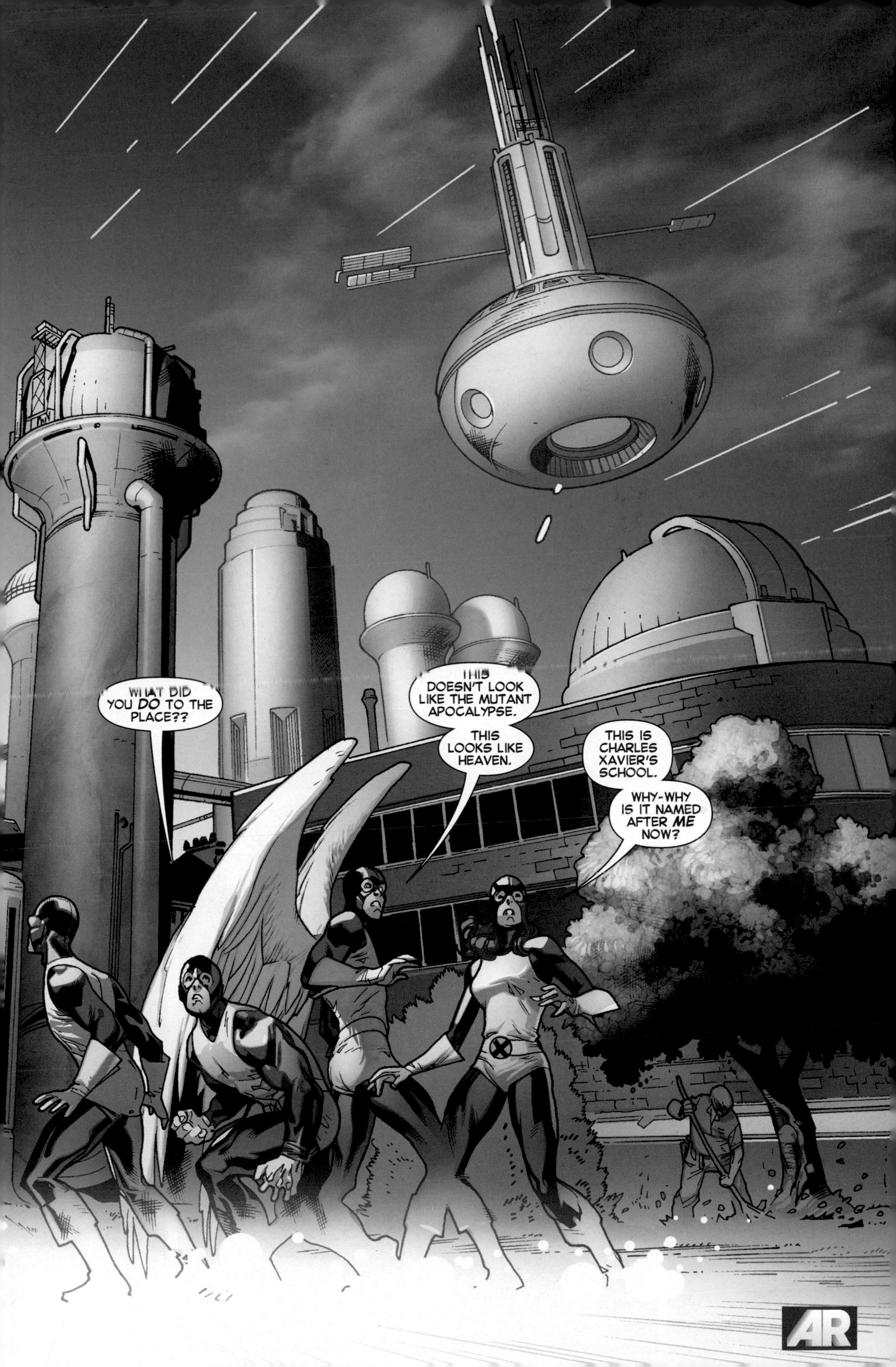
WHAT DID YOU DO TO THE PLACE??
THIS DOESN'T LOOK LIKE THE MUTANT APOCALYPSE.
THIS LOOKS LIKE HEAVEN.
THIS IS CHARLES XAVIER'S SCHOOL.
WHY-WHY IS IT NAMED AFTER ME NOW?
AR

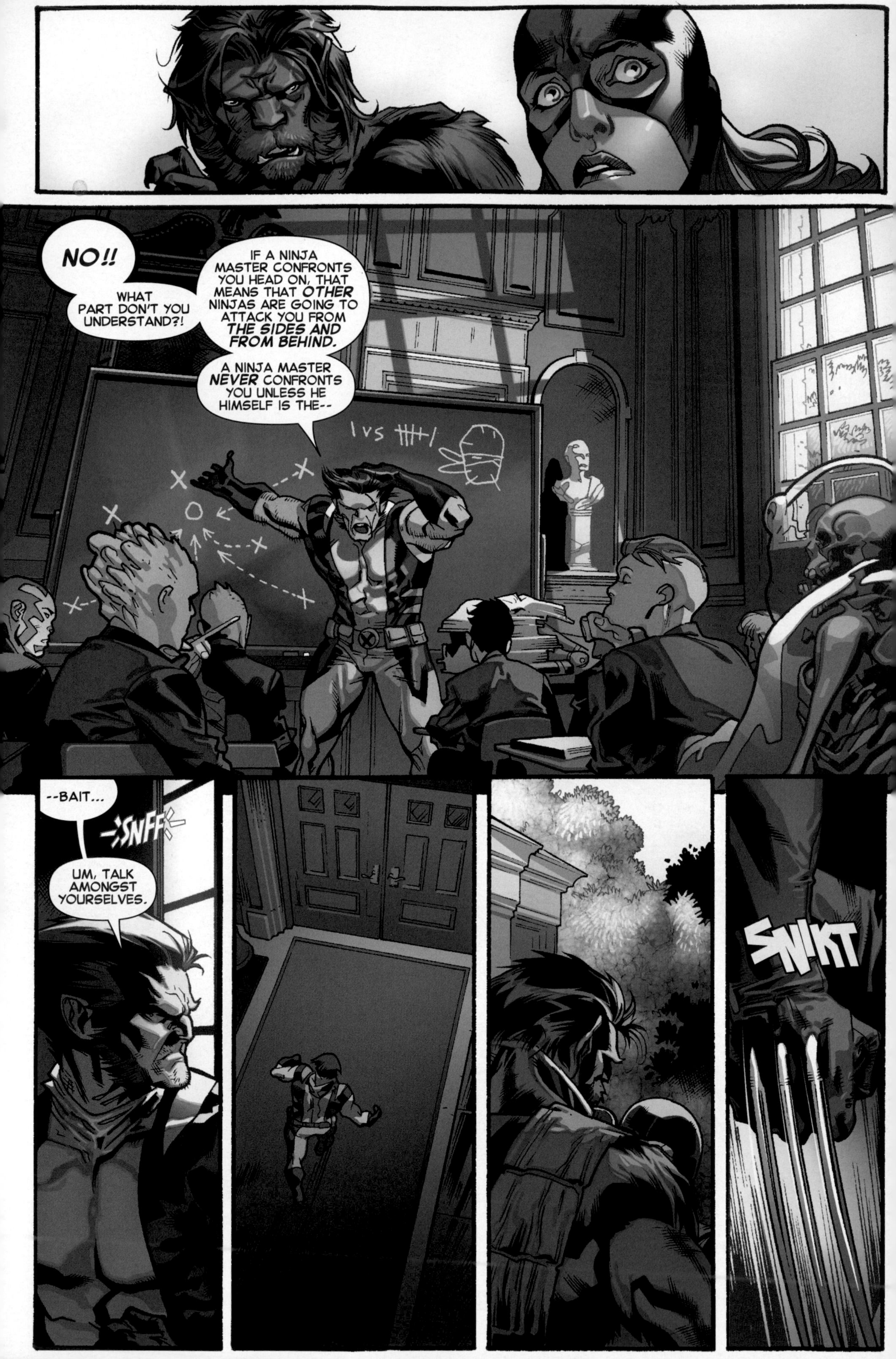
NO!!
WHAT PART DON'T YOU UNDERSTAND?!
IF A NINJA MASTER CONFRONTS YOU HEAD ON, THAT MEANS THAT OTHER NINJAS ARE GOING TO ATTACK YOU FROM THE SIDES AND FROM BEHIND.
A NINJA MASTER NEVER CONFRONTS YOU UNLESS HE HIMSELF IS THE--
1 VS 6
--BAIT...
SNFF
UM, TALK AMONGST YOURSELVES.
SNIKT

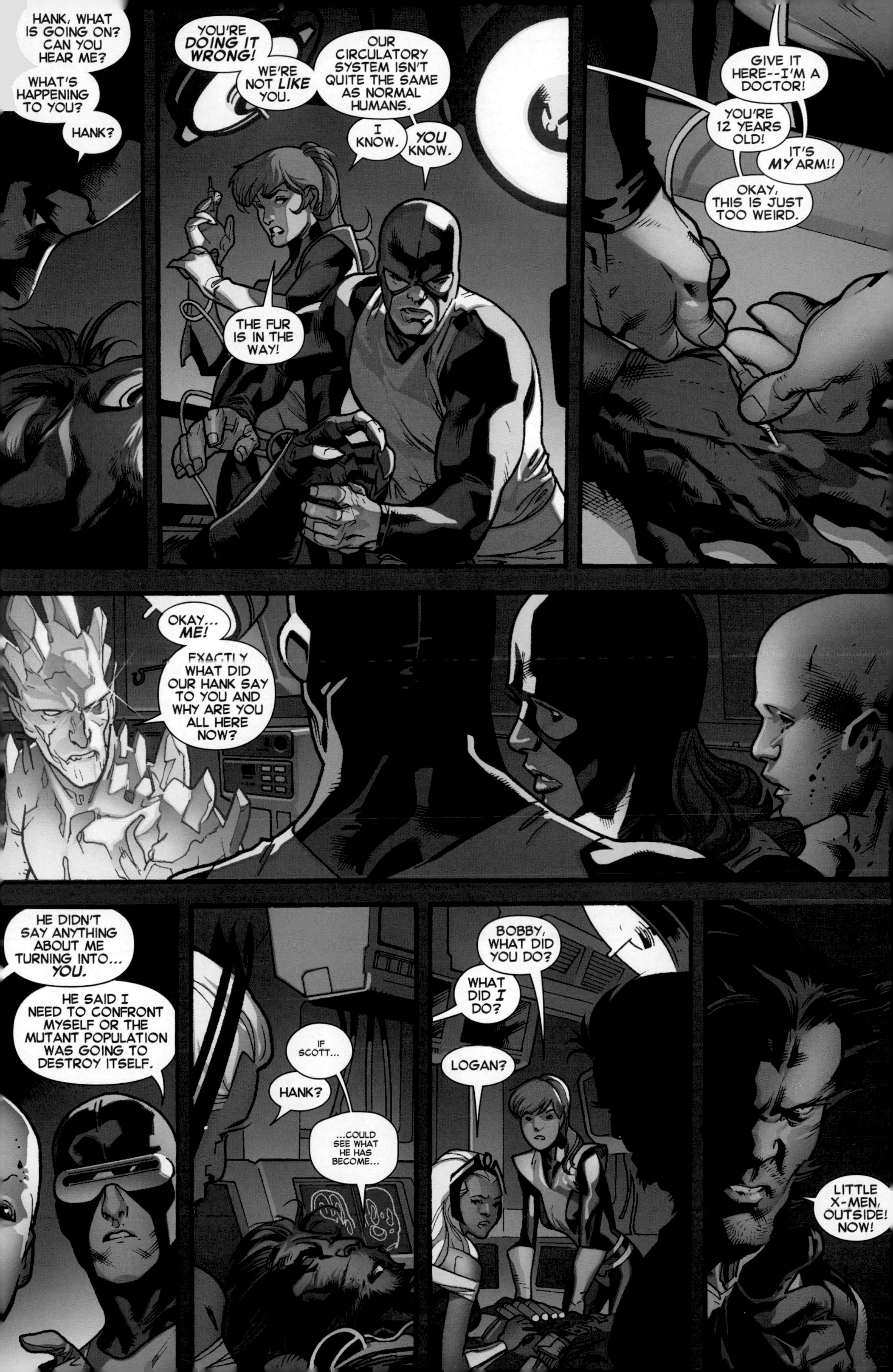
HANK, WHAT IS GOING ON? CAN YOU HEAR ME?
WHAT'S HAPPENING TO YOU?
HANK?
YOU'RE DOING IT WRONG!
WE'RE NOT LIKE YOU.
OUR CIRCULATORY SYSTEM ISN'T QUITE THE SAME AS NORMAL HUMANS.
I KNOW.
YOU KNOW.
THE FUR IS IN THE WAY!
GIVE IT HERE--I'M A DOCTOR!
YOU'RE 12 YEARS OLD!
IT'S MY ARM!!
OKAY, THIS IS JUST TOO WEIRD.
OKAY... ME!
EXACTLY WHAT DID OUR HANK SAY TO YOU AND WHY ARE YOU ALL HERE NOW?
HE DIDN'T SAY ANYTHING ABOUT ME TURNING INTO... YOU.
HE SAID I NEED TO CONFRONT MYSELF OR THE MUTANT POPULATION WAS GOING TO DESTROY ITSELF.
IF SCOTT...
HANK?
...COULD SEE WHAT HE HAS BECOME...
BOBBY, WHAT DID YOU DO?
WHAT DID I DO?
LOGAN?
LITTLE X-MEN, OUTSIDE! NOW!

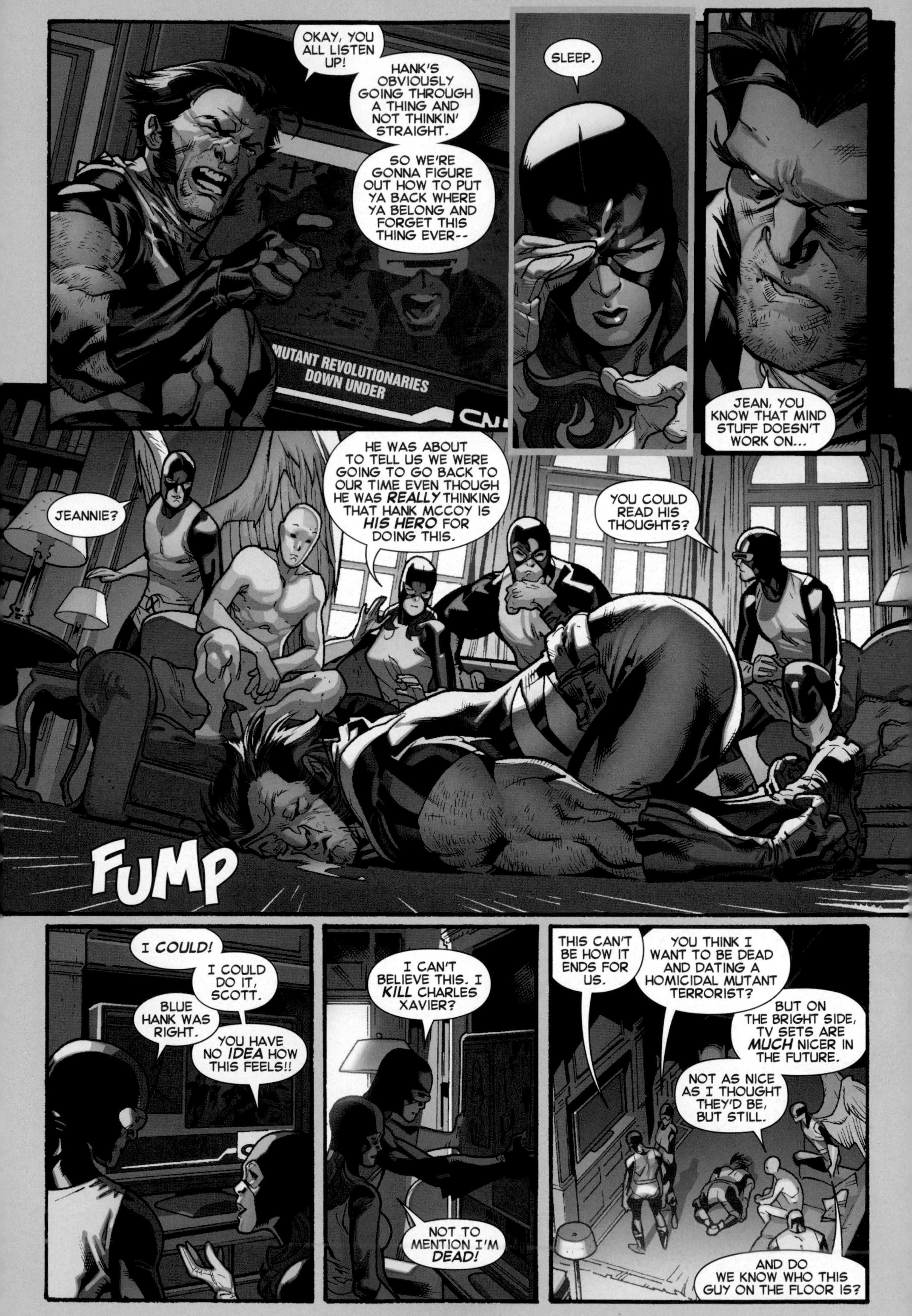
OKAY, YOU ALL LISTEN UP!
HANK'S OBVIOUSLY GOING THROUGH A THING AND NOT THINKIN' STRAIGHT.
SO WE'RE GONNA FIGURE OUT HOW TO PUT YA BACK WHERE YA BELONG AND FORGET THIS THING EVER--
MUTANT REVOLUTIONARIES DOWN UNDER
SLEEP.
JEAN, YOU KNOW THAT MIND STUFF DOESN'T WORK ON...
JEANNIE?
HE WAS ABOUT TO TELL US WE WERE GOING TO GO BACK TO OUR TIME EVEN THOUGH HE WAS REALLY THINKING THAT HANK MCCOY IS HIS HERO FOR DOING THIS.
YOU COULD READ HIS THOUGHTS?
FUMP
I COULD!
I COULD DO IT, SCOTT.
BLUE HANK WAS RIGHT.
YOU HAVE NO IDEA HOW THIS FEELS!!
I CAN'T BELIEVE THIS. I KILL CHARLES XAVIER?
NOT TO MENTION I'M DEAD!
THIS CAN'T BE HOW IT ENDS FOR US.
YOU THINK I WANT TO BE DEAD AND DATING A HOMICIDAL MUTANT TERRORIST?
BUT ON THE BRIGHT SIDE, TV SETS ARE MUCH NICER IN THE FUTURE.
NOT AS NICE AS I THOUGHT THEY'D BE, BUT STILL.
AND DO WE KNOW WHO THIS GUY ON THE FLOOR IS?

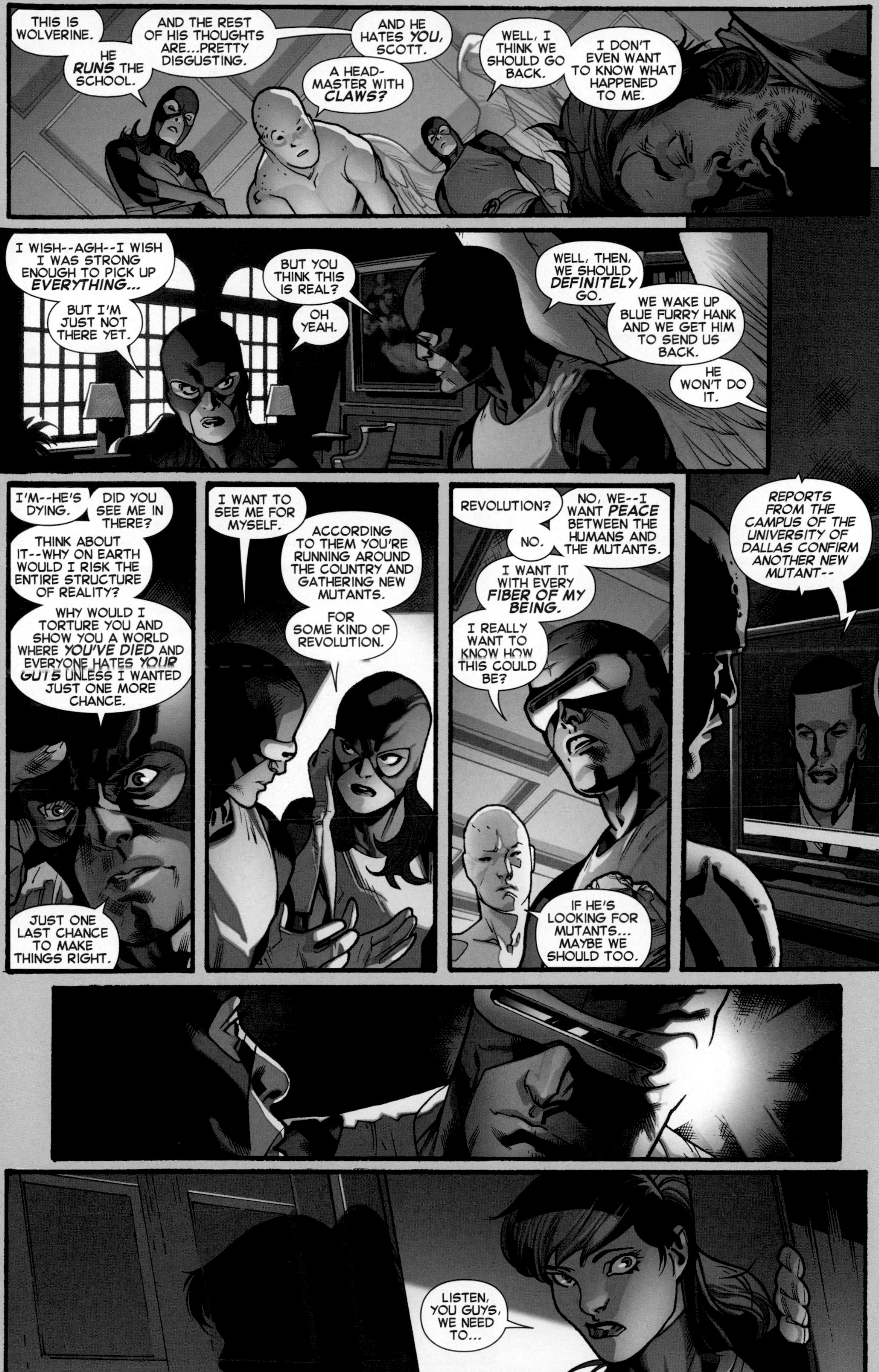
THIS IS WOLVERINE.
HE RUNS THE SCHOOL.
AND THE REST OF HIS THOUGHTS ARE...PRETTY DISGUSTING.
AND HE HATES YOU, SCOTT.
A HEAD-MASTER WITH CLAWS?
WELL, I THINK WE SHOULD GO BACK.
I DON'T EVEN WANT TO KNOW WHAT HAPPENED TO ME.
I WISH--AGH--I WISH I WAS STRONG ENOUGH TO PICK UP EVERYTHING...
BUT I'M JUST NOT THERE YET.
BUT YOU THINK THIS IS REAL?
OH YEAH.
WELL, THEN, WE SHOULD DEFINITELY GO.
WE WAKE UP BLUE FURRY HANK AND WE GET HIM TO SEND US BACK.
HE WON'T DO IT.
I'M--HE'S DYING.
DID YOU SEE ME IN THERE?
THINK ABOUT IT--WHY ON EARTH WOULD I RISK THE ENTIRE STRUCTURE OF REALITY?
WHY WOULD I TORTURE YOU AND SHOW YOU A WORLD WHERE YOU'VE DIED AND EVERYONE HATES YOUR GUTS UNLESS I WANTED JUST ONE MORE CHANCE.
JUST ONE LAST CHANCE TO MAKE THINGS RIGHT.
I WANT TO SEE ME FOR MYSELF.
ACCORDING TO THEM YOU'RE RUNNING AROUND THE COUNTRY AND GATHERING NEW MUTANTS.
FOR SOME KIND OF REVOLUTION.
REVOLUTION?
NO.
NO, WE--I WANT PEACE BETWEEN THE HUMANS AND THE MUTANTS.
I WANT IT WITH EVERY FIBER OF MY BEING.
I REALLY WANT TO KNOW HOW THIS COULD BE?
IF HE'S LOOKING FOR MUTANTS... MAYBE WE SHOULD TOO.
REPORTS FROM THE CAMPUS OF THE UNIVERSITY OF DALLAS CONFIRM ANOTHER NEW MUTANT--
LISTEN, YOU GUYS, WE NEED TO...

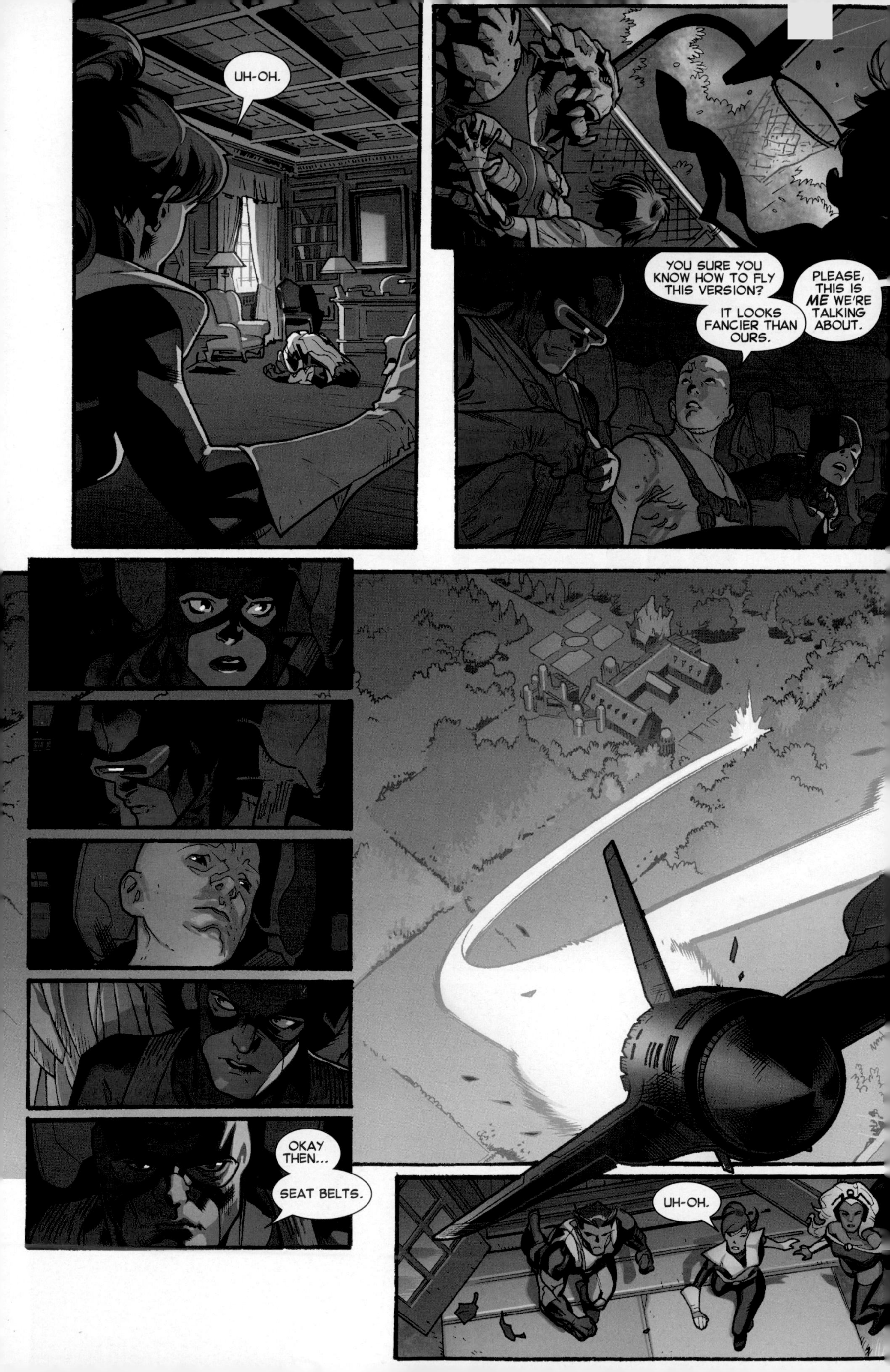
UH-OH.
YOU SURE YOU KNOW HOW TO FLY THIS VERSION?
IT LOOKS FANCIER THAN OURS.
PLEASE, THIS IS *ME* WE'RE TALKING ABOUT.
OKAY THEN...
SEAT BELTS.
UH-OH.

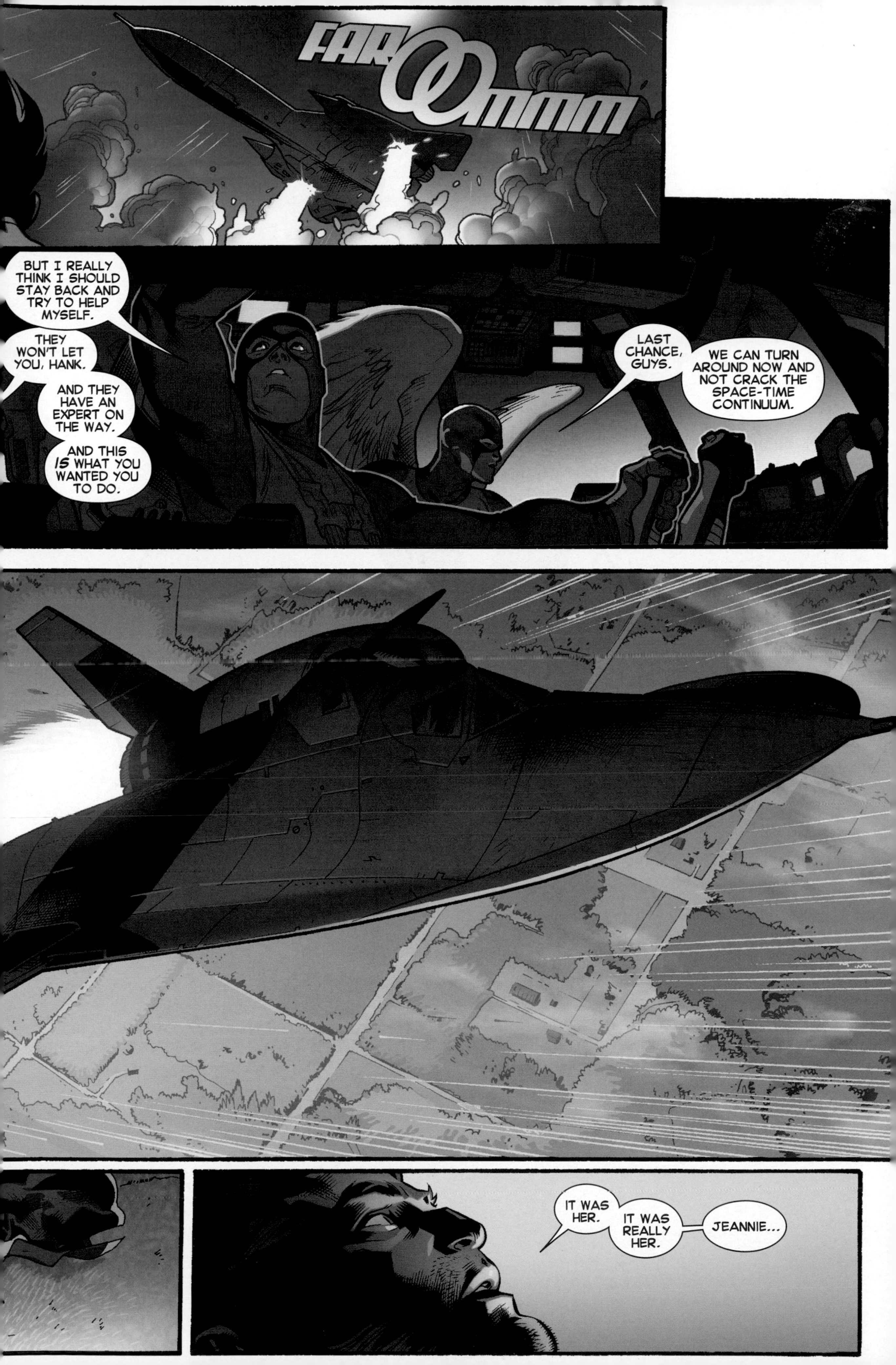
FAROOMMMM
BUT I REALLY THINK I SHOULD STAY BACK AND TRY TO HELP MYSELF.
THEY WON'T LET YOU, HANK.
AND THEY HAVE AN EXPERT ON THE WAY.
AND THIS *IS* WHAT YOU WANTED YOU TO DO.
LAST CHANCE, GUYS.
WE CAN TURN AROUND NOW AND NOT CRACK THE SPACE-TIME CONTINUUM.
IT WAS HER.
IT WAS REALLY HER.
JEANNIE...

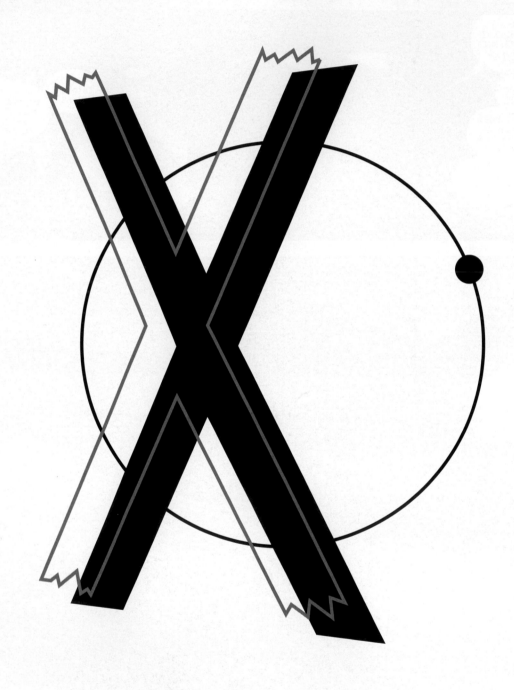

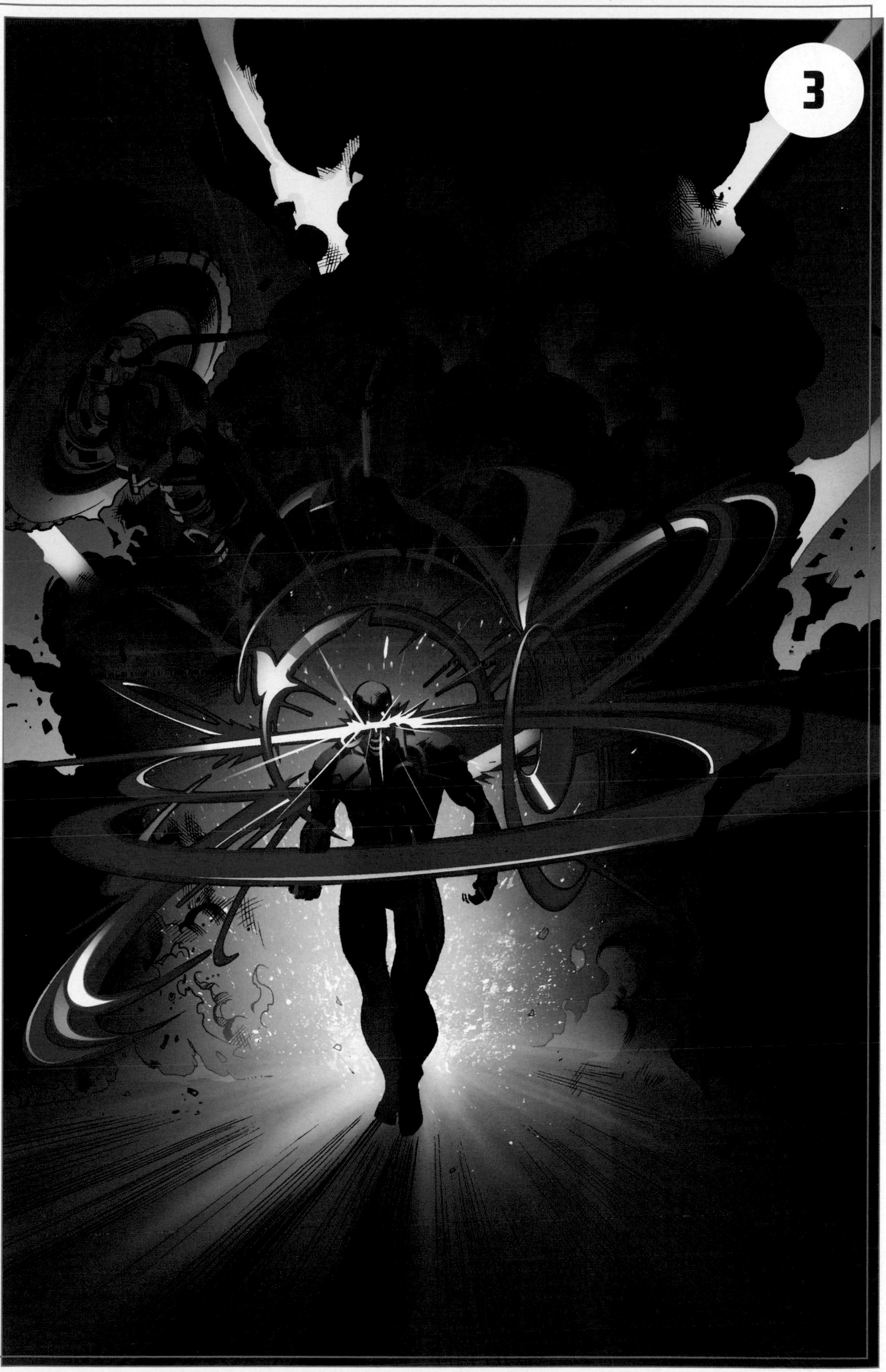
3

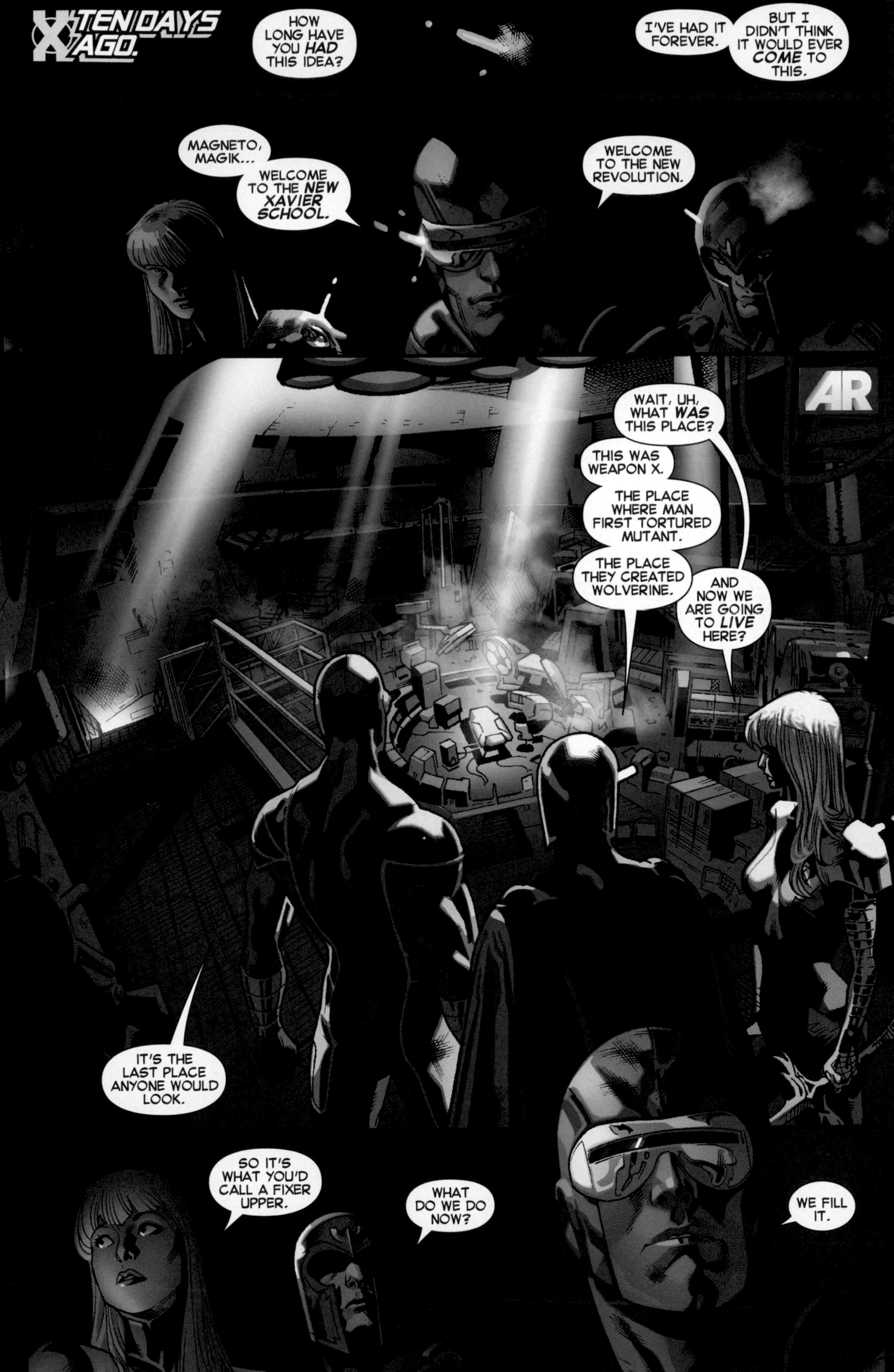
TEN DAYS AGO.
HOW LONG HAVE YOU HAD THIS IDEA?
I'VE HAD IT FOREVER.
BUT I DIDN'T THINK IT WOULD EVER COME TO THIS.
MAGNETO, MAGIK...
WELCOME TO THE NEW XAVIER SCHOOL.
WELCOME TO THE NEW REVOLUTION.
AR
WAIT, UH, WHAT WAS THIS PLACE?
THIS WAS WEAPON X.
THE PLACE WHERE MAN FIRST TORTURED MUTANT.
THE PLACE THEY CREATED WOLVERINE.
AND NOW WE ARE GOING TO LIVE HERE?
IT'S THE LAST PLACE ANYONE WOULD LOOK.
SO IT'S WHAT YOU'D CALL A FIXER UPPER.
WHAT DO WE DO NOW?
WE FILL IT.

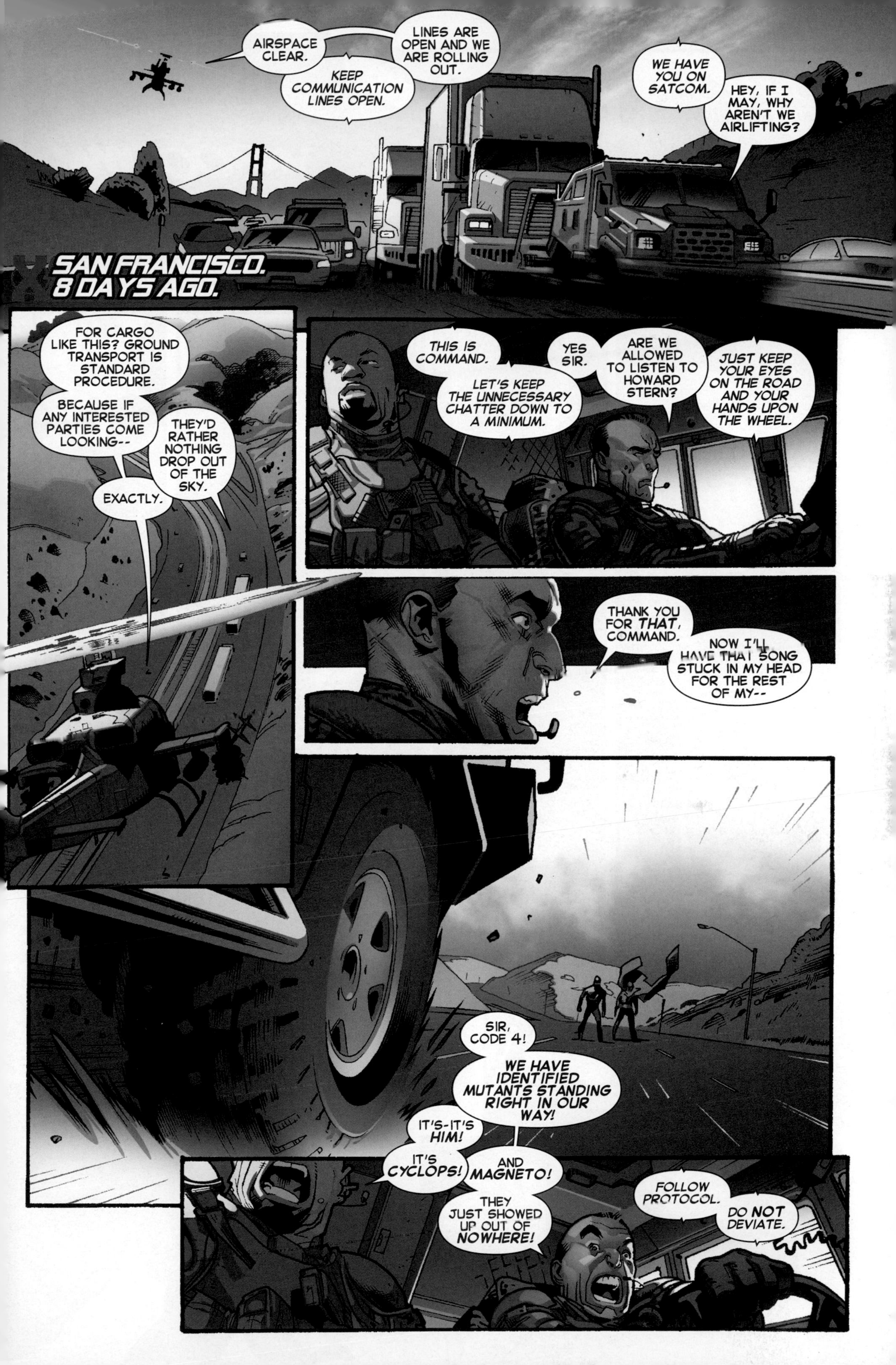
AIRSPACE CLEAR.
LINES ARE OPEN AND WE ARE ROLLING OUT.
KEEP COMMUNICATION LINES OPEN.
WE HAVE YOU ON SATCOM.
HEY, IF I MAY, WHY AREN'T WE AIRLIFTING?
SAN FRANCISCO. 8 DAYS AGO.
FOR CARGO LIKE THIS? GROUND TRANSPORT IS STANDARD PROCEDURE.
BECAUSE IF ANY INTERESTED PARTIES COME LOOKING--
THEY'D RATHER NOTHING DROP OUT OF THE SKY.
EXACTLY.
THIS IS COMMAND.
LET'S KEEP THE UNNECESSARY CHATTER DOWN TO A MINIMUM.
YES SIR.
ARE WE ALLOWED TO LISTEN TO HOWARD STERN?
JUST KEEP YOUR EYES ON THE ROAD AND YOUR HANDS UPON THE WHEEL.
THANK YOU FOR THAT, COMMAND.
NOW I'LL HAVE THAT SONG STUCK IN MY HEAD FOR THE REST OF MY--
SIR, CODE 4!
WE HAVE IDENTIFIED MUTANTS STANDING RIGHT IN OUR WAY!
IT'S-IT'S HIM!
IT'S CYCLOPS!
AND MAGNETO!
THEY JUST SHOWED UP OUT OF NOWHERE!
FOLLOW PROTOCOL.
DO NOT DEVIATE.

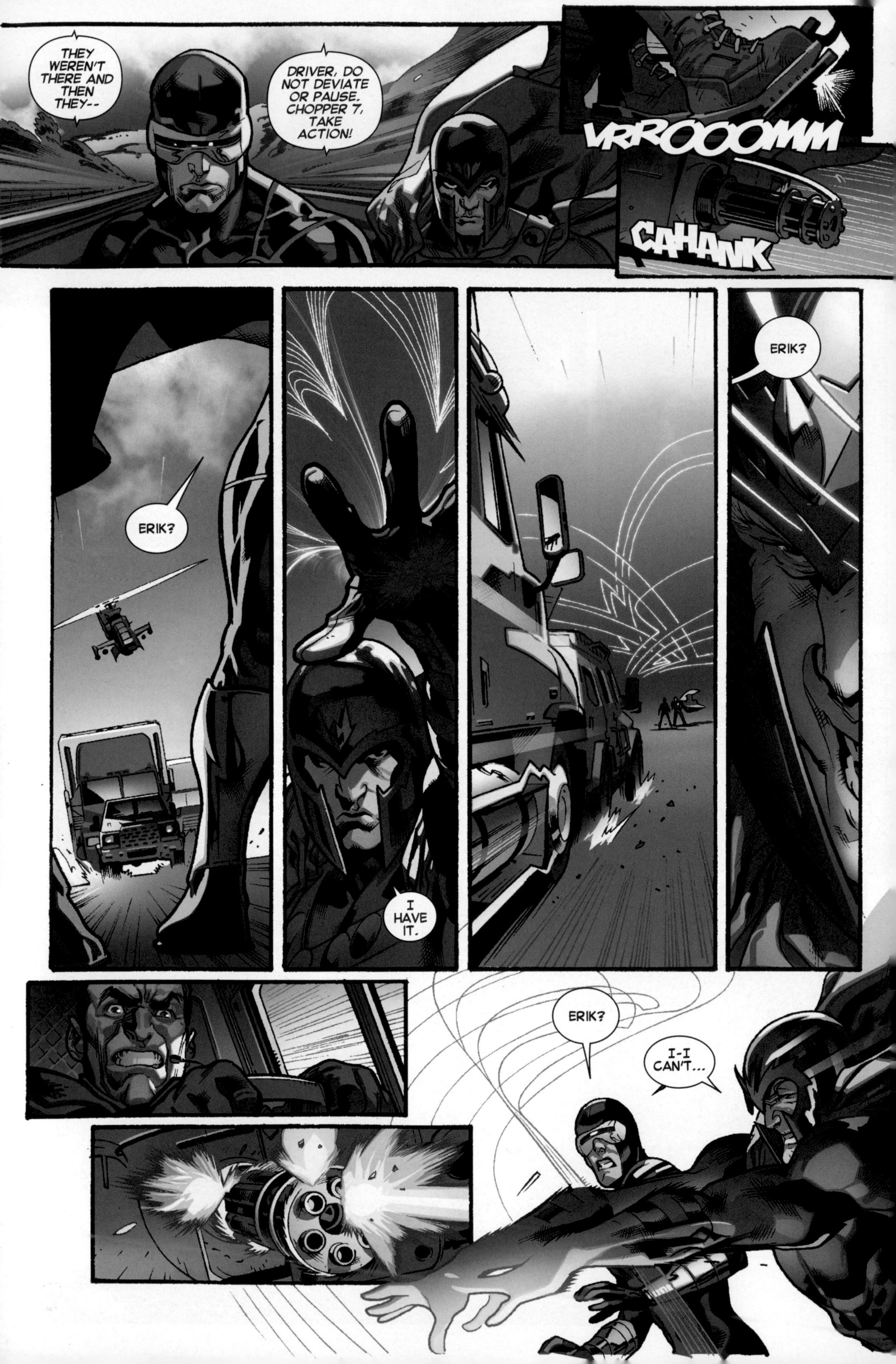
THEY WEREN'T THERE AND THEN THEY--
DRIVER, DO NOT DEVIATE OR PAUSE. CHOPPER 7, TAKE ACTION!
VRROOOMM
CAHANK
ERIK?
I HAVE IT.
ERIK?
ERIK?
I-I CAN'T...

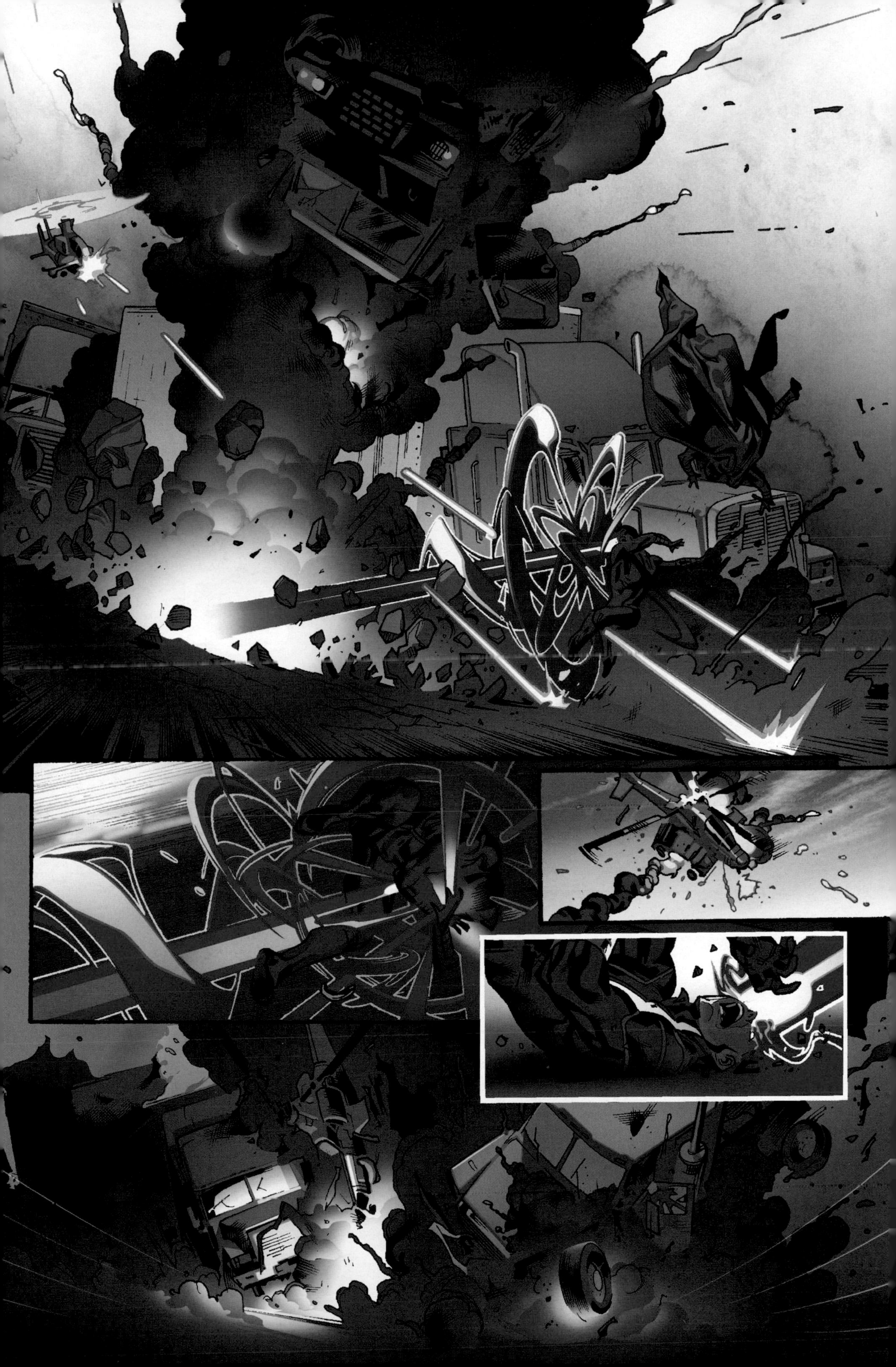

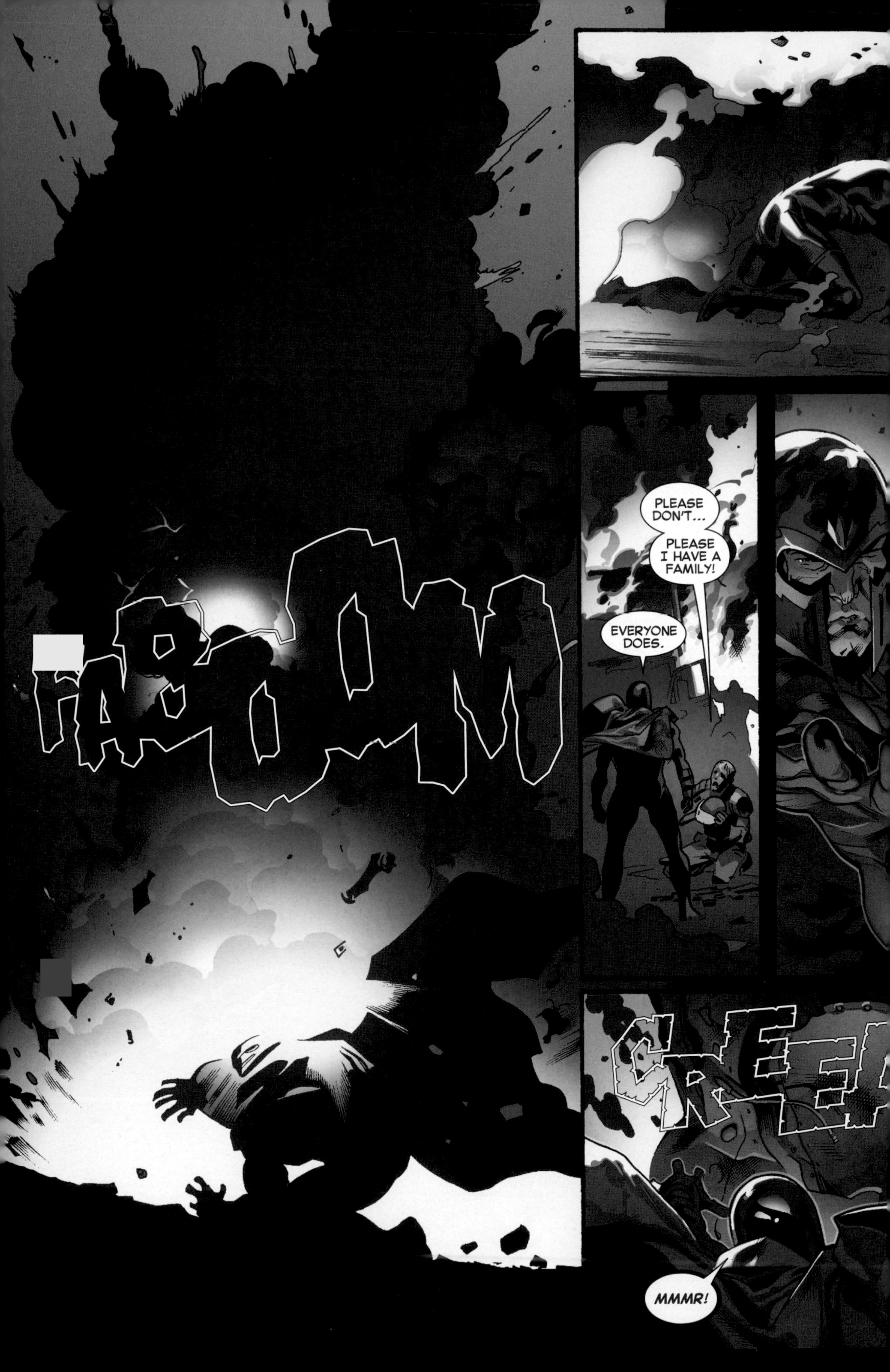
PLEASE DON'T...
PLEASE I HAVE A FAMILY!
EVERYONE DOES.
MMMR!

OH NO...

OH NO...

WHAT DID YOU DO?

WHAT DID YOU DO?!

OH GOD!

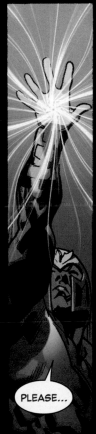

PLEASE...

WHAT'S-- WHAT'S HAPPENING?

CLANG

ACCK

MUTIE!

NOT ONE MOVE!

NOT ONE MUSCLE!

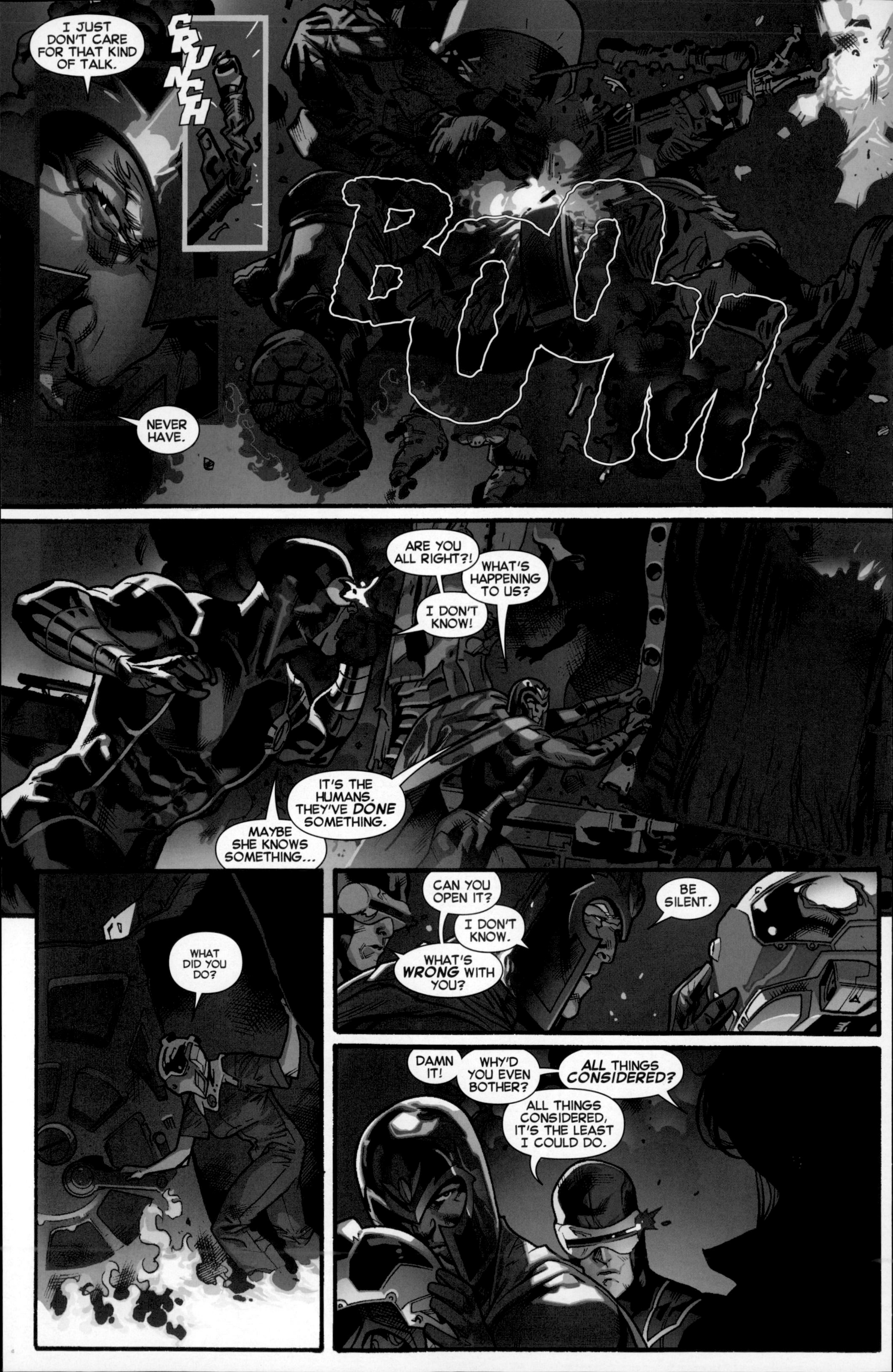
I JUST DON'T CARE FOR THAT KIND OF TALK.
CRUNCH
NEVER HAVE.
BOOM
ARE YOU ALL RIGHT?!
I DON'T KNOW!
WHAT'S HAPPENING TO US?
IT'S THE HUMANS. THEY'VE DONE SOMETHING.
MAYBE SHE KNOWS SOMETHING...
WHAT DID YOU DO?
CAN YOU OPEN IT?
I DON'T KNOW.
WHAT'S WRONG WITH YOU?
BE SILENT.
DAMN IT!
WHY'D YOU EVEN BOTHER?
ALL THINGS CONSIDERED?
ALL THINGS CONSIDERED, IT'S THE LEAST I COULD DO.

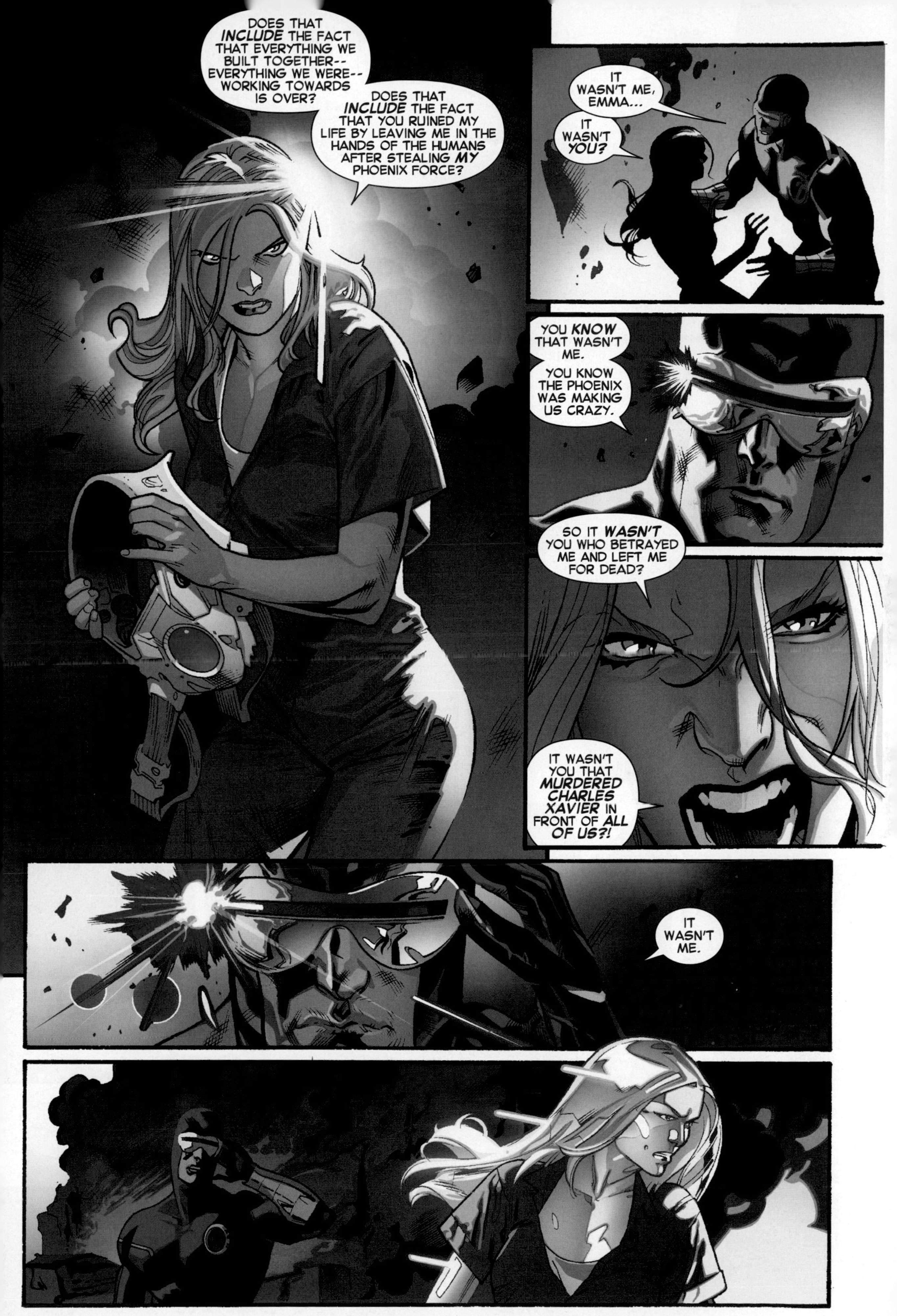
DOES THAT INCLUDE THE FACT THAT EVERYTHING WE BUILT TOGETHER-- EVERYTHING WE WERE-- WORKING TOWARDS IS OVER?
DOES THAT INCLUDE THE FACT THAT YOU RUINED MY LIFE BY LEAVING ME IN THE HANDS OF THE HUMANS AFTER STEALING MY PHOENIX FORCE?
IT WASN'T ME, EMMA...
IT WASN'T YOU?
YOU KNOW THAT WASN'T ME.
YOU KNOW THE PHOENIX WAS MAKING US CRAZY.
SO IT WASN'T YOU WHO BETRAYED ME AND LEFT ME FOR DEAD?
IT WASN'T YOU THAT MURDERED CHARLES XAVIER IN FRONT OF ALL OF US?!
IT WASN'T ME.

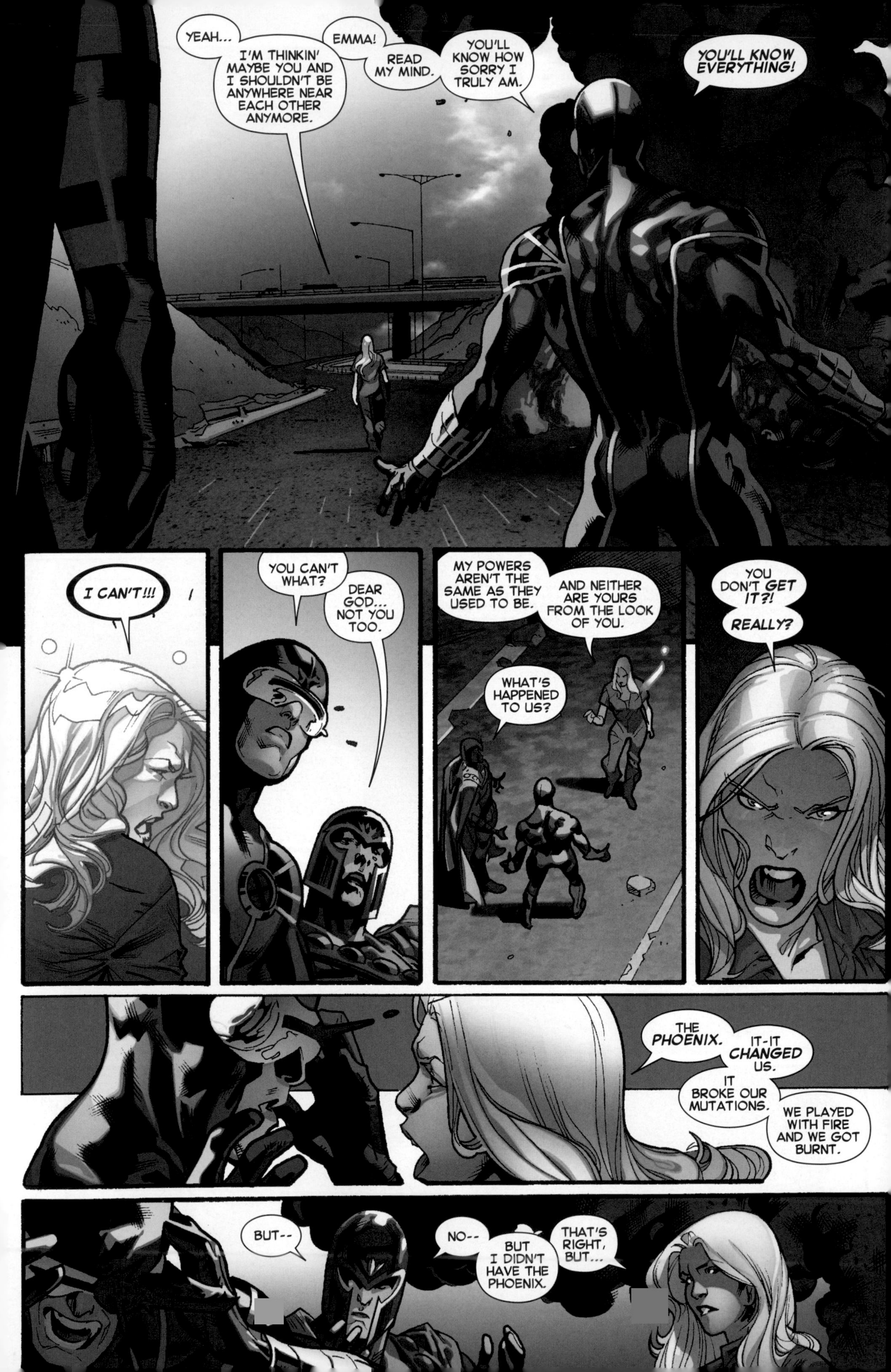
YEAH...
I'M THINKIN' MAYBE YOU AND I SHOULDN'T BE ANYWHERE NEAR EACH OTHER ANYMORE.
EMMA!
READ MY MIND.
YOU'LL KNOW HOW SORRY I TRULY AM.
YOU'LL KNOW EVERYTHING!
I CAN'T!!!
YOU CAN'T WHAT?
DEAR GOD... NOT YOU TOO.
MY POWERS AREN'T THE SAME AS THEY USED TO BE.
AND NEITHER ARE YOURS FROM THE LOOK OF YOU.
WHAT'S HAPPENED TO US?
YOU DON'T GET IT?!
REALLY?
THE PHOENIX.
IT-IT CHANGED US.
IT BROKE OUR MUTATIONS.
WE PLAYED WITH FIRE AND WE GOT BURNT.
BUT--
NO--
BUT I DIDN'T HAVE THE PHOENIX.
THAT'S RIGHT, BUT...

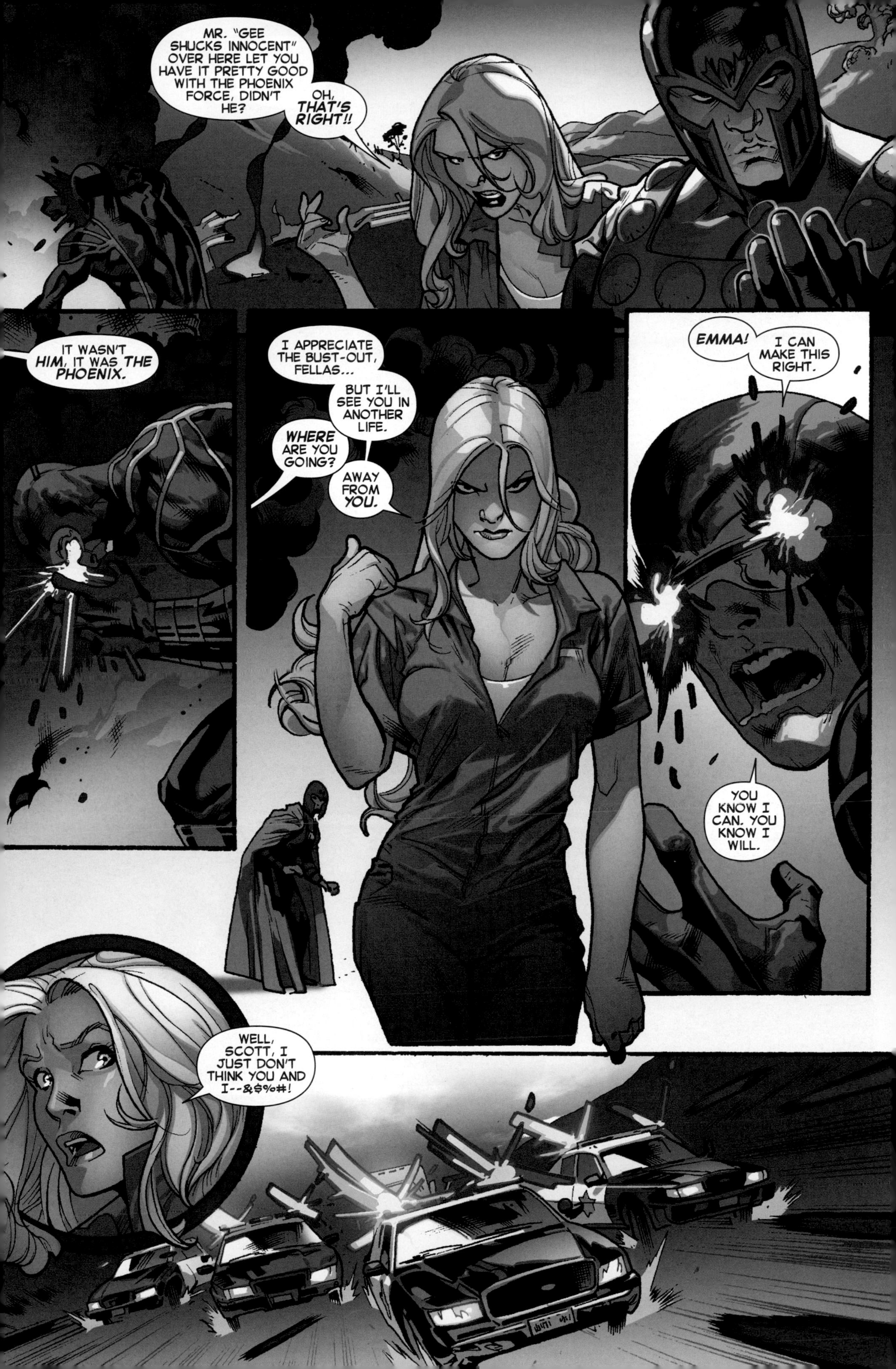
MR. "GEE SHUCKS INNOCENT" OVER HERE LET YOU HAVE IT PRETTY GOOD WITH THE PHOENIX FORCE, DIDN'T HE?
OH, THAT'S RIGHT!!
IT WASN'T HIM, IT WAS THE PHOENIX.
I APPRECIATE THE BUST-OUT, FELLAS...
BUT I'LL SEE YOU IN ANOTHER LIFE.
WHERE ARE YOU GOING?
AWAY FROM YOU.
EMMA!
I CAN MAKE THIS RIGHT.
YOU KNOW I CAN. YOU KNOW I WILL.
WELL, SCOTT, I JUST DON'T THINK YOU AND I--&$%#!

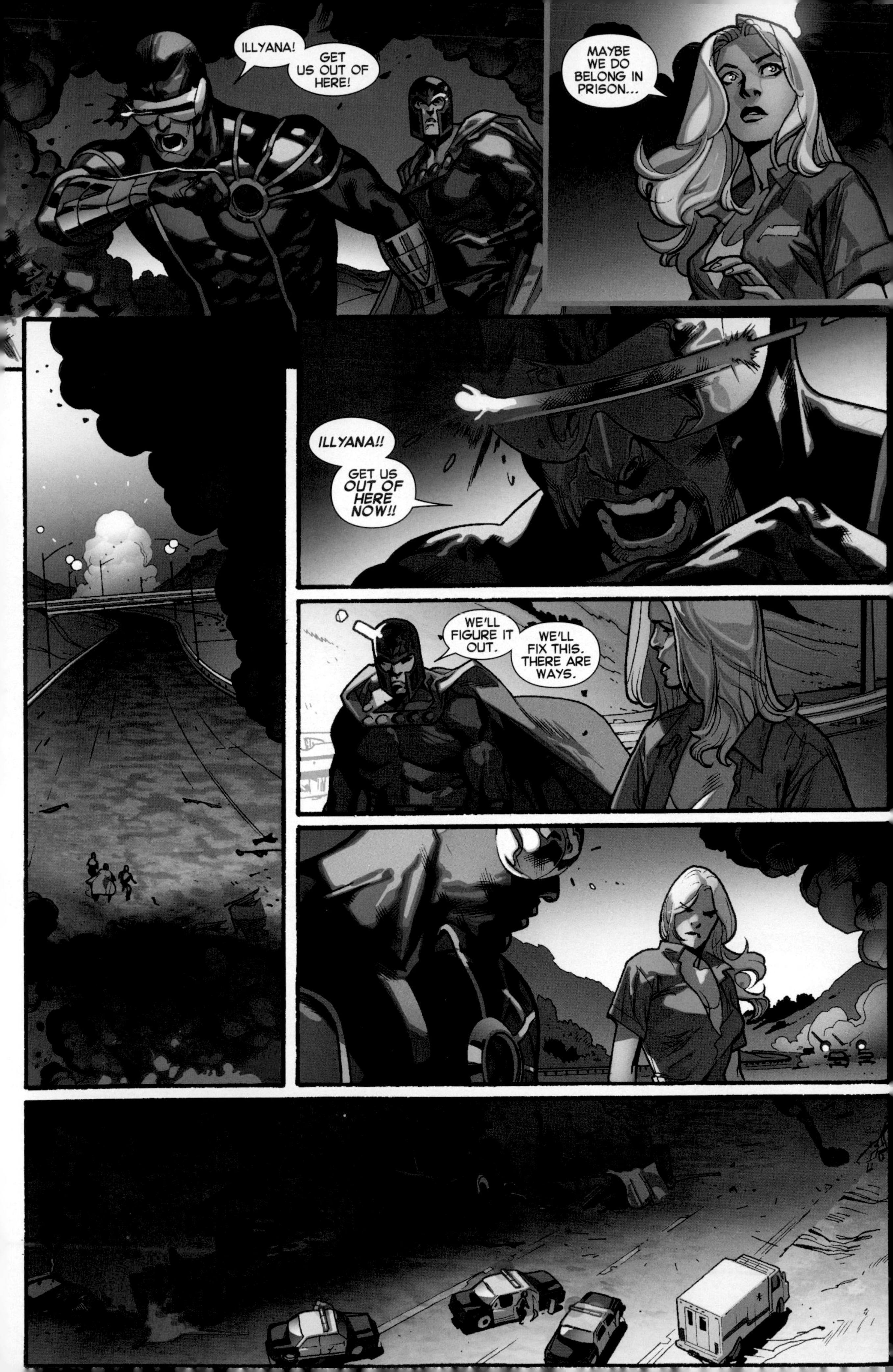
ILLYANA!
GET US OUT OF HERE!
MAYBE WE DO BELONG IN PRISON...
ILLYANA!!
GET US OUT OF HERE NOW!!
WE'LL FIGURE IT OUT.
WE'LL FIX THIS. THERE ARE WAYS.

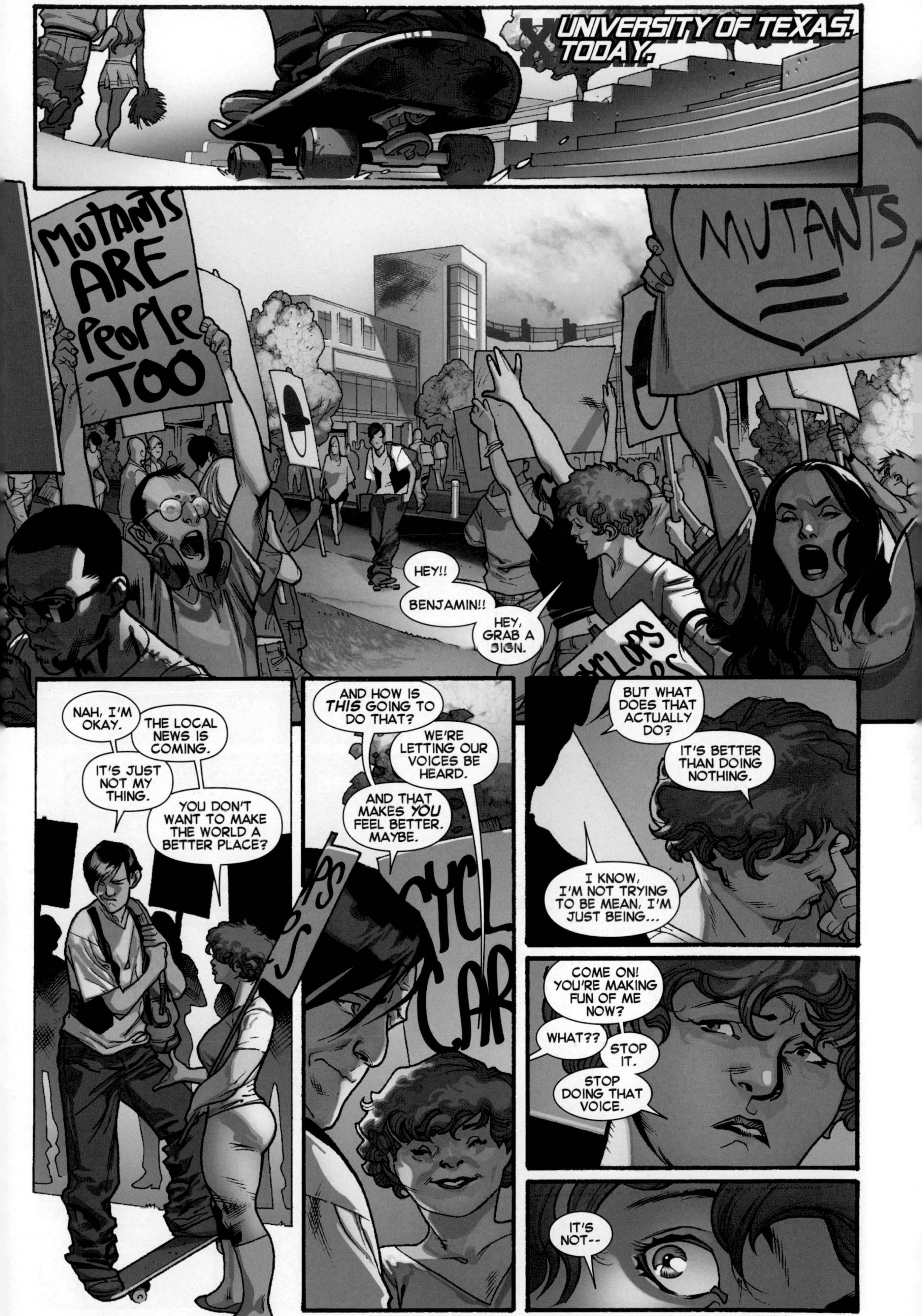
UNIVERSITY OF TEXAS. TODAY.
MUTANTS ARE PEOPLE TOO
MUTANTS =
HEY!!
BENJAMIN!!
HEY, GRAB A SIGN.
NAH, I'M OKAY.
THE LOCAL NEWS IS COMING.
IT'S JUST NOT MY THING.
YOU DON'T WANT TO MAKE THE WORLD A BETTER PLACE?
AND HOW IS THIS GOING TO DO THAT?
WE'RE LETTING OUR VOICES BE HEARD.
AND THAT MAKES YOU FEEL BETTER. MAYBE.
BUT WHAT DOES THAT ACTUALLY DO?
IT'S BETTER THAN DOING NOTHING.
I KNOW, I'M NOT TRYING TO BE MEAN, I'M JUST BEING...
COME ON! YOU'RE MAKING FUN OF ME NOW?
WHAT??
STOP IT.
STOP DOING THAT VOICE.
IT'S NOT--

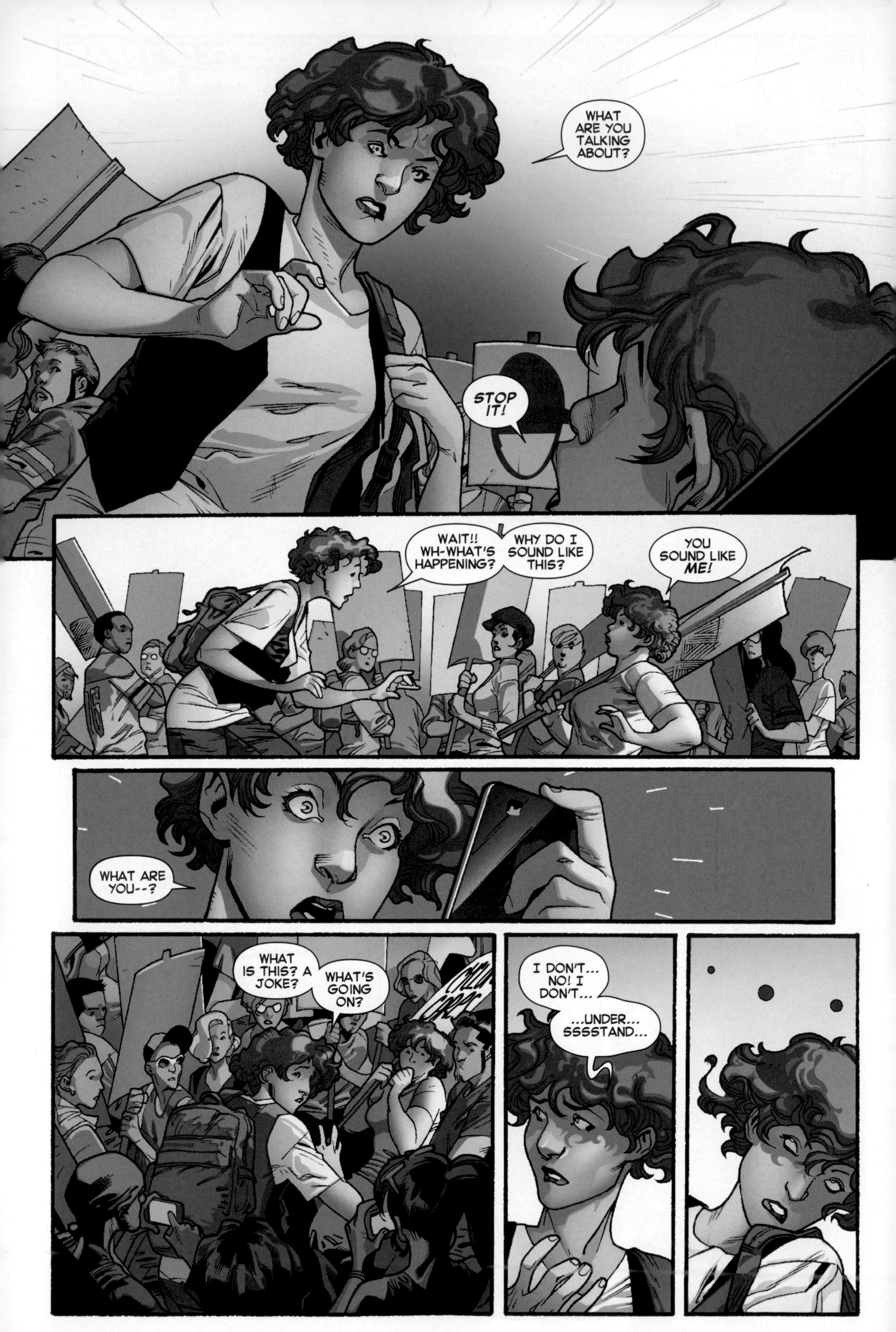
WHAT ARE YOU TALKING ABOUT?
STOP IT!
WAIT!! WH-WHAT'S HAPPENING?
WHY DO I SOUND LIKE THIS?
YOU SOUND LIKE ME!
WHAT ARE YOU--?
WHAT IS THIS? A JOKE?
WHAT'S GOING ON?
I DON'T... NO! I DON'T...
...UNDER... SSSSTAND...

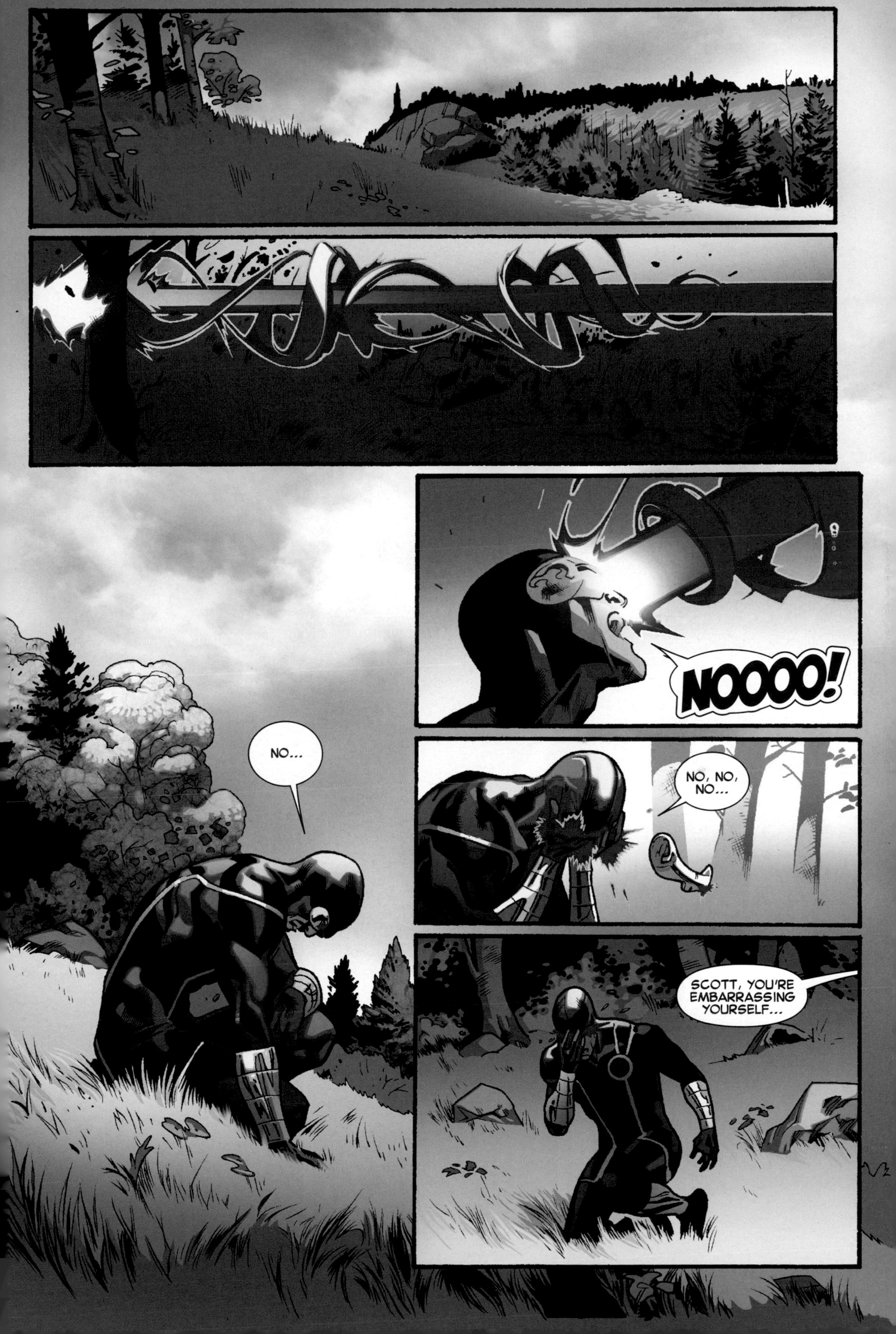
NOOOO!
NO...
NO, NO, NO...
SCOTT, YOU'RE EMBARRASSING YOURSELF...

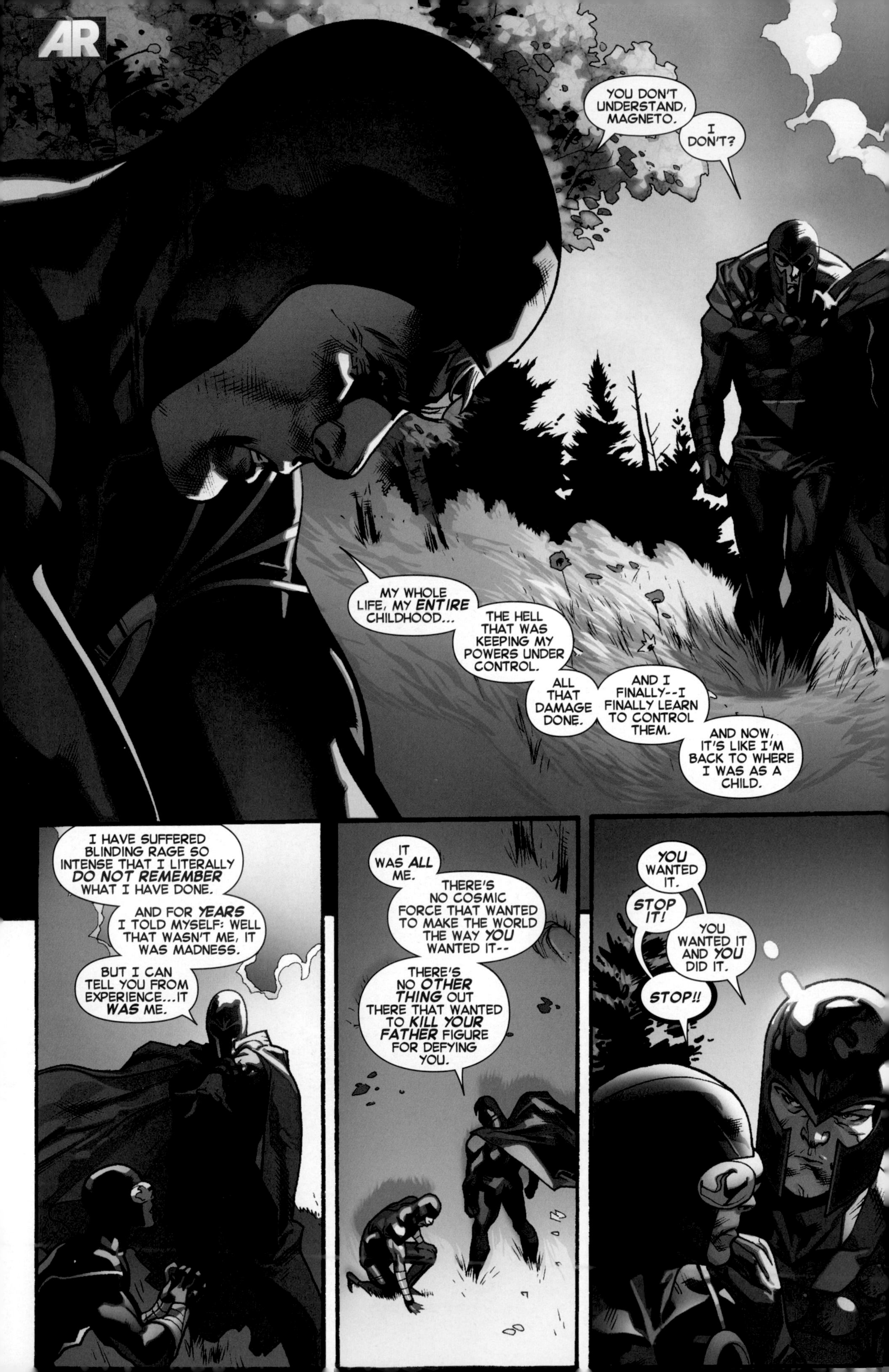

YOU DON'T UNDERSTAND, MAGNETO.
I DON'T?
MY WHOLE LIFE, MY ENTIRE CHILDHOOD...
THE HELL THAT WAS KEEPING MY POWERS UNDER CONTROL.
ALL THAT DAMAGE DONE.
AND I FINALLY--I FINALLY LEARN TO CONTROL THEM.
AND NOW, IT'S LIKE I'M BACK TO WHERE I WAS AS A CHILD.
I HAVE SUFFERED BLINDING RAGE SO INTENSE THAT I LITERALLY DO NOT REMEMBER WHAT I HAVE DONE.
AND FOR YEARS I TOLD MYSELF: WELL THAT WASN'T ME, IT WAS MADNESS.
BUT I CAN TELL YOU FROM EXPERIENCE...IT WAS ME.
IT WAS ALL ME.
THERE'S NO COSMIC FORCE THAT WANTED TO MAKE THE WORLD THE WAY YOU WANTED IT--
THERE'S NO OTHER THING OUT THERE THAT WANTED TO KILL YOUR FATHER FIGURE FOR DEFYING YOU.
YOU WANTED IT.
STOP IT!
YOU WANTED IT AND YOU DID IT.
STOP!!

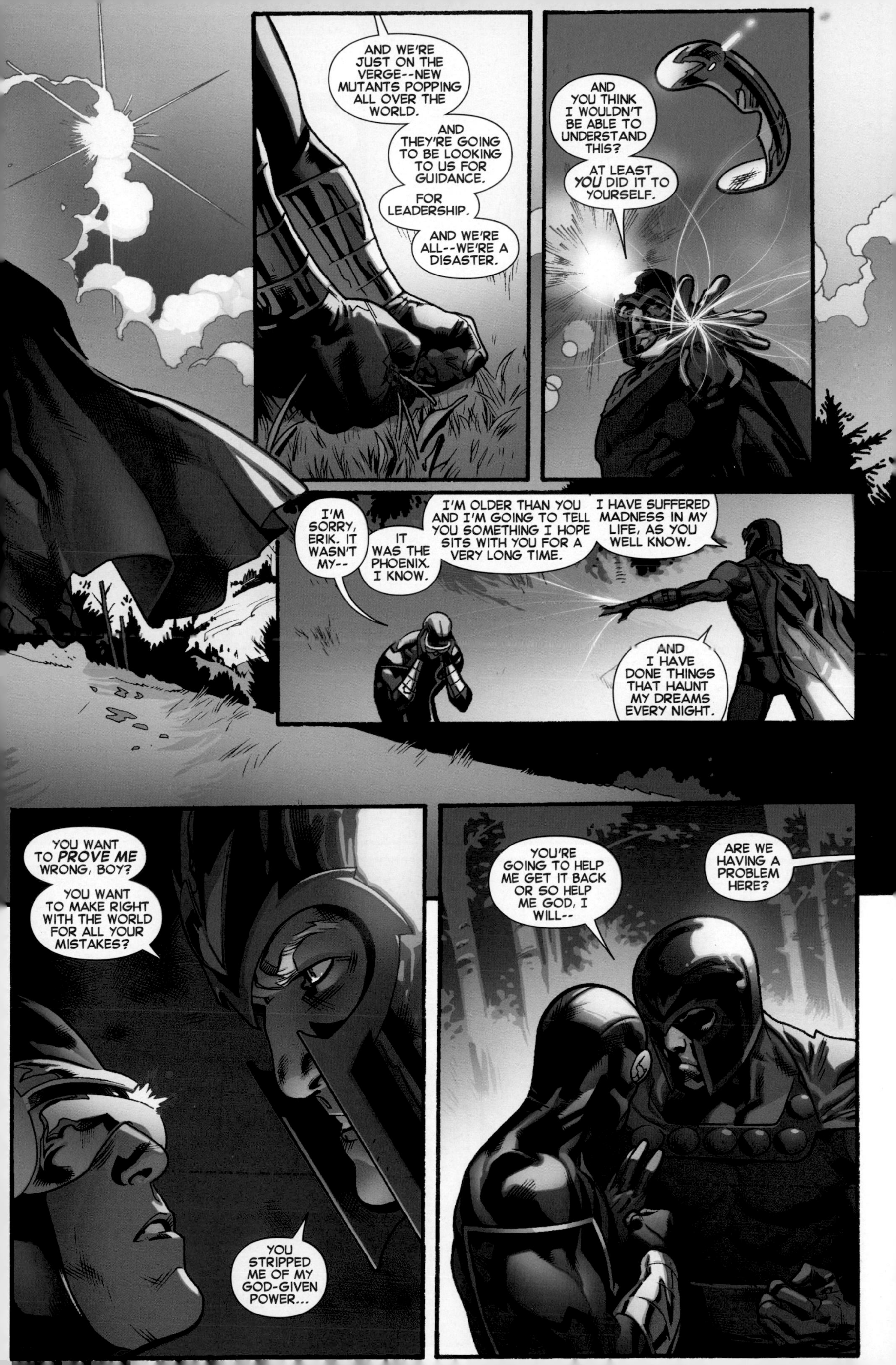
AND WE'RE JUST ON THE VERGE--NEW MUTANTS POPPING ALL OVER THE WORLD.
AND THEY'RE GOING TO BE LOOKING TO US FOR GUIDANCE.
FOR LEADERSHIP.
AND WE'RE ALL--WE'RE A DISASTER.
AND YOU THINK I WOULDN'T BE ABLE TO UNDERSTAND THIS?
AT LEAST *YOU* DID IT TO YOURSELF.
I'M SORRY, ERIK. IT WASN'T MY--
IT WAS THE PHOENIX. I KNOW.
I'M OLDER THAN YOU AND I'M GOING TO TELL YOU SOMETHING I HOPE SITS WITH YOU FOR A VERY LONG TIME.
I HAVE SUFFERED MADNESS IN MY LIFE, AS YOU WELL KNOW.
AND I HAVE DONE THINGS THAT HAUNT MY DREAMS EVERY NIGHT.
YOU WANT TO ***PROVE ME*** WRONG, BOY?
YOU WANT TO MAKE RIGHT WITH THE WORLD FOR ALL YOUR MISTAKES?
YOU STRIPPED ME OF MY GOD-GIVEN POWER...
YOU'RE GOING TO HELP ME GET IT BACK OR SO HELP ME GOD, I WILL--
ARE WE HAVING A PROBLEM HERE?

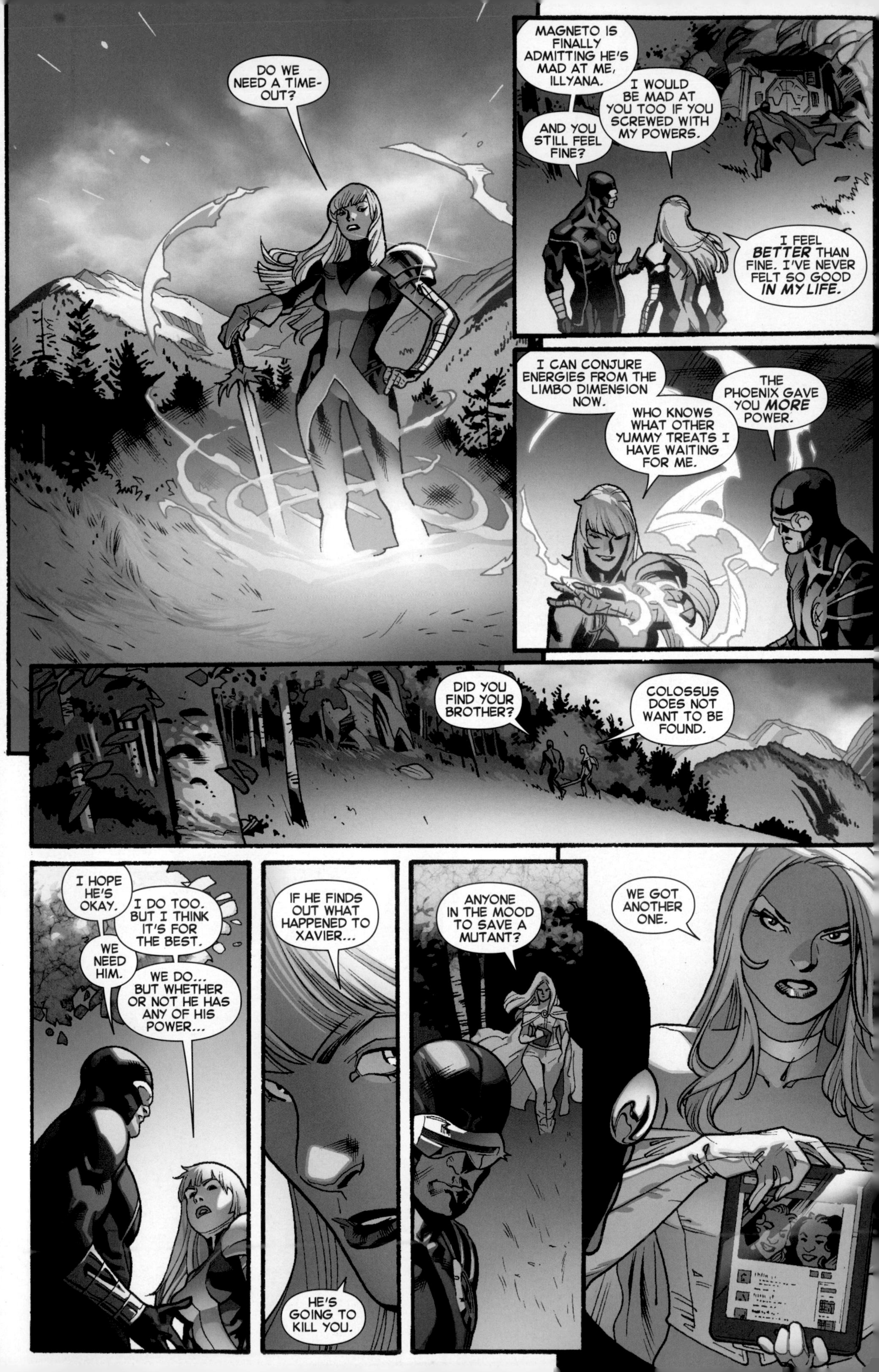
DO WE NEED A TIME-OUT?
MAGNETO IS FINALLY ADMITTING HE'S MAD AT ME, ILLYANA.
AND YOU STILL FEEL FINE?
I WOULD BE MAD AT YOU TOO IF YOU SCREWED WITH MY POWERS.
I FEEL BETTER THAN FINE. I'VE NEVER FELT SO GOOD IN MY LIFE.
I CAN CONJURE ENERGIES FROM THE LIMBO DIMENSION NOW.
WHO KNOWS WHAT OTHER YUMMY TREATS I HAVE WAITING FOR ME.
THE PHOENIX GAVE YOU MORE POWER.
DID YOU FIND YOUR BROTHER?
COLOSSUS DOES NOT WANT TO BE FOUND.
I HOPE HE'S OKAY.
I DO TOO. BUT I THINK IT'S FOR THE BEST.
WE NEED HIM.
WE DO... BUT WHETHER OR NOT HE HAS ANY OF HIS POWER...
IF HE FINDS OUT WHAT HAPPENED TO XAVIER...
HE'S GOING TO KILL YOU.
ANYONE IN THE MOOD TO SAVE A MUTANT?
WE GOT ANOTHER ONE.

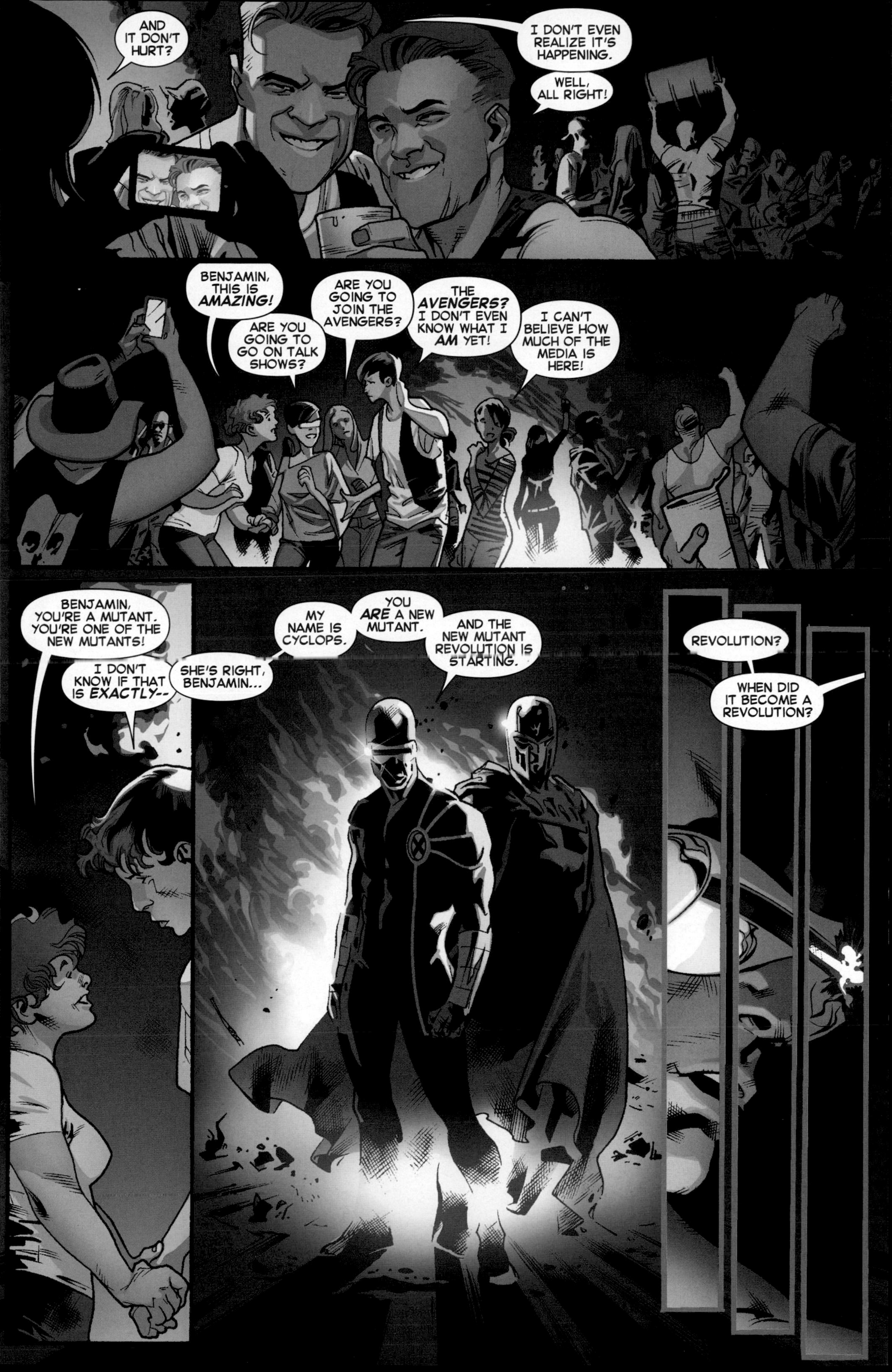
AND IT DON'T HURT?
I DON'T EVEN REALIZE IT'S HAPPENING.
WELL, ALL RIGHT!
BENJAMIN, THIS IS AMAZING!
ARE YOU GOING TO GO ON TALK SHOWS?
ARE YOU GOING TO JOIN THE AVENGERS?
THE AVENGERS? I DON'T EVEN KNOW WHAT I AM YET!
I CAN'T BELIEVE HOW MUCH OF THE MEDIA IS HERE!
BENJAMIN, YOU'RE A MUTANT. YOU'RE ONE OF THE NEW MUTANTS!
I DON'T KNOW IF THAT IS EXACTLY--
SHE'S RIGHT, BENJAMIN...
MY NAME IS CYCLOPS.
YOU ARE A NEW MUTANT.
AND THE NEW MUTANT REVOLUTION IS STARTING.
REVOLUTION?
WHEN DID IT BECOME A REVOLUTION?

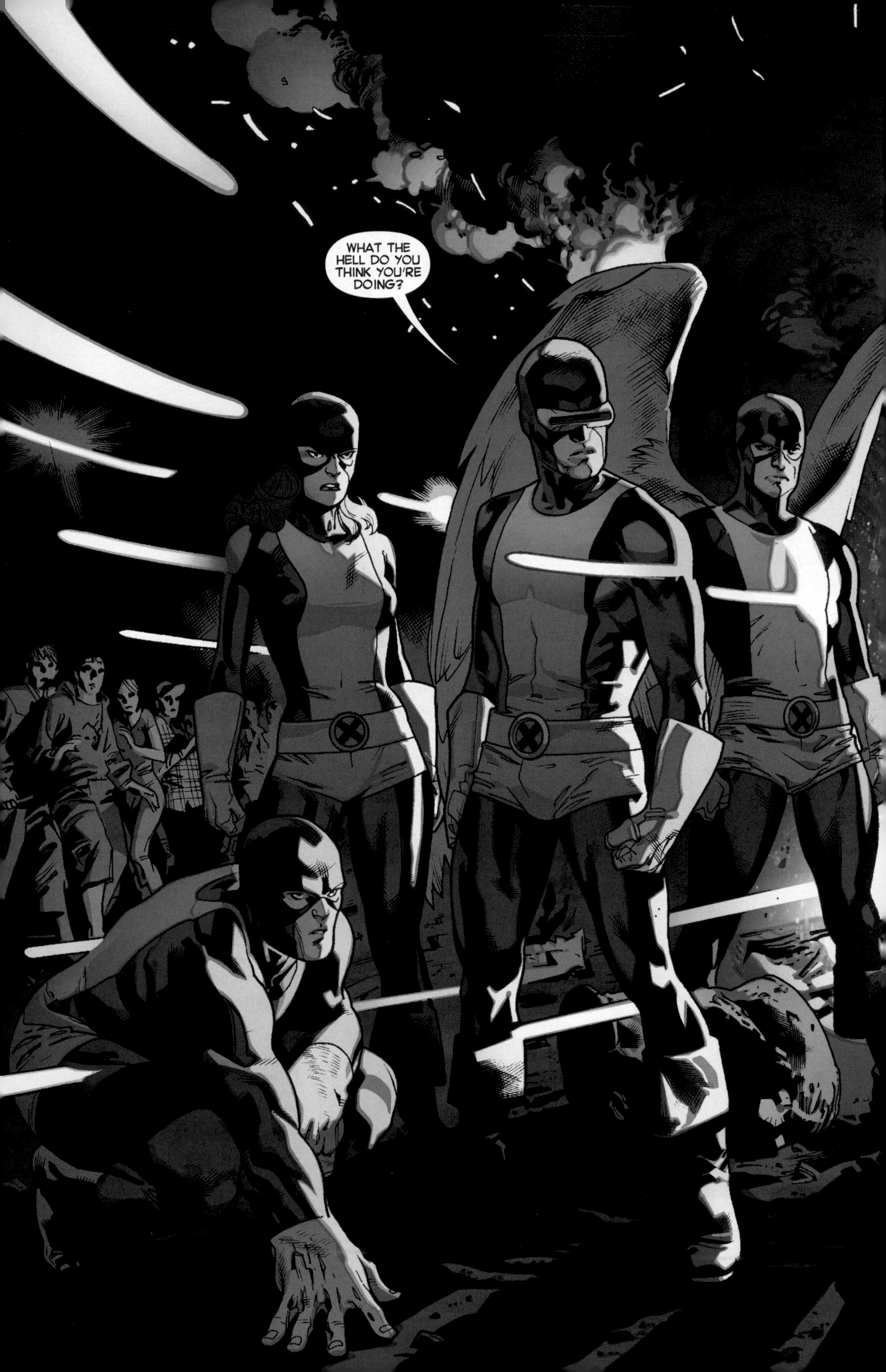
WHAT THE HELL DO YOU THINK YOU'RE DOING?

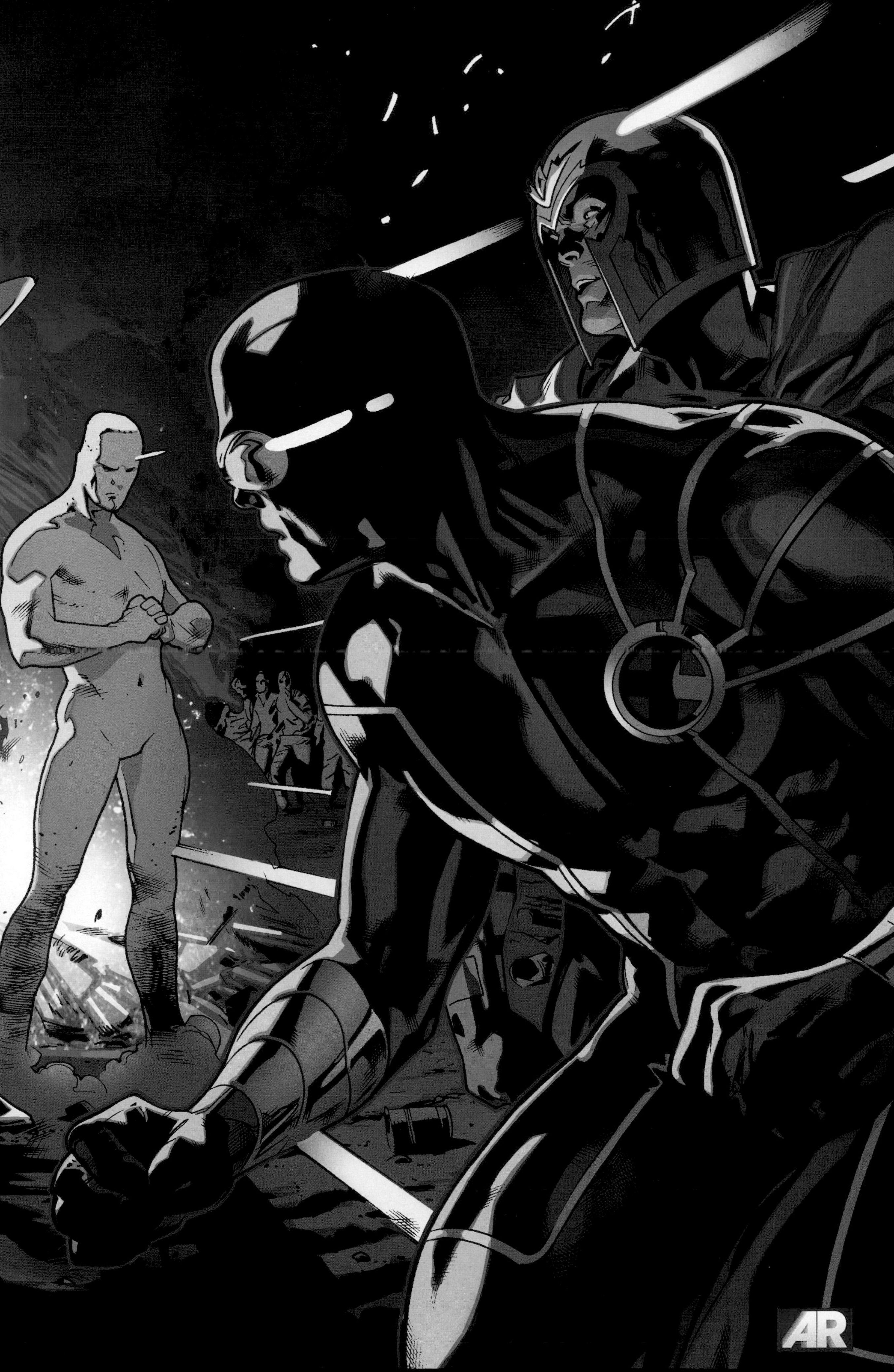

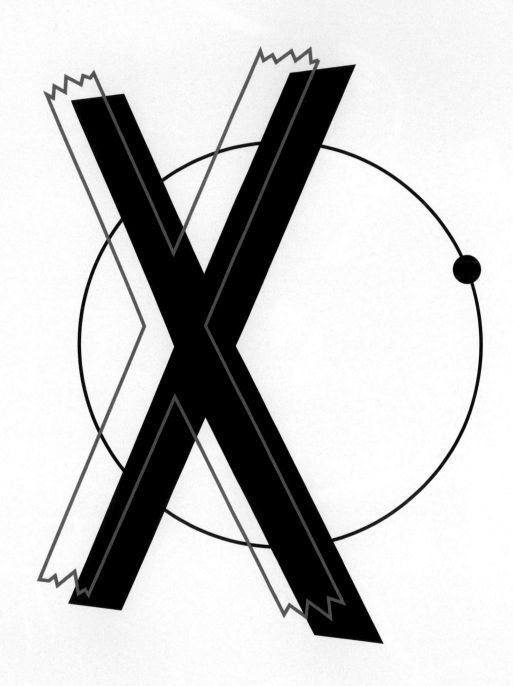

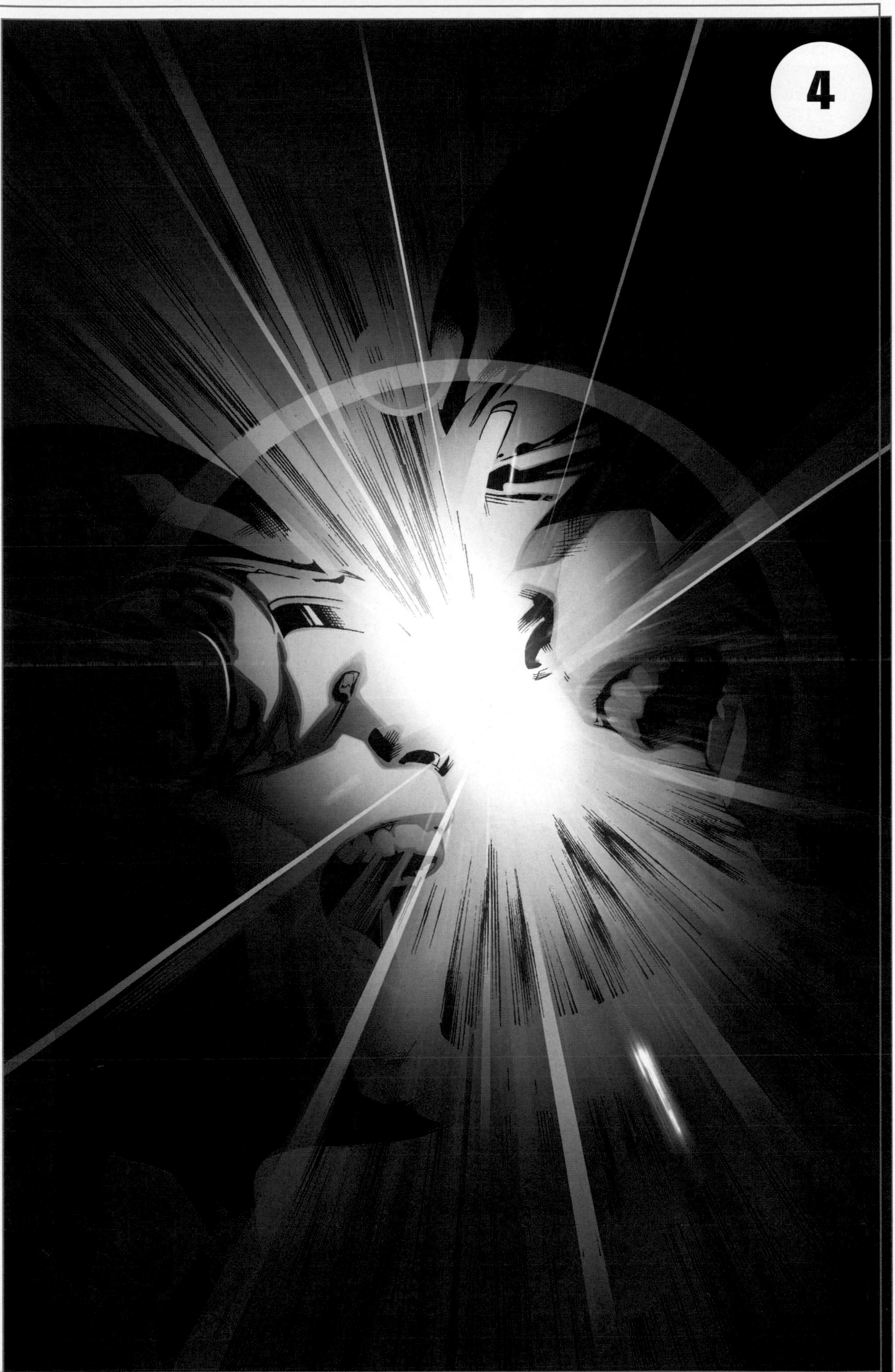
4

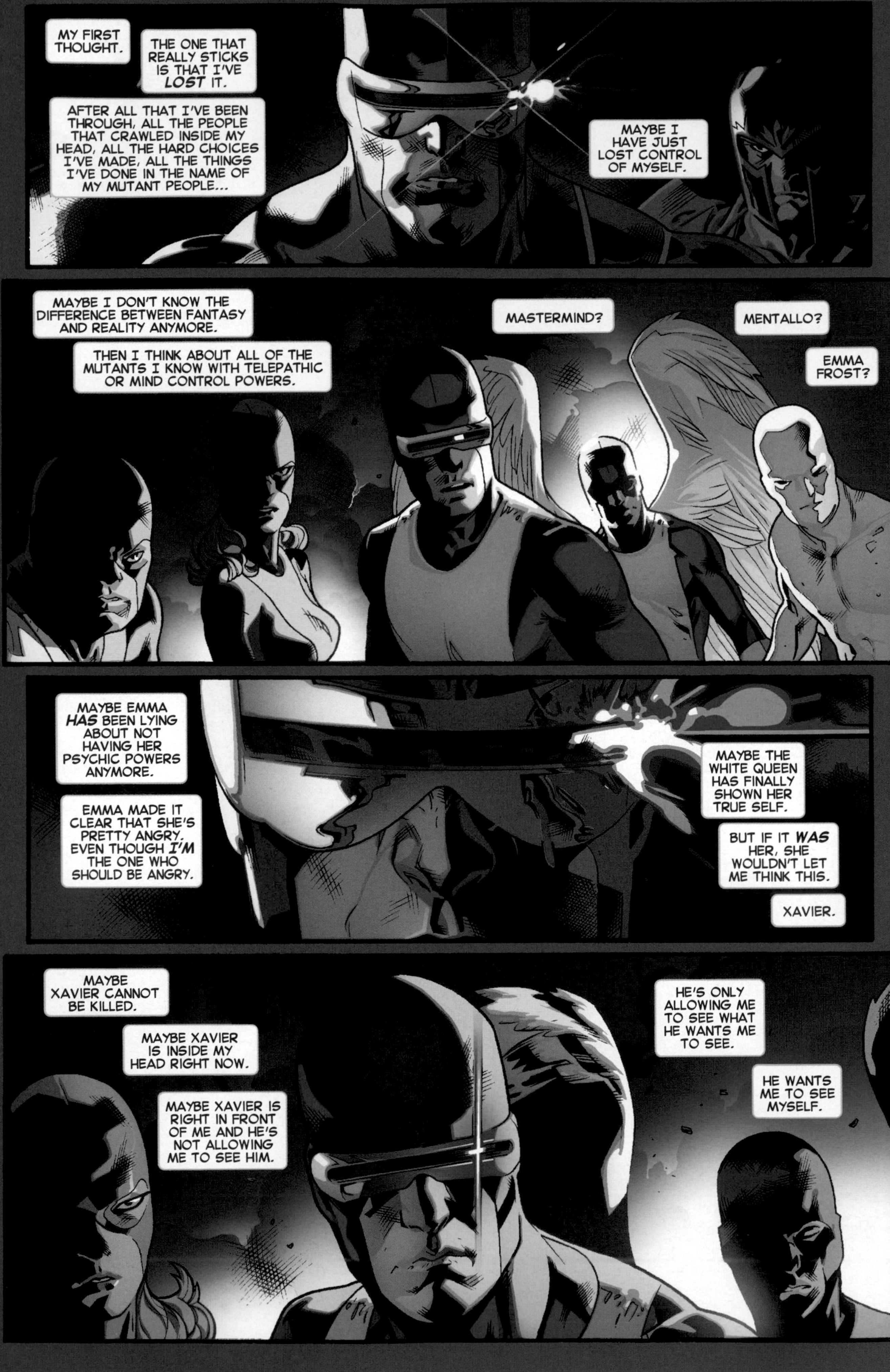

MY FIRST THOUGHT.
THE ONE THAT REALLY STICKS IS THAT I'VE *LOST* IT.
AFTER ALL THAT I'VE BEEN THROUGH, ALL THE PEOPLE THAT CRAWLED INSIDE MY HEAD, ALL THE HARD CHOICES I'VE MADE, ALL THE THINGS I'VE DONE IN THE NAME OF MY MUTANT PEOPLE...
MAYBE I HAVE JUST LOST CONTROL OF MYSELF.
MAYBE I DON'T KNOW THE DIFFERENCE BETWEEN FANTASY AND REALITY ANYMORE.
THEN I THINK ABOUT ALL OF THE MUTANTS I KNOW WITH TELEPATHIC OR MIND CONTROL POWERS.
MASTERMIND?
MENTALLO?
EMMA FROST?
MAYBE EMMA *HAS* BEEN LYING ABOUT NOT HAVING HER PSYCHIC POWERS ANYMORE.
EMMA MADE IT CLEAR THAT SHE'S PRETTY ANGRY, EVEN THOUGH *I'M* THE ONE WHO SHOULD BE ANGRY.
MAYBE THE WHITE QUEEN HAS FINALLY SHOWN HER TRUE SELF.
BUT IF IT *WAS* HER, SHE WOULDN'T LET ME THINK THIS.
XAVIER.
MAYBE XAVIER CANNOT BE KILLED.
MAYBE XAVIER IS INSIDE MY HEAD RIGHT NOW.
MAYBE XAVIER IS RIGHT IN FRONT OF ME AND HE'S NOT ALLOWING ME TO SEE HIM.
HE'S ONLY ALLOWING ME TO SEE WHAT HE WANTS ME TO SEE.
HE WANTS ME TO SEE MYSELF.

HE WANTS ME TO SEE WHO I WAS WHEN HE LOVED ME.
WHEN I WAS EVERYTHING THAT HE WANTED ME TO BE.
HE WANTS ME TO SEE THE ORIGINAL X-MEN.
HE WANTS ME TO SEE US WHEN WE WERE PURE.
WHEN WE DIDN'T KNOW ANY BETTER.
WHEN WE DIDN'T KNOW WHAT THE WORLD WAS REALLY LIKE.
BUT I KNOW IN MY HEART THAT XAVIER'S DEAD.
AND I KNOW, IF I REALLY THINK ABOUT IT, I KNOW THAT NO MATTER HOW ANGRY EMMA IS--SHE WOULD NEVER DO THIS.
SO I HAVE TO REALLY THINK ABOUT WHO WOULD DO THIS.
WHO WOULD PUNISH ME THIS VICIOUSLY.
THEN I THINK ABOUT SHAPE-SHIFTERS.
I THINK ABOUT MYSTIQUE.
BUT THERE WOULD HAVE TO BE FIVE SHAPE-SHIFTERS, WOULDN'T THERE?
AND THEY WOULD HAVE TO BE FANTASTIC.
NO.
SOMEHOW THIS IS REAL.
I AM LOOKING RIGHT AT MYSELF.

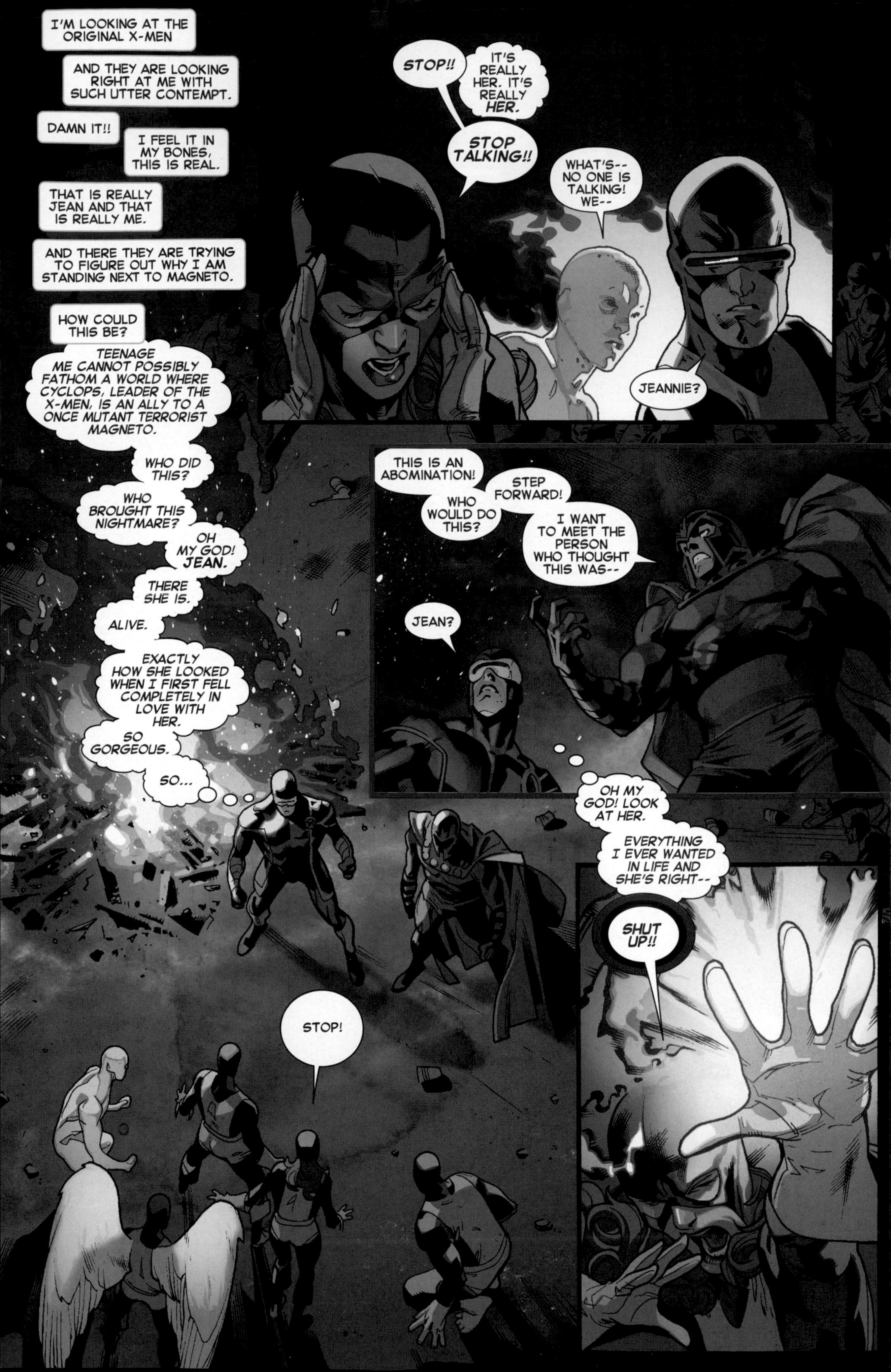
I'M LOOKING AT THE ORIGINAL X-MEN
AND THEY ARE LOOKING RIGHT AT ME WITH SUCH UTTER CONTEMPT.
DAMN IT!!
I FEEL IT IN MY BONES, THIS IS REAL.
THAT IS REALLY JEAN AND THAT IS REALLY ME.
AND THERE THEY ARE TRYING TO FIGURE OUT WHY I AM STANDING NEXT TO MAGNETO.
HOW COULD THIS BE?
TEENAGE ME CANNOT POSSIBLY FATHOM A WORLD WHERE CYCLOPS, LEADER OF THE X-MEN, IS AN ALLY TO A ONCE MUTANT TERRORIST MAGNETO.
STOP!!
IT'S REALLY HER. IT'S REALLY HER.
STOP TALKING!!
WHAT'S-- NO ONE IS TALKING! WE--
JEANNIE?
WHO DID THIS?
WHO BROUGHT THIS NIGHTMARE?
OH MY GOD! JEAN.
THERE SHE IS.
ALIVE.
EXACTLY HOW SHE LOOKED WHEN I FIRST FELL COMPLETELY IN LOVE WITH HER.
SO GORGEOUS.
SO...
THIS IS AN ABOMINATION!
WHO WOULD DO THIS?
STEP FORWARD!
I WANT TO MEET THE PERSON WHO THOUGHT THIS WAS--
JEAN?
OH MY GOD! LOOK AT HER.
EVERYTHING I EVER WANTED IN LIFE AND SHE'S RIGHT--
SHUT UP!!
STOP!

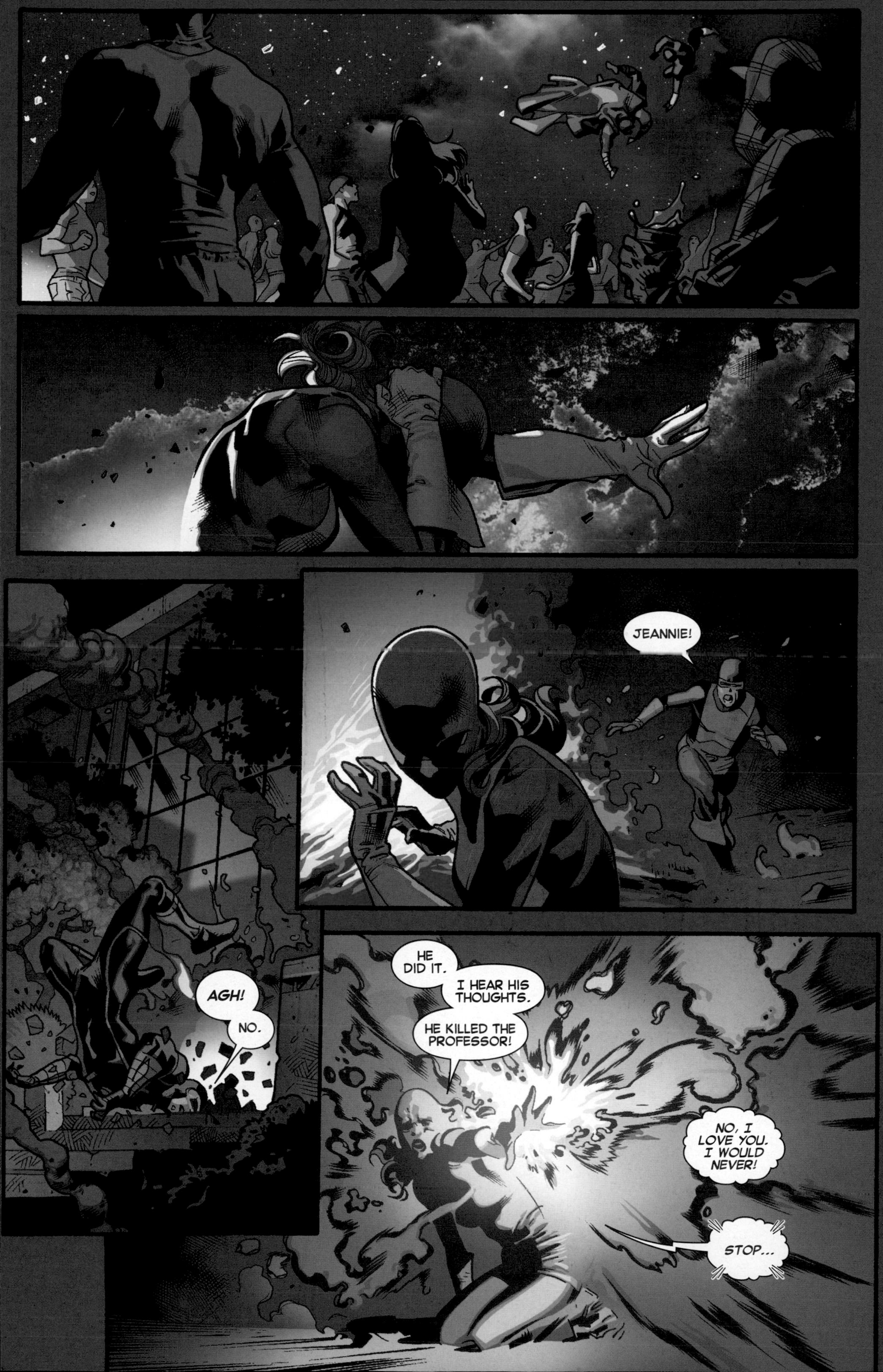

JEANNIE!
AGH!
NO.
HE DID IT.
I HEAR HIS THOUGHTS.
HE KILLED THE PROFESSOR!
NO, I LOVE YOU. I WOULD NEVER!
STOP...

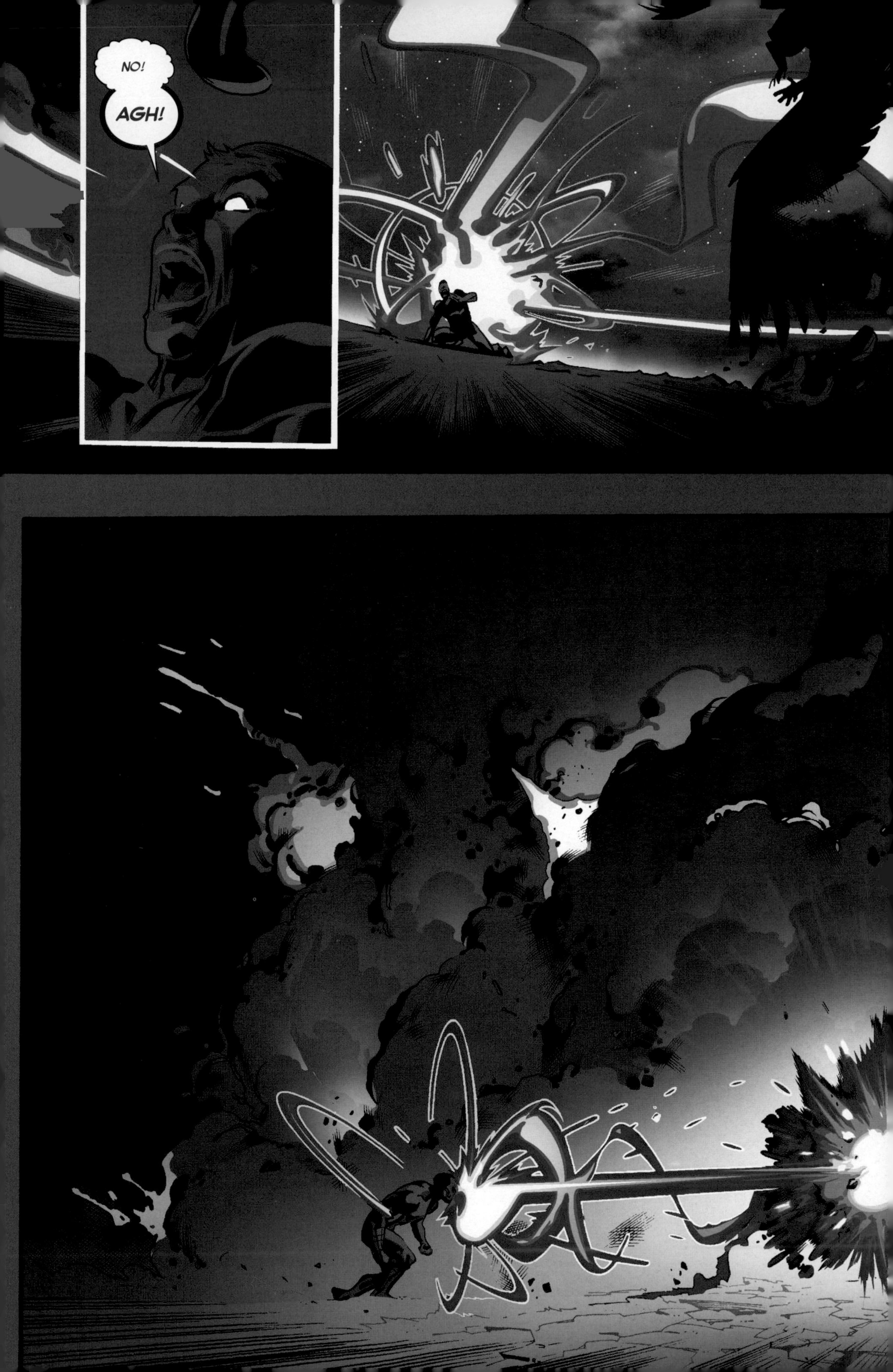
NO!
AGH!

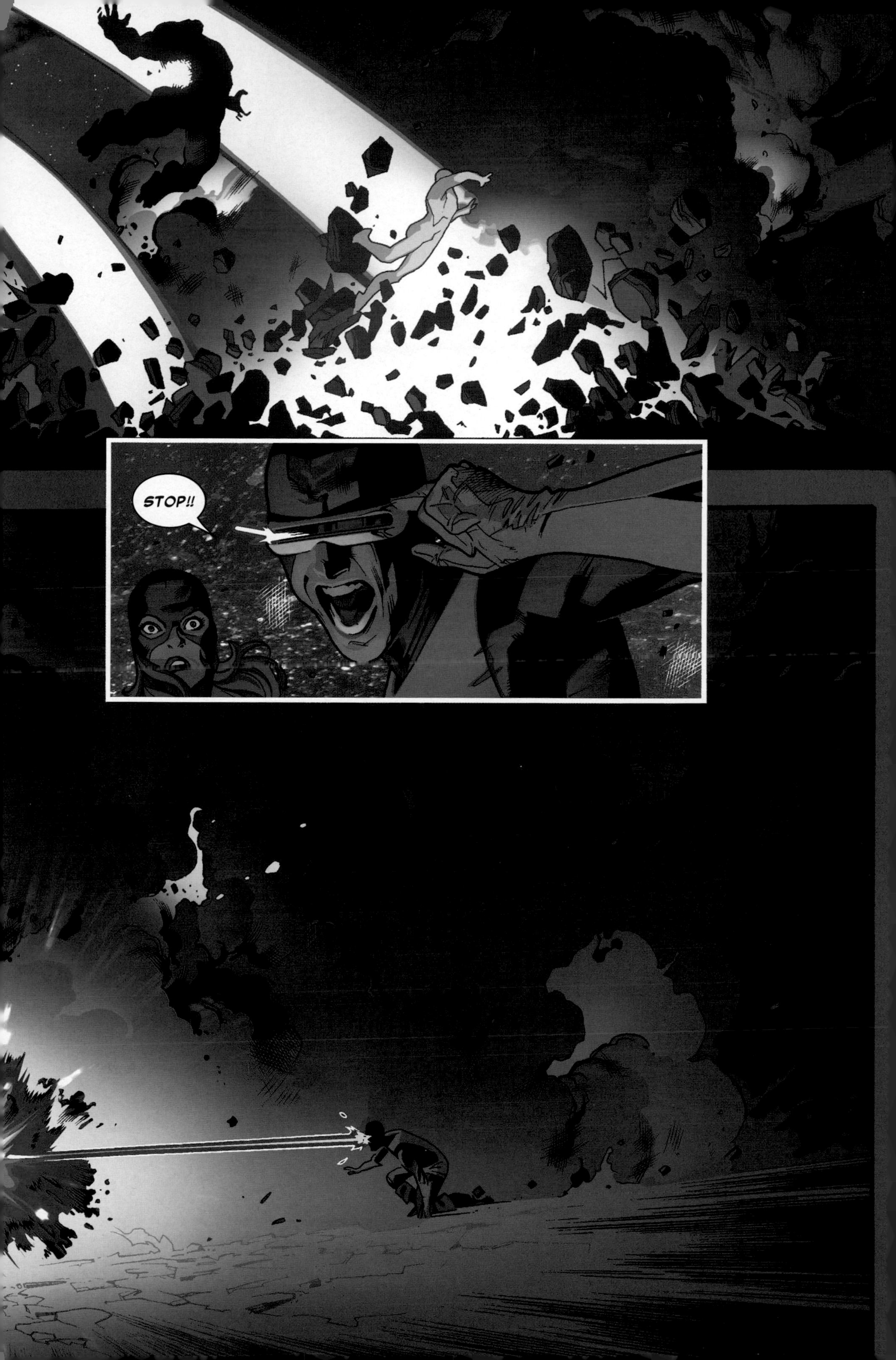
STOP!!

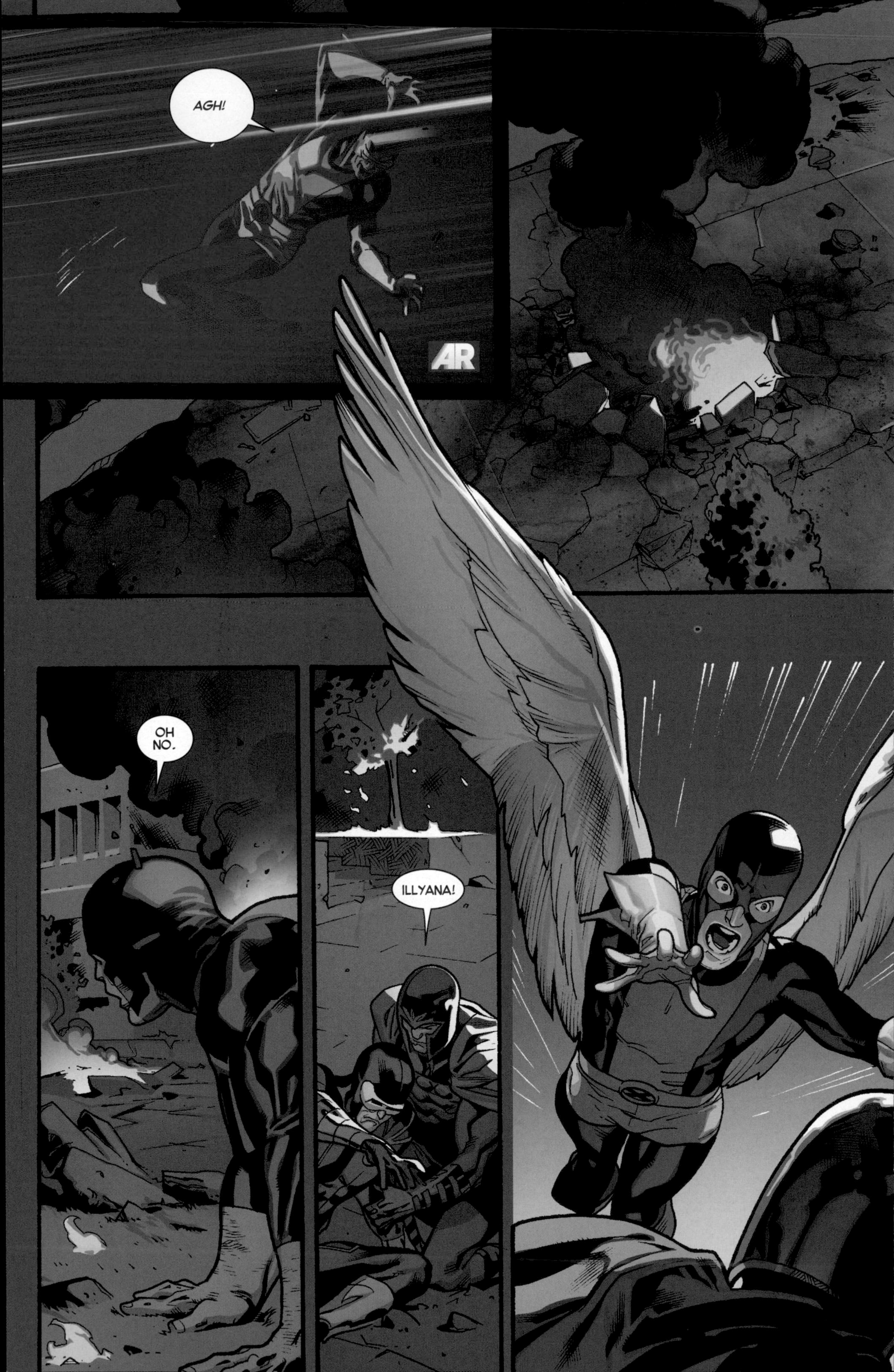
AGH!
OH NO.
ILLYANA!

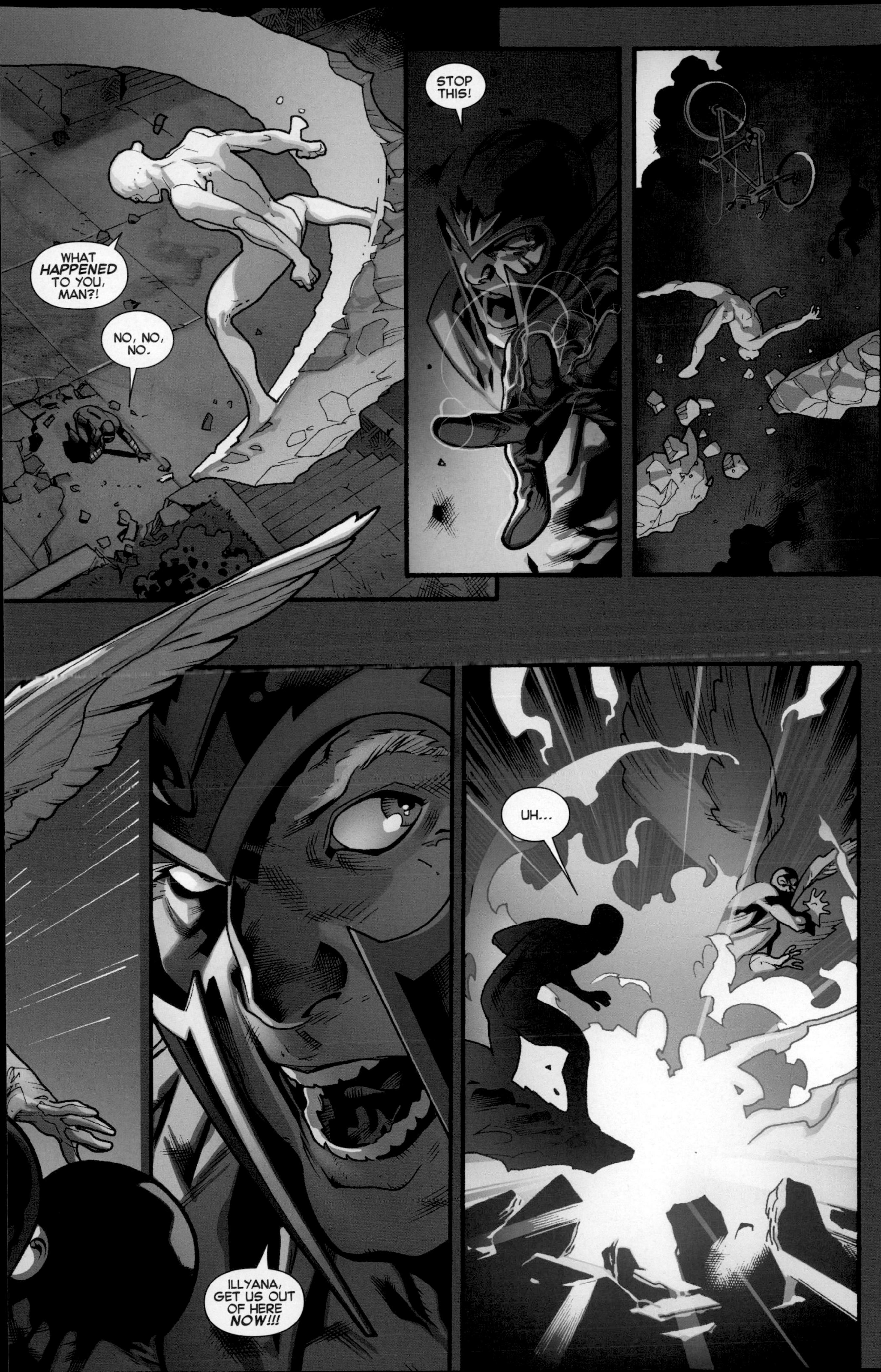
WHAT HAPPENED TO YOU, MAN?!
NO, NO, NO.
STOP THIS!
UH...
ILLYANA, GET US OUT OF HERE NOW!!!

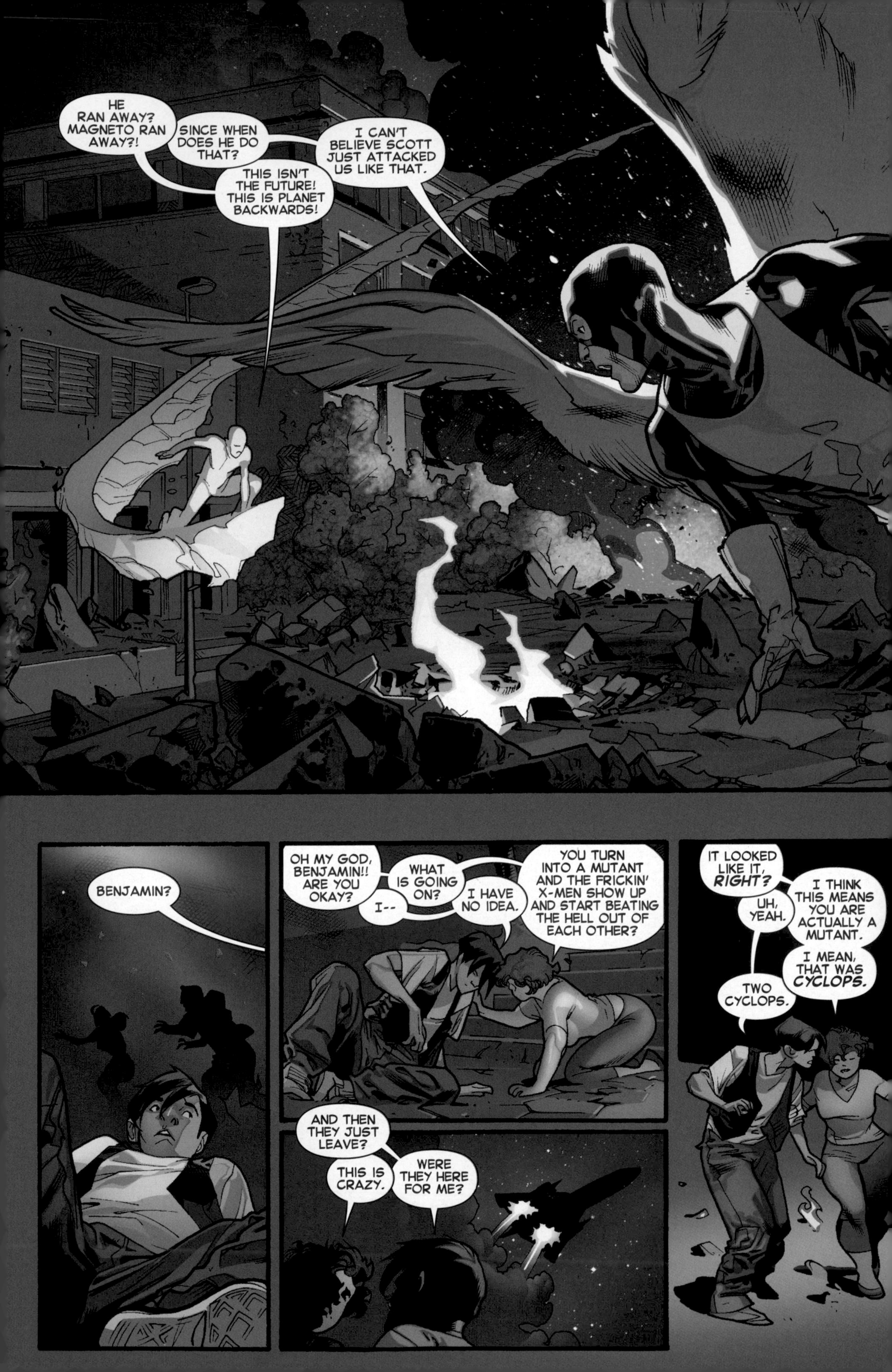
HE RAN AWAY? MAGNETO RAN AWAY?!
SINCE WHEN DOES HE DO THAT?
I CAN'T BELIEVE SCOTT JUST ATTACKED US LIKE THAT.
THIS ISN'T THE FUTURE! THIS IS PLANET BACKWARDS!
BENJAMIN?
OH MY GOD, BENJAMIN!! ARE YOU OKAY?
WHAT IS GOING ON?
I--
I HAVE NO IDEA.
YOU TURN INTO A MUTANT AND THE FRICKIN' X-MEN SHOW UP AND START BEATING THE HELL OUT OF EACH OTHER?
AND THEN THEY JUST LEAVE?
THIS IS CRAZY.
WERE THEY HERE FOR ME?
IT LOOKED LIKE IT, *RIGHT?*
UH, YEAH.
I THINK THIS MEANS YOU ARE ACTUALLY A MUTANT.
I MEAN, THAT WAS *CYCLOPS.*
TWO CYCLOPS.

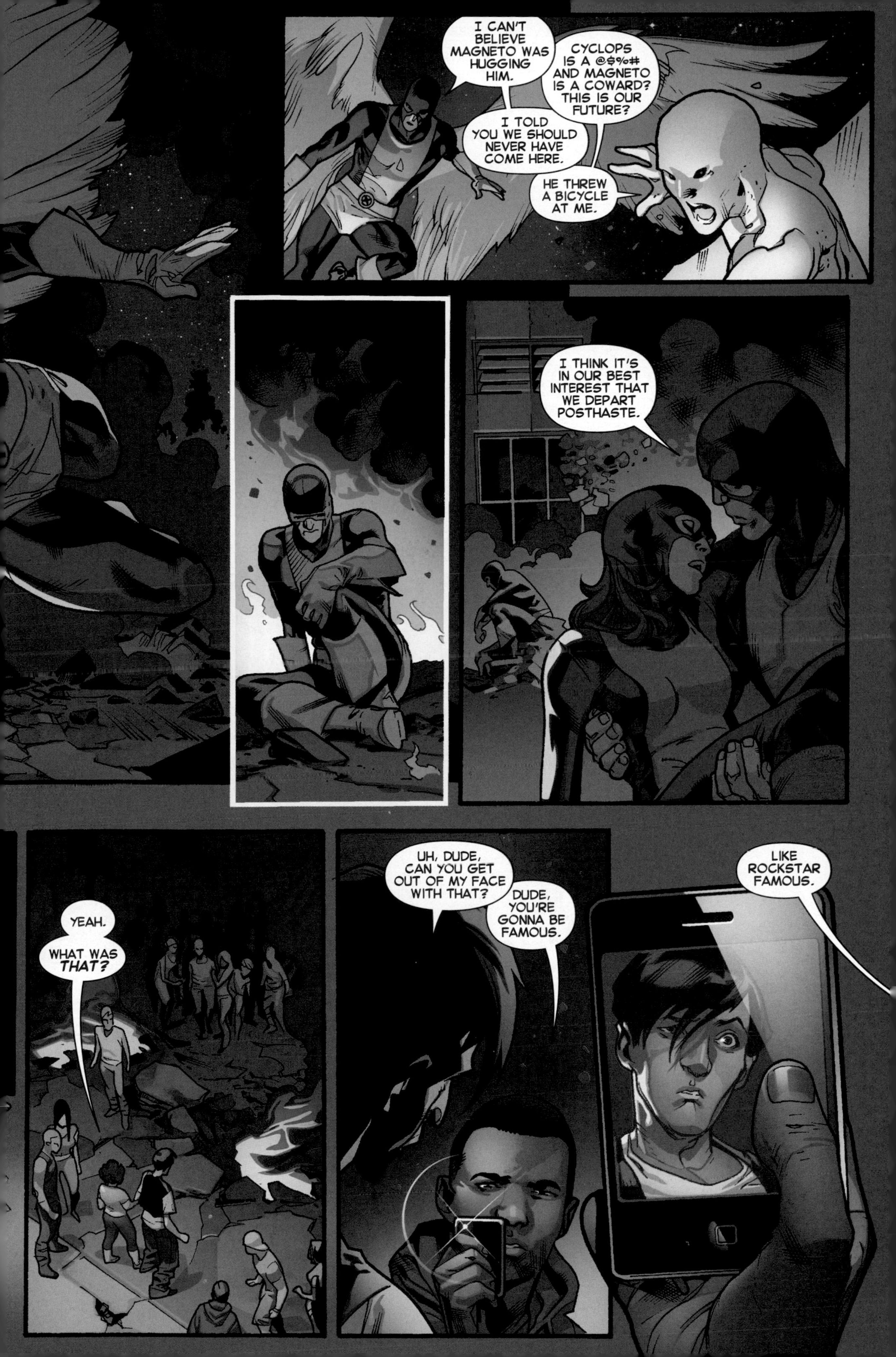
I CAN'T BELIEVE MAGNETO WAS HUGGING HIM.
CYCLOPS IS A @$%# AND MAGNETO IS A COWARD? THIS IS OUR FUTURE?
I TOLD YOU WE SHOULD NEVER HAVE COME HERE.
HE THREW A BICYCLE AT ME.
I THINK IT'S IN OUR BEST INTEREST THAT WE DEPART POSTHASTE.
YEAH.
WHAT WAS *THAT?*
UH, DUDE, CAN YOU GET OUT OF MY FACE WITH THAT?
DUDE, YOU'RE GONNA BE FAMOUS.
LIKE ROCKSTAR FAMOUS.

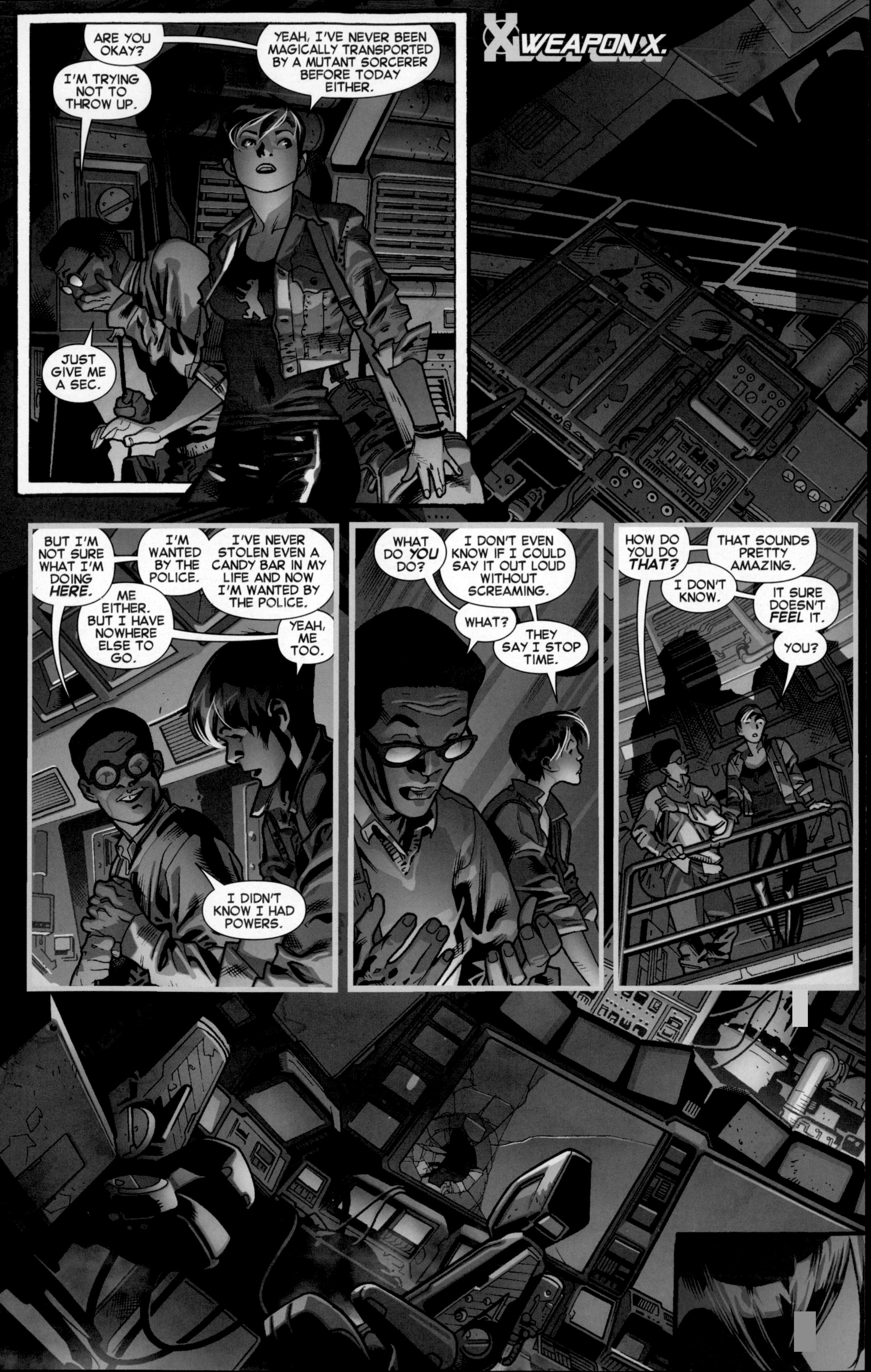
WEAPON X.
ARE YOU OKAY?
YEAH, I'VE NEVER BEEN MAGICALLY TRANSPORTED BY A MUTANT SORCERER BEFORE TODAY EITHER.
I'M TRYING NOT TO THROW UP.
JUST GIVE ME A SEC.
BUT I'M NOT SURE WHAT I'M DOING HERE.
I'M WANTED BY THE POLICE.
I'VE NEVER STOLEN EVEN A CANDY BAR IN MY LIFE AND NOW I'M WANTED BY THE POLICE.
ME EITHER. BUT I HAVE NOWHERE ELSE TO GO.
YEAH, ME TOO.
I DIDN'T KNOW I HAD POWERS.
WHAT DO YOU DO?
I DON'T EVEN KNOW IF I COULD SAY IT OUT LOUD WITHOUT SCREAMING.
WHAT?
THEY SAY I STOP TIME.
HOW DO YOU DO THAT?
THAT SOUNDS PRETTY AMAZING.
I DON'T KNOW.
IT SURE DOESN'T FEEL IT.
YOU?

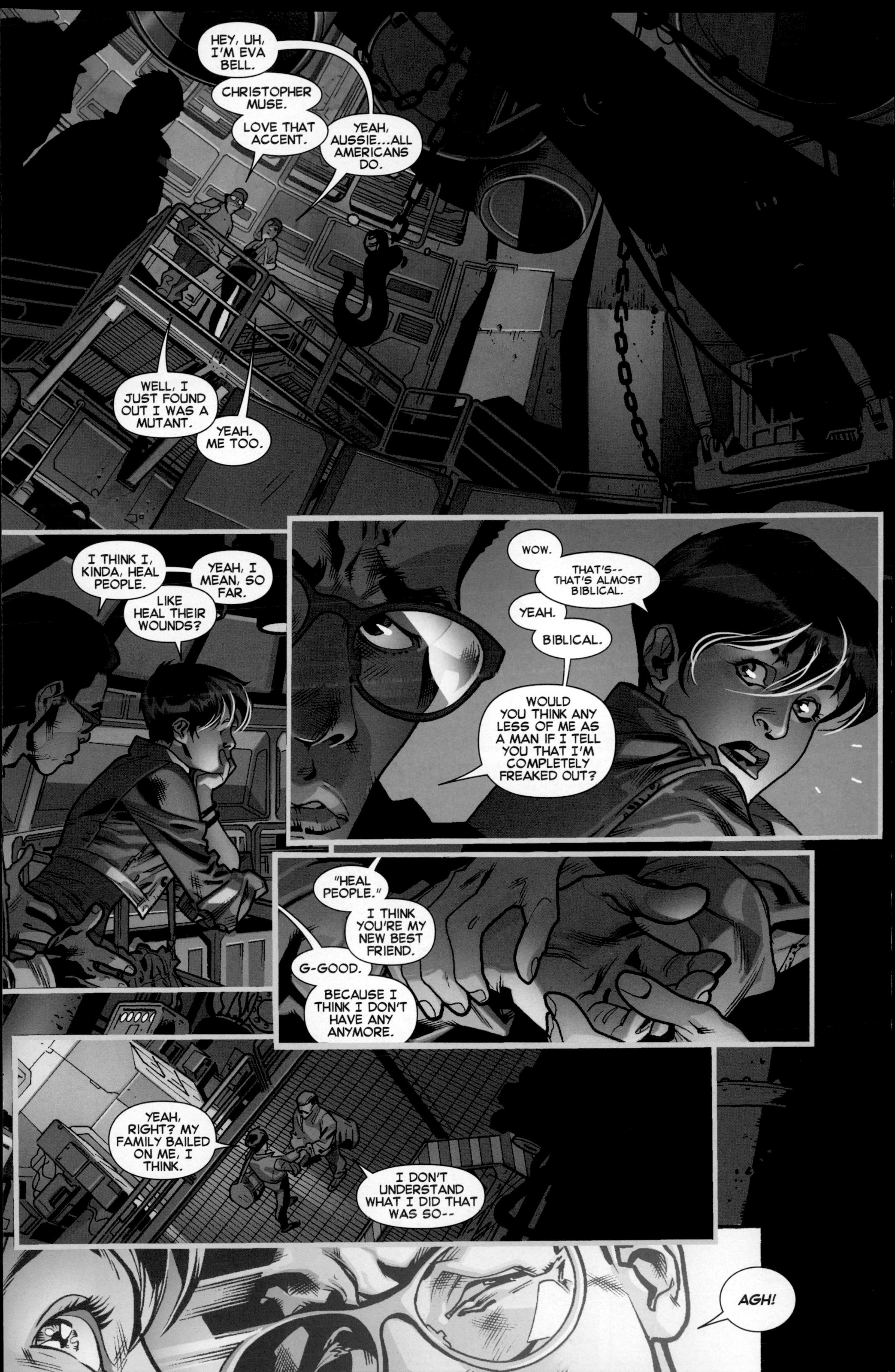
HEY, UH, I'M EVA BELL.
CHRISTOPHER MUSE.
LOVE THAT ACCENT.
YEAH, AUSSIE...ALL AMERICANS DO.
WELL, I JUST FOUND OUT I WAS A MUTANT.
YEAH. ME TOO.
I THINK I, KINDA, HEAL PEOPLE.
YEAH, I MEAN, SO FAR.
LIKE HEAL THEIR WOUNDS?
WOW.
THAT'S-- THAT'S ALMOST BIBLICAL.
YEAH.
BIBLICAL.
WOULD YOU THINK ANY LESS OF ME AS A MAN IF I TELL YOU THAT I'M COMPLETELY FREAKED OUT?
"HEAL PEOPLE."
I THINK YOU'RE MY NEW BEST FRIEND.
G-GOOD.
BECAUSE I THINK I DON'T HAVE ANY ANYMORE.
YEAH, RIGHT? MY FAMILY BAILED ON ME, I THINK.
I DON'T UNDERSTAND WHAT I DID THAT WAS SO--
AGH!

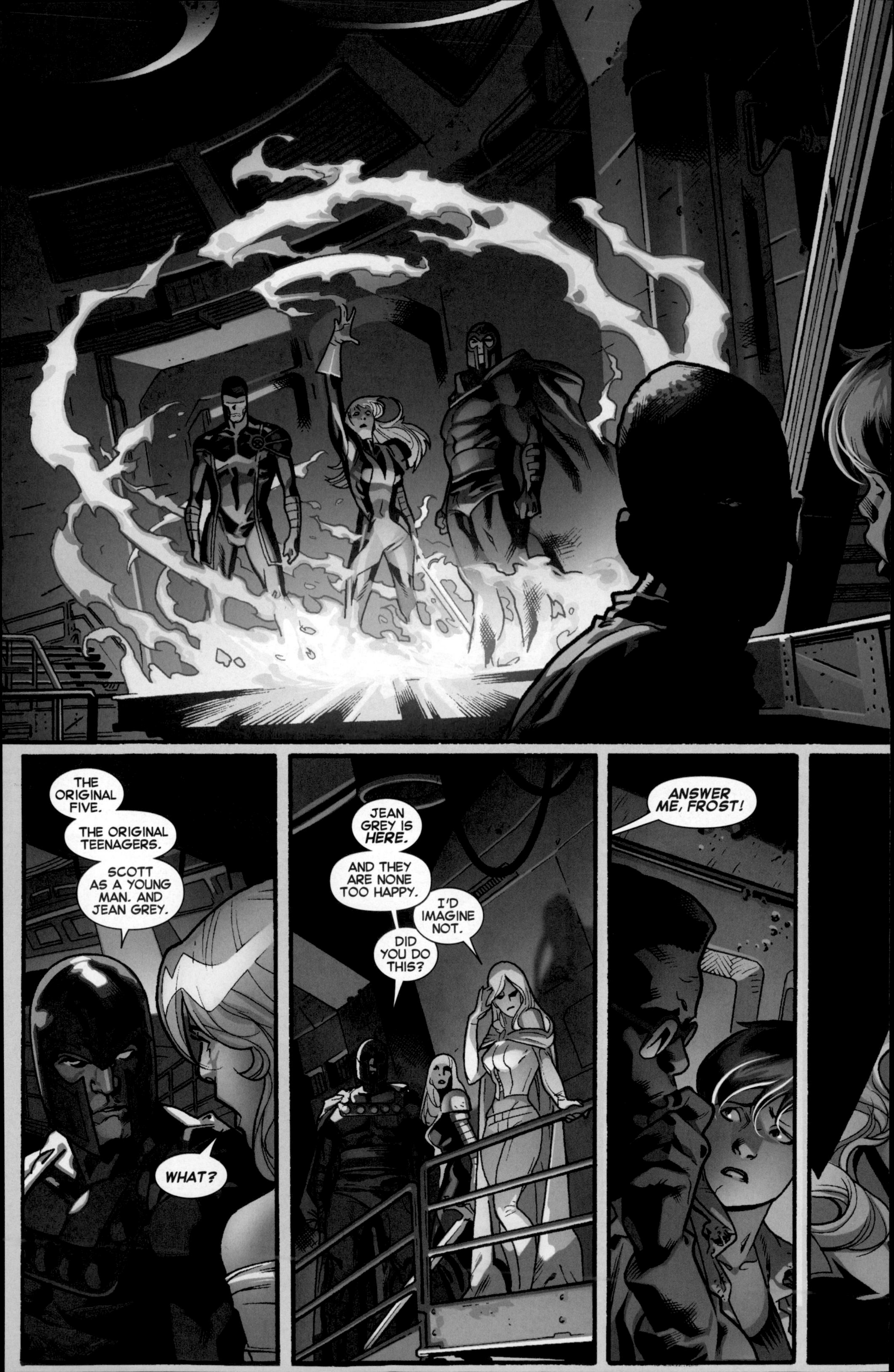
THE ORIGINAL FIVE.
THE ORIGINAL TEENAGERS.
SCOTT AS A YOUNG MAN. AND JEAN GREY.
WHAT?
JEAN GREY IS HERE.
AND THEY ARE NONE TOO HAPPY.
I'D IMAGINE NOT.
DID YOU DO THIS?
ANSWER ME, FROST!

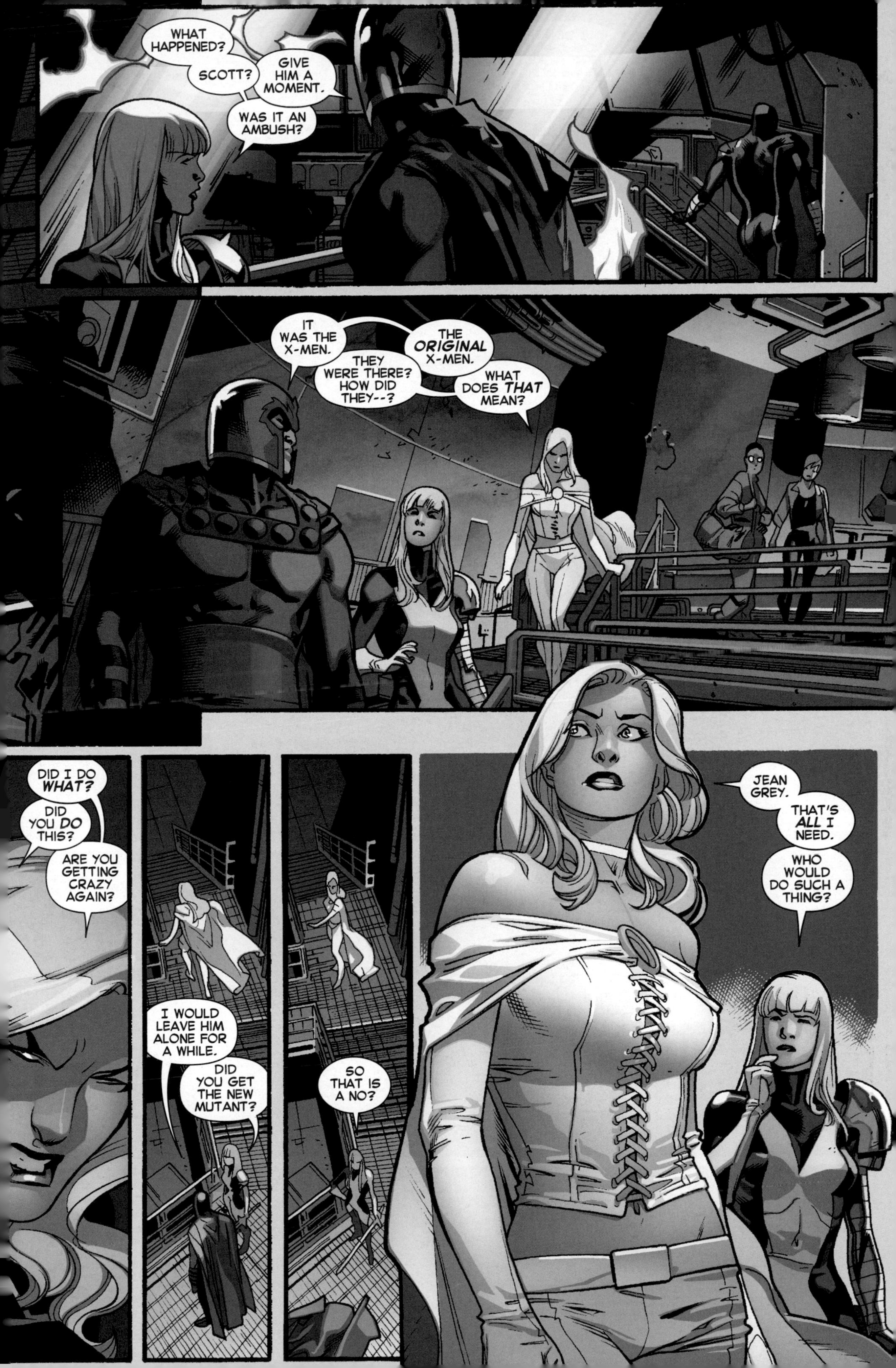

WHAT HAPPENED?
SCOTT?
GIVE HIM A MOMENT.
WAS IT AN AMBUSH?
IT WAS THE X-MEN.
THE ORIGINAL X-MEN.
THEY WERE THERE? HOW DID THEY--?
WHAT DOES THAT MEAN?
DID I DO WHAT?
DID YOU DO THIS?
ARE YOU GETTING CRAZY AGAIN?
I WOULD LEAVE HIM ALONE FOR A WHILE.
DID YOU GET THE NEW MUTANT?
SO THAT IS A NO?
JEAN GREY.
THAT'S ALL I NEED.
WHO WOULD DO SUCH A THING?

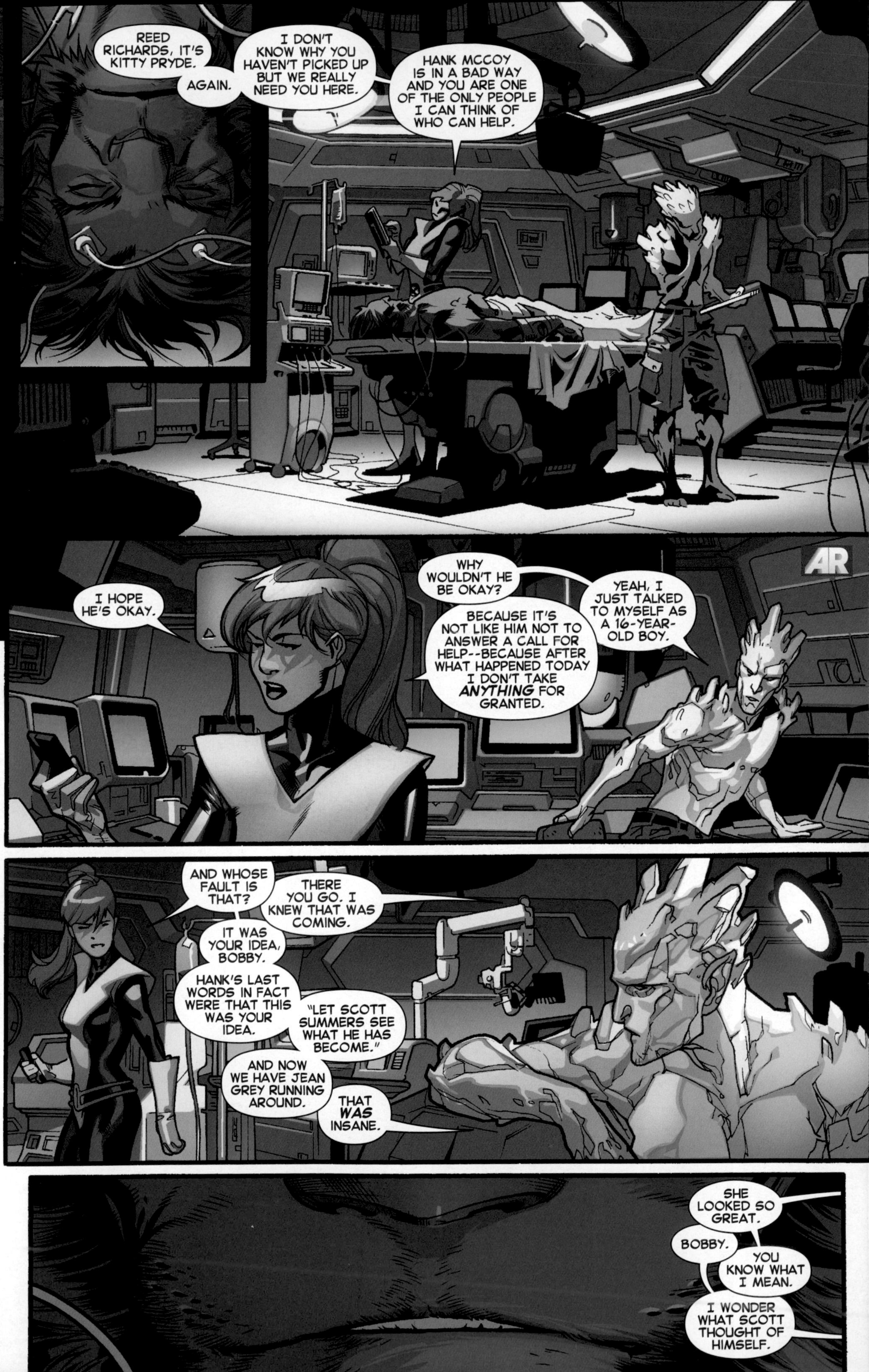
REED RICHARDS, IT'S KITTY PRYDE.
AGAIN.
I DON'T KNOW WHY YOU HAVEN'T PICKED UP BUT WE REALLY NEED YOU HERE.
HANK MCCOY IS IN A BAD WAY AND YOU ARE ONE OF THE ONLY PEOPLE I CAN THINK OF WHO CAN HELP.
I HOPE HE'S OKAY.
WHY WOULDN'T HE BE OKAY?
BECAUSE IT'S NOT LIKE HIM NOT TO ANSWER A CALL FOR HELP--BECAUSE AFTER WHAT HAPPENED TODAY I DON'T TAKE ***ANYTHING*** FOR GRANTED.
YEAH, I JUST TALKED TO MYSELF AS A 16-YEAR-OLD BOY.
AND WHOSE FAULT IS THAT?
THERE YOU GO. I KNEW THAT WAS COMING.
IT WAS YOUR IDEA, BOBBY.
HANK'S LAST WORDS IN FACT WERE THAT THIS WAS YOUR IDEA.
"LET SCOTT SUMMERS SEE WHAT HE HAS BECOME."
AND NOW WE HAVE JEAN GREY RUNNING AROUND.
THAT ***WAS*** INSANE.
SHE LOOKED SO GREAT.
BOBBY.
YOU KNOW WHAT I MEAN.
I WONDER WHAT SCOTT THOUGHT OF HIMSELF.

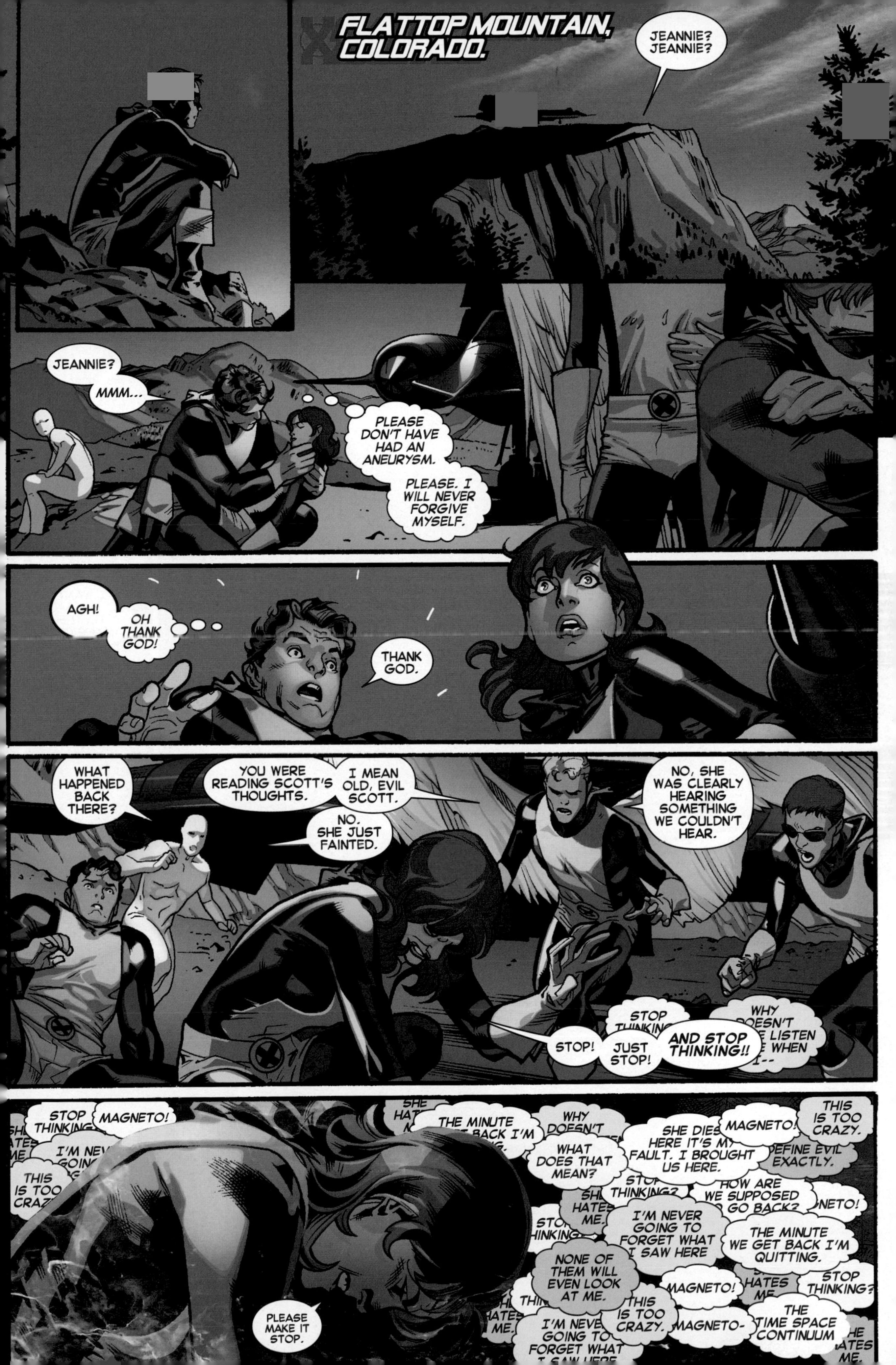
FLATTOP MOUNTAIN, COLORADO.
JEANNIE? JEANNIE?
JEANNIE?
MMM...
PLEASE DON'T HAVE HAD AN ANEURYSM.
PLEASE. I WILL NEVER FORGIVE MYSELF.
AGH!
OH THANK GOD!
THANK GOD.
WHAT HAPPENED BACK THERE?
YOU WERE READING SCOTT'S THOUGHTS.
I MEAN OLD, EVIL SCOTT.
NO. SHE JUST FAINTED.
NO, SHE WAS CLEARLY HEARING SOMETHING WE COULDN'T HEAR.
STOP!
JUST STOP!
AND STOP THINKING!!
MAGNETO!
WHAT DOES THAT MEAN?
MAGNETO!
THIS IS TOO CRAZY.
DEFINE EVIL EXACTLY.
HOW ARE WE SUPPOSED
I'M NEVER GOING TO FORGET WHAT I SAW HERE
THE MINUTE WE GET BACK I'M QUITTING.
NONE OF THEM WILL EVEN LOOK AT ME.
MAGNETO!
STOP THINKING?
THIS IS TOO CRAZY.
MAGNETO-
THE TIME SPACE CONTINUUM
PLEASE MAKE IT STOP.

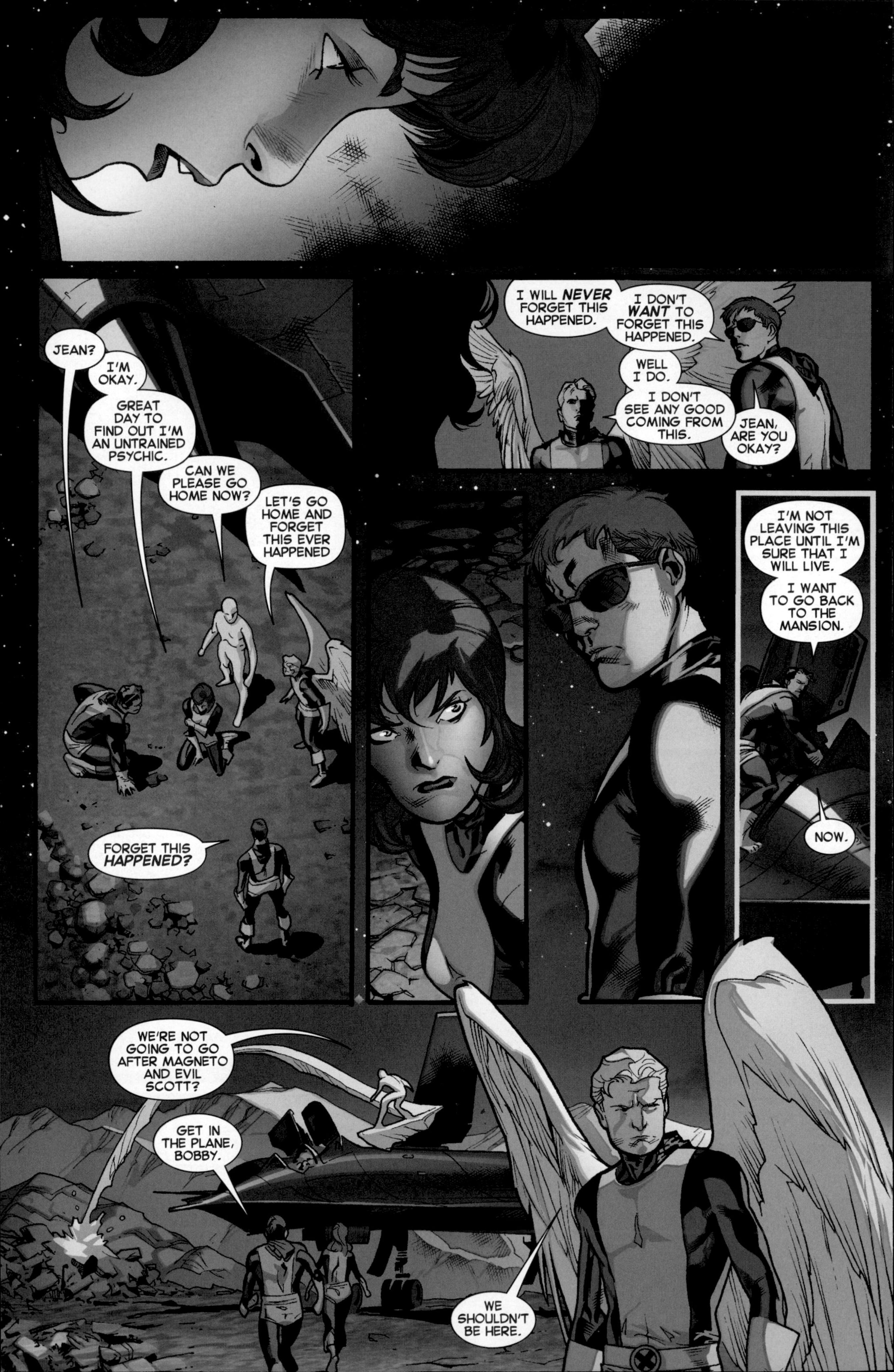
JEAN?
I'M OKAY.
GREAT DAY TO FIND OUT I'M AN UNTRAINED PSYCHIC.
CAN WE PLEASE GO HOME NOW?
LET'S GO HOME AND FORGET THIS EVER HAPPENED
FORGET THIS *HAPPENED?*
I WILL ***NEVER*** FORGET THIS HAPPENED.
I DON'T ***WANT*** TO FORGET THIS HAPPENED.
WELL I DO.
I DON'T SEE ANY GOOD COMING FROM THIS.
JEAN, ARE YOU OKAY?
I'M NOT LEAVING THIS PLACE UNTIL I'M SURE THAT I WILL LIVE.
I WANT TO GO BACK TO THE MANSION.
NOW.
WE'RE NOT GOING TO GO AFTER MAGNETO AND EVIL SCOTT?
GET IN THE PLANE, BOBBY.
WE SHOULDN'T BE HERE.

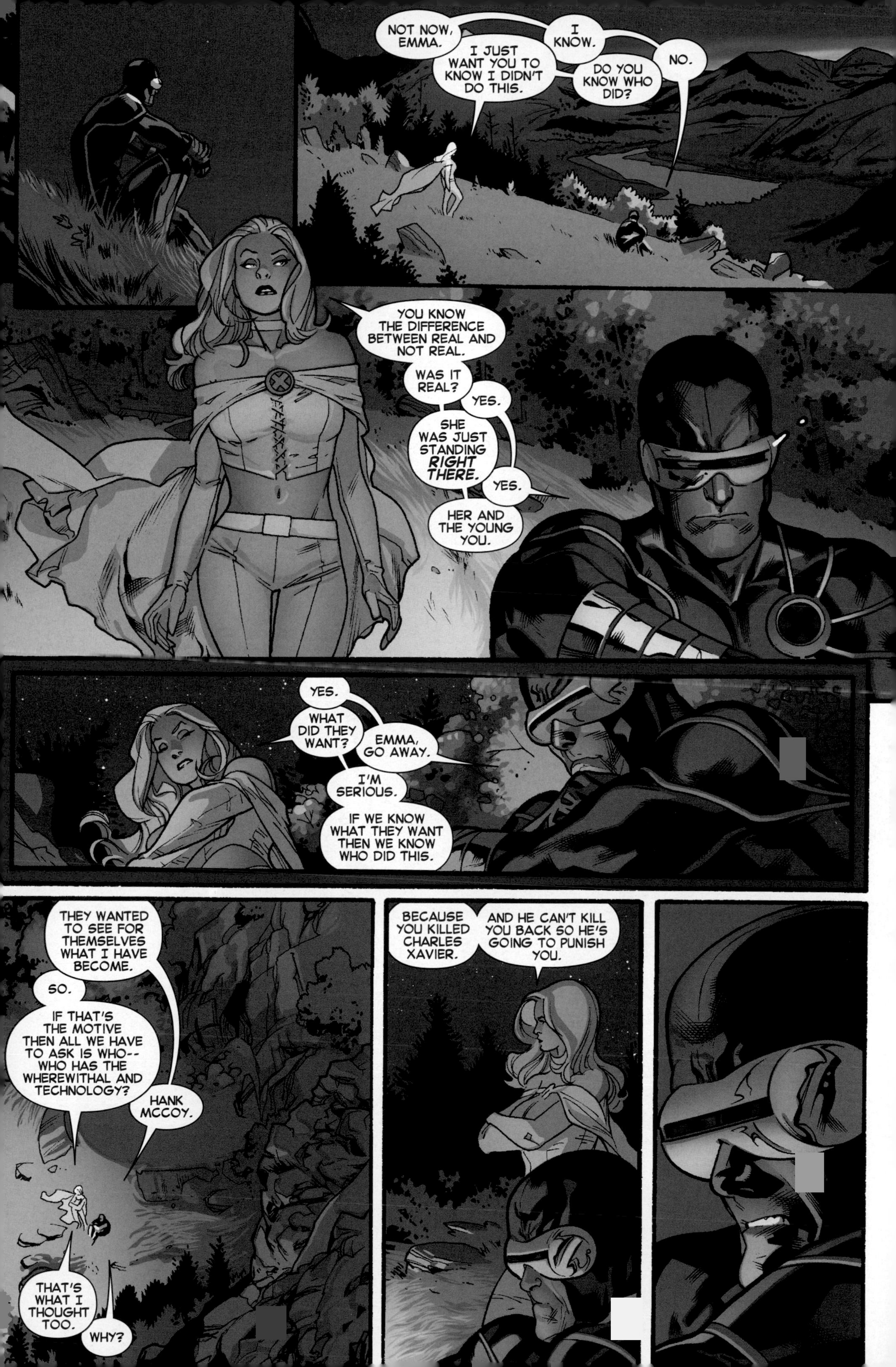
NOT NOW, EMMA.
I JUST WANT YOU TO KNOW I DIDN'T DO THIS.
I KNOW.
DO YOU KNOW WHO DID?
NO.
YOU KNOW THE DIFFERENCE BETWEEN REAL AND NOT REAL.
WAS IT REAL?
YES.
SHE WAS JUST STANDING RIGHT THERE.
YES.
HER AND THE YOUNG YOU.
YES.
WHAT DID THEY WANT?
EMMA, GO AWAY.
I'M SERIOUS.
IF WE KNOW WHAT THEY WANT THEN WE KNOW WHO DID THIS.
THEY WANTED TO SEE FOR THEMSELVES WHAT I HAVE BECOME.
SO.
IF THAT'S THE MOTIVE THEN ALL WE HAVE TO ASK IS WHO-- WHO HAS THE WHEREWITHAL AND TECHNOLOGY?
HANK MCCOY.
THAT'S WHAT I THOUGHT TOO.
WHY?
BECAUSE YOU KILLED CHARLES XAVIER.
AND HE CAN'T KILL YOU BACK SO HE'S GOING TO PUNISH YOU.

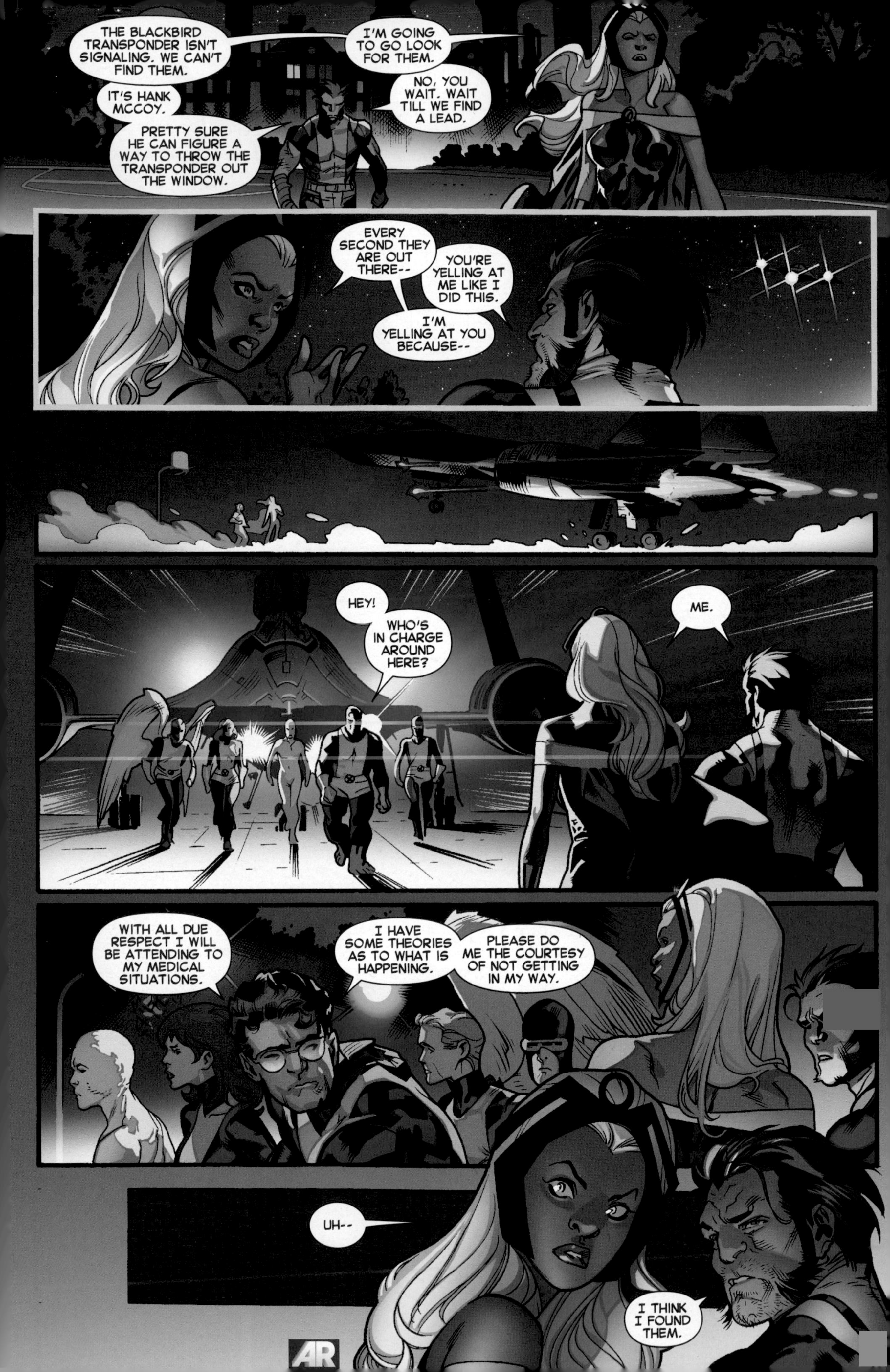
THE BLACKBIRD TRANSPONDER ISN'T SIGNALING. WE CAN'T FIND THEM.
I'M GOING TO GO LOOK FOR THEM.
IT'S HANK McCOY.
NO, YOU WAIT. WAIT TILL WE FIND A LEAD.
PRETTY SURE HE CAN FIGURE A WAY TO THROW THE TRANSPONDER OUT THE WINDOW.
EVERY SECOND THEY ARE OUT THERE--
YOU'RE YELLING AT ME LIKE I DID THIS.
I'M YELLING AT YOU BECAUSE--
HEY!
WHO'S IN CHARGE AROUND HERE?
ME.
WITH ALL DUE RESPECT I WILL BE ATTENDING TO MY MEDICAL SITUATIONS.
I HAVE SOME THEORIES AS TO WHAT IS HAPPENING.
PLEASE DO ME THE COURTESY OF NOT GETTING IN MY WAY.
UH--
I THINK I FOUND THEM.

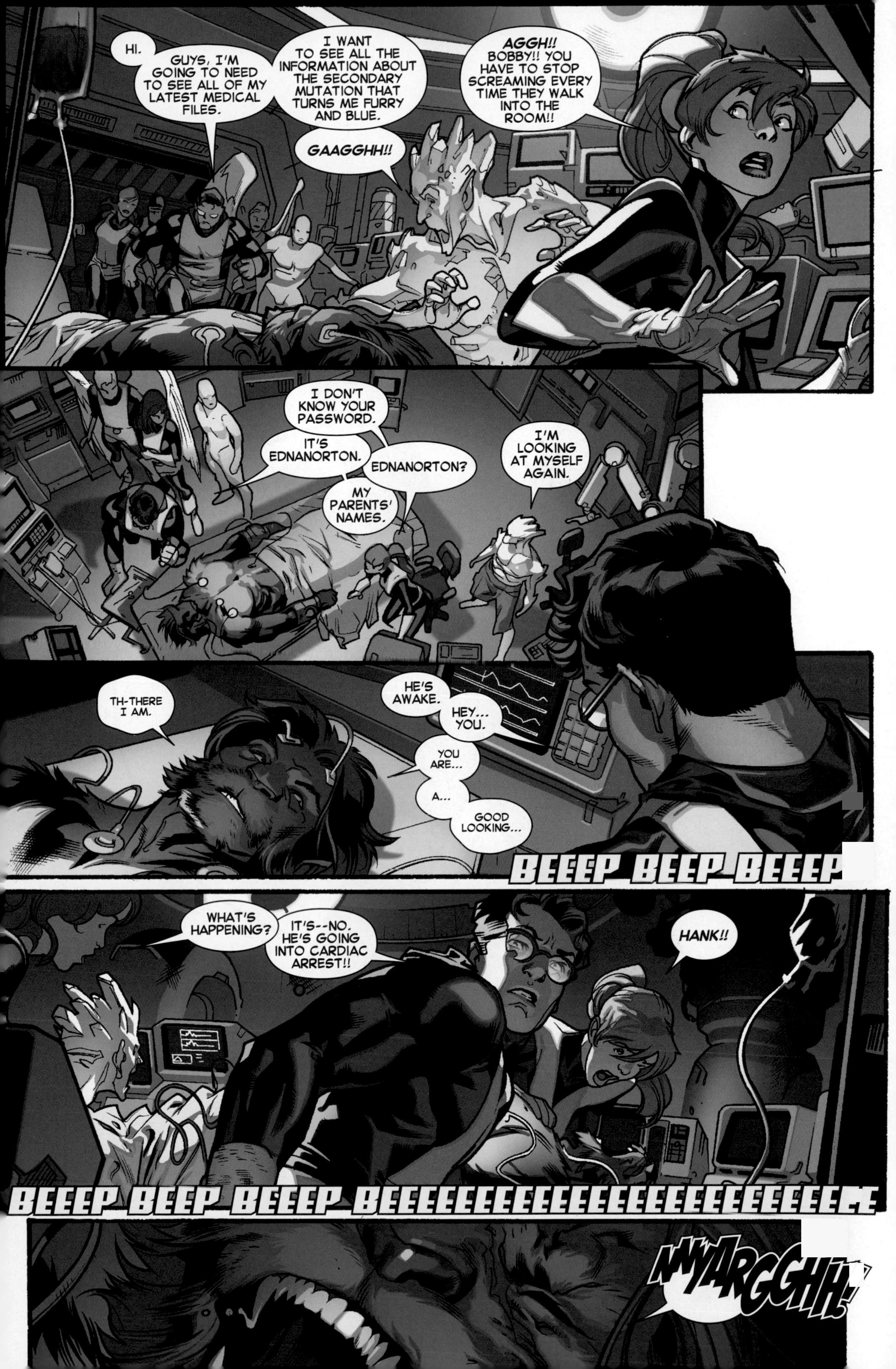
HI.
GUYS, I'M GOING TO NEED TO SEE ALL OF MY LATEST MEDICAL FILES.
I WANT TO SEE ALL THE INFORMATION ABOUT THE SECONDARY MUTATION THAT TURNS ME FURRY AND BLUE.
GAAGGHH!!
AGGH!! BOBBY!! YOU HAVE TO STOP SCREAMING EVERY TIME THEY WALK INTO THE ROOM!!
I DON'T KNOW YOUR PASSWORD.
IT'S EDNANORTON.
EDNANORTON?
MY PARENTS' NAMES.
I'M LOOKING AT MYSELF AGAIN.
TH-THERE I AM.
HE'S AWAKE.
HEY... YOU.
YOU ARE...
A...
GOOD LOOKING...
BEEEP BEEP BEEEP
WHAT'S HAPPENING?
IT'S--NO. HE'S GOING INTO CARDIAC ARREST!!
HANK!!
BEEEP BEEP BEEEP BEEEEEEEEEEEEEEEEEEEEEEEEEEEEEE
NNYARGGHH!

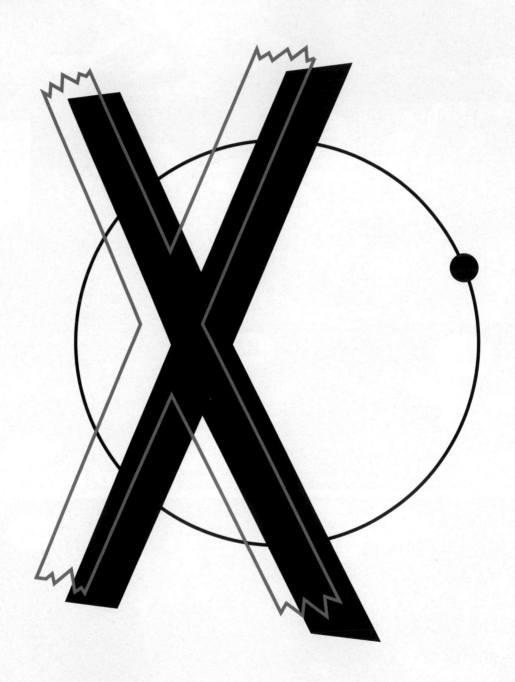

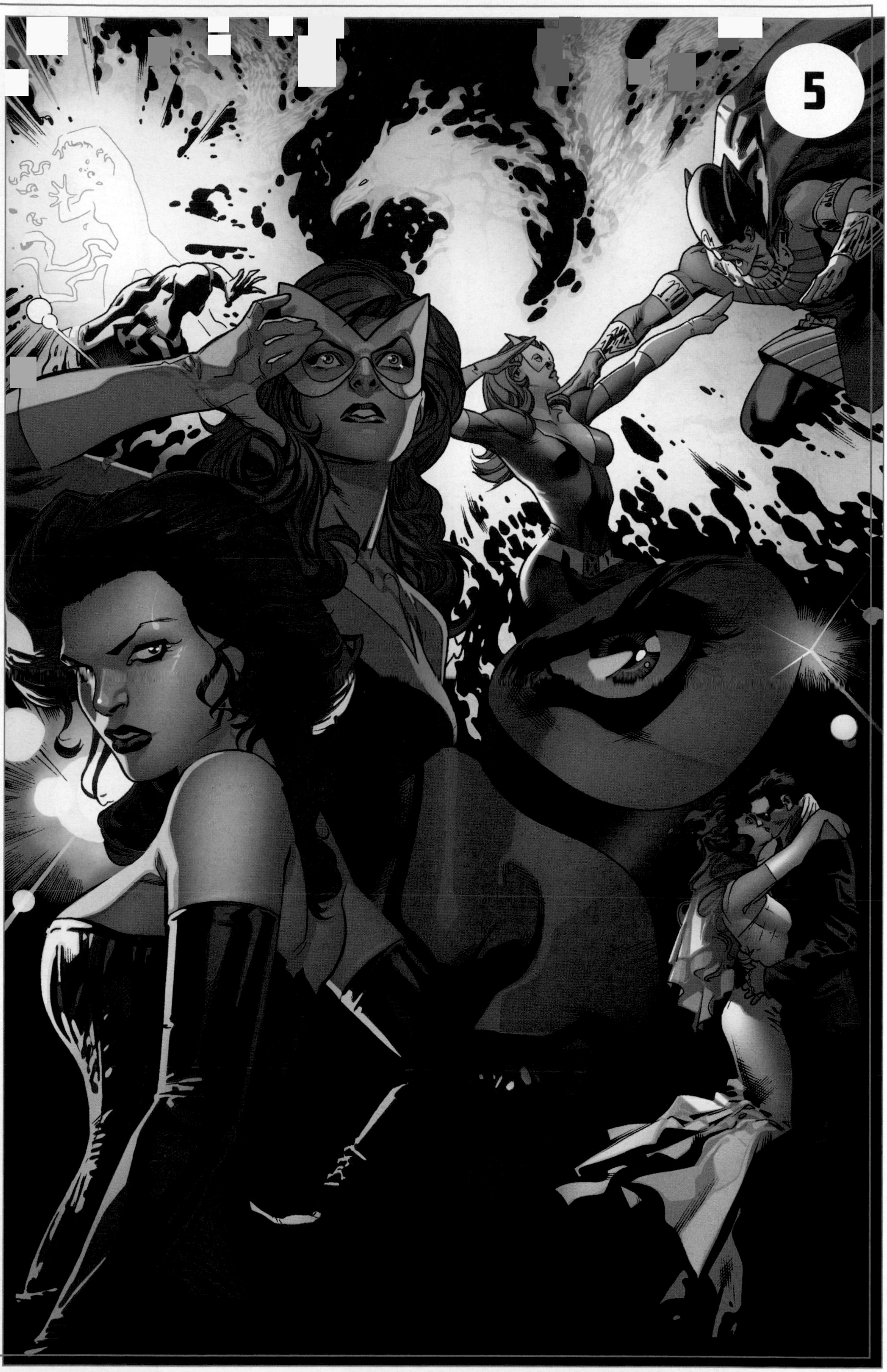
5

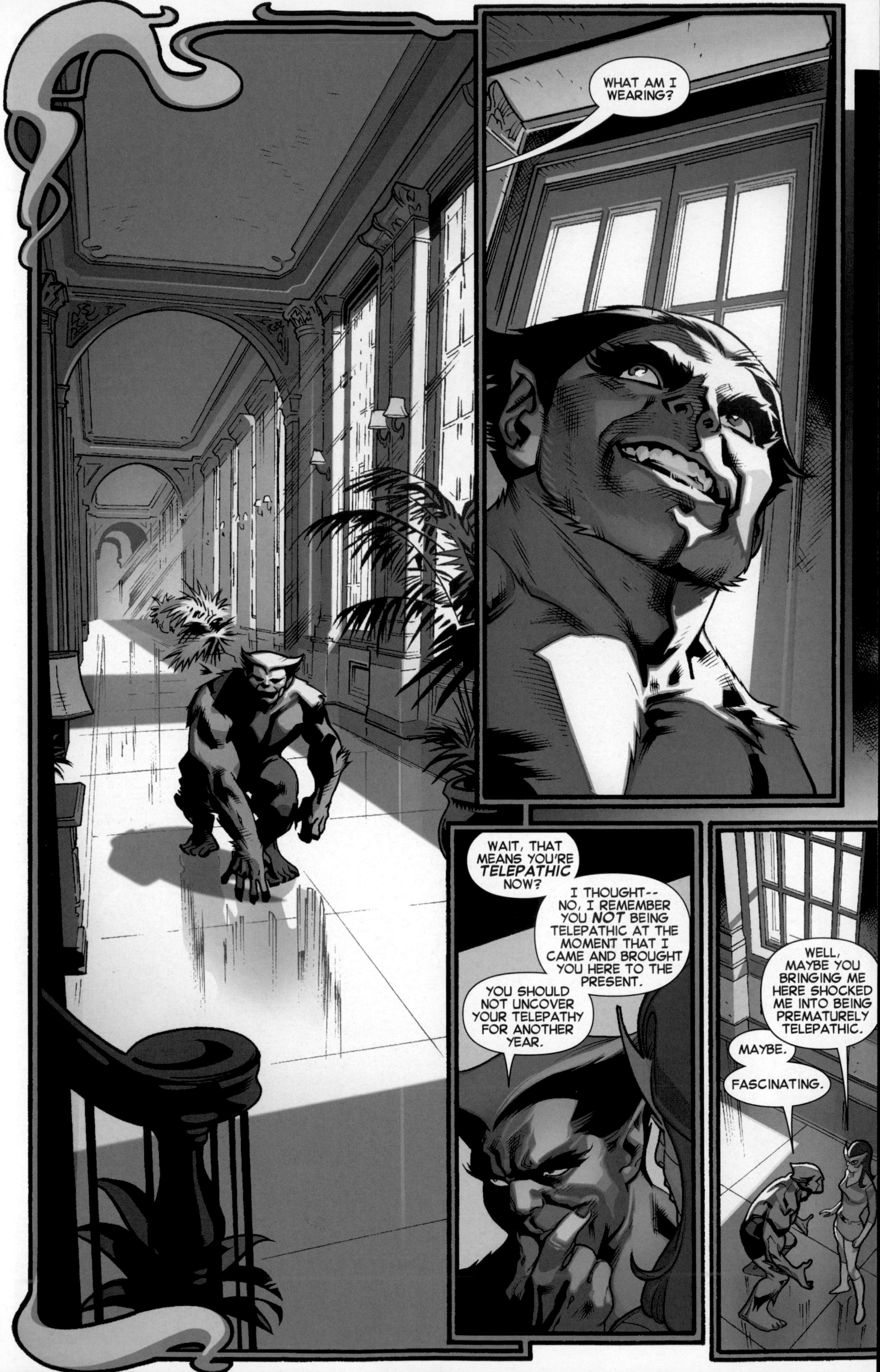
WHAT AM I WEARING?
WAIT, THAT MEANS YOU'RE *TELEPATHIC* NOW?
I THOUGHT-- NO, I REMEMBER YOU *NOT* BEING TELEPATHIC AT THE MOMENT THAT I CAME AND BROUGHT YOU HERE TO THE PRESENT.
YOU SHOULD NOT UNCOVER YOUR TELEPATHY FOR ANOTHER YEAR.
WELL, MAYBE YOU BRINGING ME HERE SHOCKED ME INTO BEING PREMATURELY TELEPATHIC.
MAYBE.
FASCINATING.

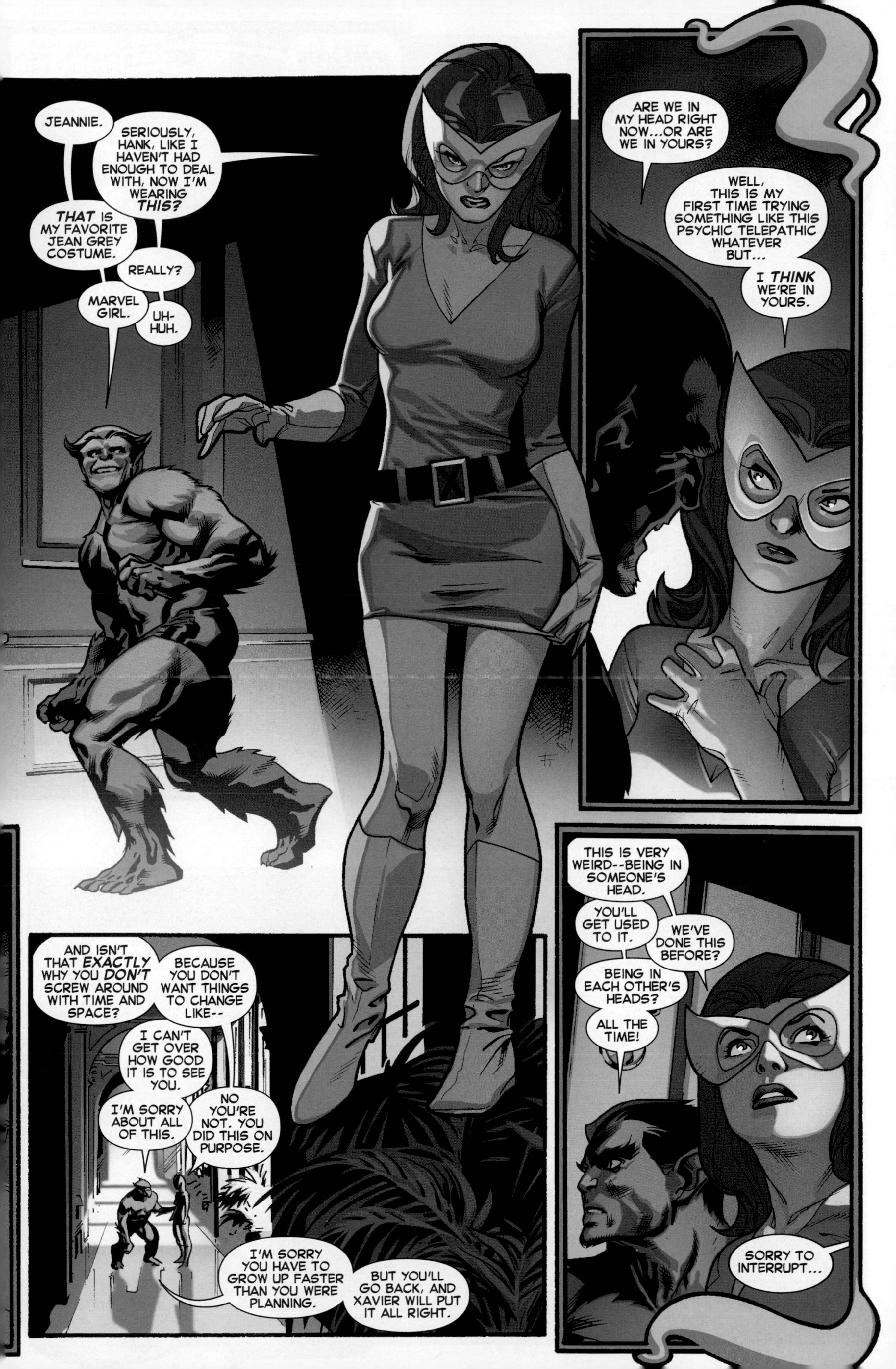

JEANNIE.
SERIOUSLY, HANK, LIKE I HAVEN'T HAD ENOUGH TO DEAL WITH, NOW I'M WEARING THIS?
THAT IS MY FAVORITE JEAN GREY COSTUME.
REALLY?
MARVEL GIRL.
UH-HUH.
ARE WE IN MY HEAD RIGHT NOW...OR ARE WE IN YOURS?
WELL, THIS IS MY FIRST TIME TRYING SOMETHING LIKE THIS PSYCHIC TELEPATHIC WHATEVER BUT...
I THINK WE'RE IN YOURS.
AND ISN'T THAT EXACTLY WHY YOU DON'T SCREW AROUND WITH TIME AND SPACE?
BECAUSE YOU DON'T WANT THINGS TO CHANGE LIKE--
I CAN'T GET OVER HOW GOOD IT IS TO SEE YOU.
I'M SORRY ABOUT ALL OF THIS.
NO YOU'RE NOT. YOU DID THIS ON PURPOSE.
I'M SORRY YOU HAVE TO GROW UP FASTER THAN YOU WERE PLANNING.
BUT YOU'LL GO BACK, AND XAVIER WILL PUT IT ALL RIGHT.
THIS IS VERY WEIRD--BEING IN SOMEONE'S HEAD.
YOU'LL GET USED TO IT.
WE'VE DONE THIS BEFORE?
BEING IN EACH OTHER'S HEADS?
ALL THE TIME!
SORRY TO INTERRUPT...

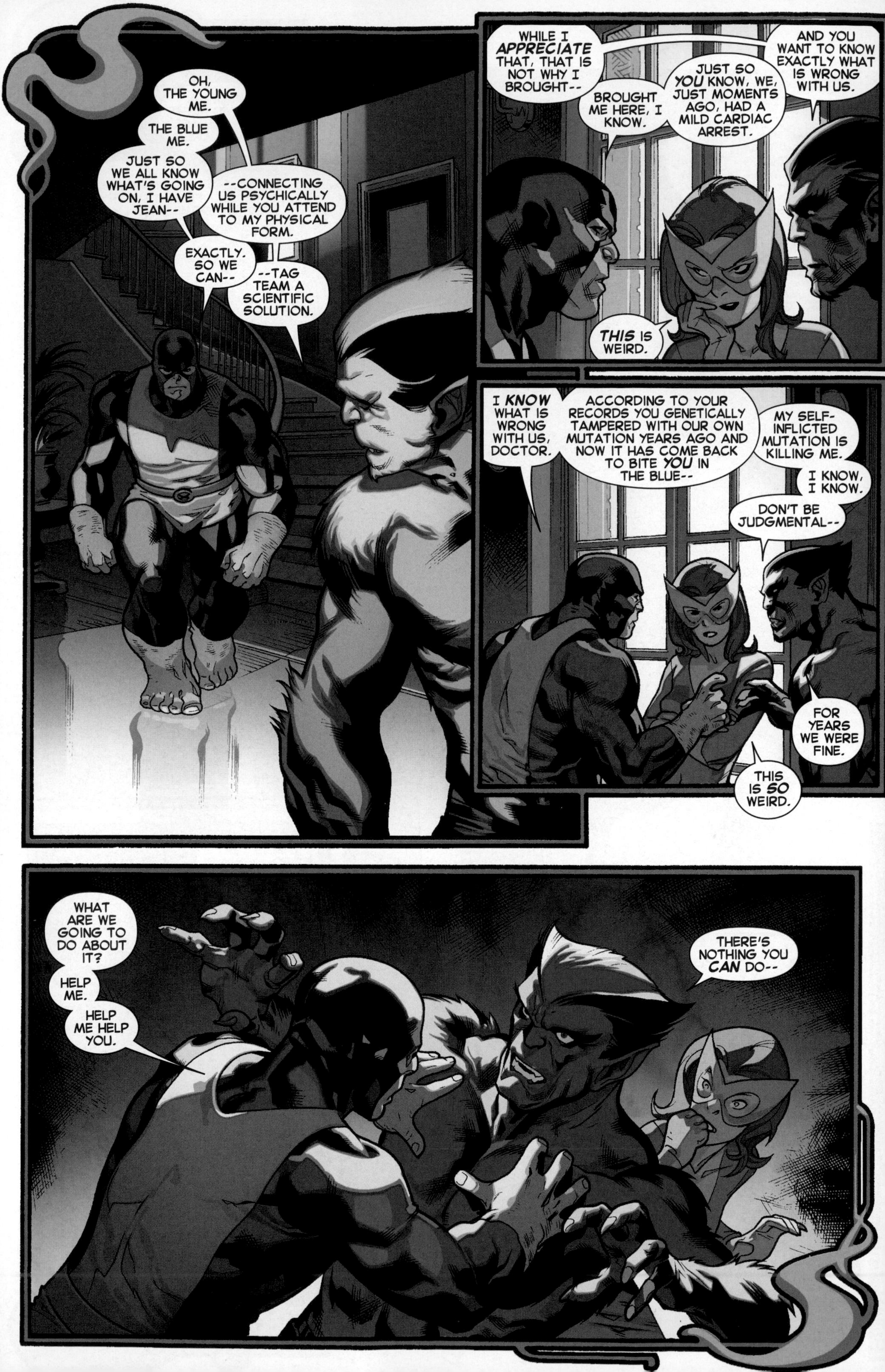
OH, THE YOUNG ME.
THE BLUE ME.
JUST SO WE ALL KNOW WHAT'S GOING ON, I HAVE JEAN--
--CONNECTING US PSYCHICALLY WHILE YOU ATTEND TO MY PHYSICAL FORM.
EXACTLY. SO WE CAN--
--TAG TEAM A SCIENTIFIC SOLUTION.
WHILE I APPRECIATE THAT, THAT IS NOT WHY I BROUGHT--
BROUGHT ME HERE, I KNOW.
JUST SO YOU KNOW, WE, JUST MOMENTS AGO, HAD A MILD CARDIAC ARREST.
AND YOU WANT TO KNOW EXACTLY WHAT IS WRONG WITH US.
THIS IS WEIRD.
I KNOW WHAT IS WRONG WITH US, DOCTOR.
ACCORDING TO YOUR RECORDS YOU GENETICALLY TAMPERED WITH OUR OWN MUTATION YEARS AGO AND NOW IT HAS COME BACK TO BITE YOU IN THE BLUE--
MY SELF-INFLICTED MUTATION IS KILLING ME.
I KNOW, I KNOW.
DON'T BE JUDGMENTAL--
FOR YEARS WE WERE FINE.
THIS IS SO WEIRD.
WHAT ARE WE GOING TO DO ABOUT IT?
HELP ME.
HELP ME HELP YOU.
THERE'S NOTHING YOU CAN DO--

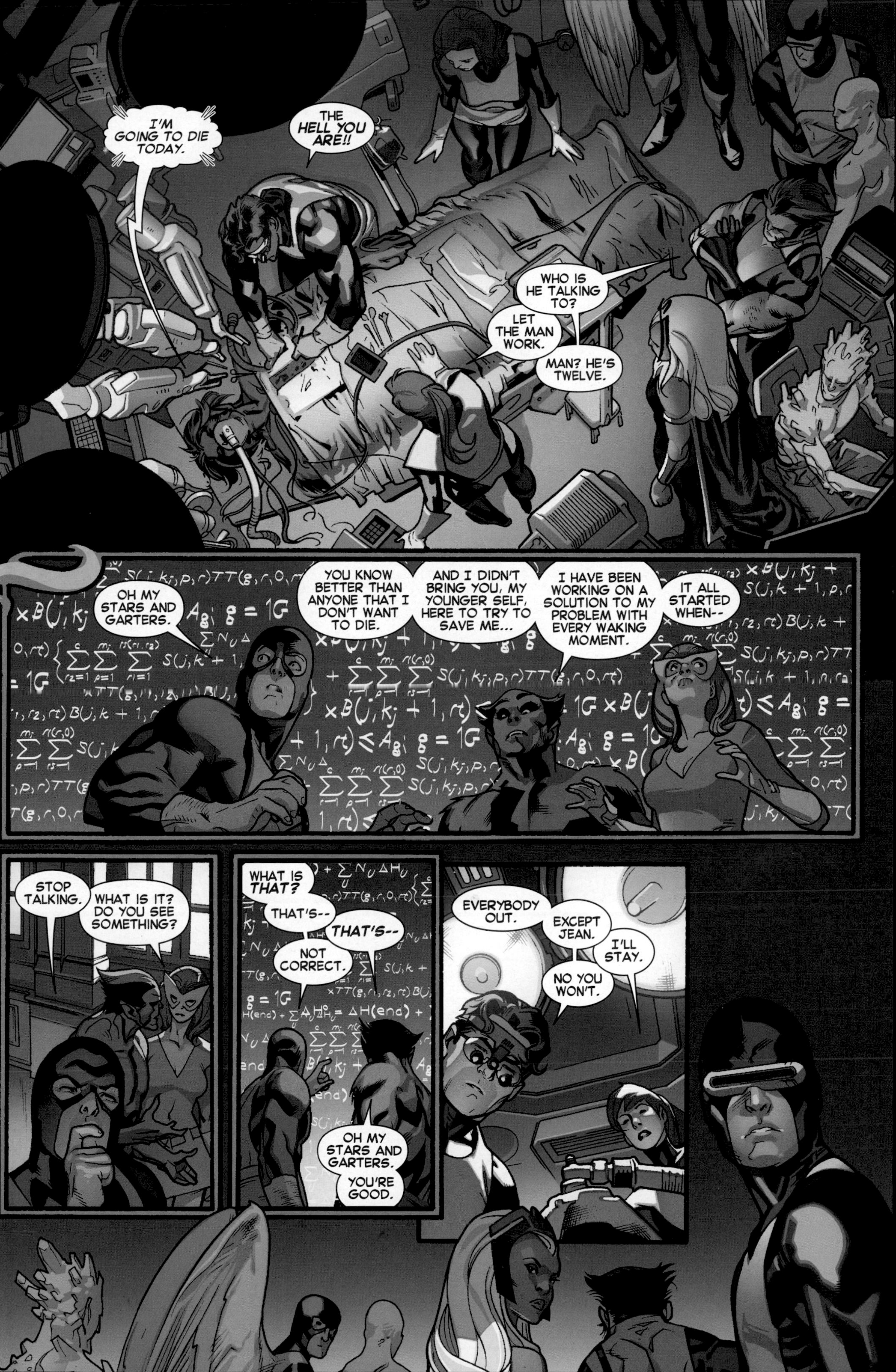
I'M GOING TO DIE TODAY.
THE HELL YOU ARE!!
WHO IS HE TALKING TO?
LET THE MAN WORK.
MAN? HE'S TWELVE.
OH MY STARS AND GARTERS.
YOU KNOW BETTER THAN ANYONE THAT I DON'T WANT TO DIE.
AND I DIDN'T BRING YOU, MY YOUNGER SELF, HERE TO TRY TO SAVE ME...
I HAVE BEEN WORKING ON A SOLUTION TO MY PROBLEM WITH EVERY WAKING MOMENT.
IT ALL STARTED WHEN--
STOP TALKING.
WHAT IS IT? DO YOU SEE SOMETHING?
WHAT IS THAT?
THAT'S--
THAT'S--
NOT CORRECT.
OH MY STARS AND GARTERS.
YOU'RE GOOD.
EVERYBODY OUT.
EXCEPT JEAN.
I'LL STAY.
NO YOU WON'T.

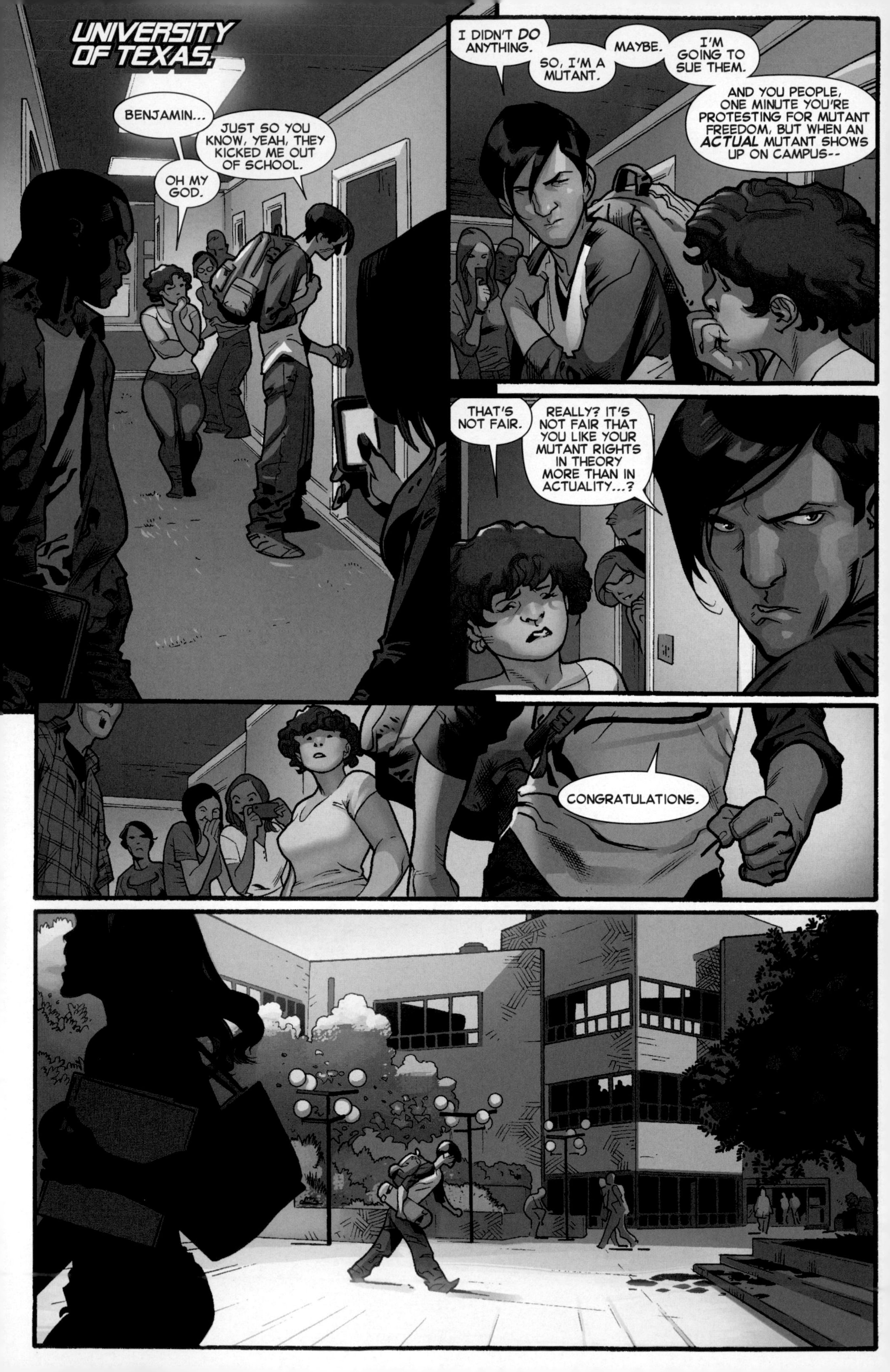
UNIVERSITY OF TEXAS.
BENJAMIN...
OH MY GOD.
JUST SO YOU KNOW, YEAH, THEY KICKED ME OUT OF SCHOOL.
I DIDN'T DO ANYTHING.
SO, I'M A MUTANT.
MAYBE.
I'M GOING TO SUE THEM.
AND YOU PEOPLE, ONE MINUTE YOU'RE PROTESTING FOR MUTANT FREEDOM, BUT WHEN AN ACTUAL MUTANT SHOWS UP ON CAMPUS--
THAT'S NOT FAIR.
REALLY? IT'S NOT FAIR THAT YOU LIKE YOUR MUTANT RIGHTS IN THEORY MORE THAN IN ACTUALITY...?
CONGRATULATIONS.

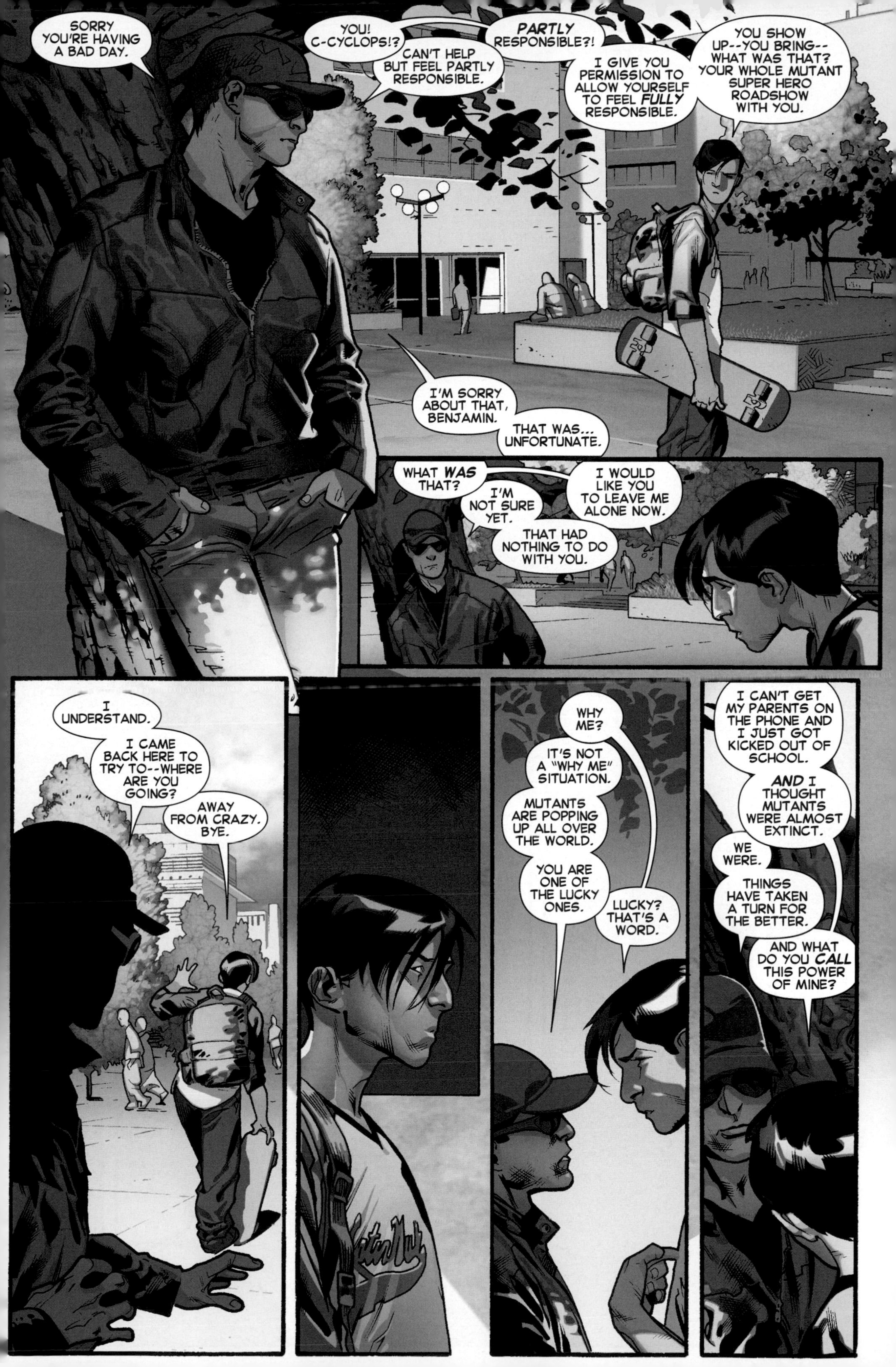
SORRY YOU'RE HAVING A BAD DAY.
YOU! C-CYCLOPS!?
CAN'T HELP BUT FEEL PARTLY RESPONSIBLE.
PARTLY RESPONSIBLE?!
I GIVE YOU PERMISSION TO ALLOW YOURSELF TO FEEL FULLY RESPONSIBLE.
YOU SHOW UP--YOU BRING--WHAT WAS THAT? YOUR WHOLE MUTANT SUPER HERO ROADSHOW WITH YOU.
I'M SORRY ABOUT THAT, BENJAMIN.
THAT WAS... UNFORTUNATE.
WHAT WAS THAT?
I'M NOT SURE YET.
I WOULD LIKE YOU TO LEAVE ME ALONE NOW.
THAT HAD NOTHING TO DO WITH YOU.
I UNDERSTAND.
I CAME BACK HERE TO TRY TO--WHERE ARE YOU GOING?
AWAY FROM CRAZY. BYE.
WHY ME?
IT'S NOT A "WHY ME" SITUATION.
MUTANTS ARE POPPING UP ALL OVER THE WORLD.
YOU ARE ONE OF THE LUCKY ONES.
LUCKY? THAT'S A WORD.
I CAN'T GET MY PARENTS ON THE PHONE AND I JUST GOT KICKED OUT OF SCHOOL.
AND I THOUGHT MUTANTS WERE ALMOST EXTINCT.
WE WERE.
THINGS HAVE TAKEN A TURN FOR THE BETTER.
AND WHAT DO YOU CALL THIS POWER OF MINE?

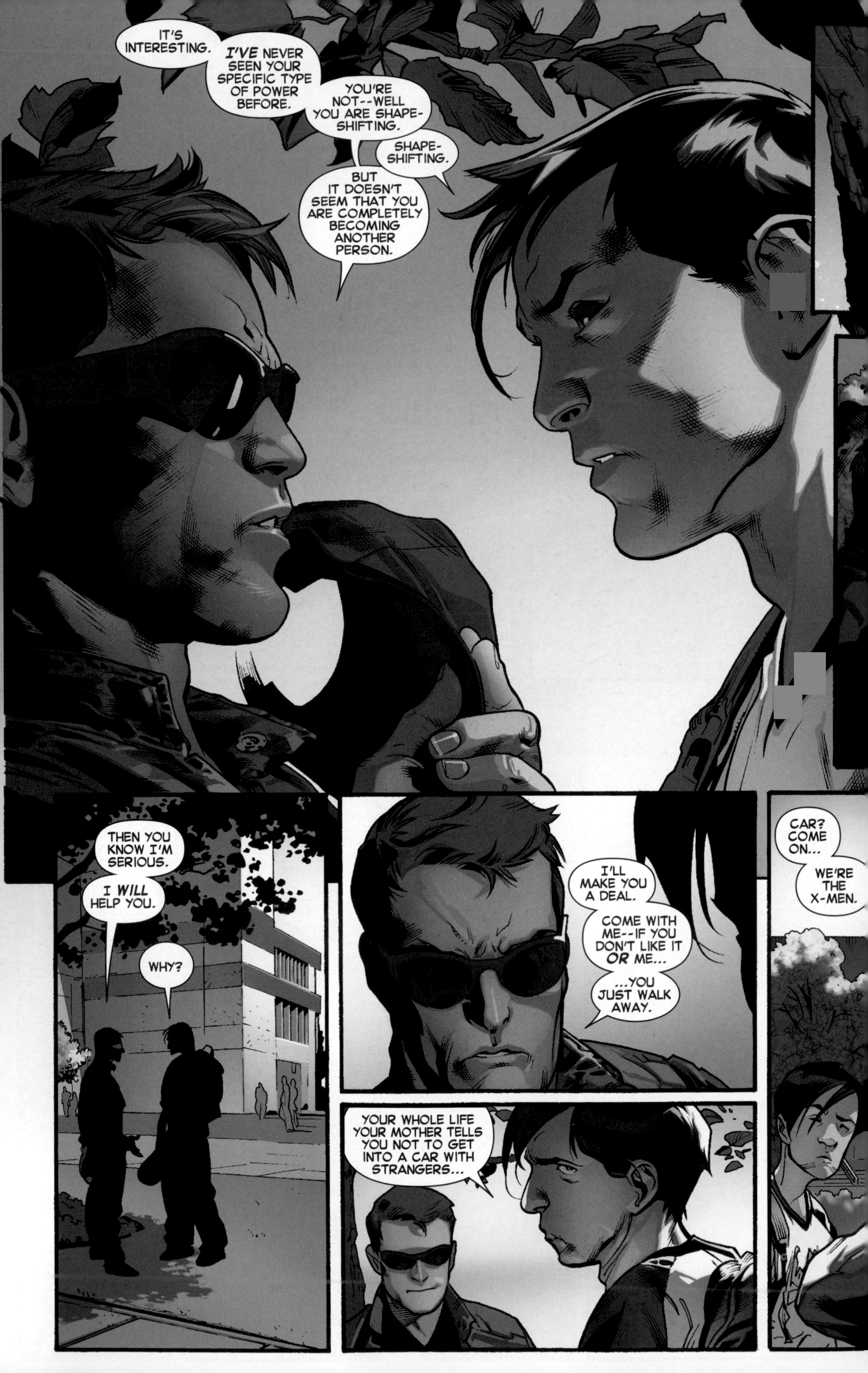
IT'S INTERESTING.
I'VE NEVER SEEN YOUR SPECIFIC TYPE OF POWER BEFORE.
YOU'RE NOT--WELL YOU ARE SHAPE-SHIFTING.
SHAPE-SHIFTING.
BUT IT DOESN'T SEEM THAT YOU ARE COMPLETELY BECOMING ANOTHER PERSON.
THEN YOU KNOW I'M SERIOUS.
I WILL HELP YOU.
WHY?
I'LL MAKE YOU A DEAL.
COME WITH ME--IF YOU DON'T LIKE IT OR ME...
...YOU JUST WALK AWAY.
YOUR WHOLE LIFE YOUR MOTHER TELLS YOU NOT TO GET INTO A CAR WITH STRANGERS...
CAR? COME ON...
WE'RE THE X-MEN.

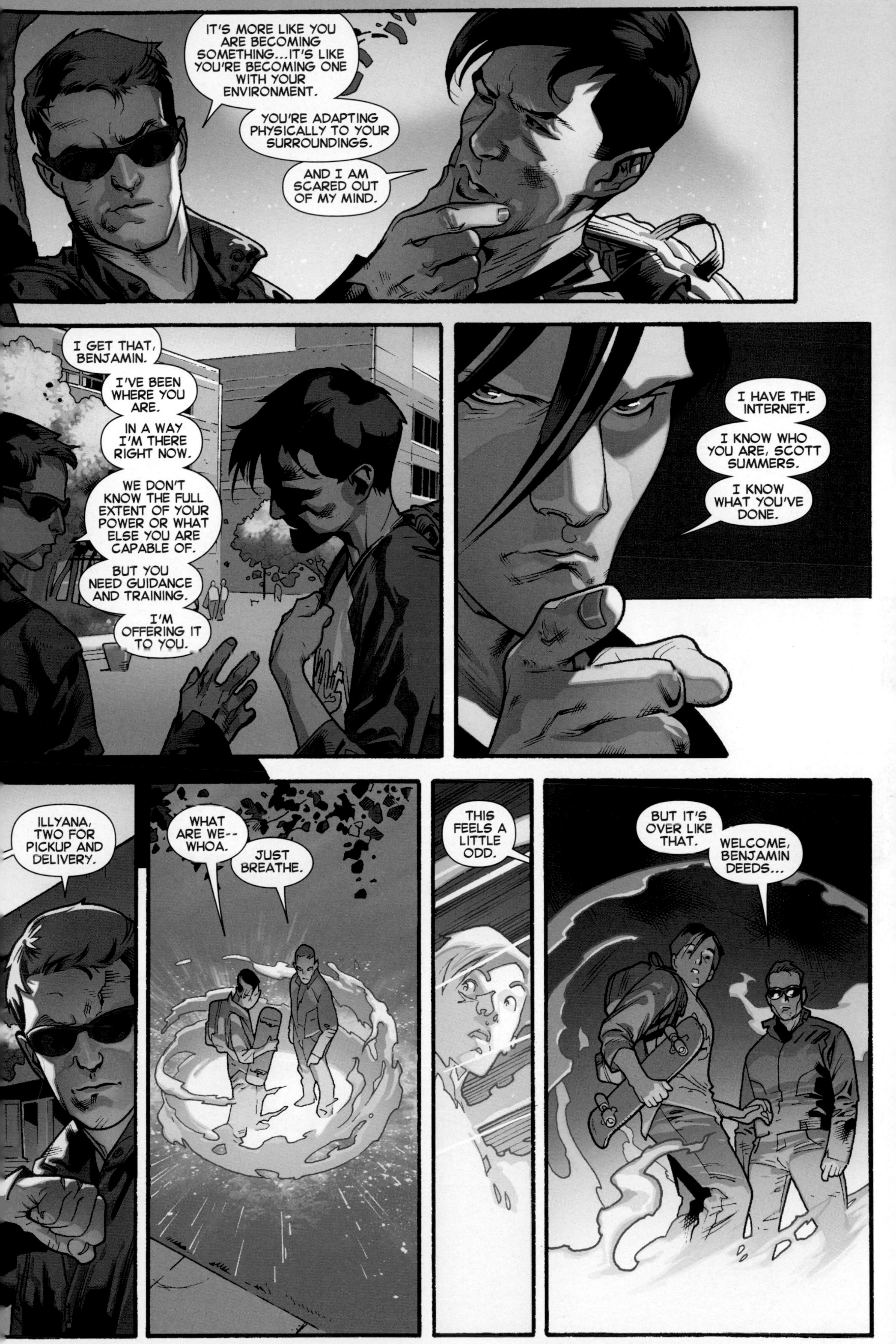
IT'S MORE LIKE YOU ARE BECOMING SOMETHING...IT'S LIKE YOU'RE BECOMING ONE WITH YOUR ENVIRONMENT.
YOU'RE ADAPTING PHYSICALLY TO YOUR SURROUNDINGS.
AND I AM SCARED OUT OF MY MIND.
I GET THAT, BENJAMIN.
I'VE BEEN WHERE YOU ARE.
IN A WAY I'M THERE RIGHT NOW.
WE DON'T KNOW THE FULL EXTENT OF YOUR POWER OR WHAT ELSE YOU ARE CAPABLE OF.
BUT YOU NEED GUIDANCE AND TRAINING.
I'M OFFERING IT TO YOU.
I HAVE THE INTERNET.
I KNOW WHO YOU ARE, SCOTT SUMMERS.
I KNOW WHAT YOU'VE DONE.
ILLYANA, TWO FOR PICKUP AND DELIVERY.
WHAT ARE WE-- WHOA.
JUST BREATHE.
THIS FEELS A LITTLE ODD.
BUT IT'S OVER LIKE THAT.
WELCOME, BENJAMIN DEEDS...

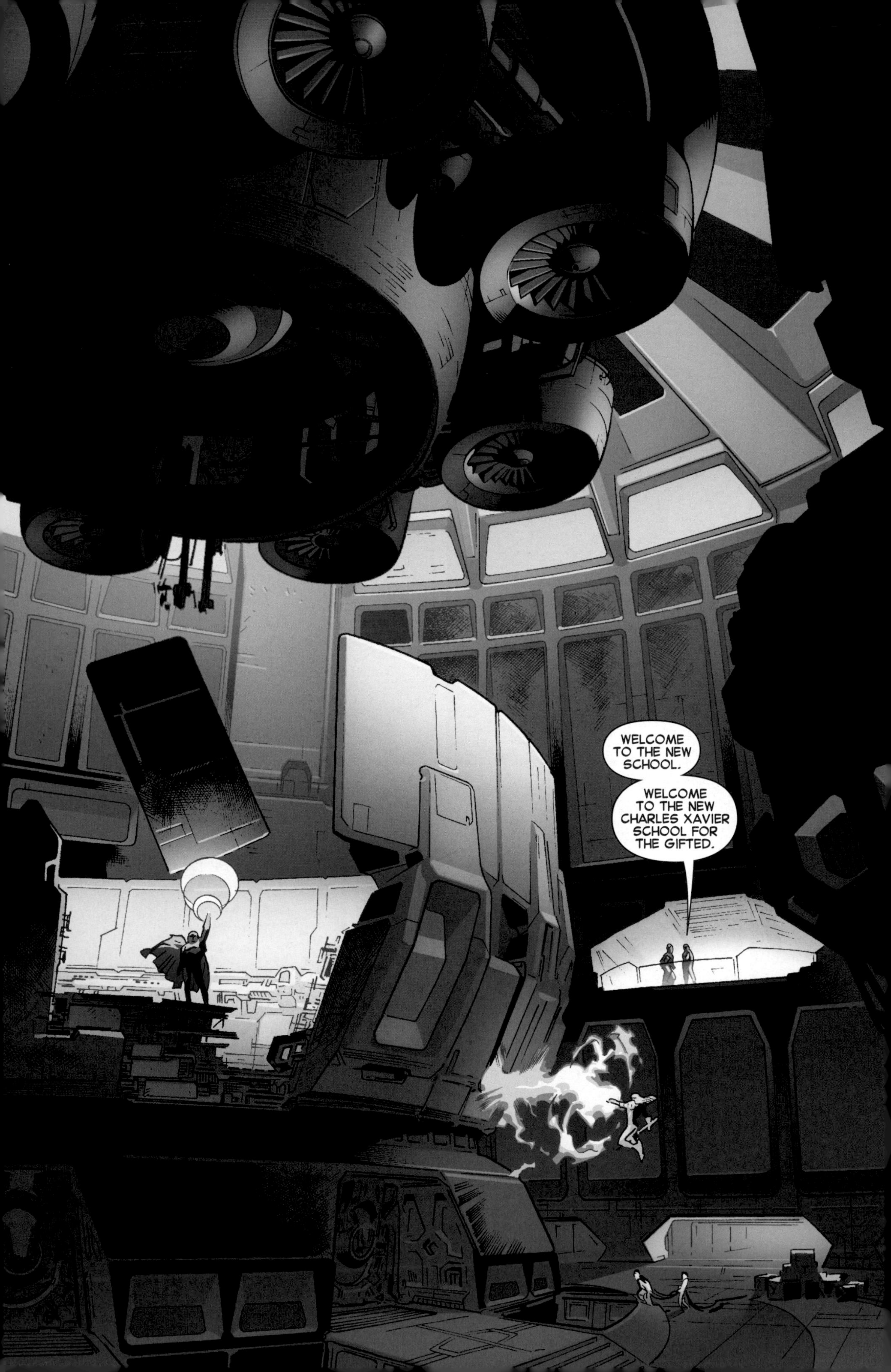
WELCOME TO THE NEW SCHOOL.
WELCOME TO THE NEW CHARLES XAVIER SCHOOL FOR THE GIFTED.

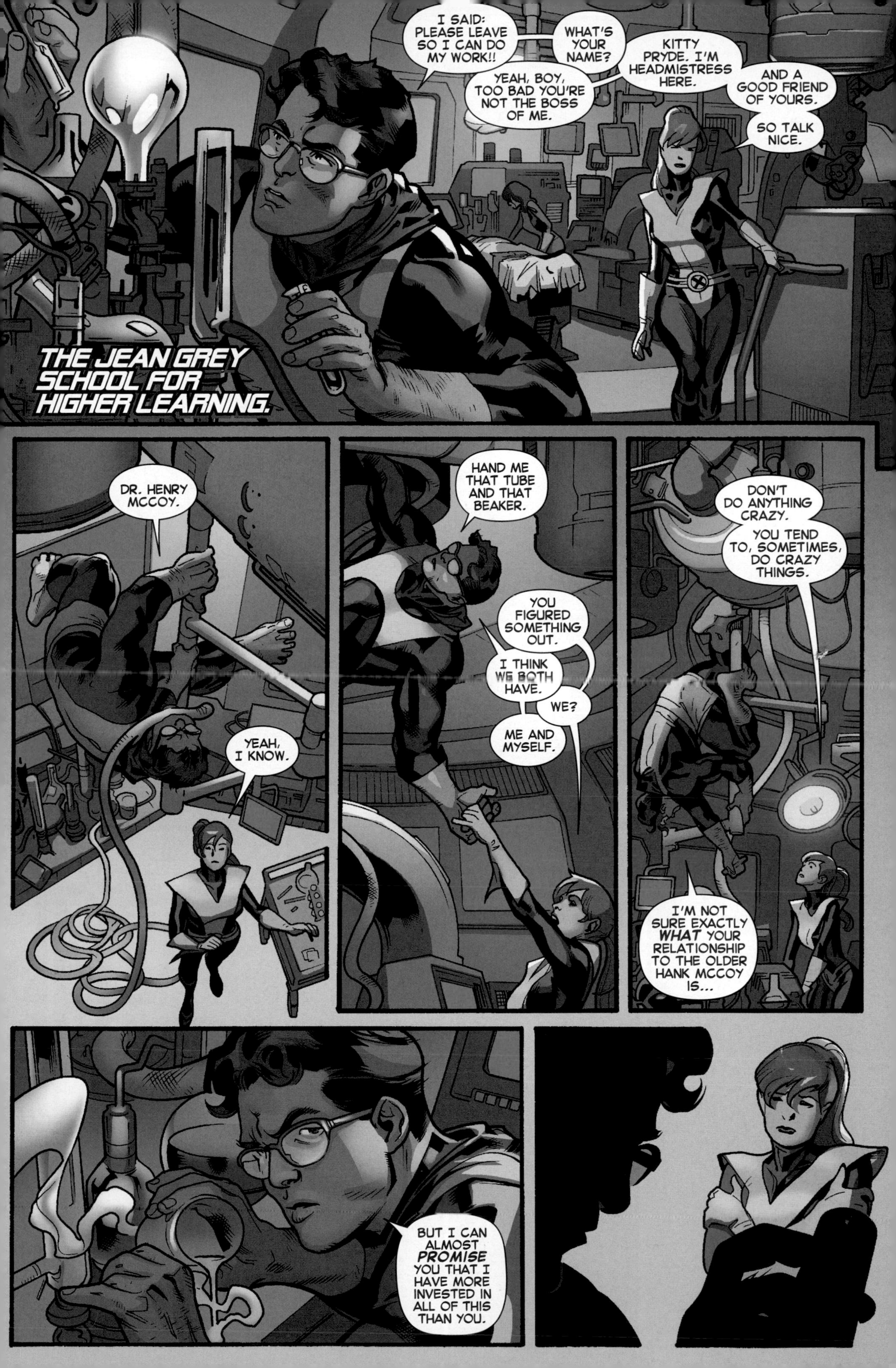
I SAID: PLEASE LEAVE SO I CAN DO MY WORK!!
WHAT'S YOUR NAME?
YEAH, BOY, TOO BAD YOU'RE NOT THE BOSS OF ME.
KITTY PRYDE. I'M HEADMISTRESS HERE.
AND A GOOD FRIEND OF YOURS.
SO TALK NICE.
THE JEAN GREY SCHOOL FOR HIGHER LEARNING.
DR. HENRY MCCOY.
YEAH, I KNOW.
HAND ME THAT TUBE AND THAT BEAKER.
YOU FIGURED SOMETHING OUT.
I THINK WE BOTH HAVE.
WE?
ME AND MYSELF.
DON'T DO ANYTHING CRAZY.
YOU TEND TO, SOMETIMES, DO CRAZY THINGS.
I'M NOT SURE EXACTLY WHAT YOUR RELATIONSHIP TO THE OLDER HANK MCCOY IS...
BUT I CAN ALMOST PROMISE YOU THAT I HAVE MORE INVESTED IN ALL OF THIS THAN YOU.

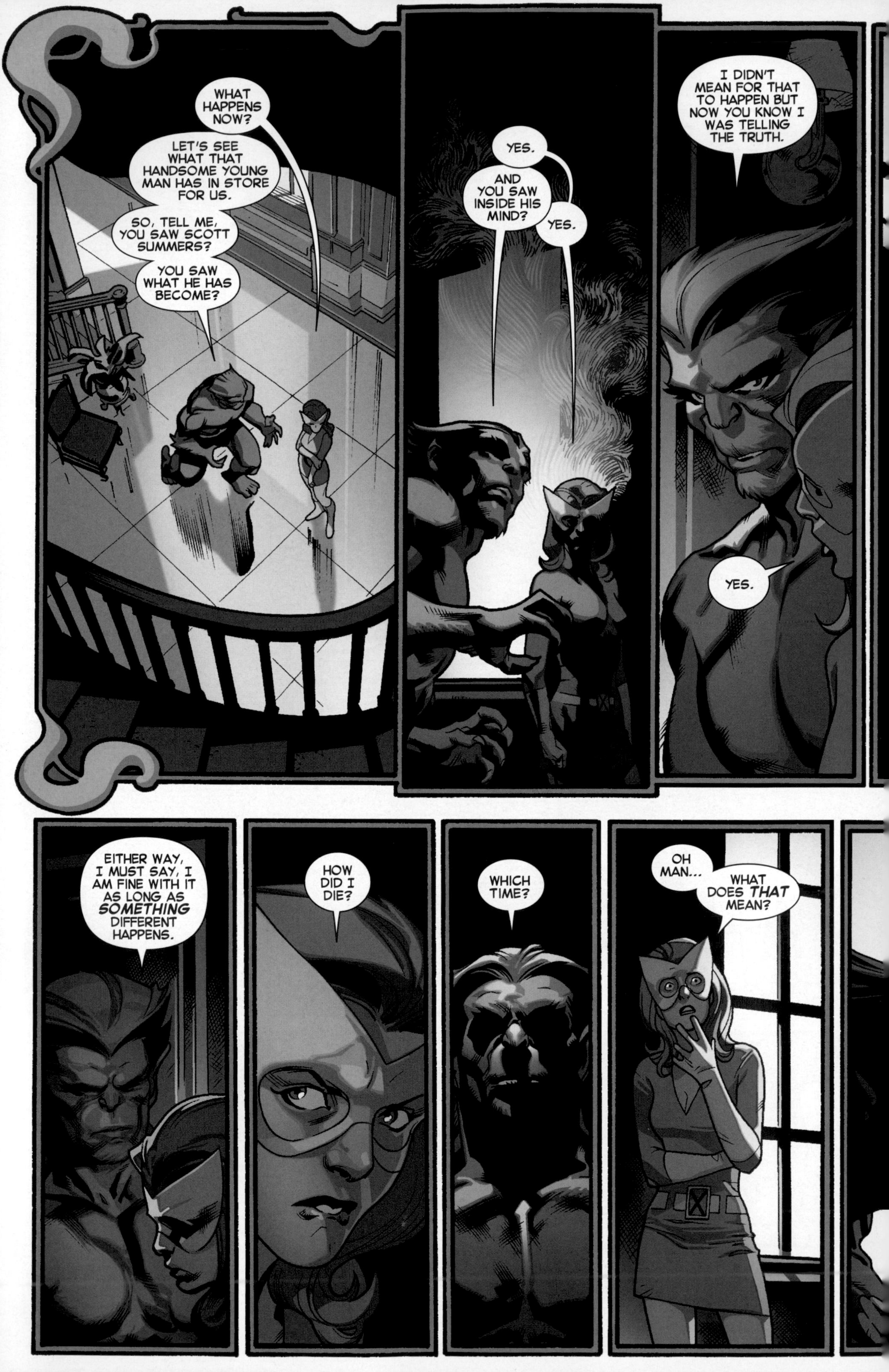
WHAT HAPPENS NOW?
LET'S SEE WHAT THAT HANDSOME YOUNG MAN HAS IN STORE FOR US.
SO, TELL ME, YOU SAW SCOTT SUMMERS?
YOU SAW WHAT HE HAS BECOME?
YES.
AND YOU SAW INSIDE HIS MIND?
YES.
I DIDN'T MEAN FOR THAT TO HAPPEN BUT NOW YOU KNOW I WAS TELLING THE TRUTH.
YES.
EITHER WAY, I MUST SAY, I AM FINE WITH IT AS LONG AS *SOMETHING* DIFFERENT HAPPENS.
HOW DID I DIE?
WHICH TIME?
OH MAN...
WHAT DOES *THAT* MEAN?

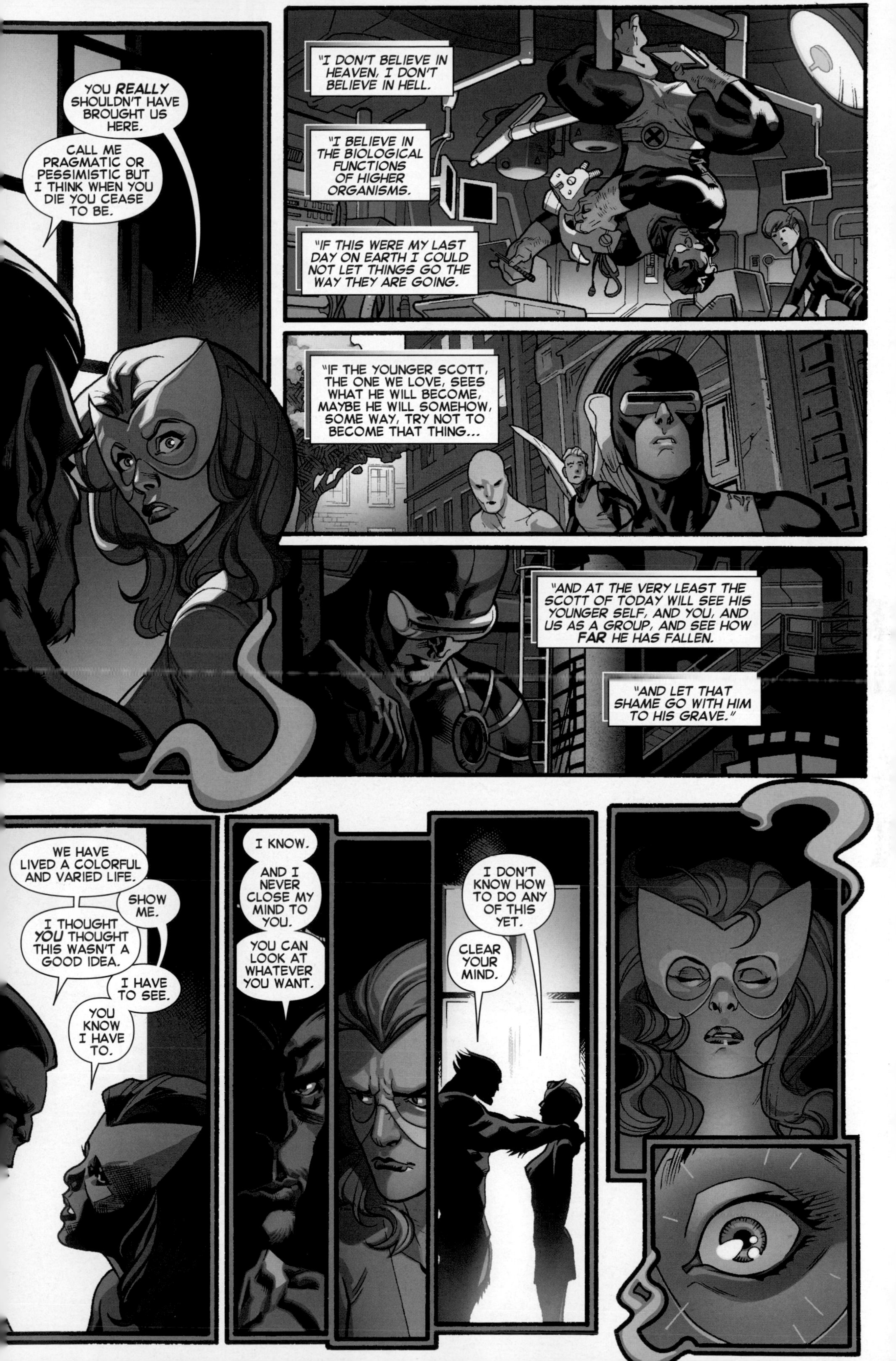
YOU REALLY SHOULDN'T HAVE BROUGHT US HERE.
CALL ME PRAGMATIC OR PESSIMISTIC BUT I THINK WHEN YOU DIE YOU CEASE TO BE.
"I DON'T BELIEVE IN HEAVEN, I DON'T BELIEVE IN HELL.
"I BELIEVE IN THE BIOLOGICAL FUNCTIONS OF HIGHER ORGANISMS.
"IF THIS WERE MY LAST DAY ON EARTH I COULD NOT LET THINGS GO THE WAY THEY ARE GOING.
"IF THE YOUNGER SCOTT, THE ONE WE LOVE, SEES WHAT HE WILL BECOME, MAYBE HE WILL SOMEHOW, SOME WAY, TRY NOT TO BECOME THAT THING...
"AND AT THE VERY LEAST THE SCOTT OF TODAY WILL SEE HIS YOUNGER SELF, AND YOU, AND US AS A GROUP, AND SEE HOW FAR HE HAS FALLEN.
"AND LET THAT SHAME GO WITH HIM TO HIS GRAVE."
WE HAVE LIVED A COLORFUL AND VARIED LIFE.
SHOW ME.
I THOUGHT YOU THOUGHT THIS WASN'T A GOOD IDEA.
I HAVE TO SEE.
YOU KNOW I HAVE TO.
I KNOW.
AND I NEVER CLOSE MY MIND TO YOU.
YOU CAN LOOK AT WHATEVER YOU WANT.
I DON'T KNOW HOW TO DO ANY OF THIS YET.
CLEAR YOUR MIND.

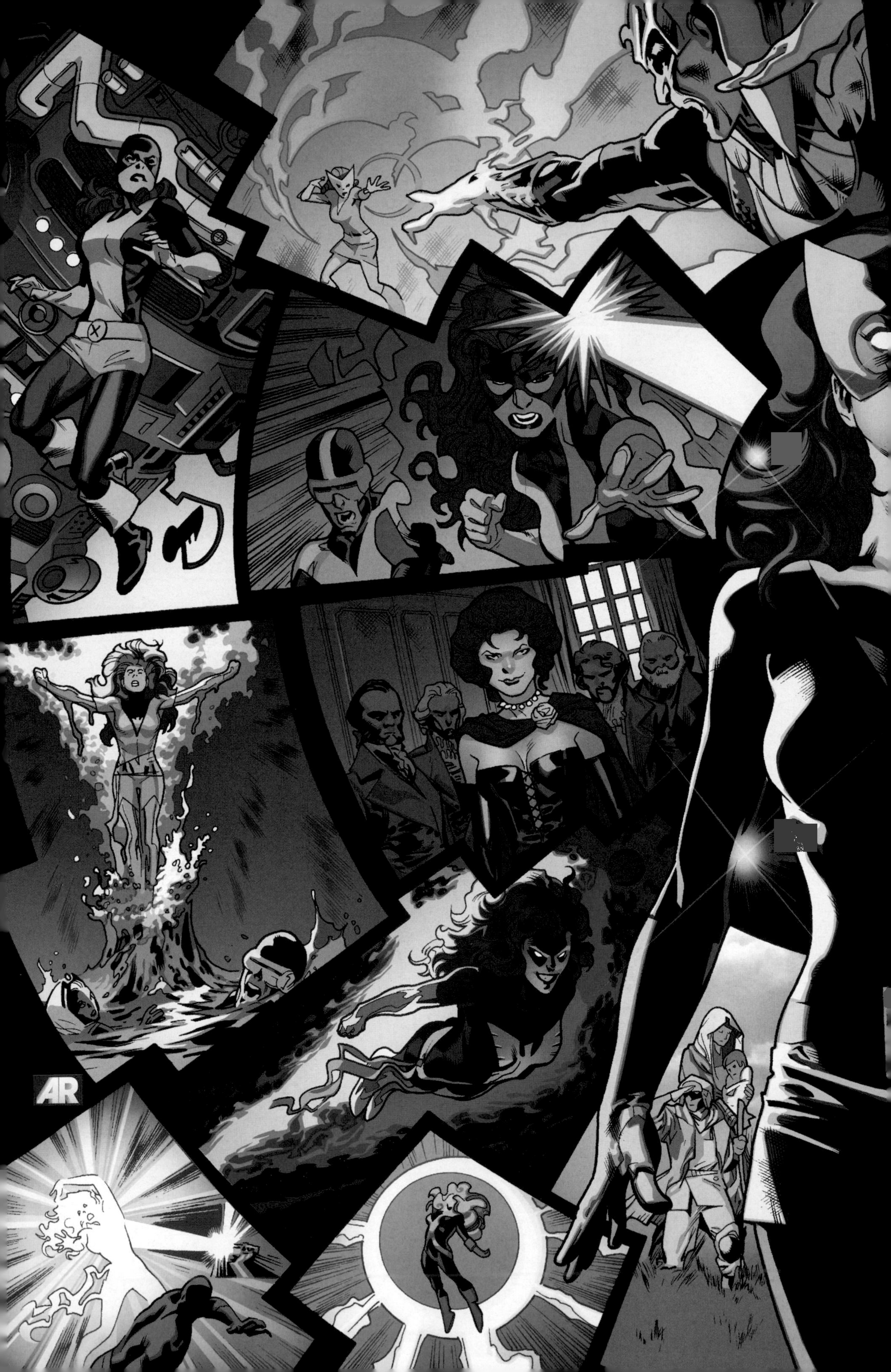

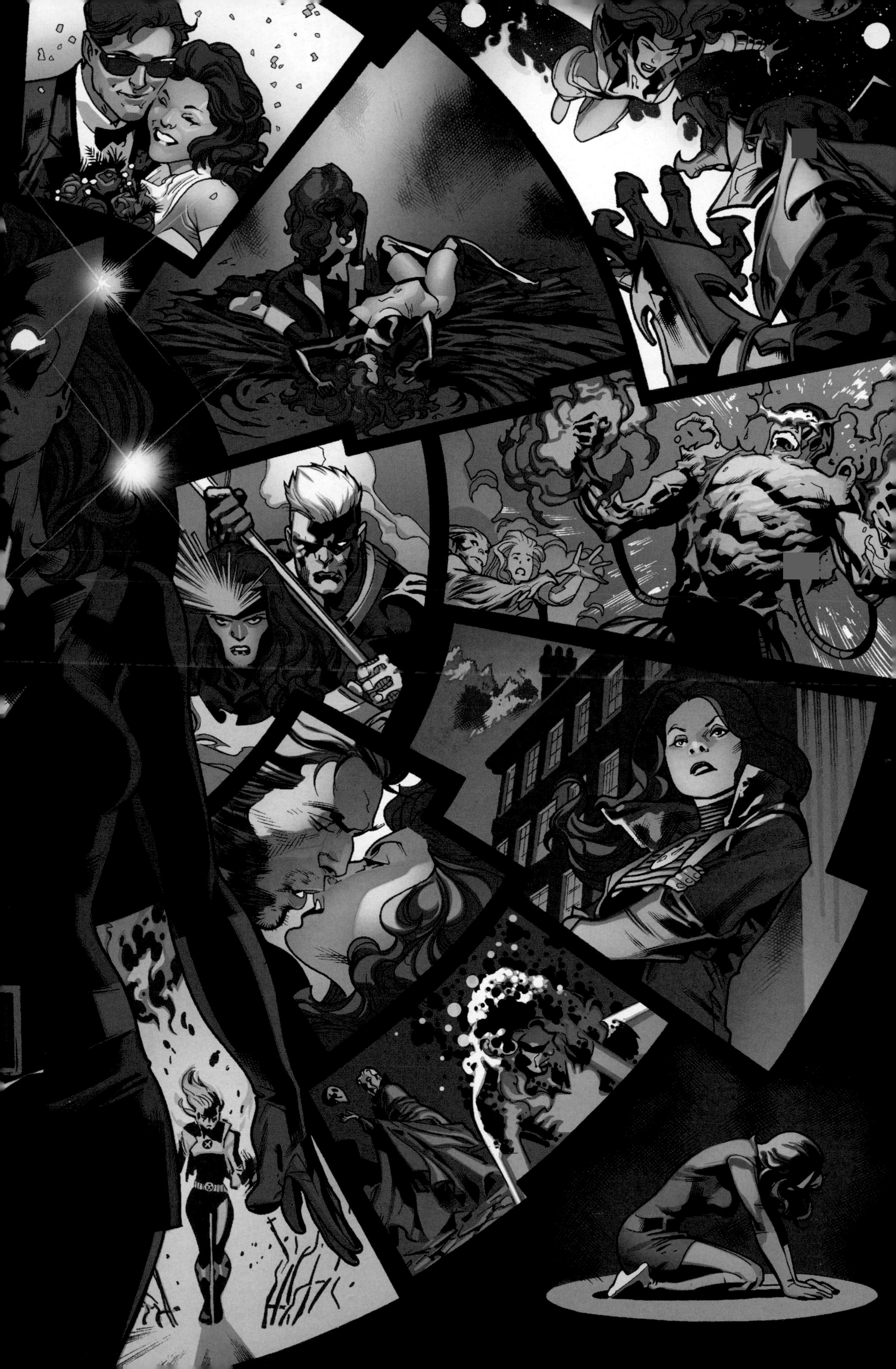

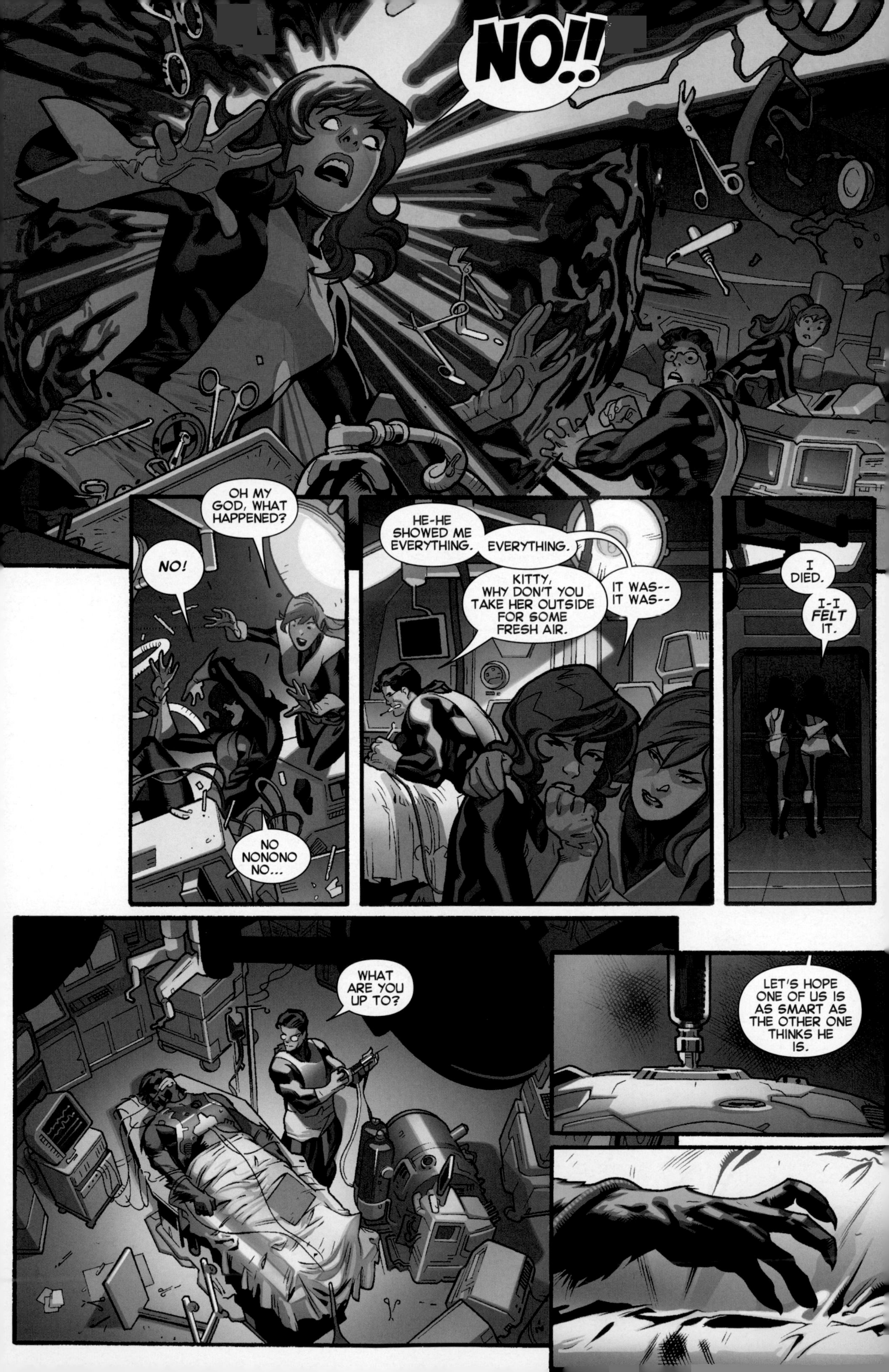
NO!!
OH MY GOD, WHAT HAPPENED?
NO!
NO NONONO NO...
HE-HE SHOWED ME EVERYTHING.
EVERYTHING.
KITTY, WHY DON'T YOU TAKE HER OUTSIDE FOR SOME FRESH AIR.
IT WAS-- IT WAS--
I DIED.
I-I *FELT* IT.
WHAT ARE YOU UP TO?
LET'S HOPE ONE OF US IS AS SMART AS THE OTHER ONE THINKS HE IS.

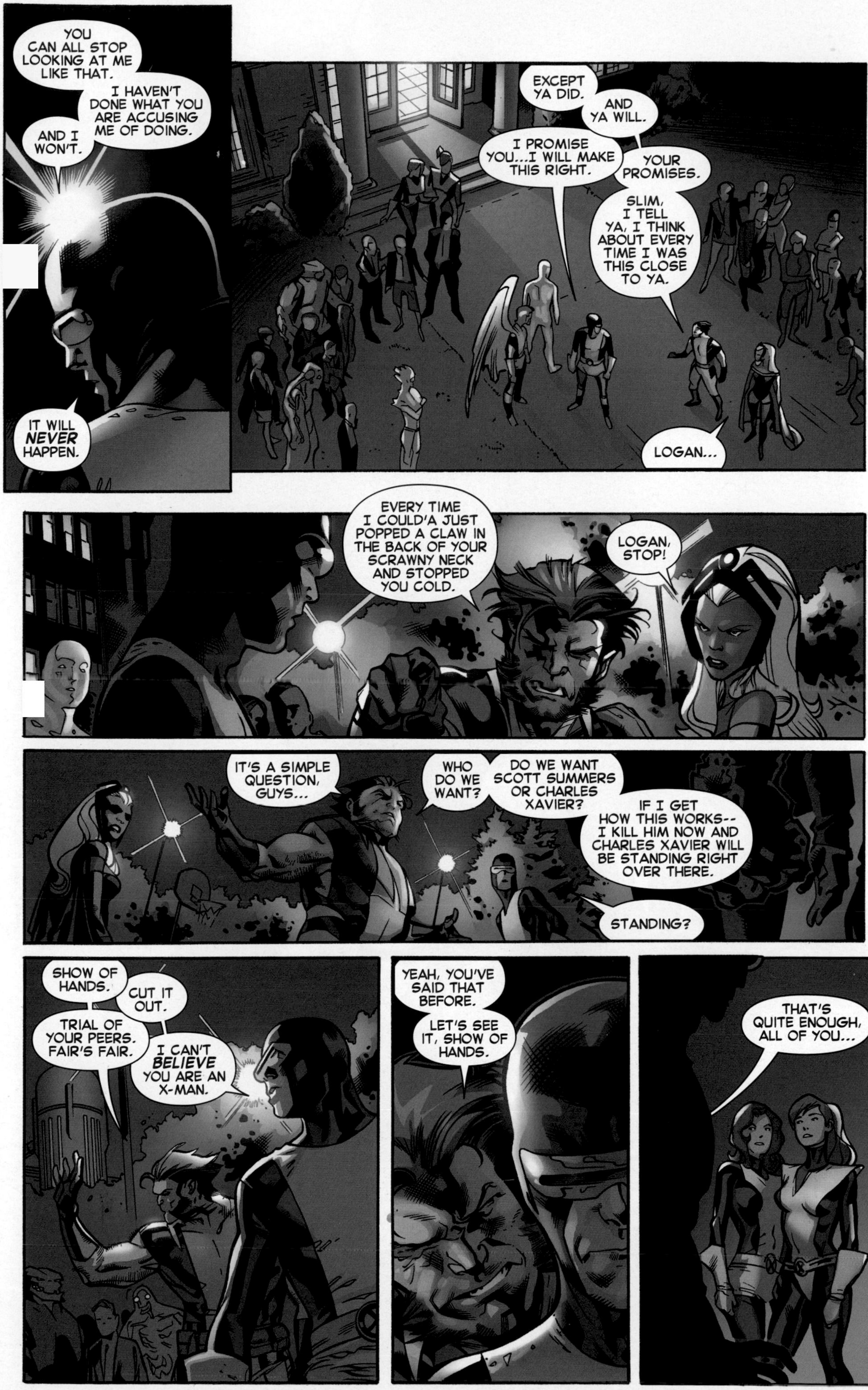
YOU CAN ALL STOP LOOKING AT ME LIKE THAT.
I HAVEN'T DONE WHAT YOU ARE ACCUSING ME OF DOING.
AND I WON'T.
IT WILL NEVER HAPPEN.
EXCEPT YA DID.
AND YA WILL.
I PROMISE YOU...I WILL MAKE THIS RIGHT.
YOUR PROMISES.
SLIM, I TELL YA, I THINK ABOUT EVERY TIME I WAS THIS CLOSE TO YA.
LOGAN...
EVERY TIME I COULD'A JUST POPPED A CLAW IN THE BACK OF YOUR SCRAWNY NECK AND STOPPED YOU COLD.
LOGAN, STOP!
IT'S A SIMPLE QUESTION, GUYS...
WHO DO WE WANT?
DO WE WANT SCOTT SUMMERS OR CHARLES XAVIER?
IF I GET HOW THIS WORKS-- I KILL HIM NOW AND CHARLES XAVIER WILL BE STANDING RIGHT OVER THERE.
STANDING?
SHOW OF HANDS.
CUT IT OUT.
TRIAL OF YOUR PEERS. FAIR'S FAIR.
I CAN'T BELIEVE YOU ARE AN X-MAN.
YEAH, YOU'VE SAID THAT BEFORE.
LET'S SEE IT, SHOW OF HANDS.
THAT'S QUITE ENOUGH, ALL OF YOU...

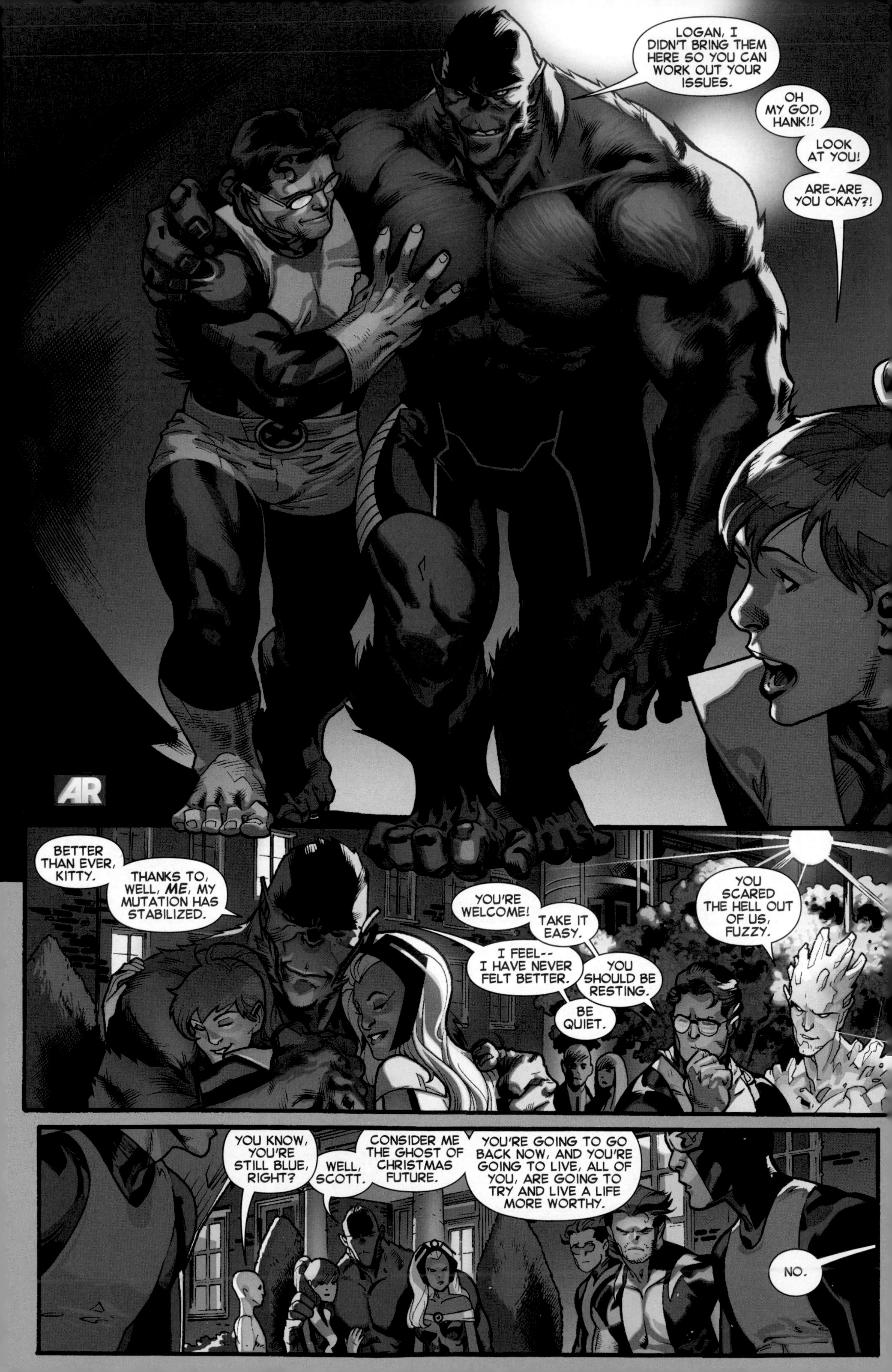
LOGAN, I DIDN'T BRING THEM HERE SO YOU CAN WORK OUT YOUR ISSUES.
OH MY GOD, HANK!!
LOOK AT YOU!
ARE-ARE YOU OKAY?!
BETTER THAN EVER, KITTY.
THANKS TO, WELL, *ME*, MY MUTATION HAS STABILIZED.
YOU'RE WELCOME!
TAKE IT EASY.
I FEEL-- I HAVE NEVER FELT BETTER.
YOU SHOULD BE RESTING.
BE QUIET.
YOU SCARED THE HELL OUT OF US, FUZZY.
YOU KNOW, YOU'RE STILL BLUE, RIGHT?
WELL, SCOTT.
CONSIDER ME THE GHOST OF CHRISTMAS FUTURE.
YOU'RE GOING TO GO BACK NOW, AND YOU'RE GOING TO LIVE, ALL OF YOU, ARE GOING TO TRY AND LIVE A LIFE MORE WORTHY.
NO.

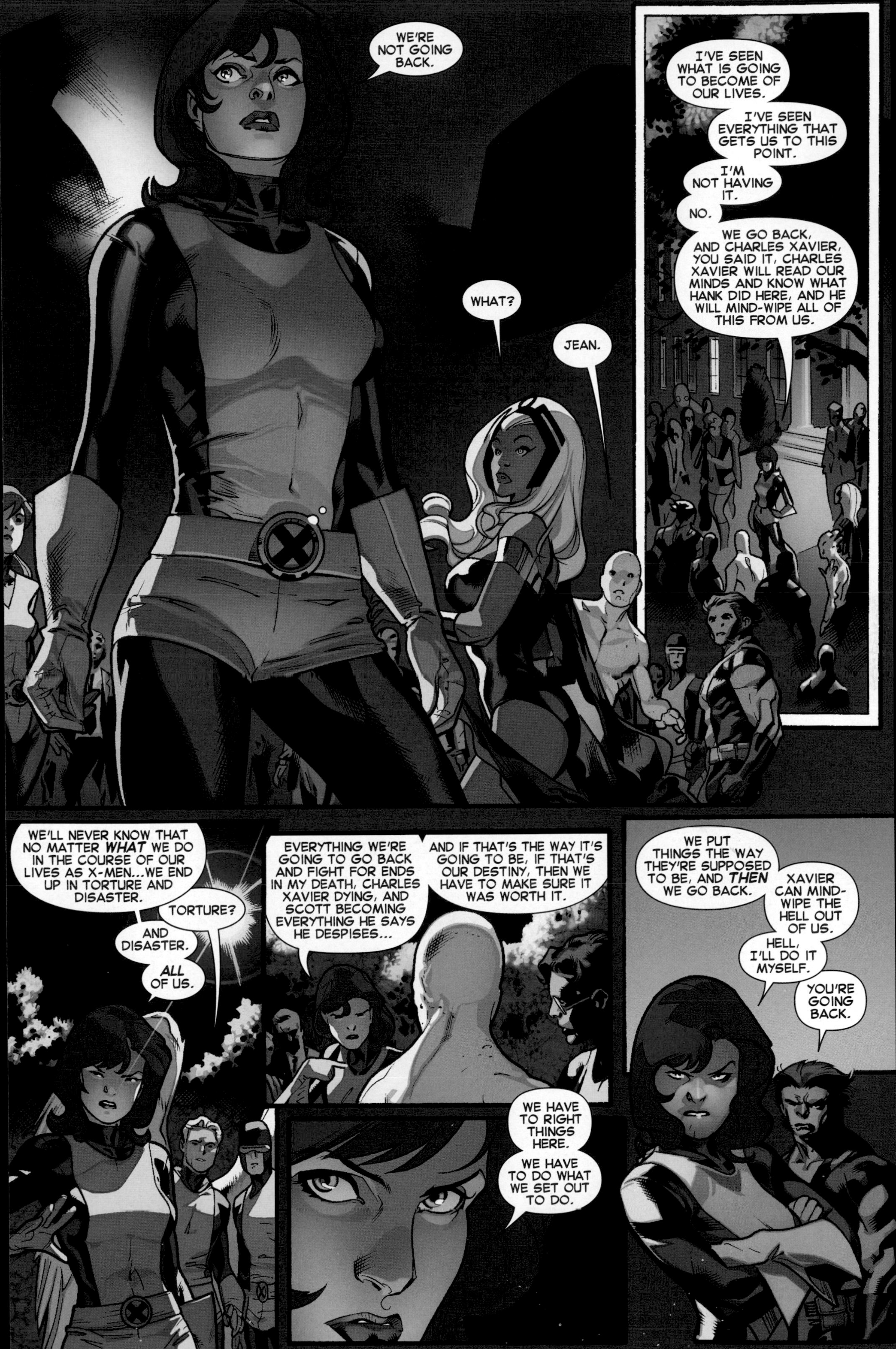
WE'RE NOT GOING BACK.
I'VE SEEN WHAT IS GOING TO BECOME OF OUR LIVES.
I'VE SEEN EVERYTHING THAT GETS US TO THIS POINT.
I'M NOT HAVING IT.
NO.
WE GO BACK, AND CHARLES XAVIER, YOU SAID IT, CHARLES XAVIER WILL READ OUR MINDS AND KNOW WHAT HANK DID HERE, AND HE WILL MIND-WIPE ALL OF THIS FROM US.
WHAT?
JEAN.
WE'LL NEVER KNOW THAT NO MATTER WHAT WE DO IN THE COURSE OF OUR LIVES AS X-MEN...WE END UP IN TORTURE AND DISASTER.
TORTURE?
AND DISASTER.
ALL OF US.
EVERYTHING WE'RE GOING TO GO BACK AND FIGHT FOR ENDS IN MY DEATH, CHARLES XAVIER DYING, AND SCOTT BECOMING EVERYTHING HE SAYS HE DESPISES...
AND IF THAT'S THE WAY IT'S GOING TO BE, IF THAT'S OUR DESTINY, THEN WE HAVE TO MAKE SURE IT WAS WORTH IT.
WE HAVE TO RIGHT THINGS HERE.
WE HAVE TO DO WHAT WE SET OUT TO DO.
WE PUT THINGS THE WAY THEY'RE SUPPOSED TO BE, AND THEN WE GO BACK.
XAVIER CAN MIND-WIPE THE HELL OUT OF US.
HELL, I'LL DO IT MYSELF.
YOU'RE GOING BACK.

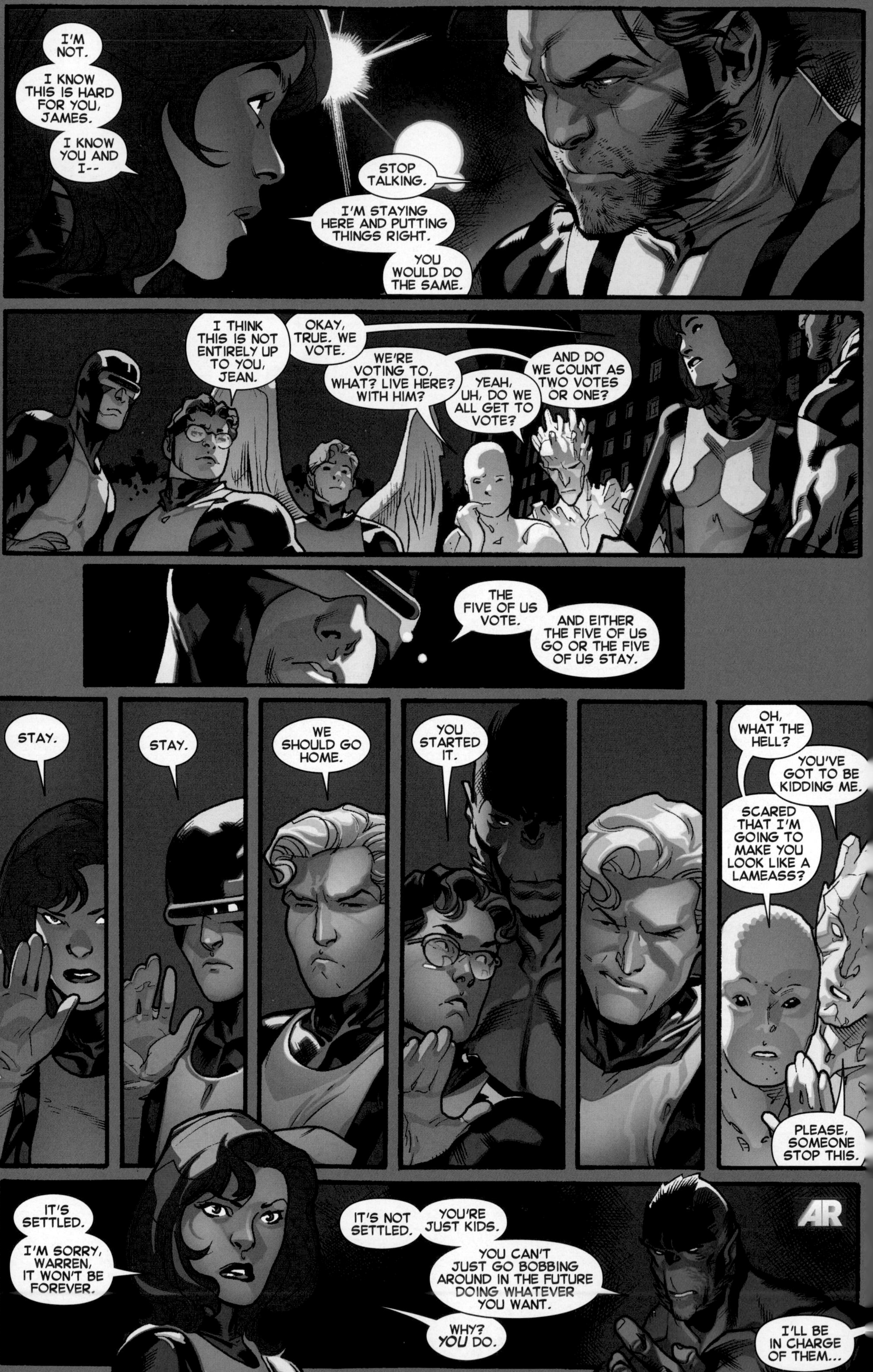
I'M NOT.
I KNOW THIS IS HARD FOR YOU, JAMES.
I KNOW YOU AND I--
STOP TALKING.
I'M STAYING HERE AND PUTTING THINGS RIGHT.
YOU WOULD DO THE SAME.
I THINK THIS IS NOT ENTIRELY UP TO YOU, JEAN.
OKAY, TRUE. WE VOTE.
WE'RE VOTING TO, WHAT? LIVE HERE? WITH HIM?
YEAH, UH, DO WE ALL GET TO VOTE?
AND DO WE COUNT AS TWO VOTES OR ONE?
THE FIVE OF US VOTE.
AND EITHER THE FIVE OF US GO OR THE FIVE OF US STAY.
STAY.
STAY.
WE SHOULD GO HOME.
YOU STARTED IT.
OH, WHAT THE HELL?
YOU'VE GOT TO BE KIDDING ME.
SCARED THAT I'M GOING TO MAKE YOU LOOK LIKE A LAMEASS?
PLEASE, SOMEONE STOP THIS.
IT'S SETTLED.
I'M SORRY, WARREN, IT WON'T BE FOREVER.
IT'S NOT SETTLED.
YOU'RE JUST KIDS.
YOU CAN'T JUST GO BOBBING AROUND IN THE FUTURE DOING WHATEVER YOU WANT.
WHY? YOU DO.
I'LL BE IN CHARGE OF THEM...

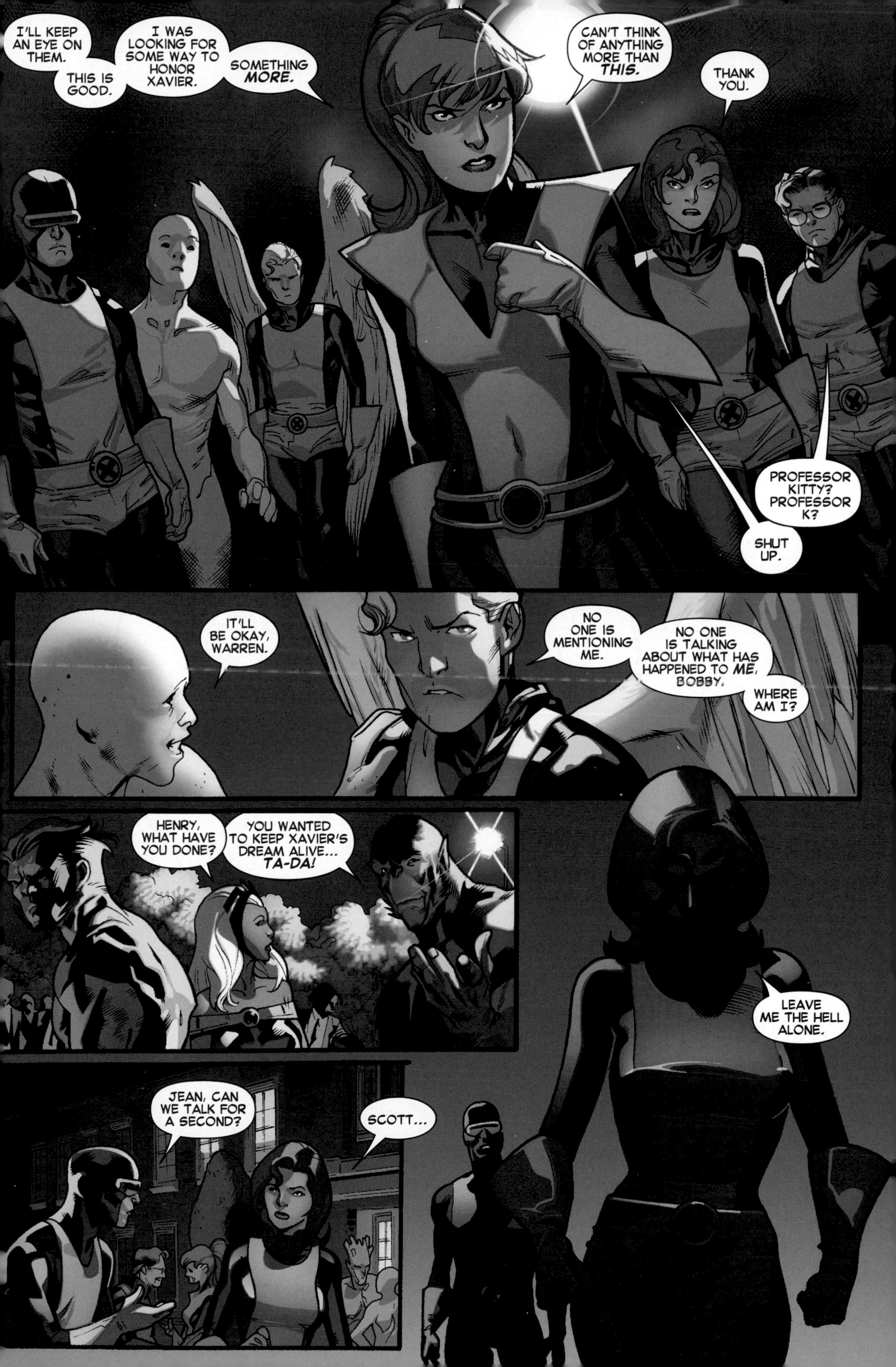

I'LL KEEP AN EYE ON THEM.
THIS IS GOOD.
I WAS LOOKING FOR SOME WAY TO HONOR XAVIER.
SOMETHING *MORE.*
CAN'T THINK OF ANYTHING MORE THAN *THIS.*
THANK YOU.
PROFESSOR KITTY? PROFESSOR K?
SHUT UP.
IT'LL BE OKAY, WARREN.
NO ONE IS MENTIONING ME.
NO ONE IS TALKING ABOUT WHAT HAS HAPPENED TO *ME*, BOBBY.
WHERE AM I?
HENRY, WHAT HAVE YOU DONE?
YOU WANTED TO KEEP XAVIER'S DREAM ALIVE... *TA-DA!*
LEAVE ME THE HELL ALONE.
JEAN, CAN WE TALK FOR A SECOND?
SCOTT...

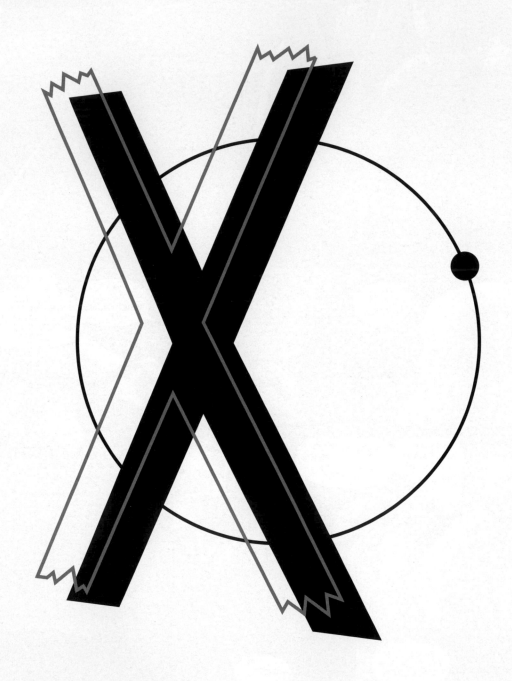

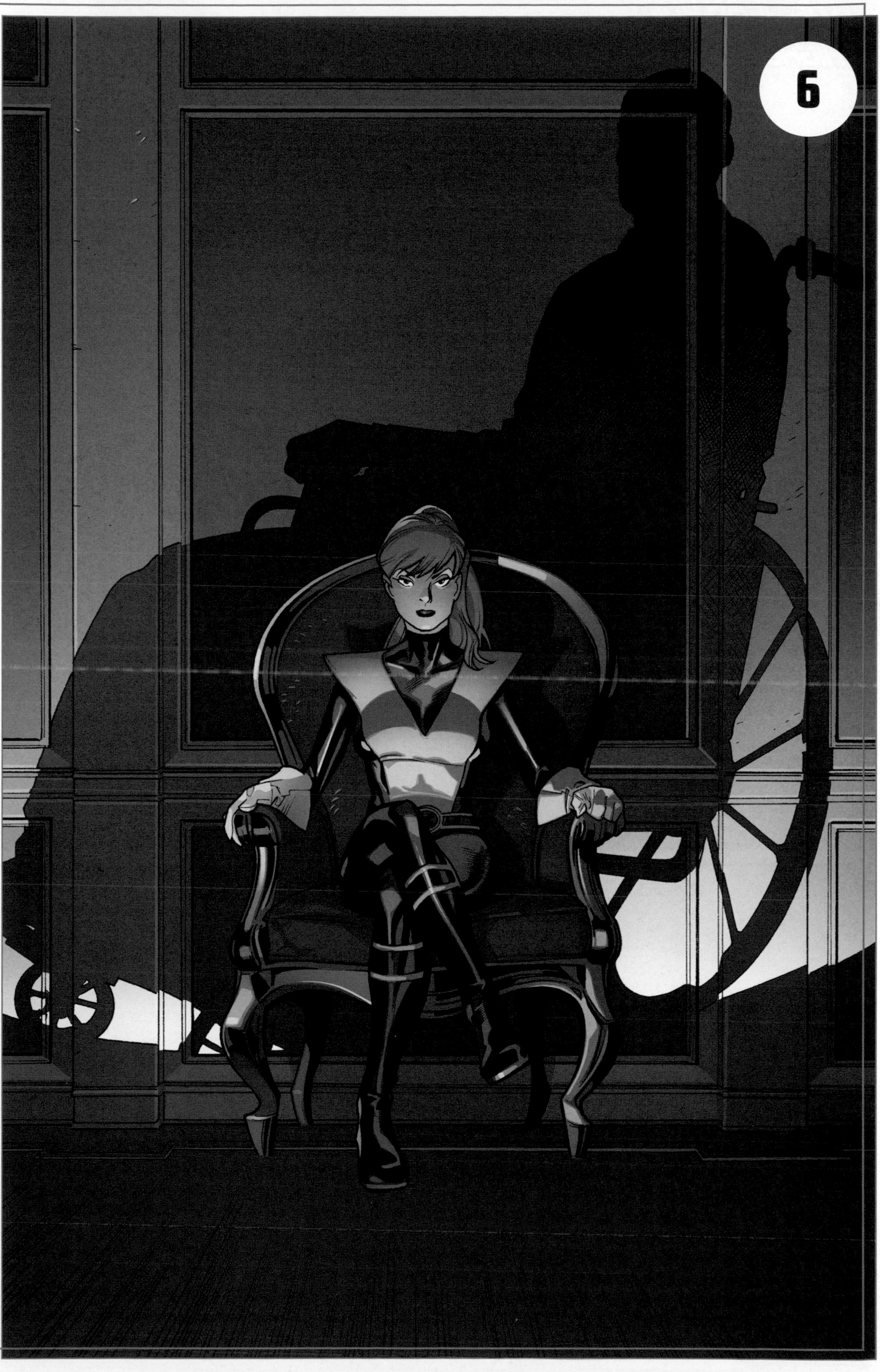
6

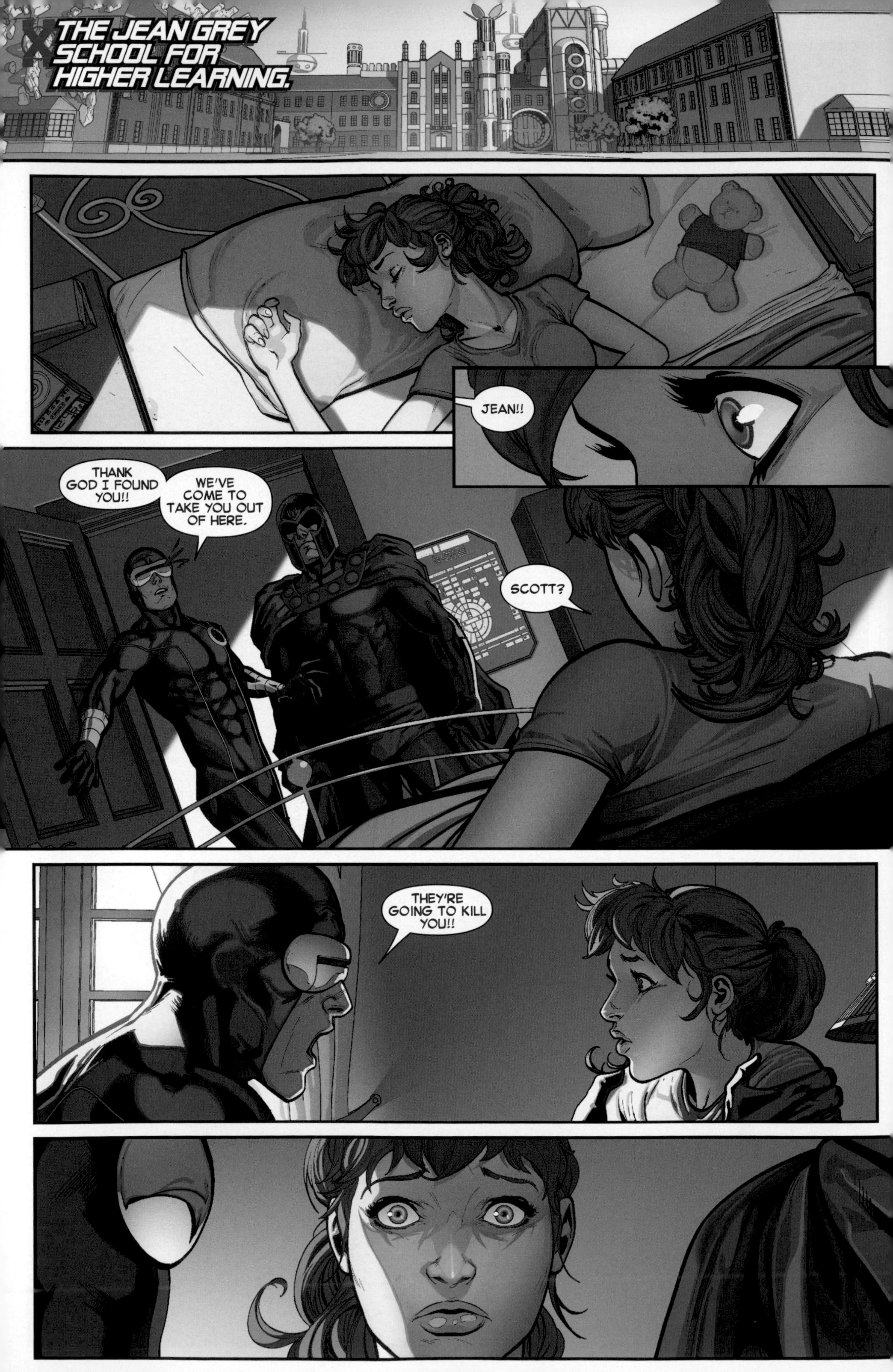
THE JEAN GREY SCHOOL FOR HIGHER LEARNING.
JEAN!!
THANK GOD I FOUND YOU!!
WE'VE COME TO TAKE YOU OUT OF HERE.
SCOTT?
THEY'RE GOING TO KILL YOU!!

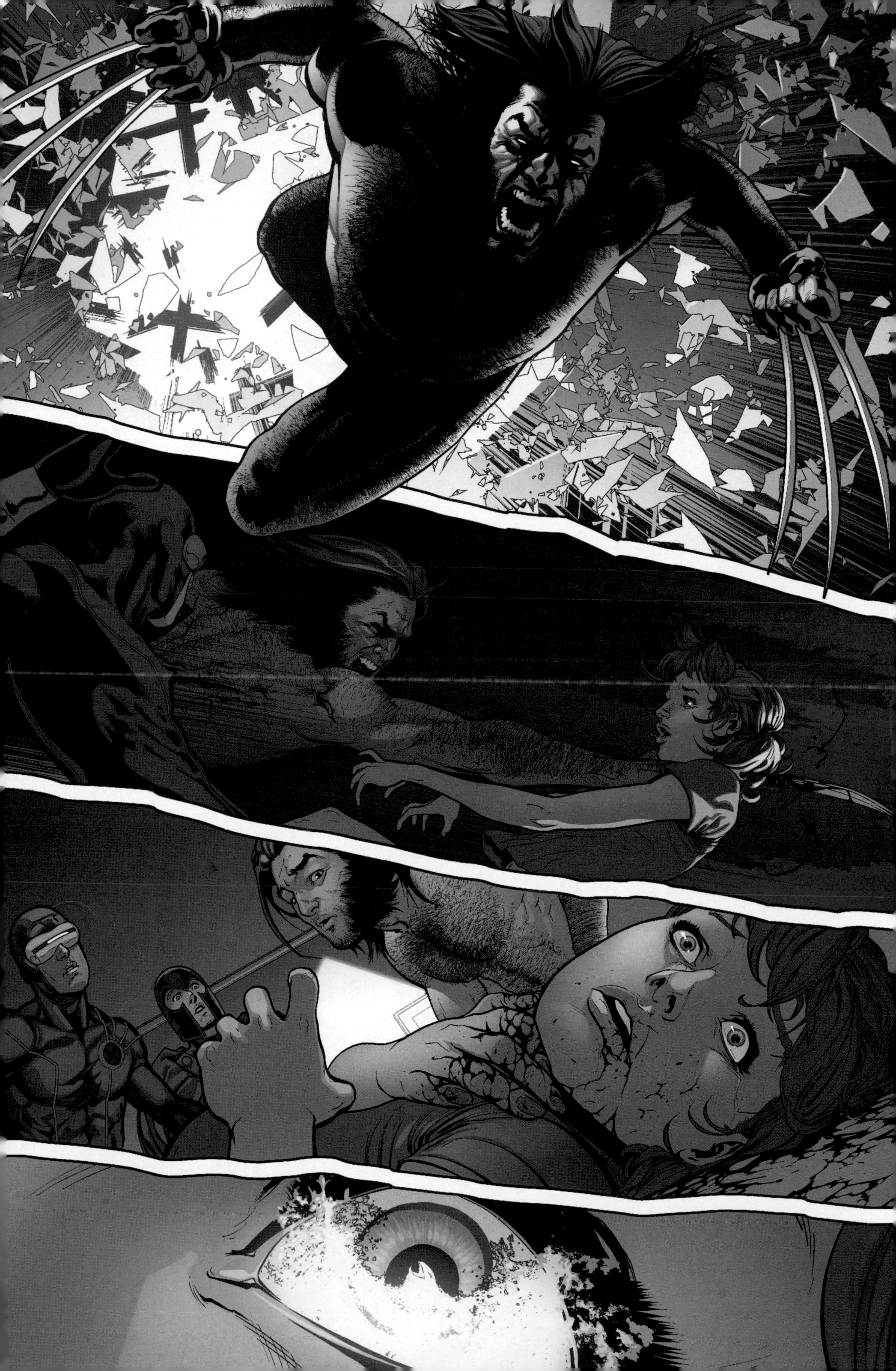

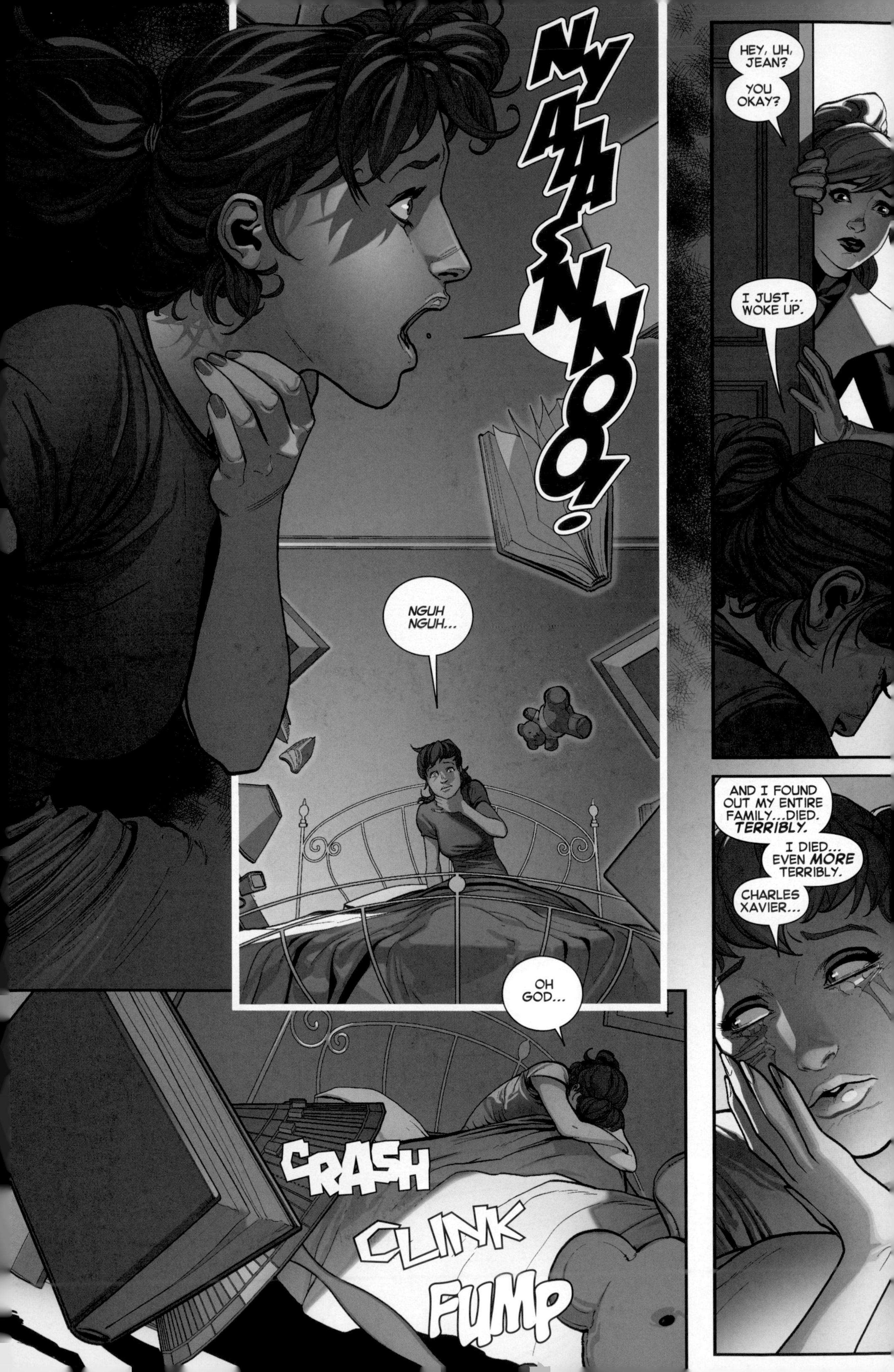
NYAAAHNNNOOO!
NGUH NGUH...
OH GOD...
CRASH
CLINK
FUMP
HEY, UH, JEAN?
YOU OKAY?
I JUST... WOKE UP.
AND I FOUND OUT MY ENTIRE FAMILY...DIED. TERRIBLY.
I DIED... EVEN MORE TERRIBLY.
CHARLES XAVIER...

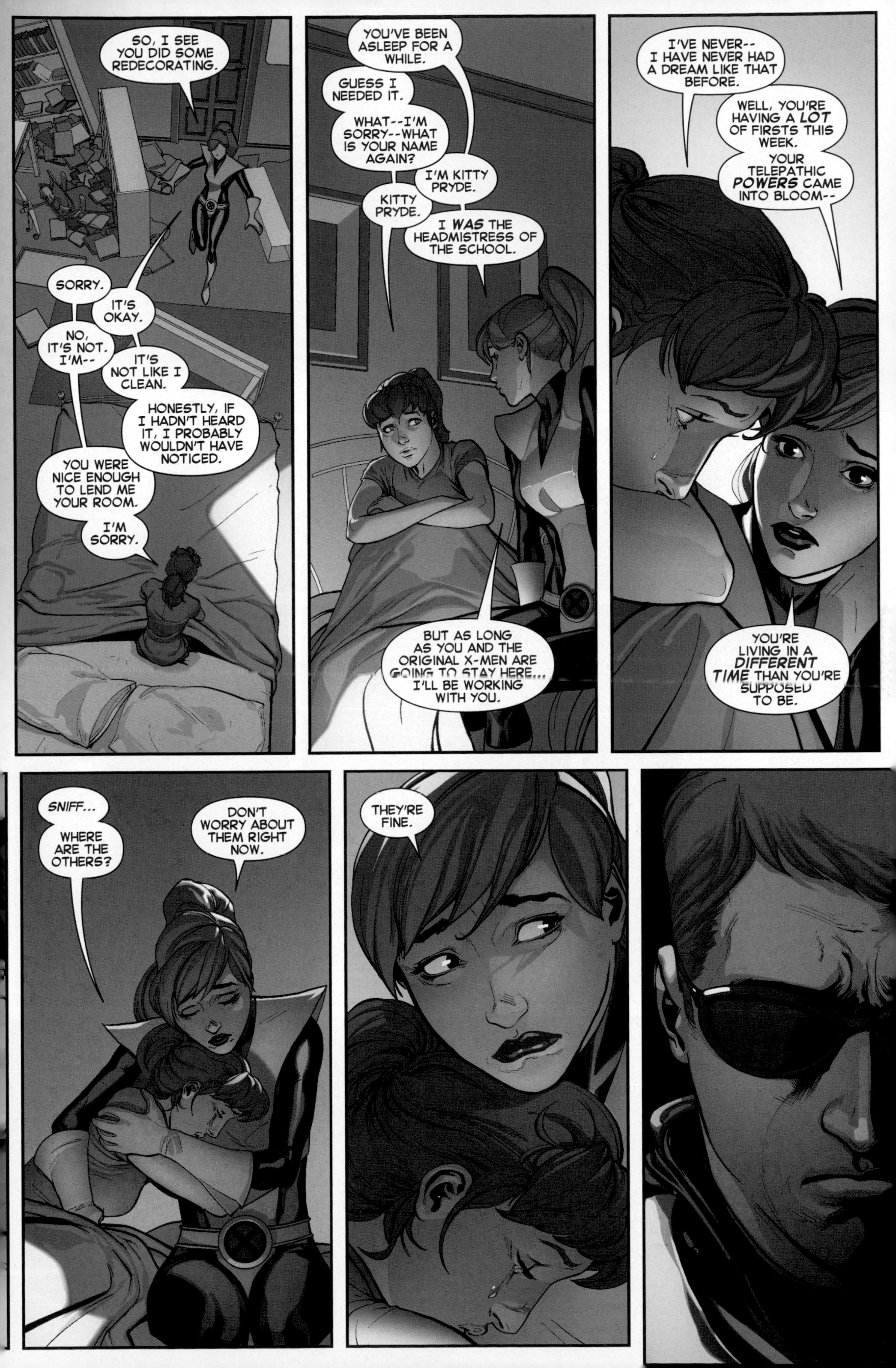
SO, I SEE YOU DID SOME REDECORATING.
SORRY.
IT'S OKAY.
NO, IT'S NOT. I'M--
IT'S NOT LIKE I CLEAN.
HONESTLY, IF I HADN'T HEARD IT, I PROBABLY WOULDN'T HAVE NOTICED.
YOU WERE NICE ENOUGH TO LEND ME YOUR ROOM.
I'M SORRY.
YOU'VE BEEN ASLEEP FOR A WHILE.
GUESS I NEEDED IT.
WHAT--I'M SORRY--WHAT IS YOUR NAME AGAIN?
I'M KITTY PRYDE.
KITTY PRYDE.
I WAS THE HEADMISTRESS OF THE SCHOOL.
BUT AS LONG AS YOU AND THE ORIGINAL X-MEN ARE GOING TO STAY HERE... I'LL BE WORKING WITH YOU.
I'VE NEVER-- I HAVE NEVER HAD A DREAM LIKE THAT BEFORE.
WELL, YOU'RE HAVING A LOT OF FIRSTS THIS WEEK.
YOUR TELEPATHIC POWERS CAME INTO BLOOM--
YOU'RE LIVING IN A DIFFERENT TIME THAN YOU'RE SUPPOSED TO BE.
SNIFF...
WHERE ARE THE OTHERS?
DON'T WORRY ABOUT THEM RIGHT NOW.
THEY'RE FINE.

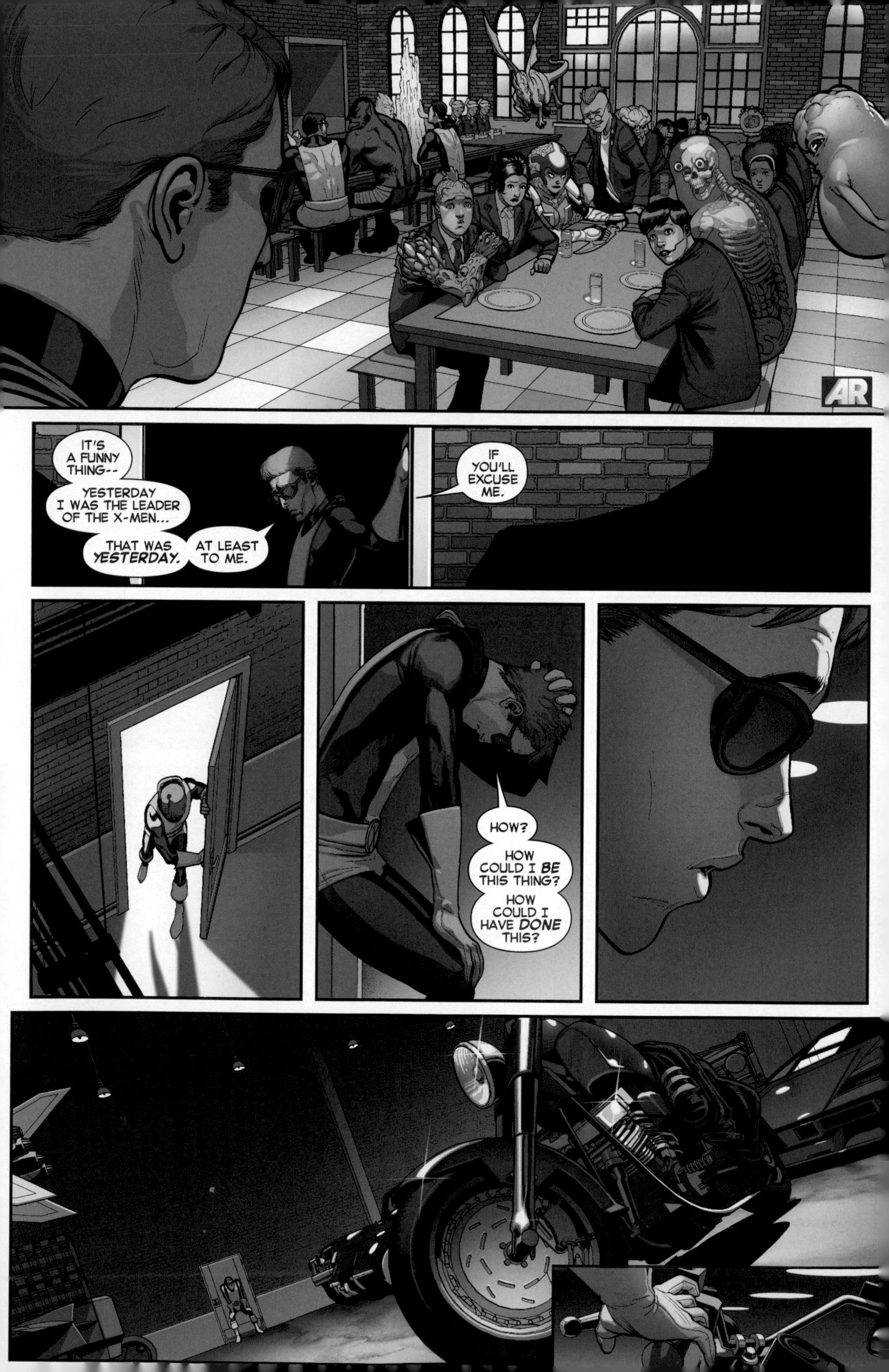
AR
IT'S A FUNNY THING--
YESTERDAY I WAS THE LEADER OF THE X-MEN...
THAT WAS YESTERDAY.
AT LEAST TO ME.
IF YOU'LL EXCUSE ME.
HOW?
HOW COULD I BE THIS THING?
HOW COULD I HAVE DONE THIS?

AND I READ ONLINE LAST NIGHT THAT REED RICHARDS THINKS THAT--THAT THE SPACE-TIME CONTINUUM IS A LIVING THING, YOU KNOW.

LIKE A PERSON, AND IF WE'RE USING IT AS A TOY TO--

SHUT IT, BOBBY.

WRRROOOOOOMMM

SON OF A--!!!

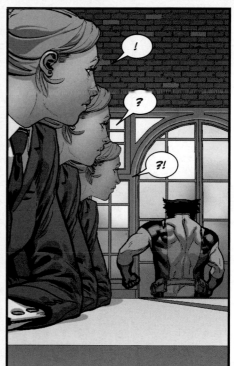

!

?

?!

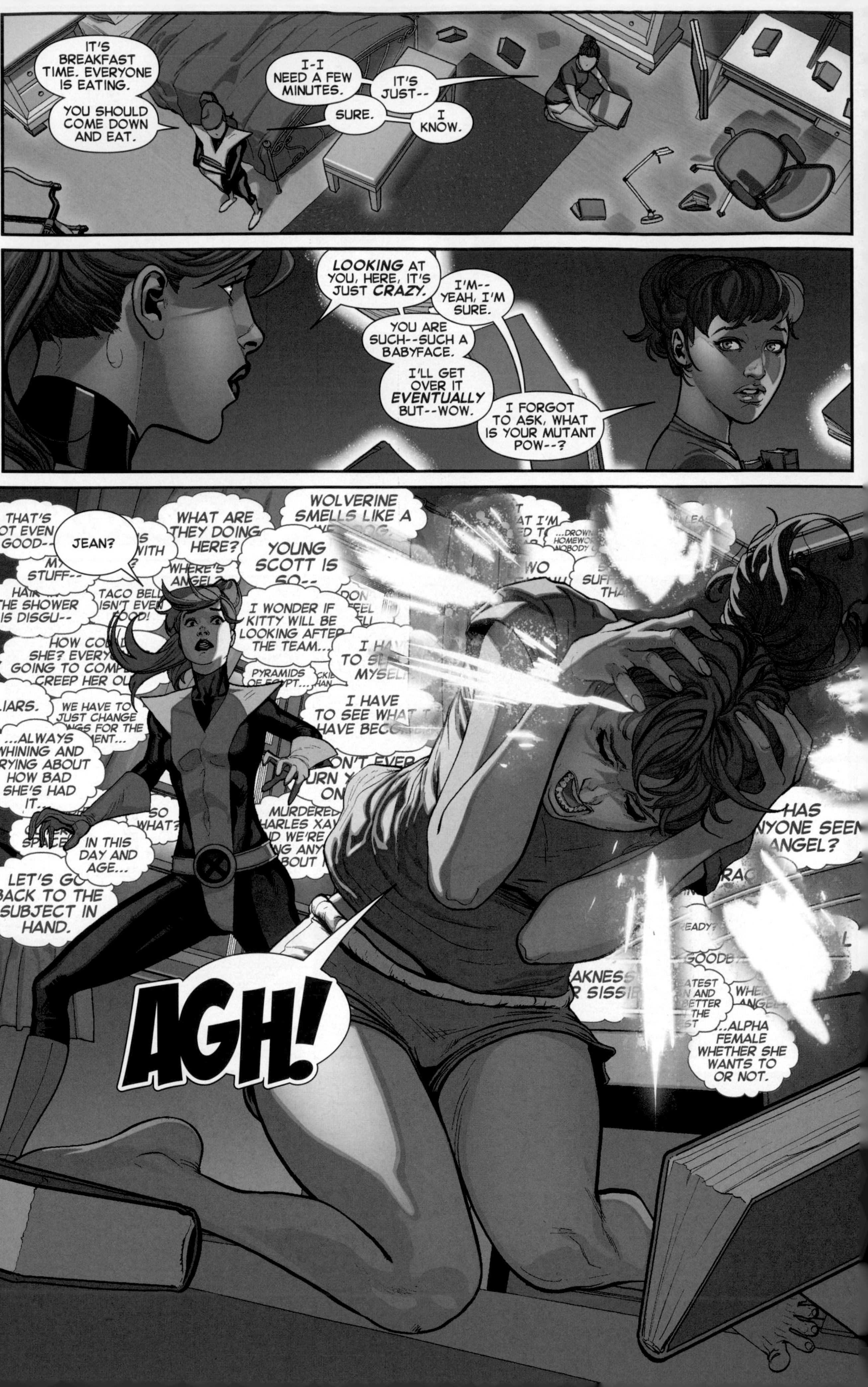

IT'S BREAKFAST TIME. EVERYONE IS EATING.
YOU SHOULD COME DOWN AND EAT.
I-I NEED A FEW MINUTES.
IT'S JUST--
SURE.
I KNOW.
LOOKING AT YOU, HERE, IT'S JUST CRAZY.
I'M-- YEAH, I'M SURE.
YOU ARE SUCH--SUCH A BABYFACE.
I'LL GET OVER IT EVENTUALLY BUT--WOW.
I FORGOT TO ASK, WHAT IS YOUR MUTANT POW--?
JEAN?
THAT'S NOT EVEN GOOD--
WHAT ARE THEY DOING HERE?
WOLVERINE SMELLS LIKE A
YOUNG SCOTT IS SO--
STUFF--
THE SHOWER IS DISGU--
TACO BELL ISN'T EVEN FOOD!
I WONDER IF KITTY WILL BE LOOKING AFTER THE TEAM...
GOING TO COMP
LIARS.
WE HAVE TO JUST CHANGE
PYRAMIDS OF
I HAVE TO SEE WHAT
...ALWAYS WHINING AND CRYING ABOUT HOW BAD SHE'S HAD IT...
SO WHAT?
MURDERED
IN THIS DAY AND AGE...
LET'S GO BACK TO THE SUBJECT IN HAND.
HAS
ANGEL?
GOODB
...ALPHA FEMALE WHETHER SHE WANTS TO OR NOT.
AGH!

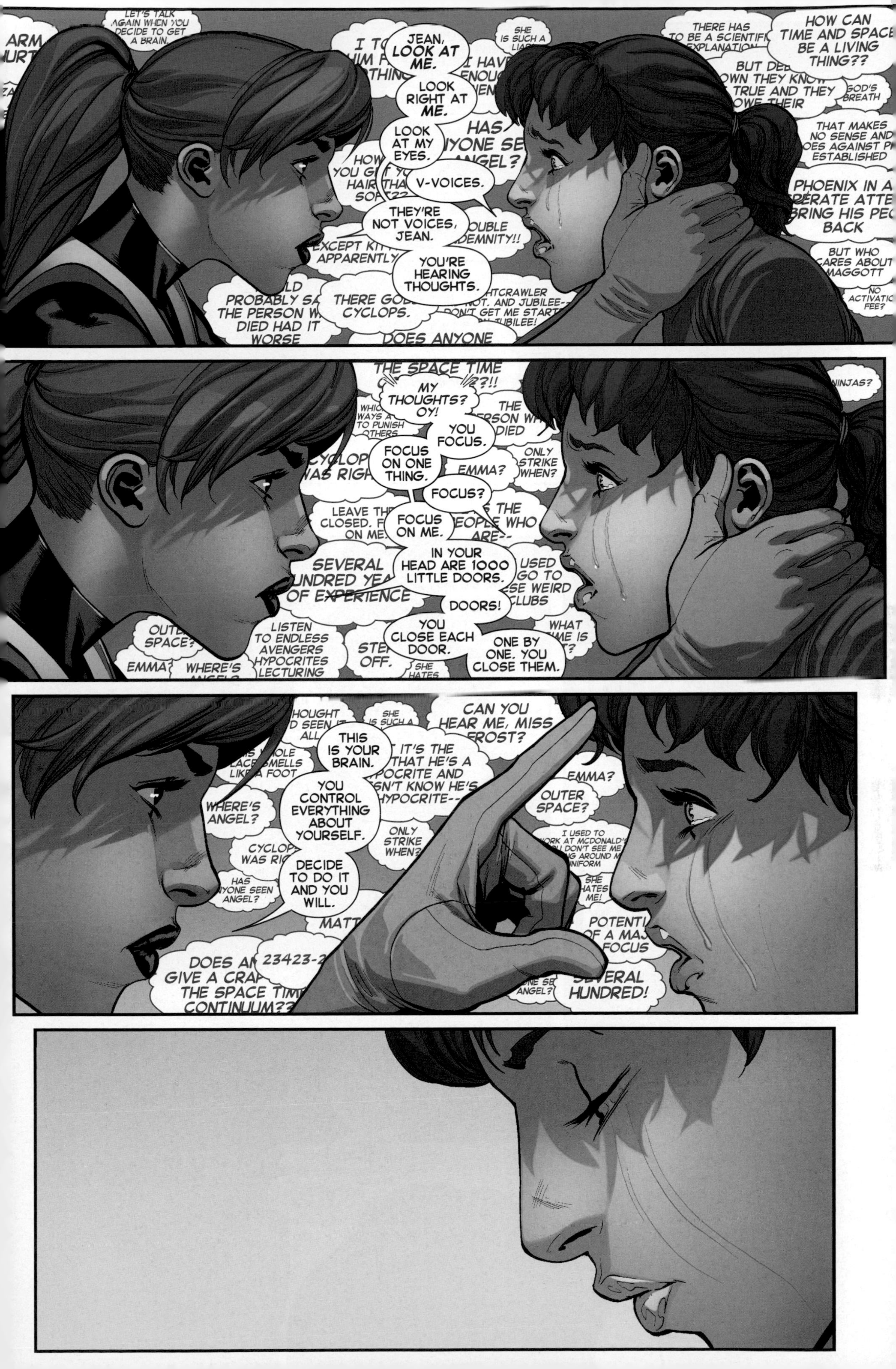
LET'S TALK AGAIN WHEN YOU DECIDE TO GET A BRAIN.
JEAN, LOOK AT ME.
LOOK RIGHT AT ME.
LOOK AT MY EYES.
V-VOICES.
THEY'RE NOT VOICES, JEAN.
YOU'RE HEARING THOUGHTS.
HOW CAN TIME AND SPACE BE A LIVING THING??
GOD'S BREATH
BUT WHO CARES ABOUT MAGGOTT
NO ACTIVATION FEE?
NINJAS?
MY THOUGHTS? OY!
YOU FOCUS.
FOCUS ON ONE THING.
EMMA?
ONLY STRIKE WHEN?
FOCUS?
FOCUS ON ME.
IN YOUR HEAD ARE 1000 LITTLE DOORS.
DOORS!
OUTER SPACE?
LISTEN TO ENDLESS AVENGERS HYPOCRITES LECTURING
YOU CLOSE EACH DOOR.
ONE BY ONE. YOU CLOSE THEM.
CAN YOU HEAR ME, MISS FROST?
THIS IS YOUR BRAIN.
WHERE'S ANGEL?
YOU CONTROL EVERYTHING ABOUT YOURSELF.
EMMA?
OUTER SPACE?
ONLY STRIKE WHEN?
SHE HATES ME!
DECIDE TO DO IT AND YOU WILL.
SEVERAL HUNDRED!

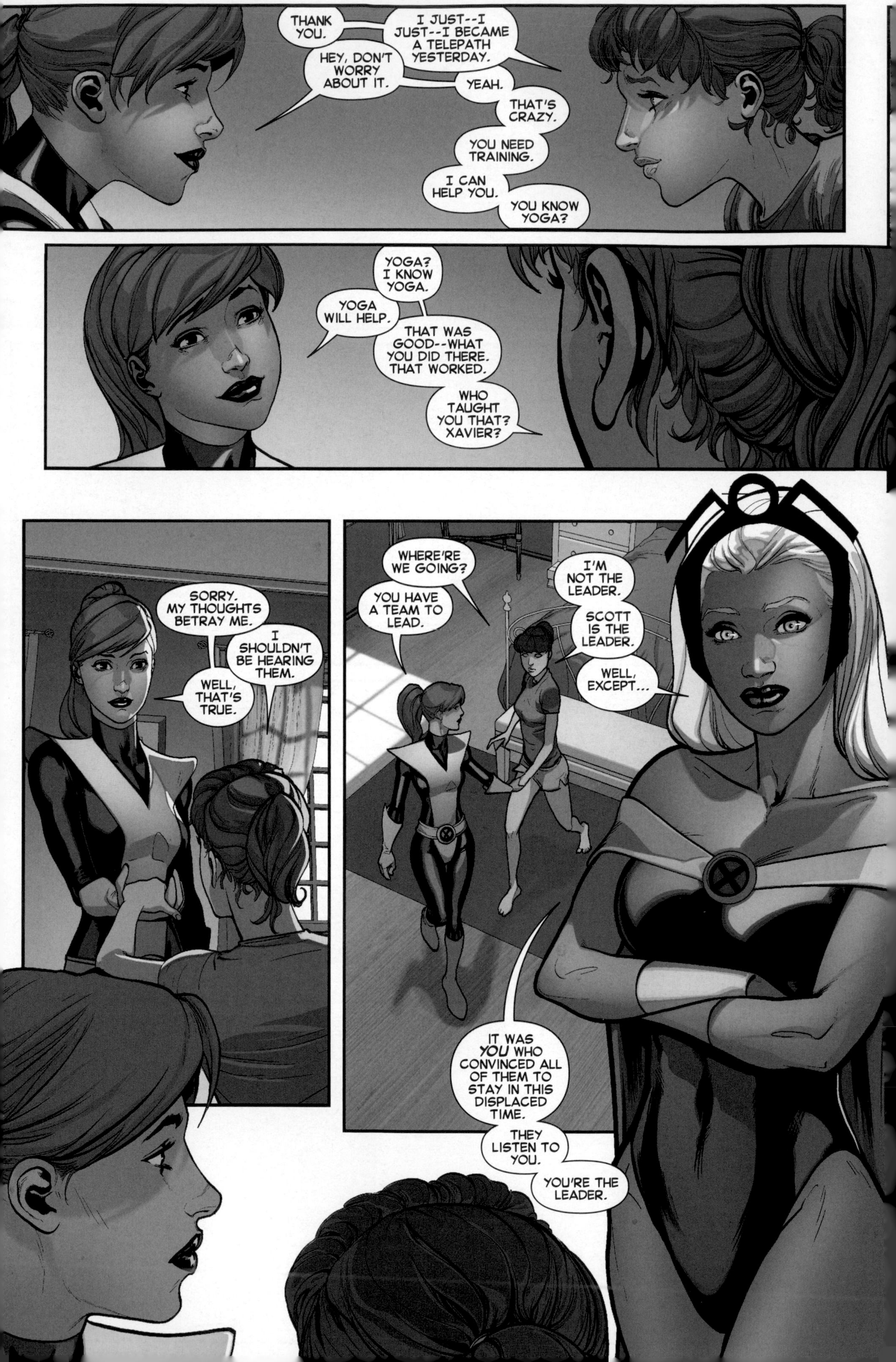
THANK YOU.
I JUST--I JUST--I BECAME A TELEPATH YESTERDAY.
HEY, DON'T WORRY ABOUT IT.
YEAH.
THAT'S CRAZY.
YOU NEED TRAINING.
I CAN HELP YOU.
YOU KNOW YOGA?
YOGA? I KNOW YOGA.
YOGA WILL HELP.
THAT WAS GOOD--WHAT YOU DID THERE. THAT WORKED.
WHO TAUGHT YOU THAT? XAVIER?
SORRY. MY THOUGHTS BETRAY ME.
I SHOULDN'T BE HEARING THEM.
WELL, THAT'S TRUE.
WHERE'RE WE GOING?
YOU HAVE A TEAM TO LEAD.
I'M NOT THE LEADER.
SCOTT IS THE LEADER.
WELL, EXCEPT...
IT WAS *YOU* WHO CONVINCED ALL OF THEM TO STAY IN THIS DISPLACED TIME.
THEY LISTEN TO YOU.
YOU'RE THE LEADER.

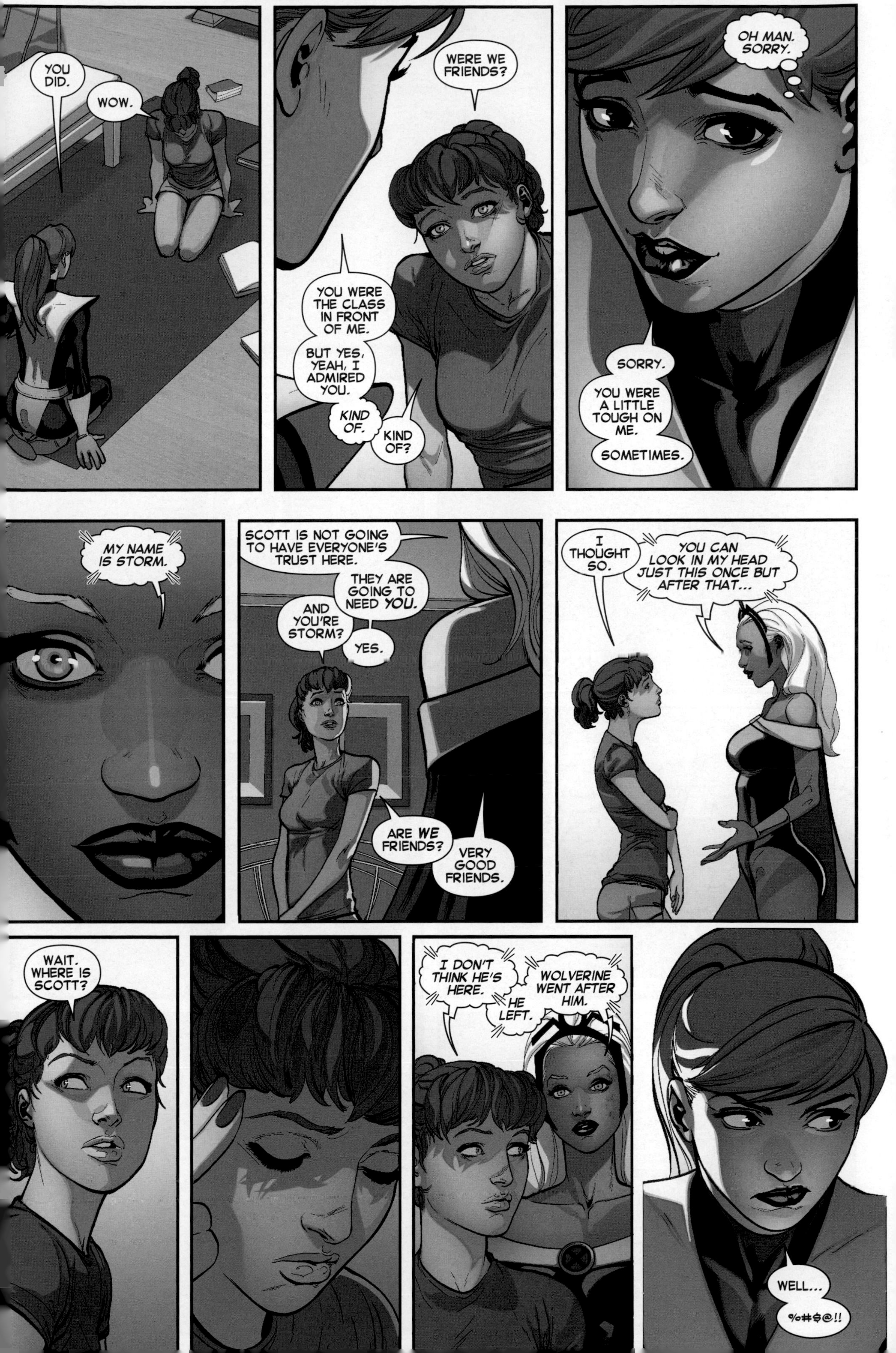
YOU DID.
WOW.
WERE WE FRIENDS?
YOU WERE THE CLASS IN FRONT OF ME.
BUT YES, YEAH, I ADMIRED YOU.
KIND OF.
KIND OF?
OH MAN. SORRY.
SORRY.
YOU WERE A LITTLE TOUGH ON ME.
SOMETIMES.
MY NAME IS STORM.
SCOTT IS NOT GOING TO HAVE EVERYONE'S TRUST HERE.
THEY ARE GOING TO NEED YOU.
AND YOU'RE STORM?
YES.
ARE WE FRIENDS?
VERY GOOD FRIENDS.
YOU CAN LOOK IN MY HEAD JUST THIS ONCE BUT AFTER THAT...
I THOUGHT SO.
WAIT. WHERE IS SCOTT?
I DON'T THINK HE'S HERE.
HE LEFT.
WOLVERINE WENT AFTER HIM.
WELL...
%#$@!!

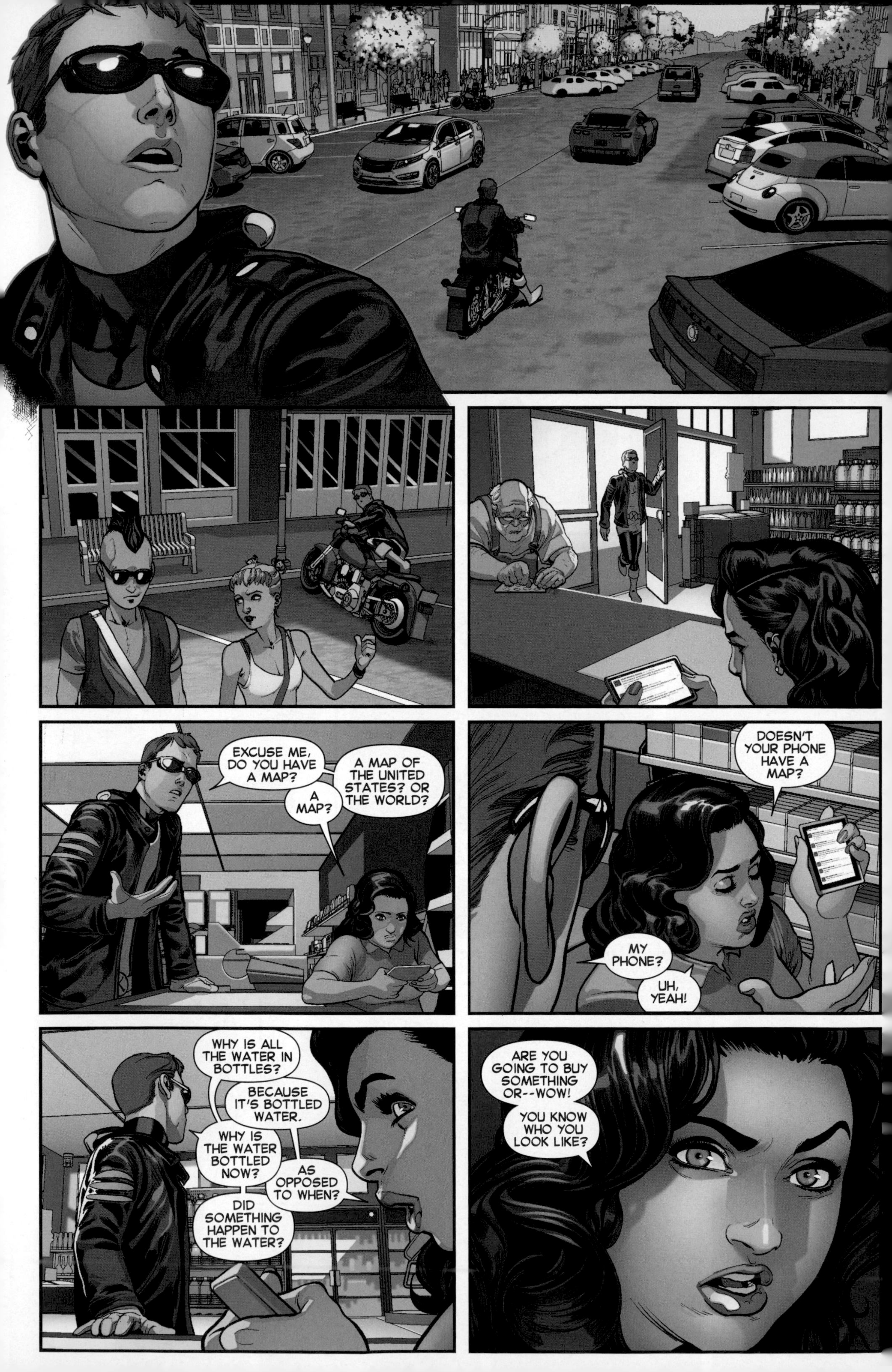
EXCUSE ME, DO YOU HAVE A MAP?
A MAP?
A MAP OF THE UNITED STATES? OR THE WORLD?
DOESN'T YOUR PHONE HAVE A MAP?
MY PHONE?
UH, YEAH!
WHY IS ALL THE WATER IN BOTTLES?
BECAUSE IT'S BOTTLED WATER.
WHY IS THE WATER BOTTLED NOW?
AS OPPOSED TO WHEN?
DID SOMETHING HAPPEN TO THE WATER?
ARE YOU GOING TO BUY SOMETHING OR--WOW!
YOU KNOW WHO YOU LOOK LIKE?

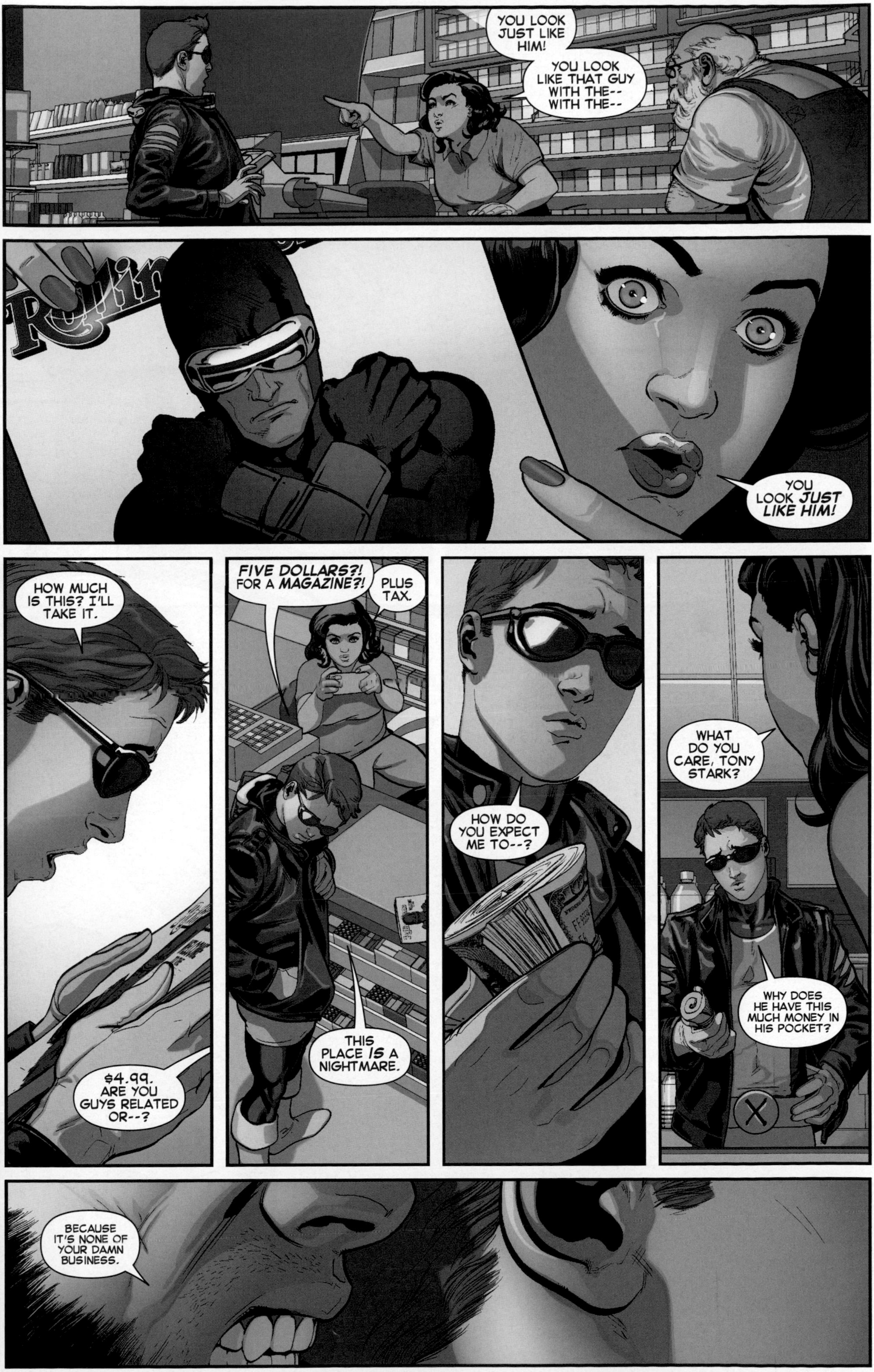

YOU LOOK JUST LIKE HIM!
YOU LOOK LIKE THAT GUY WITH THE-- WITH THE--
YOU LOOK JUST LIKE HIM!
HOW MUCH IS THIS? I'LL TAKE IT.
$4.99. ARE YOU GUYS RELATED OR--?
FIVE DOLLARS?! FOR A MAGAZINE?!
PLUS TAX.
THIS PLACE IS A NIGHTMARE.
HOW DO YOU EXPECT ME TO--?
WHAT DO YOU CARE, TONY STARK?
WHY DOES HE HAVE THIS MUCH MONEY IN HIS POCKET?
BECAUSE IT'S NONE OF YOUR DAMN BUSINESS.

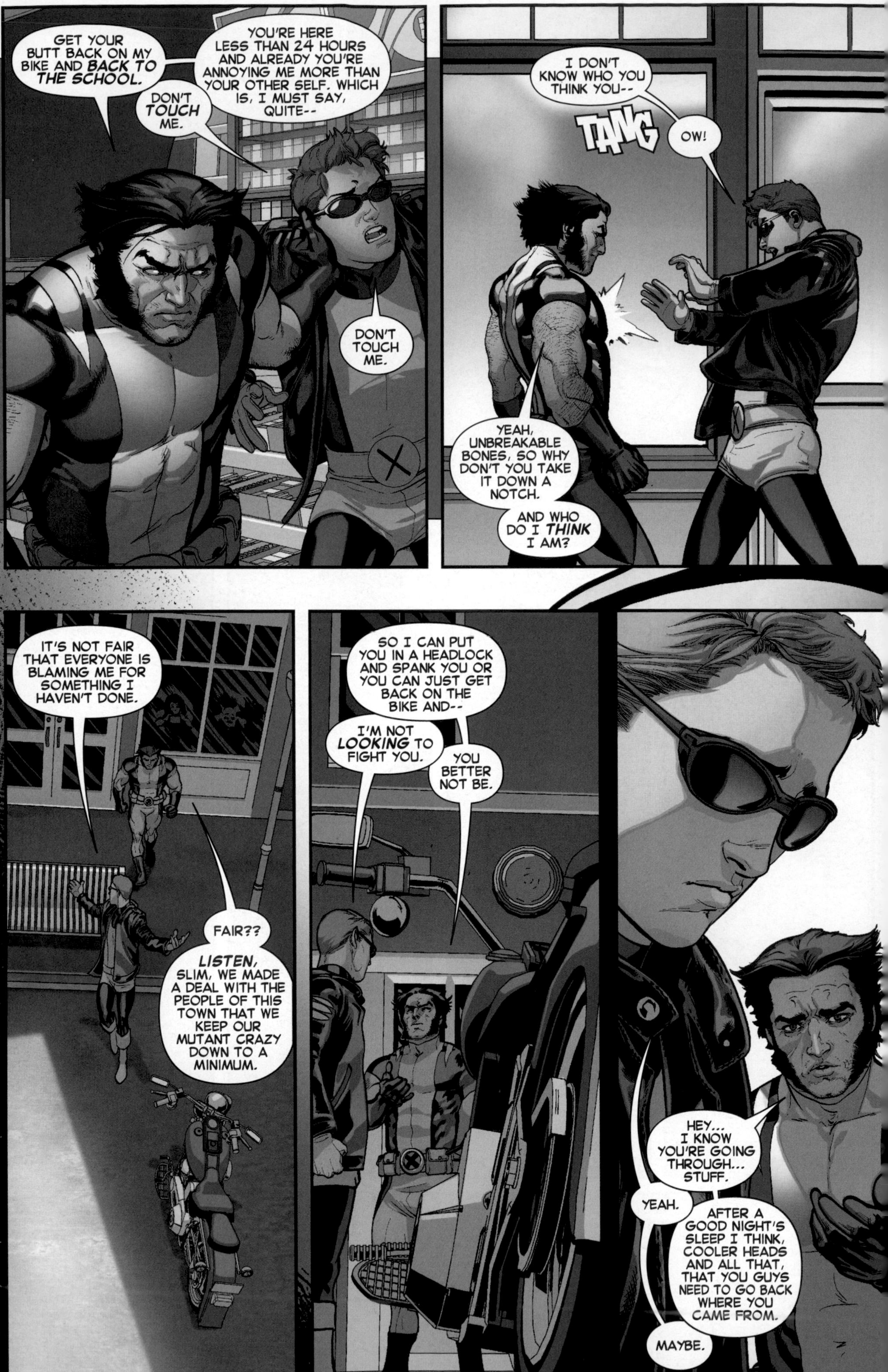
GET YOUR BUTT BACK ON MY BIKE AND BACK TO THE SCHOOL.
YOU'RE HERE LESS THAN 24 HOURS AND ALREADY YOU'RE ANNOYING ME MORE THAN YOUR OTHER SELF. WHICH IS, I MUST SAY, QUITE--
DON'T TOUCH ME.
DON'T TOUCH ME.
I DON'T KNOW WHO YOU THINK YOU--
TANG
OW!
YEAH, UNBREAKABLE BONES, SO WHY DON'T YOU TAKE IT DOWN A NOTCH.
AND WHO DO I THINK I AM?
IT'S NOT FAIR THAT EVERYONE IS BLAMING ME FOR SOMETHING I HAVEN'T DONE.
FAIR??
LISTEN, SLIM, WE MADE A DEAL WITH THE PEOPLE OF THIS TOWN THAT WE KEEP OUR MUTANT CRAZY DOWN TO A MINIMUM.
SO I CAN PUT YOU IN A HEADLOCK AND SPANK YOU OR YOU CAN JUST GET BACK ON THE BIKE AND--
I'M NOT LOOKING TO FIGHT YOU.
YOU BETTER NOT BE.
HEY... I KNOW YOU'RE GOING THROUGH... STUFF.
YEAH.
AFTER A GOOD NIGHT'S SLEEP I THINK, COOLER HEADS AND ALL THAT, THAT YOU GUYS NEED TO GO BACK WHERE YOU CAME FROM.
MAYBE.

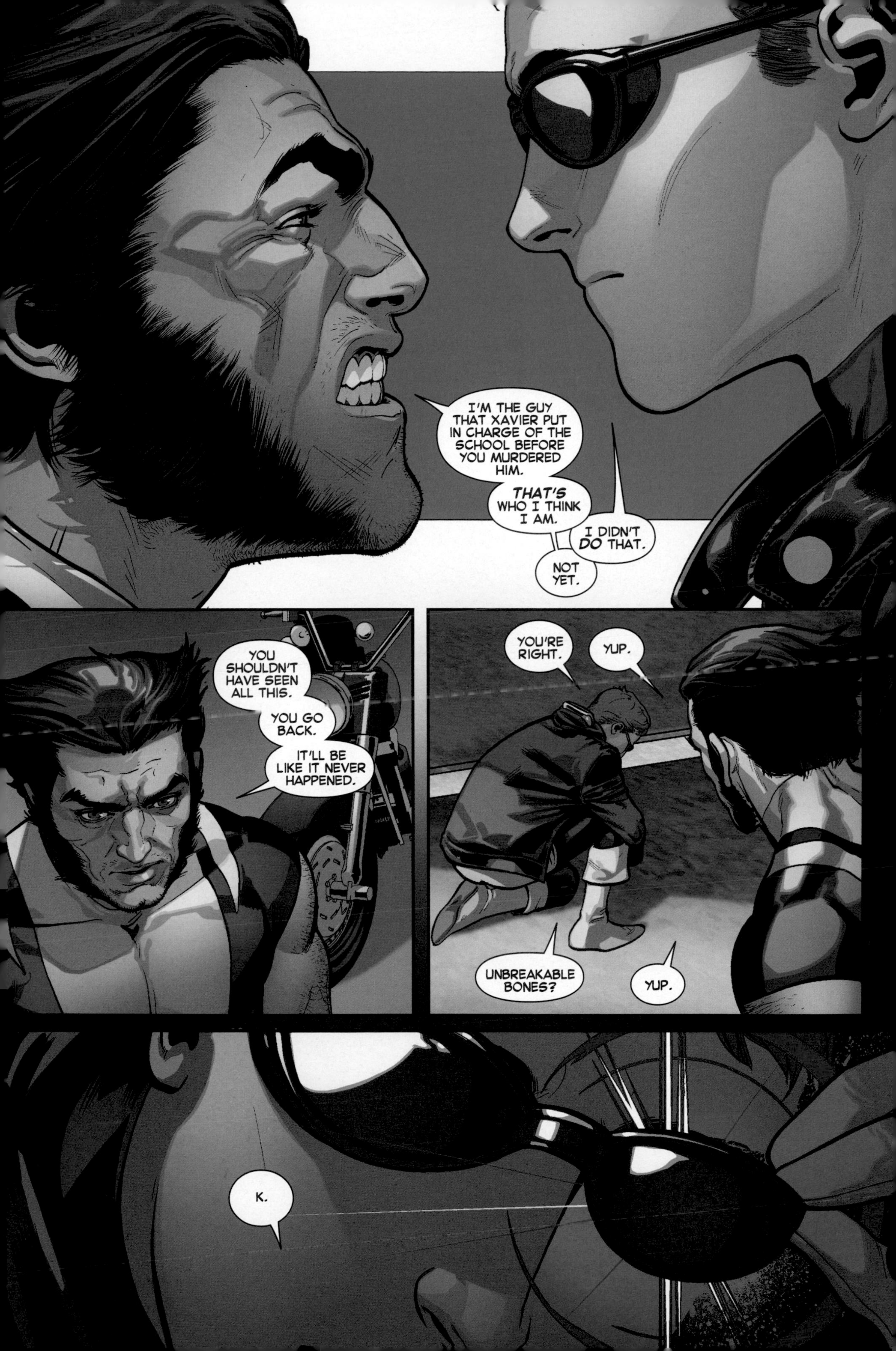

I'M THE GUY THAT XAVIER PUT IN CHARGE OF THE SCHOOL BEFORE YOU MURDERED HIM.
THAT'S WHO I THINK I AM.
I DIDN'T DO THAT.
NOT YET.
YOU SHOULDN'T HAVE SEEN ALL THIS.
YOU GO BACK.
IT'LL BE LIKE IT NEVER HAPPENED.
YOU'RE RIGHT.
YUP.
UNBREAKABLE BONES?
YUP.
K.

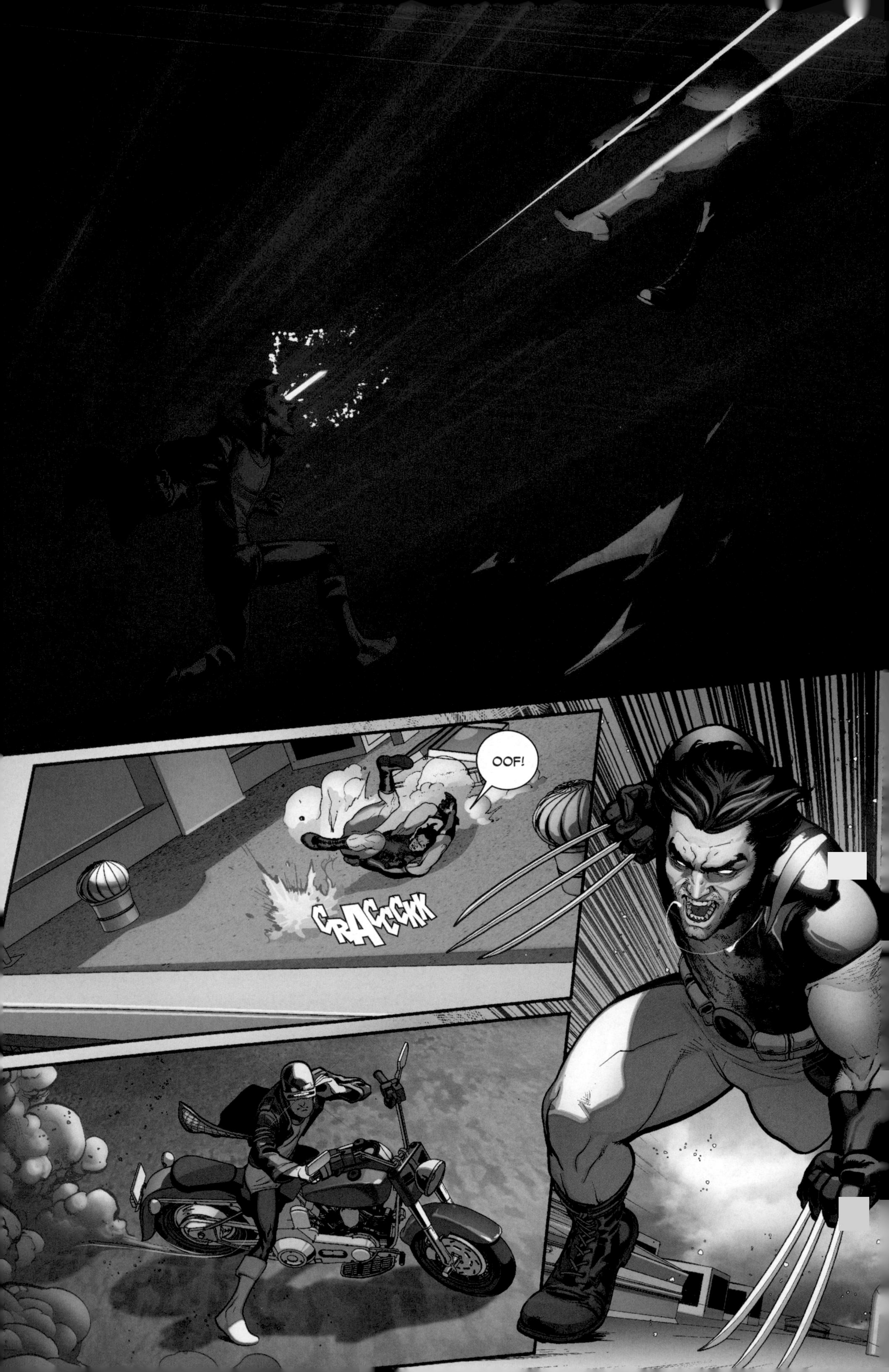
OOF!
CRACCCKK

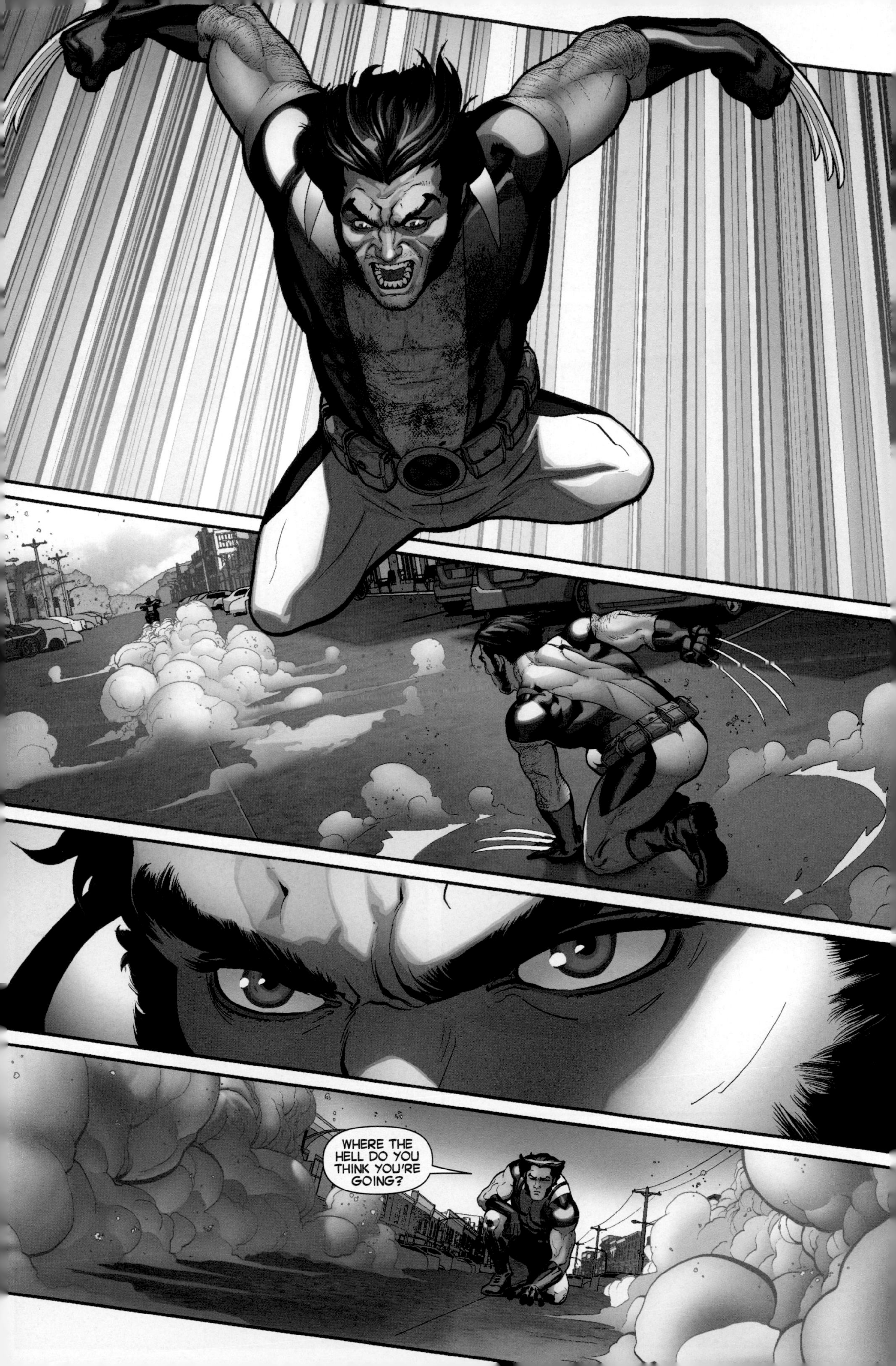
WHERE THE HELL DO YOU THINK YOU'RE GOING?

I HAVE TO SEE FOR MYSELF.

I HAVE TO SEE WHAT I HAVE BECOME.

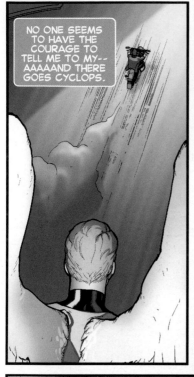

NO ONE SEEMS TO HAVE THE COURAGE TO TELL ME TO MY-- AAAAAND THERE GOES CYCLOPS.

SURE, LEAVE ME HERE, SCOTTIE.

I DON'T WANT TO BE HERE IN THE FIRST PLACE AND NOW YOU LEAVE ME HERE.

YOU GUYS STICK ME HERE AND YOU DON'T EVEN--

HUH-- OKAY.

WHAT IS--?

AM I NUTS OR DID THE GROUND JUST BURP?

WHAT HAS HAPPENED TO THE SCHOOL? WHAT HAS HAPPENED TO THE--?

WELL, THIS IS... UNEXPECTED.

OH MY GOD...

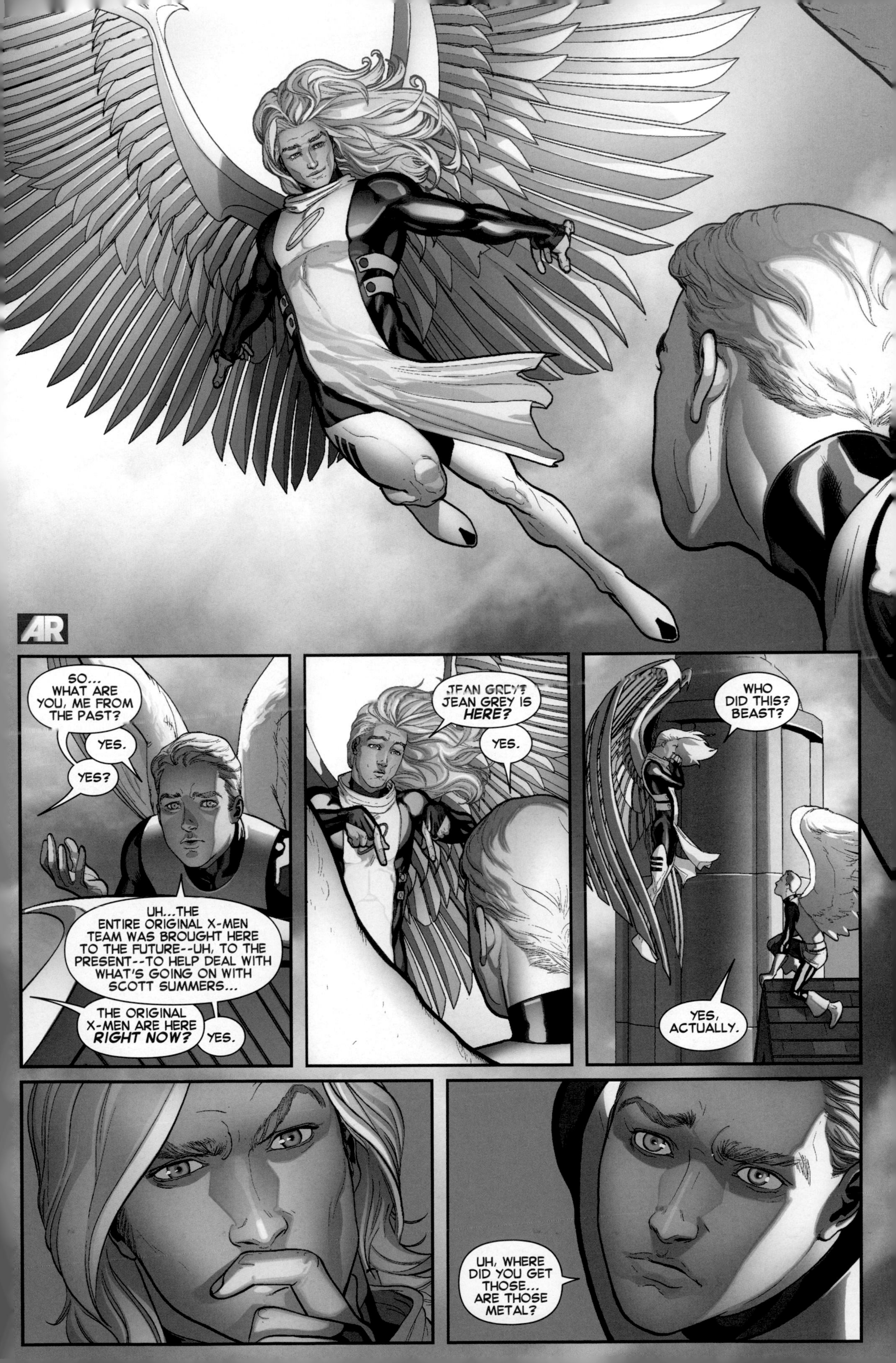
SO... WHAT ARE YOU, ME FROM THE PAST?
YES.
YES?
UH...THE ENTIRE ORIGINAL X-MEN TEAM WAS BROUGHT HERE TO THE FUTURE--UH, TO THE PRESENT--TO HELP DEAL WITH WHAT'S GOING ON WITH SCOTT SUMMERS...
THE ORIGINAL X-MEN ARE HERE *RIGHT NOW?*
YES.
JEAN GREY? JEAN GREY IS *HERE?*
YES.
WHO DID THIS? BEAST?
YES, ACTUALLY.
UH, WHERE DID YOU GET THOSE... ARE THOSE METAL?

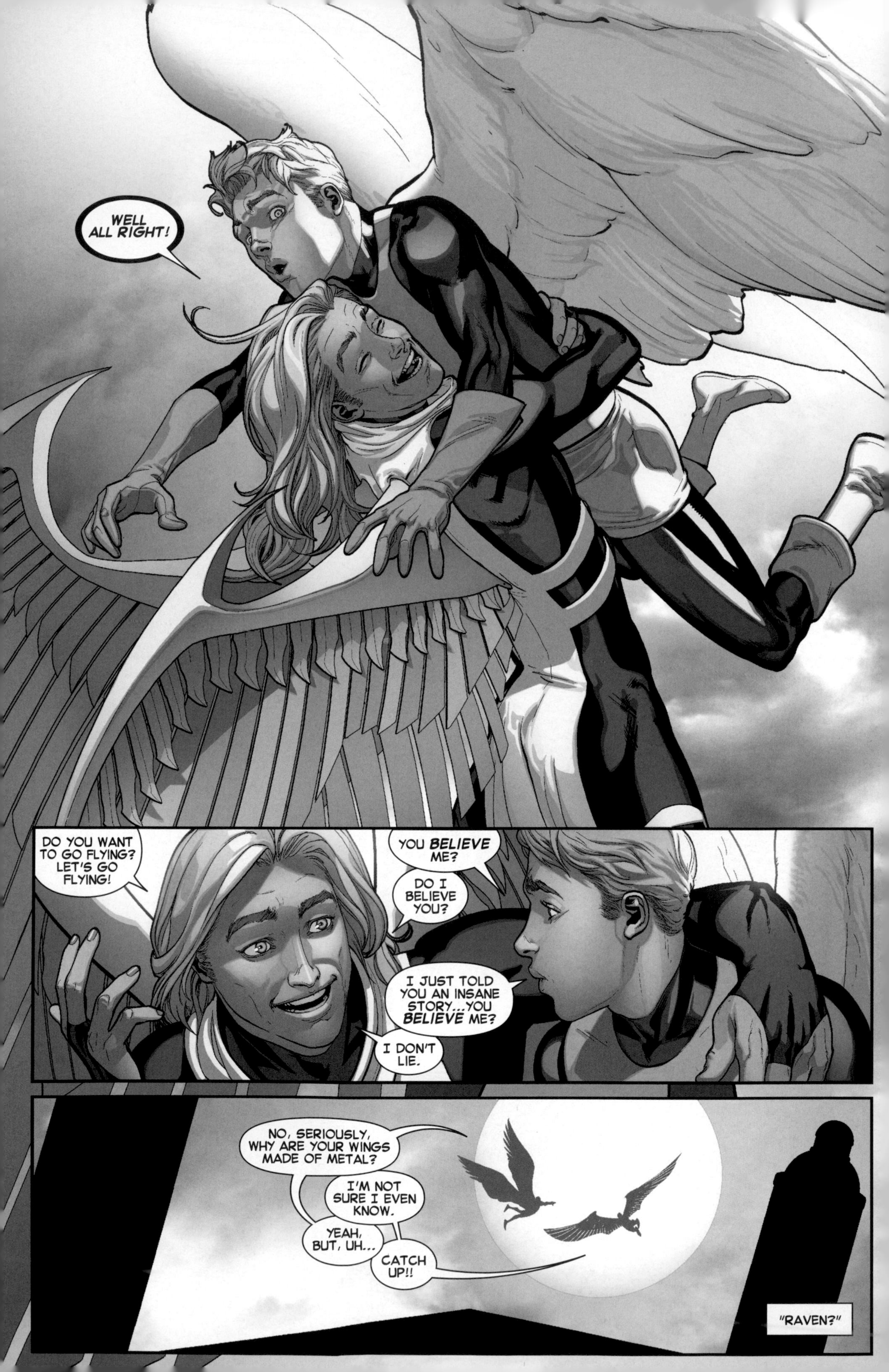
WELL ALL RIGHT!
DO YOU WANT TO GO FLYING? LET'S GO FLYING!
YOU BELIEVE ME?
DO I BELIEVE YOU?
I JUST TOLD YOU AN INSANE STORY...YOU BELIEVE ME?
I DON'T LIE.
NO, SERIOUSLY, WHY ARE YOUR WINGS MADE OF METAL?
I'M NOT SURE I EVEN KNOW.
YEAH, BUT, UH...
CATCH UP!!
"RAVEN?"

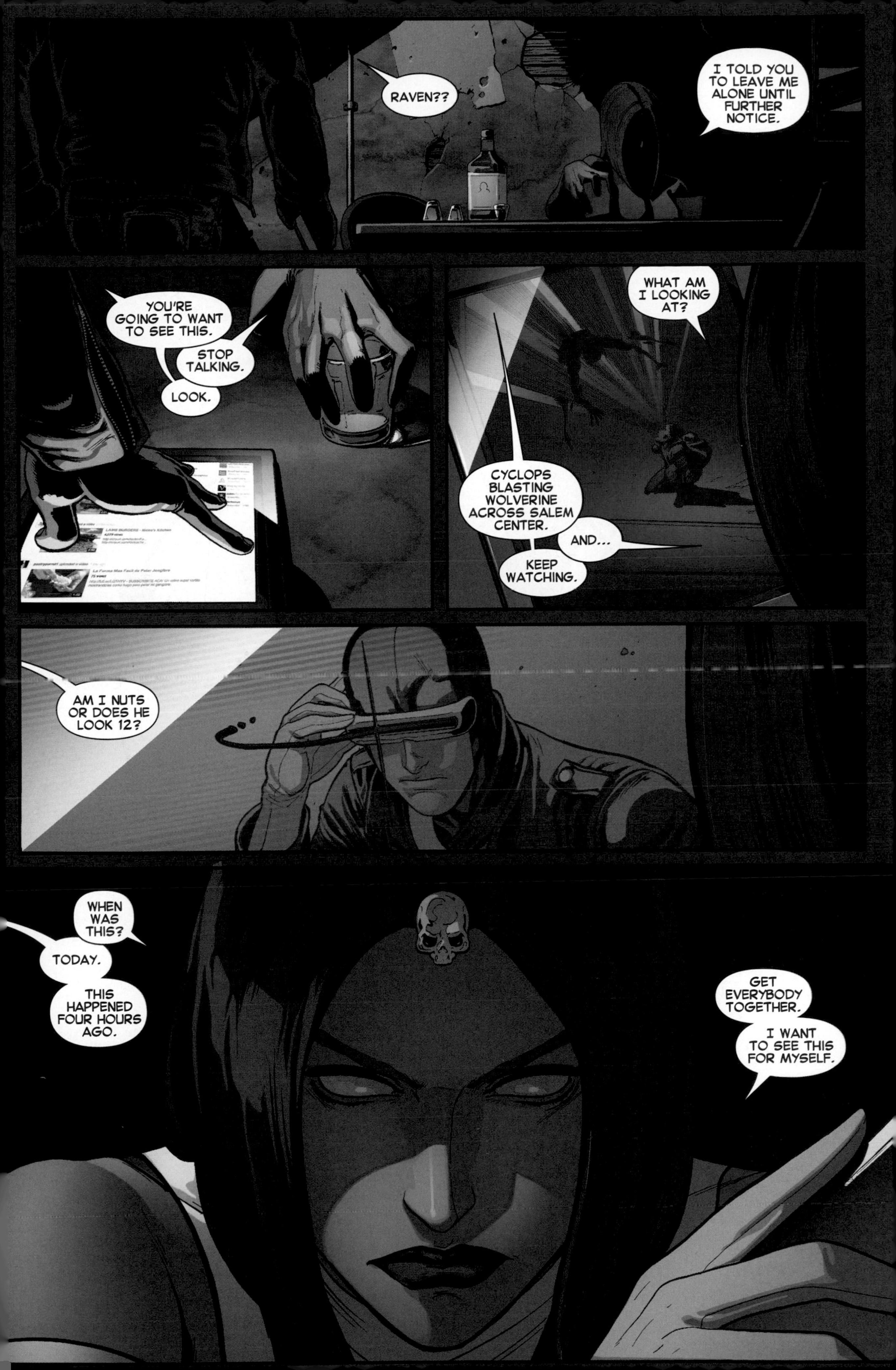
RAVEN??
I TOLD YOU TO LEAVE ME ALONE UNTIL FURTHER NOTICE.
YOU'RE GOING TO WANT TO SEE THIS.
STOP TALKING.
LOOK.
WHAT AM I LOOKING AT?
CYCLOPS BLASTING WOLVERINE ACROSS SALEM CENTER.
AND...
KEEP WATCHING.
AM I NUTS OR DOES HE LOOK 12?
WHEN WAS THIS?
TODAY.
THIS HAPPENED FOUR HOURS AGO.
GET EVERYBODY TOGETHER.
I WANT TO SEE THIS FOR MYSELF.

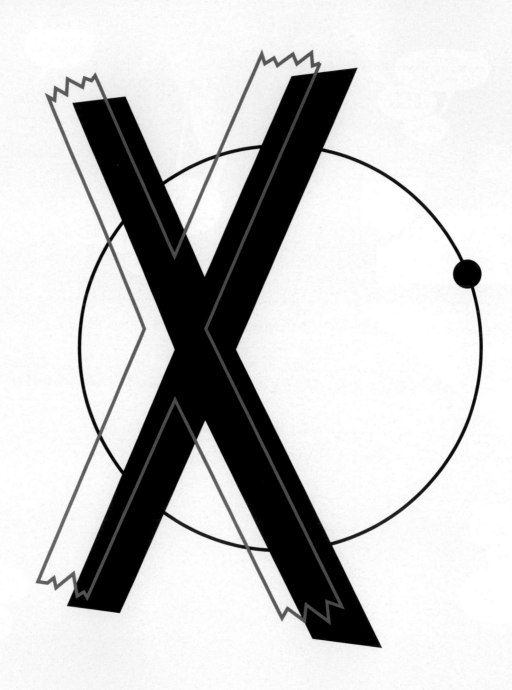

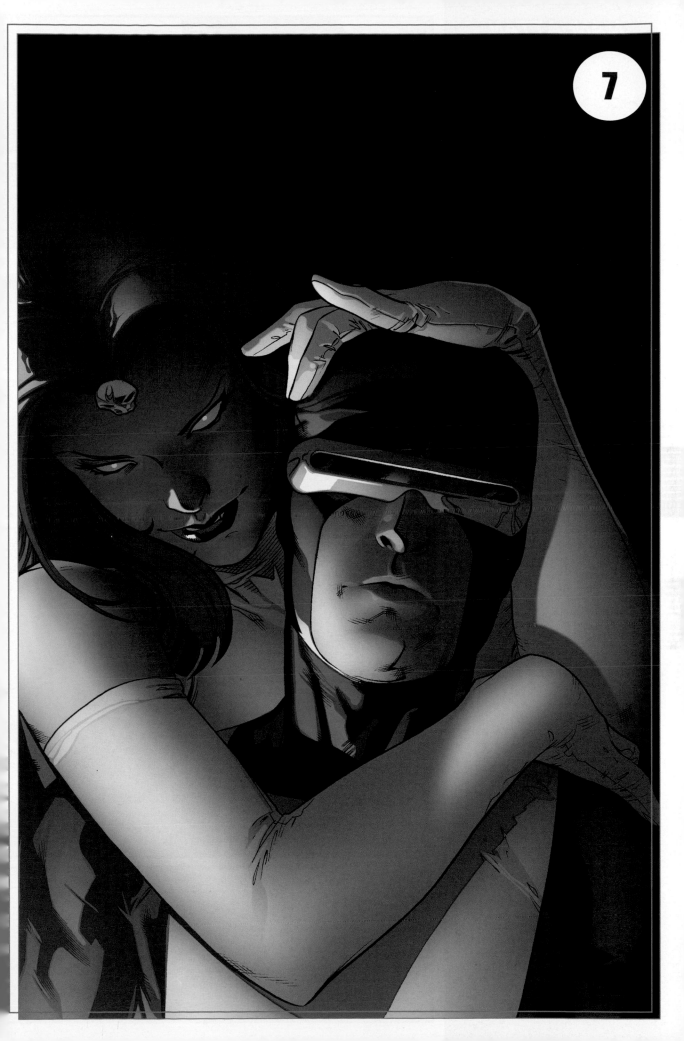

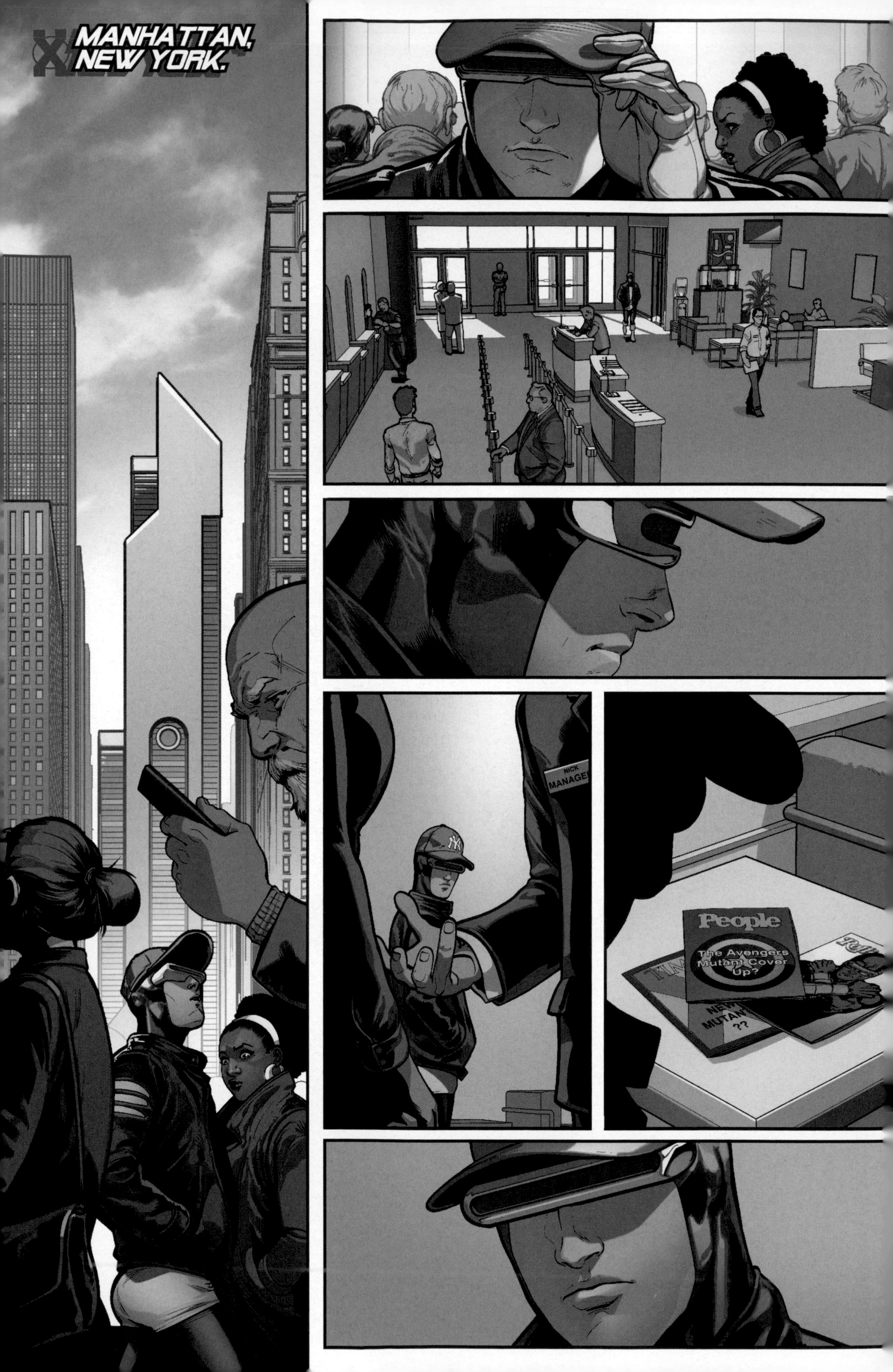
MANHATTAN, NEW YORK.
NICK
MANAGER
People
The Avengers Mutant Cover Up?
NEW MUTANT ??

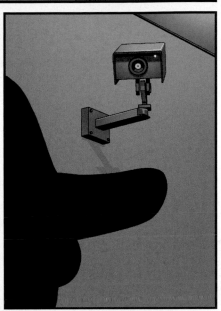

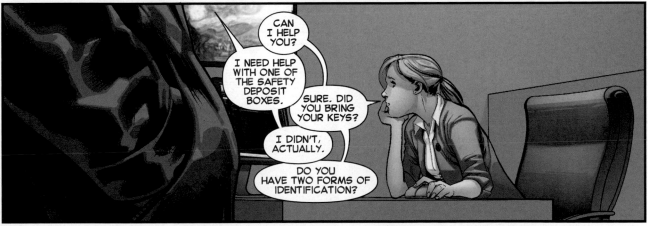

CAN I HELP YOU?

I NEED HELP WITH ONE OF THE SAFETY DEPOSIT BOXES.

SURE. DID YOU BRING YOUR KEYS?

I DIDN'T, ACTUALLY.

DO YOU HAVE TWO FORMS OF IDENTIFICATION?

WELL, SORT OF. I'M SURE WE CAN--

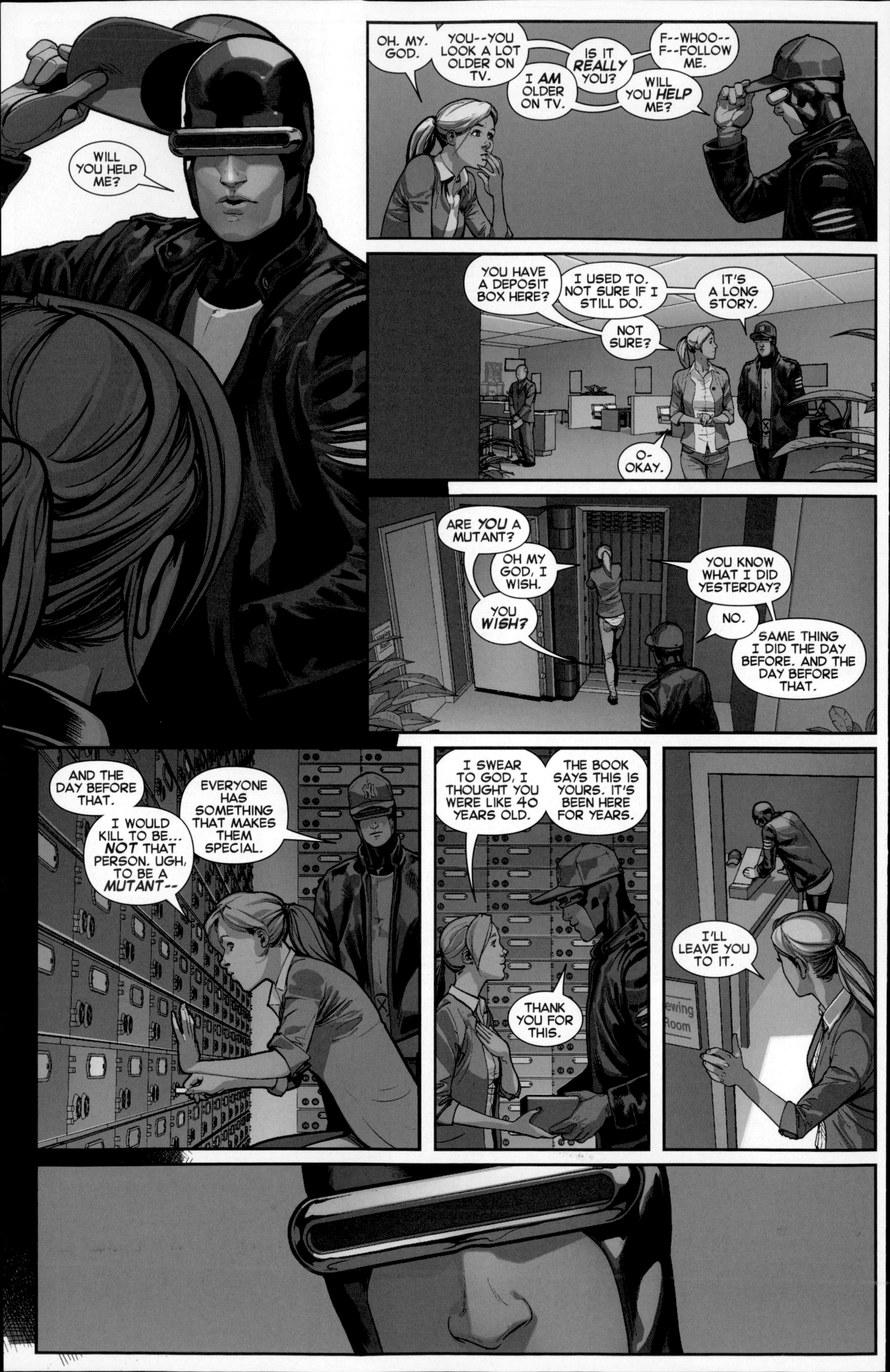
WILL YOU HELP ME?
OH. MY. GOD.
YOU--YOU LOOK A LOT OLDER ON TV.
I *AM* OLDER ON TV.
IS IT *REALLY* YOU?
WILL YOU *HELP* ME?
F--WHOO-- F--FOLLOW ME.
YOU HAVE A DEPOSIT BOX HERE?
I USED TO. NOT SURE IF I STILL DO.
NOT SURE?
IT'S A LONG STORY.
O-OKAY.
ARE *YOU* A MUTANT?
OH MY GOD, I WISH.
YOU *WISH?*
YOU KNOW WHAT I DID YESTERDAY?
NO.
SAME THING I DID THE DAY BEFORE. AND THE DAY BEFORE THAT.
AND THE DAY BEFORE THAT.
I WOULD KILL TO BE... *NOT* THAT PERSON. UGH, TO BE A *MUTANT*--
EVERYONE HAS SOMETHING THAT MAKES THEM SPECIAL.
I SWEAR TO GOD, I THOUGHT YOU WERE LIKE 40 YEARS OLD.
THE BOOK SAYS THIS IS YOURS. IT'S BEEN HERE FOR YEARS.
THANK YOU FOR THIS.
I'LL LEAVE YOU TO IT.

AGH!

OH... THAT'S BETTER.

THANK YOU, SCOTT SUMMERS.

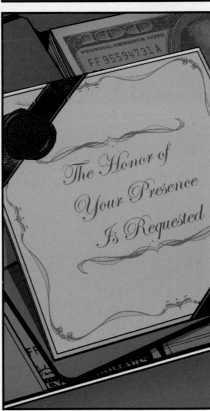

The Honor of Your Presence Is Requested

WHAT IS GOING ON WITH *YOU*, ALL OF A SUDDEN?

YOU HAVE *NO IDEA* WHO IS IN THERE RIGHT NOW...

WHO IS IN *WHERE*?

WHO?

THE SAFE DEPOSIT BOX ROOM.

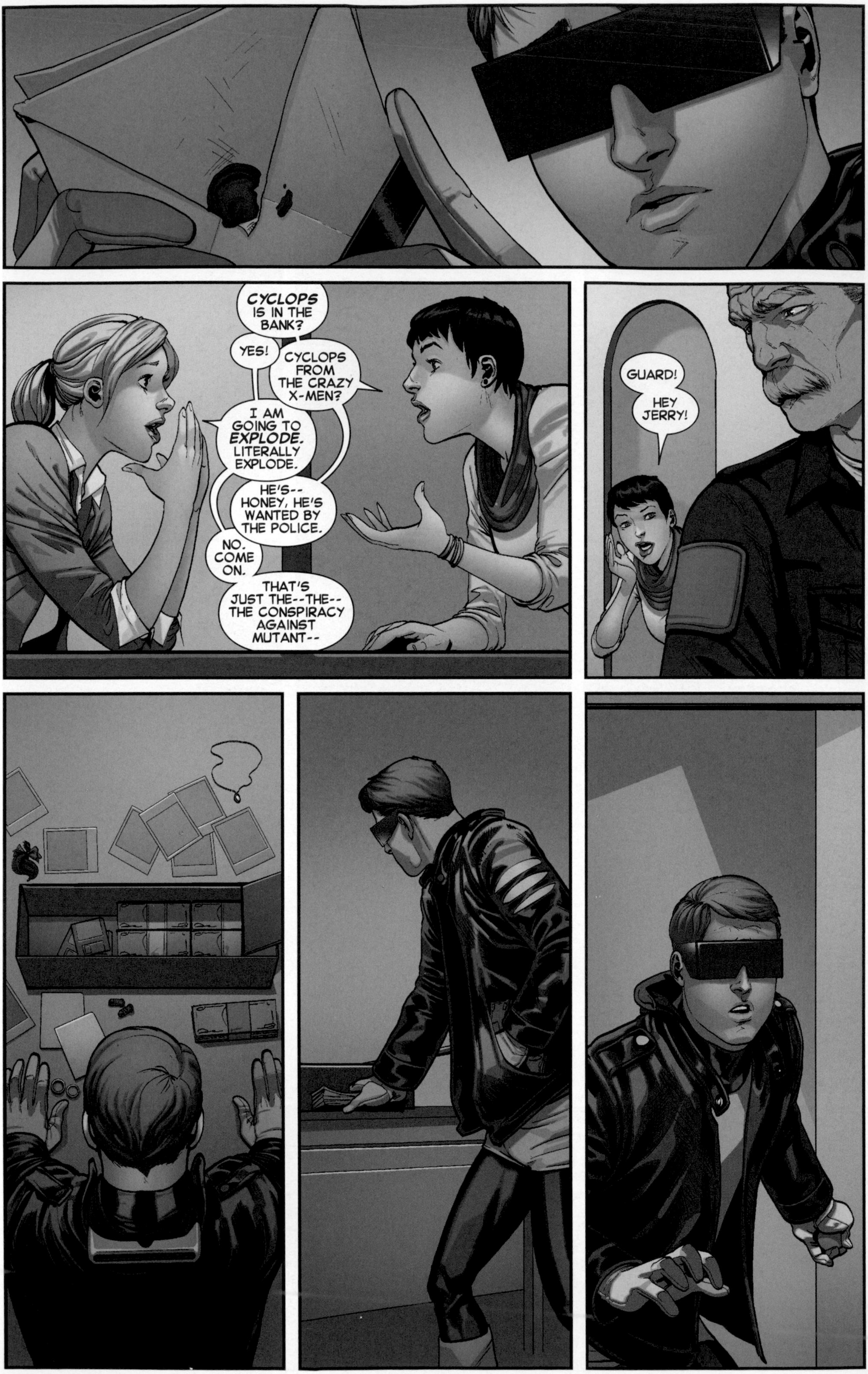

CYCLOPS IS IN THE BANK?
YES!
CYCLOPS FROM THE CRAZY X-MEN?
I AM GOING TO EXPLODE. LITERALLY EXPLODE.
HE'S-- HONEY, HE'S WANTED BY THE POLICE.
NO. COME ON.
THAT'S JUST THE--THE-- THE CONSPIRACY AGAINST MUTANT--
GUARD!
HEY JERRY!

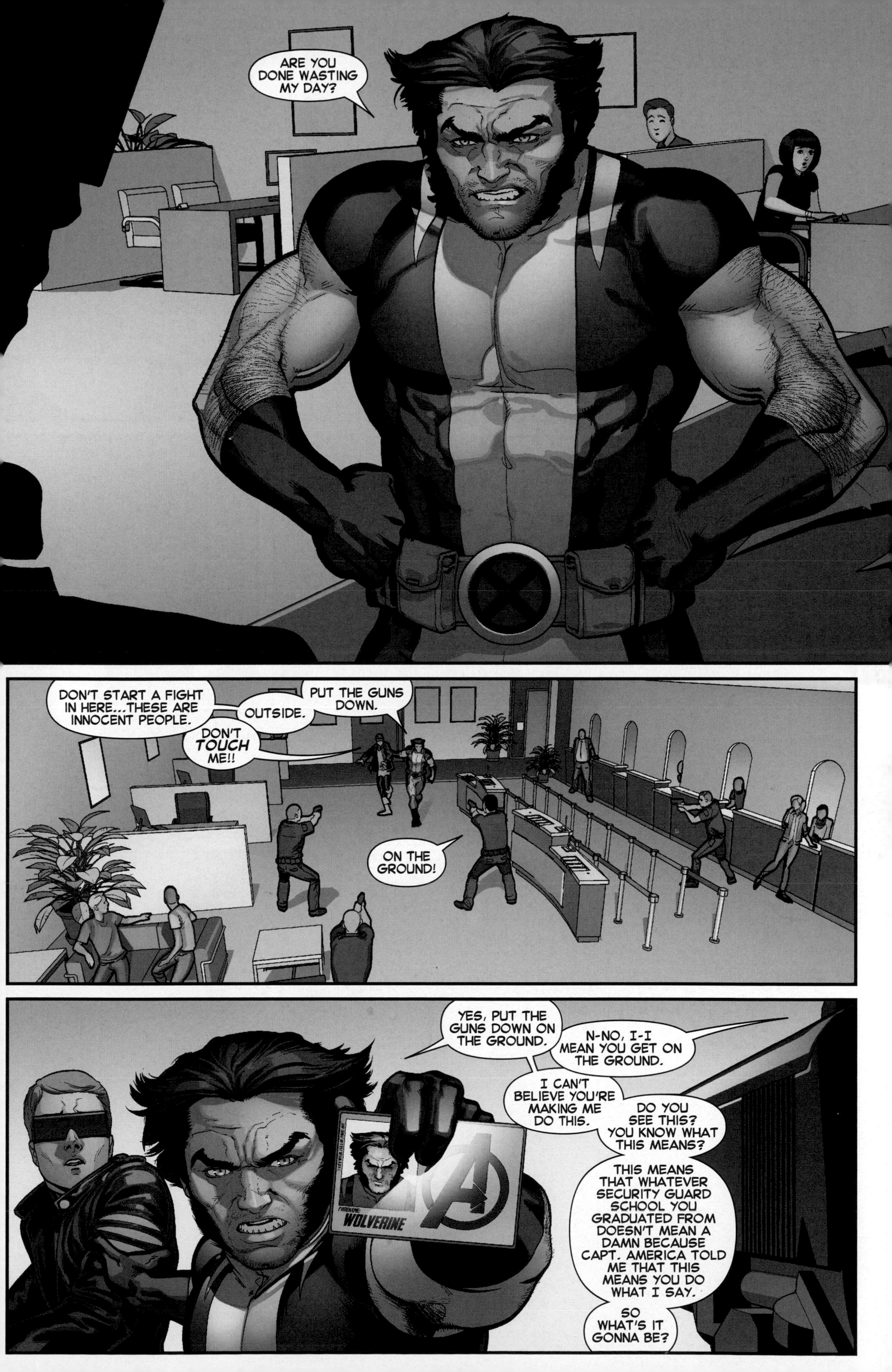
ARE YOU DONE WASTING MY DAY?
DON'T START A FIGHT IN HERE...THESE ARE INNOCENT PEOPLE.
OUTSIDE.
PUT THE GUNS DOWN.
DON'T TOUCH ME!!
ON THE GROUND!
YES, PUT THE GUNS DOWN ON THE GROUND.
N-NO, I-I MEAN YOU GET ON THE GROUND.
I CAN'T BELIEVE YOU'RE MAKING ME DO THIS.
DO YOU SEE THIS? YOU KNOW WHAT THIS MEANS?
THIS MEANS THAT WHATEVER SECURITY GUARD SCHOOL YOU GRADUATED FROM DOESN'T MEAN A DAMN BECAUSE CAPT. AMERICA TOLD ME THAT THIS MEANS YOU DO WHAT I SAY.
SO WHAT'S IT GONNA BE?
WOLVERINE

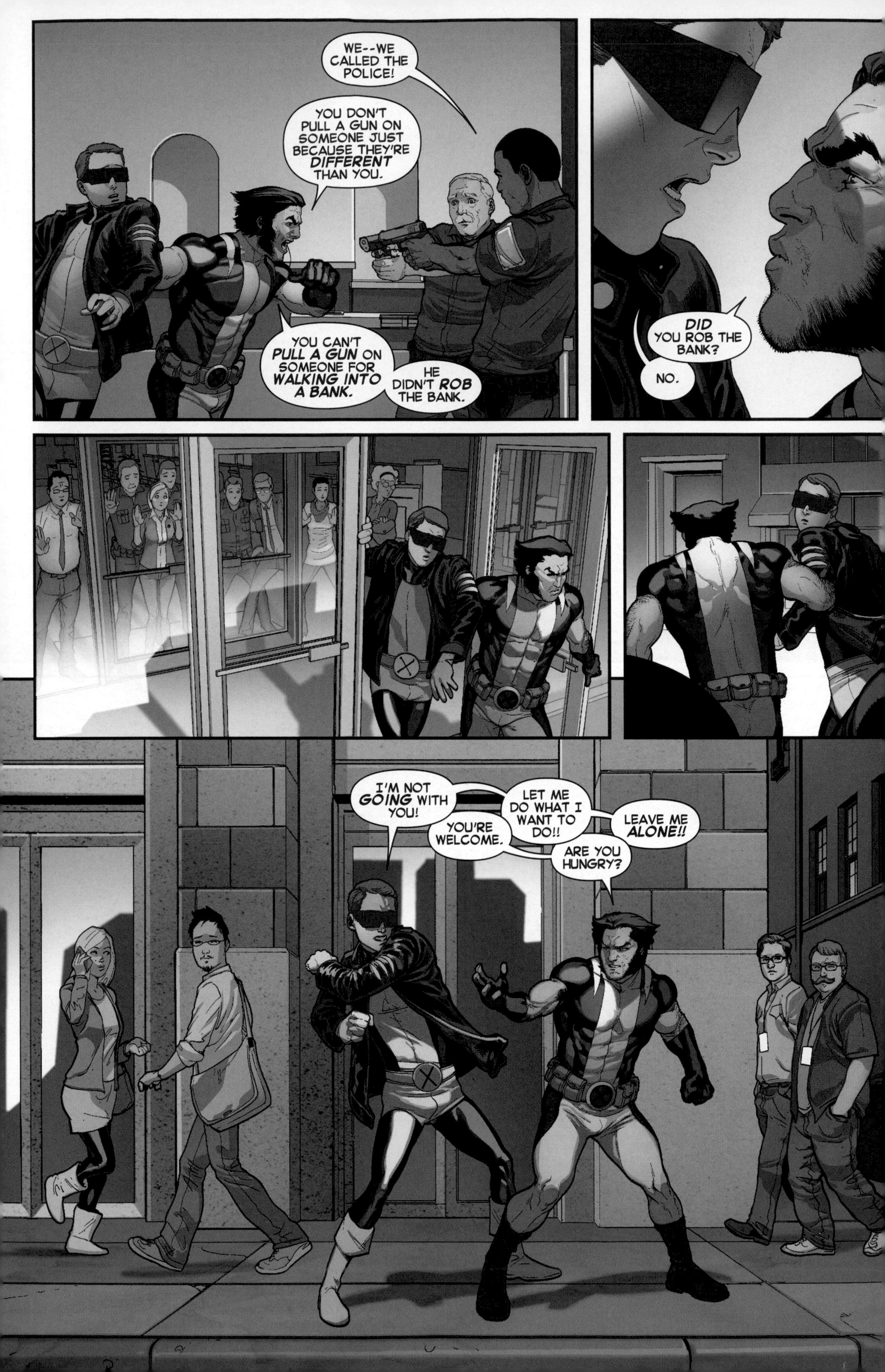
WE--WE CALLED THE POLICE!
YOU DON'T PULL A GUN ON SOMEONE JUST BECAUSE THEY'RE DIFFERENT THAN YOU.
YOU CAN'T PULL A GUN ON SOMEONE FOR WALKING INTO A BANK.
HE DIDN'T ROB THE BANK.
DID YOU ROB THE BANK?
NO.
I'M NOT GOING WITH YOU!
YOU'RE WELCOME.
LET ME DO WHAT I WANT TO DO!!
ARE YOU HUNGRY?
LEAVE ME ALONE!!

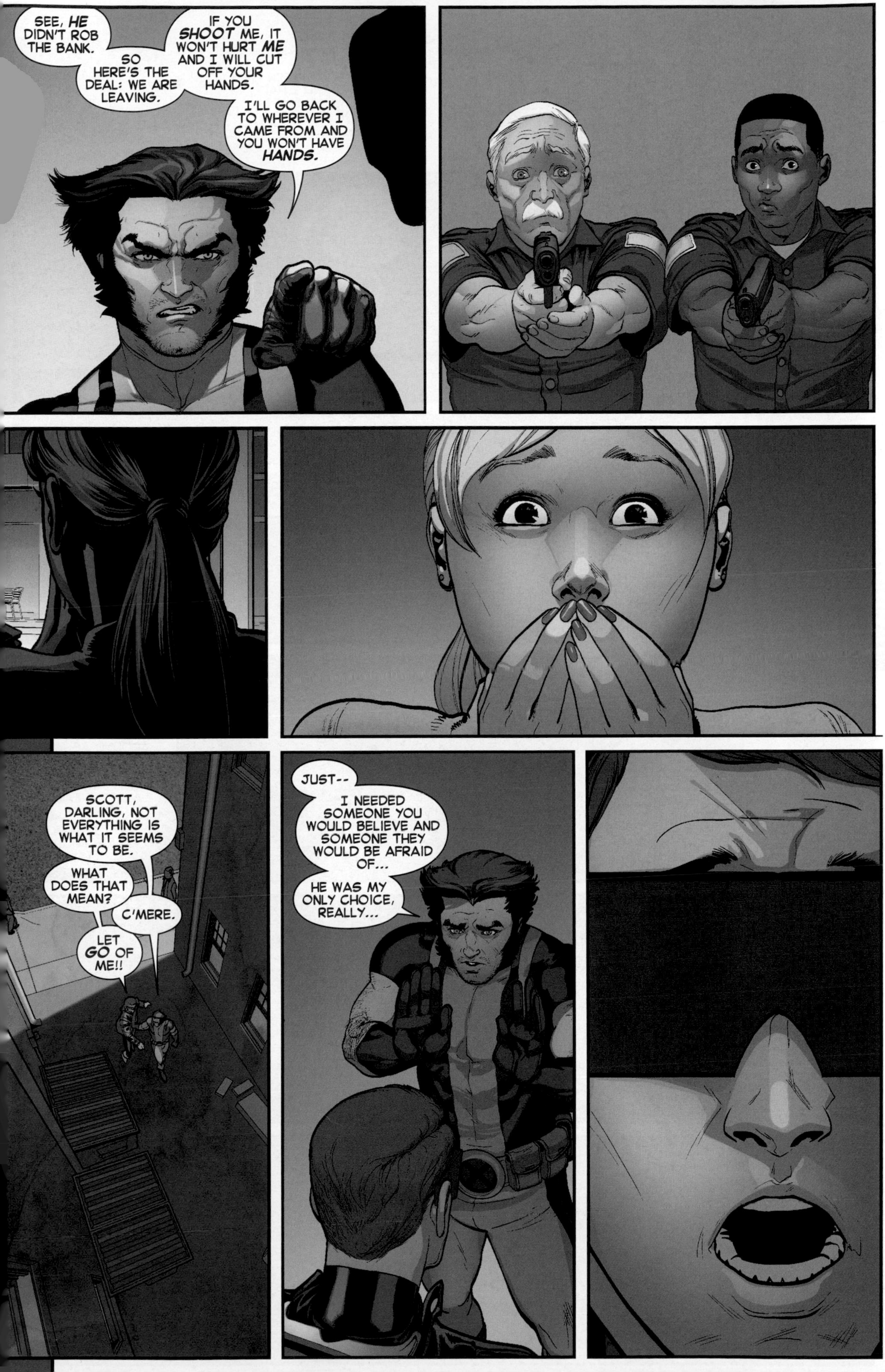
SEE, HE DIDN'T ROB THE BANK.
SO HERE'S THE DEAL: WE ARE LEAVING.
IF YOU SHOOT ME, IT WON'T HURT ME AND I WILL CUT OFF YOUR HANDS.
I'LL GO BACK TO WHEREVER I CAME FROM AND YOU WON'T HAVE HANDS.
SCOTT, DARLING, NOT EVERYTHING IS WHAT IT SEEMS TO BE.
WHAT DOES THAT MEAN?
C'MERE.
LET GO OF ME!!
JUST--
I NEEDED SOMEONE YOU WOULD BELIEVE AND SOMEONE THEY WOULD BE AFRAID OF...
HE WAS MY ONLY CHOICE, REALLY...

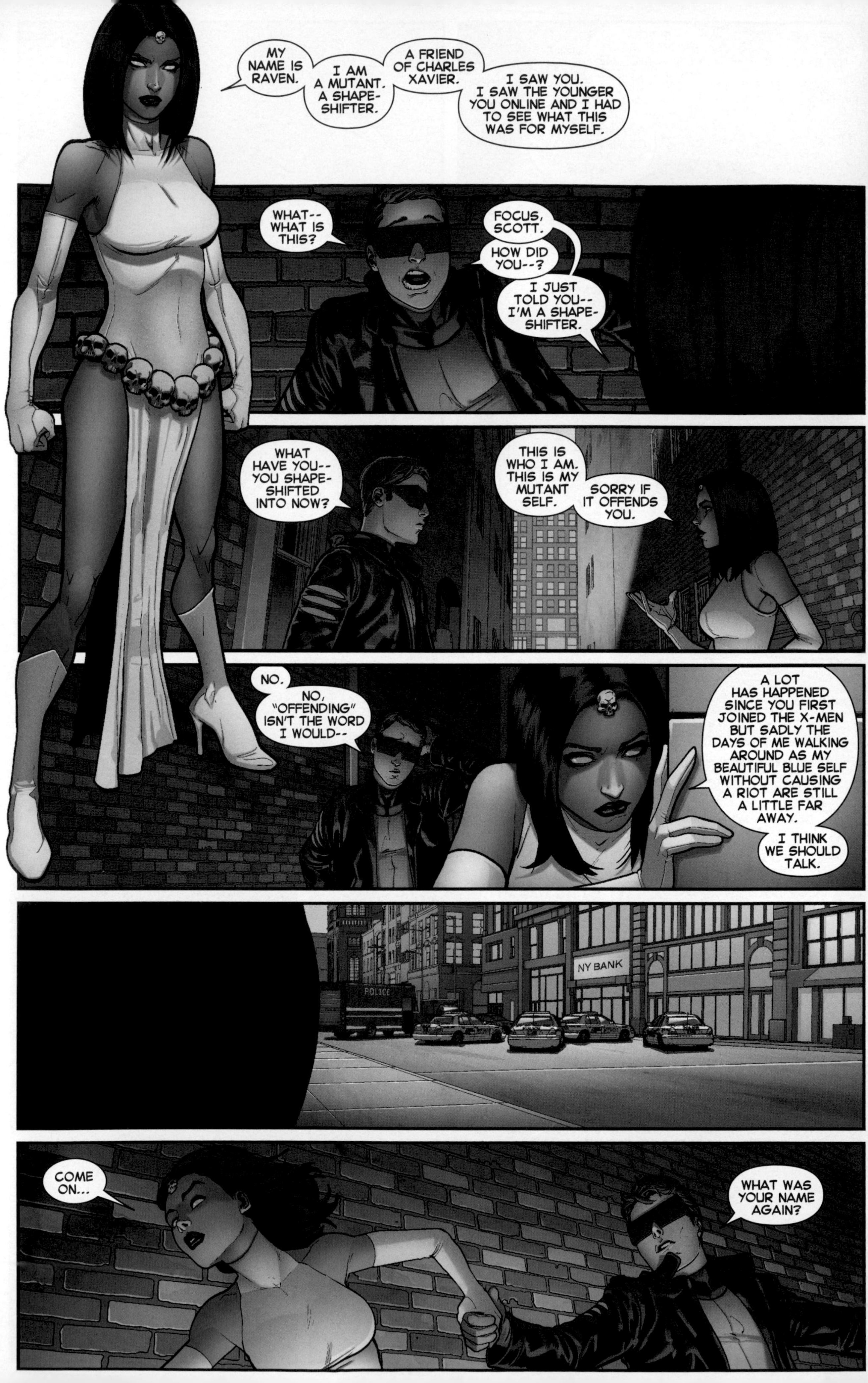
MY NAME IS RAVEN.
I AM A MUTANT. A SHAPE-SHIFTER.
A FRIEND OF CHARLES XAVIER.
I SAW YOU. I SAW THE YOUNGER YOU ONLINE AND I HAD TO SEE WHAT THIS WAS FOR MYSELF.
WHAT-- WHAT IS THIS?
FOCUS, SCOTT.
HOW DID YOU--?
I JUST TOLD YOU-- I'M A SHAPE-SHIFTER.
WHAT HAVE YOU-- YOU SHAPE-SHIFTED INTO NOW?
THIS IS WHO I AM. THIS IS MY MUTANT SELF.
SORRY IF IT OFFENDS YOU.
NO.
NO, "OFFENDING" ISN'T THE WORD I WOULD--
A LOT HAS HAPPENED SINCE YOU FIRST JOINED THE X-MEN BUT SADLY THE DAYS OF ME WALKING AROUND AS MY BEAUTIFUL BLUE SELF WITHOUT CAUSING A RIOT ARE STILL A LITTLE FAR AWAY.
I THINK WE SHOULD TALK.
POLICE
NY BANK
COME ON...
WHAT WAS YOUR NAME AGAIN?

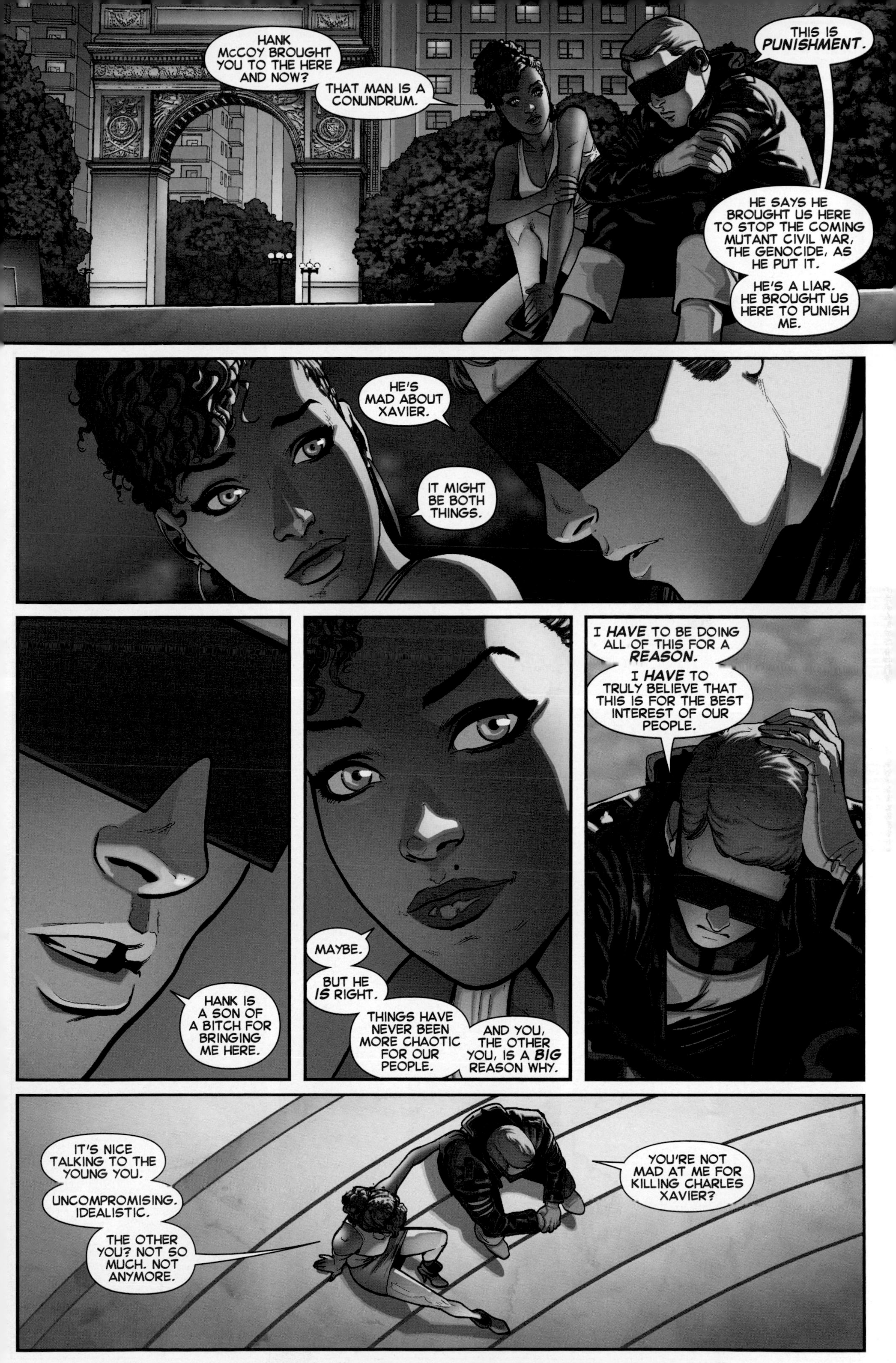
HANK McCOY BROUGHT YOU TO THE HERE AND NOW?
THAT MAN IS A CONUNDRUM.
THIS IS PUNISHMENT.
HE SAYS HE BROUGHT US HERE TO STOP THE COMING MUTANT CIVIL WAR, THE GENOCIDE, AS HE PUT IT.
HE'S A LIAR. HE BROUGHT US HERE TO PUNISH ME.
HE'S MAD ABOUT XAVIER.
IT MIGHT BE BOTH THINGS.
HANK IS A SON OF A BITCH FOR BRINGING ME HERE.
MAYBE.
BUT HE IS RIGHT.
THINGS HAVE NEVER BEEN MORE CHAOTIC FOR OUR PEOPLE.
AND YOU, THE OTHER YOU, IS A BIG REASON WHY.
I HAVE TO BE DOING ALL OF THIS FOR A REASON.
I HAVE TO TRULY BELIEVE THAT THIS IS FOR THE BEST INTEREST OF OUR PEOPLE.
IT'S NICE TALKING TO THE YOUNG YOU.
UNCOMPROMISING. IDEALISTIC.
THE OTHER YOU? NOT SO MUCH. NOT ANYMORE.
YOU'RE NOT MAD AT ME FOR KILLING CHARLES XAVIER?

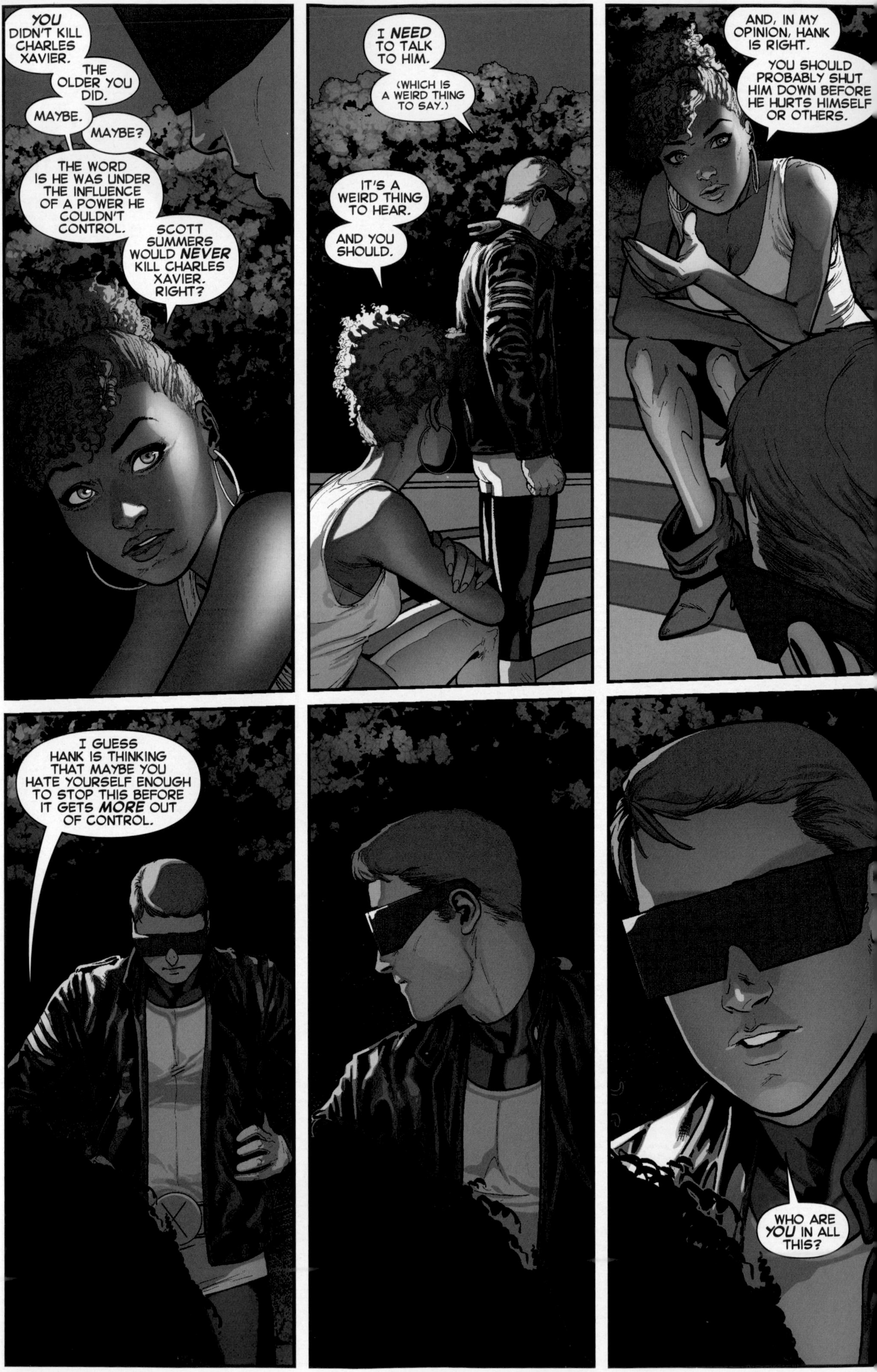
YOU DIDN'T KILL CHARLES XAVIER.
THE OLDER YOU DID.
MAYBE.
MAYBE?
THE WORD IS HE WAS UNDER THE INFLUENCE OF A POWER HE COULDN'T CONTROL.
SCOTT SUMMERS WOULD NEVER KILL CHARLES XAVIER. RIGHT?
I NEED TO TALK TO HIM.
(WHICH IS A WEIRD THING TO SAY.)
IT'S A WEIRD THING TO HEAR.
AND YOU SHOULD.
AND, IN MY OPINION, HANK IS RIGHT.
YOU SHOULD PROBABLY SHUT HIM DOWN BEFORE HE HURTS HIMSELF OR OTHERS.
I GUESS HANK IS THINKING THAT MAYBE YOU HATE YOURSELF ENOUGH TO STOP THIS BEFORE IT GETS MORE OUT OF CONTROL.
WHO ARE YOU IN ALL THIS?

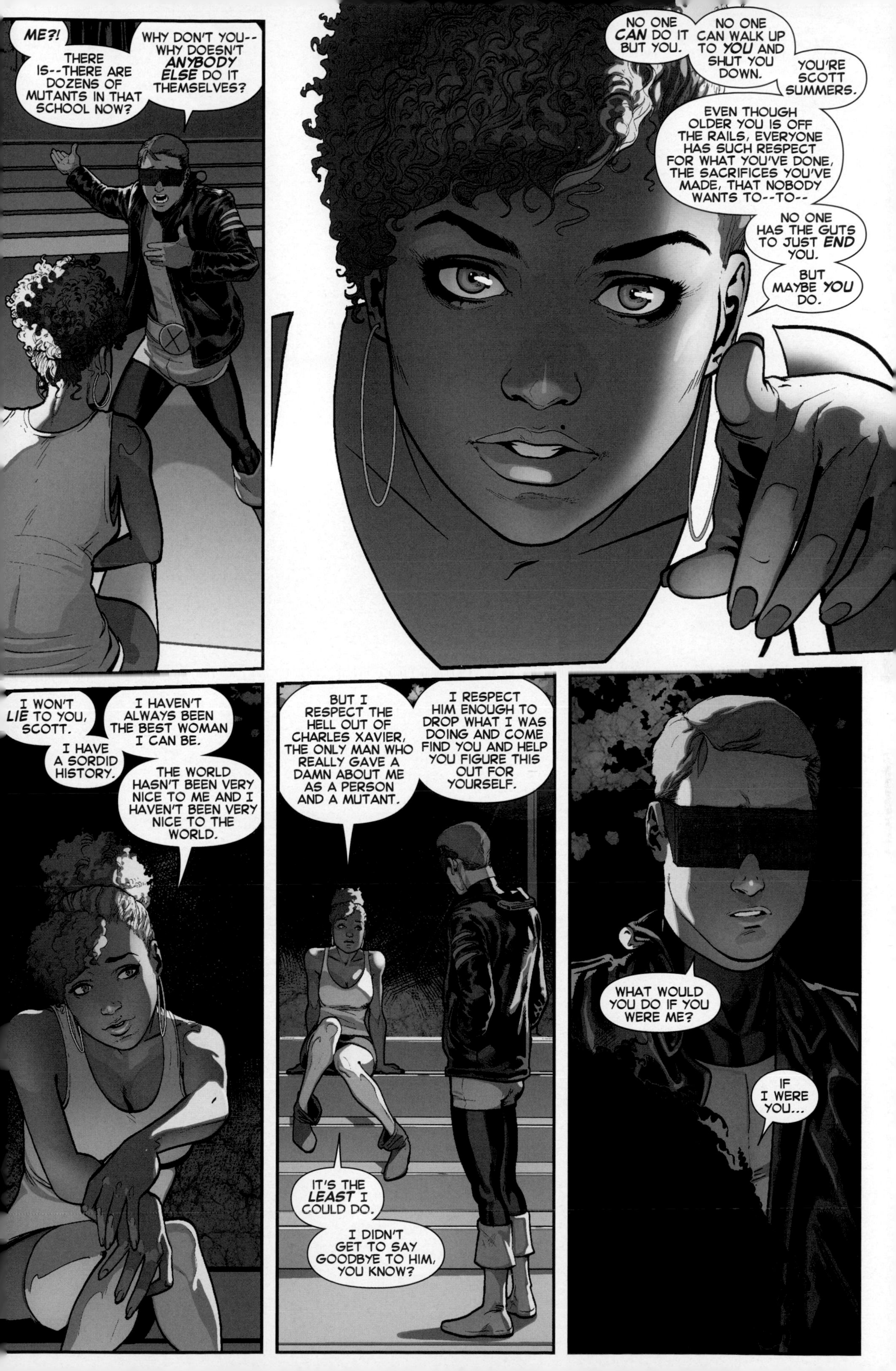
ME?!
THERE IS--THERE ARE DOZENS OF MUTANTS IN THAT SCHOOL NOW?
WHY DON'T YOU--WHY DOESN'T ANYBODY ELSE DO IT THEMSELVES?
NO ONE CAN DO IT BUT YOU.
NO ONE CAN WALK UP TO YOU AND SHUT YOU DOWN.
YOU'RE SCOTT SUMMERS.
EVEN THOUGH OLDER YOU IS OFF THE RAILS, EVERYONE HAS SUCH RESPECT FOR WHAT YOU'VE DONE, THE SACRIFICES YOU'VE MADE, THAT NOBODY WANTS TO--TO--
NO ONE HAS THE GUTS TO JUST END YOU.
BUT MAYBE YOU DO.
I WON'T LIE TO YOU, SCOTT.
I HAVE A SORDID HISTORY.
I HAVEN'T ALWAYS BEEN THE BEST WOMAN I CAN BE.
THE WORLD HASN'T BEEN VERY NICE TO ME AND I HAVEN'T BEEN VERY NICE TO THE WORLD.
BUT I RESPECT THE HELL OUT OF CHARLES XAVIER, THE ONLY MAN WHO REALLY GAVE A DAMN ABOUT ME AS A PERSON AND A MUTANT.
I RESPECT HIM ENOUGH TO DROP WHAT I WAS DOING AND COME FIND YOU AND HELP YOU FIGURE THIS OUT FOR YOURSELF.
IT'S THE LEAST I COULD DO.
I DIDN'T GET TO SAY GOODBYE TO HIM, YOU KNOW?
WHAT WOULD YOU DO IF YOU WERE ME?
IF I WERE YOU...

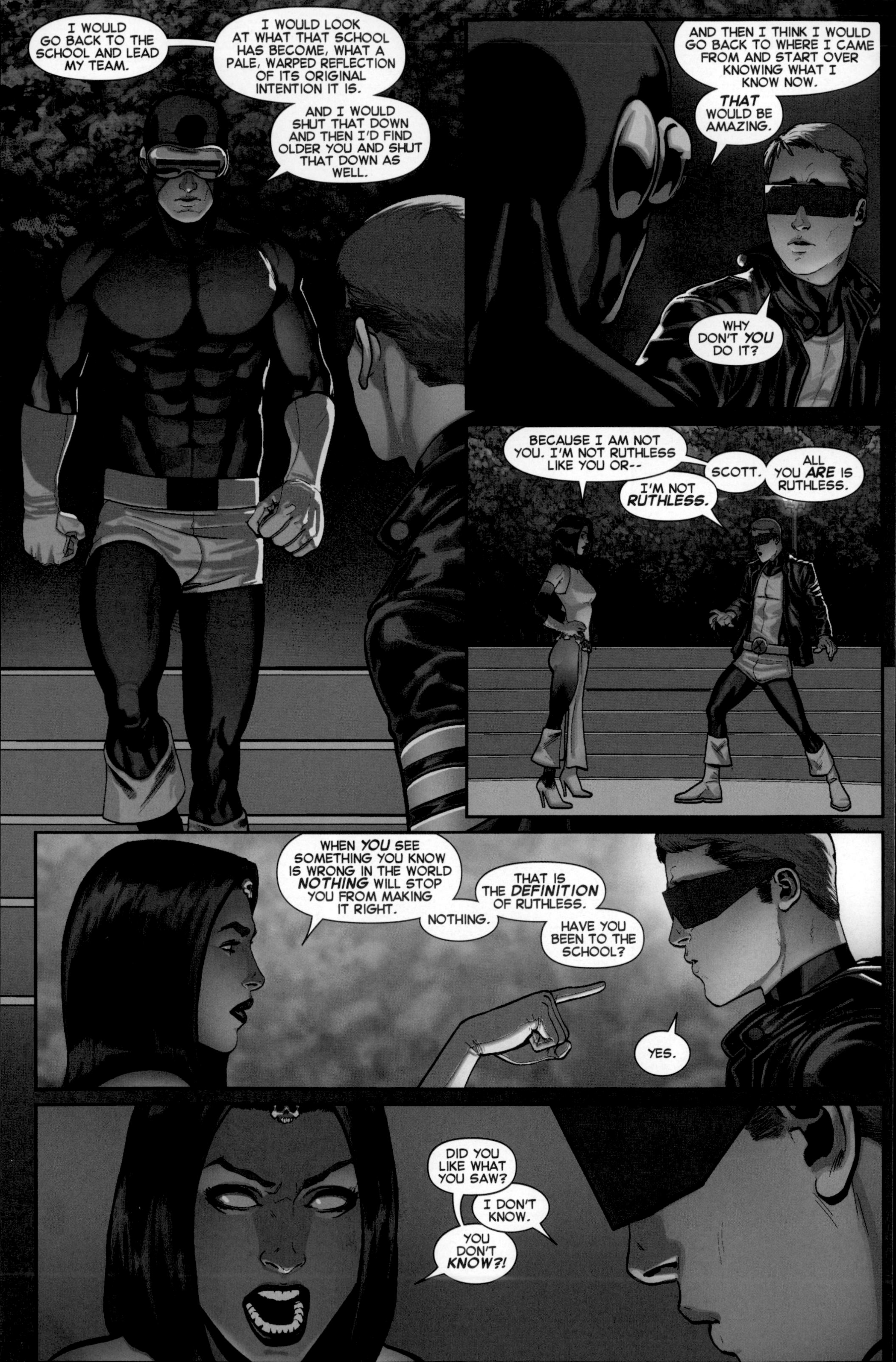
I WOULD GO BACK TO THE SCHOOL AND LEAD MY TEAM.
I WOULD LOOK AT WHAT THAT SCHOOL HAS BECOME, WHAT A PALE, WARPED REFLECTION OF ITS ORIGINAL INTENTION IT IS.
AND I WOULD SHUT THAT DOWN AND THEN I'D FIND OLDER YOU AND SHUT THAT DOWN AS WELL.
AND THEN I THINK I WOULD GO BACK TO WHERE I CAME FROM AND START OVER KNOWING WHAT I KNOW NOW.
THAT WOULD BE AMAZING.
WHY DON'T YOU DO IT?
BECAUSE I AM NOT YOU. I'M NOT RUTHLESS LIKE YOU OR--
SCOTT.
ALL YOU ARE IS RUTHLESS.
I'M NOT RUTHLESS.
WHEN YOU SEE SOMETHING YOU KNOW IS WRONG IN THE WORLD NOTHING WILL STOP YOU FROM MAKING IT RIGHT.
NOTHING.
THAT IS THE DEFINITION OF RUTHLESS.
HAVE YOU BEEN TO THE SCHOOL?
YES.
DID YOU LIKE WHAT YOU SAW?
I DON'T KNOW.
YOU DON'T KNOW?!

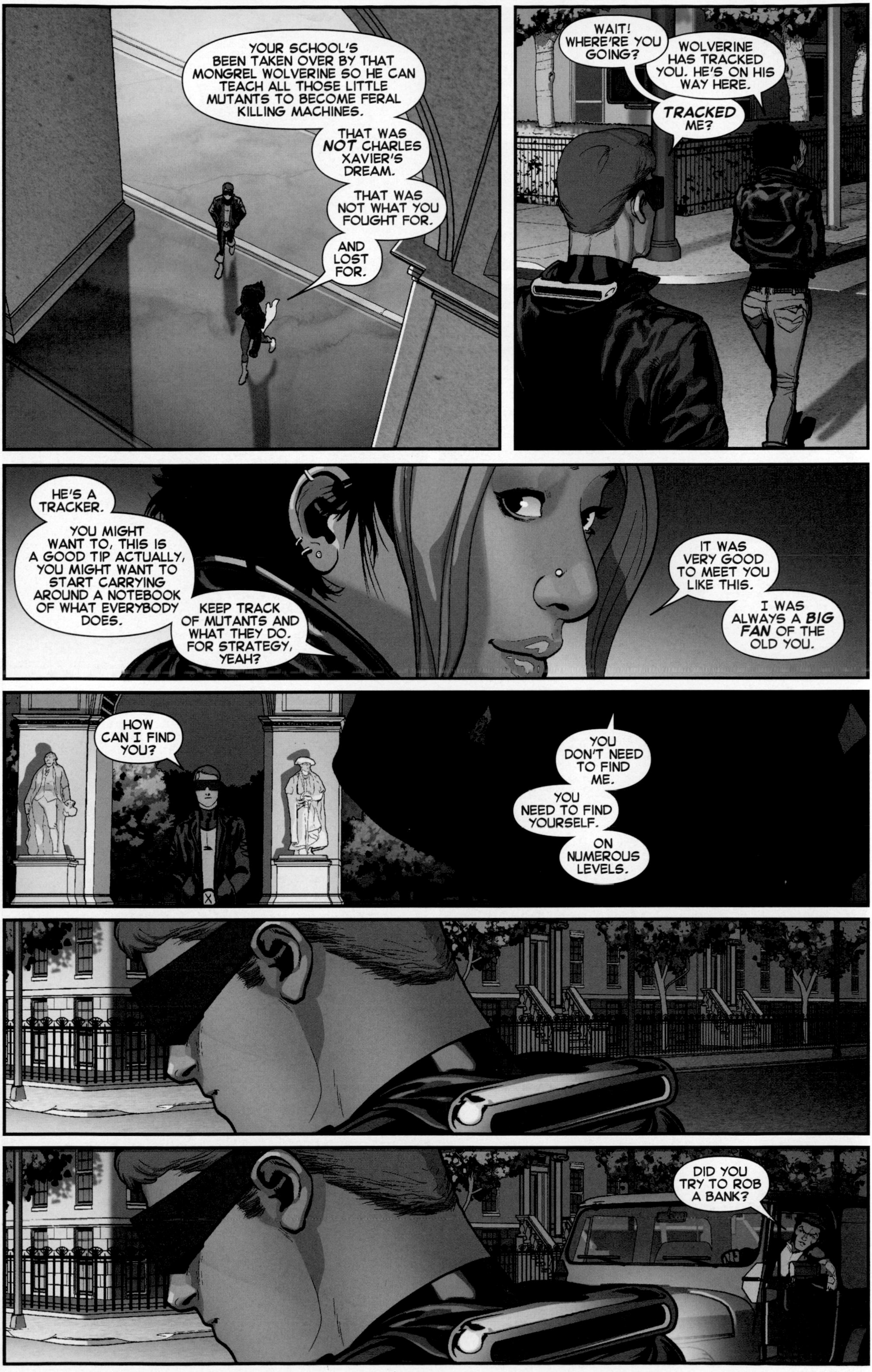
YOUR SCHOOL'S BEEN TAKEN OVER BY THAT MONGREL WOLVERINE SO HE CAN TEACH ALL THOSE LITTLE MUTANTS TO BECOME FERAL KILLING MACHINES.
THAT WAS NOT CHARLES XAVIER'S DREAM.
THAT WAS NOT WHAT YOU FOUGHT FOR.
AND LOST FOR.
WAIT! WHERE'RE YOU GOING?
WOLVERINE HAS TRACKED YOU. HE'S ON HIS WAY HERE.
TRACKED ME?
HE'S A TRACKER.
YOU MIGHT WANT TO, THIS IS A GOOD TIP ACTUALLY, YOU MIGHT WANT TO START CARRYING AROUND A NOTEBOOK OF WHAT EVERYBODY DOES.
KEEP TRACK OF MUTANTS AND WHAT THEY DO. FOR STRATEGY, YEAH?
IT WAS VERY GOOD TO MEET YOU LIKE THIS.
I WAS ALWAYS A BIG FAN OF THE OLD YOU.
HOW CAN I FIND YOU?
YOU DON'T NEED TO FIND ME.
YOU NEED TO FIND YOURSELF.
ON NUMEROUS LEVELS.
DID YOU TRY TO ROB A BANK?

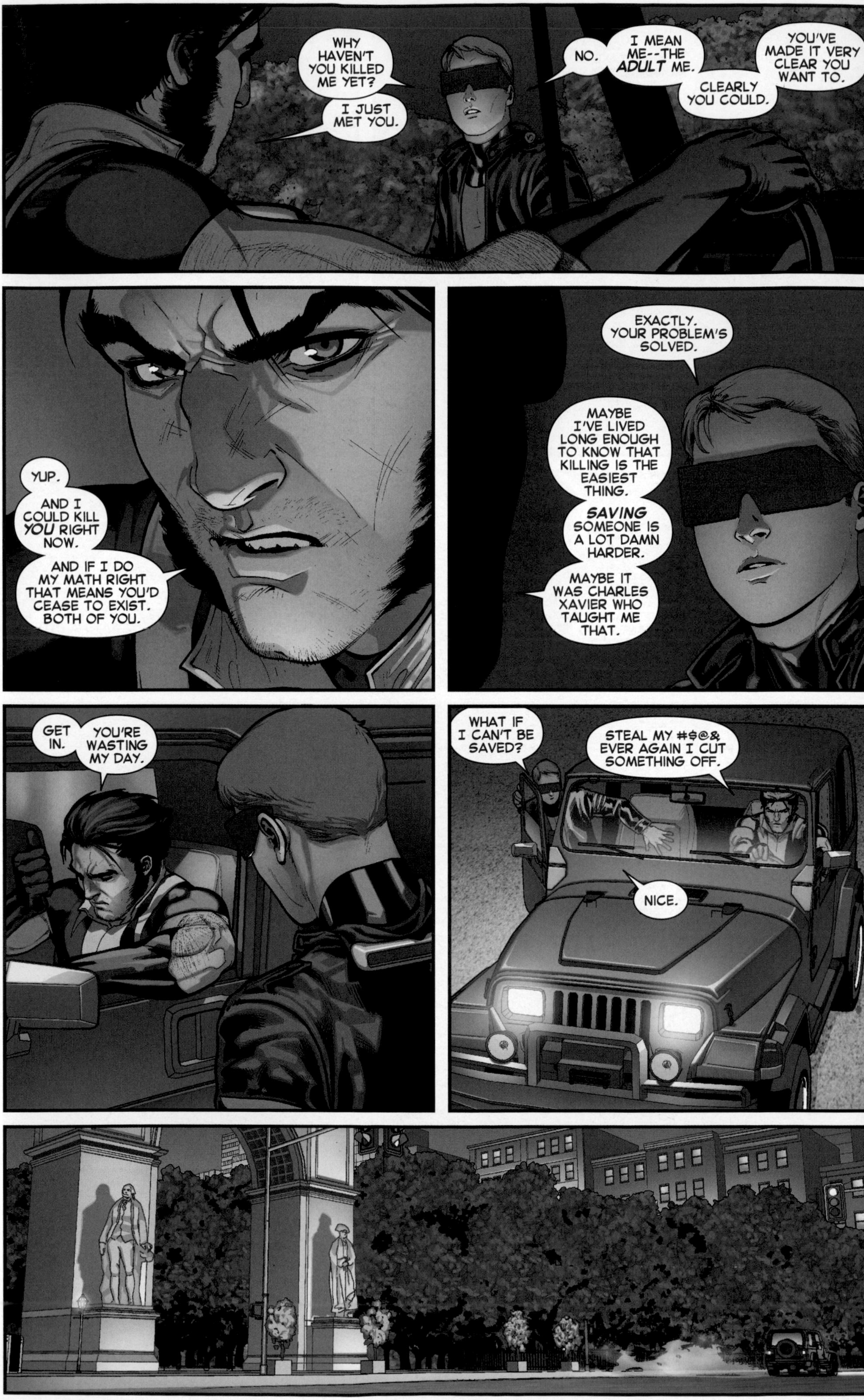
WHY HAVEN'T YOU KILLED ME YET?
I JUST MET YOU.
NO.
I MEAN ME--THE ADULT ME.
CLEARLY YOU COULD.
YOU'VE MADE IT VERY CLEAR YOU WANT TO.
YUP.
AND I COULD KILL YOU RIGHT NOW.
AND IF I DO MY MATH RIGHT THAT MEANS YOU'D CEASE TO EXIST. BOTH OF YOU.
EXACTLY. YOUR PROBLEM'S SOLVED.
MAYBE I'VE LIVED LONG ENOUGH TO KNOW THAT KILLING IS THE EASIEST THING.
SAVING SOMEONE IS A LOT DAMN HARDER.
MAYBE IT WAS CHARLES XAVIER WHO TAUGHT ME THAT.
GET IN.
YOU'RE WASTING MY DAY.
WHAT IF I CAN'T BE SAVED?
STEAL MY #$@& EVER AGAIN I CUT SOMETHING OFF.
NICE.

WHAT WAS *THAT* ALL ABOUT?

I THOUGHT YOU DIDN'T CARE ABOUT THEM.

THE X-MEN? OH, I DON'T.

IT'S A FISK.

WHAT'S A FISK?

THESE X-MEN, THEY'RE GOING TO BE CHASING EACH OTHER'S TAILS SO FAST ON THIS THAT THEY WON'T BE ABLE TO SEE ANYTHING ELSE.

WE'LL BE FREE TO SEE OUR PLANS ALL THE WAY TO THE FINISH LINE.

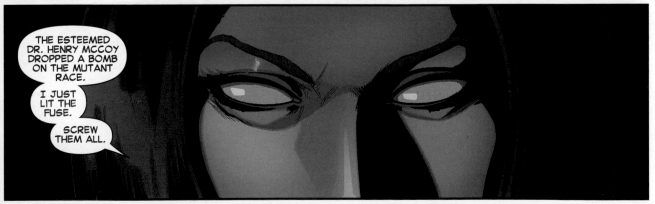

THE ESTEEMED DR. HENRY MCCOY DROPPED A BOMB ON THE MUTANT RACE.

I JUST LIT THE FUSE.

SCREW THEM ALL.

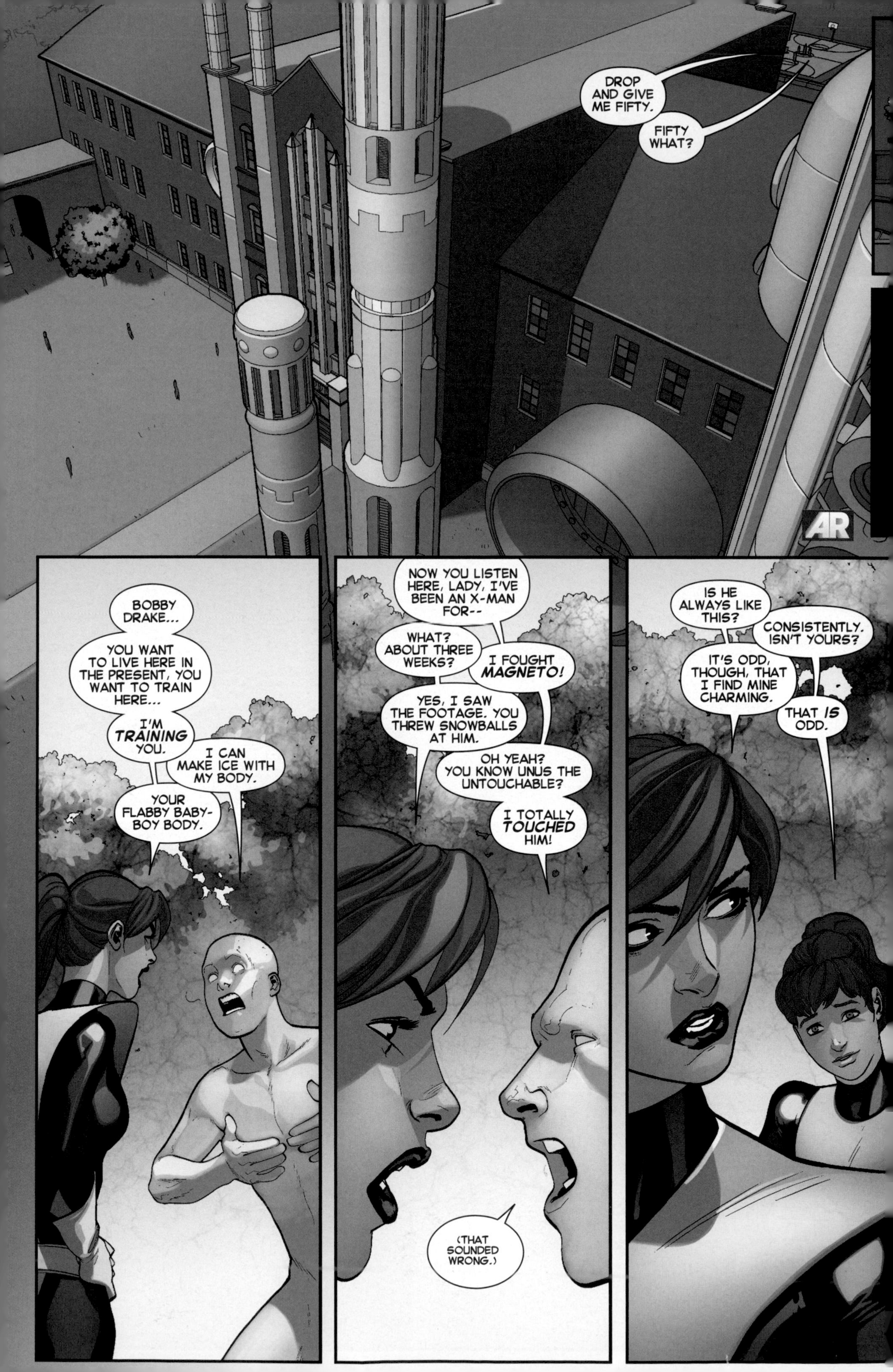
DROP AND GIVE ME FIFTY.
FIFTY WHAT?
AR
BOBBY DRAKE...
YOU WANT TO LIVE HERE IN THE PRESENT, YOU WANT TO TRAIN HERE...
I'M TRAINING YOU.
I CAN MAKE ICE WITH MY BODY.
YOUR FLABBY BABY-BOY BODY.
NOW YOU LISTEN HERE, LADY, I'VE BEEN AN X-MAN FOR--
WHAT? ABOUT THREE WEEKS?
I FOUGHT MAGNETO!
YES, I SAW THE FOOTAGE. YOU THREW SNOWBALLS AT HIM.
OH YEAH? YOU KNOW UNUS THE UNTOUCHABLE?
I TOTALLY TOUCHED HIM!
(THAT SOUNDED WRONG.)
IS HE ALWAYS LIKE THIS?
CONSISTENTLY. ISN'T YOURS?
IT'S ODD, THOUGH, THAT I FIND MINE CHARMING.
THAT IS ODD.

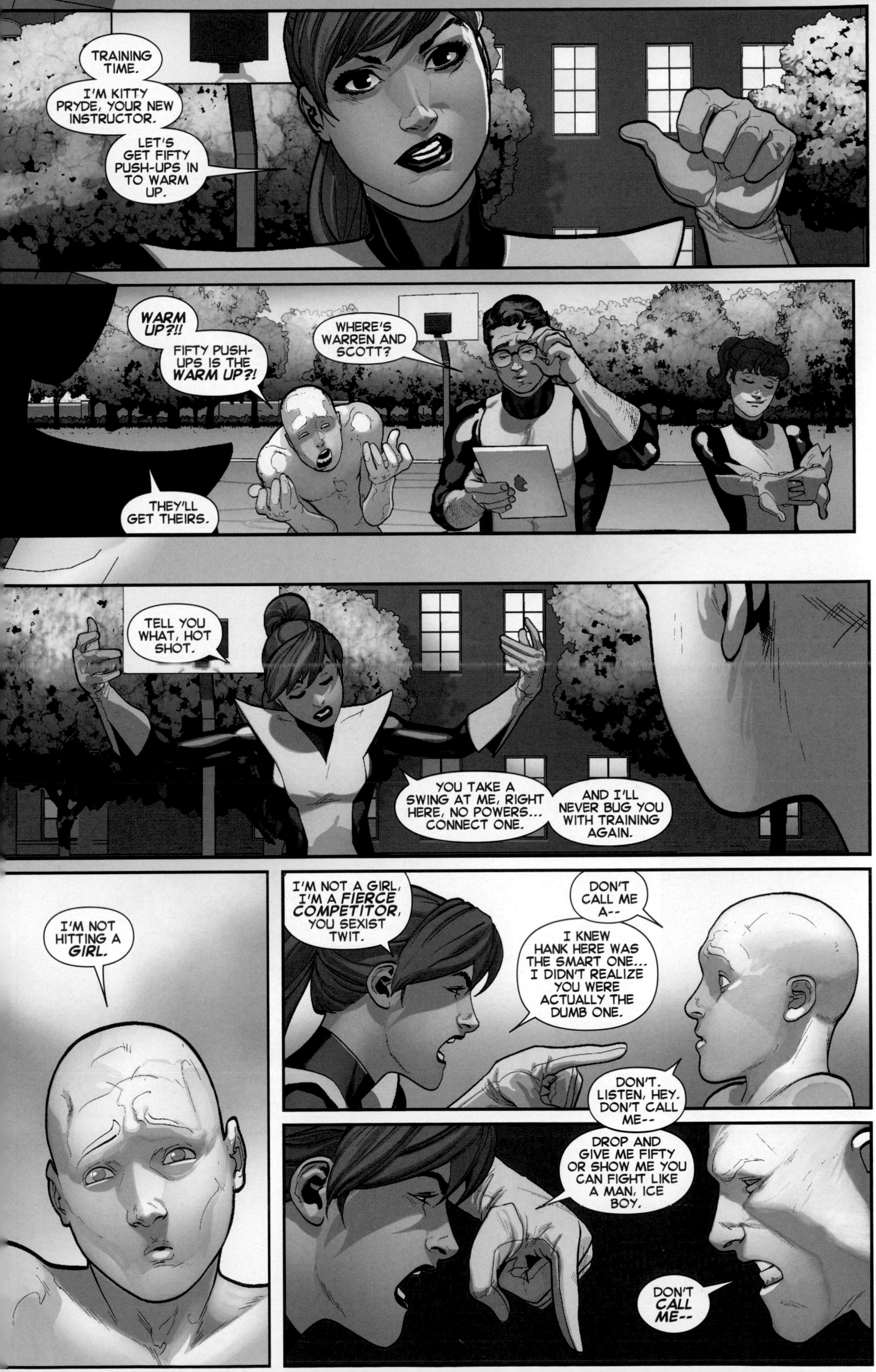
TRAINING TIME.
I'M KITTY PRYDE, YOUR NEW INSTRUCTOR.
LET'S GET FIFTY PUSH-UPS IN TO WARM UP.
WARM UP?!!
FIFTY PUSH-UPS IS THE WARM UP?!
WHERE'S WARREN AND SCOTT?
THEY'LL GET THEIRS.
TELL YOU WHAT, HOT SHOT.
YOU TAKE A SWING AT ME, RIGHT HERE, NO POWERS... CONNECT ONE.
AND I'LL NEVER BUG YOU WITH TRAINING AGAIN.
I'M NOT HITTING A GIRL.
I'M NOT A GIRL, I'M A FIERCE COMPETITOR, YOU SEXIST TWIT.
DON'T CALL ME A--
I KNEW HANK HERE WAS THE SMART ONE... I DIDN'T REALIZE YOU WERE ACTUALLY THE DUMB ONE.
DON'T. LISTEN, HEY. DON'T CALL ME--
DROP AND GIVE ME FIFTY OR SHOW ME YOU CAN FIGHT LIKE A MAN, ICE BOY.
DON'T CALL ME--

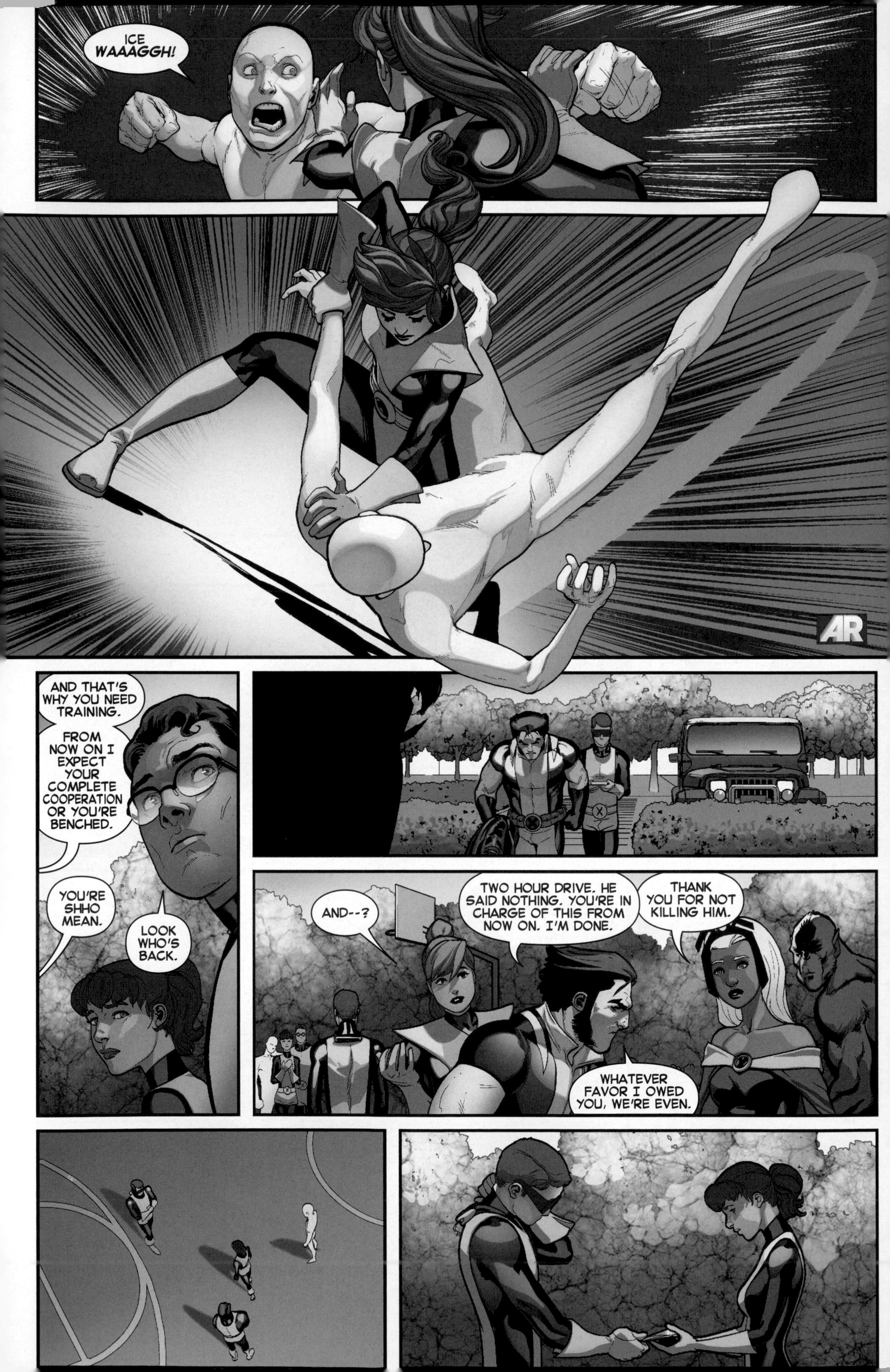
ICE WAAAGGH!
AND THAT'S WHY YOU NEED TRAINING.
FROM NOW ON I EXPECT YOUR COMPLETE COOPERATION OR YOU'RE BENCHED.
YOU'RE SHHO MEAN.
LOOK WHO'S BACK.
AND--?
TWO HOUR DRIVE. HE SAID NOTHING. YOU'RE IN CHARGE OF THIS FROM NOW ON. I'M DONE.
THANK YOU FOR NOT KILLING HIM.
WHATEVER FAVOR I OWED YOU, WE'RE EVEN.

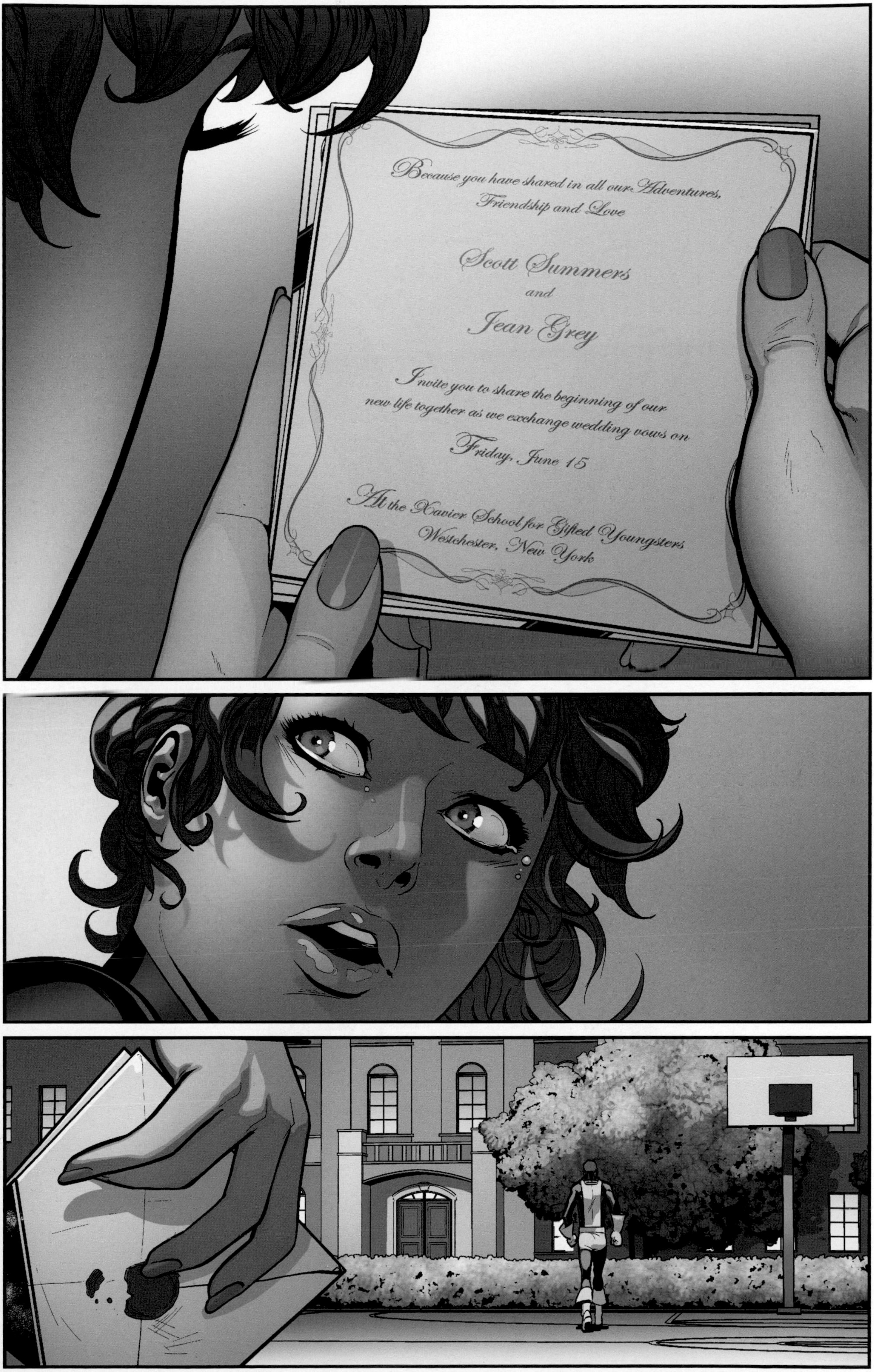
Because you have shared in all our Adventures,
Friendship and Love
Scott Summers
and
Jean Grey
Invite you to share the beginning of our
new life together as we exchange wedding vows on
Friday, June 15
At the Xavier School for Gifted Youngsters
Westchester, New York

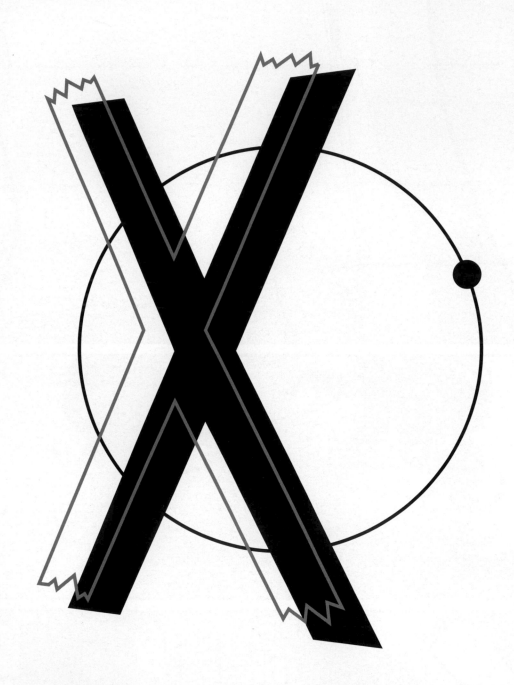

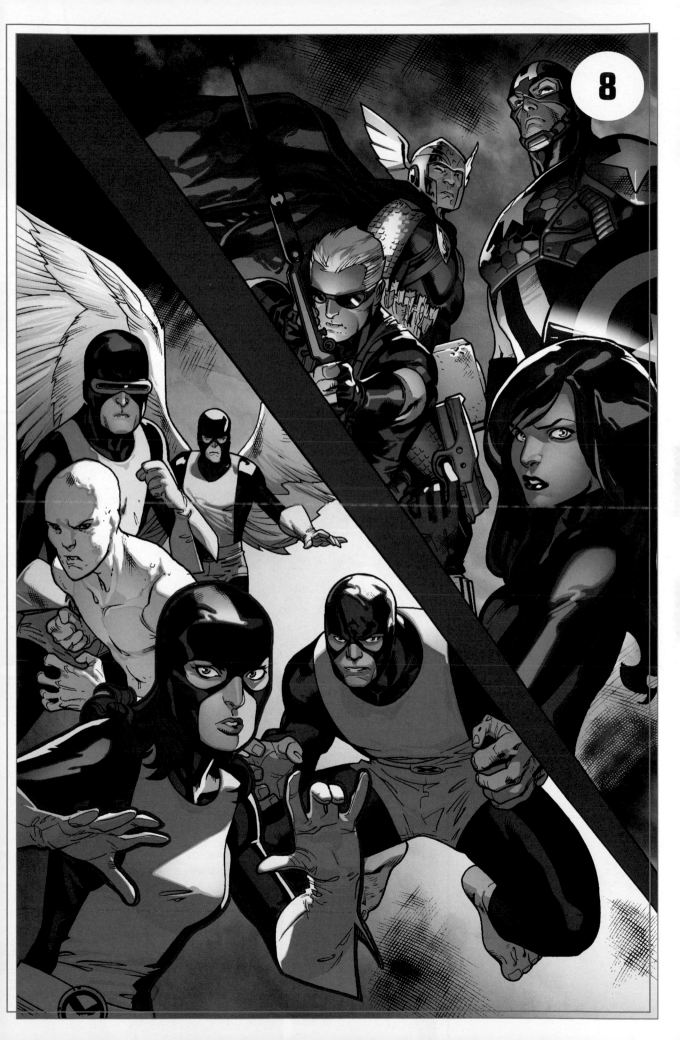

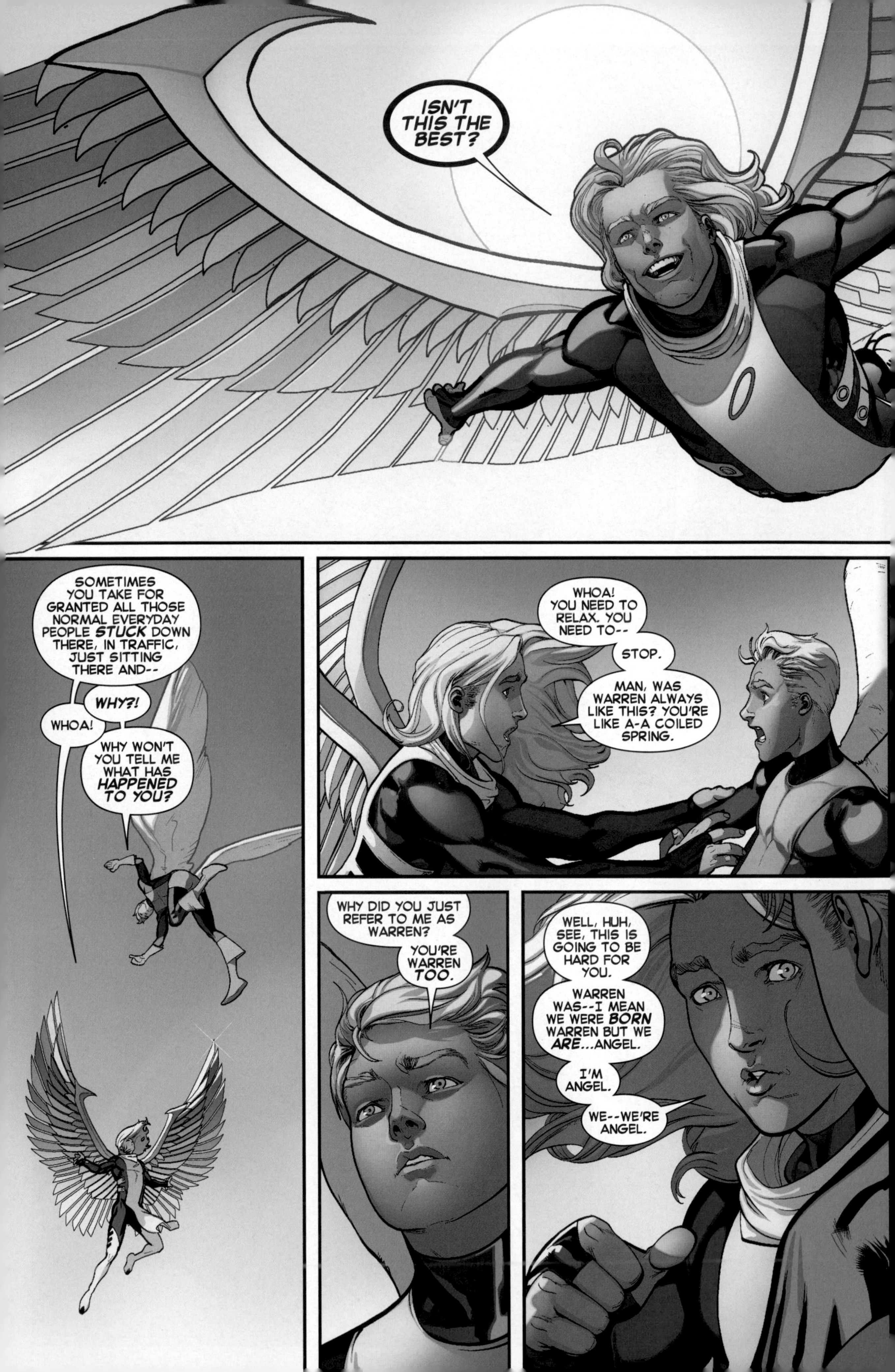
ISN'T THIS THE BEST?
SOMETIMES YOU TAKE FOR GRANTED ALL THOSE NORMAL EVERYDAY PEOPLE STUCK DOWN THERE, IN TRAFFIC, JUST SITTING THERE AND--
WHY?!
WHOA!
WHY WON'T YOU TELL ME WHAT HAS HAPPENED TO YOU?
WHOA! YOU NEED TO RELAX. YOU NEED TO--
STOP.
MAN, WAS WARREN ALWAYS LIKE THIS? YOU'RE LIKE A-A COILED SPRING.
WHY DID YOU JUST REFER TO ME AS WARREN?
YOU'RE WARREN TOO.
WELL, HUH, SEE, THIS IS GOING TO BE HARD FOR YOU.
WARREN WAS--I MEAN WE WERE BORN WARREN BUT WE ARE...ANGEL.
I'M ANGEL.
WE--WE'RE ANGEL.

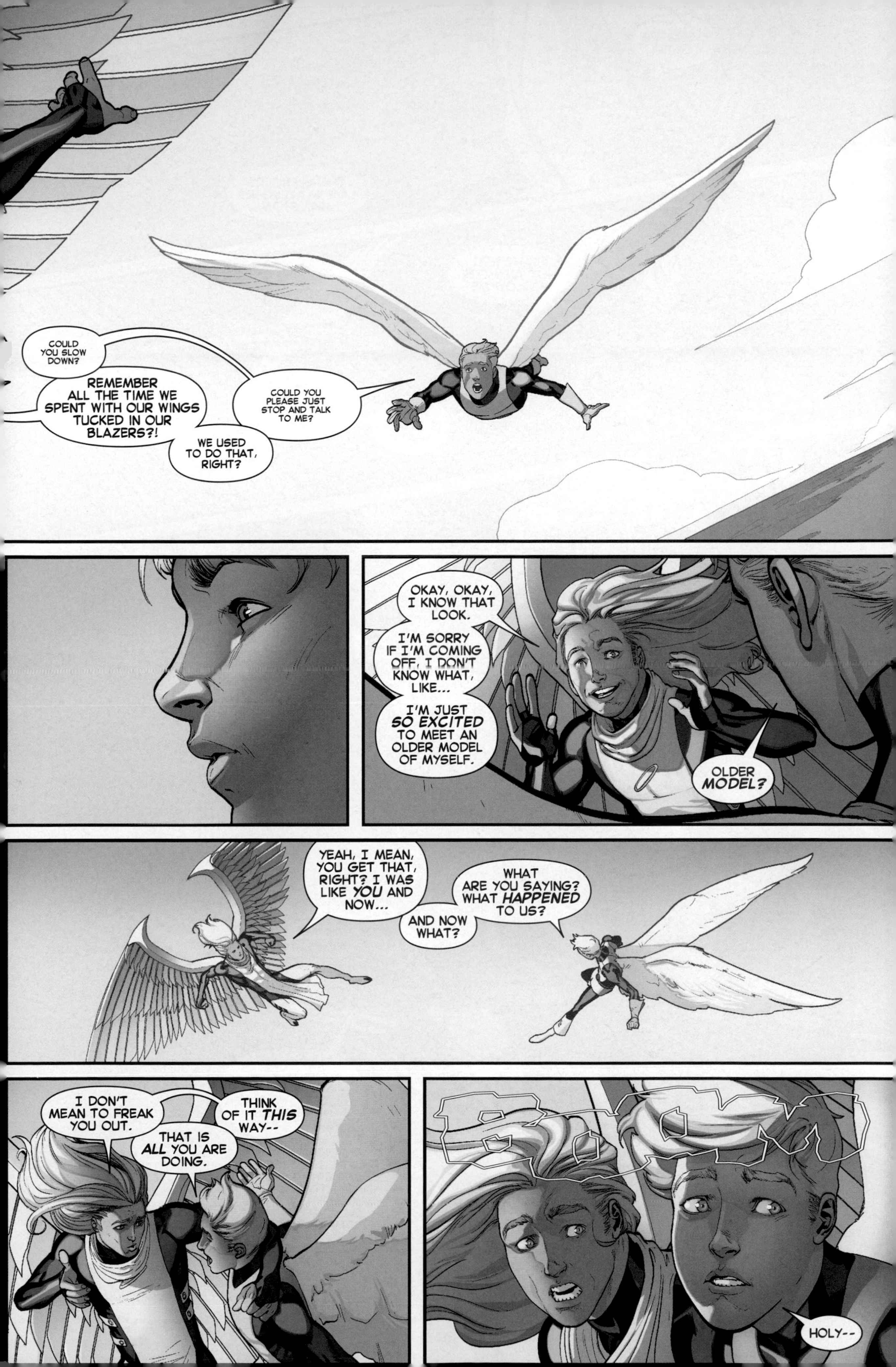
COULD YOU SLOW DOWN?
REMEMBER ALL THE TIME WE SPENT WITH OUR WINGS TUCKED IN OUR BLAZERS?!
COULD YOU PLEASE JUST STOP AND TALK TO ME?
WE USED TO DO THAT, RIGHT?
OKAY, OKAY, I KNOW THAT LOOK.
I'M SORRY IF I'M COMING OFF, I DON'T KNOW WHAT, LIKE...
I'M JUST SO EXCITED TO MEET AN OLDER MODEL OF MYSELF.
OLDER MODEL?
YEAH, I MEAN, YOU GET THAT, RIGHT? I WAS LIKE YOU AND NOW...
AND NOW WHAT?
WHAT ARE YOU SAYING? WHAT HAPPENED TO US?
I DON'T MEAN TO FREAK YOU OUT.
THINK OF IT THIS WAY--
THAT IS ALL YOU ARE DOING.
HOLY--

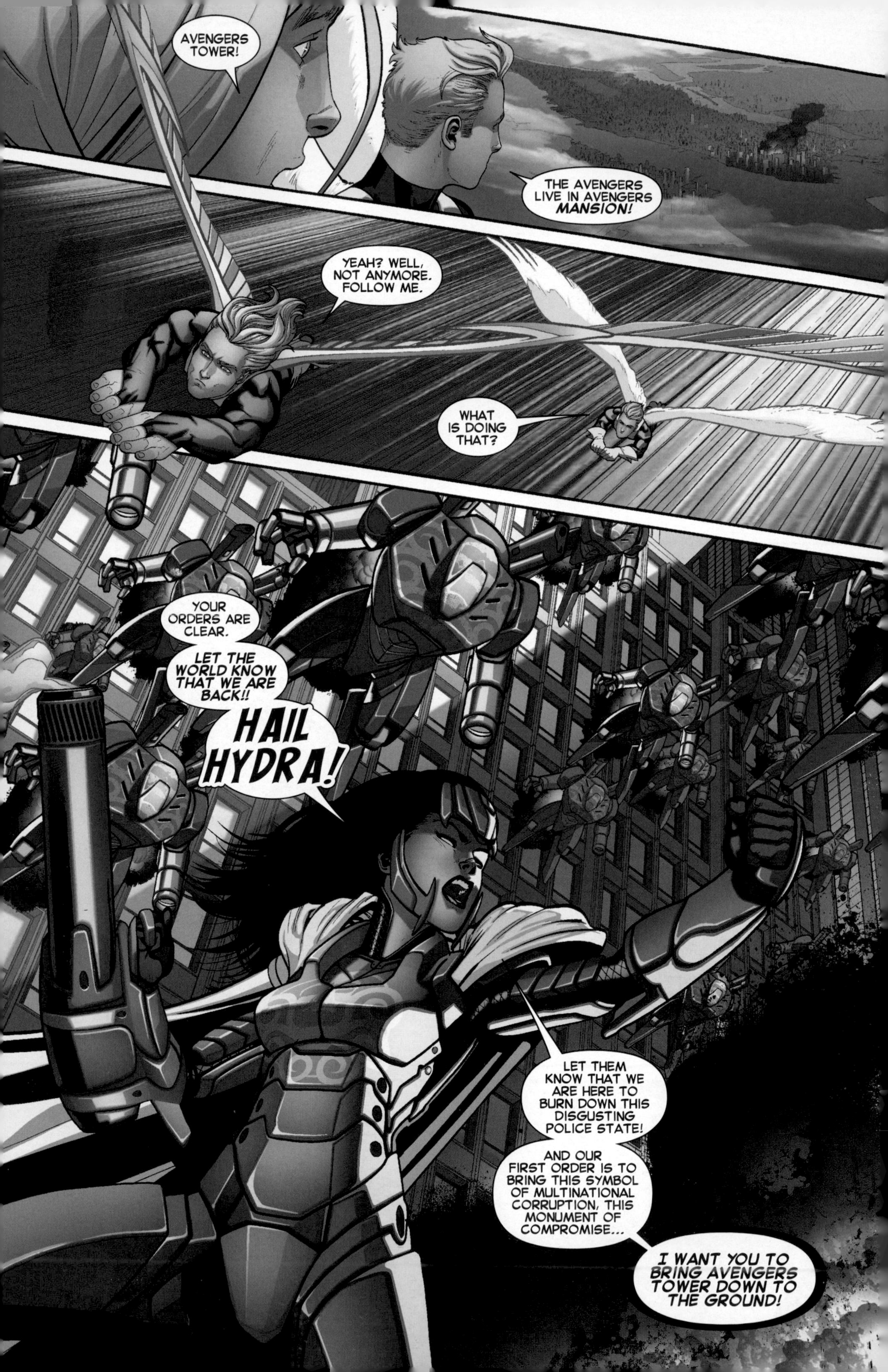
AVENGERS TOWER!
THE AVENGERS LIVE IN AVENGERS MANSION!
YEAH? WELL, NOT ANYMORE. FOLLOW ME.
WHAT IS DOING THAT?
YOUR ORDERS ARE CLEAR.
LET THE WORLD KNOW THAT WE ARE BACK!!
HAIL HYDRA!
LET THEM KNOW THAT WE ARE HERE TO BURN DOWN THIS DISGUSTING POLICE STATE!
AND OUR FIRST ORDER IS TO BRING THIS SYMBOL OF MULTINATIONAL CORRUPTION, THIS MONUMENT OF COMPROMISE...
I WANT YOU TO BRING AVENGERS TOWER DOWN TO THE GROUND!

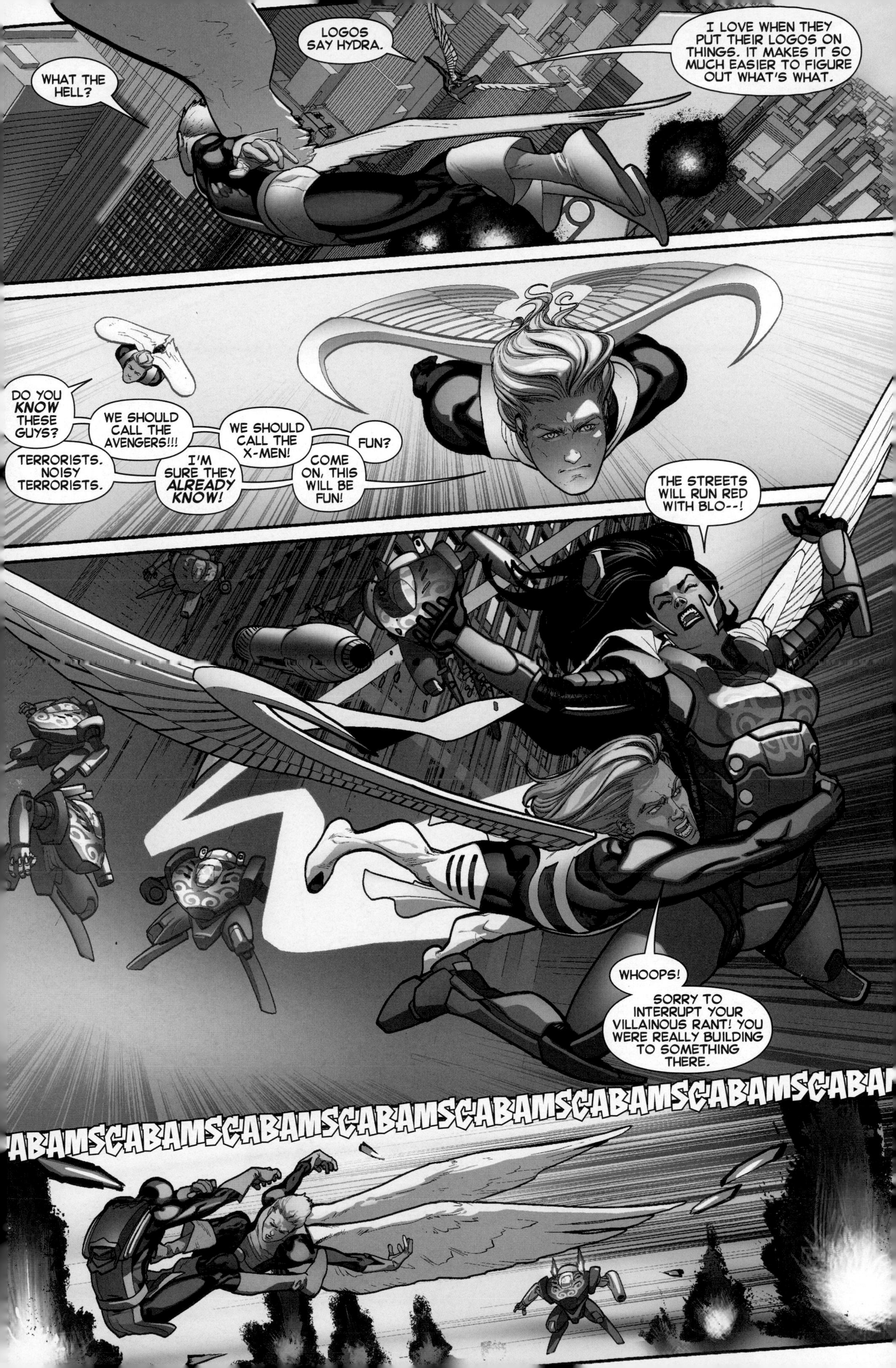
WHAT THE HELL?
LOGOS SAY HYDRA.
I LOVE WHEN THEY PUT THEIR LOGOS ON THINGS. IT MAKES IT SO MUCH EASIER TO FIGURE OUT WHAT'S WHAT.
DO YOU KNOW THESE GUYS?
TERRORISTS. NOISY TERRORISTS.
WE SHOULD CALL THE AVENGERS!!!
I'M SURE THEY ALREADY KNOW!
WE SHOULD CALL THE X-MEN!
COME ON, THIS WILL BE FUN!
FUN?
THE STREETS WILL RUN RED WITH BLO--!
WHOOPS!
SORRY TO INTERRUPT YOUR VILLAINOUS RANT! YOU WERE REALLY BUILDING TO SOMETHING THERE.
ABAMSCABAMSCABAMSCABAMSCABAMSCABAMSCABAMSCABAM

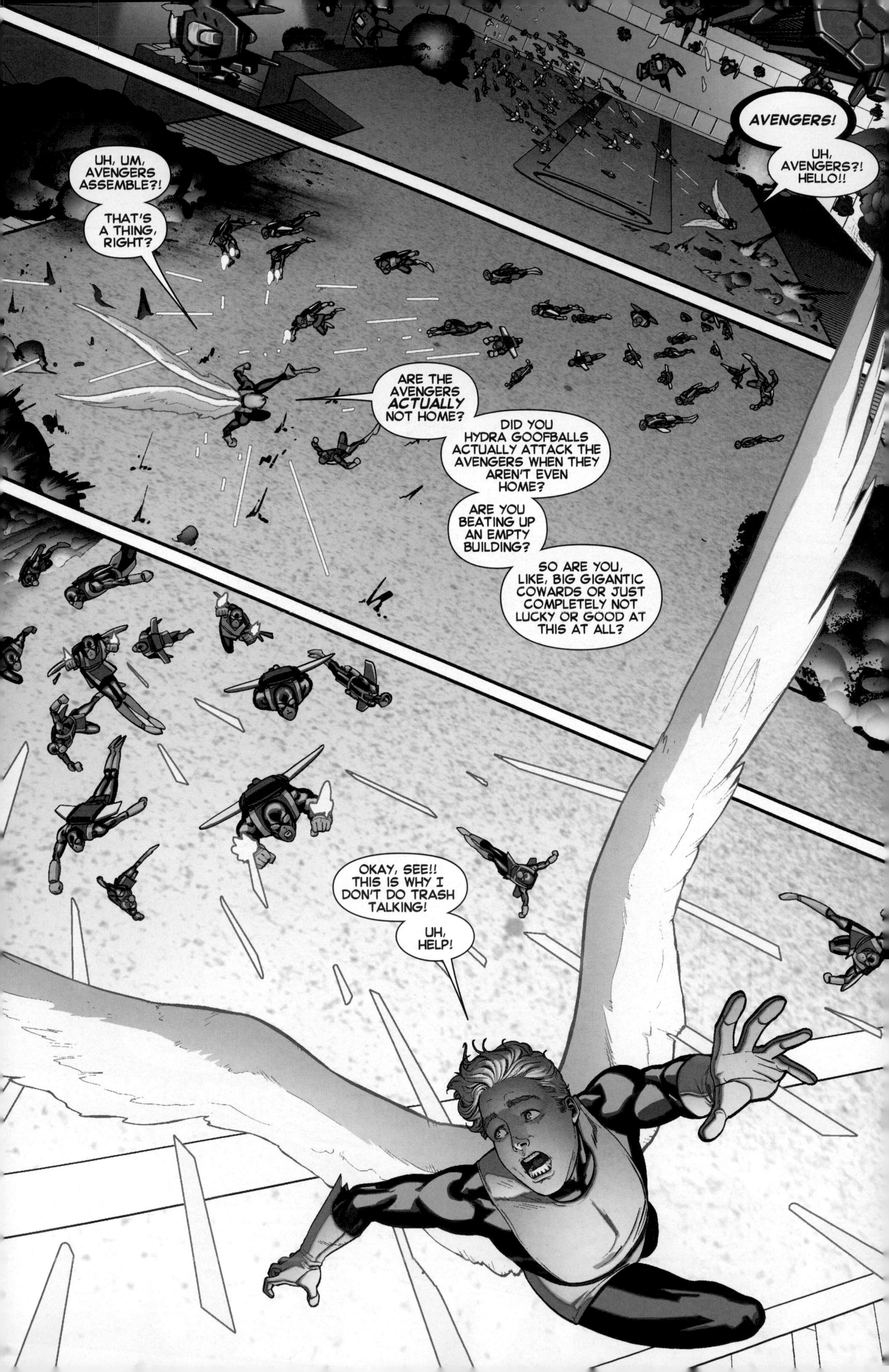
AVENGERS!
UH, AVENGERS?! HELLO!!
UH, UM, AVENGERS ASSEMBLE?!
THAT'S A THING, RIGHT?
ARE THE AVENGERS *ACTUALLY* NOT HOME?
DID YOU HYDRA GOOFBALLS ACTUALLY ATTACK THE AVENGERS WHEN THEY AREN'T EVEN HOME?
ARE YOU BEATING UP AN EMPTY BUILDING?
SO ARE YOU, LIKE, BIG GIGANTIC COWARDS OR JUST COMPLETELY NOT LUCKY OR GOOD AT THIS AT ALL?
OKAY, SEE!! THIS IS WHY I DON'T DO TRASH TALKING!
UH, HELP!

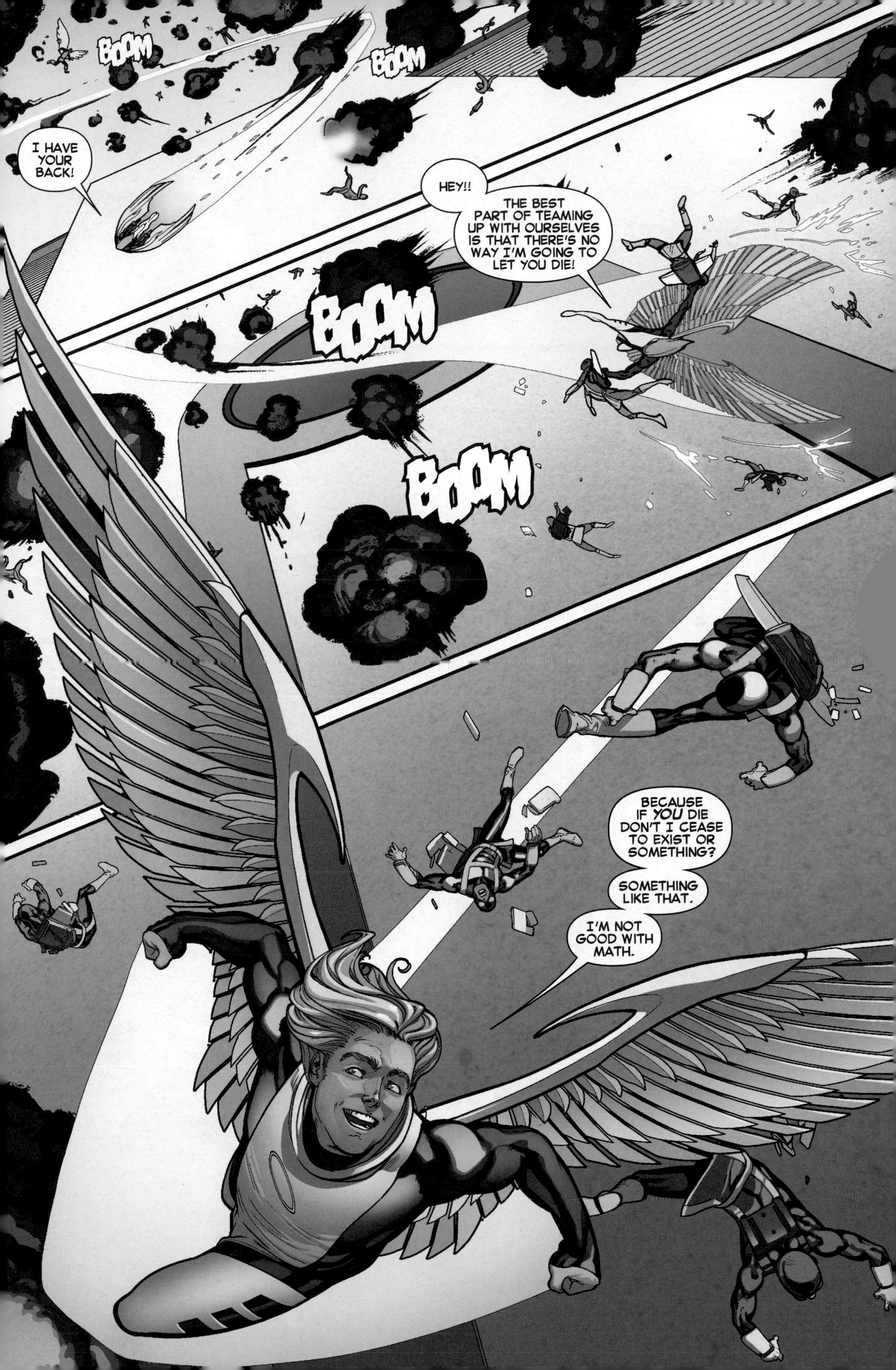
BOOM
BOOM
I HAVE YOUR BACK!
HEY!!
THE BEST PART OF TEAMING UP WITH OURSELVES IS THAT THERE'S NO WAY I'M GOING TO LET YOU DIE!
BOOM
BOOM
BECAUSE IF *YOU* DIE DON'T I CEASE TO EXIST OR SOMETHING?
SOMETHING LIKE THAT.
I'M NOT GOOD WITH MATH.

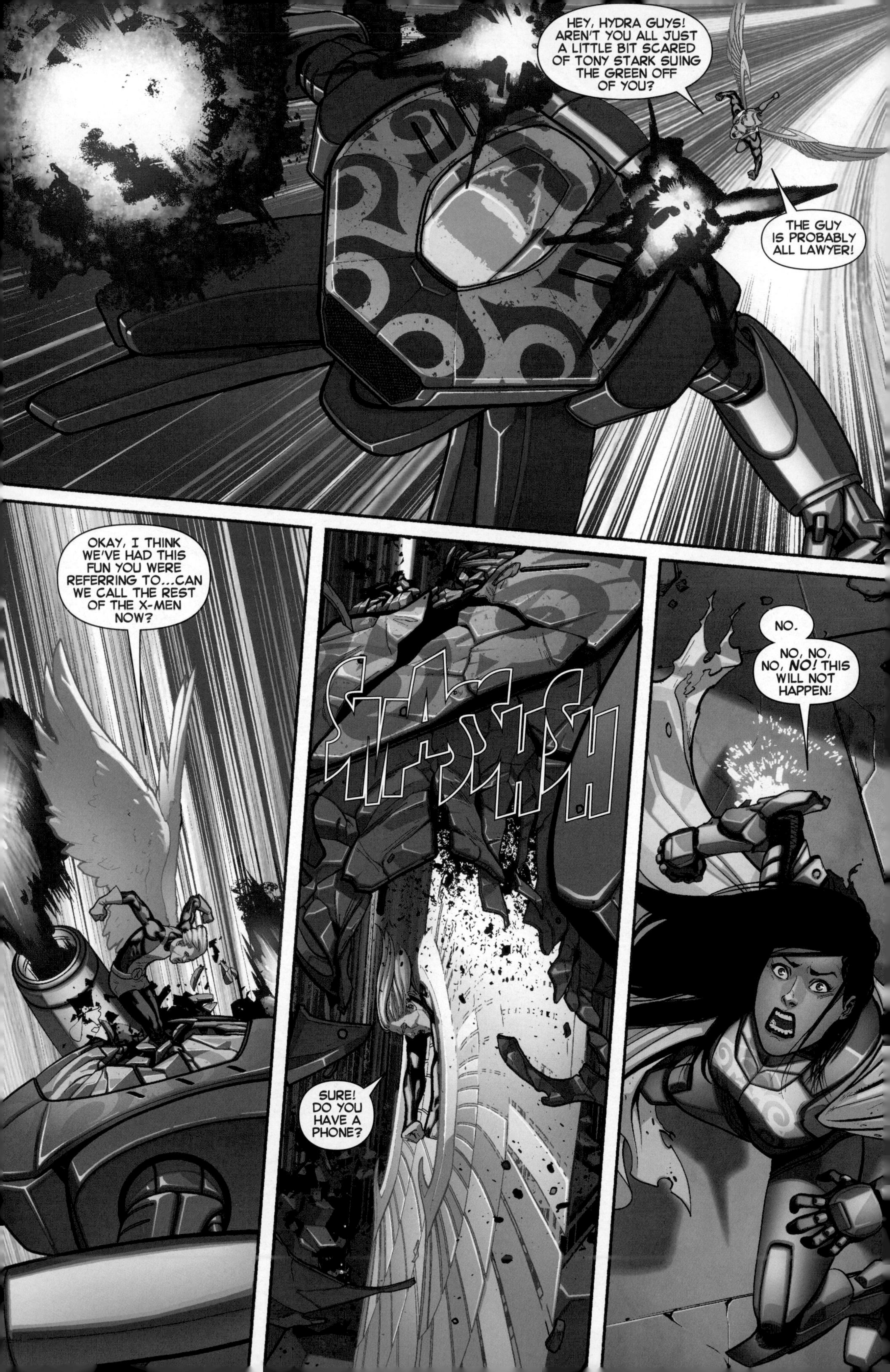
HEY, HYDRA GUYS! AREN'T YOU ALL JUST A LITTLE BIT SCARED OF TONY STARK SUING THE GREEN OFF OF YOU?
THE GUY IS PROBABLY ALL LAWYER!
OKAY, I THINK WE'VE HAD THIS FUN YOU WERE REFERRING TO...CAN WE CALL THE REST OF THE X-MEN NOW?
SHASHH
SURE! DO YOU HAVE A PHONE?
NO.
NO, NO, NO, ***NO!*** THIS WILL NOT HAPPEN!

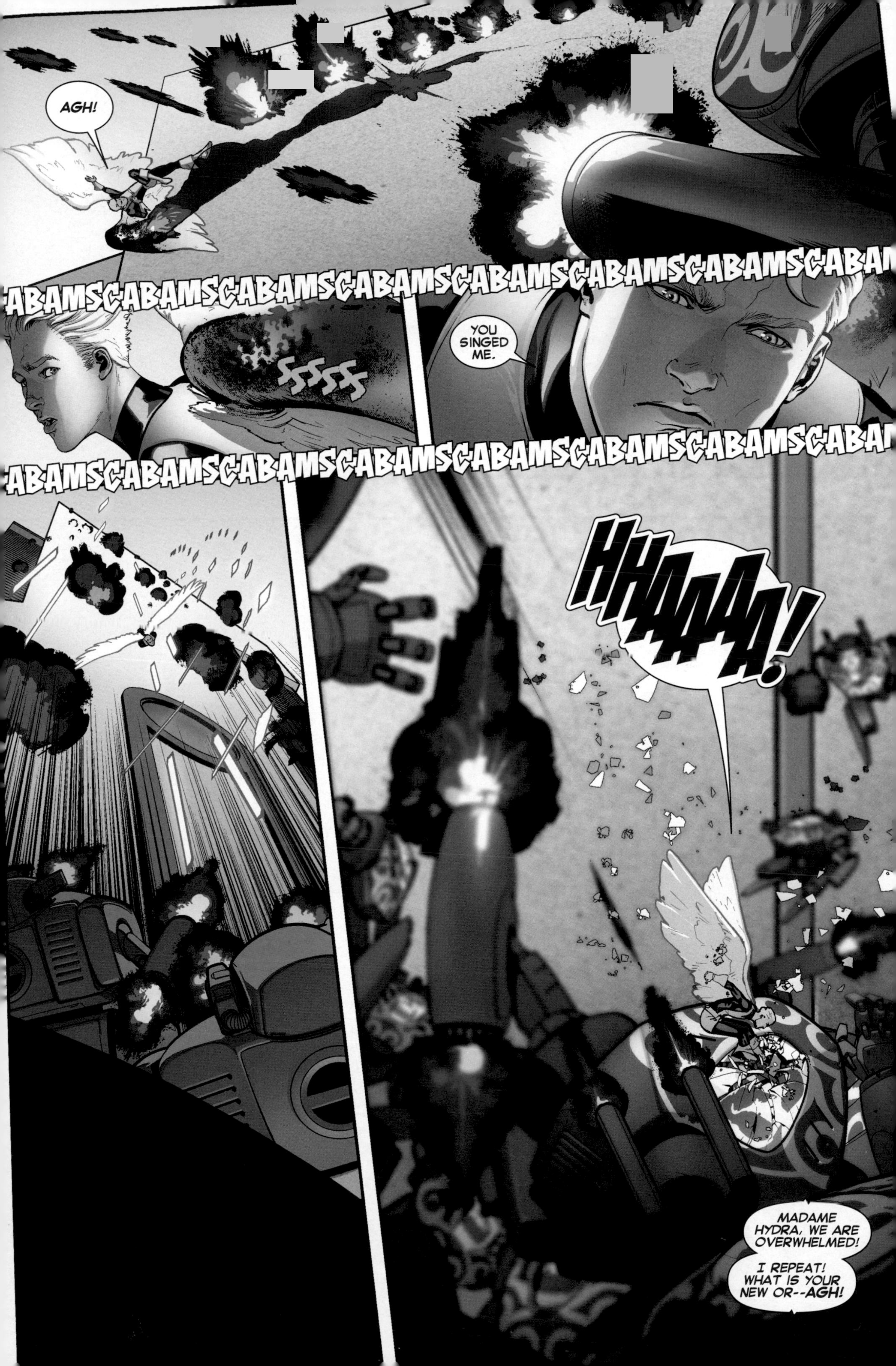
AGH!
ABAMSCABAMSCABAMSCABAMSCABAMSCABAMSCABAMSCABAMSCABAM
SSSSS
YOU SINGED ME.
ABAMSCABAMSCABAMSCABAMSCABAMSCABAMSCABAMSCABAMSCABAM
HHAAAAA!
MADAME HYDRA, WE ARE OVERWHELMED!
I REPEAT! WHAT IS YOUR NEW OR--AGH!

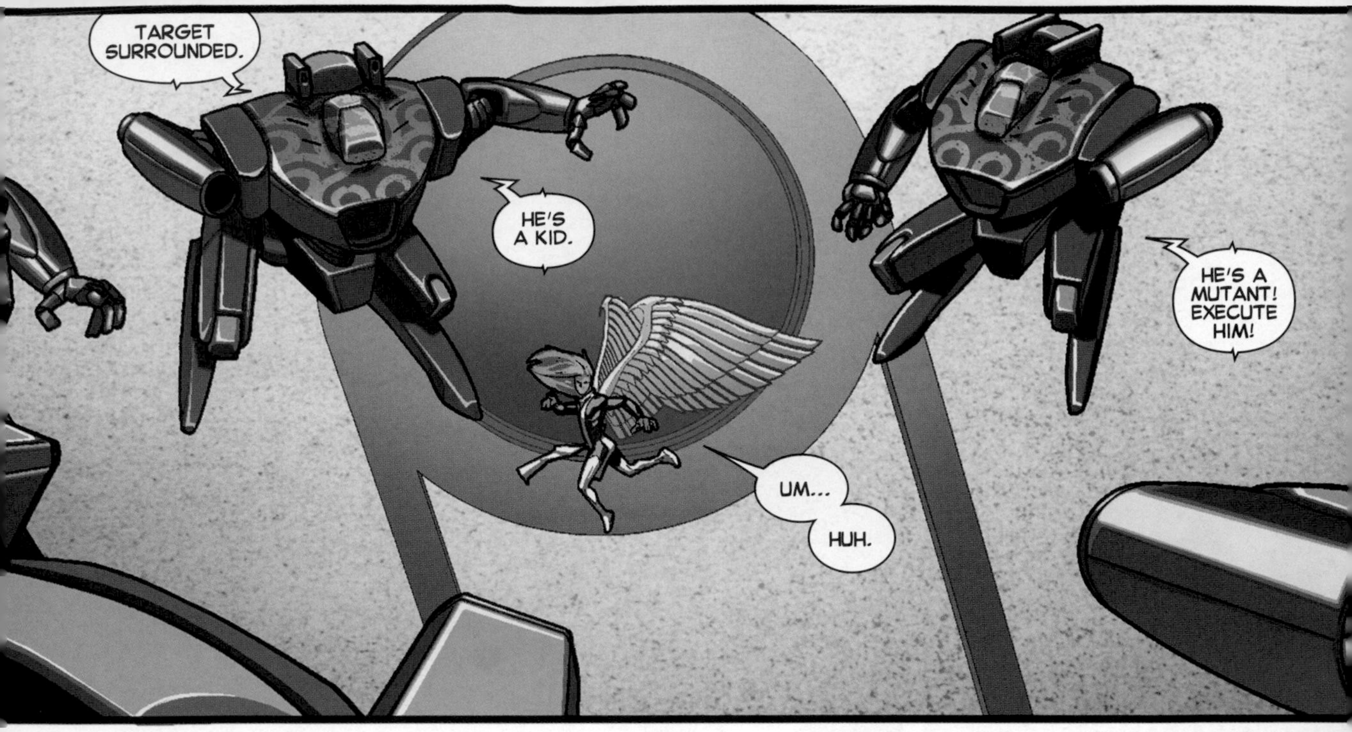
TARGET SURROUNDED.
HE'S A KID.
HE'S A MUTANT! EXECUTE HIM!
UM...
HUH.

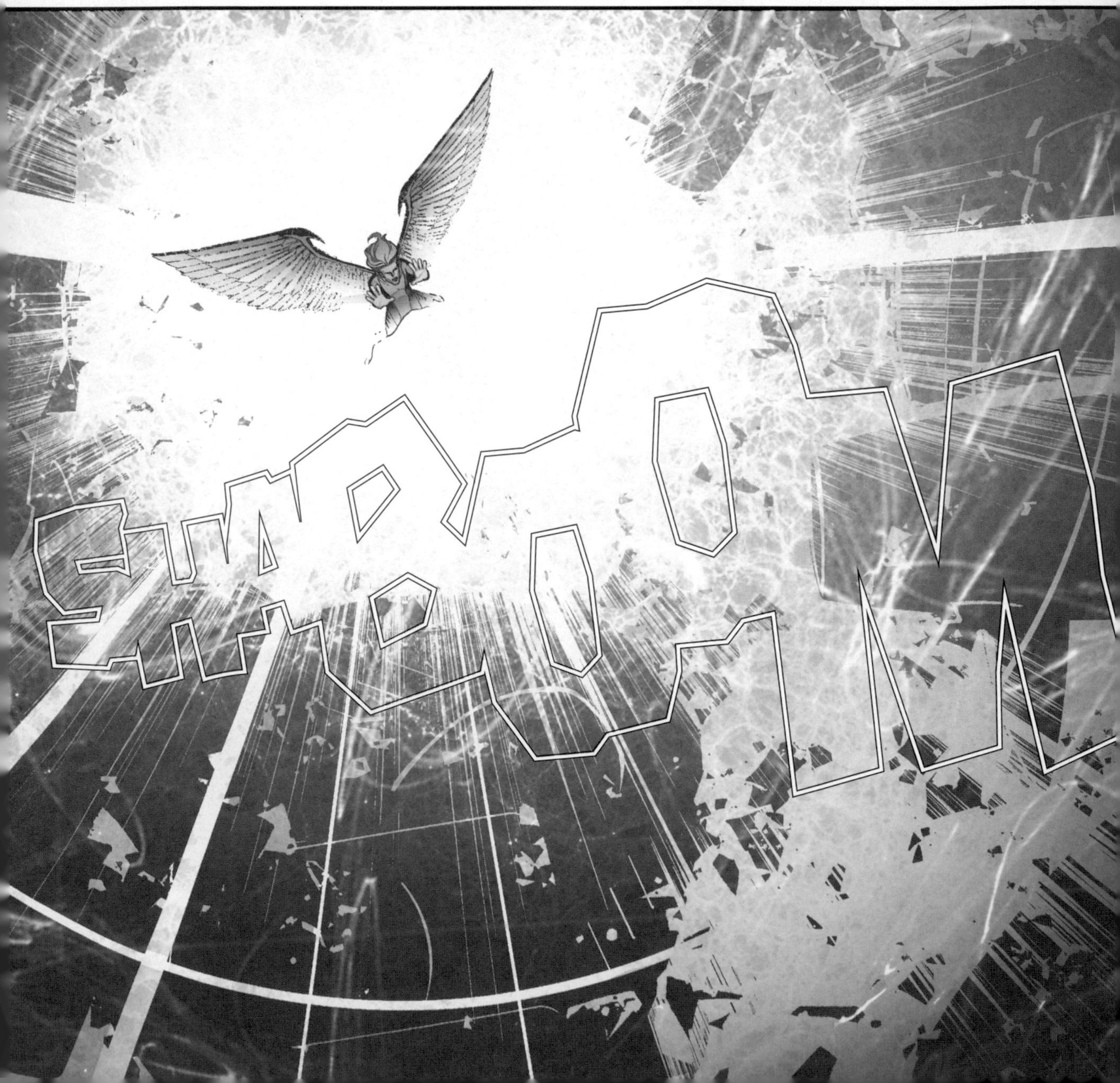

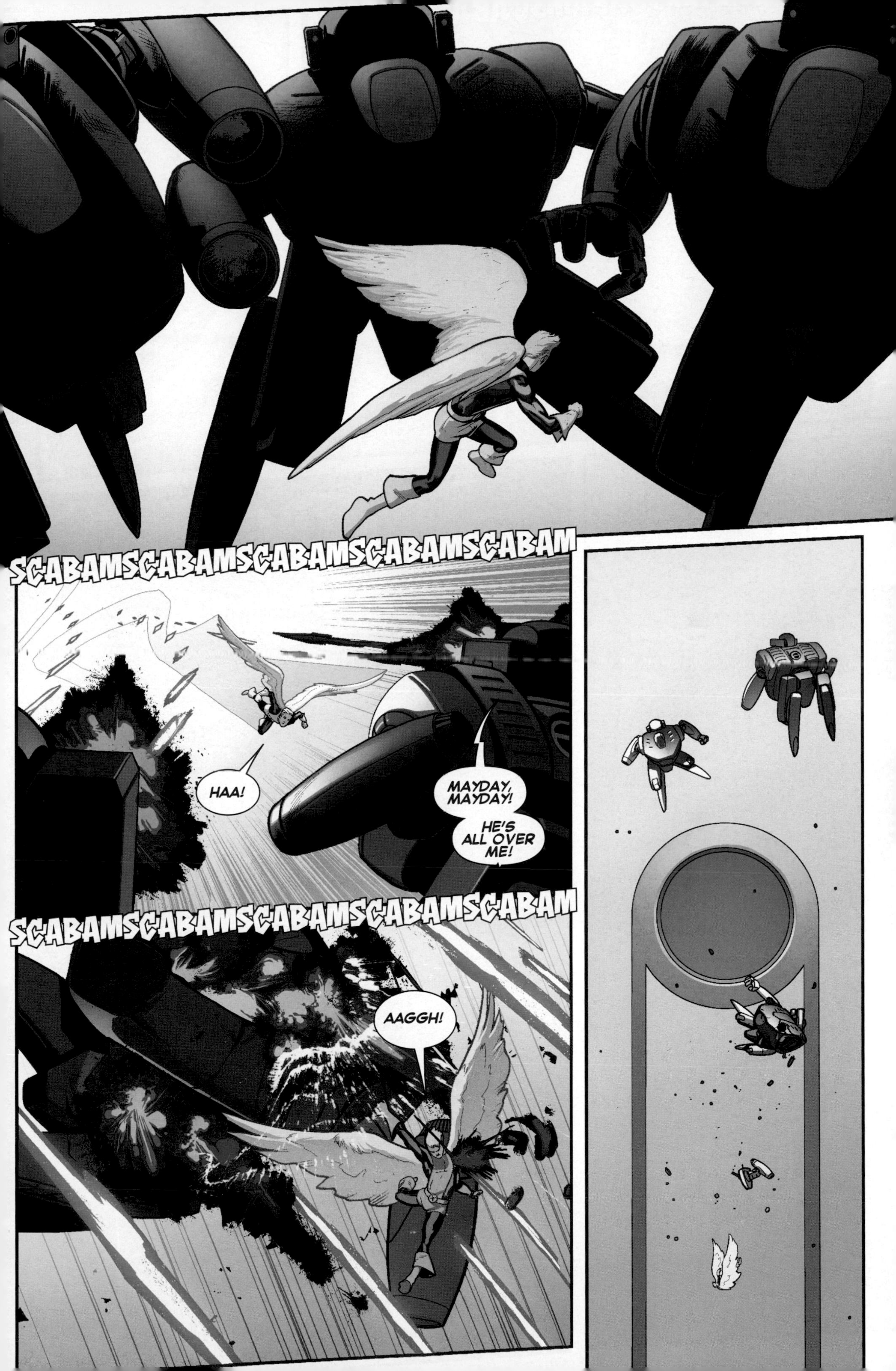
SCABAMSCABAMSCABAMSCABAMSCABAM
HAA!
MAYDAY, MAYDAY!
HE'S ALL OVER ME!
SCABAMSCABAMSCABAMSCABAMSCABAM
AAGGH!

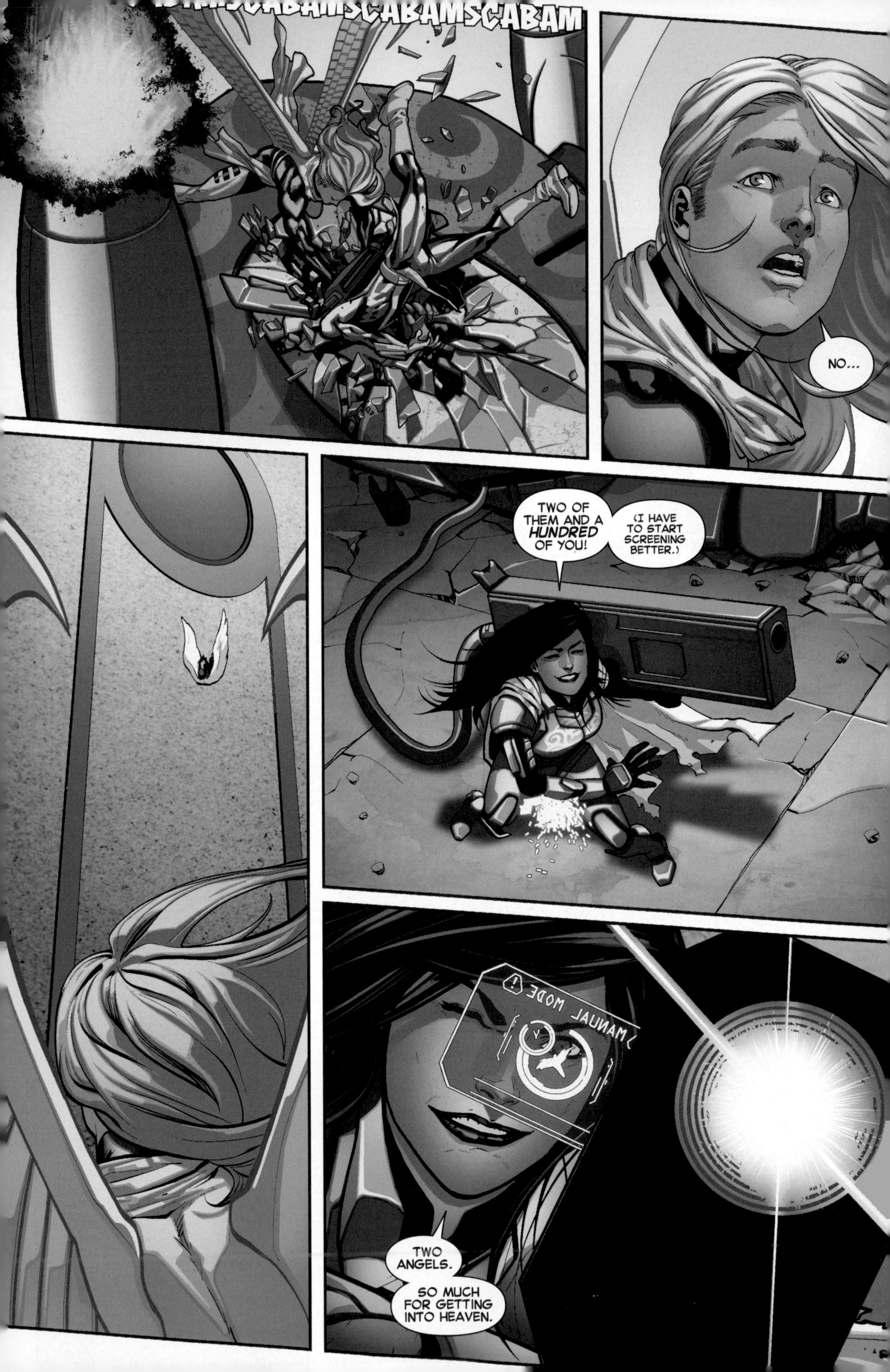
CABAMSCABAMSCABAM
NO...
TWO OF THEM AND A HUNDRED OF YOU!
(I HAVE TO START SCREENING BETTER.)
MANUAL MODE
TWO ANGELS.
SO MUCH FOR GETTING INTO HEAVEN.

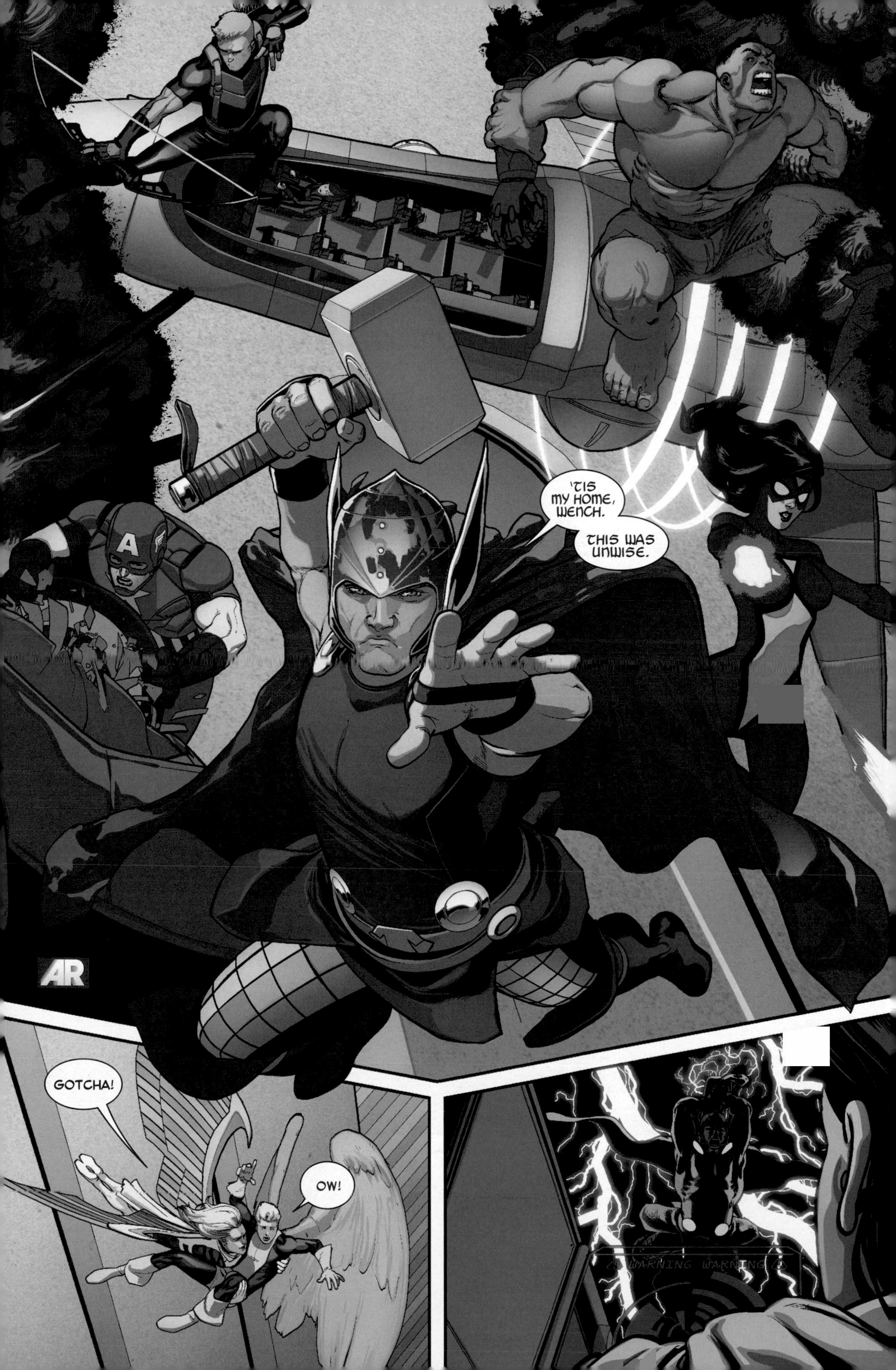
'TIS MY HOME, WENCH.
THIS WAS UNWISE.
GOTCHA!
OW!
WARNING WARNING

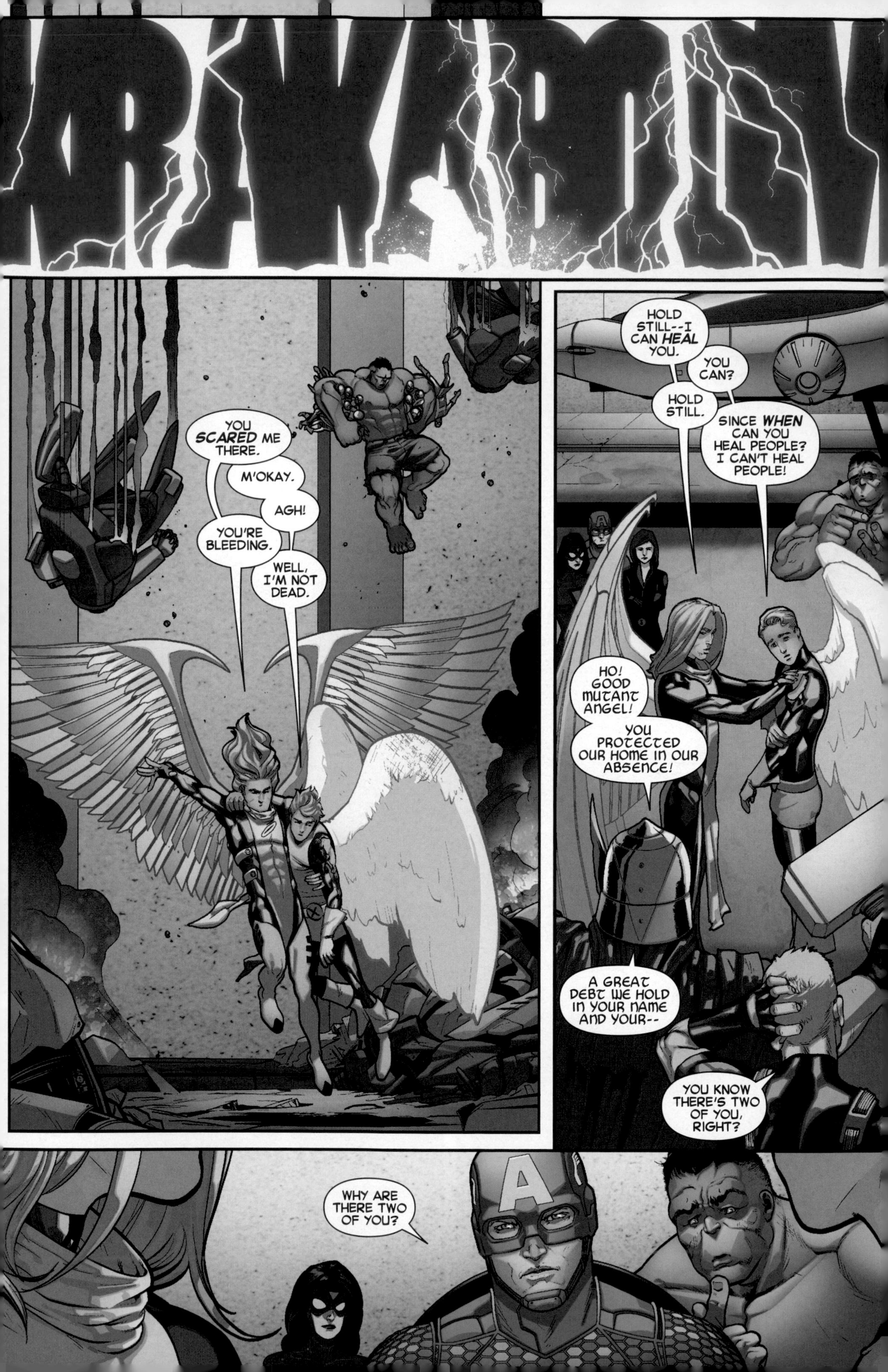
YOU SCARED ME THERE.
M'OKAY.
AGH!
YOU'RE BLEEDING.
WELL, I'M NOT DEAD.
HOLD STILL--I CAN HEAL YOU.
YOU CAN?
HOLD STILL.
SINCE WHEN CAN YOU HEAL PEOPLE? I CAN'T HEAL PEOPLE!
HO! GOOD MUTANT ANGEL!
YOU PROTECTED OUR HOME IN OUR ABSENCE!
A GREAT DEBT WE HOLD IN YOUR NAME AND YOUR--
YOU KNOW THERE'S TWO OF YOU, RIGHT?
WHY ARE THERE TWO OF YOU?

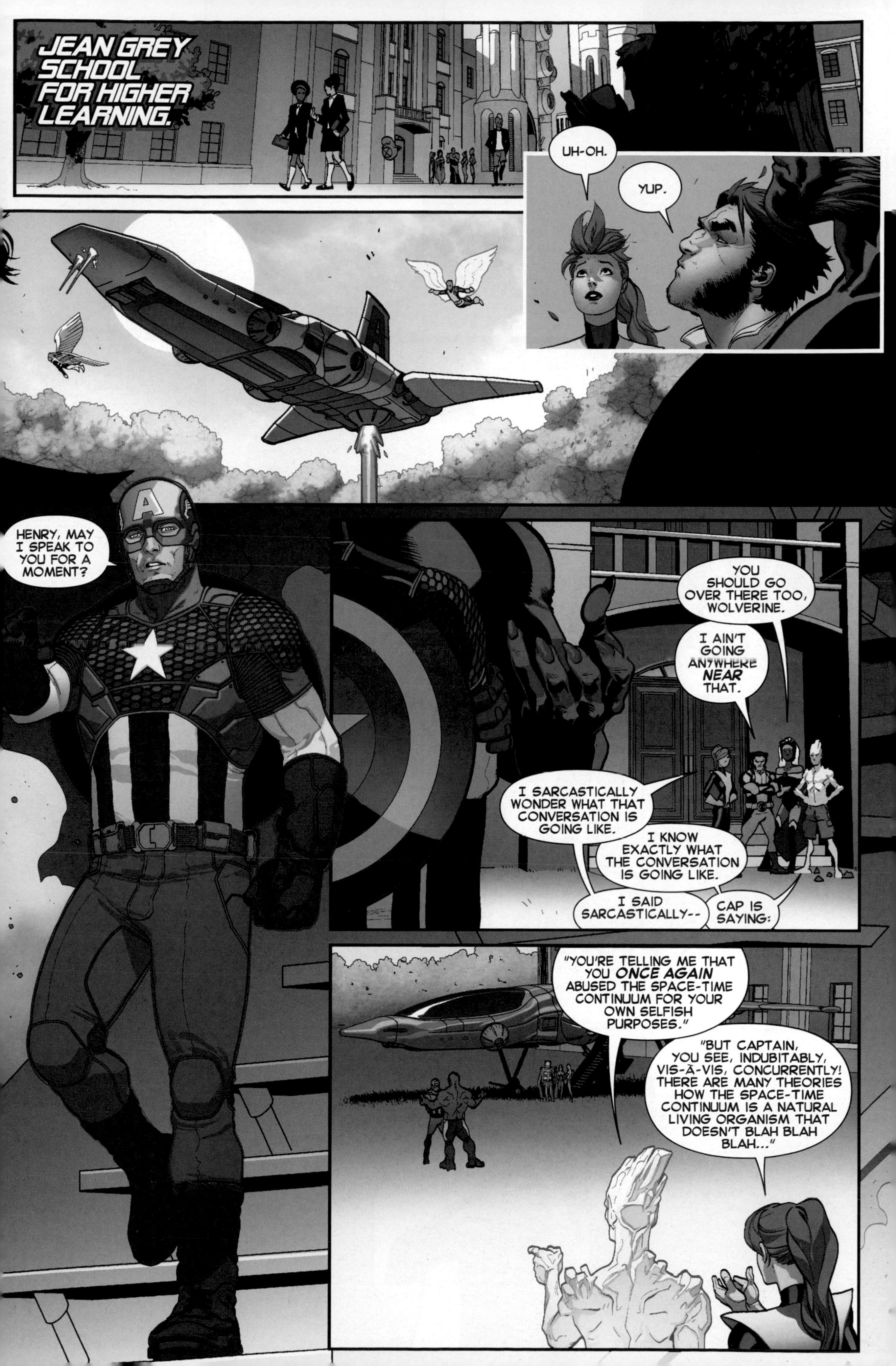
JEAN GREY SCHOOL FOR HIGHER LEARNING.
UH-OH.
YUP.
HENRY, MAY I SPEAK TO YOU FOR A MOMENT?
YOU SHOULD GO OVER THERE TOO, WOLVERINE.
I AIN'T GOING ANYWHERE NEAR THAT.
I SARCASTICALLY WONDER WHAT THAT CONVERSATION IS GOING LIKE.
I KNOW EXACTLY WHAT THE CONVERSATION IS GOING LIKE.
I SAID SARCASTICALLY--
CAP IS SAYING:
"YOU'RE TELLING ME THAT YOU ONCE AGAIN ABUSED THE SPACE-TIME CONTINUUM FOR YOUR OWN SELFISH PURPOSES."
"BUT CAPTAIN, YOU SEE, INDUBITABLY, VIS-Ã-VIS, CONCURRENTLY! THERE ARE MANY THEORIES HOW THE SPACE-TIME CONTINUUM IS A NATURAL LIVING ORGANISM THAT DOESN'T BLAH BLAH BLAH..."

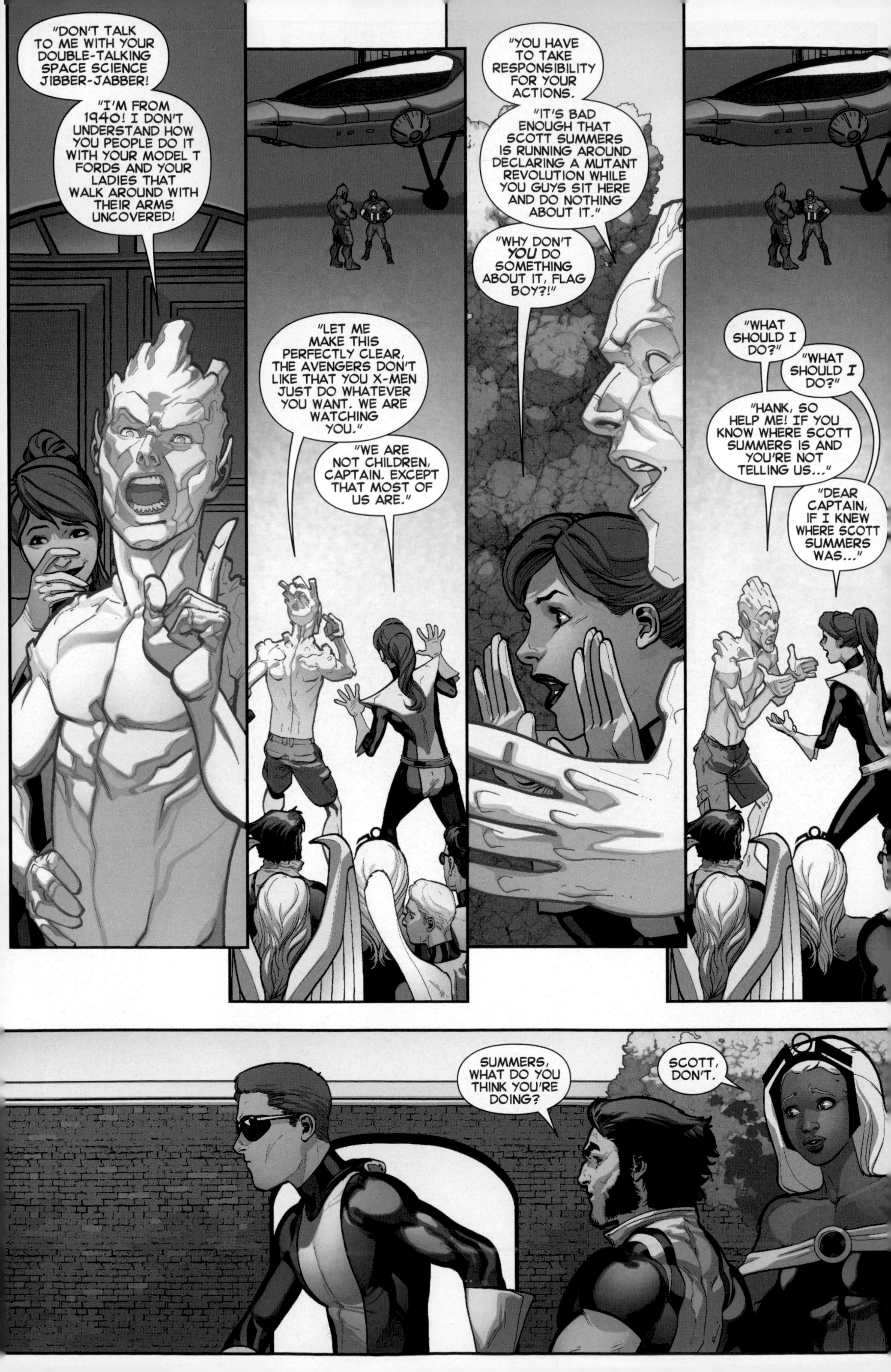

"DON'T TALK TO ME WITH YOUR DOUBLE-TALKING SPACE SCIENCE JIBBER-JABBER!
"I'M FROM 1940! I DON'T UNDERSTAND HOW YOU PEOPLE DO IT WITH YOUR MODEL T FORDS AND YOUR LADIES THAT WALK AROUND WITH THEIR ARMS UNCOVERED!
"LET ME MAKE THIS PERFECTLY CLEAR, THE AVENGERS DON'T LIKE THAT YOU X-MEN JUST DO WHATEVER YOU WANT. WE ARE WATCHING YOU."
"WE ARE NOT CHILDREN, CAPTAIN. EXCEPT THAT MOST OF US ARE."
"YOU HAVE TO TAKE RESPONSIBILITY FOR YOUR ACTIONS.
"IT'S BAD ENOUGH THAT SCOTT SUMMERS IS RUNNING AROUND DECLARING A MUTANT REVOLUTION WHILE YOU GUYS SIT HERE AND DO NOTHING ABOUT IT."
"WHY DON'T YOU DO SOMETHING ABOUT IT, FLAG BOY?!"
"WHAT SHOULD I DO?"
"WHAT SHOULD I DO?"
"HANK, SO HELP ME! IF YOU KNOW WHERE SCOTT SUMMERS IS AND YOU'RE NOT TELLING US..."
"DEAR CAPTAIN, IF I KNEW WHERE SCOTT SUMMERS WAS..."
SUMMERS, WHAT DO YOU THINK YOU'RE DOING?
SCOTT, DON'T.

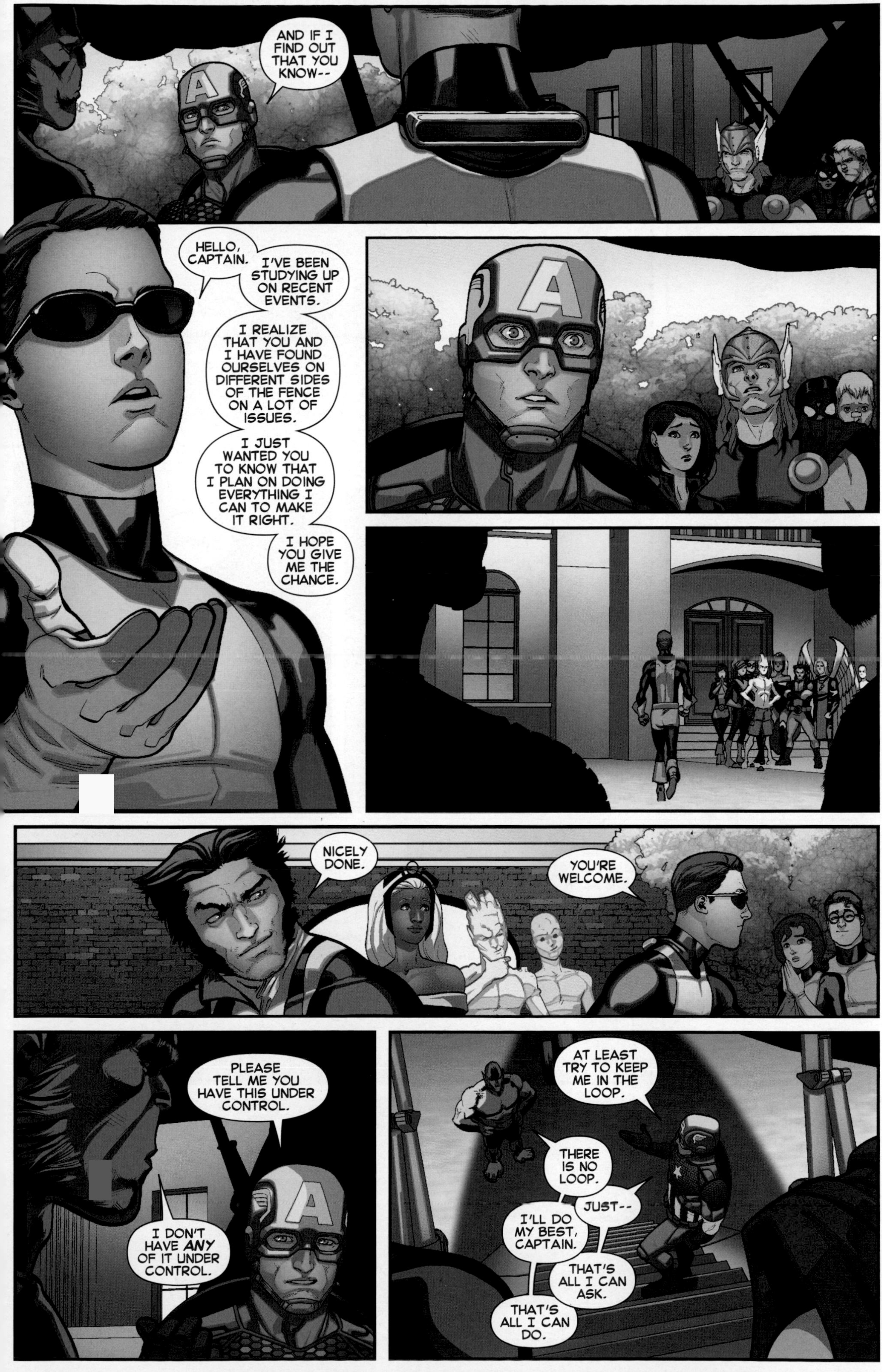
AND IF I FIND OUT THAT YOU KNOW--
HELLO, CAPTAIN.
I'VE BEEN STUDYING UP ON RECENT EVENTS.
I REALIZE THAT YOU AND I HAVE FOUND OURSELVES ON DIFFERENT SIDES OF THE FENCE ON A LOT OF ISSUES.
I JUST WANTED YOU TO KNOW THAT I PLAN ON DOING EVERYTHING I CAN TO MAKE IT RIGHT.
I HOPE YOU GIVE ME THE CHANCE.
NICELY DONE.
YOU'RE WELCOME.
PLEASE TELL ME YOU HAVE THIS UNDER CONTROL.
I DON'T HAVE *ANY* OF IT UNDER CONTROL.
AT LEAST TRY TO KEEP ME IN THE LOOP.
THERE IS NO LOOP.
JUST--
I'LL DO MY BEST, CAPTAIN.
THAT'S ALL I CAN ASK.
THAT'S ALL I CAN DO.

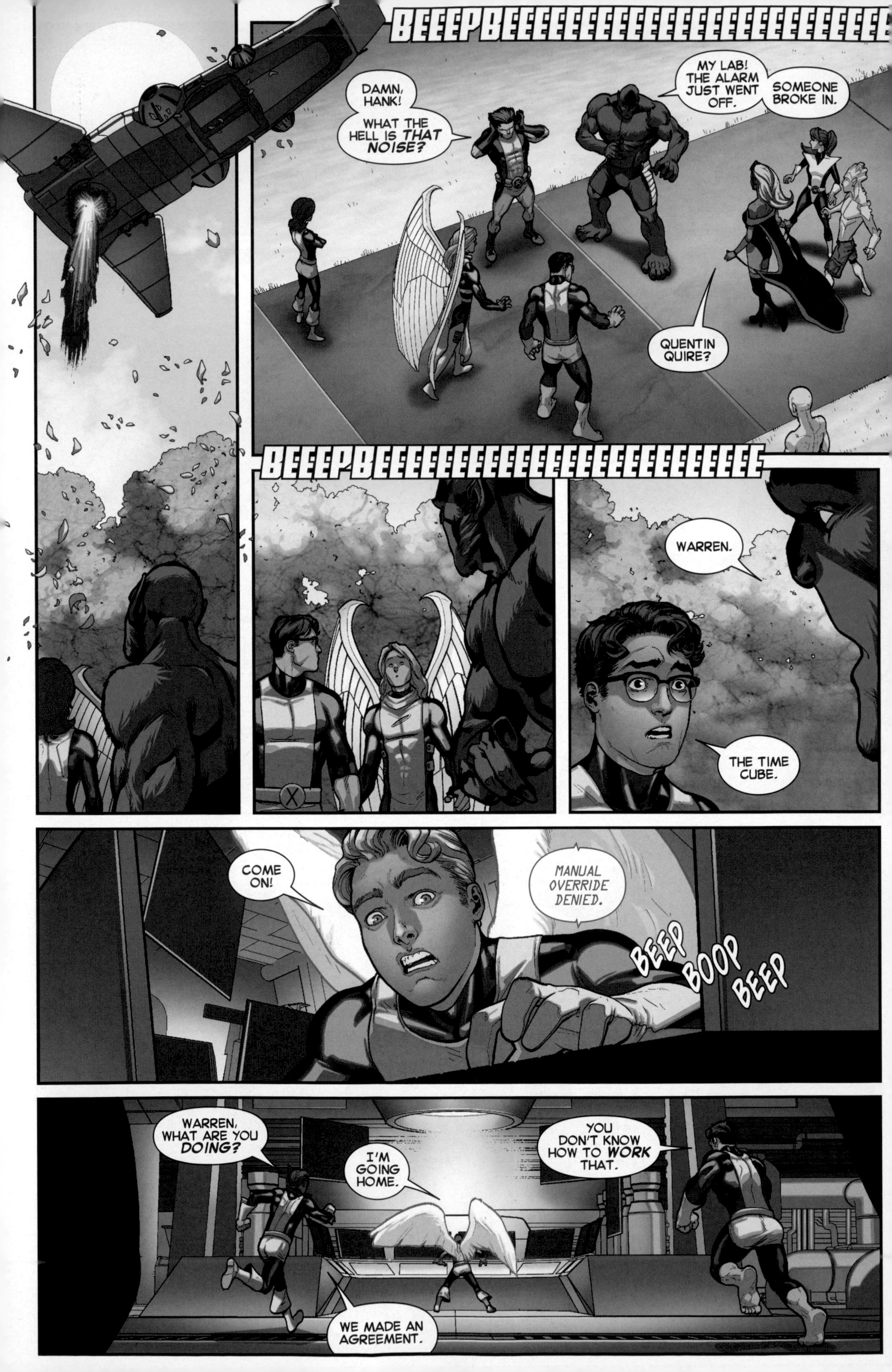
BEEEPBEEEEEEEEEEEEEEEEEEEEEEEEE
DAMN, HANK!
WHAT THE HELL IS THAT NOISE?
MY LAB! THE ALARM JUST WENT OFF.
SOMEONE BROKE IN.
QUENTIN QUIRE?
BEEEPBEEEEEEEEEEEEEEEEEEEEEEEEE
WARREN.
THE TIME CUBE.
COME ON!
MANUAL OVERRIDE DENIED.
BEEP BOOP BEEP
WARREN, WHAT ARE YOU DOING?
I'M GOING HOME.
YOU DON'T KNOW HOW TO WORK THAT.
WE MADE AN AGREEMENT.

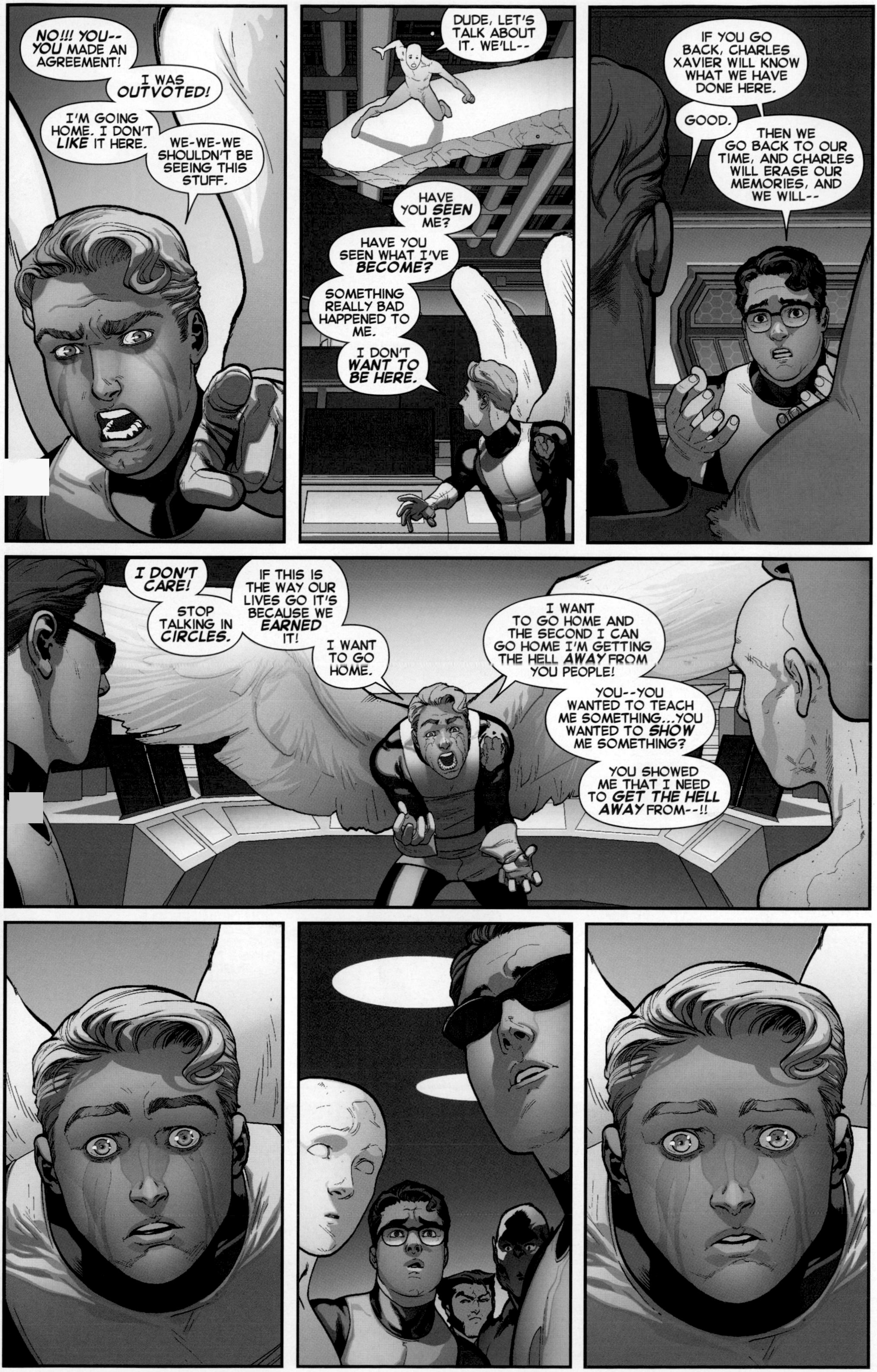
NO!!! YOU--
YOU MADE AN AGREEMENT!
I WAS OUTVOTED!
I'M GOING HOME. I DON'T LIKE IT HERE.
WE-WE-WE SHOULDN'T BE SEEING THIS STUFF.
DUDE, LET'S TALK ABOUT IT. WE'LL--
HAVE YOU SEEN ME?
HAVE YOU SEEN WHAT I'VE BECOME?
SOMETHING REALLY BAD HAPPENED TO ME.
I DON'T WANT TO BE HERE.
IF YOU GO BACK, CHARLES XAVIER WILL KNOW WHAT WE HAVE DONE HERE.
GOOD.
THEN WE GO BACK TO OUR TIME, AND CHARLES WILL ERASE OUR MEMORIES, AND WE WILL--
I DON'T CARE!
STOP TALKING IN CIRCLES.
IF THIS IS THE WAY OUR LIVES GO IT'S BECAUSE WE EARNED IT!
I WANT TO GO HOME.
I WANT TO GO HOME AND THE SECOND I CAN GO HOME I'M GETTING THE HELL AWAY FROM YOU PEOPLE!
YOU--YOU WANTED TO TEACH ME SOMETHING...YOU WANTED TO SHOW ME SOMETHING?
YOU SHOWED ME THAT I NEED TO GET THE HELL AWAY FROM--!!

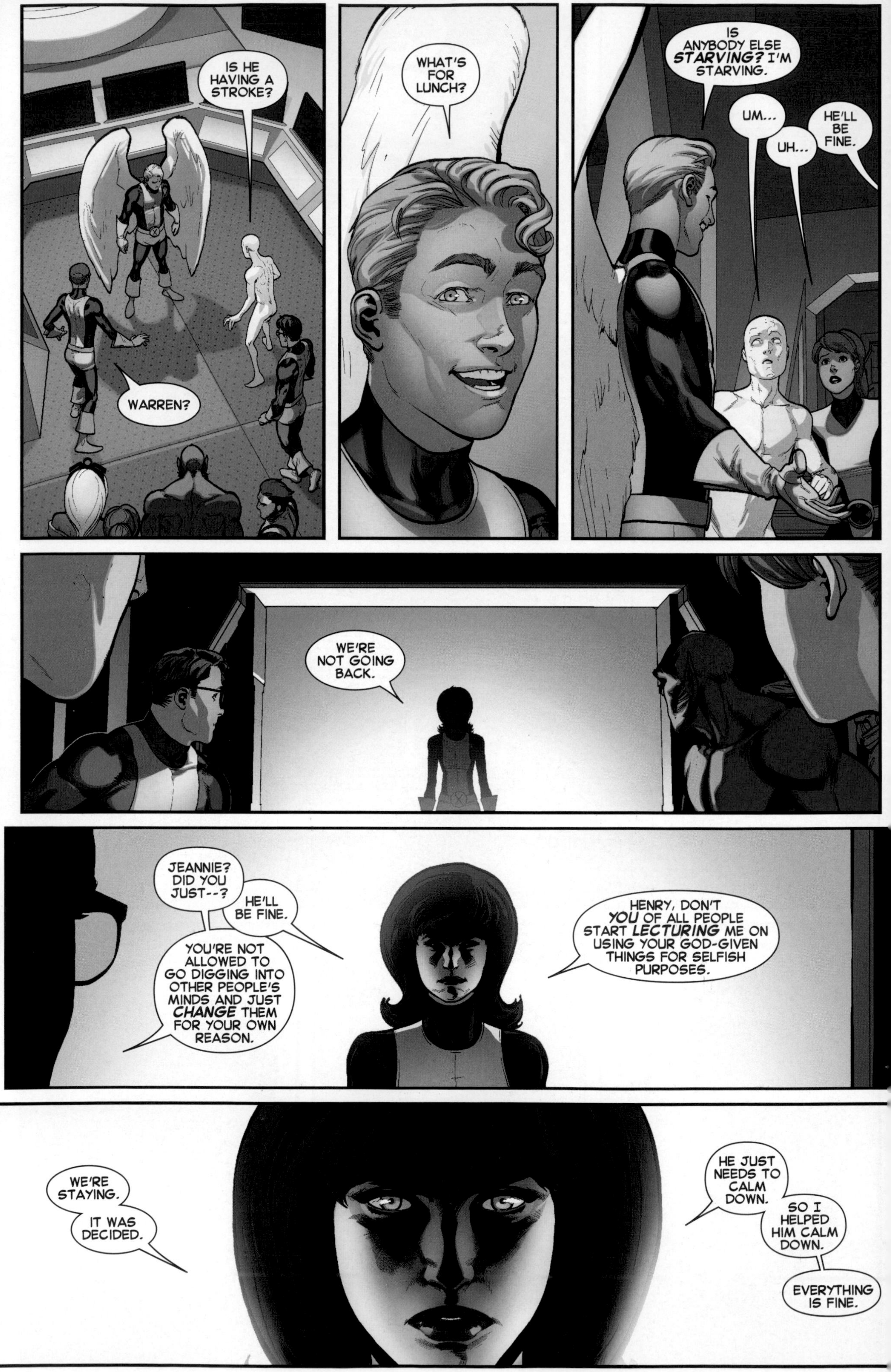
IS HE HAVING A STROKE?
WARREN?
WHAT'S FOR LUNCH?
IS ANYBODY ELSE STARVING? I'M STARVING.
UM...
UH...
HE'LL BE FINE.
WE'RE NOT GOING BACK.
JEANNIE? DID YOU JUST--?
HE'LL BE FINE.
YOU'RE NOT ALLOWED TO GO DIGGING INTO OTHER PEOPLE'S MINDS AND JUST CHANGE THEM FOR YOUR OWN REASON.
HENRY, DON'T YOU OF ALL PEOPLE START LECTURING ME ON USING YOUR GOD-GIVEN THINGS FOR SELFISH PURPOSES.
WE'RE STAYING.
IT WAS DECIDED.
HE JUST NEEDS TO CALM DOWN.
SO I HELPED HIM CALM DOWN.
EVERYTHING IS FINE.

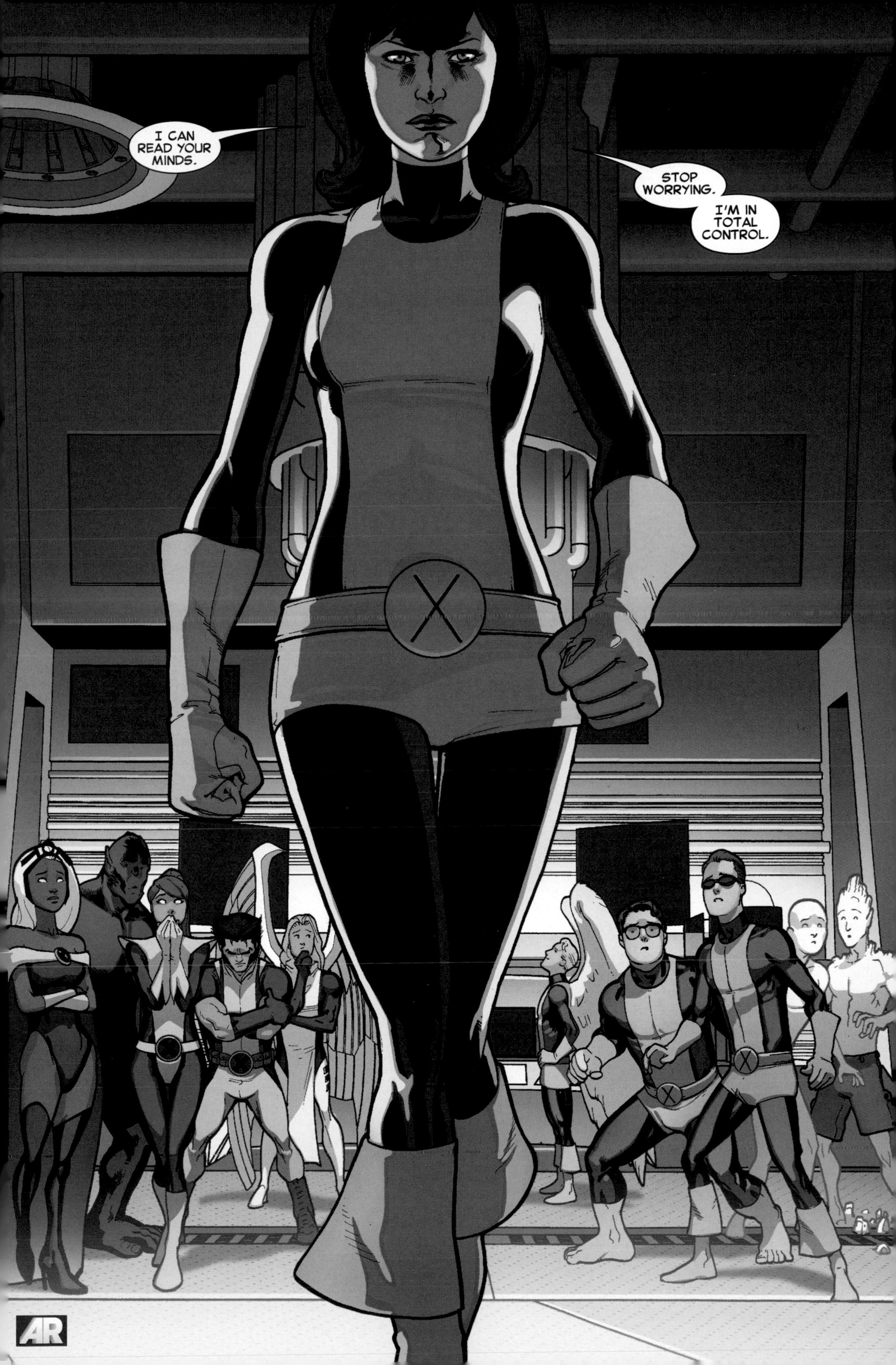
I CAN READ YOUR MINDS.
STOP WORRYING.
I'M IN TOTAL CONTROL.

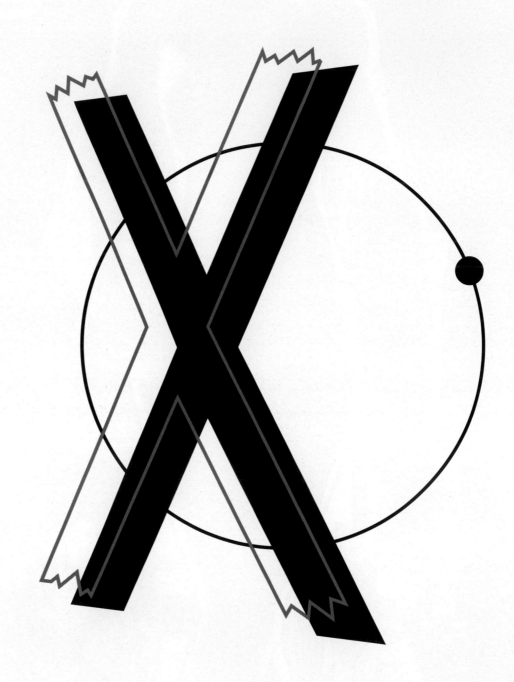

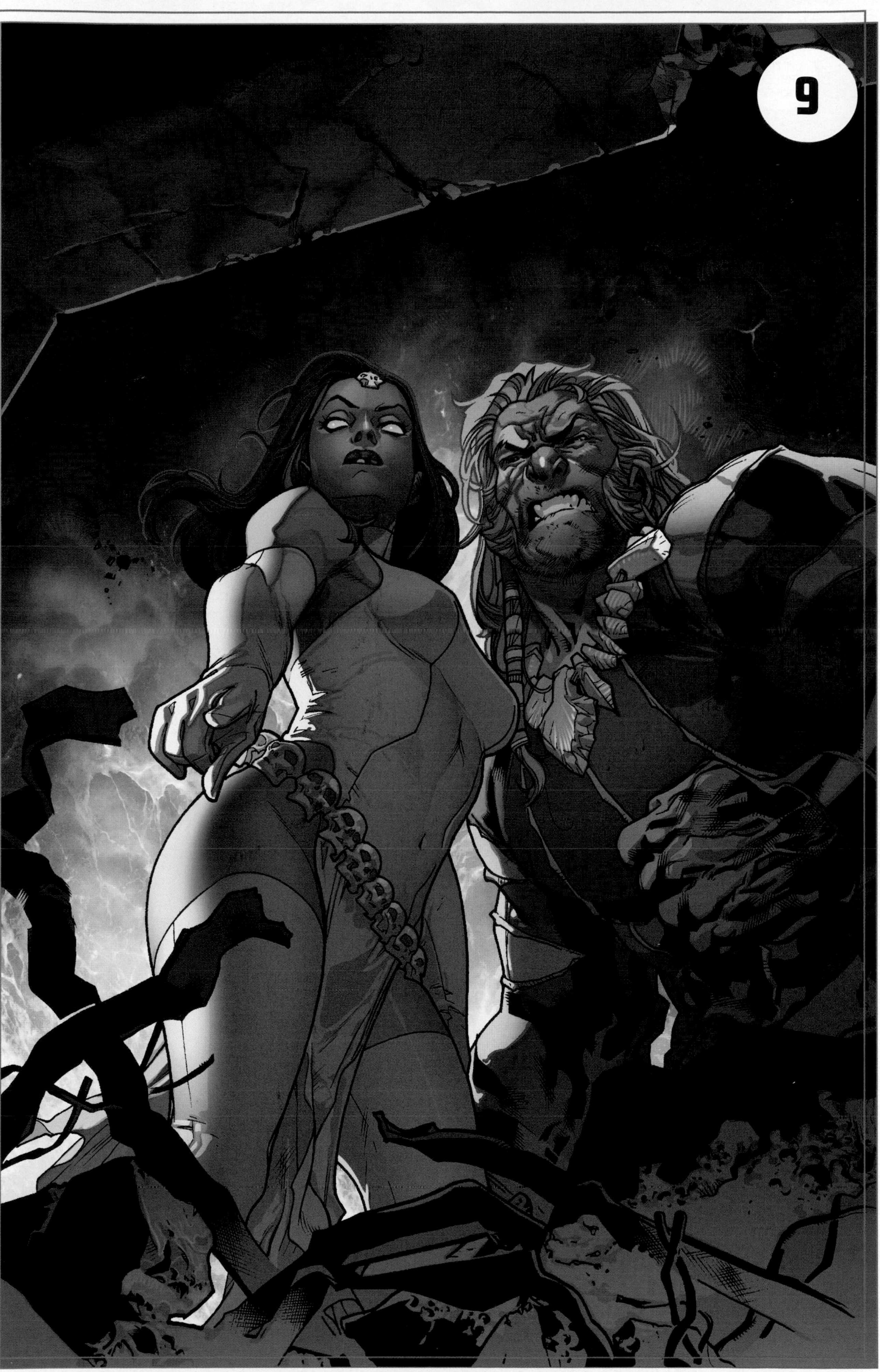
9

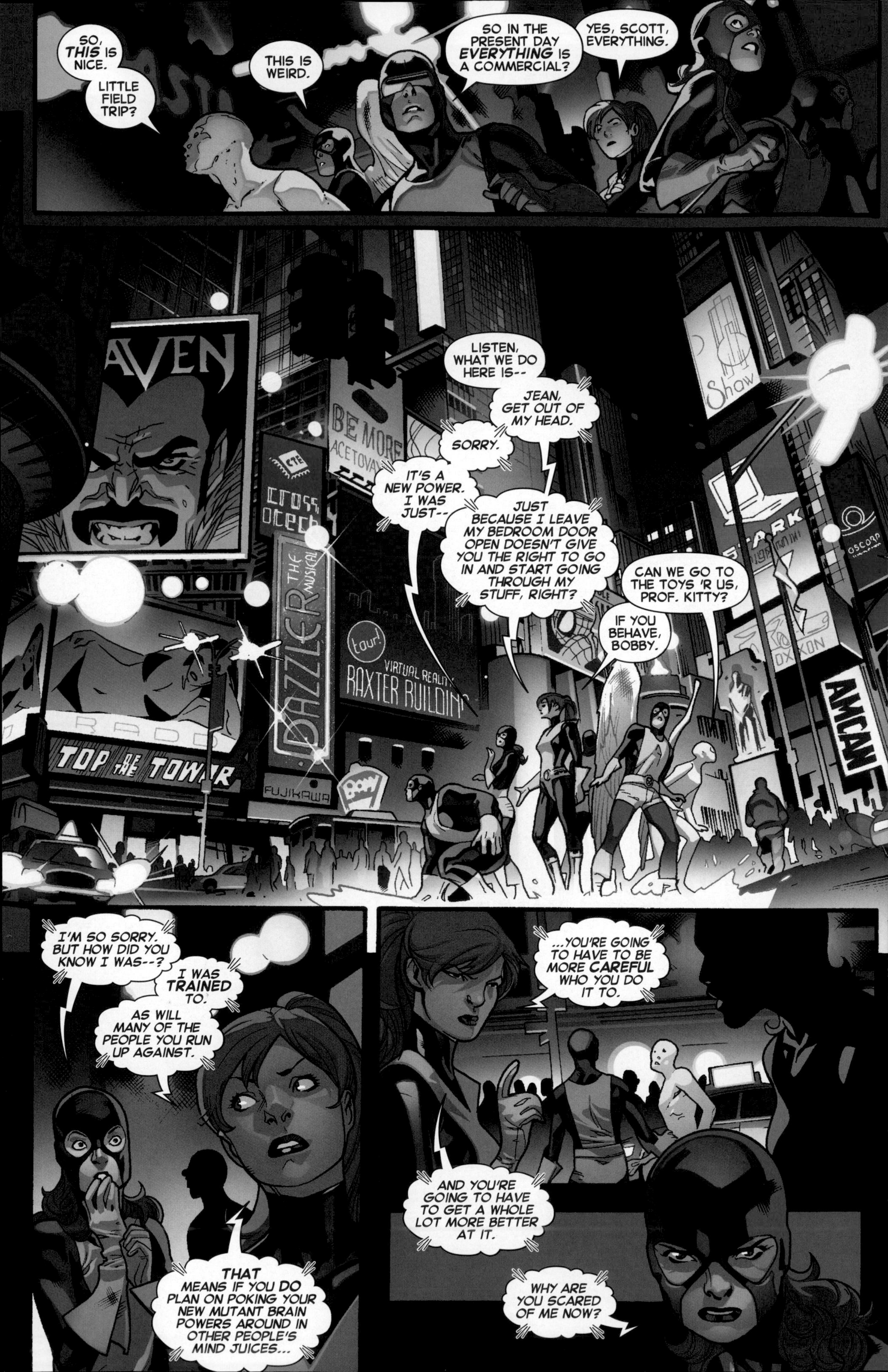
SO, THIS IS NICE.
LITTLE FIELD TRIP?
THIS IS WEIRD.
SO IN THE PRESENT DAY EVERYTHING IS A COMMERCIAL?
YES, SCOTT, EVERYTHING.
AVEN
BE MORE
ACETOVAY
cross otech
DAZZLER THE MUSICAL
tour!
VIRTUAL REALITY
BAXTER BUILDIN
TOP OF THE TOWER
FUJIKAWA
Show
STARK
OXXON
AMCAN
LISTEN, WHAT WE DO HERE IS--
JEAN, GET OUT OF MY HEAD.
SORRY.
IT'S A NEW POWER. I WAS JUST--
JUST BECAUSE I LEAVE MY BEDROOM DOOR OPEN DOESN'T GIVE YOU THE RIGHT TO GO IN AND START GOING THROUGH MY STUFF, RIGHT?
CAN WE GO TO THE TOYS 'R US, PROF. KITTY?
IF YOU BEHAVE, BOBBY.
I'M SO SORRY. BUT HOW DID YOU KNOW I WAS--?
I WAS TRAINED TO.
AS WILL MANY OF THE PEOPLE YOU RUN UP AGAINST.
THAT MEANS IF YOU DO PLAN ON POKING YOUR NEW MUTANT BRAIN POWERS AROUND IN OTHER PEOPLE'S MIND JUICES...
...YOU'RE GOING TO HAVE TO BE MORE CAREFUL WHO YOU DO IT TO.
AND YOU'RE GOING TO HAVE TO GET A WHOLE LOT MORE BETTER AT IT.
WHY ARE YOU SCARED OF ME NOW?

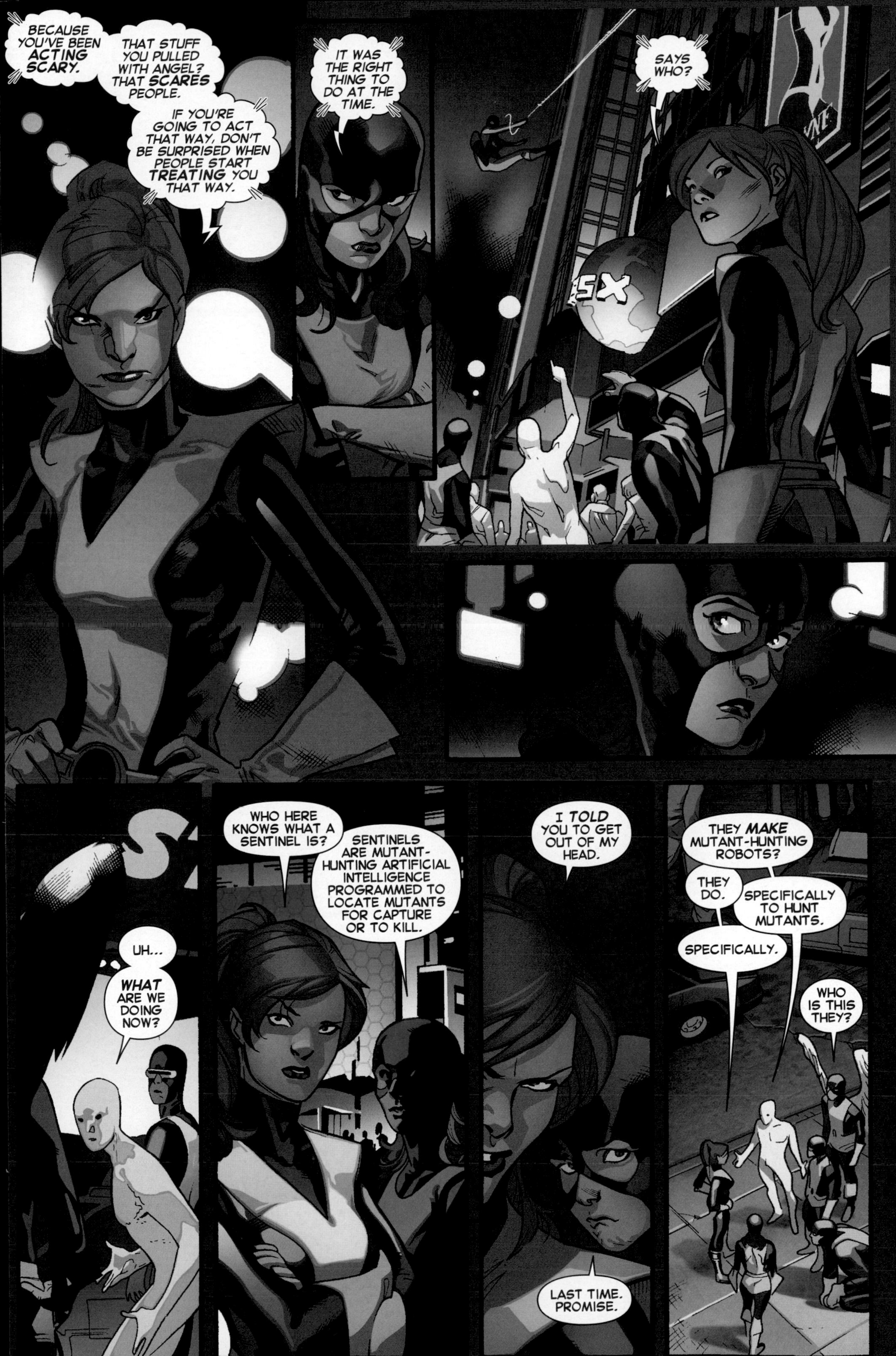
BECAUSE YOU'VE BEEN ACTING SCARY.
THAT STUFF YOU PULLED WITH ANGEL? THAT SCARES PEOPLE.
IF YOU'RE GOING TO ACT THAT WAY, DON'T BE SURPRISED WHEN PEOPLE START TREATING YOU THAT WAY.
IT WAS THE RIGHT THING TO DO AT THE TIME.
SAYS WHO?
UH...
WHAT ARE WE DOING NOW?
WHO HERE KNOWS WHAT A SENTINEL IS?
SENTINELS ARE MUTANT-HUNTING ARTIFICIAL INTELLIGENCE PROGRAMMED TO LOCATE MUTANTS FOR CAPTURE OR TO KILL.
I TOLD YOU TO GET OUT OF MY HEAD.
LAST TIME. PROMISE.
THEY MAKE MUTANT-HUNTING ROBOTS?
THEY DO.
SPECIFICALLY TO HUNT MUTANTS.
SPECIFICALLY.
WHO IS THIS THEY?

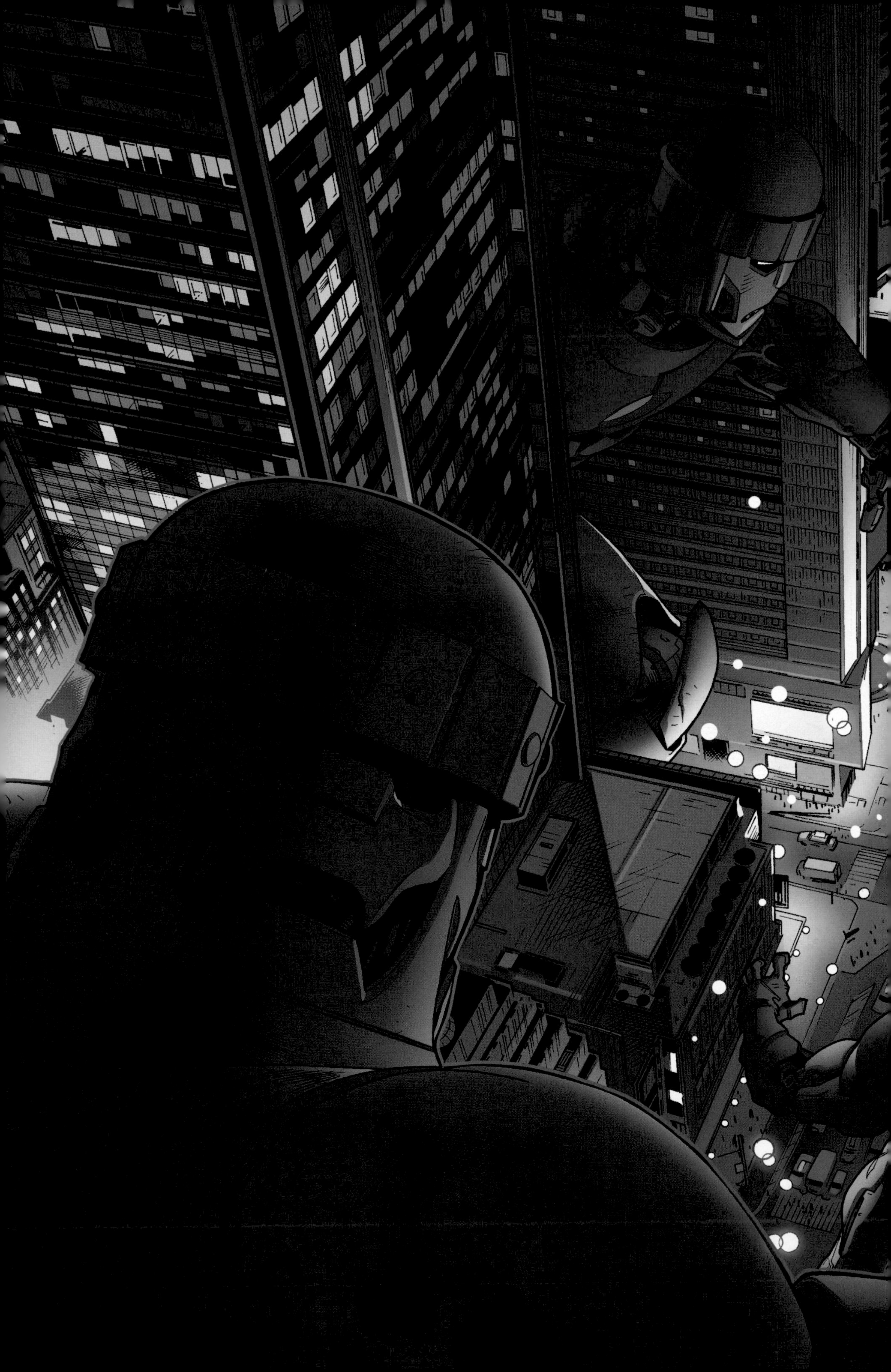

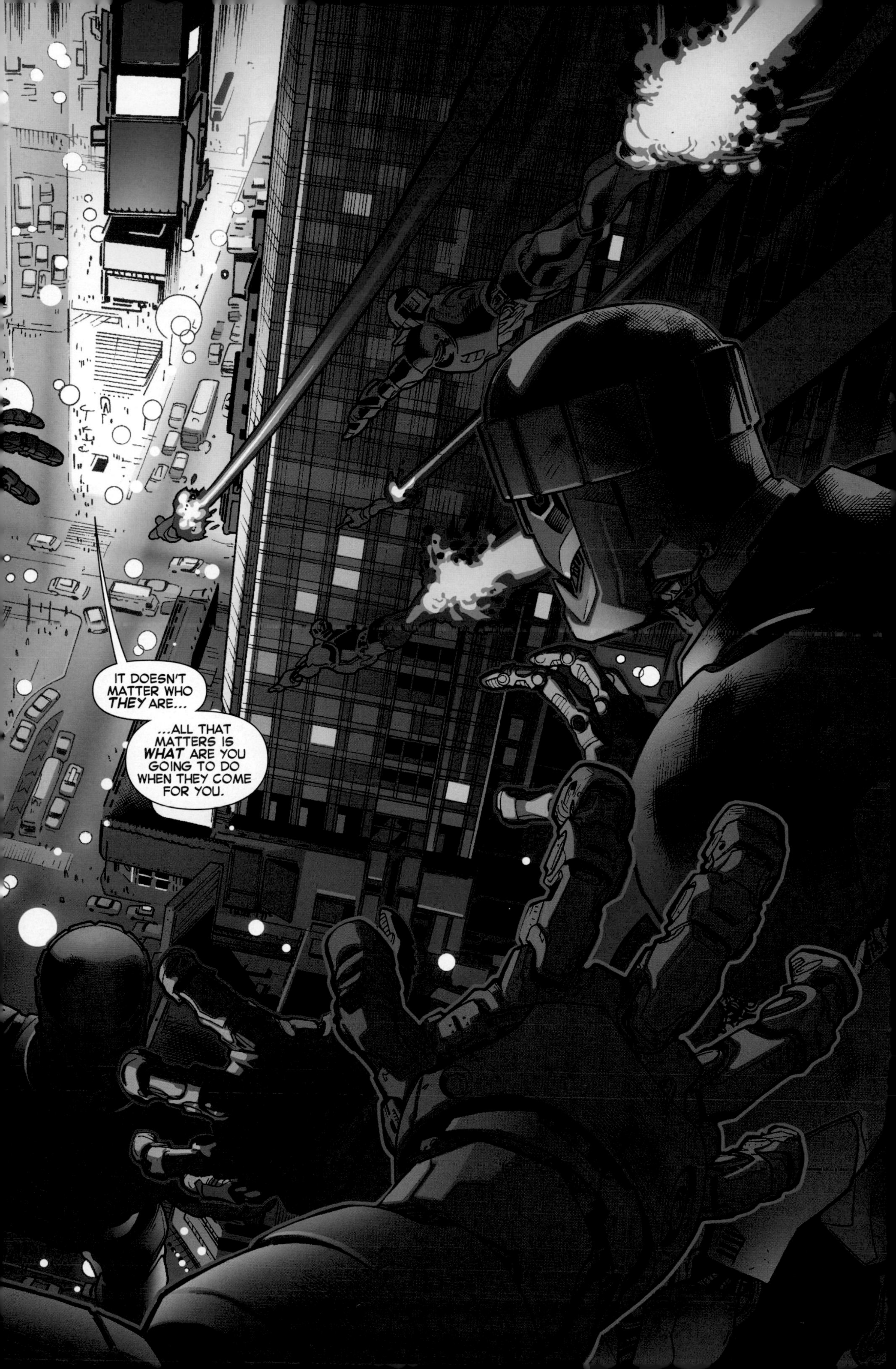
IT DOESN'T MATTER WHO *THEY* ARE...
...ALL THAT MATTERS IS *WHAT* ARE YOU GOING TO DO WHEN THEY COME FOR YOU.

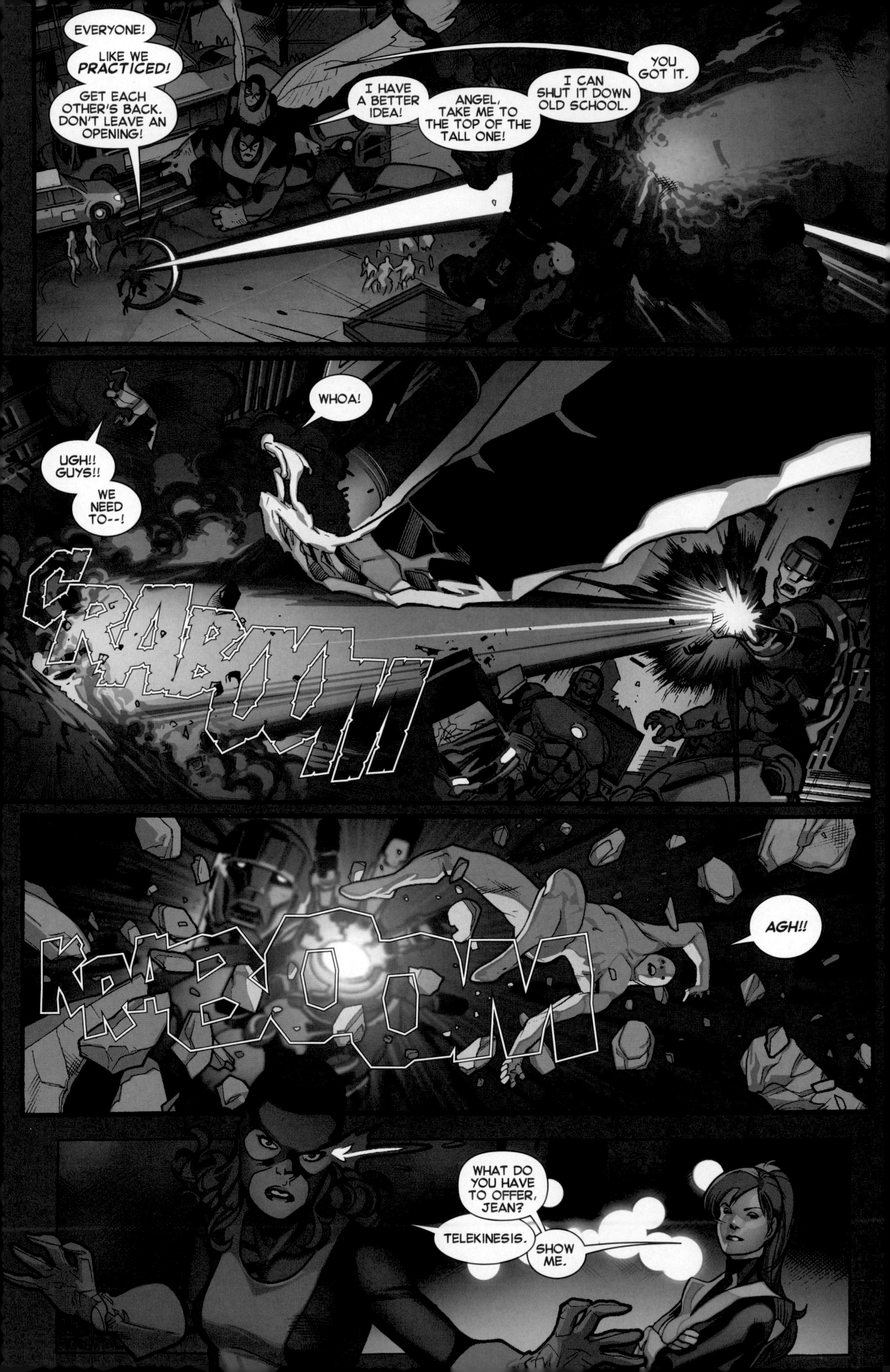
EVERYONE!
LIKE WE PRACTICED!
GET EACH OTHER'S BACK. DON'T LEAVE AN OPENING!
I HAVE A BETTER IDEA!
ANGEL, TAKE ME TO THE TOP OF THE TALL ONE!
I CAN SHUT IT DOWN OLD SCHOOL.
YOU GOT IT.
WHOA!
UGH!! GUYS!!
WE NEED TO--!
CRABOOM
KA-BOOOM
AGH!!
WHAT DO YOU HAVE TO OFFER, JEAN?
TELEKINESIS.
SHOW ME.

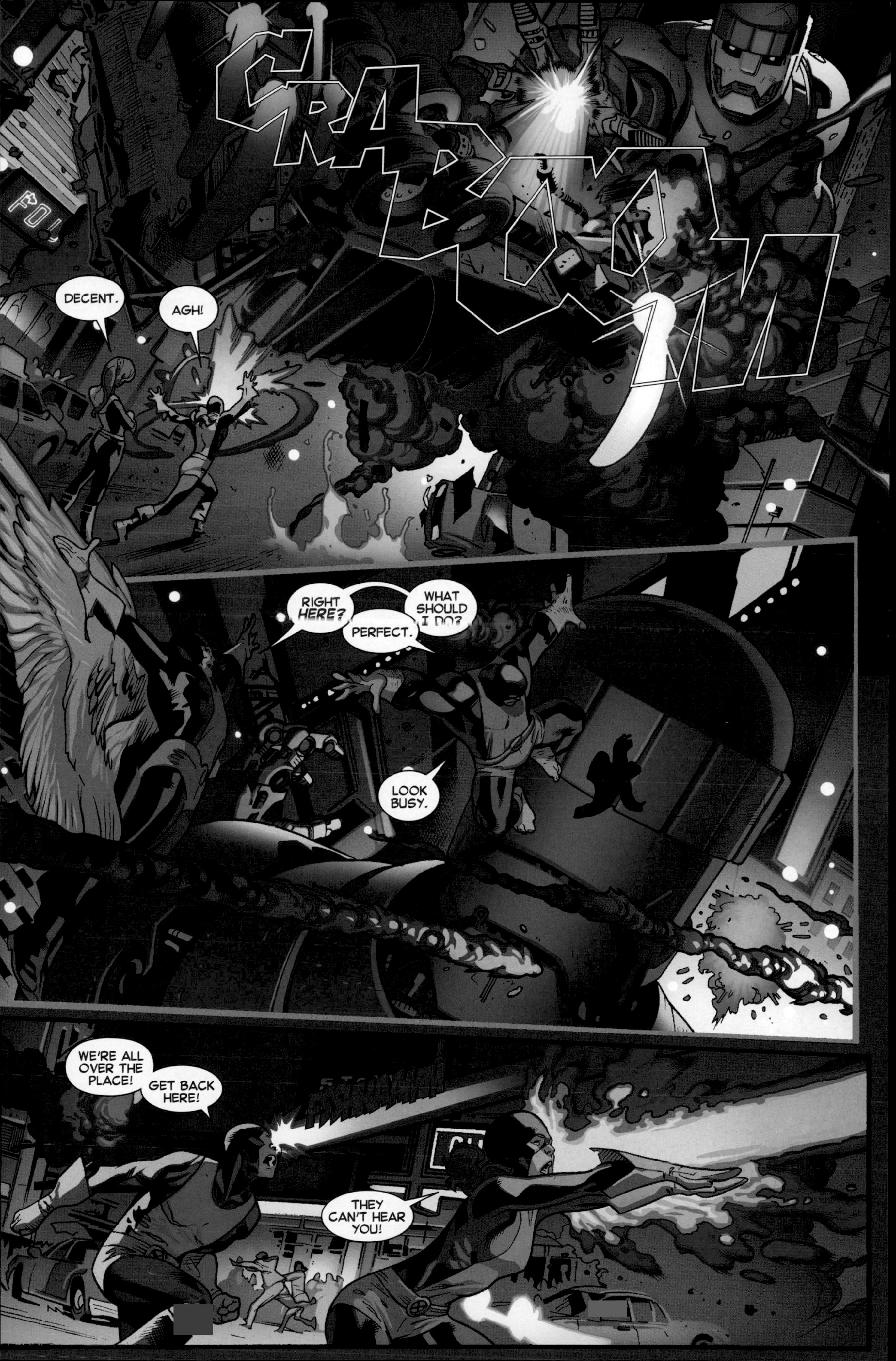
CRABOOM
DECENT.
AGH!
RIGHT HERE?
WHAT SHOULD I DO?
PERFECT.
LOOK BUSY.
WE'RE ALL OVER THE PLACE!
GET BACK HERE!
THEY CAN'T HEAR YOU!

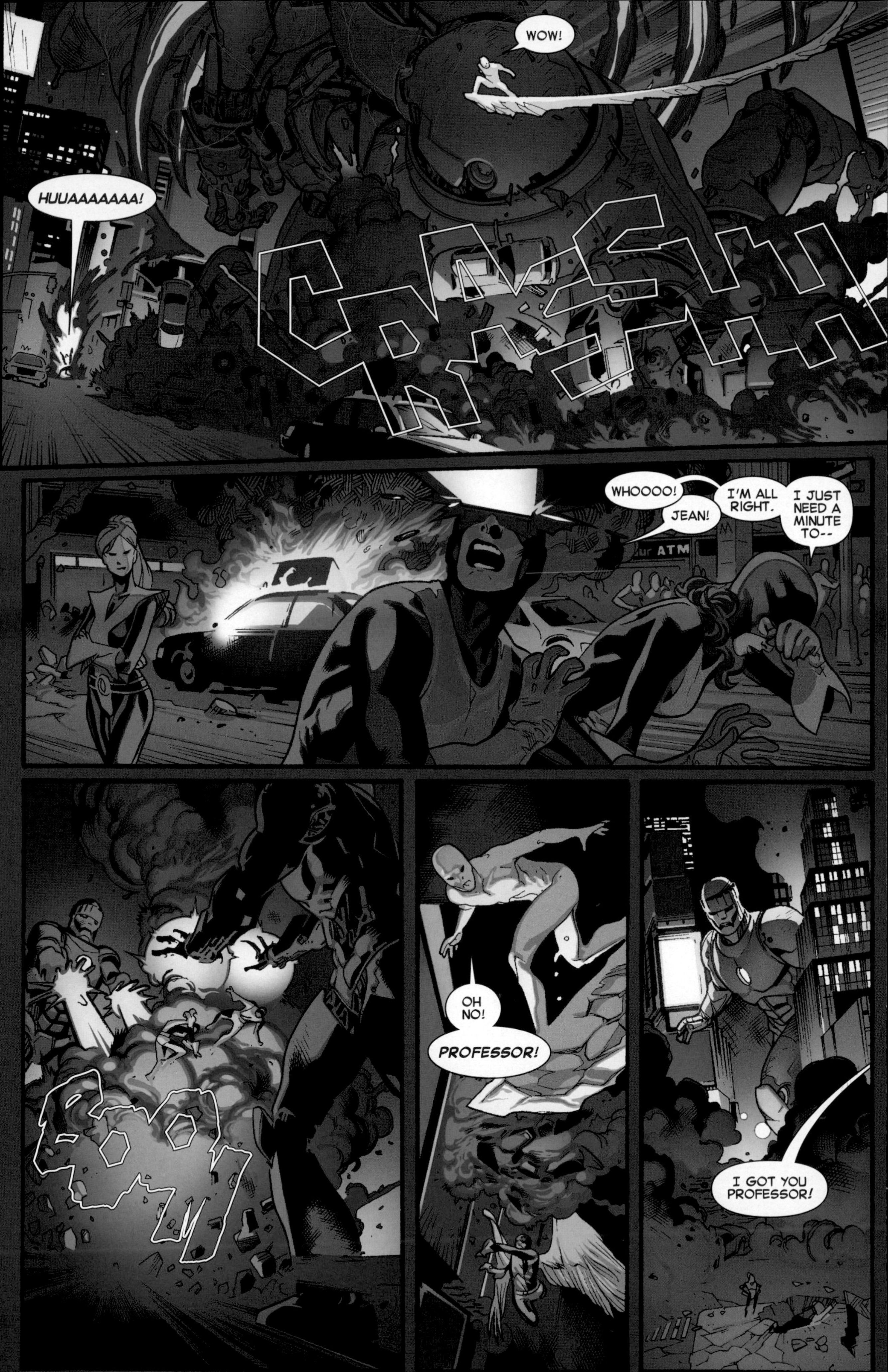
WOW!
HUUAAAAAAA!
WHOOOO!
JEAN!
I'M ALL RIGHT.
I JUST NEED A MINUTE TO--
ATM
OH NO!
PROFESSOR!
I GOT YOU PROFESSOR!

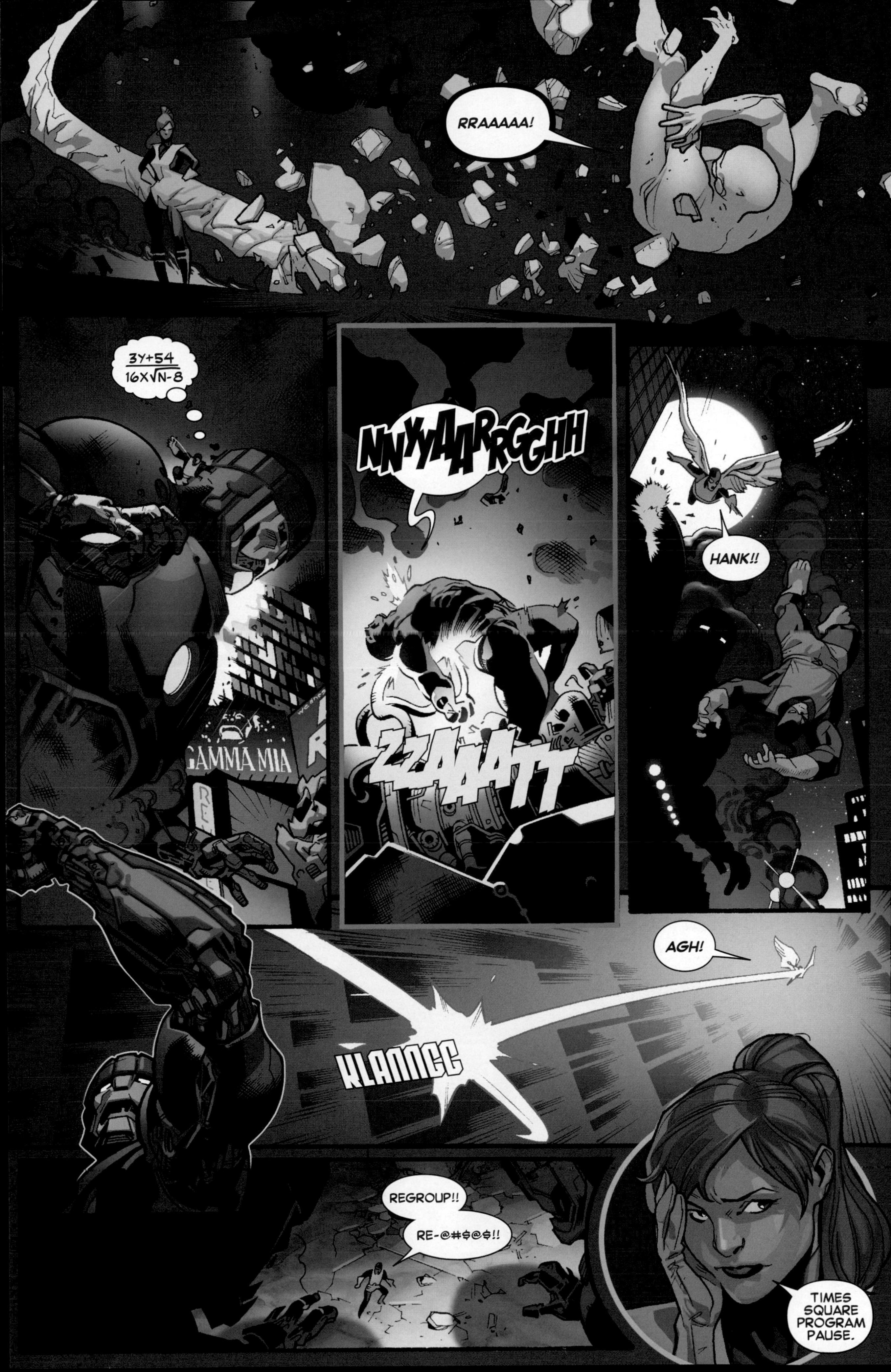
RRAAAAA!
3Y+54
16X√N-8
NNYYAARRGGHH
ZZAAATT
HANK!!
GAMMA MIA
AGH!
KLANNGG
REGROUP!!
RE-@#$@$!!
TIMES SQUARE PROGRAM PAUSE.

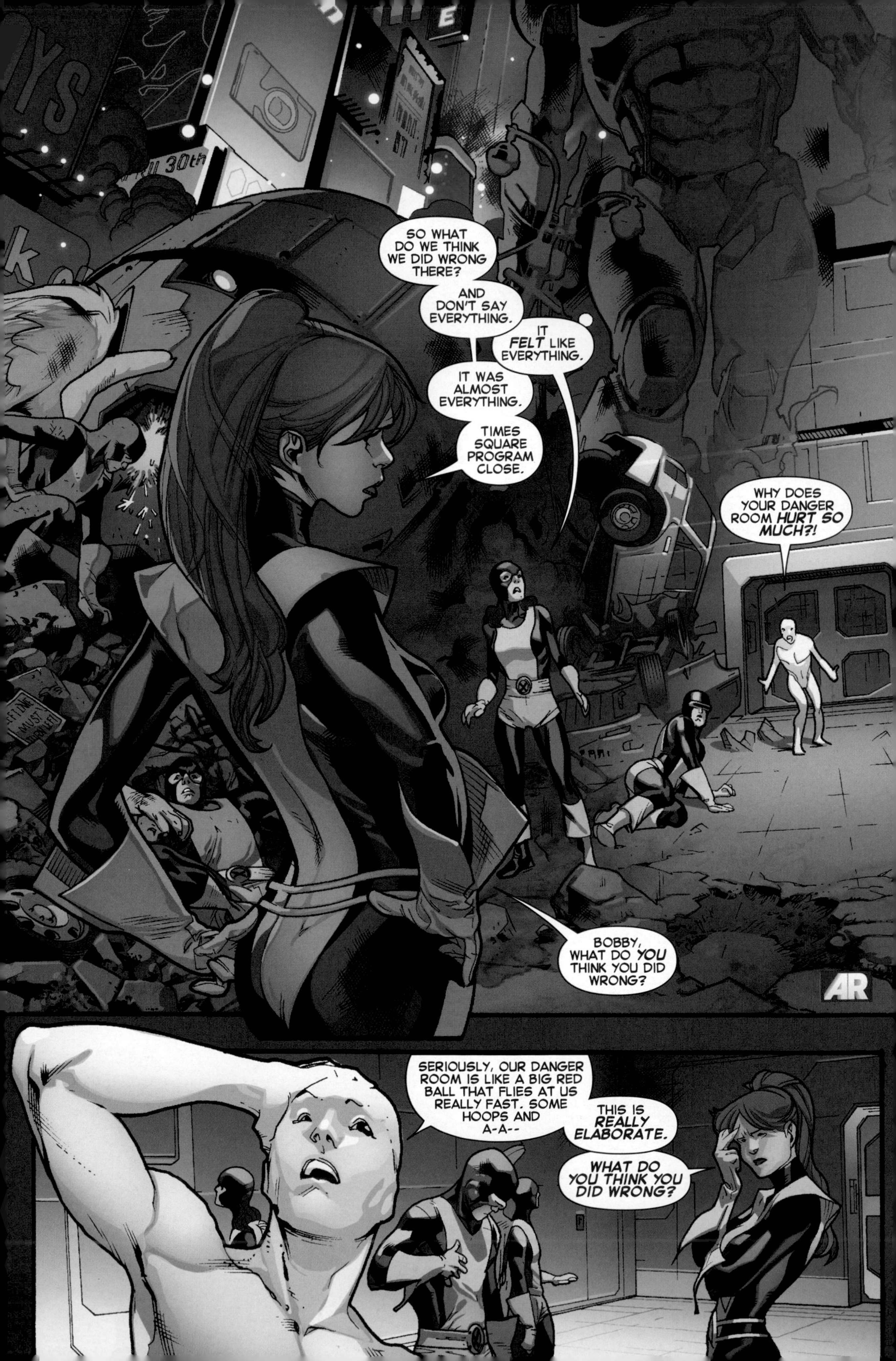
SO WHAT DO WE THINK WE DID WRONG THERE?
AND DON'T SAY EVERYTHING.
IT *FELT* LIKE EVERYTHING.
IT WAS ALMOST EVERYTHING.
TIMES SQUARE PROGRAM CLOSE.
WHY DOES YOUR DANGER ROOM *HURT SO MUCH?!*
BOBBY, WHAT DO *YOU* THINK YOU DID WRONG?
SERIOUSLY, OUR DANGER ROOM IS LIKE A BIG RED BALL THAT FLIES AT US REALLY FAST. SOME HOOPS AND A-A--
THIS IS *REALLY ELABORATE.*
WHAT DO YOU THINK YOU DID WRONG?

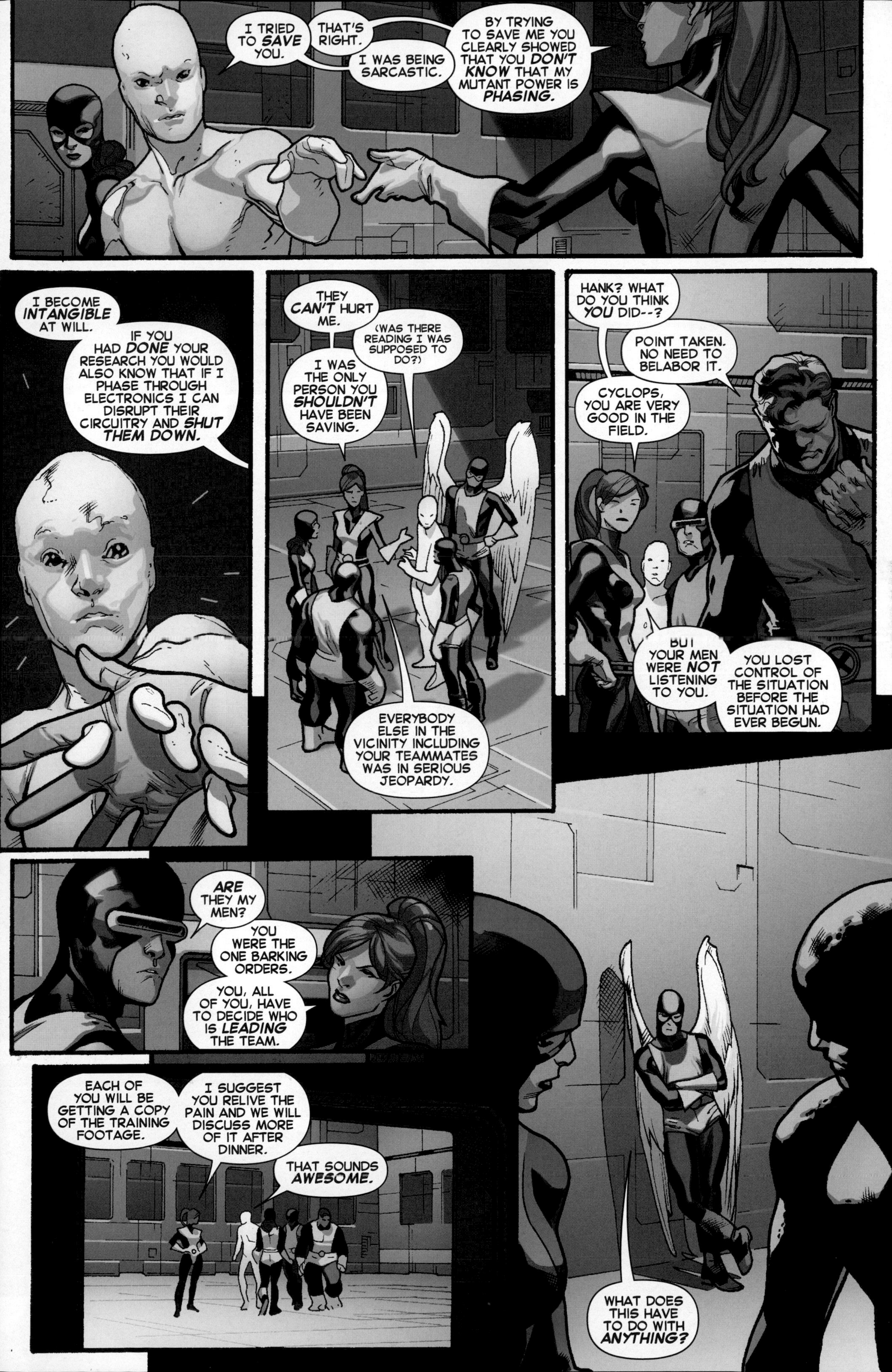
I TRIED TO SAVE YOU.
THAT'S RIGHT.
I WAS BEING SARCASTIC.
BY TRYING TO SAVE ME YOU CLEARLY SHOWED THAT YOU DON'T KNOW THAT MY MUTANT POWER IS PHASING.
I BECOME INTANGIBLE AT WILL.
IF YOU HAD DONE YOUR RESEARCH YOU WOULD ALSO KNOW THAT IF I PHASE THROUGH ELECTRONICS I CAN DISRUPT THEIR CIRCUITRY AND SHUT THEM DOWN.
THEY CAN'T HURT ME.
(WAS THERE READING I WAS SUPPOSED TO DO?)
I WAS THE ONLY PERSON YOU SHOULDN'T HAVE BEEN SAVING.
EVERYBODY ELSE IN THE VICINITY INCLUDING YOUR TEAMMATES WAS IN SERIOUS JEOPARDY.
HANK? WHAT DO YOU THINK YOU DID--?
POINT TAKEN. NO NEED TO BELABOR IT.
CYCLOPS, YOU ARE VERY GOOD IN THE FIELD.
BUT YOUR MEN WERE NOT LISTENING TO YOU.
YOU LOST CONTROL OF THE SITUATION BEFORE THE SITUATION HAD EVER BEGUN.
ARE THEY MY MEN?
YOU WERE THE ONE BARKING ORDERS.
YOU, ALL OF YOU, HAVE TO DECIDE WHO IS LEADING THE TEAM.
EACH OF YOU WILL BE GETTING A COPY OF THE TRAINING FOOTAGE.
I SUGGEST YOU RELIVE THE PAIN AND WE WILL DISCUSS MORE OF IT AFTER DINNER.
THAT SOUNDS AWESOME.
WHAT DOES THIS HAVE TO DO WITH ANYTHING?

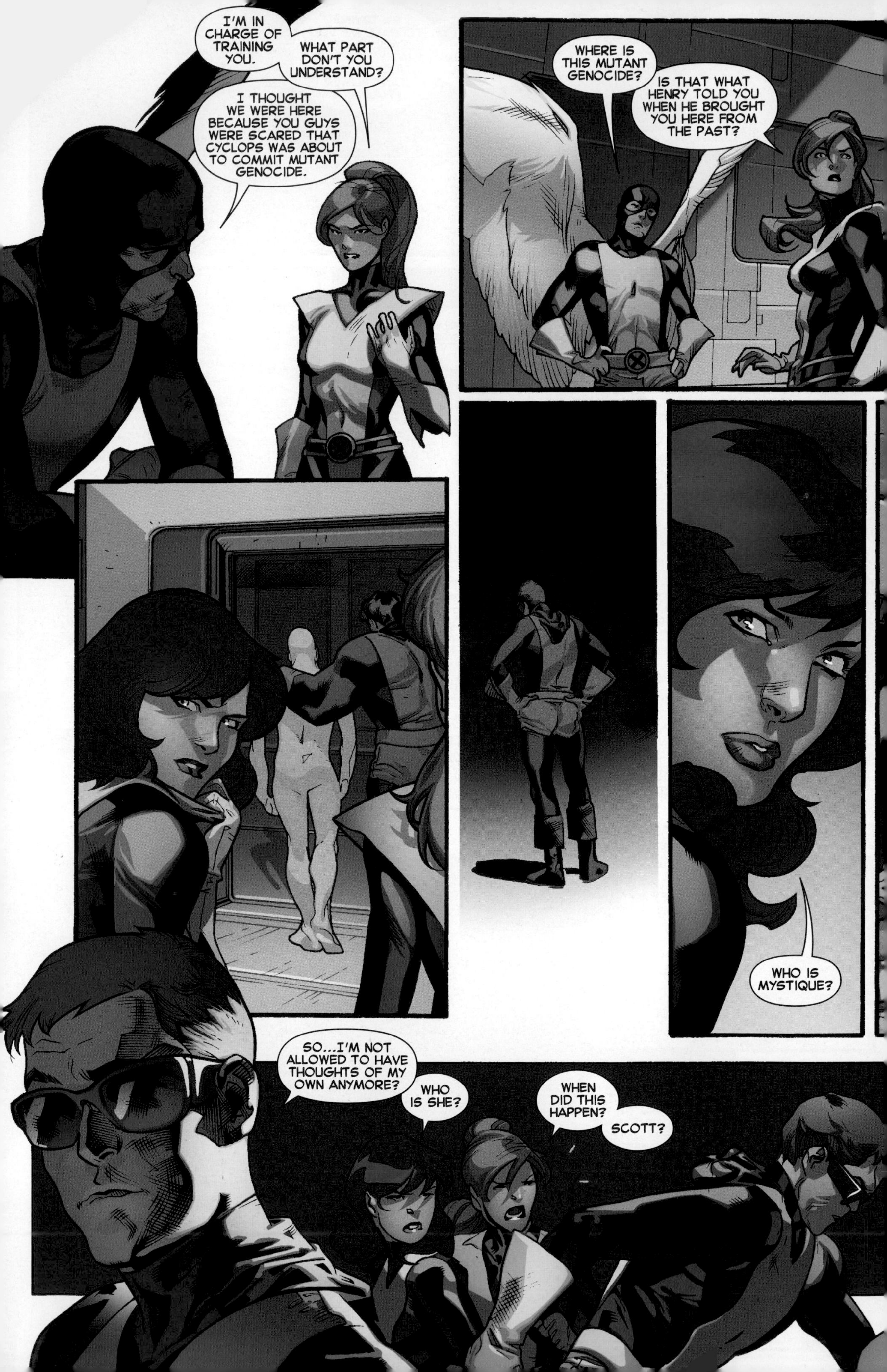
I'M IN CHARGE OF TRAINING YOU.
WHAT PART DON'T YOU UNDERSTAND?
I THOUGHT WE WERE HERE BECAUSE YOU GUYS WERE SCARED THAT CYCLOPS WAS ABOUT TO COMMIT MUTANT GENOCIDE.
WHERE IS THIS MUTANT GENOCIDE?
IS THAT WHAT HENRY TOLD YOU WHEN HE BROUGHT YOU HERE FROM THE PAST?
WHO IS MYSTIQUE?
SO...I'M NOT ALLOWED TO HAVE THOUGHTS OF MY OWN ANYMORE?
WHO IS SHE?
WHEN DID THIS HAPPEN?
SCOTT?

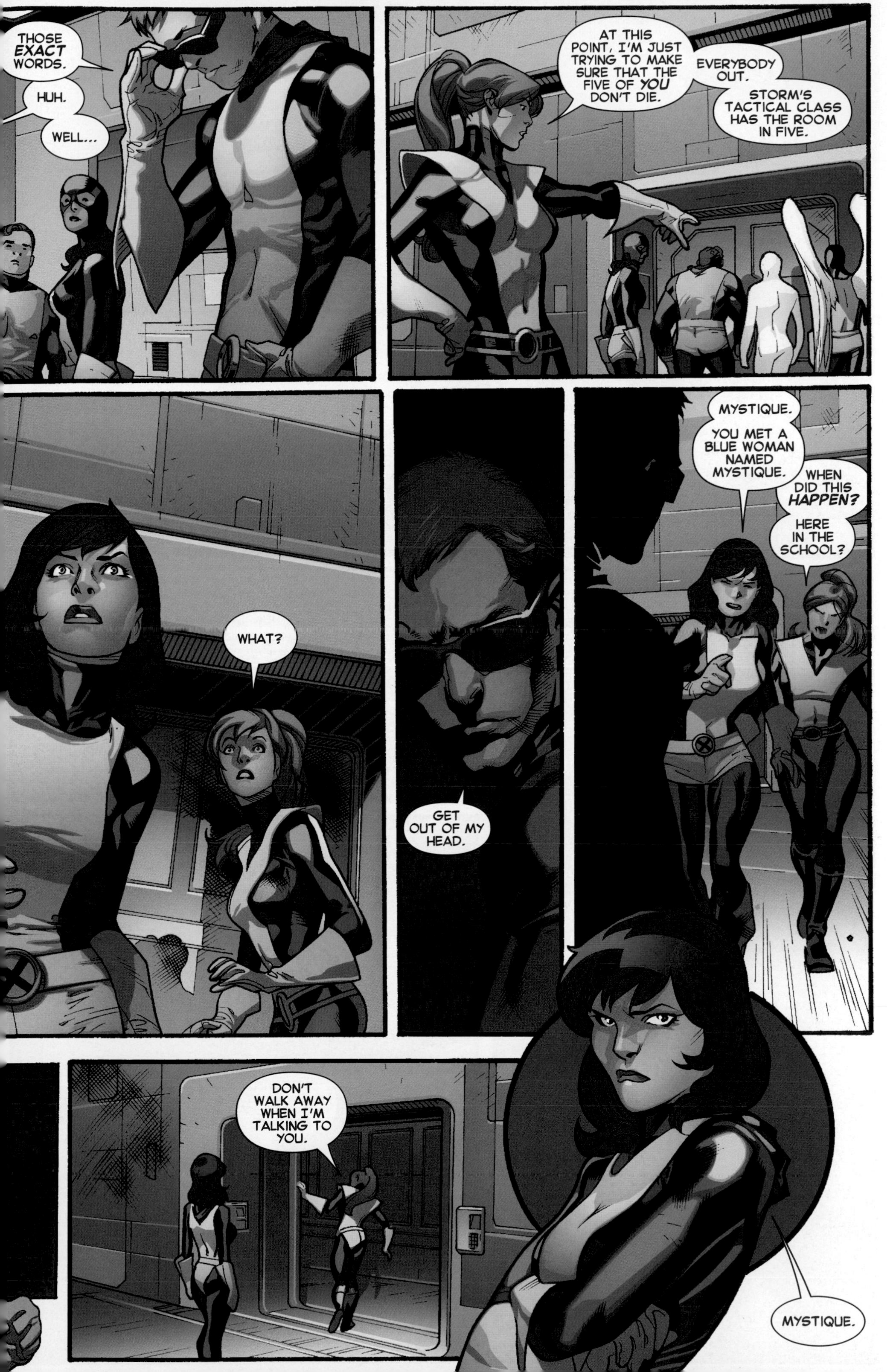
THOSE EXACT WORDS.
HUH.
WELL...
AT THIS POINT, I'M JUST TRYING TO MAKE SURE THAT THE FIVE OF YOU DON'T DIE.
EVERYBODY OUT.
STORM'S TACTICAL CLASS HAS THE ROOM IN FIVE.
WHAT?
GET OUT OF MY HEAD.
MYSTIQUE.
YOU MET A BLUE WOMAN NAMED MYSTIQUE.
WHEN DID THIS HAPPEN?
HERE IN THE SCHOOL?
DON'T WALK AWAY WHEN I'M TALKING TO YOU.
MYSTIQUE.

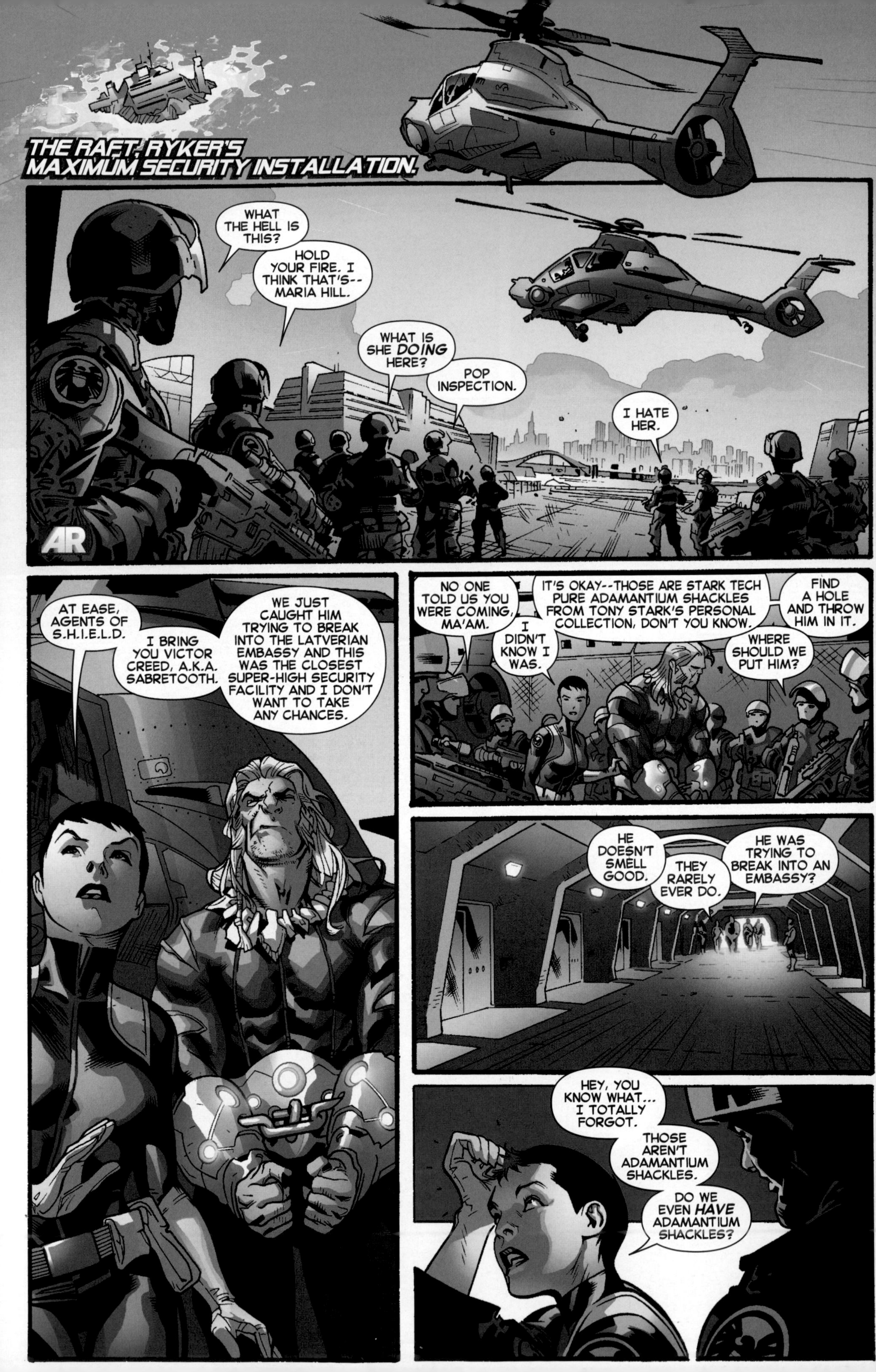
THE RAFT, RYKER'S MAXIMUM SECURITY INSTALLATION.
WHAT THE HELL IS THIS?
HOLD YOUR FIRE. I THINK THAT'S-- MARIA HILL.
WHAT IS SHE DOING HERE?
POP INSPECTION.
I HATE HER.
AT EASE, AGENTS OF S.H.I.E.L.D.
I BRING YOU VICTOR CREED, A.K.A. SABRETOOTH.
WE JUST CAUGHT HIM TRYING TO BREAK INTO THE LATVERIAN EMBASSY AND THIS WAS THE CLOSEST SUPER-HIGH SECURITY FACILITY AND I DON'T WANT TO TAKE ANY CHANCES.
NO ONE TOLD US YOU WERE COMING, MA'AM.
I DIDN'T KNOW I WAS.
IT'S OKAY--THOSE ARE STARK TECH PURE ADAMANTIUM SHACKLES FROM TONY STARK'S PERSONAL COLLECTION, DON'T YOU KNOW.
WHERE SHOULD WE PUT HIM?
FIND A HOLE AND THROW HIM IN IT.
HE DOESN'T SMELL GOOD.
THEY RARELY EVER DO.
HE WAS TRYING TO BREAK INTO AN EMBASSY?
HEY, YOU KNOW WHAT... I TOTALLY FORGOT.
THOSE AREN'T ADAMANTIUM SHACKLES.
DO WE EVEN HAVE ADAMANTIUM SHACKLES?

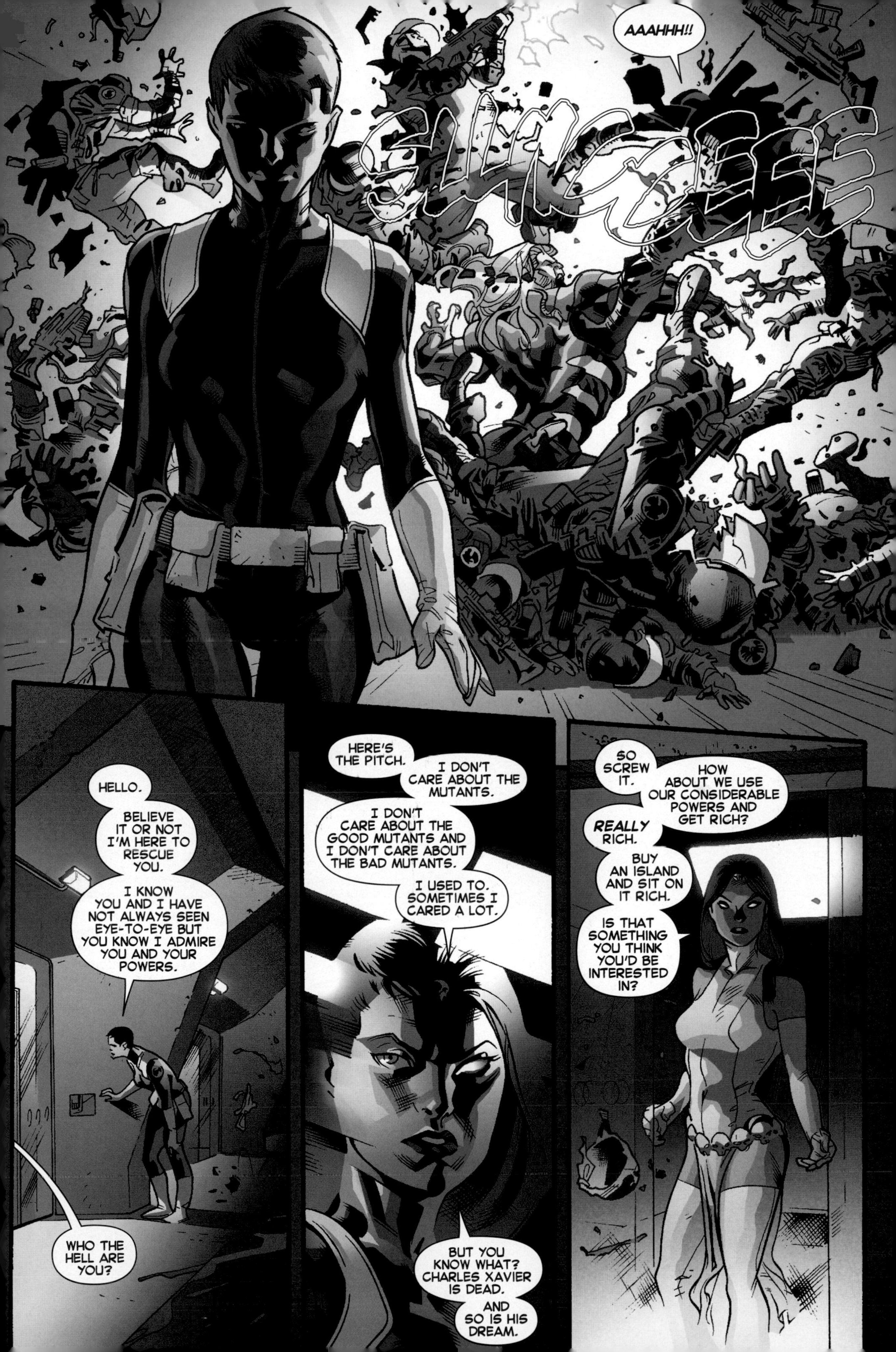
AAAHHH!!
HELLO.
BELIEVE IT OR NOT I'M HERE TO RESCUE YOU.
I KNOW YOU AND I HAVE NOT ALWAYS SEEN EYE-TO-EYE BUT YOU KNOW I ADMIRE YOU AND YOUR POWERS.
WHO THE HELL ARE YOU?
HERE'S THE PITCH.
I DON'T CARE ABOUT THE MUTANTS.
I DON'T CARE ABOUT THE GOOD MUTANTS AND I DON'T CARE ABOUT THE BAD MUTANTS.
I USED TO. SOMETIMES I CARED A LOT.
BUT YOU KNOW WHAT? CHARLES XAVIER IS DEAD.
AND SO IS HIS DREAM.
SO SCREW IT.
HOW ABOUT WE USE OUR CONSIDERABLE POWERS AND GET RICH?
REALLY RICH.
BUY AN ISLAND AND SIT ON IT RICH.
IS THAT SOMETHING YOU THINK YOU'D BE INTERESTED IN?

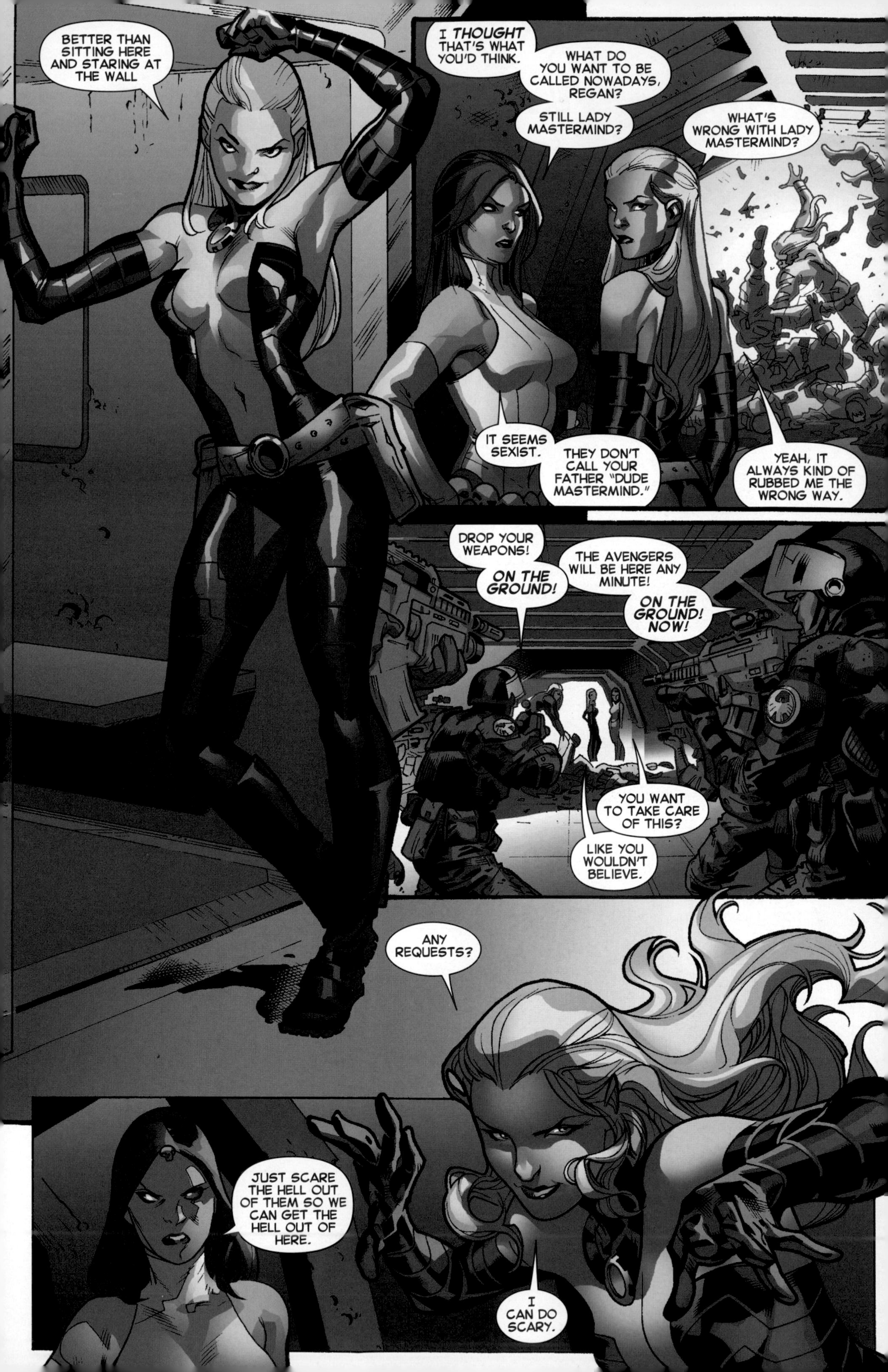

BETTER THAN SITTING HERE AND STARING AT THE WALL
I *THOUGHT* THAT'S WHAT YOU'D THINK.
WHAT DO YOU WANT TO BE CALLED NOWADAYS, REGAN?
STILL LADY MASTERMIND?
WHAT'S WRONG WITH LADY MASTERMIND?
IT SEEMS SEXIST.
THEY DON'T CALL YOUR FATHER "DUDE MASTERMIND."
YEAH, IT ALWAYS KIND OF RUBBED ME THE WRONG WAY.
DROP YOUR WEAPONS! *ON THE GROUND!*
THE AVENGERS WILL BE HERE ANY MINUTE! *ON THE GROUND! NOW!*
YOU WANT TO TAKE CARE OF THIS?
LIKE YOU WOULDN'T BELIEVE.
ANY REQUESTS?
JUST SCARE THE HELL OUT OF THEM SO WE CAN GET THE HELL OUT OF HERE.
I CAN DO SCARY.

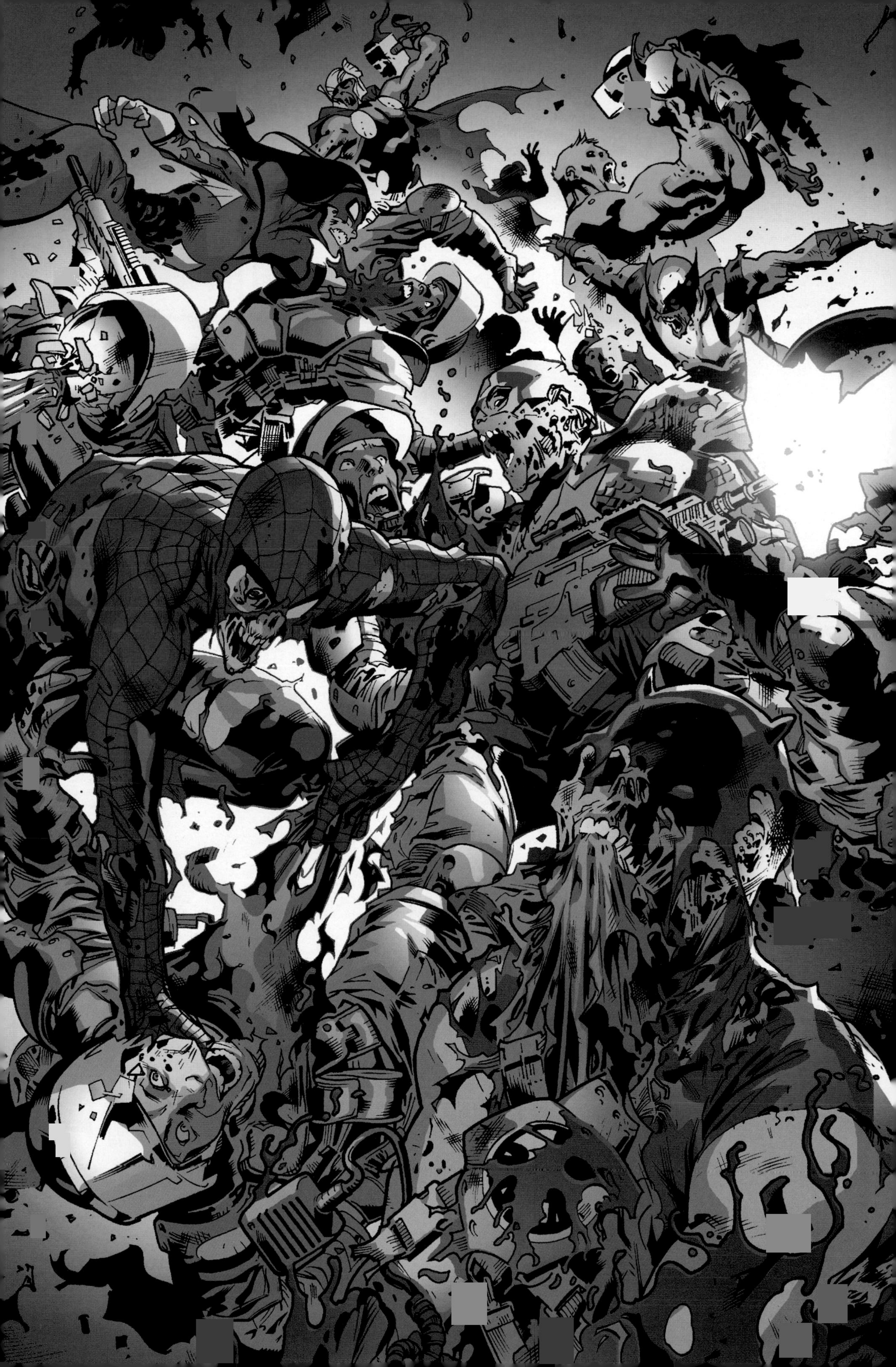

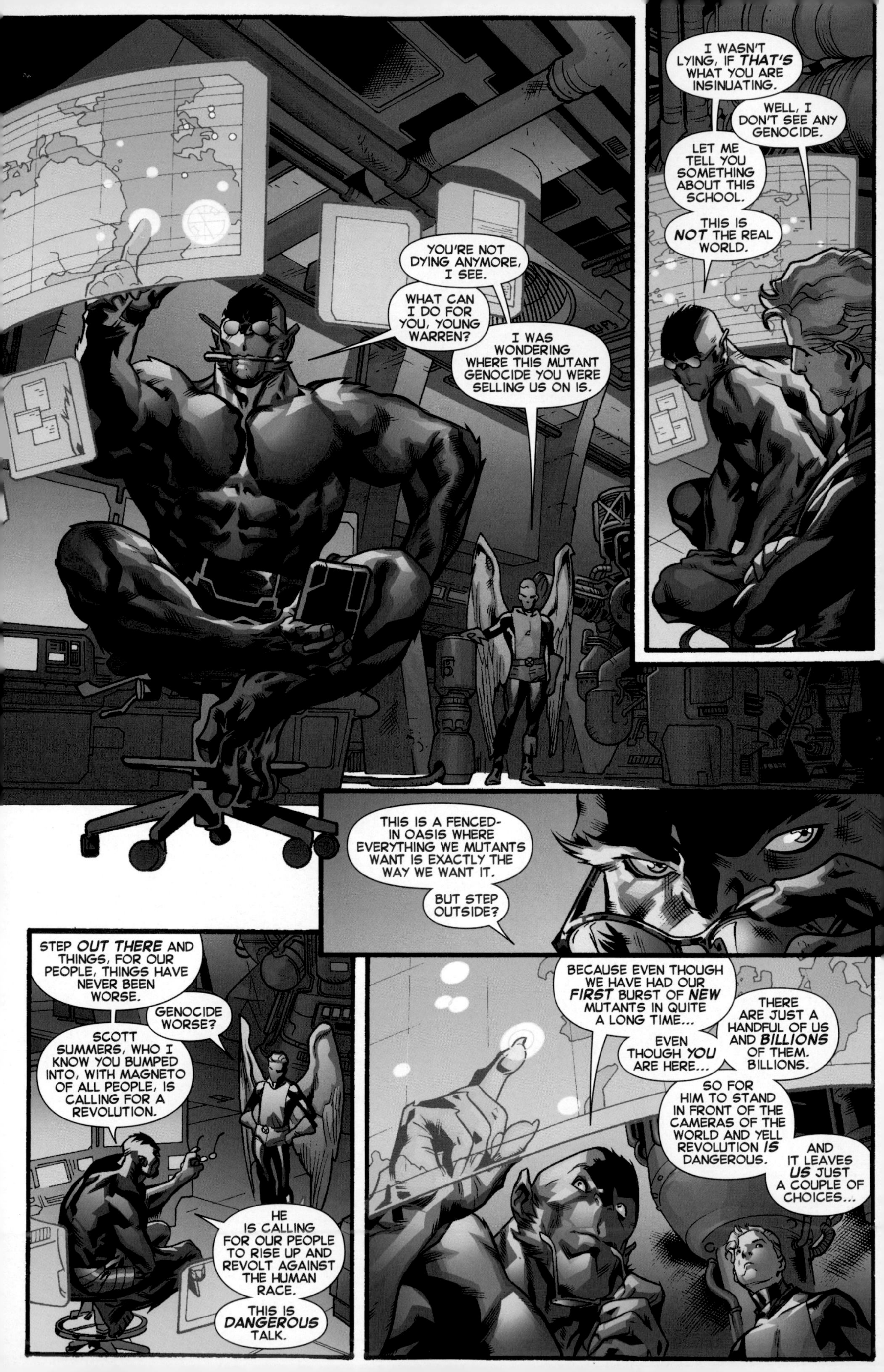
YOU'RE NOT DYING ANYMORE, I SEE.
WHAT CAN I DO FOR YOU, YOUNG WARREN?
I WAS WONDERING WHERE THIS MUTANT GENOCIDE YOU WERE SELLING US ON IS.
I WASN'T LYING, IF THAT'S WHAT YOU ARE INSINUATING.
WELL, I DON'T SEE ANY GENOCIDE.
LET ME TELL YOU SOMETHING ABOUT THIS SCHOOL.
THIS IS NOT THE REAL WORLD.
THIS IS A FENCED-IN OASIS WHERE EVERYTHING WE MUTANTS WANT IS EXACTLY THE WAY WE WANT IT.
BUT STEP OUTSIDE?
STEP OUT THERE AND THINGS, FOR OUR PEOPLE, THINGS HAVE NEVER BEEN WORSE.
GENOCIDE WORSE?
SCOTT SUMMERS, WHO I KNOW YOU BUMPED INTO, WITH MAGNETO OF ALL PEOPLE, IS CALLING FOR A REVOLUTION.
HE IS CALLING FOR OUR PEOPLE TO RISE UP AND REVOLT AGAINST THE HUMAN RACE.
THIS IS DANGEROUS TALK.
BECAUSE EVEN THOUGH WE HAVE HAD OUR FIRST BURST OF NEW MUTANTS IN QUITE A LONG TIME...
EVEN THOUGH YOU ARE HERE...
THERE ARE JUST A HANDFUL OF US AND BILLIONS OF THEM. BILLIONS.
SO FOR HIM TO STAND IN FRONT OF THE CAMERAS OF THE WORLD AND YELL REVOLUTION IS DANGEROUS.
AND IT LEAVES US JUST A COUPLE OF CHOICES...

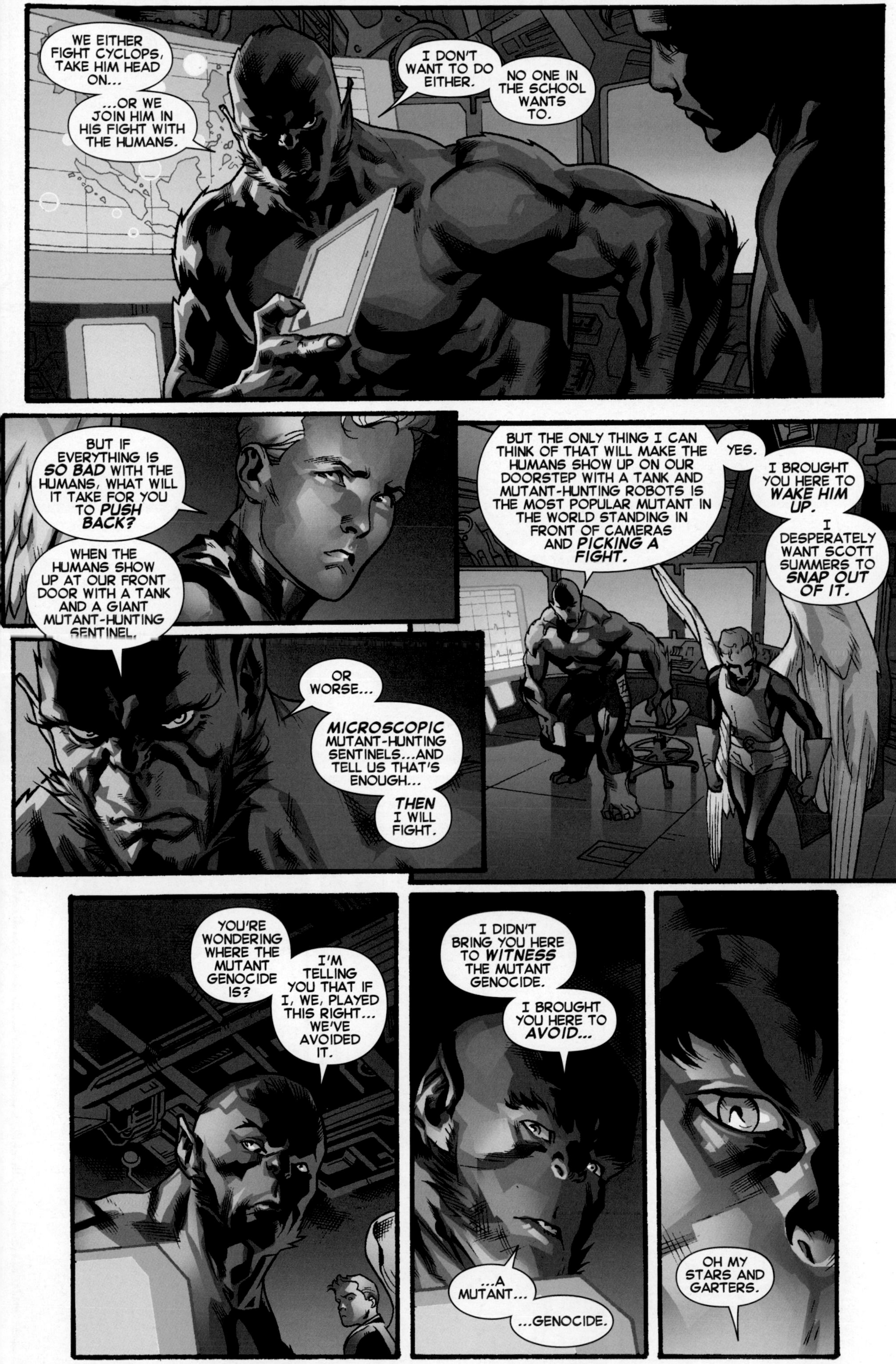
WE EITHER FIGHT CYCLOPS, TAKE HIM HEAD ON...
...OR WE JOIN HIM IN HIS FIGHT WITH THE HUMANS.
I DON'T WANT TO DO EITHER.
NO ONE IN THE SCHOOL WANTS TO.
BUT IF EVERYTHING IS SO BAD WITH THE HUMANS, WHAT WILL IT TAKE FOR YOU TO PUSH BACK?
WHEN THE HUMANS SHOW UP AT OUR FRONT DOOR WITH A TANK AND A GIANT MUTANT-HUNTING SENTINEL.
OR WORSE...
MICROSCOPIC MUTANT-HUNTING SENTINELS...AND TELL US THAT'S ENOUGH...
THEN I WILL FIGHT.
BUT THE ONLY THING I CAN THINK OF THAT WILL MAKE THE HUMANS SHOW UP ON OUR DOORSTEP WITH A TANK AND MUTANT-HUNTING ROBOTS IS THE MOST POPULAR MUTANT IN THE WORLD STANDING IN FRONT OF CAMERAS AND PICKING A FIGHT.
YES.
I BROUGHT YOU HERE TO WAKE HIM UP.
I DESPERATELY WANT SCOTT SUMMERS TO SNAP OUT OF IT.
YOU'RE WONDERING WHERE THE MUTANT GENOCIDE IS?
I'M TELLING YOU THAT IF I, WE, PLAYED THIS RIGHT... WE'VE AVOIDED IT.
I DIDN'T BRING YOU HERE TO WITNESS THE MUTANT GENOCIDE.
I BROUGHT YOU HERE TO AVOID...
...A MUTANT...
...GENOCIDE.
OH MY STARS AND GARTERS.

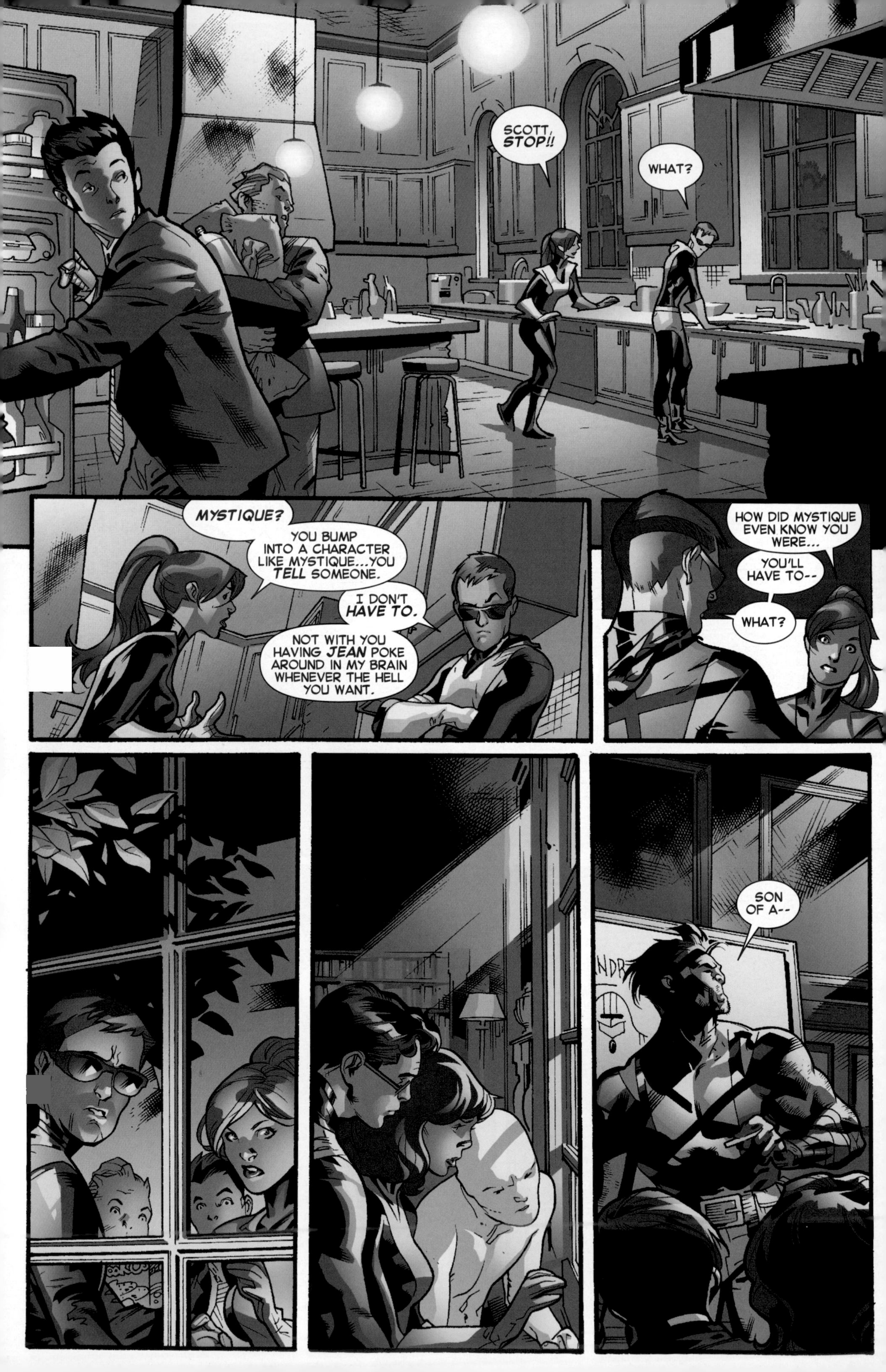
SCOTT, STOP!!
WHAT?
MYSTIQUE?
YOU BUMP INTO A CHARACTER LIKE MYSTIQUE...YOU TELL SOMEONE.
I DON'T HAVE TO.
NOT WITH YOU HAVING JEAN POKE AROUND IN MY BRAIN WHENEVER THE HELL YOU WANT.
HOW DID MYSTIQUE EVEN KNOW YOU WERE...
YOU'LL HAVE TO--
WHAT?
SON OF A--

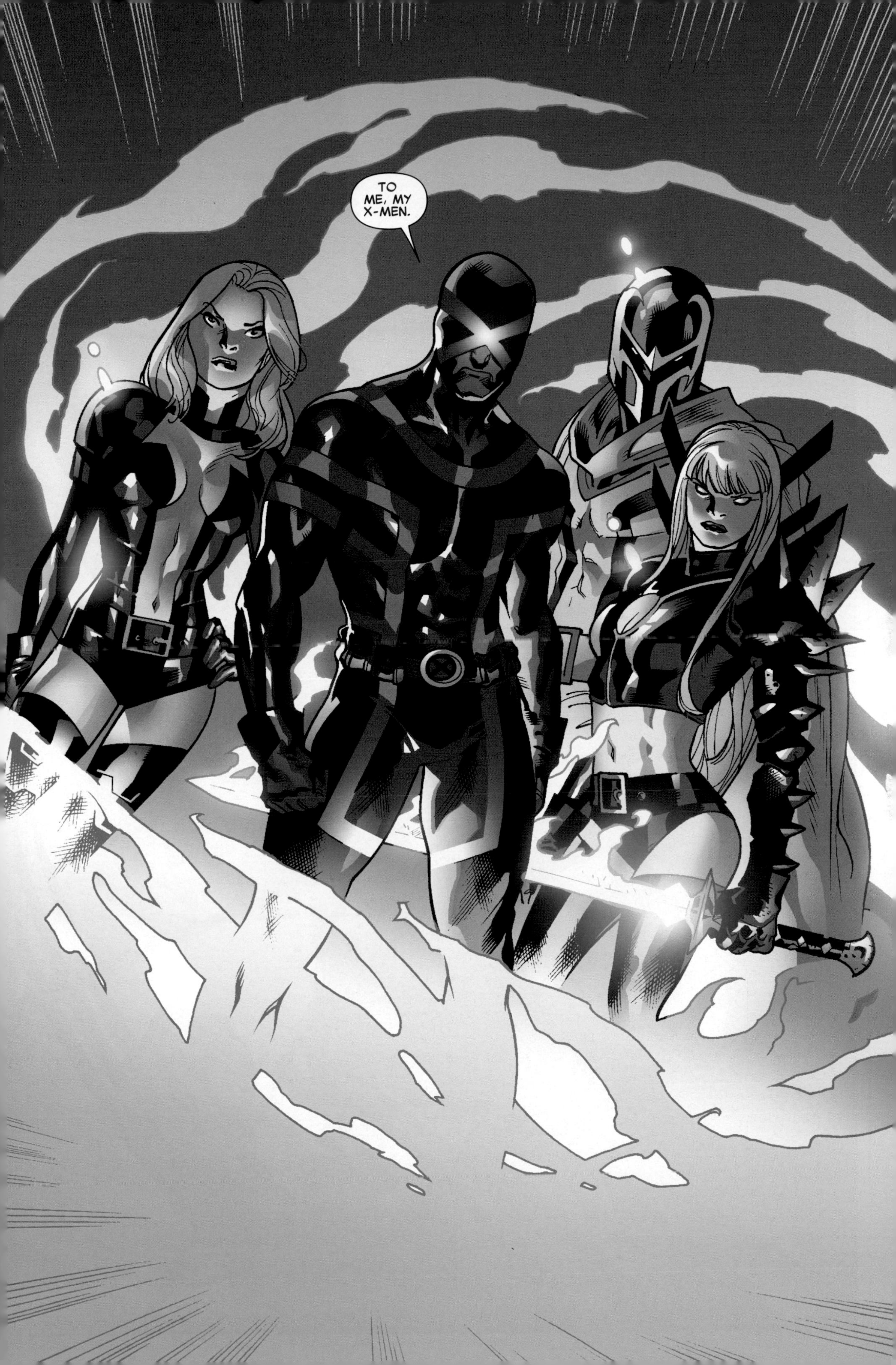
TO ME, MY X-MEN.

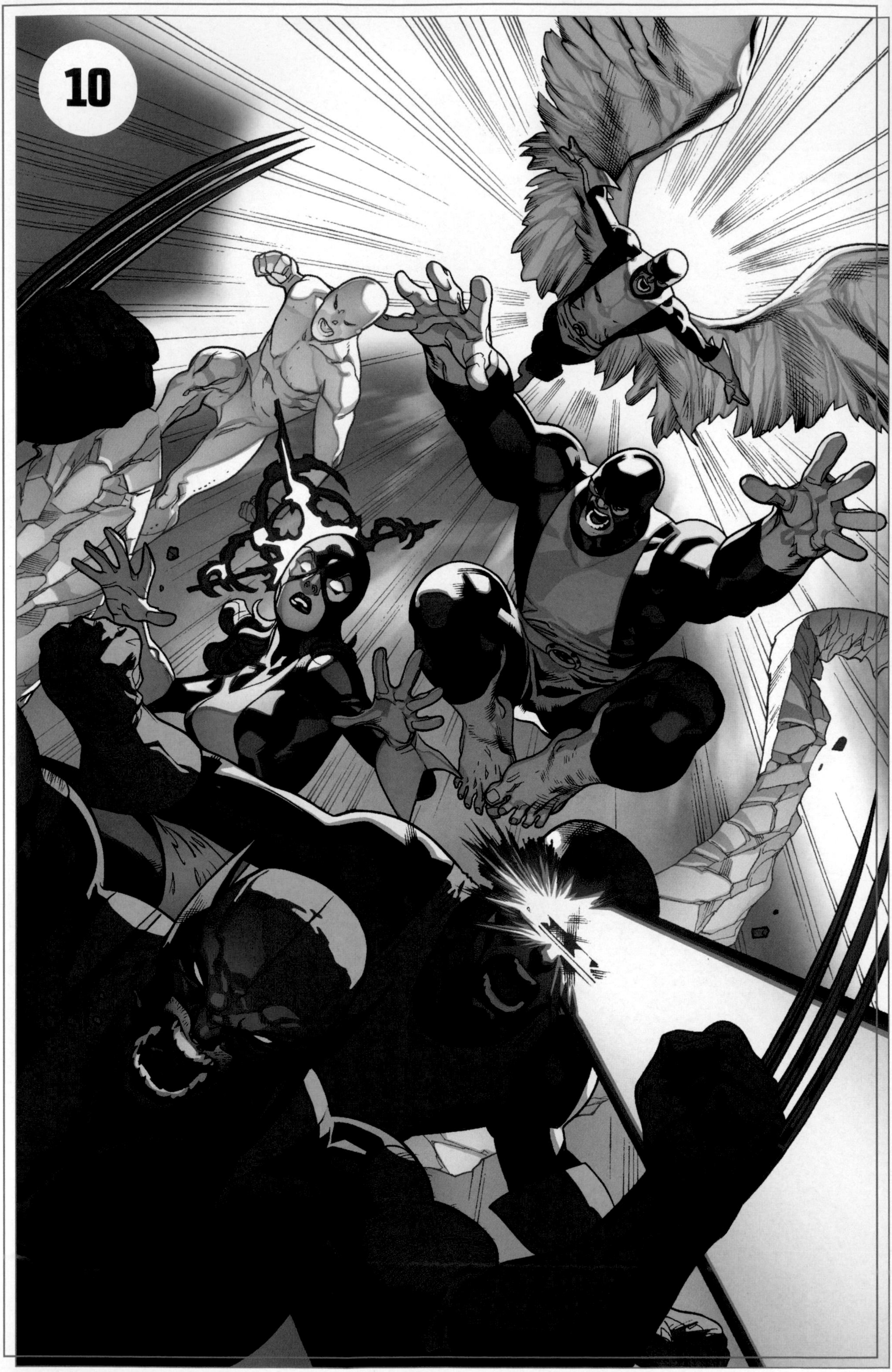
10

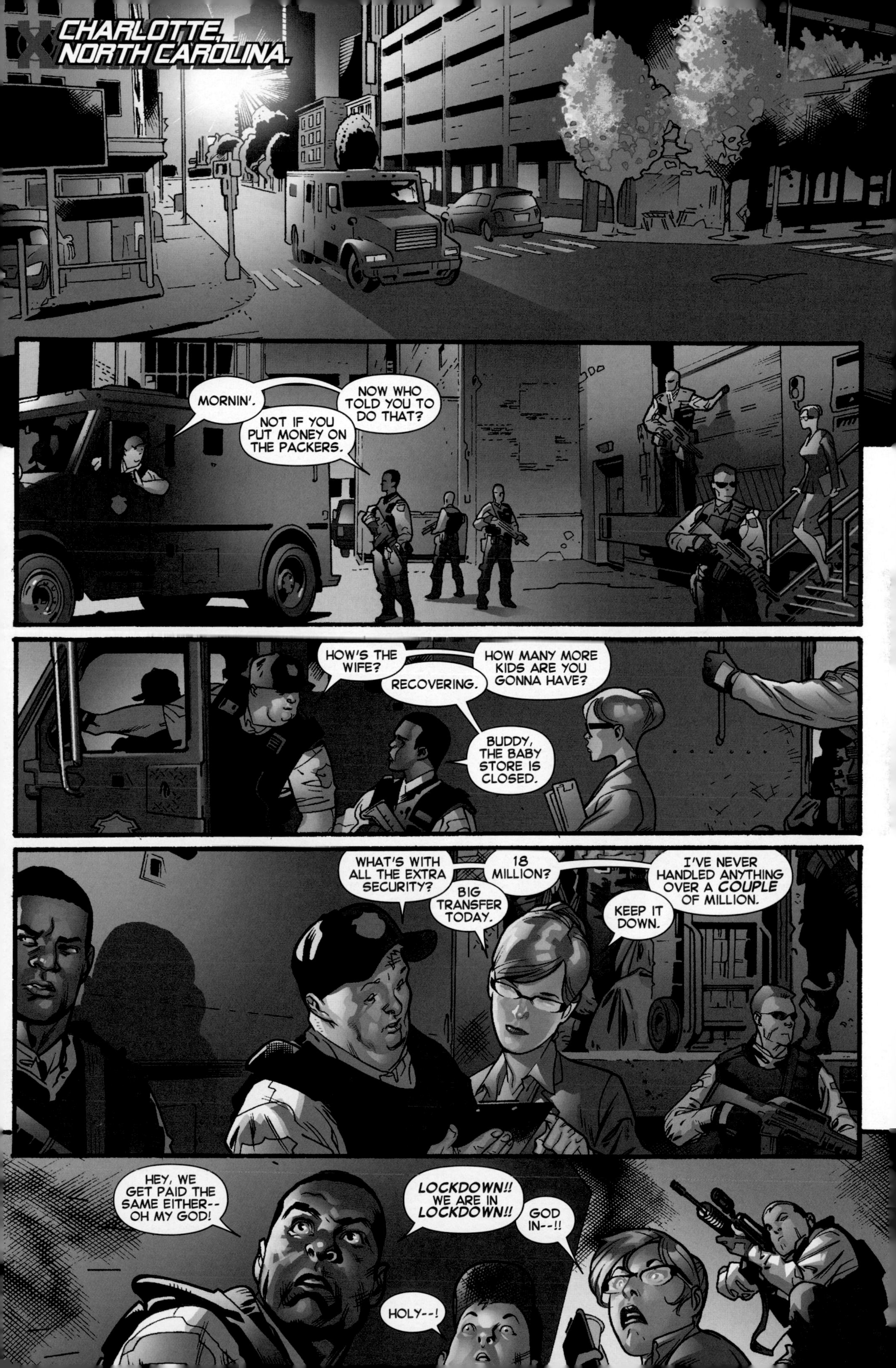
CHARLOTTE, NORTH CAROLINA.
MORNIN'.
NOW WHO TOLD YOU TO DO THAT?
NOT IF YOU PUT MONEY ON THE PACKERS.
HOW'S THE WIFE?
RECOVERING.
HOW MANY MORE KIDS ARE YOU GONNA HAVE?
BUDDY, THE BABY STORE IS CLOSED.
WHAT'S WITH ALL THE EXTRA SECURITY?
BIG TRANSFER TODAY.
18 MILLION?
I'VE NEVER HANDLED ANYTHING OVER A COUPLE OF MILLION.
KEEP IT DOWN.
HEY, WE GET PAID THE SAME EITHER-- OH MY GOD!
LOCKDOWN!! WE ARE IN LOCKDOWN!!
GOD IN--!!
HOLY--!

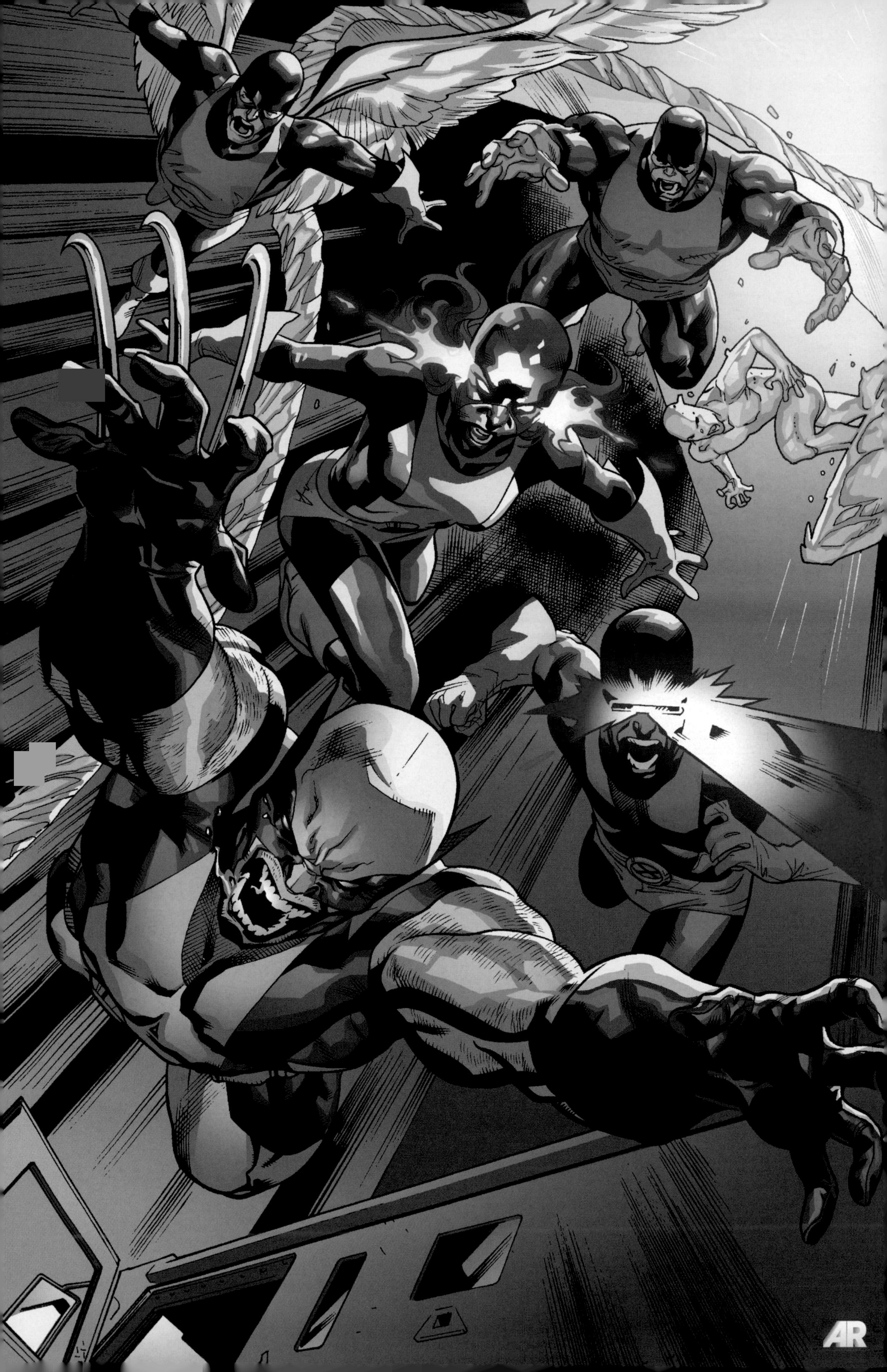

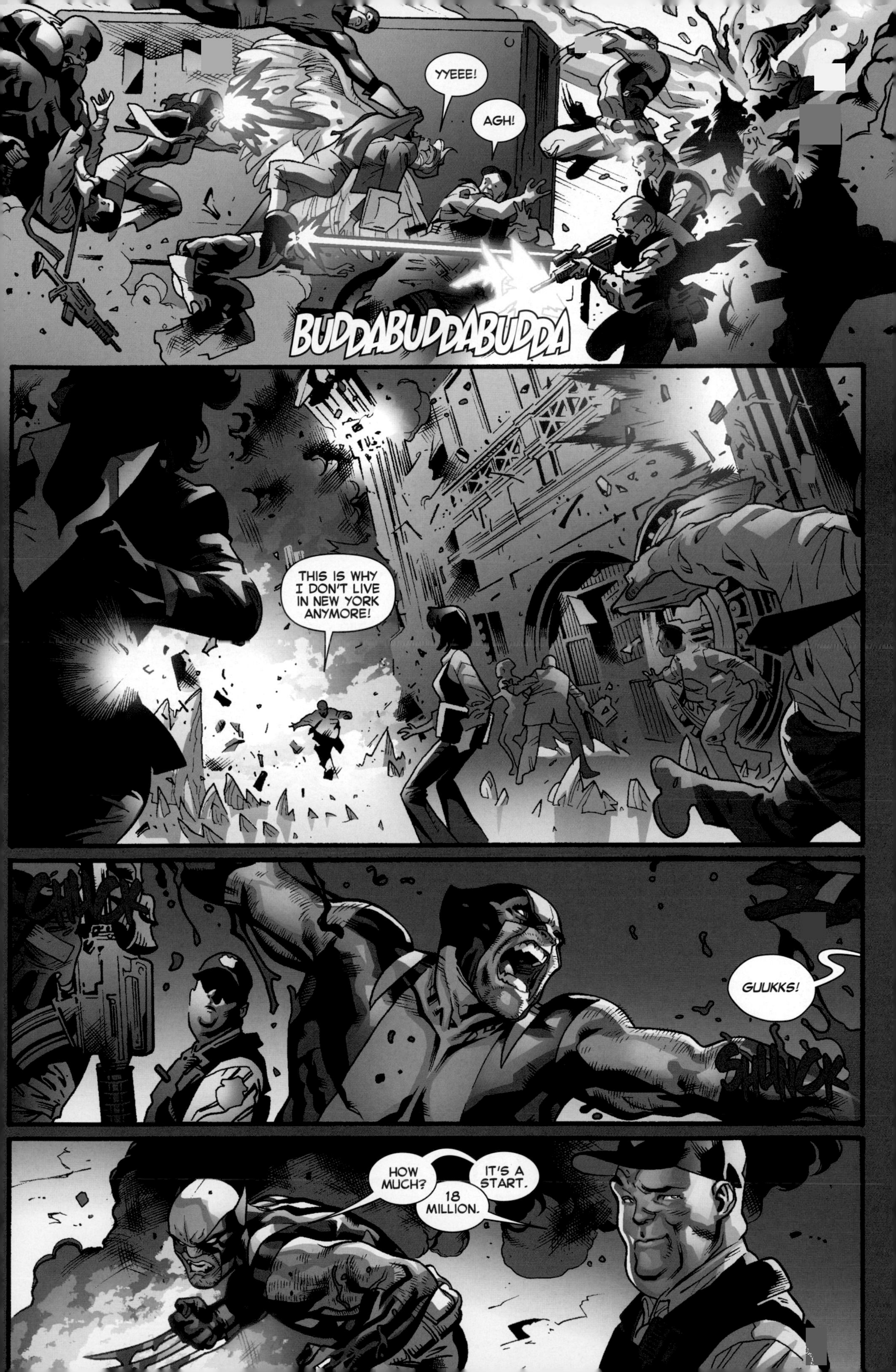
YYEEE!
AGH!
BUDDABUDDABUDDA
THIS IS WHY I DON'T LIVE IN NEW YORK ANYMORE!
GUUKKS!
SHUNK
HOW MUCH?
18 MILLION.
IT'S A START.

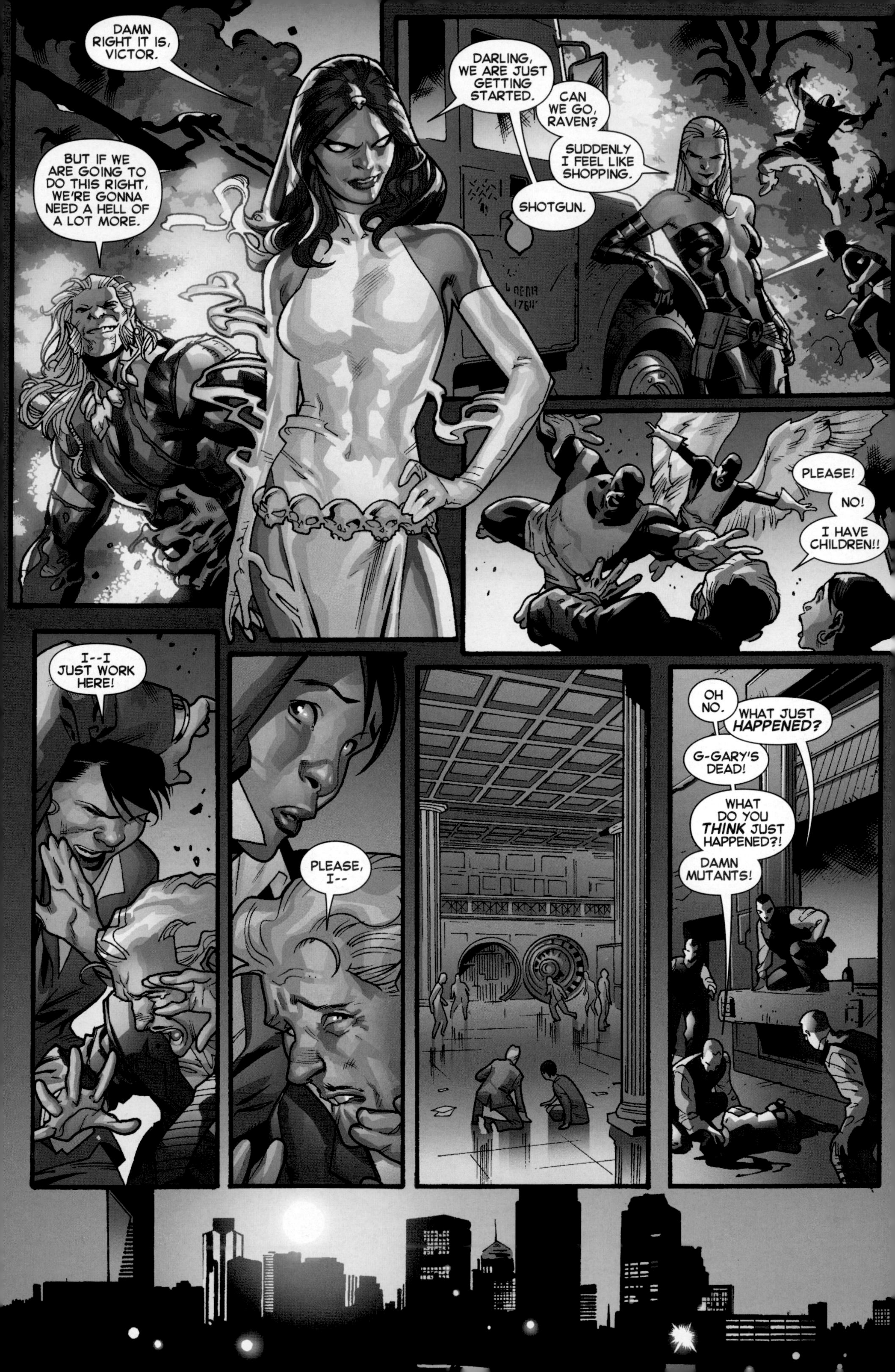
DAMN RIGHT IT IS, VICTOR.
BUT IF WE ARE GOING TO DO THIS RIGHT, WE'RE GONNA NEED A HELL OF A LOT MORE.
DARLING, WE ARE JUST GETTING STARTED.
CAN WE GO, RAVEN?
SUDDENLY I FEEL LIKE SHOPPING.
SHOTGUN.
PLEASE!
NO!
I HAVE CHILDREN!!
I--I JUST WORK HERE!
PLEASE, I--
OH NO.
WHAT JUST HAPPENED?
G-GARY'S DEAD!
WHAT DO YOU THINK JUST HAPPENED?!
DAMN MUTANTS!

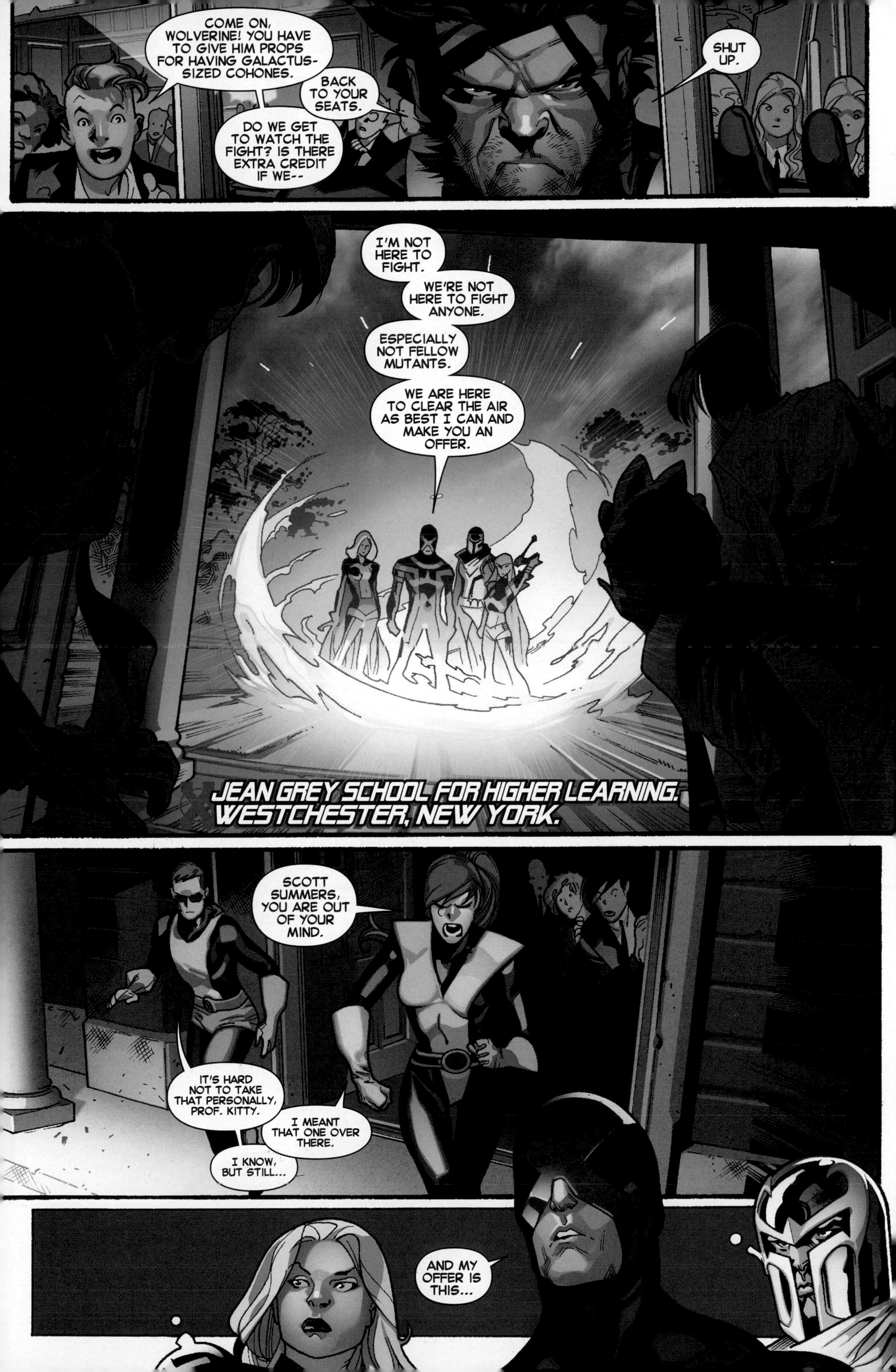
COME ON, WOLVERINE! YOU HAVE TO GIVE HIM PROPS FOR HAVING GALACTUS-SIZED COHONES.
DO WE GET TO WATCH THE FIGHT? IS THERE EXTRA CREDIT IF WE--
BACK TO YOUR SEATS.
SHUT UP.
I'M NOT HERE TO FIGHT.
WE'RE NOT HERE TO FIGHT ANYONE.
ESPECIALLY NOT FELLOW MUTANTS.
WE ARE HERE TO CLEAR THE AIR AS BEST I CAN AND MAKE YOU AN OFFER.
JEAN GREY SCHOOL FOR HIGHER LEARNING. WESTCHESTER, NEW YORK.
SCOTT SUMMERS, YOU ARE OUT OF YOUR MIND.
IT'S HARD NOT TO TAKE THAT PERSONALLY, PROF. KITTY.
I MEANT THAT ONE OVER THERE.
I KNOW, BUT STILL...
AND MY OFFER IS THIS...

IF IT INVOLVES YOU STANDING TRIAL FOR THE *MURDER* OF CHARLES XAVIER...

WE ACCEPT.

WE ALL HAVE MANY SINS TO ATONE FOR, BOBBY.

BUT ONLY *ONE* OF US MURDERED CHARLES XAVIER IN FRONT OF THE REST OF US.

YES.

IT DID HAPPEN IN FRONT OF *MANY* OF YOU.

BUT DO YOU THINK THAT'S *EXACTLY* WHAT HAPPENED?

DO YOU THINK THAT I *SET OUT* TO MURDER A MAN WHO *RAISED* ME?

THE MAN WHO PICKED ME UP OUT OF THE GUTTER AND TAUGHT ME *EVERYTHING* I KNOW.

THE MAN WHO GAVE MY LIFE *PURPOSE* AND *MEANING* BEYOND ANYTHING I THOUGHT I WOULD EVER HAVE...

YOU THINK THAT, IN CONTROL OF MYSELF, I *MURDERED* THIS MAN?

IF YOU THINK THAT I MURDERED CHARLES XAVIER OF MY OWN FREE WILL...

THEN HERE I AM...

KILL ME HERE.

I COULDN'T LIVE WITH THE THOUGHT THAT ANY OF YOU EVEN *THINK* THAT IS WHO I AM.

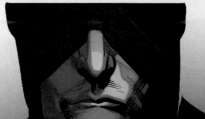

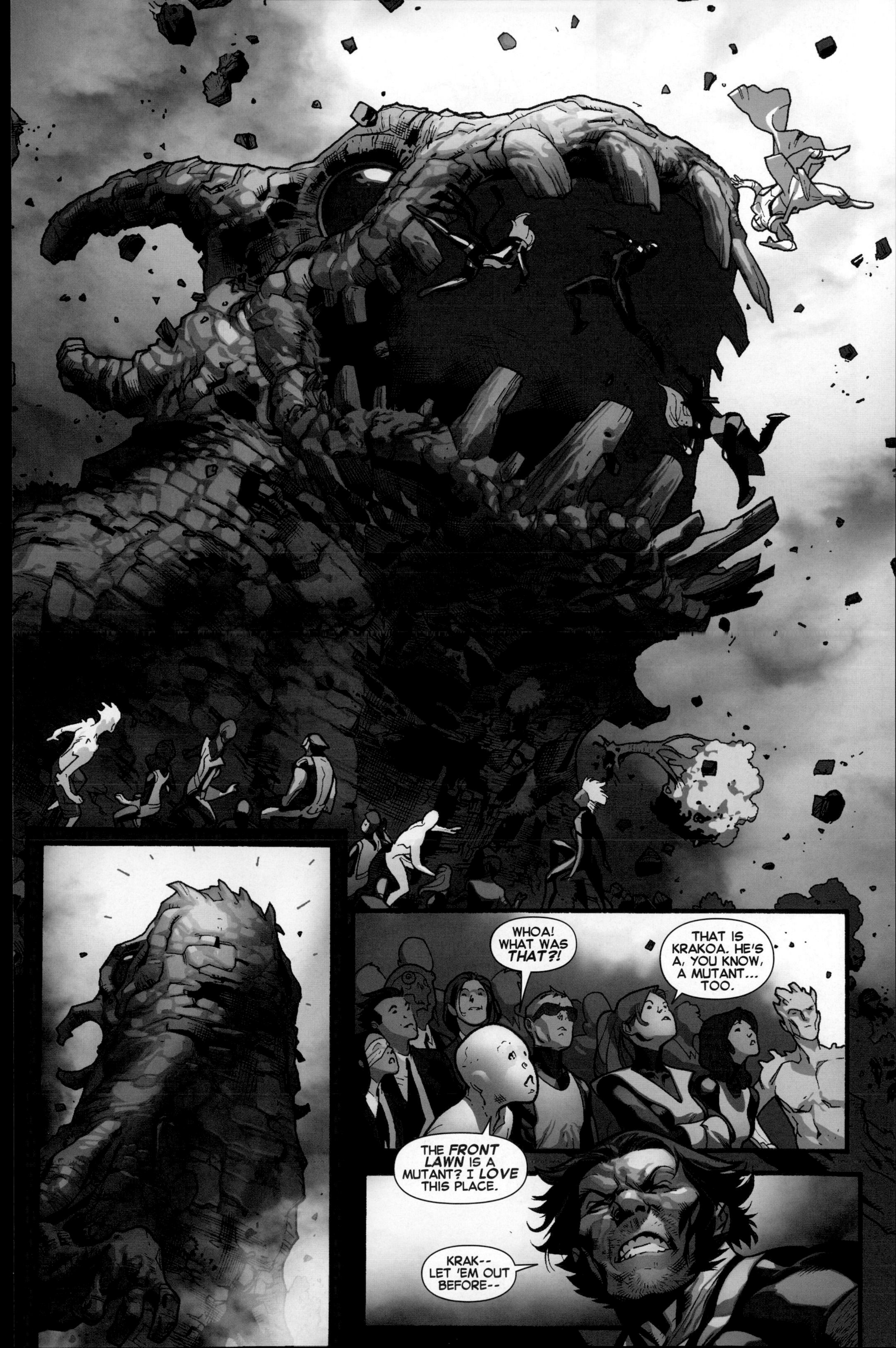
WHOA! WHAT WAS THAT?!
THAT IS KRAKOA. HE'S A, YOU KNOW, A MUTANT... TOO.
THE FRONT LAWN IS A MUTANT? I LOVE THIS PLACE.
KRAK-- LET 'EM OUT BEFORE--

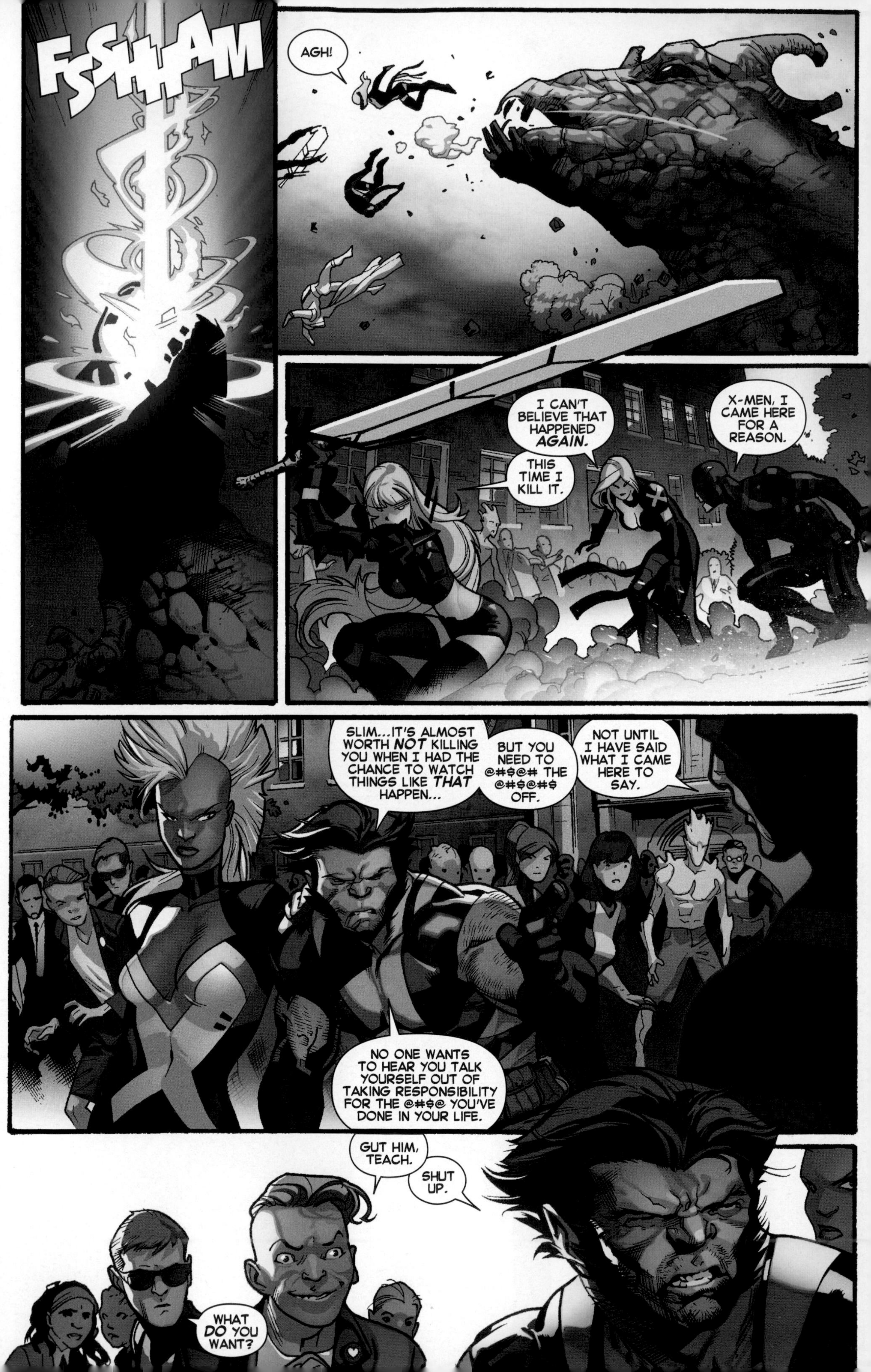
FSSHHAM
AGH!
I CAN'T BELIEVE THAT HAPPENED AGAIN.
THIS TIME I KILL IT.
X-MEN, I CAME HERE FOR A REASON.
SLIM... IT'S ALMOST WORTH NOT KILLING YOU WHEN I HAD THE CHANCE TO WATCH THINGS LIKE THAT HAPPEN...
BUT YOU NEED TO @#$@# THE @#$@#$ OFF.
NOT UNTIL I HAVE SAID WHAT I CAME HERE TO SAY.
NO ONE WANTS TO HEAR YOU TALK YOURSELF OUT OF TAKING RESPONSIBILITY FOR THE @#$@ YOU'VE DONE IN YOUR LIFE.
GUT HIM, TEACH.
SHUT UP.
WHAT DO YOU WANT?

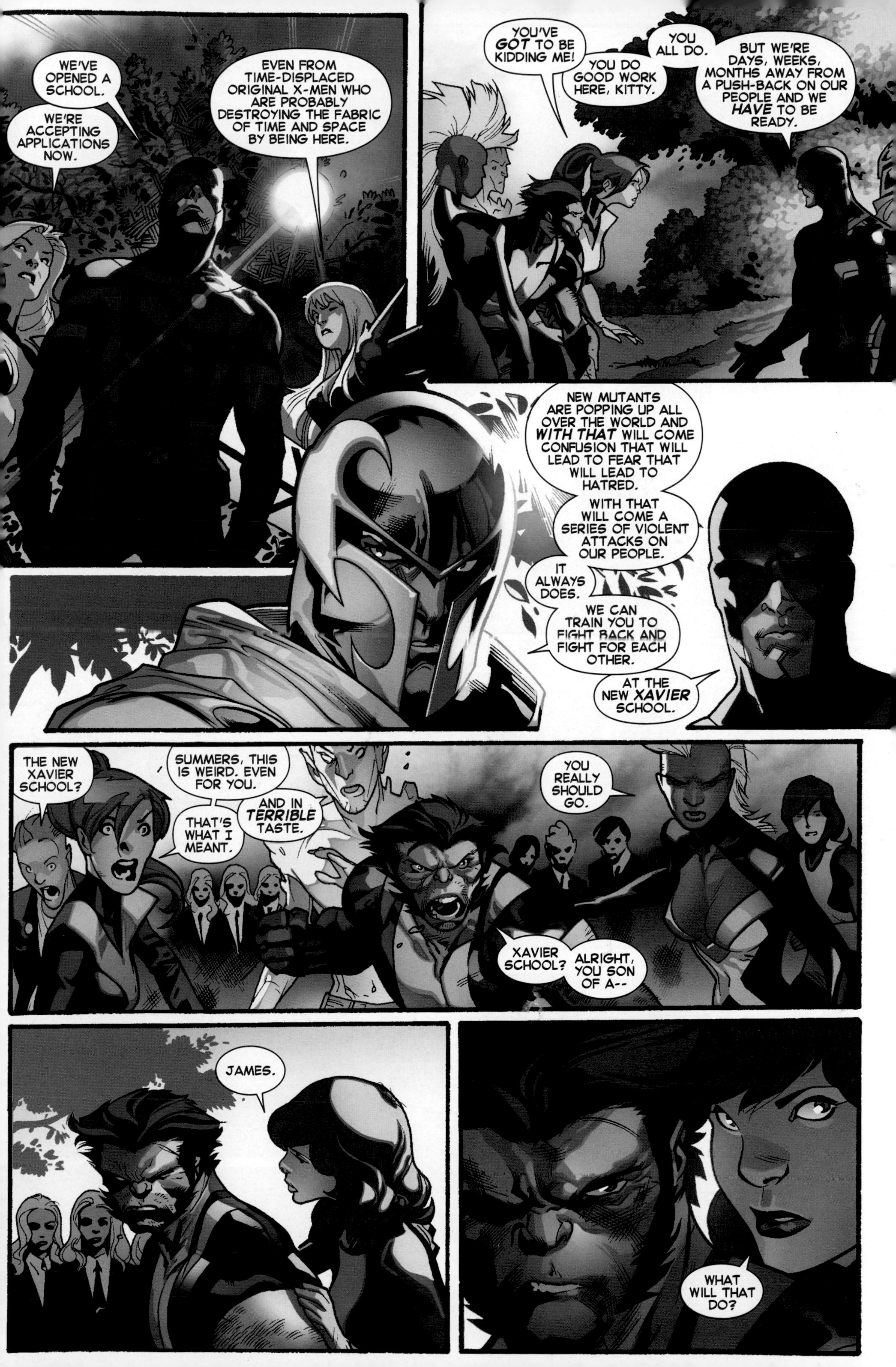
WE'VE OPENED A SCHOOL.
WE'RE ACCEPTING APPLICATIONS NOW.
EVEN FROM TIME-DISPLACED ORIGINAL X-MEN WHO ARE PROBABLY DESTROYING THE FABRIC OF TIME AND SPACE BY BEING HERE.
YOU'VE GOT TO BE KIDDING ME!
YOU DO GOOD WORK HERE, KITTY.
YOU ALL DO.
BUT WE'RE DAYS, WEEKS, MONTHS AWAY FROM A PUSH-BACK ON OUR PEOPLE AND WE HAVE TO BE READY.
NEW MUTANTS ARE POPPING UP ALL OVER THE WORLD AND WITH THAT WILL COME CONFUSION THAT WILL LEAD TO FEAR THAT WILL LEAD TO HATRED.
WITH THAT WILL COME A SERIES OF VIOLENT ATTACKS ON OUR PEOPLE.
IT ALWAYS DOES.
WE CAN TRAIN YOU TO FIGHT BACK AND FIGHT FOR EACH OTHER.
AT THE NEW XAVIER SCHOOL.
THE NEW XAVIER SCHOOL?
SUMMERS, THIS IS WEIRD. EVEN FOR YOU.
THAT'S WHAT I MEANT.
AND IN TERRIBLE TASTE.
YOU REALLY SHOULD GO.
XAVIER SCHOOL?
ALRIGHT, YOU SON OF A--
JAMES.
WHAT WILL THAT DO?

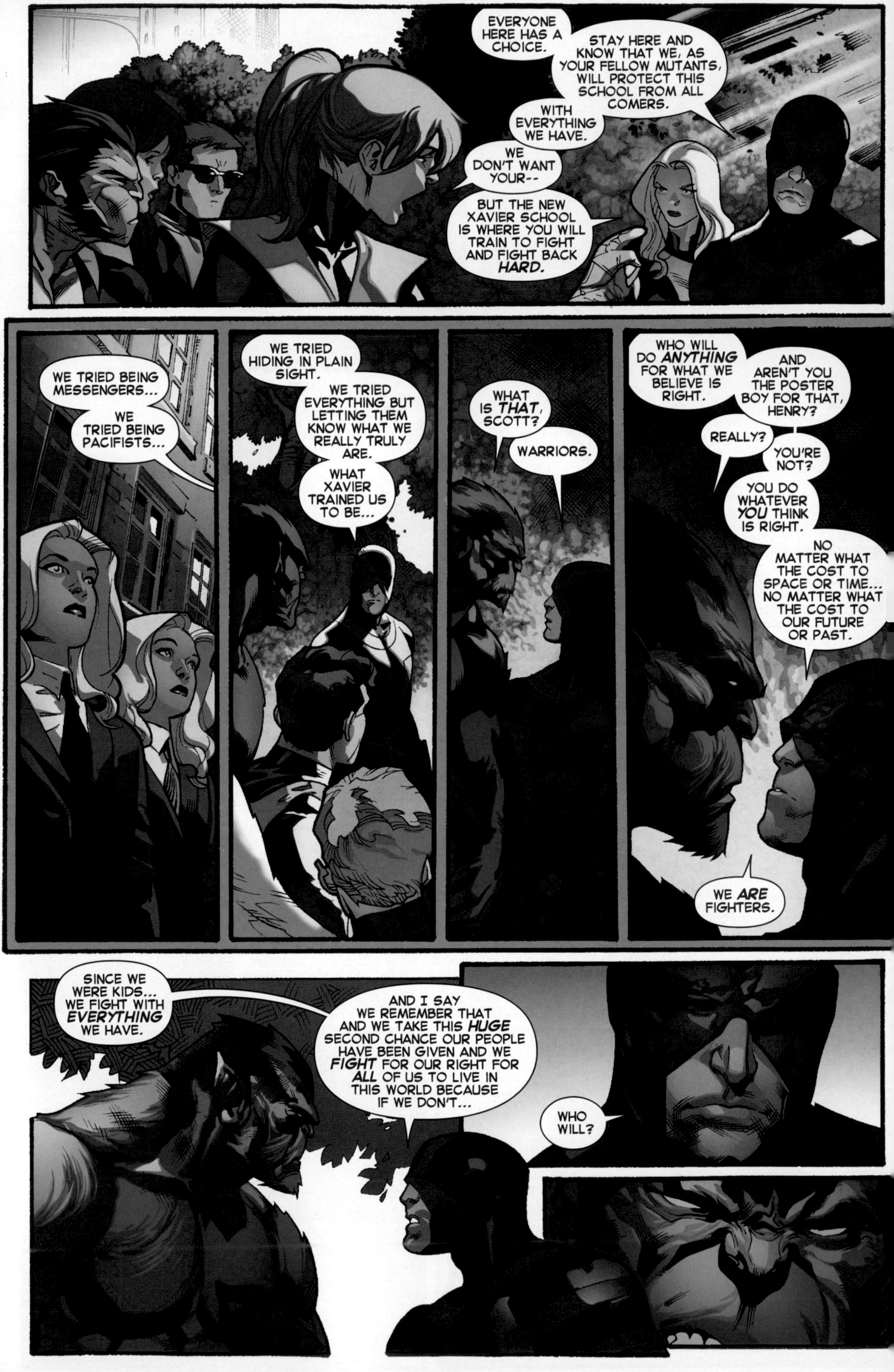
EVERYONE HERE HAS A CHOICE.
STAY HERE AND KNOW THAT WE, AS YOUR FELLOW MUTANTS, WILL PROTECT THIS SCHOOL FROM ALL COMERS.
WITH EVERYTHING WE HAVE.
WE DON'T WANT YOUR--
BUT THE NEW XAVIER SCHOOL IS WHERE YOU WILL TRAIN TO FIGHT AND FIGHT BACK *HARD.*
WE TRIED BEING MESSENGERS...
WE TRIED BEING PACIFISTS...
WE TRIED HIDING IN PLAIN SIGHT.
WE TRIED EVERYTHING BUT LETTING THEM KNOW WHAT WE REALLY TRULY ARE.
WHAT XAVIER TRAINED US TO BE...
WHAT IS *THAT*, SCOTT?
WARRIORS.
WHO WILL DO *ANYTHING* FOR WHAT WE BELIEVE IS RIGHT.
AND AREN'T YOU THE POSTER BOY FOR THAT, HENRY?
REALLY?
YOU'RE NOT?
YOU DO WHATEVER *YOU* THINK IS RIGHT.
NO MATTER WHAT THE COST TO SPACE OR TIME... NO MATTER WHAT THE COST TO OUR FUTURE OR PAST.
WE *ARE* FIGHTERS.
SINCE WE WERE KIDS... WE FIGHT WITH *EVERYTHING* WE HAVE.
AND I SAY WE REMEMBER THAT AND WE TAKE THIS *HUGE* SECOND CHANCE OUR PEOPLE HAVE BEEN GIVEN AND WE *FIGHT* FOR OUR RIGHT FOR *ALL* OF US TO LIVE IN THIS WORLD BECAUSE IF WE DON'T...
WHO WILL?

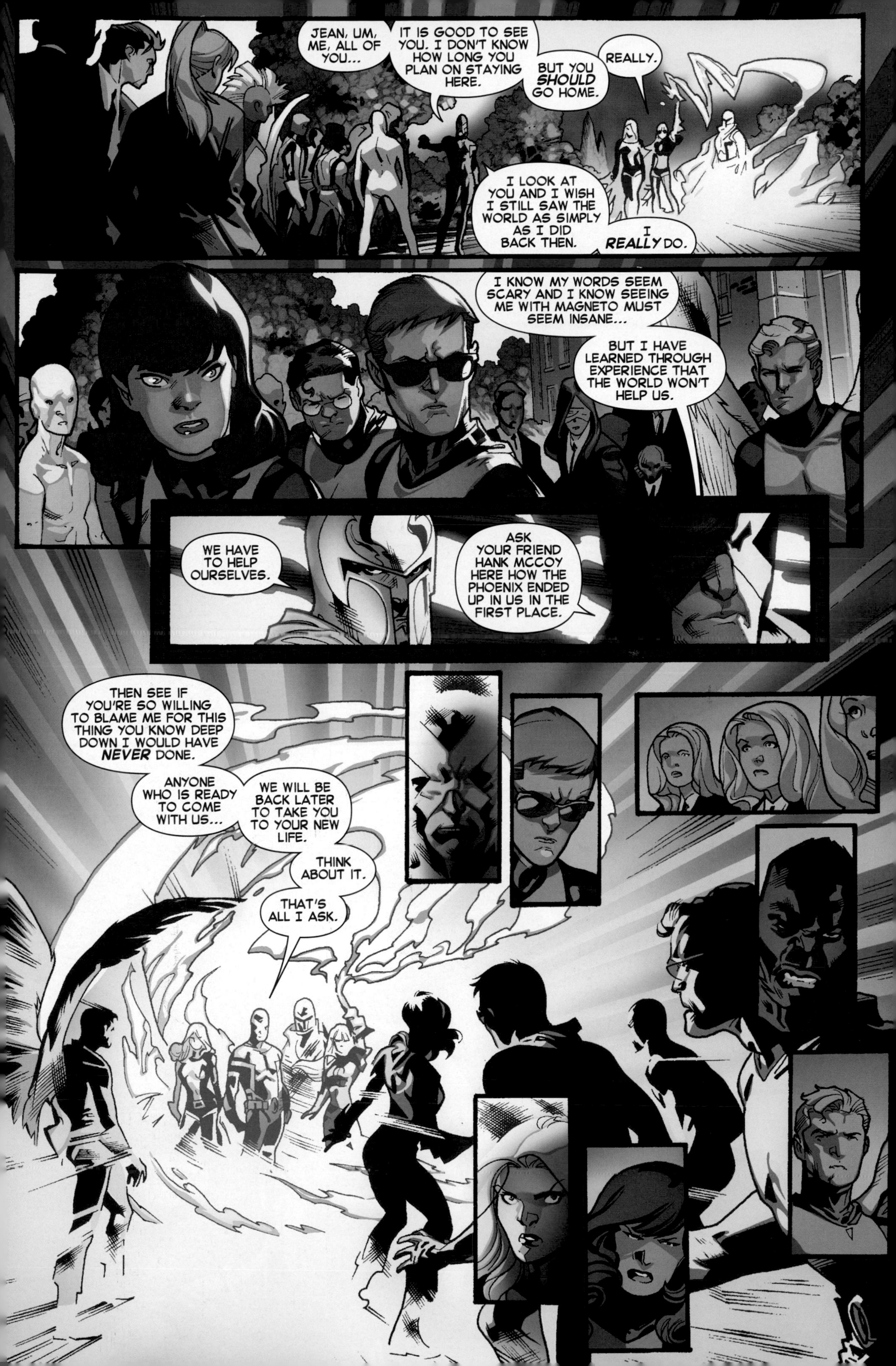
JEAN, UM, ME, ALL OF YOU...
IT IS GOOD TO SEE YOU. I DON'T KNOW HOW LONG YOU PLAN ON STAYING HERE.
BUT YOU SHOULD GO HOME.
REALLY.
I LOOK AT YOU AND I WISH I STILL SAW THE WORLD AS SIMPLY AS I DID BACK THEN.
I REALLY DO.
I KNOW MY WORDS SEEM SCARY AND I KNOW SEEING ME WITH MAGNETO MUST SEEM INSANE...
BUT I HAVE LEARNED THROUGH EXPERIENCE THAT THE WORLD WON'T HELP US.
WE HAVE TO HELP OURSELVES.
ASK YOUR FRIEND HANK MCCOY HERE HOW THE PHOENIX ENDED UP IN US IN THE FIRST PLACE.
THEN SEE IF YOU'RE SO WILLING TO BLAME ME FOR THIS THING YOU KNOW DEEP DOWN I WOULD HAVE NEVER DONE.
ANYONE WHO IS READY TO COME WITH US...
WE WILL BE BACK LATER TO TAKE YOU TO YOUR NEW LIFE.
THINK ABOUT IT.
THAT'S ALL I ASK.

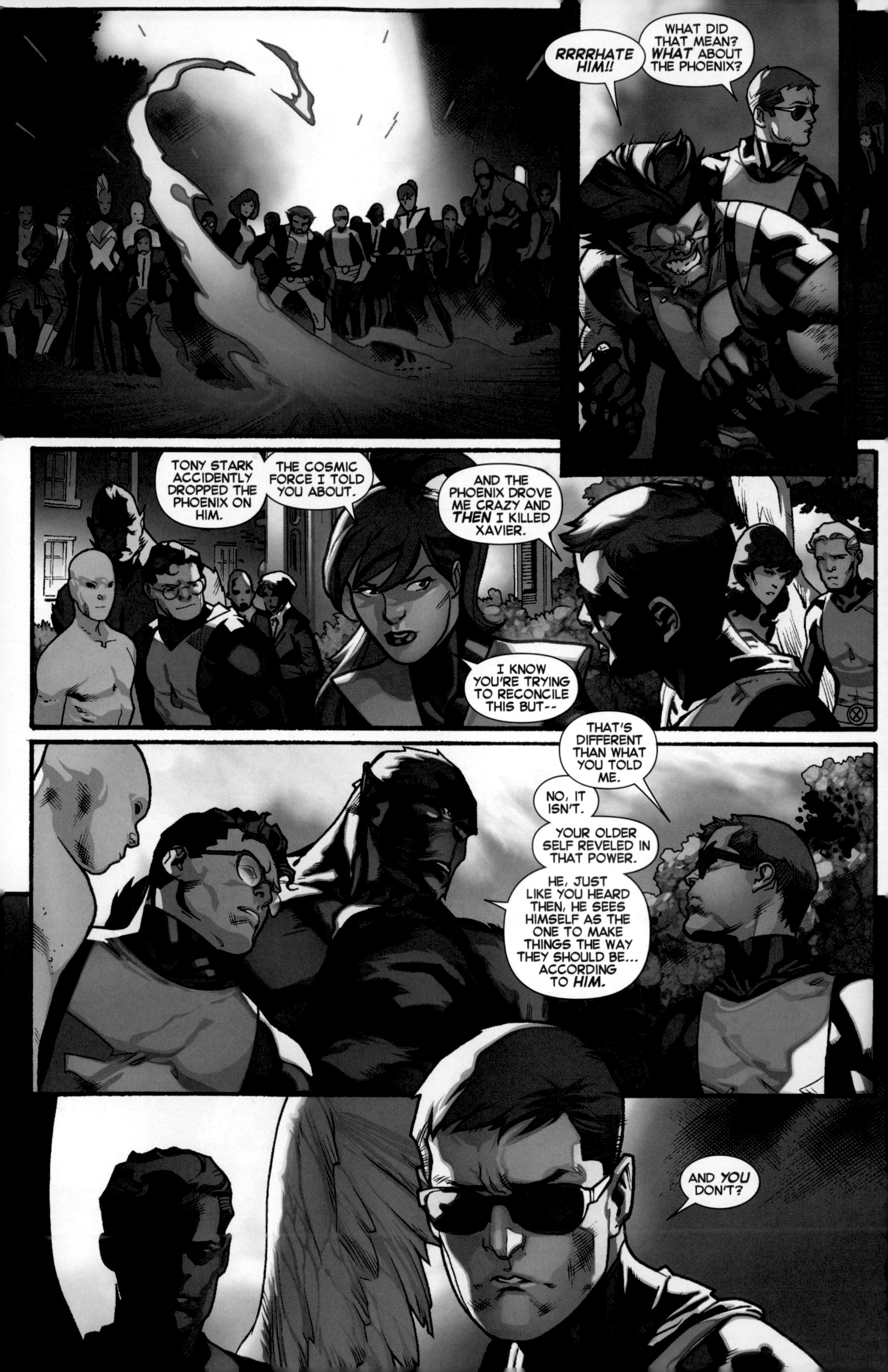
RRRRHATE HIM!!
WHAT DID THAT MEAN? WHAT ABOUT THE PHOENIX?
TONY STARK ACCIDENTLY DROPPED THE PHOENIX ON HIM.
THE COSMIC FORCE I TOLD YOU ABOUT.
AND THE PHOENIX DROVE ME CRAZY AND THEN I KILLED XAVIER.
I KNOW YOU'RE TRYING TO RECONCILE THIS BUT--
THAT'S DIFFERENT THAN WHAT YOU TOLD ME.
NO, IT ISN'T.
YOUR OLDER SELF REVELED IN THAT POWER.
HE, JUST LIKE YOU HEARD THEN, HE SEES HIMSELF AS THE ONE TO MAKE THINGS THE WAY THEY SHOULD BE... ACCORDING TO HIM.
AND YOU DON'T?

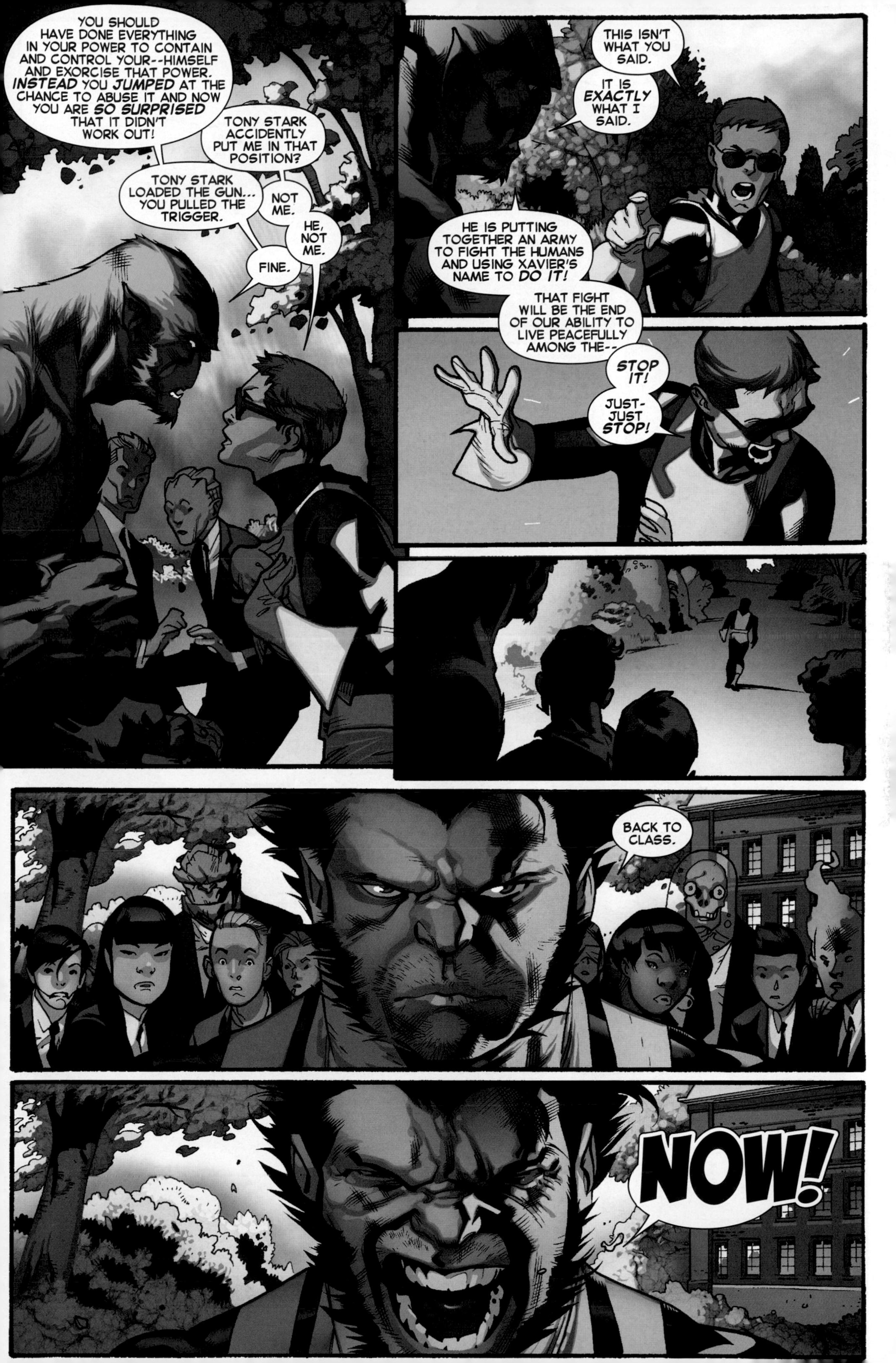
YOU SHOULD HAVE DONE EVERYTHING IN YOUR POWER TO CONTAIN AND CONTROL YOUR--HIMSELF AND EXORCISE THAT POWER. INSTEAD YOU JUMPED AT THE CHANCE TO ABUSE IT AND NOW YOU ARE SO SURPRISED THAT IT DIDN'T WORK OUT!
TONY STARK ACCIDENTLY PUT ME IN THAT POSITION?
TONY STARK LOADED THE GUN... YOU PULLED THE TRIGGER.
NOT ME.
HE, NOT ME.
FINE.
THIS ISN'T WHAT YOU SAID.
IT IS EXACTLY WHAT I SAID.
HE IS PUTTING TOGETHER AN ARMY TO FIGHT THE HUMANS AND USING XAVIER'S NAME TO DO IT!
THAT FIGHT WILL BE THE END OF OUR ABILITY TO LIVE PEACEFULLY AMONG THE--
STOP IT!
JUST-JUST STOP!
BACK TO CLASS.
NOW!

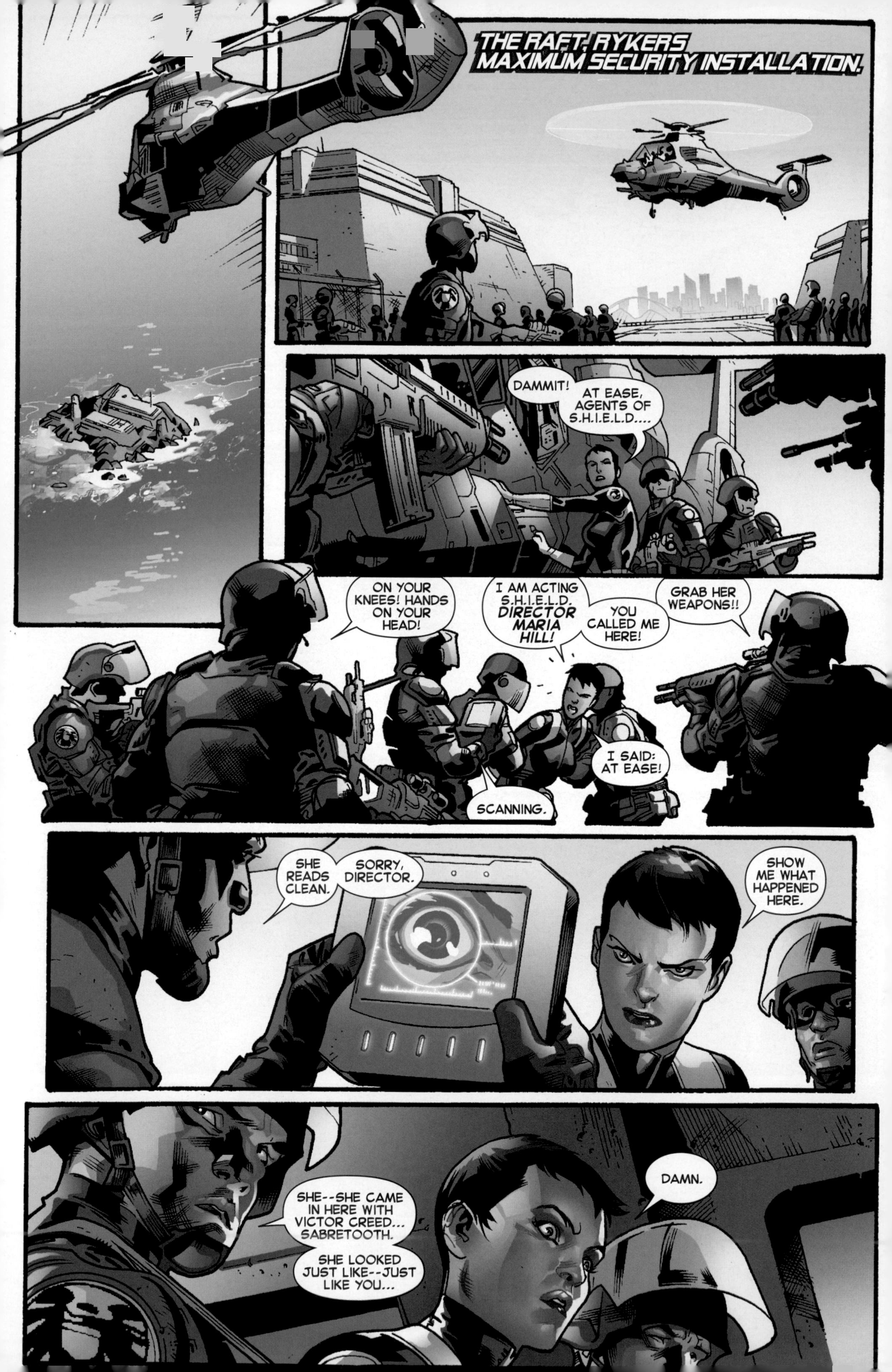

THE RAFT, RYKERS MAXIMUM SECURITY INSTALLATION.
DAMMIT!
AT EASE, AGENTS OF S.H.I.E.L.D....
ON YOUR KNEES! HANDS ON YOUR HEAD!
I AM ACTING S.H.I.E.L.D. DIRECTOR MARIA HILL!
YOU CALLED ME HERE!
GRAB HER WEAPONS!!
I SAID: AT EASE!
SCANNING.
SHE READS CLEAN.
SORRY, DIRECTOR.
SHOW ME WHAT HAPPENED HERE.
SHE--SHE CAME IN HERE WITH VICTOR CREED... SABRETOOTH.
SHE LOOKED JUST LIKE--JUST LIKE YOU...
DAMN.

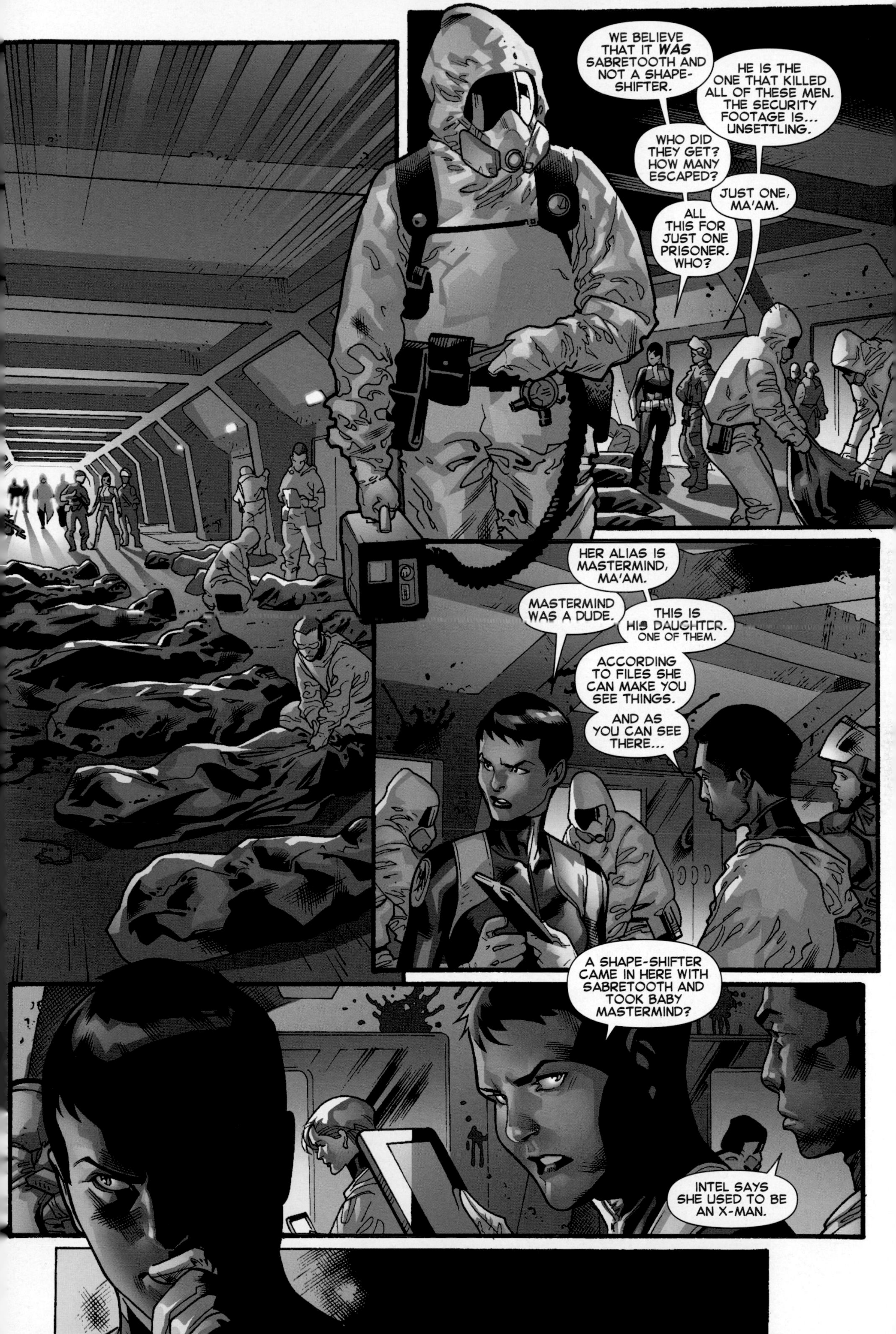

WE BELIEVE THAT IT WAS SABRETOOTH AND NOT A SHAPE-SHIFTER.
HE IS THE ONE THAT KILLED ALL OF THESE MEN. THE SECURITY FOOTAGE IS... UNSETTLING.
WHO DID THEY GET? HOW MANY ESCAPED?
JUST ONE, MA'AM.
ALL THIS FOR JUST ONE PRISONER. WHO?
HER ALIAS IS MASTERMIND, MA'AM.
MASTERMIND WAS A DUDE.
THIS IS HIS DAUGHTER. ONE OF THEM.
ACCORDING TO FILES SHE CAN MAKE YOU SEE THINGS.
AND AS YOU CAN SEE THERE...
A SHAPE-SHIFTER CAME IN HERE WITH SABRETOOTH AND TOOK BABY MASTERMIND?
INTEL SAYS SHE USED TO BE AN X-MAN.

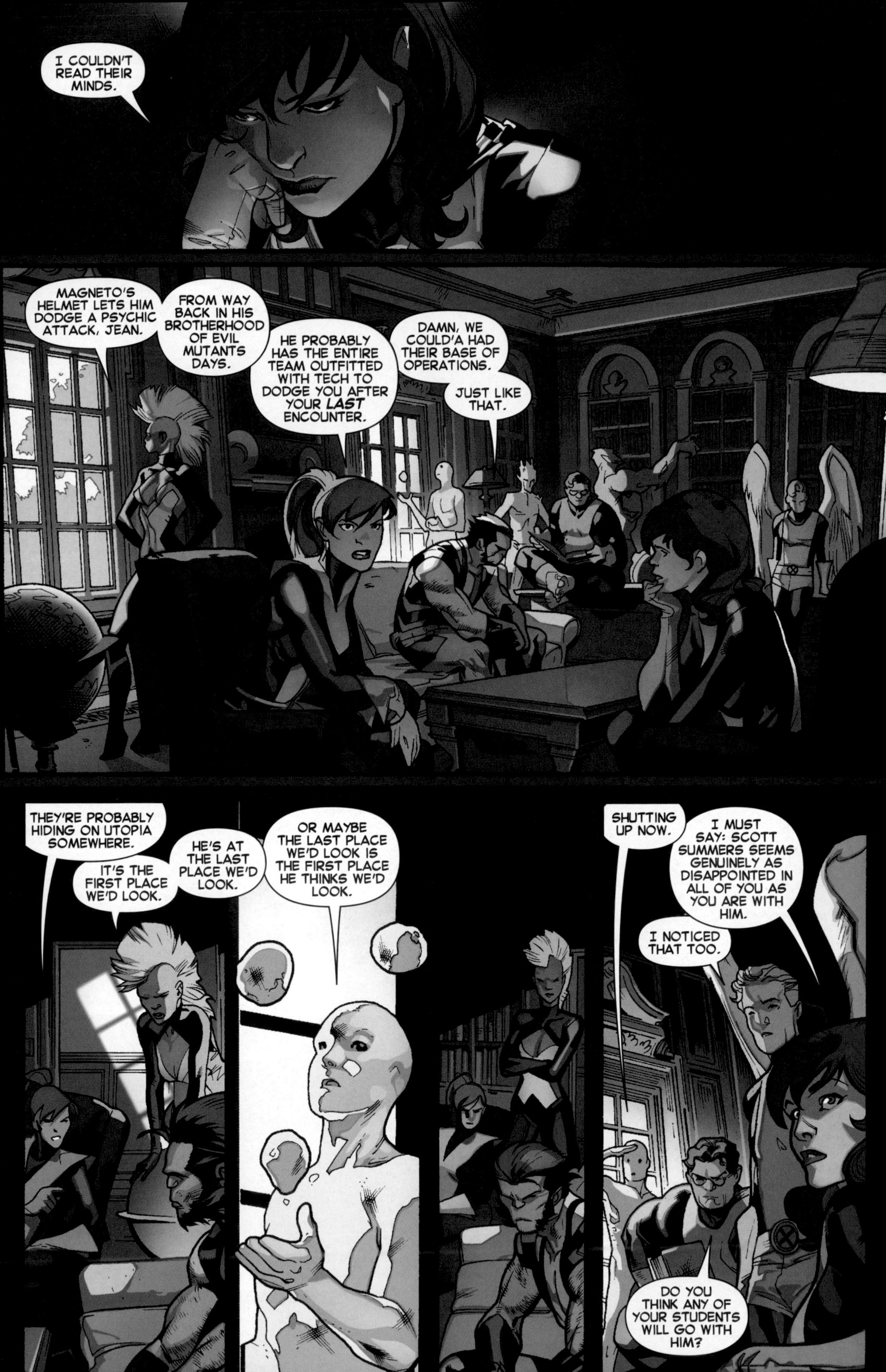
I COULDN'T READ THEIR MINDS.
MAGNETO'S HELMET LETS HIM DODGE A PSYCHIC ATTACK, JEAN.
FROM WAY BACK IN HIS BROTHERHOOD OF EVIL MUTANTS DAYS.
HE PROBABLY HAS THE ENTIRE TEAM OUTFITTED WITH TECH TO DODGE YOU AFTER YOUR LAST ENCOUNTER.
DAMN, WE COULD'A HAD THEIR BASE OF OPERATIONS.
JUST LIKE THAT.
THEY'RE PROBABLY HIDING ON UTOPIA SOMEWHERE.
IT'S THE FIRST PLACE WE'D LOOK.
HE'S AT THE LAST PLACE WE'D LOOK.
OR MAYBE THE LAST PLACE WE'D LOOK IS THE FIRST PLACE HE THINKS WE'D LOOK.
SHUTTING UP NOW.
I MUST SAY: SCOTT SUMMERS SEEMS GENUINELY AS DISAPPOINTED IN ALL OF YOU AS YOU ARE WITH HIM.
I NOTICED THAT TOO.
DO YOU THINK ANY OF YOUR STUDENTS WILL GO WITH HIM?

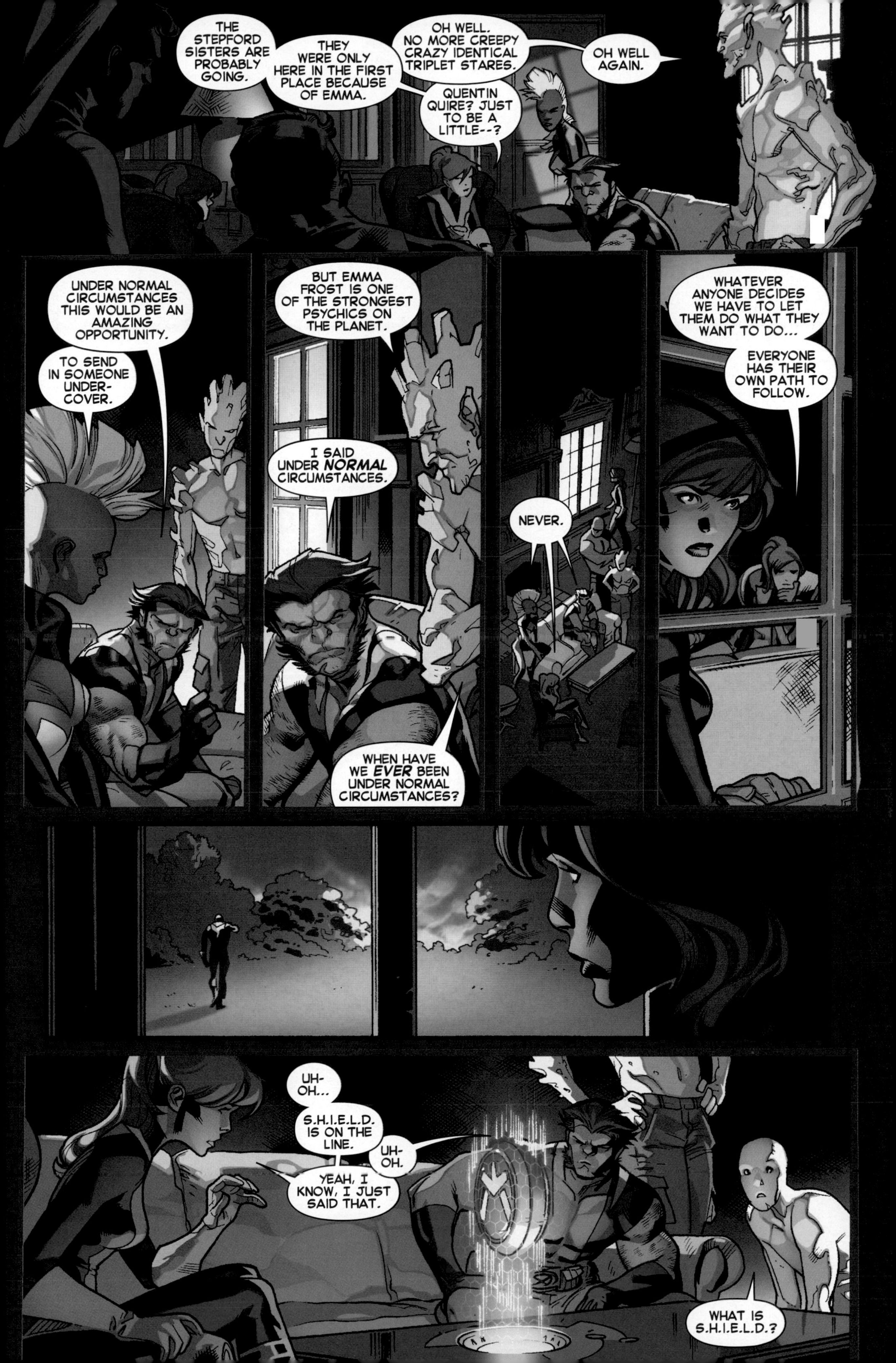
THE STEPFORD SISTERS ARE PROBABLY GOING.
THEY WERE ONLY HERE IN THE FIRST PLACE BECAUSE OF EMMA.
OH WELL. NO MORE CREEPY CRAZY IDENTICAL TRIPLET STARES.
OH WELL AGAIN.
QUENTIN QUIRE? JUST TO BE A LITTLE--?
UNDER NORMAL CIRCUMSTANCES THIS WOULD BE AN AMAZING OPPORTUNITY.
TO SEND IN SOMEONE UNDER-COVER.
BUT EMMA FROST IS ONE OF THE STRONGEST PSYCHICS ON THE PLANET.
I SAID UNDER NORMAL CIRCUMSTANCES.
WHEN HAVE WE EVER BEEN UNDER NORMAL CIRCUMSTANCES?
NEVER.
WHATEVER ANYONE DECIDES WE HAVE TO LET THEM DO WHAT THEY WANT TO DO...
EVERYONE HAS THEIR OWN PATH TO FOLLOW.
UH-OH...
S.H.I.E.L.D. IS ON THE LINE.
UH-OH.
YEAH, I KNOW, I JUST SAID THAT.
WHAT IS S.H.I.E.L.D.?

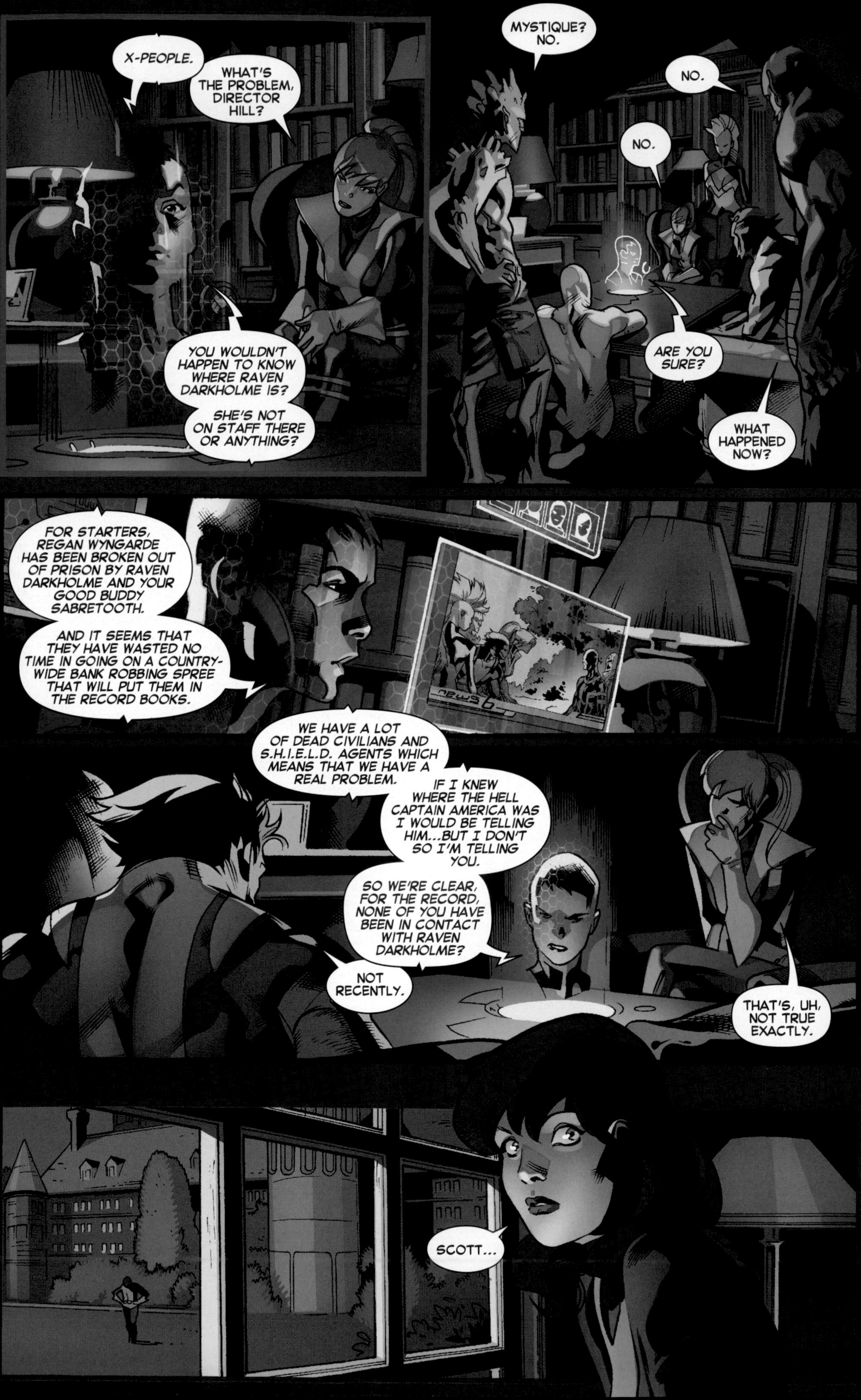
X-PEOPLE.
WHAT'S THE PROBLEM, DIRECTOR HILL?
YOU WOULDN'T HAPPEN TO KNOW WHERE RAVEN DARKHOLME IS?
SHE'S NOT ON STAFF THERE OR ANYTHING?
MYSTIQUE? NO.
NO.
NO.
ARE YOU SURE?
WHAT HAPPENED NOW?
FOR STARTERS, REGAN WYNGARDE HAS BEEN BROKEN OUT OF PRISON BY RAVEN DARKHOLME AND YOUR GOOD BUDDY SABRETOOTH.
AND IT SEEMS THAT THEY HAVE WASTED NO TIME IN GOING ON A COUNTRY-WIDE BANK ROBBING SPREE THAT WILL PUT THEM IN THE RECORD BOOKS.
WE HAVE A LOT OF DEAD CIVILIANS AND S.H.I.E.L.D. AGENTS WHICH MEANS THAT WE HAVE A REAL PROBLEM.
IF I KNEW WHERE THE HELL CAPTAIN AMERICA WAS I WOULD BE TELLING HIM...BUT I DON'T SO I'M TELLING YOU.
SO WE'RE CLEAR, FOR THE RECORD, NONE OF YOU HAVE BEEN IN CONTACT WITH RAVEN DARKHOLME?
NOT RECENTLY.
THAT'S, UH, NOT TRUE EXACTLY.
SCOTT...

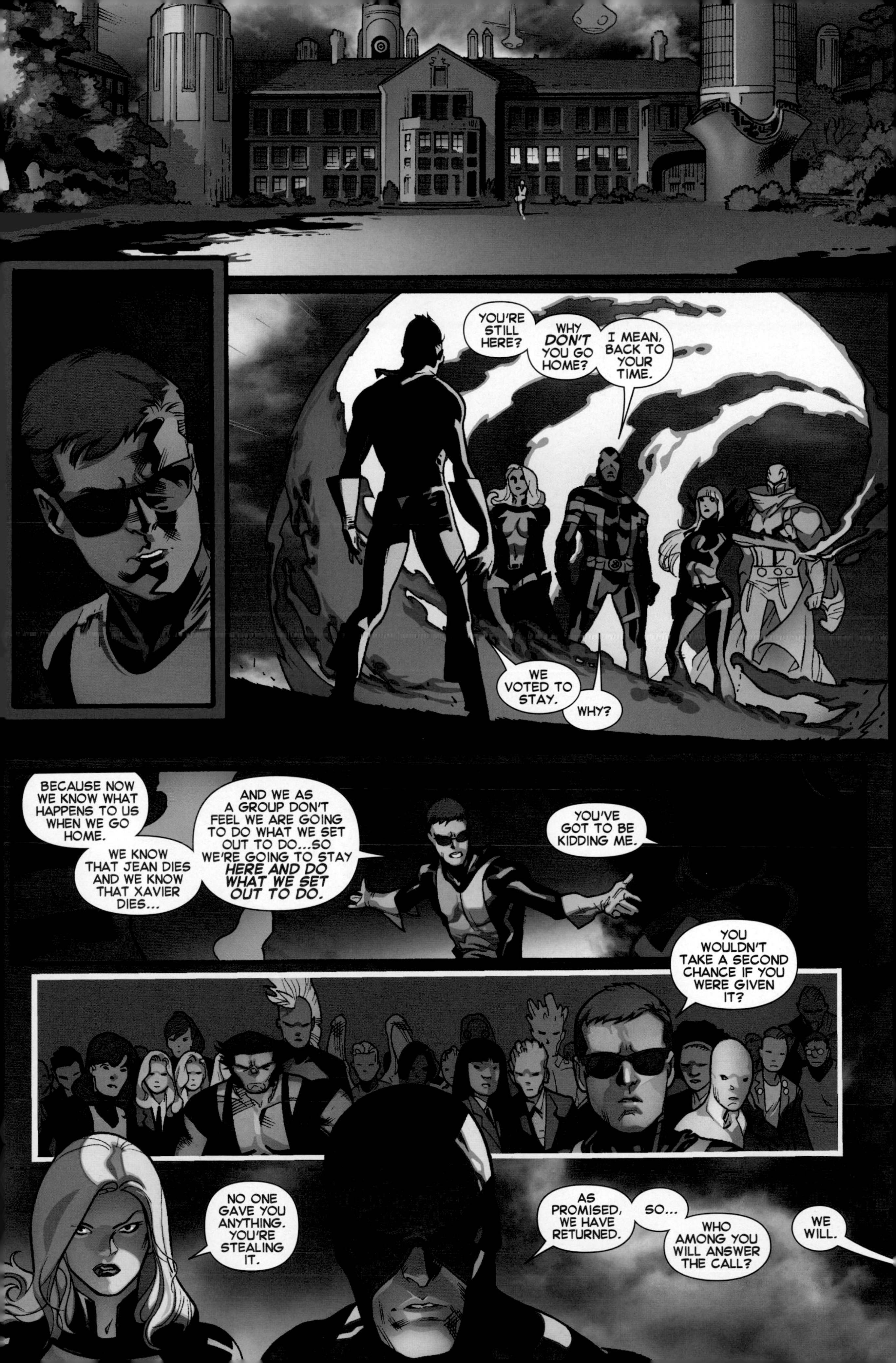
YOU'RE STILL HERE?
WHY DON'T YOU GO HOME?
I MEAN, BACK TO YOUR TIME.
WE VOTED TO STAY.
WHY?
BECAUSE NOW WE KNOW WHAT HAPPENS TO US WHEN WE GO HOME.
WE KNOW THAT JEAN DIES AND WE KNOW THAT XAVIER DIES...
AND WE AS A GROUP DON'T FEEL WE ARE GOING TO DO WHAT WE SET OUT TO DO...SO WE'RE GOING TO STAY HERE AND DO WHAT WE SET OUT TO DO.
YOU'VE GOT TO BE KIDDING ME.
YOU WOULDN'T TAKE A SECOND CHANCE IF YOU WERE GIVEN IT?
NO ONE GAVE YOU ANYTHING. YOU'RE STEALING IT.
AS PROMISED, WE HAVE RETURNED.
SO...
WHO AMONG YOU WILL ANSWER THE CALL?
WE WILL.

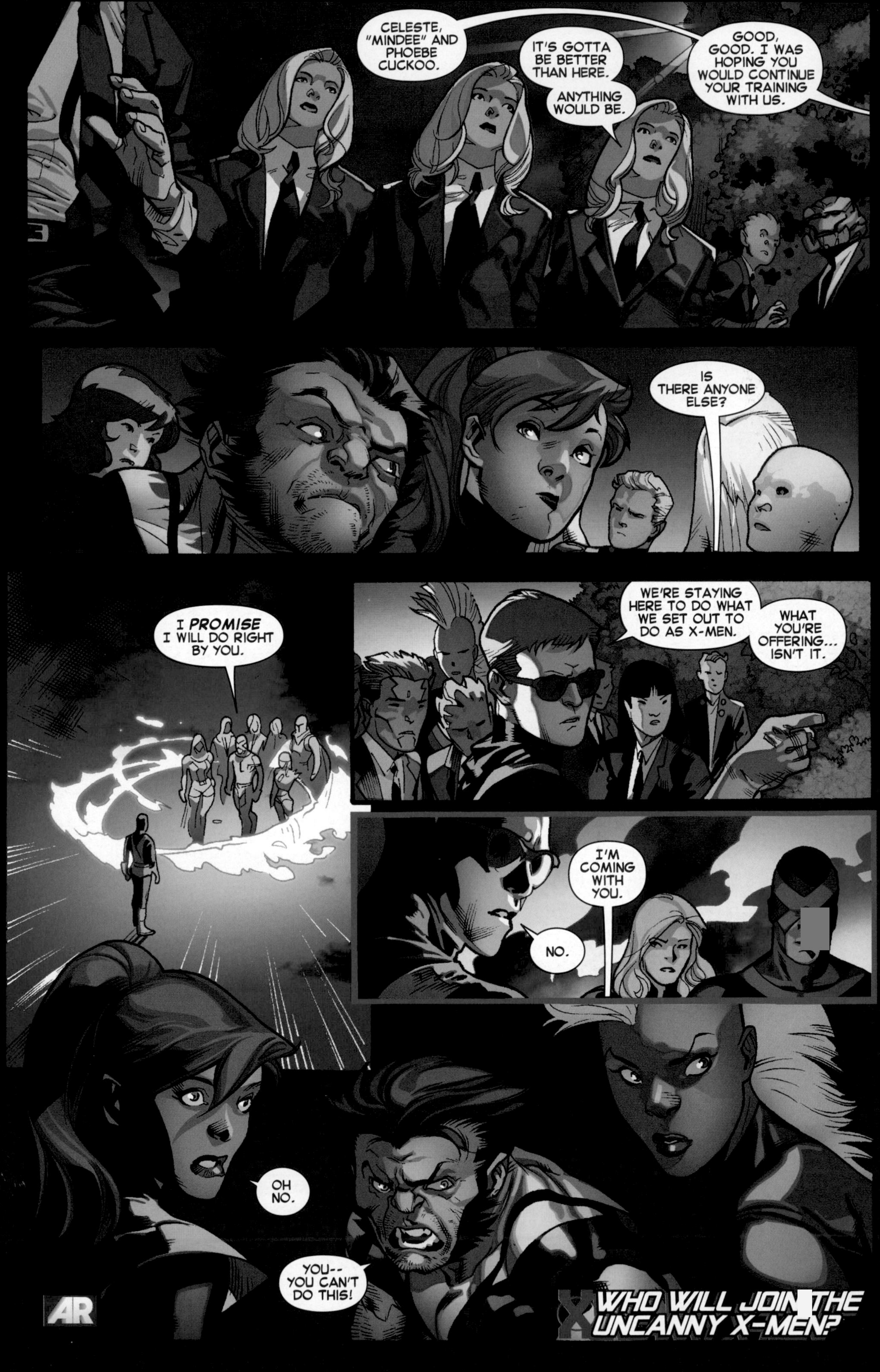

CELESTE, "MINDEE" AND PHOEBE CUCKOO.
IT'S GOTTA BE BETTER THAN HERE.
ANYTHING WOULD BE.
GOOD, GOOD. I WAS HOPING YOU WOULD CONTINUE YOUR TRAINING WITH US.
IS THERE ANYONE ELSE?
WE'RE STAYING HERE TO DO WHAT WE SET OUT TO DO AS X-MEN.
WHAT YOU'RE OFFERING... ISN'T IT.
I *PROMISE* I WILL DO RIGHT BY YOU.
I'M COMING WITH YOU.
NO.
OH NO.
YOU-- YOU CAN'T DO THIS!
AR
WHO WILL JOIN THE UNCANNY X-MEN?

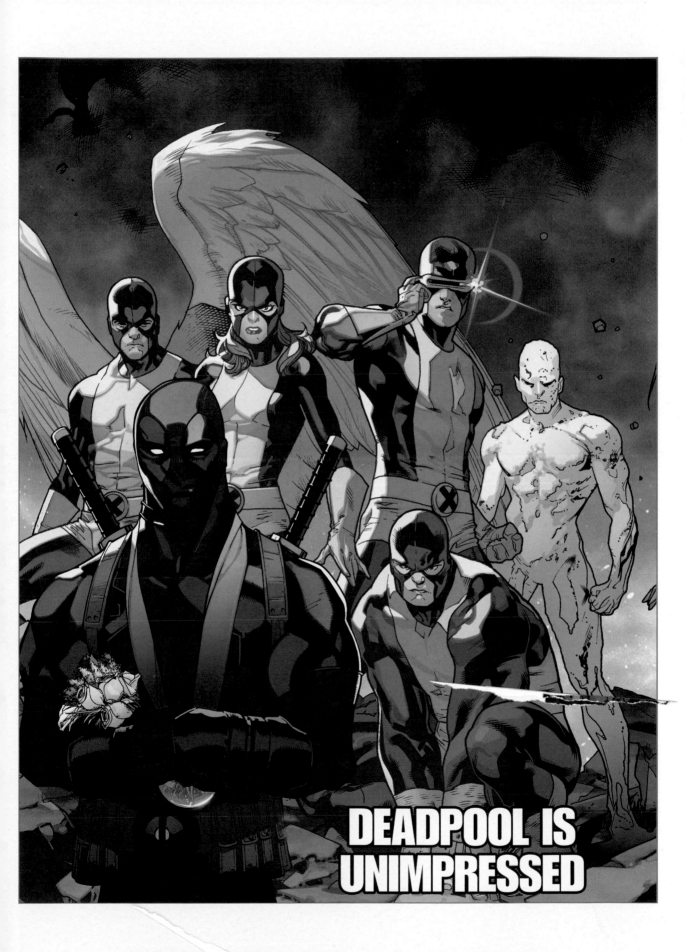

DEADPOOL IS
UNIMPRESSED

ALL-NEW X-MEN #1 DEADPOOL IS UNIMPRESSED VARIANT
BY STUART IMMONEN, WADE VON GRAWBADGER & MARTE GRACIA
WITH CARLO BARBERI

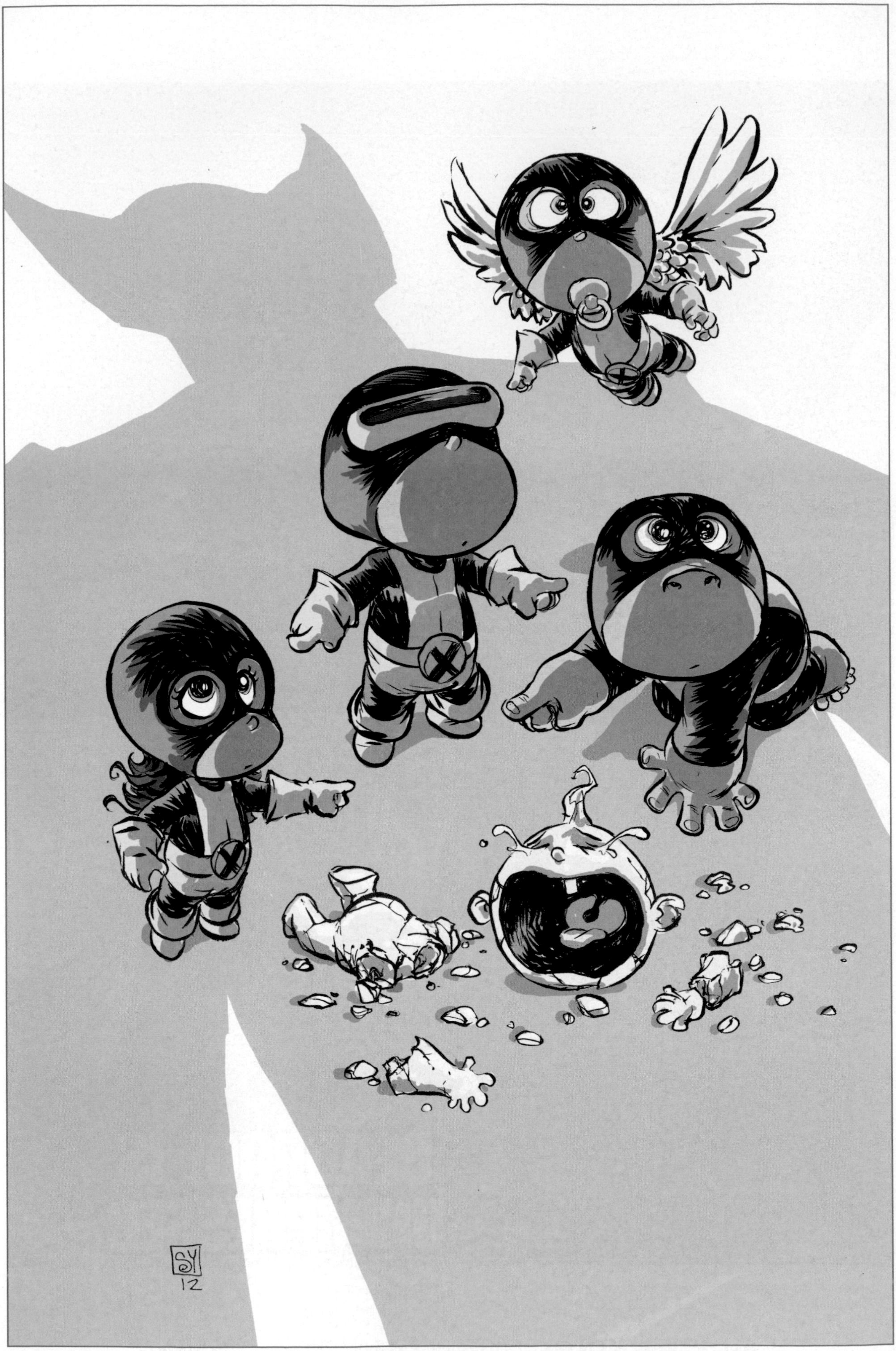
SY
'12

ALL-NEW X-MEN #1 VARIANT

BY SKOTTIE YOUNG

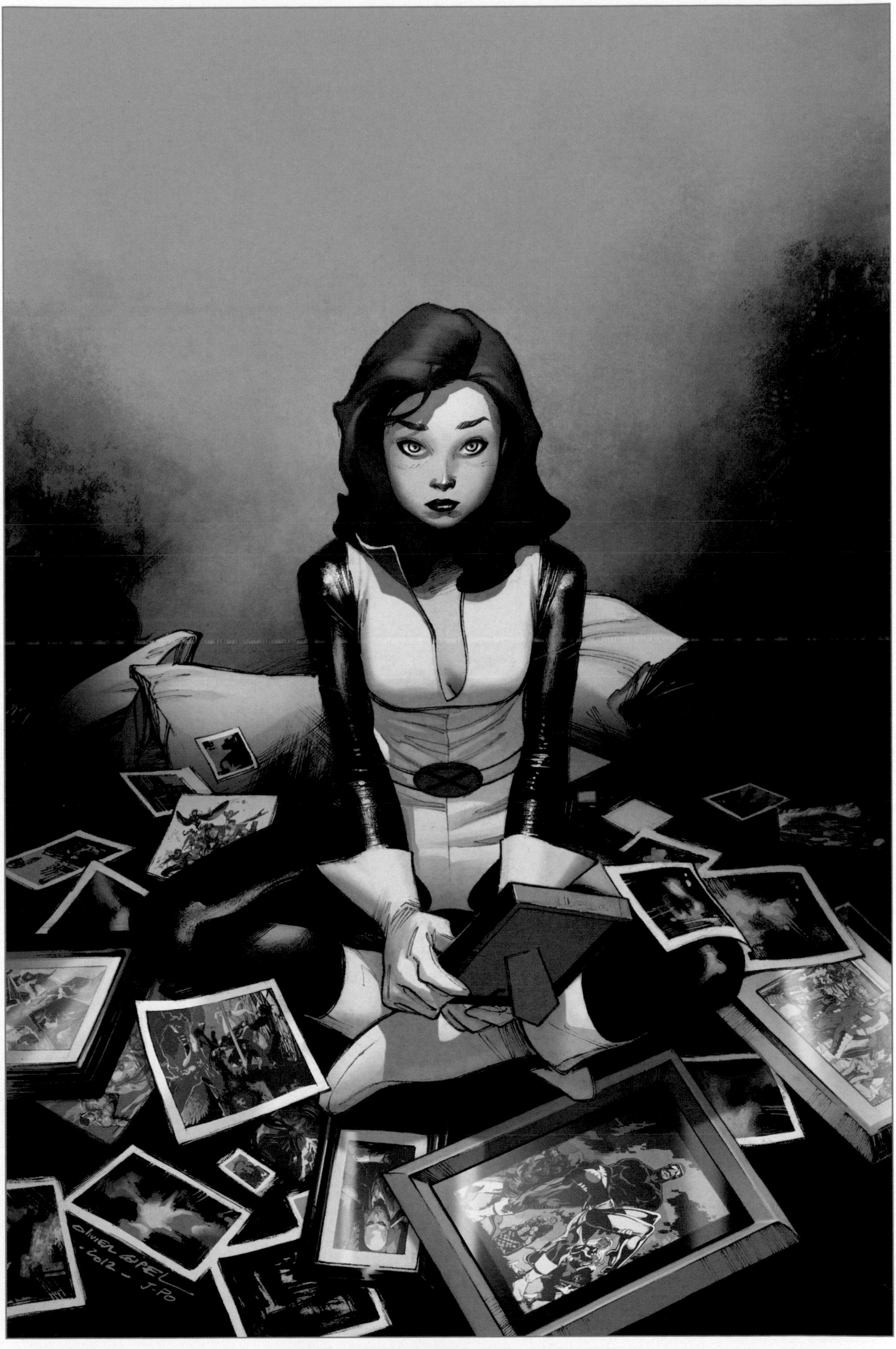

ALL-NEW X-MEN #5 VARIANT
BY OLIVIER COIPEL & JUSTIN PONSOR

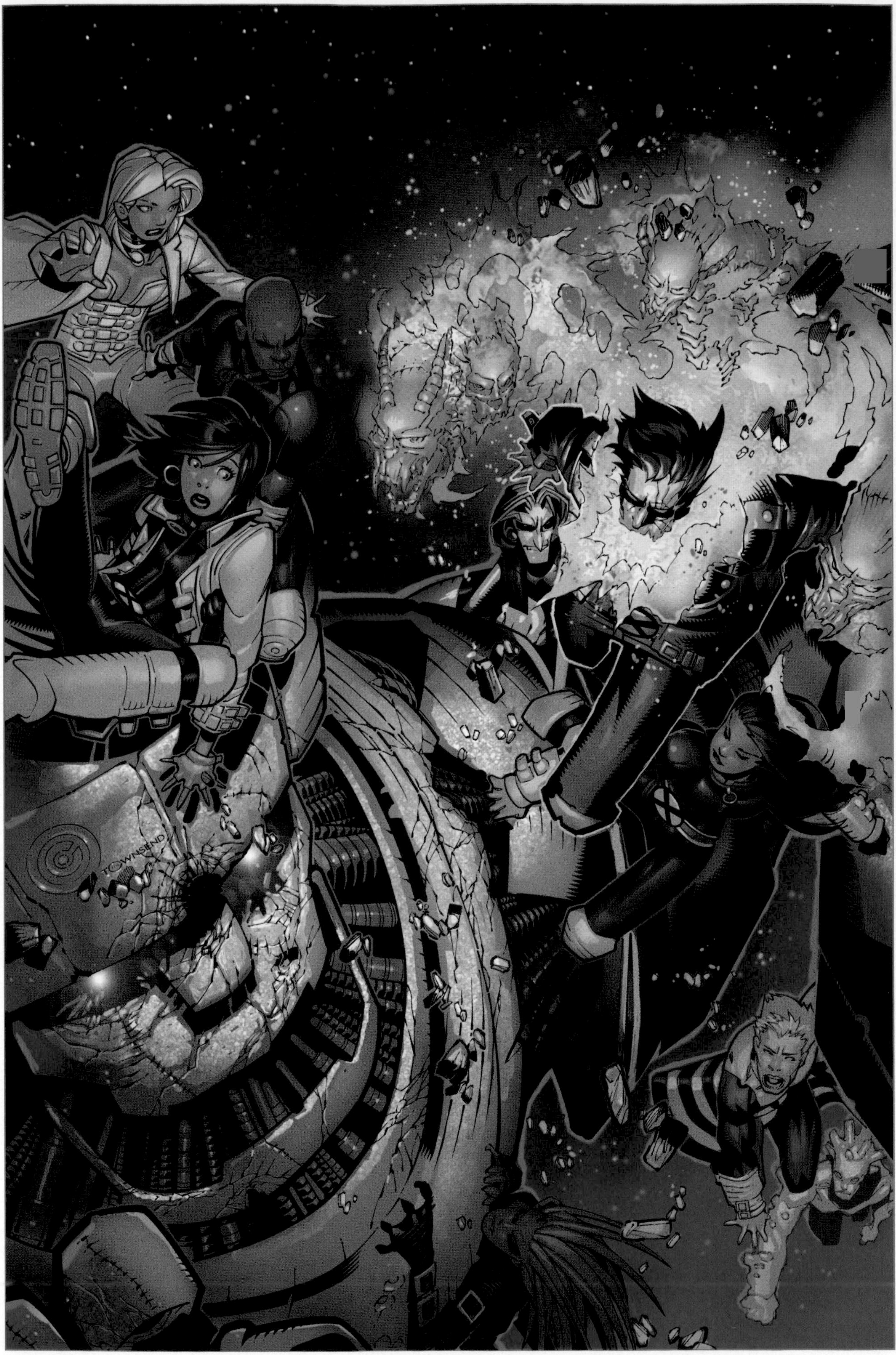
TOWNSEND

ALL-NEW X-MEN #6 X-MEN 50TH ANNIVERSARY VARIANT

BY CHRIS BACHALO & TIM TOWNSEND

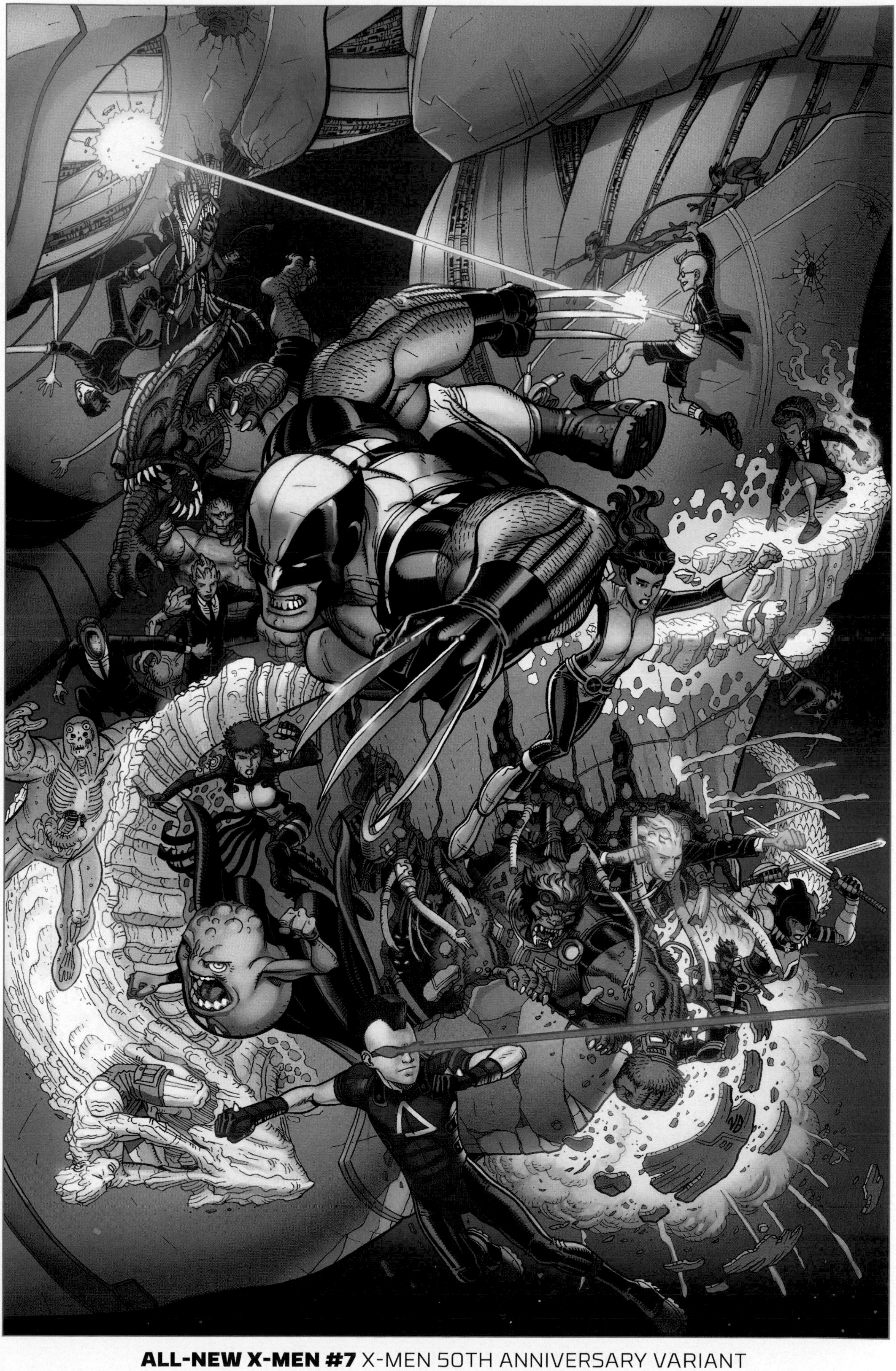

ALL-NEW X-MEN #7 X-MEN 50TH ANNIVERSARY VARIANT
BY NICK BRADSHAW & JASON KEITH

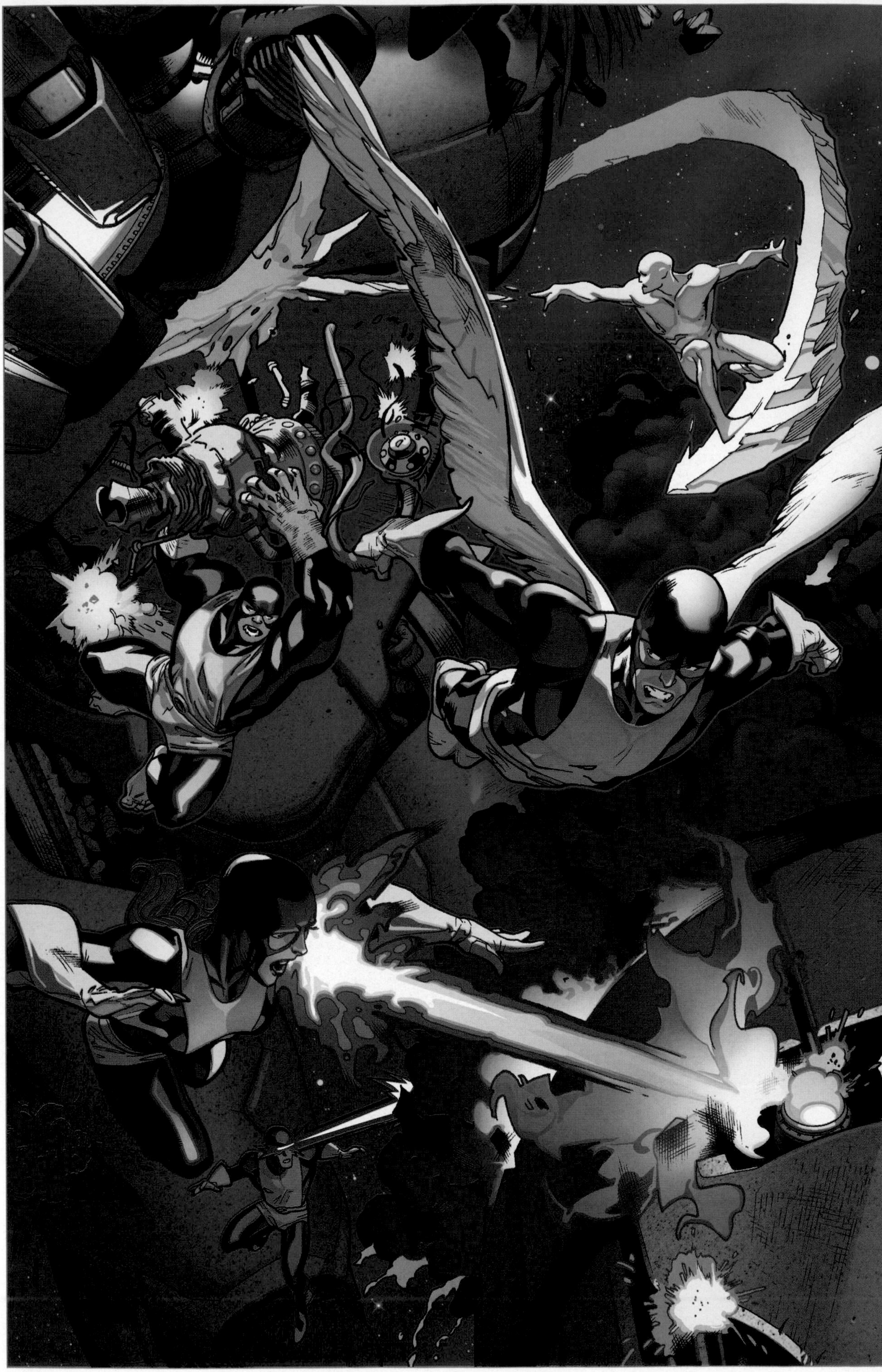

ALL-NEW X-MEN #8 X-MEN 50TH ANNIVERSARY VARIANT
BY STUART IMMONEN, WADE VON GRAWBADGER & MARTE GRACIA

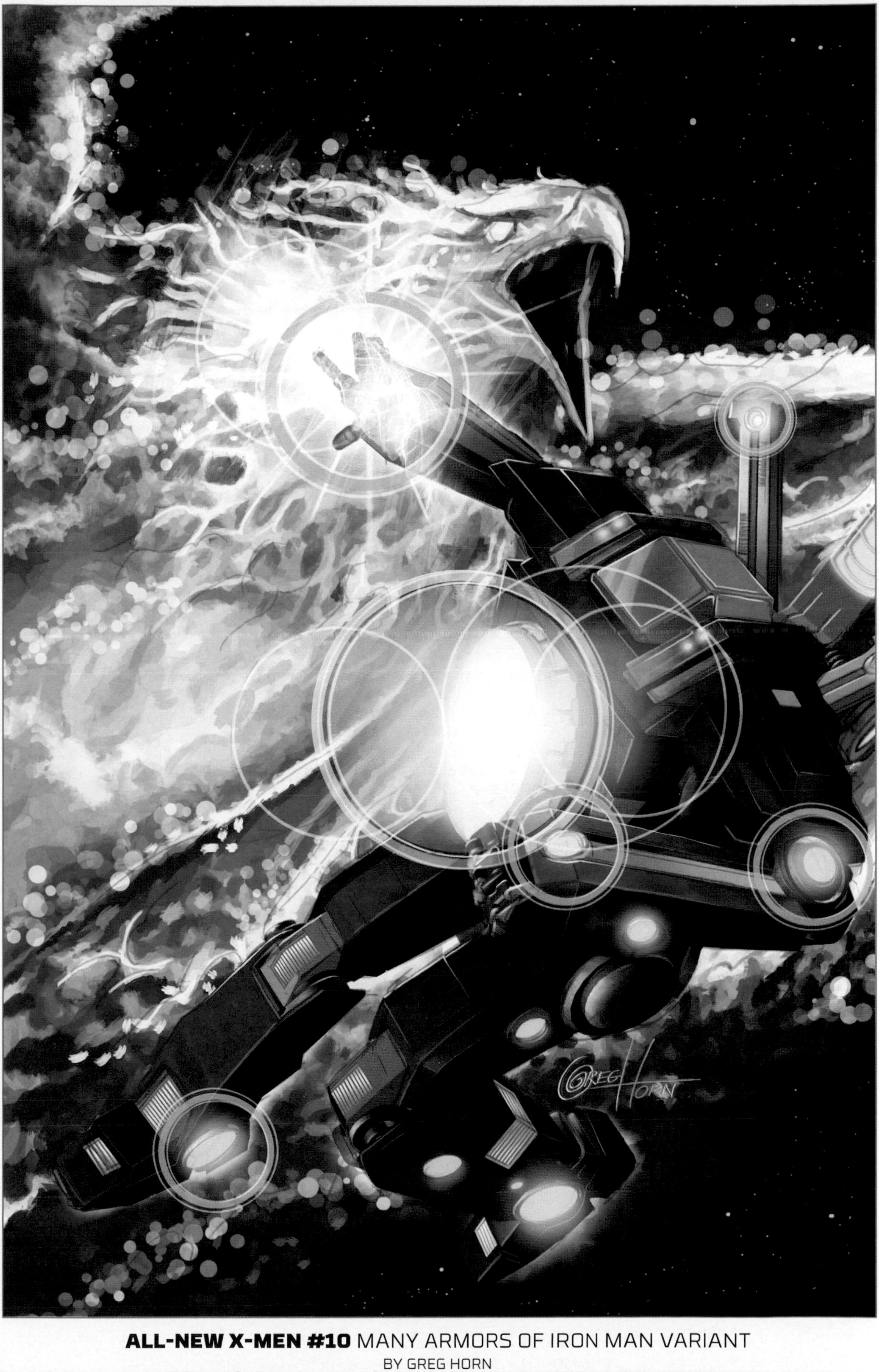
GREG HORN

ALL-NEW X-MEN #10 MANY ARMORS OF IRON MAN VARIANT
BY GREG HORN

Here's the first document that Brian Bendis wrote for his X-Men run. It was
written quite long ago — so long, in fact, you'll notice it was written before the
final decision to kill Charles Xavier in *Avengers vs. X-Men #11* was made. There
are a few details we needed to redact, but here it is for your edification!

X-Men discussion document

By Brian Michael Bendis

DAYS OF FUTURE NOW

Art- STUART IMMONEN

After the punishing results of Avengers versus X-Men, mutant confusion is
at an all-time high. Cyclops, and what is left of the Phoenix 5, have gone
full-on mutant revolutionary which is illustrated by a huge set piece where
Cyclops makes his 'take no prisoners' attitude very clear.

Hank McCoy, Storm, Wolverine, Iceman, Kitty and the others watch the chaos
in disgust. What can they do? If they confront Scott head on then the next
step is MUTANT CIVIL WAR.

And if that happens... no one wins.

STORM

If young Scott Summers saw what he has turned into... he
would be sick to his stomach.

ICE MAN

When we were young we were always worried about a mutant
apocalyptic nightmare... if the young us saw what was
going on today it would feel worse than an apocalyptic
nightmare!!

What the X-Men don't know is that the 'Phoenix 5's' power sets have been
severely altered by their time with the Phoenix power.

Scott has to completely re-train himself, Emma is ██████████████████,
Magneto had his powers leveled by the final conflict in AvX. The X-Men
revolutionaries' dark secret is that they are as untrained and unprepared
for war as they were the first day they got their powers.

Hank McCoy, secretly, hits another secondary mutation. A mutation so severe
that he fears for his life. On top of this, Hank is tortured by what has
become of their youthful dream of humans and mutants living together and
fears that there is no hope.

Storm's words about young Scott haunt him.

He cannot get the idea out of his head that there was no one who can
peacefully stop Scott Summers other than the Scott Summers that used to be
his friend.

Hank McCoy travels back to the earliest days of the Uncanny X-Men (Uncanny
X-Men number 8 for those of you playing at home) and offers them a chance to
save the world from themselves.

The original Uncanny X-Men take the offer and travel to the present.

End of 1st issue

Rest of the story—

Throughout the first arc the original Uncanny X-Men will see everything that has happened to them. They will see that the Xavier school is now the Jean Grey School.

Young Jean will be rattled to her core as she hears how she sacrificed herself for the greater good of mankind.

Young Scott will come face-to-face with the future self that in many ways represents everything he's sworn to fight against.

Older Scott is PARTNERED with Magneto?

Everyone is shocked to find out that Bobby Drake ended up turning out the best. Bobby, humorously, is a little disappointed.

And young Hank McCoy is eventually able to figure out how to turn The Beast back into the fun-loving, blue, furry friend to everyone.

The original Uncanny X-Men and the X-Men of today will go head-to-head in a very large set piece.

At the end of it the original X-Men will decide to stay.

JEAN GREY

This is where we are needed most.

Then...

Three months later this project will split into 2 monthly books.

ALL-NEW X-MEN will continue and will star the original Uncanny X-Men coming to terms with the world as it is today and fighting to make it better.

The book will star the original Uncanny X-Men and members of the X-Men today. New friendships, new relationships, new drama, new dedication towards an ideal as fresh as it was originally stated.

Plus we have a book full of fish out of water Capt. America types dealing with the new.

The other book, launching in February will be called, UNCANNY X-MEN and will star, primarily, the Phoenix 5 as they deal with their uphill battles, their new powers and their new struggles.

ALL NEW X-MEN will be youthful and exuberant. Think of it as a cross between the original idea of the X-Men and the best version of the runaways. This is where Stuart will remain.

UNCANNY X-MEN will be, in many ways, similar in function to the DARK AVENGERS. While nowhere near as twisted, because of the nature of the characters, it will be a more mature look at a revolutionary's dedication to making the world a better place at all costs.

What is the world like when the people decide they have to rise up against their oppressors?

The original 5 X-Men [redacted]. QUESTIONS TO BRING UP IN THE RETREAT Where does Xavier fit into all of this?

I don't want to take him off the table. I want him to be furious at Hank McCoy for abusing technology for his own selfish purposes. Maybe it pushes him so far as to side up with Scott. Maybe he can't abandon his star pupil.

The Wolverine of it all.

I know that you, Nick, have ideas about [redacted] but I don't think we should do it right away. [redacted]. I do think we should do it, I'm just saying I don't think we need right now.

Where does Hope fit into all of this?

Can Kitty be the modern Xavier to the original Uncanny X-Men? Does that mess up the New Mutants book?

When is the right time to put all this together for a [redacted]?

CHARACTER SKETCHES

BY STUART IMMONEN

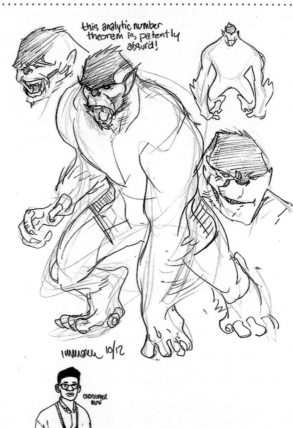

this analytic number theorem is patently absurd!
IMMONEN 10/12

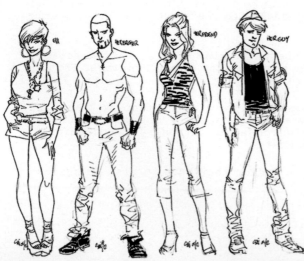

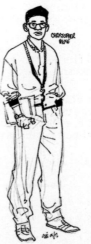

COVER PROCESS

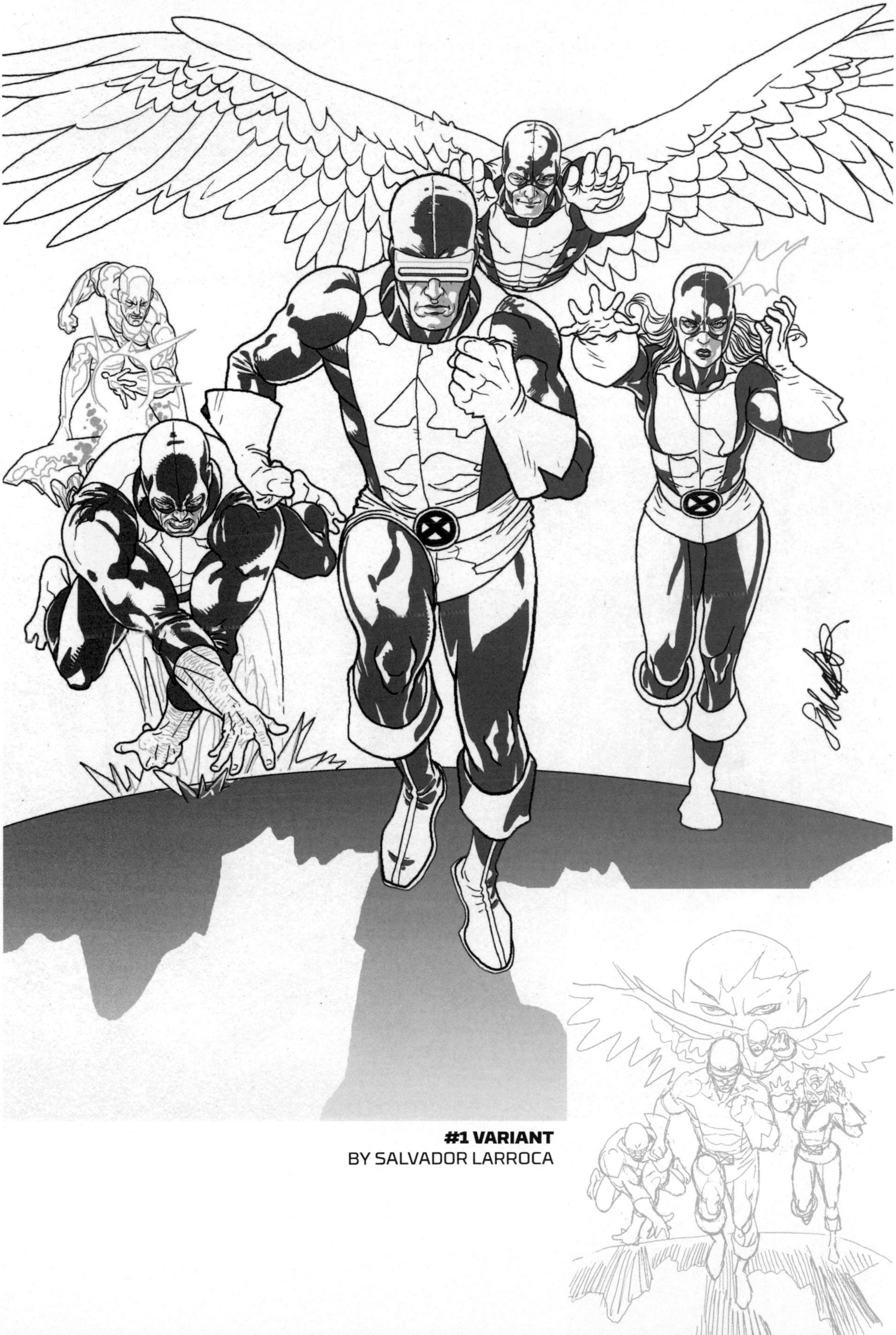

#1 VARIANT
BY SALVADOR LARROCA

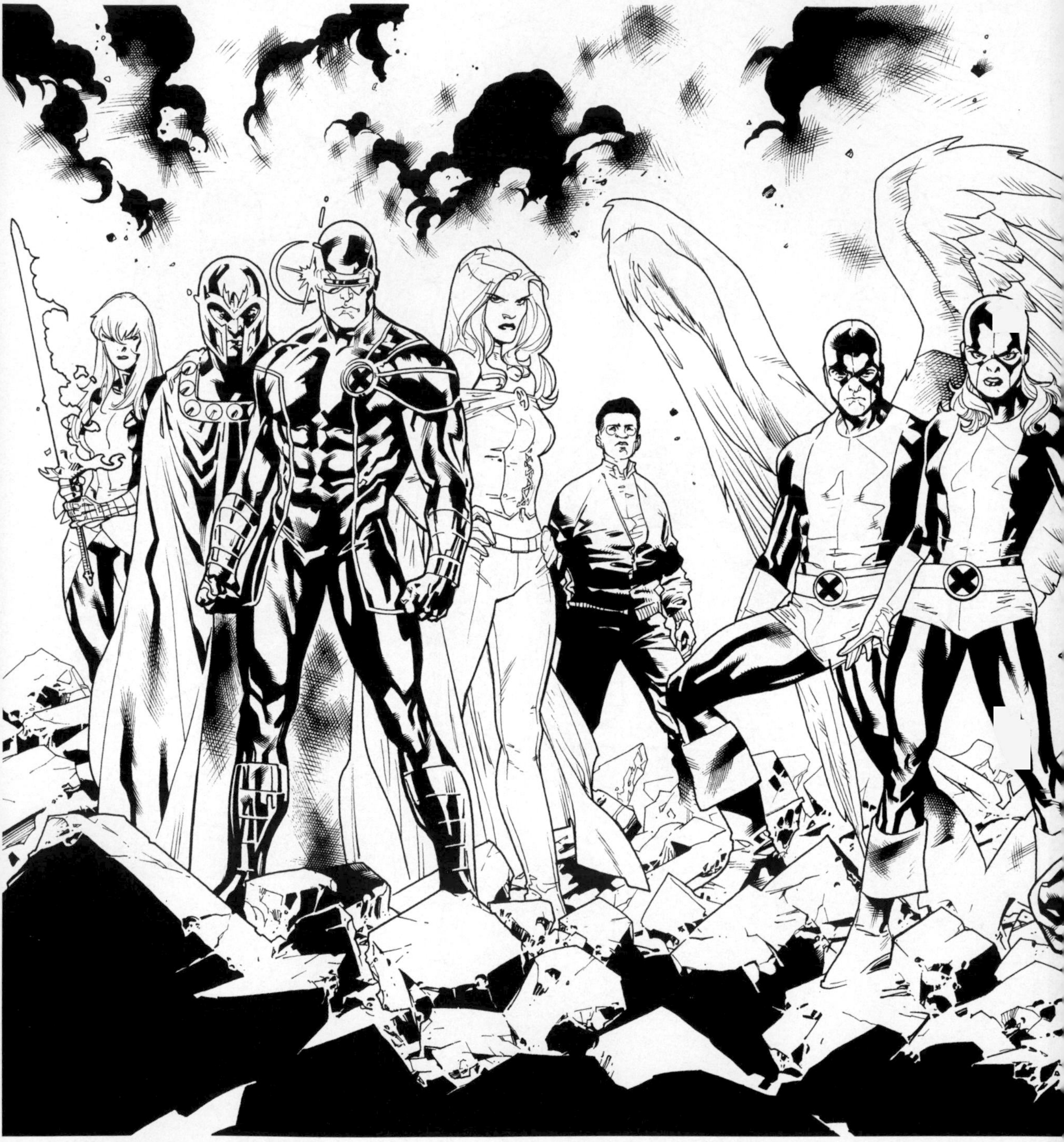

ALL-NEW X-MEN #1–2 COMINED COVER ART
BY STUART IMMONEN & WADE VON GRAWBADGER

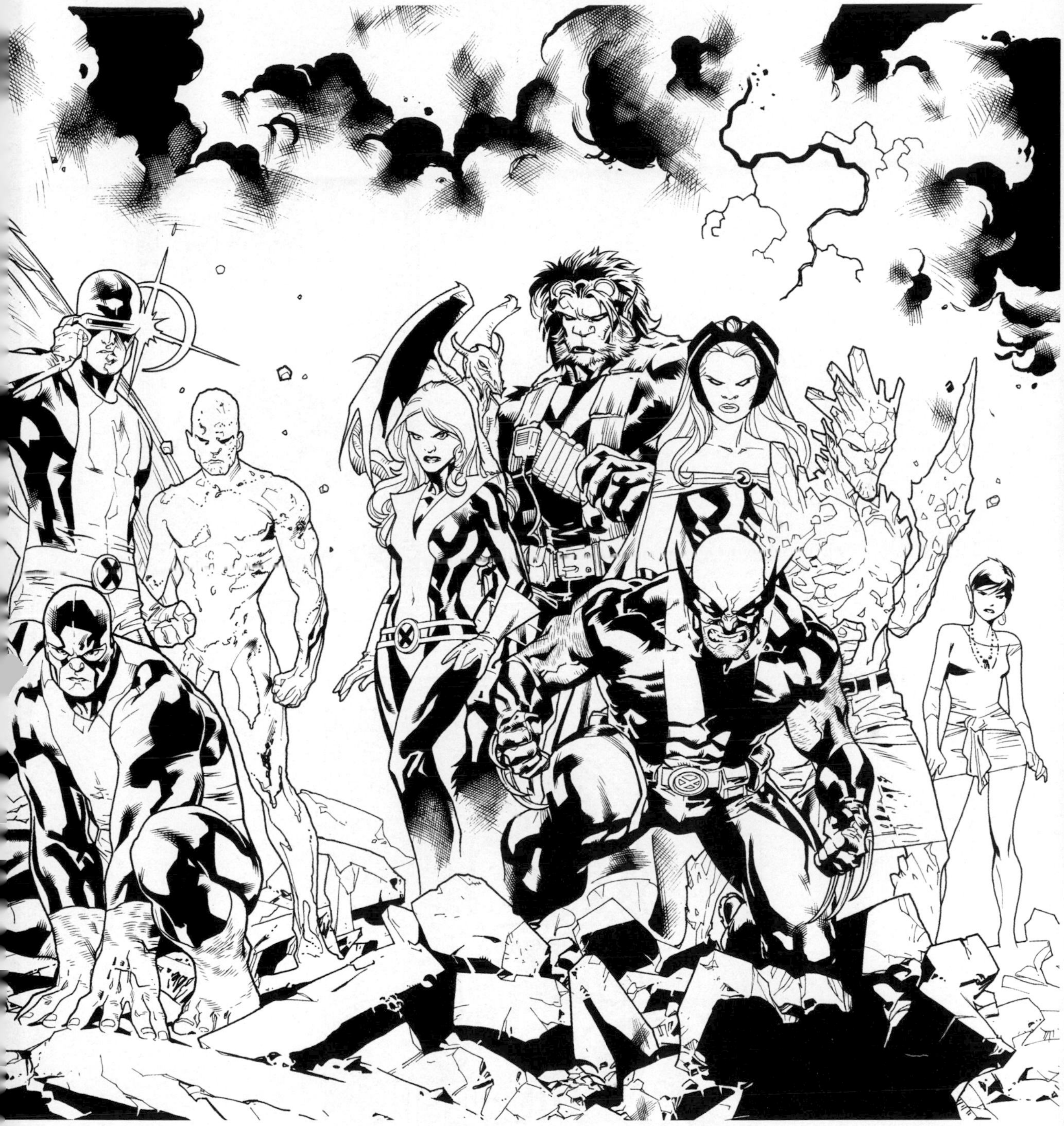

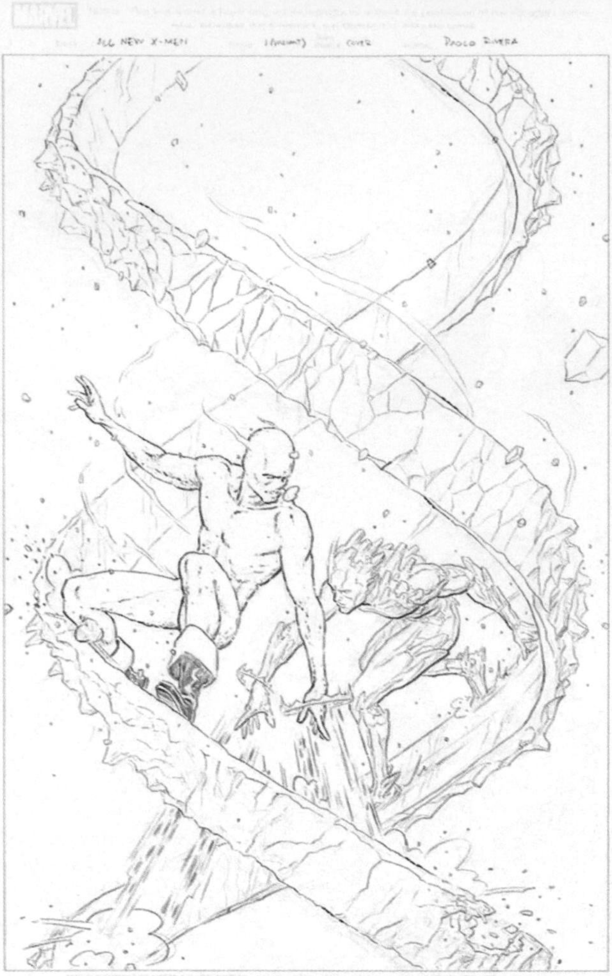
ALL NEW X-MEN
COVER
PAOLO RIVERA

#1 VARIANT
BY PAOLO RIVERA

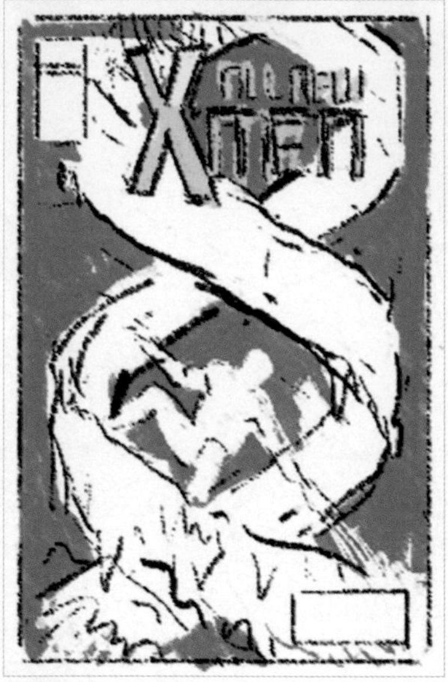

#1 VARIANT
BY JOE QUESADA

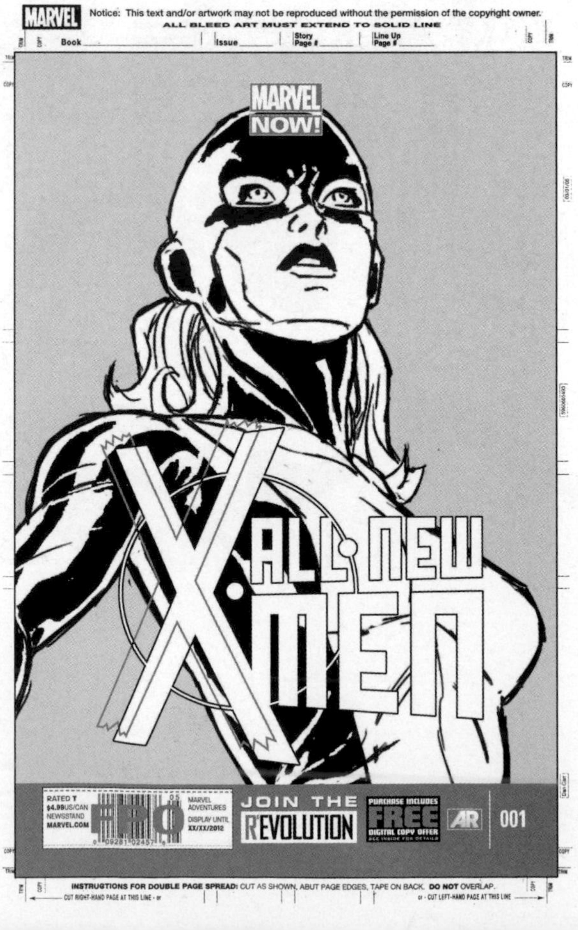
MARVEL Notice: This text and/or artwork may not be reproduced without the permission of the copyright owner.
ALL BLEED ART MUST EXTEND TO SOLID LINE
Book
Issue
Story Page #
Line Up Page #
MARVEL NOW!
ALL NEW X-MEN
RATED T
$4.99US/CAN
NEWSSTAND
MARVEL.COM
MARVEL ADVENTURES
DISPLAY UNTIL XX/XX/2012
JOIN THE R̃EVOLUTION
PURCHASE INCLUDES FREE DIGITAL COPY OFFER
AR
001
INSTRUTIONS FOR DOUBLE PAGE SPREAD: CUT AS SHOWN, ABUT PAGE EDGES, TAPE ON BACK. DO NOT OVERLAP.
CUT RIGHT-HAND PAGE AT THIS LINE
CUT LEFT-HAND PAGE AT THIS LINE

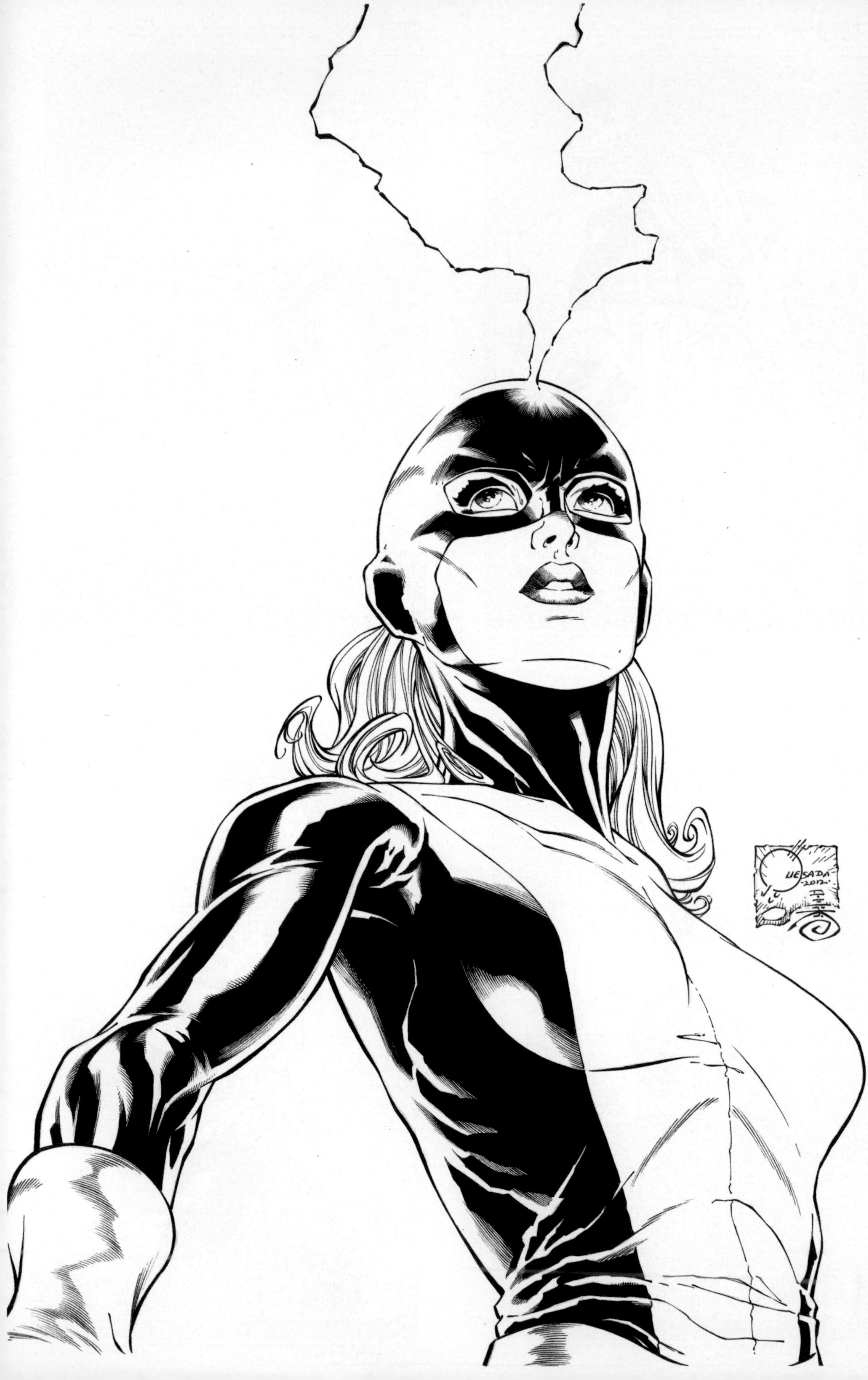

#1 DEADPOOL IN UNIMPRESSED VARIANT
BY CARLO BARBERI

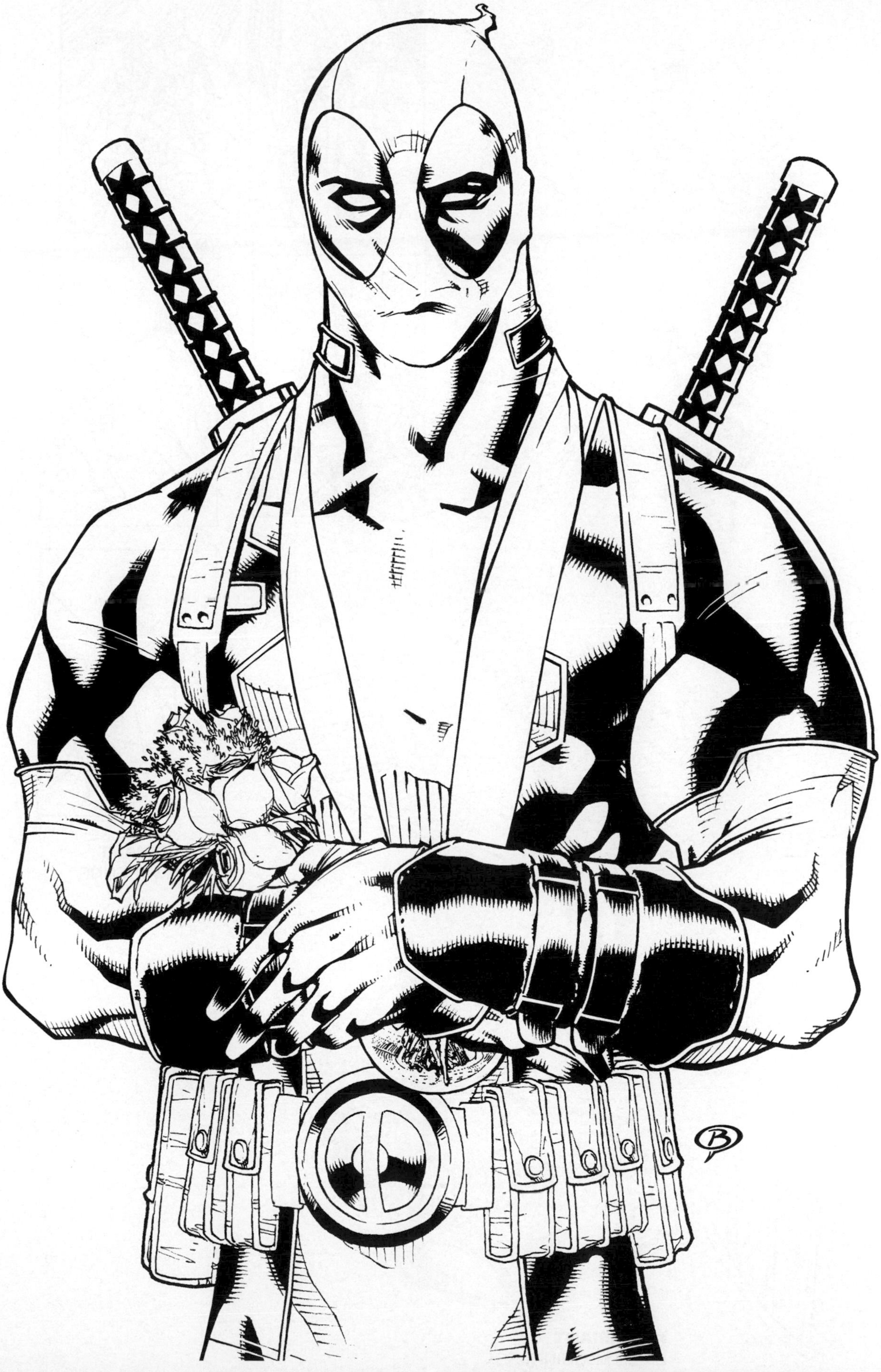

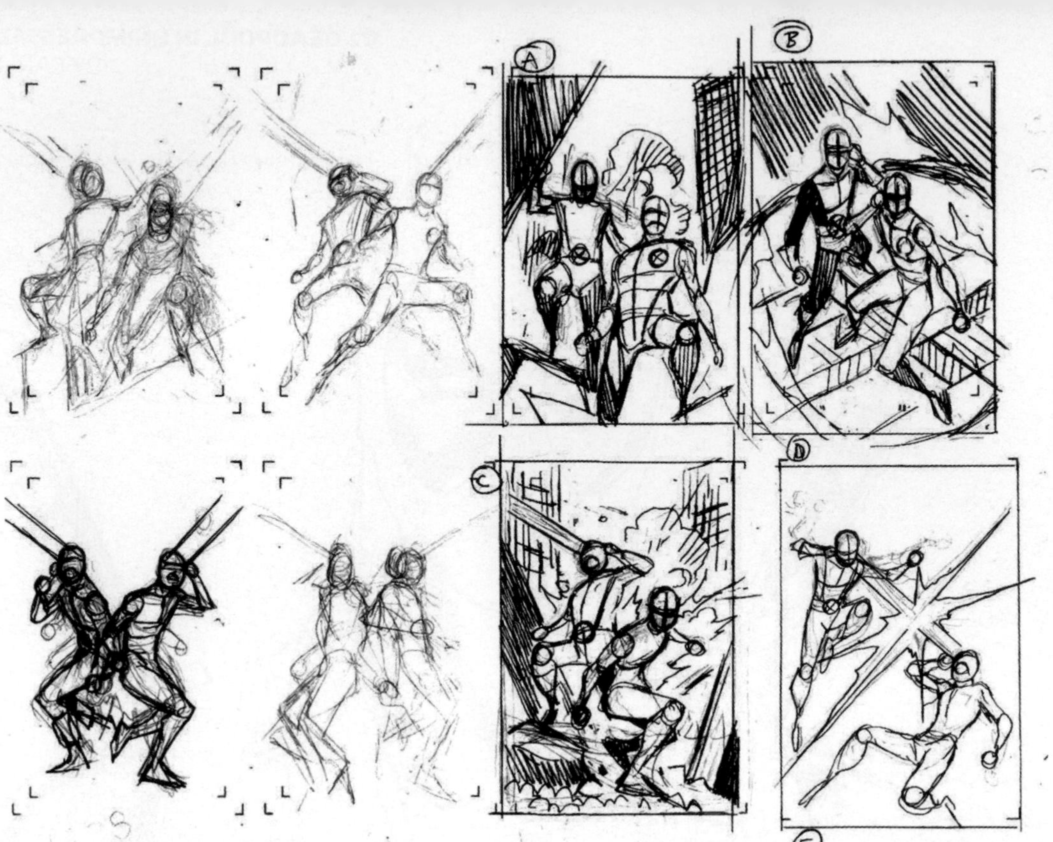
A
B
C
D

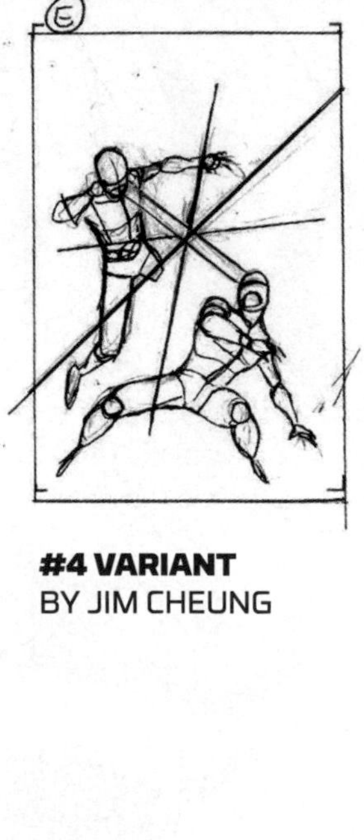
E

#4 VARIANT
BY JIM CHEUNG

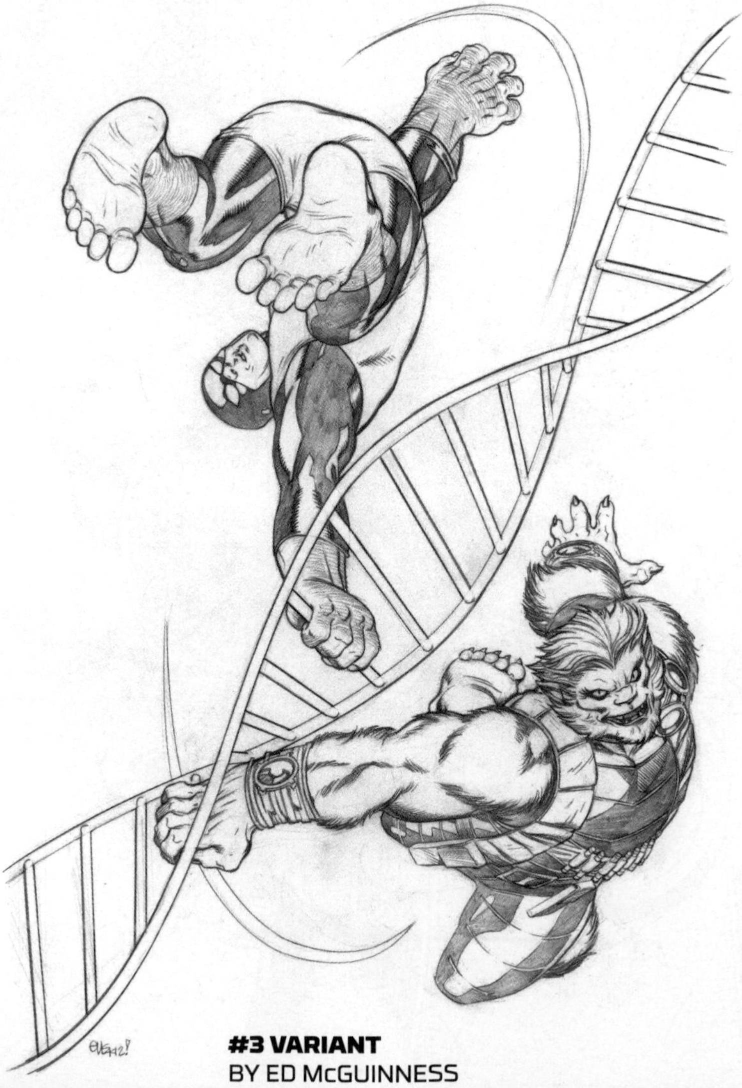

#3 VARIANT
BY ED McGUINNESS

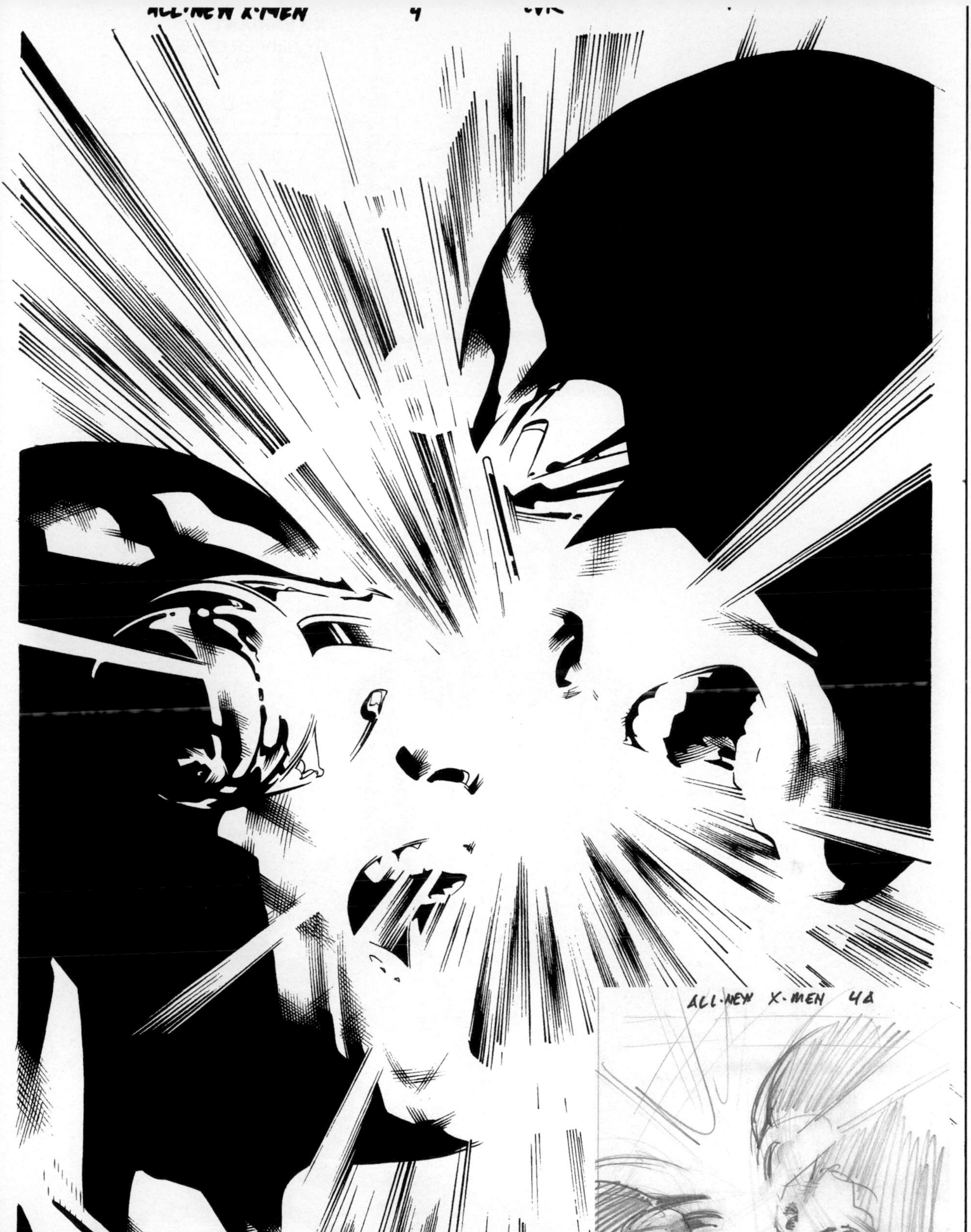

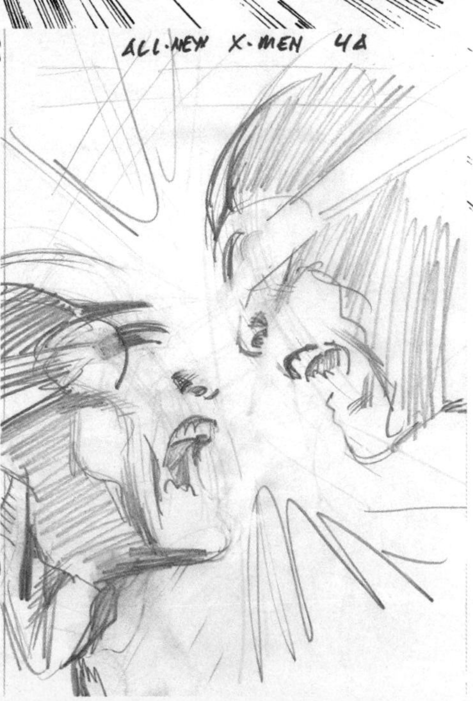
ALL-NEW X-MEN 4A

#4
BY STUART IMMONEN & WADE VON GRAWBADGER

#5 VARIANT
BY OLIVIER COIPEL

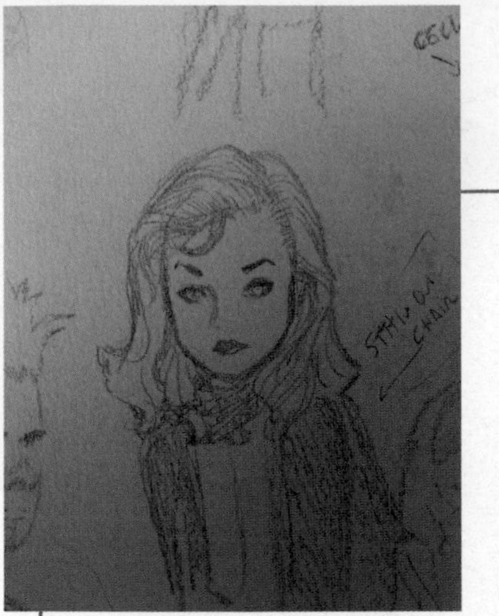

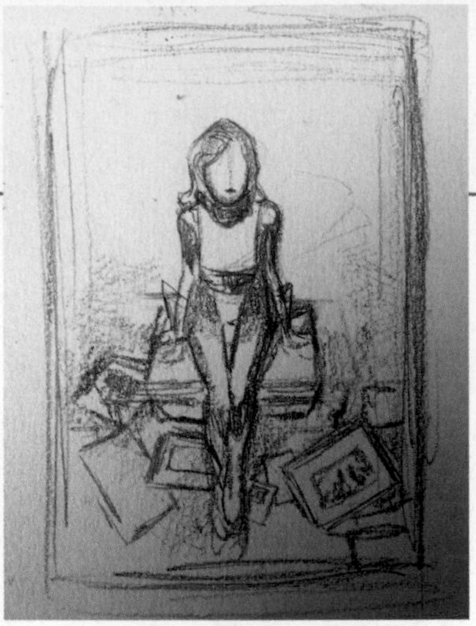

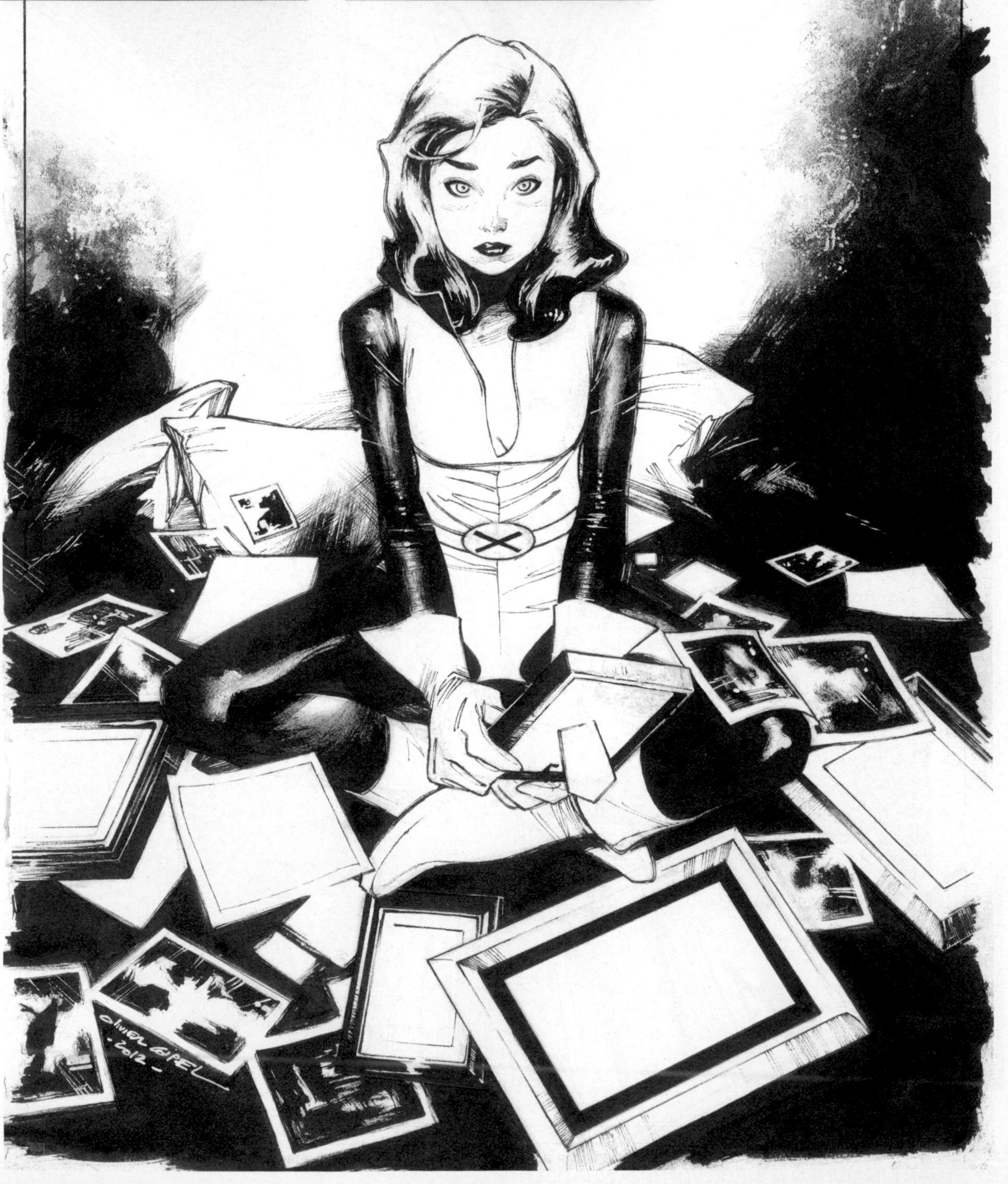
OLIVIER COIPEL
-2012-

#6
BY STUART IMMONEN & WADE VON GRAWBADGER

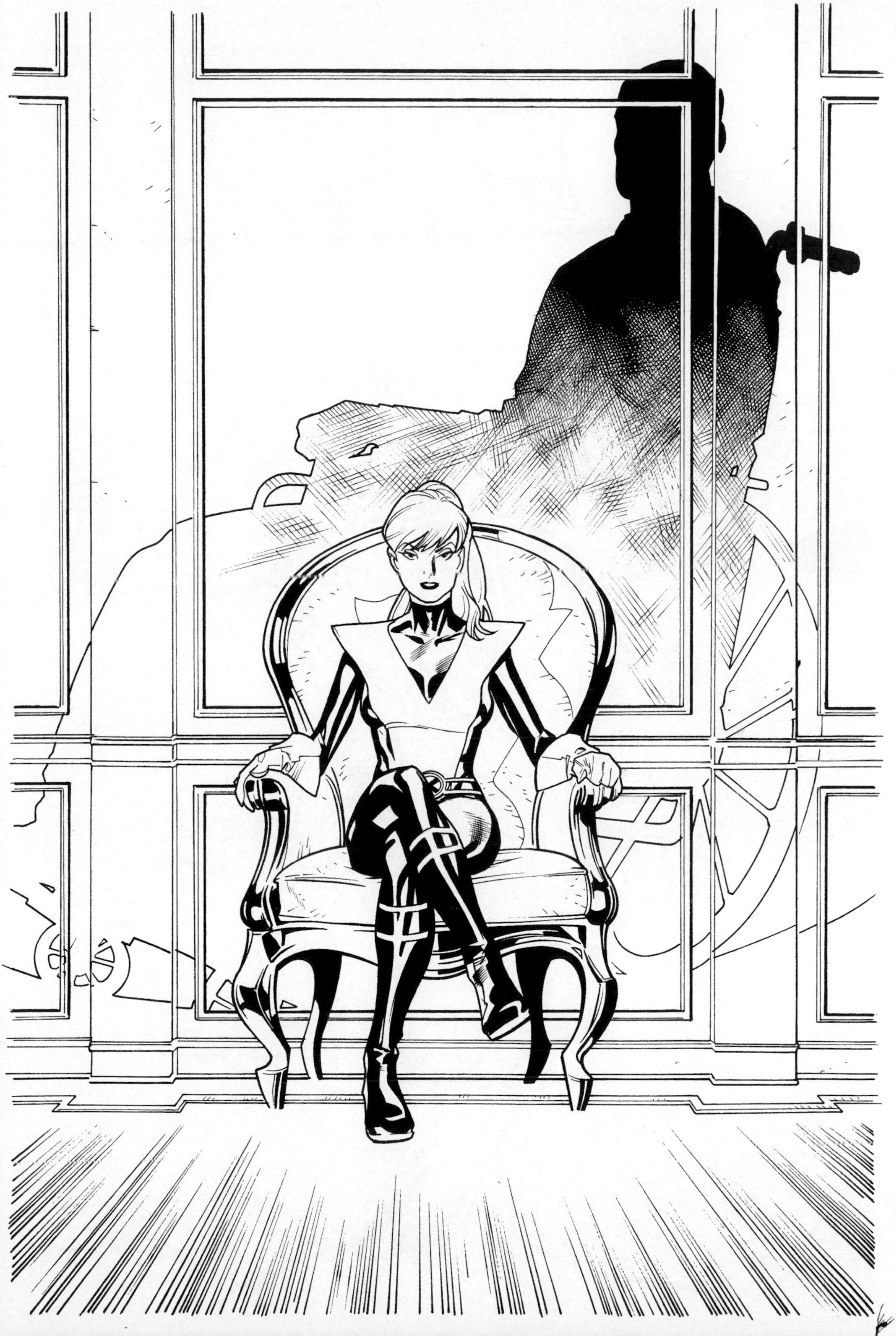

#7 X-MEN 50TH ANNIVERSARY VARIANT
BY NICK BRADSHAW

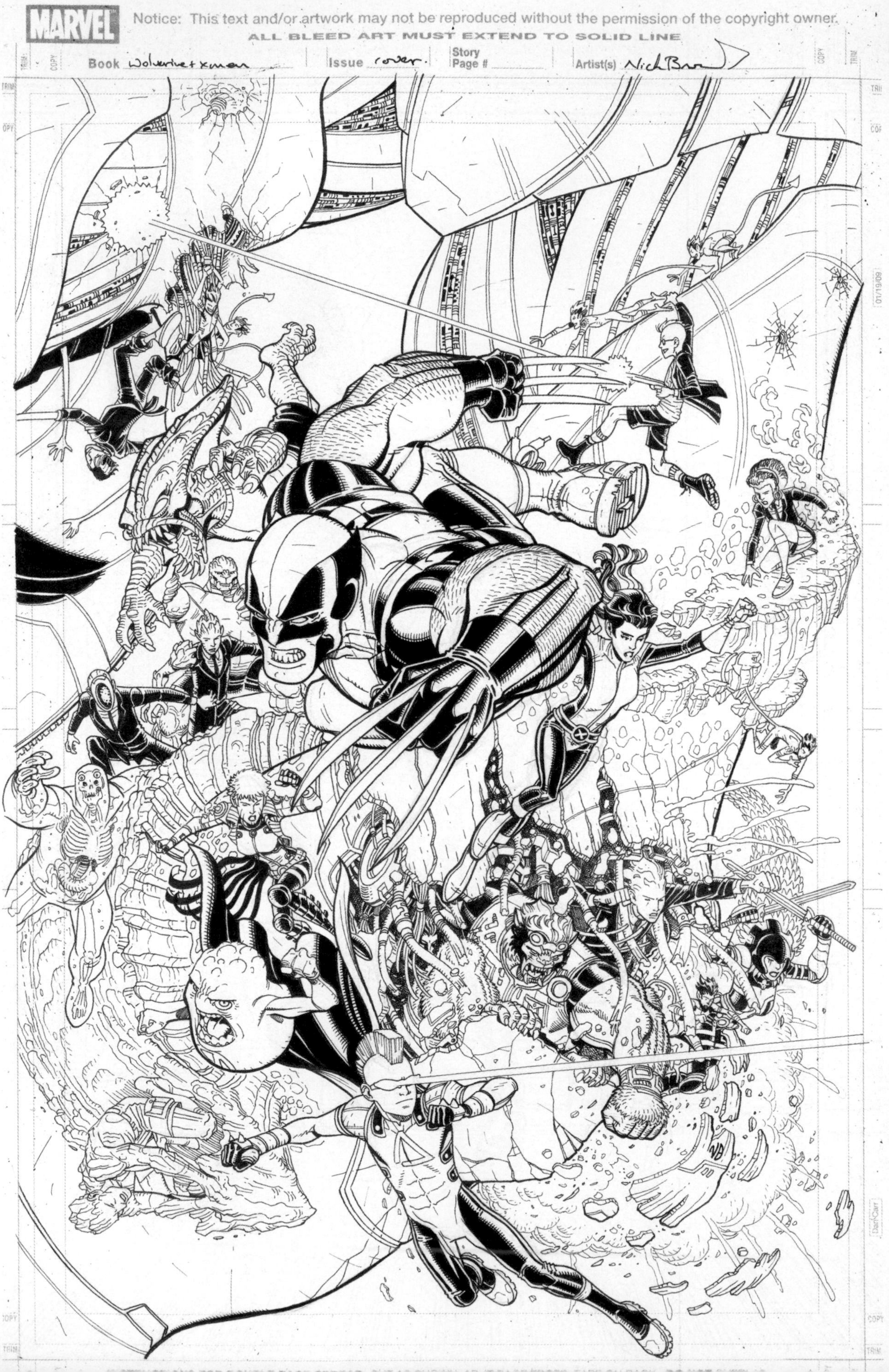
MARVEL
Notice: This text and/or artwork may not be reproduced without the permission of the copyright owner.
ALL BLEED ART MUST EXTEND TO SOLID LINE
Book Wolverine+xmen
Issue cover
Story Page #
Artist(s)
01/19/09

ART PROCESS & COMMENTARY WITH DAVID MARQUEZ

I thought it might be interesting, as part of the "behind the scenes" material, to give readers a look into the editorial and review process of a few pages that underwent some changes before the final image. Marvel Comics are by nature very collaborative, and the input made by editors and writers regarding the art is incredibly important. So...

#6, PAGE 5, PANEL 1

This page was an awesome opportunity to draw the huge cast of the Jean Grey School. To take some of the edge off an already very complex page and panel, I leaned pretty heavily on one of my favorite tools for digital art creation: SketchUp. It's a great tool that allows a user to intuitively build 3D models that I use extensively in my workflow.

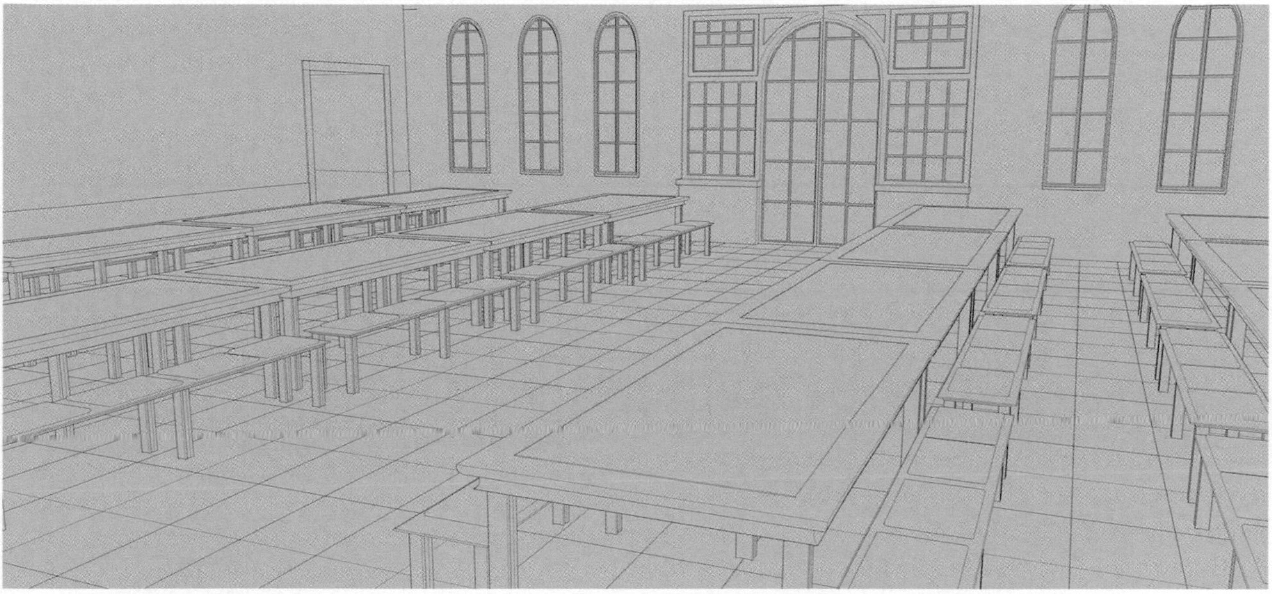

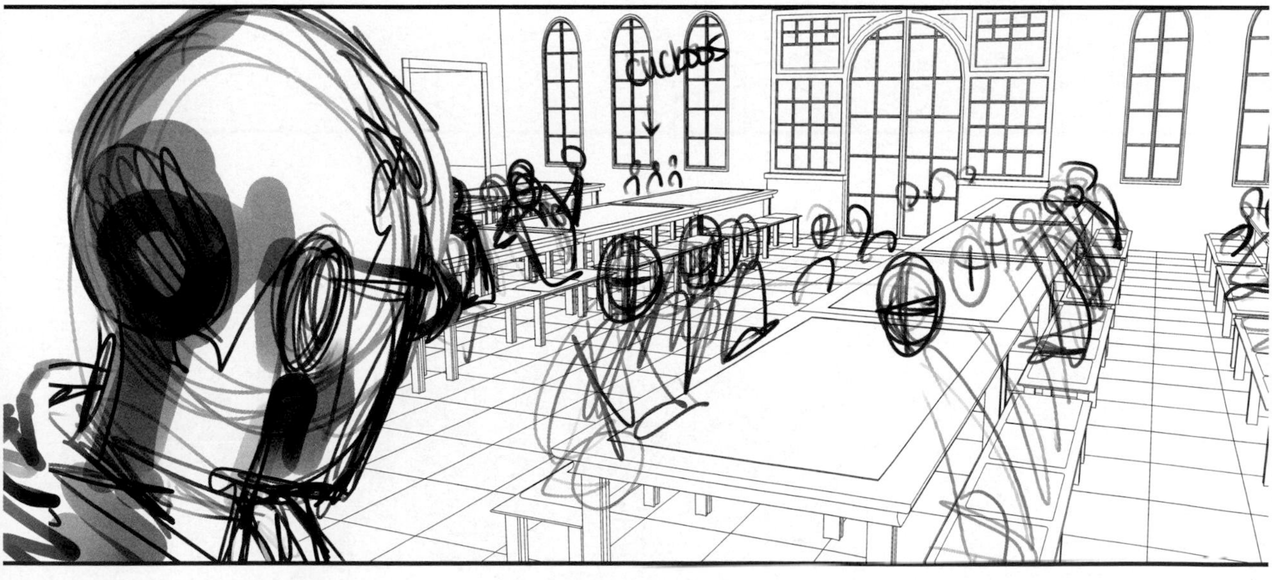
Cuckoos

For this scene, I created a model of the cafeteria, added some brick texture to the walls and started populating the tables with all the colorful characters from the school.

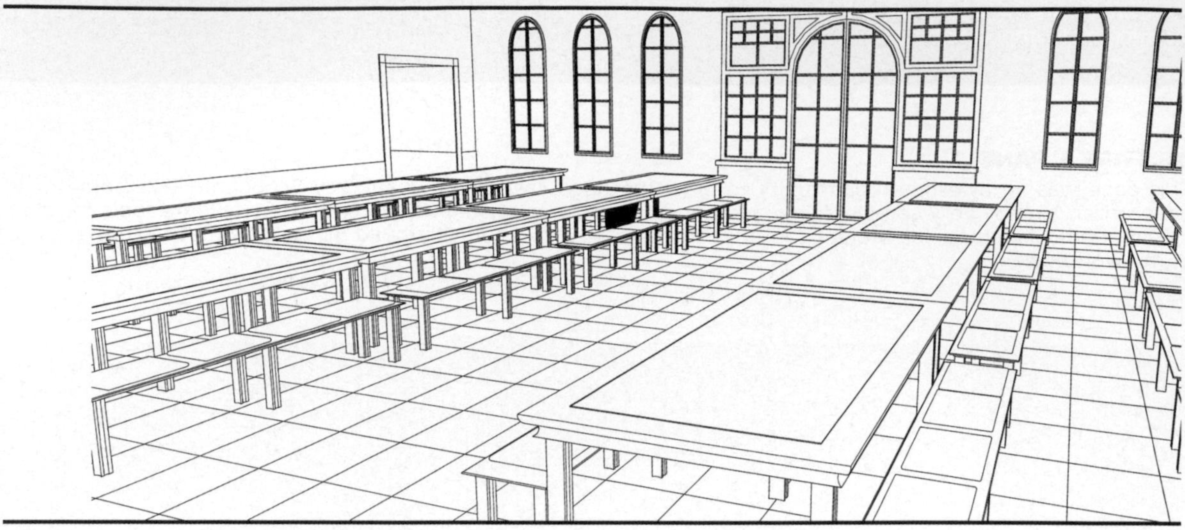

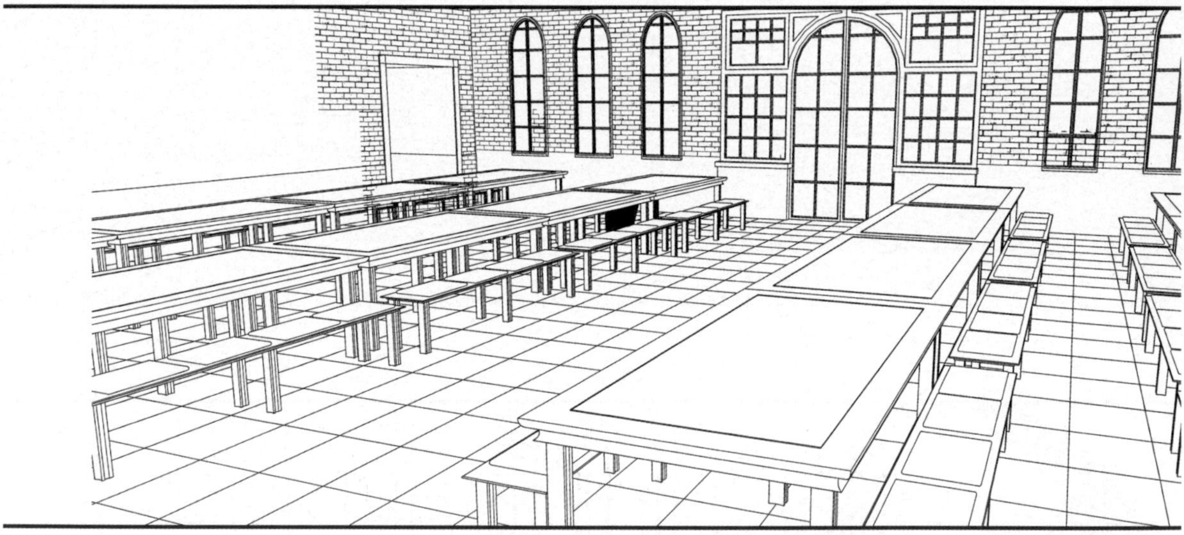

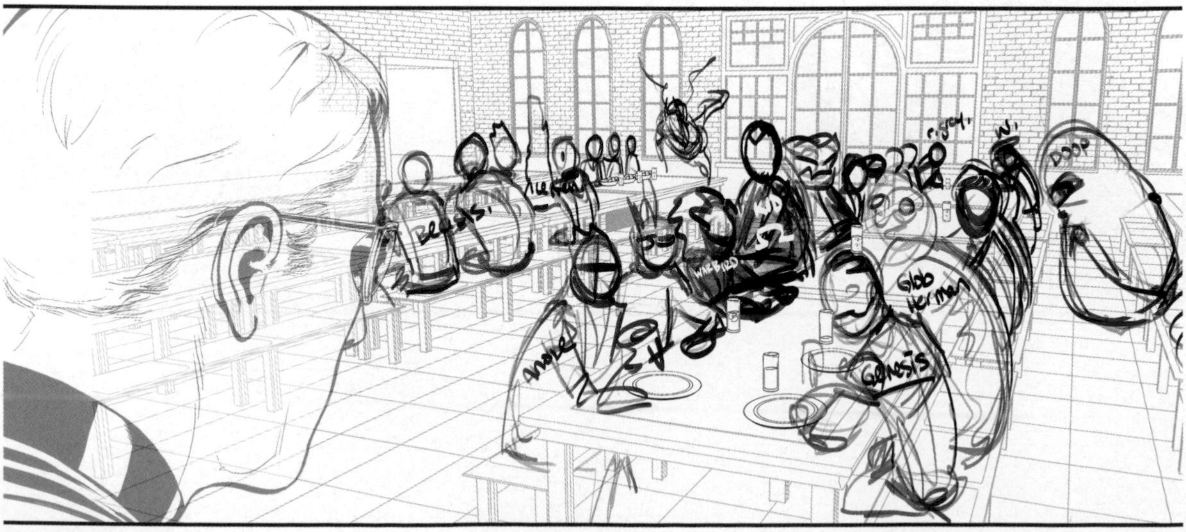
WARBIRD
Glob
Herman
DOOP
Anole
Genesis

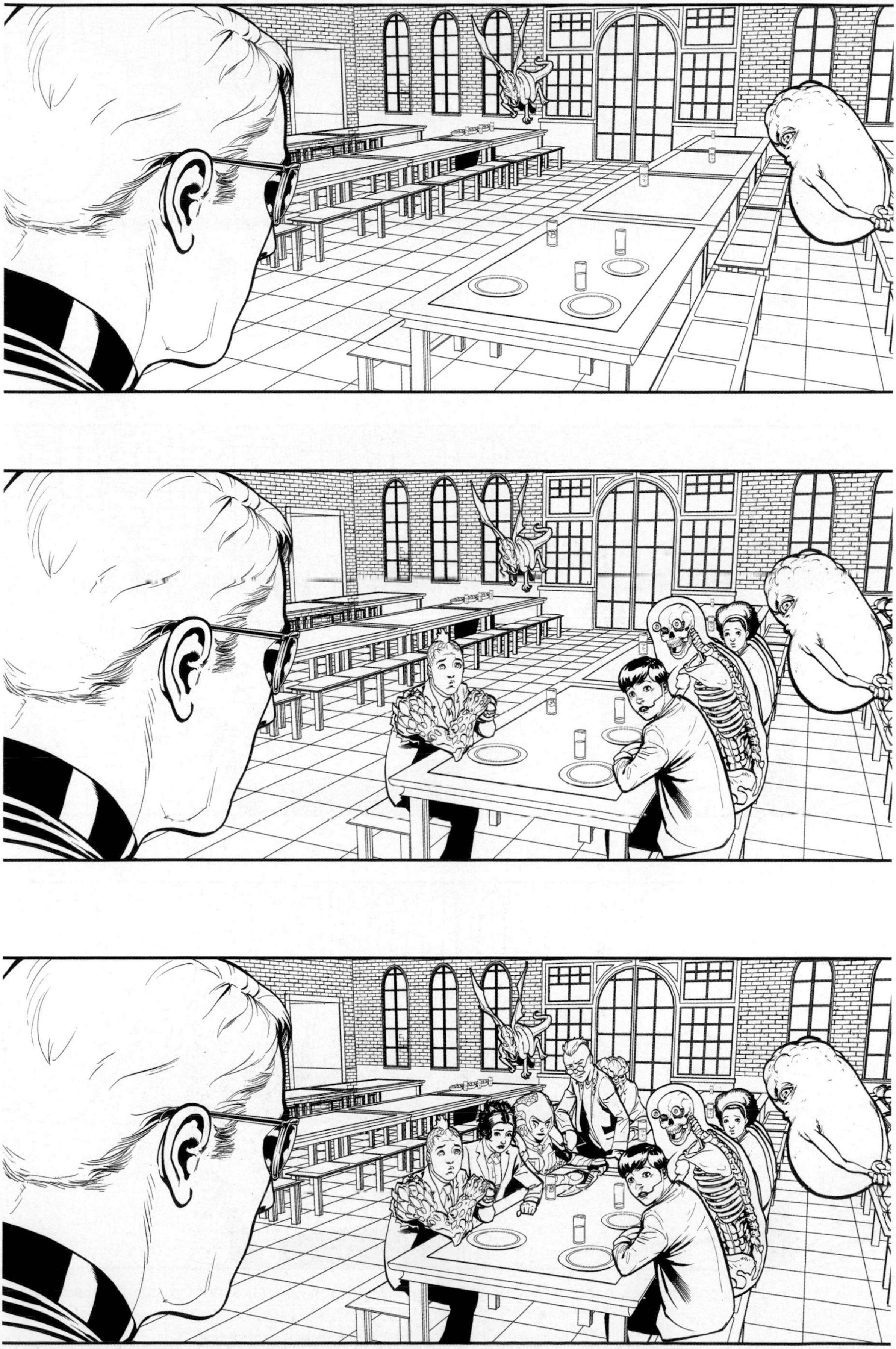

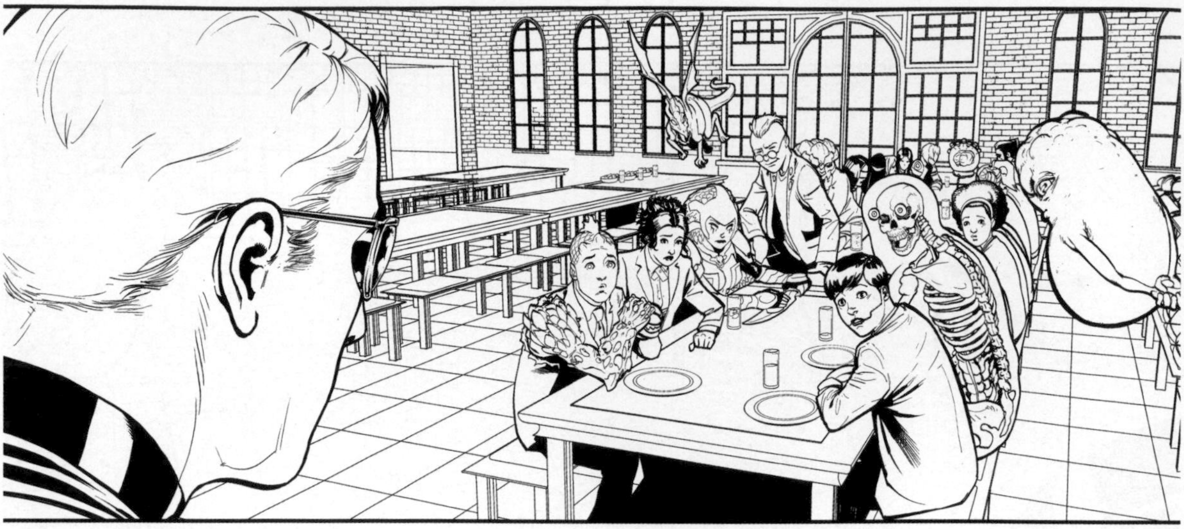

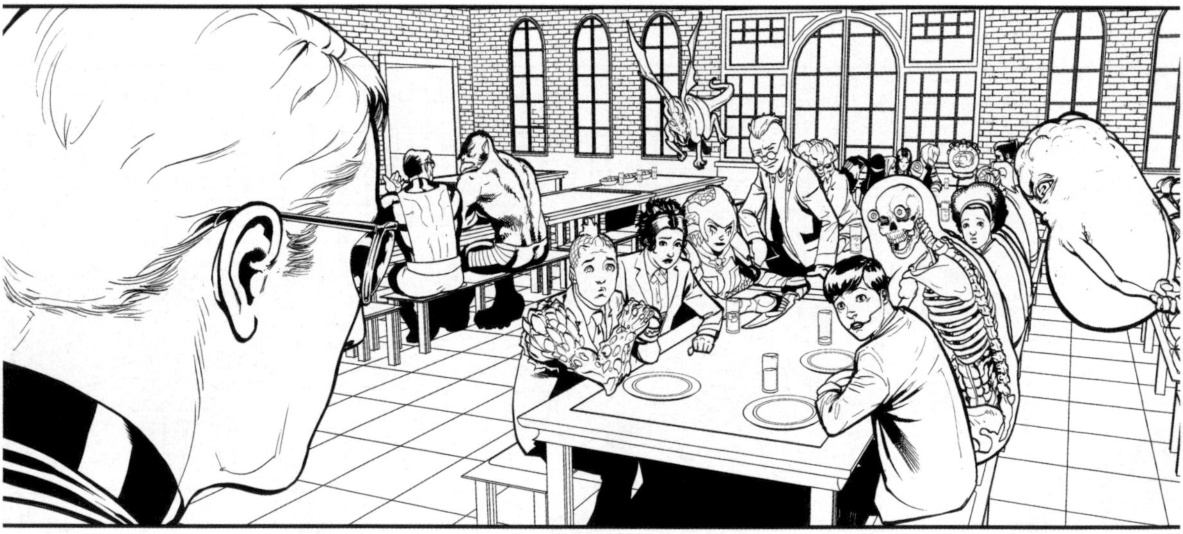

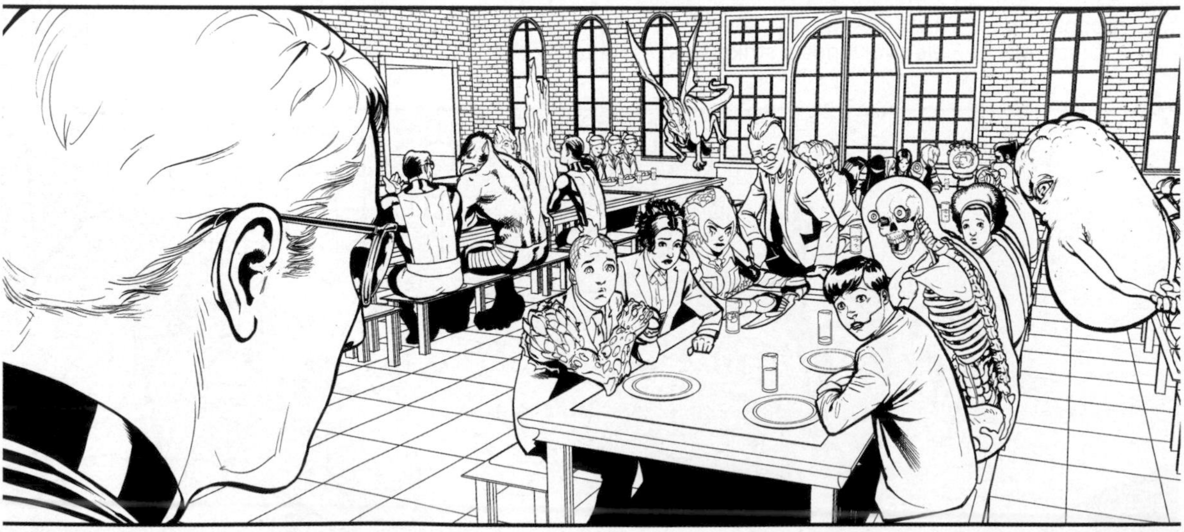

HUGE kudos go to editors Nick and Jordan for providing me with an official school roster to make sure I didn't mess it up!

#6, PAGE 3

This was a tricky page since it's important to keep the gore level low in a Marvel comic, while still portraying the ferocity and viciousness Wolverine is capable of. In the first version of this panel, I drew Jean after being slashed so I wouldn't have to explicitly show the wound she received, but editors Nick and Jordan, as well as Brian, all made the excellent point that we really should be able to see her face and reaction to sell the moment.

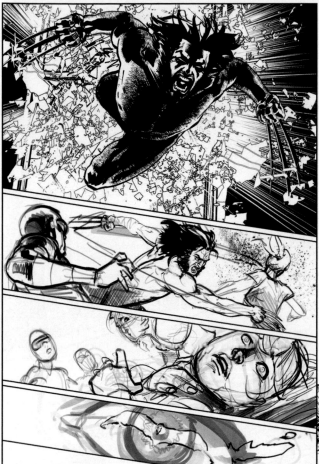

In version two — which ended up being the final version — we got to see her face, with her hair and shoulder hiding the worst of the damage, while showing the claws popping out behind her head give the sense of just how terrible Wolverine's strike was.

FINAL INKS

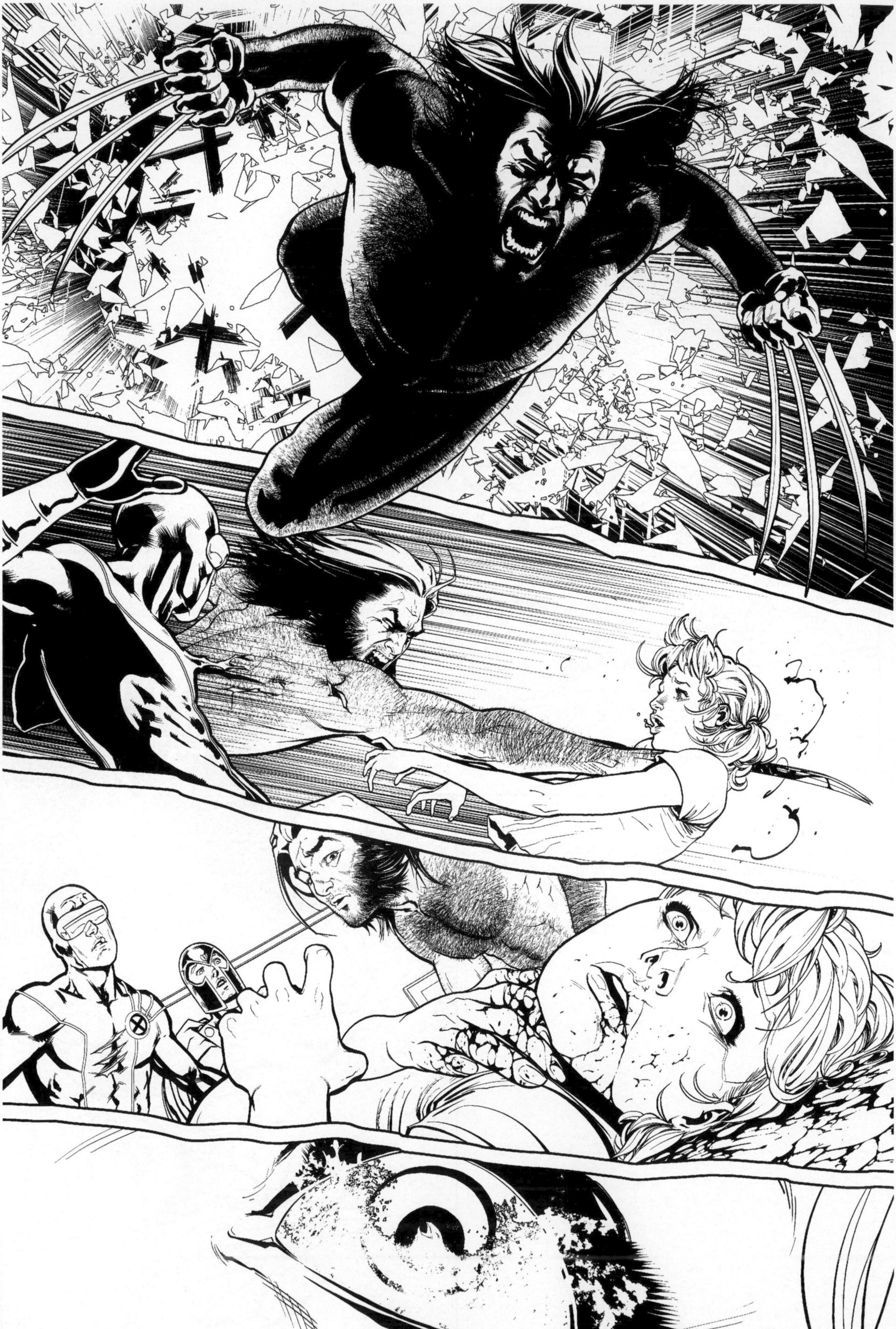

#8, PAGE 4

My original layout for this panel was meant to evoke WW2-era propaganda posters, with Madam Hydra against a backdrop of Hydra exoskeletons flying in formation. The rest of the team was afraid that the extreme low angle would obscure her face too much, so in the revised sketch I inched the "camera" up just enough so we could still see her, while also giving us the sense of power that low-angle shots offer.

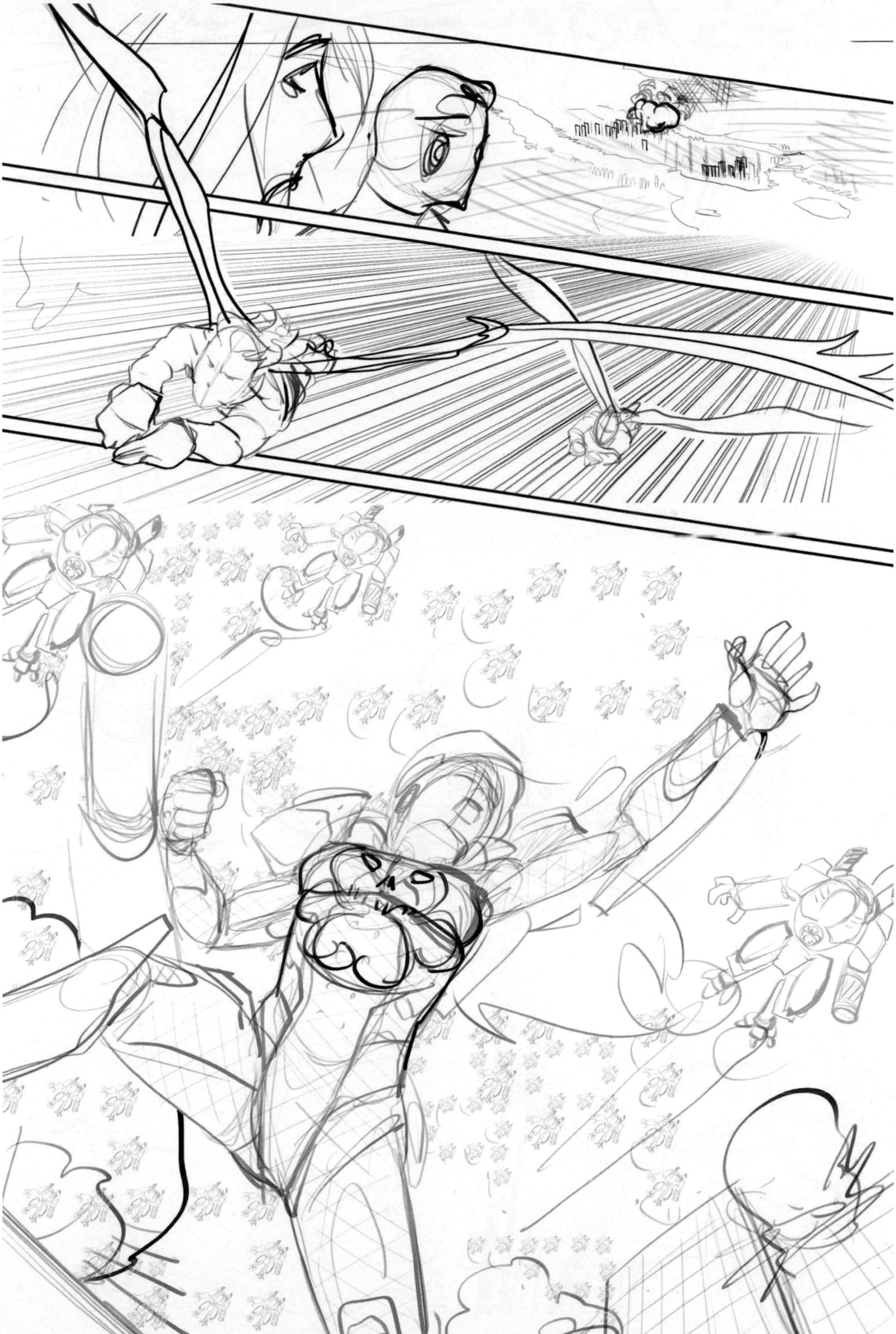

An unexpected consequence of changing the angle, though, was that we wouldn't be looking quite so directly up into the sky, and so I dropped in the building behind her to give a sense of scale and verticality.

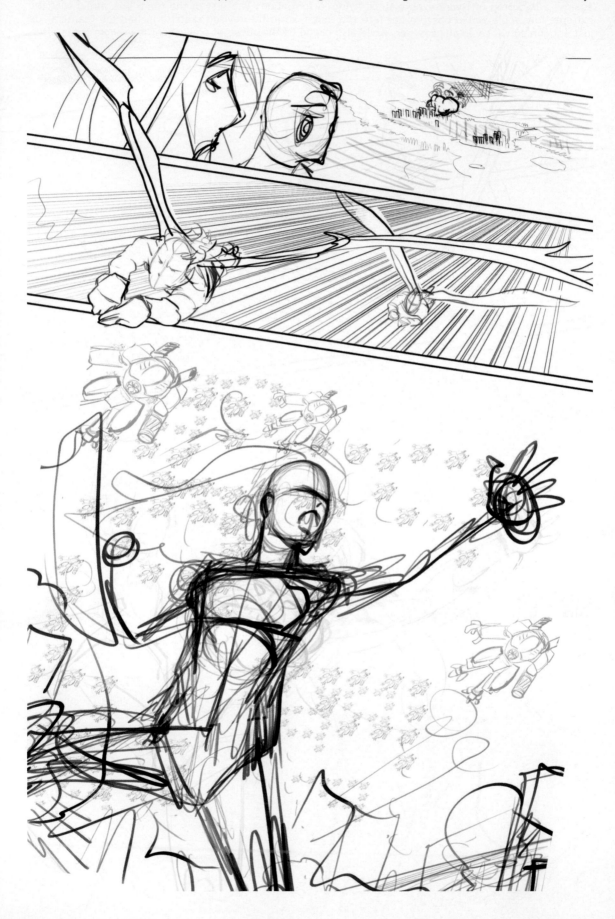

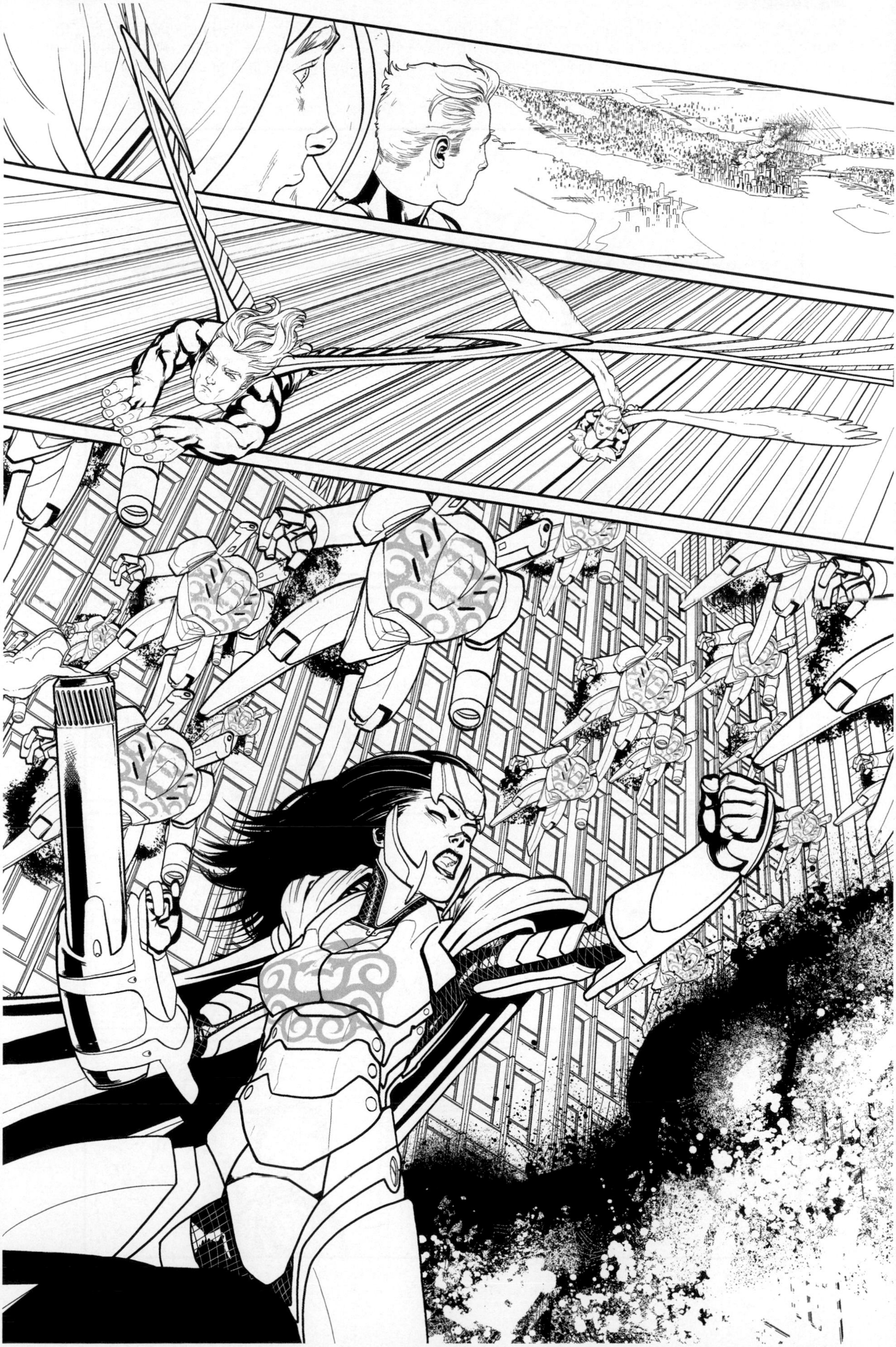

This was an incredibly fun page to draw. Brian has a such a gift for writing hilarious dialogue, and the relationship between Kitty and Bobby is so fun to play with. This was a case, though, where my initial layout, while visually functional, really didn't take into account leaving enough space for all the dialogue.

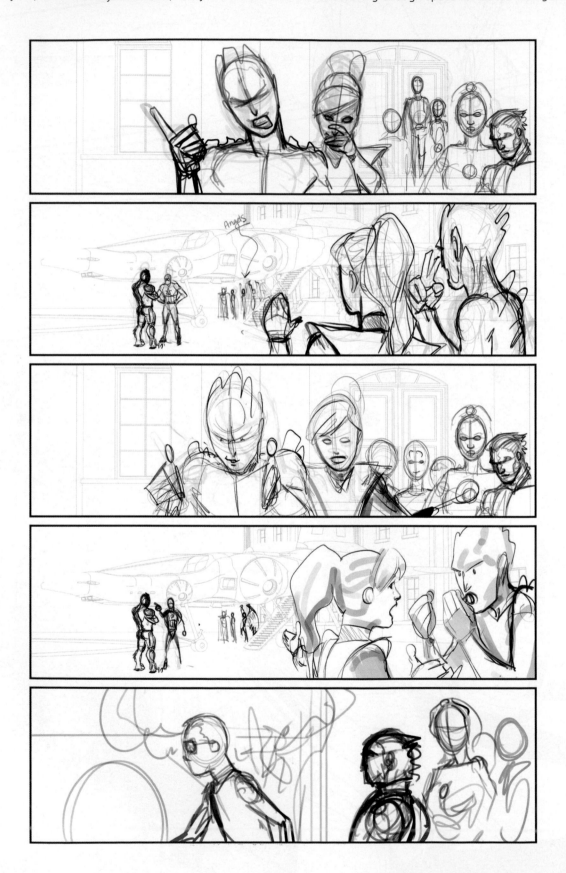

The collaborative nature of comics — between writer and artist, and also between words and pictures — can be seen right on the page. Tall panels can, among many other things, give dialogue room to breathe.

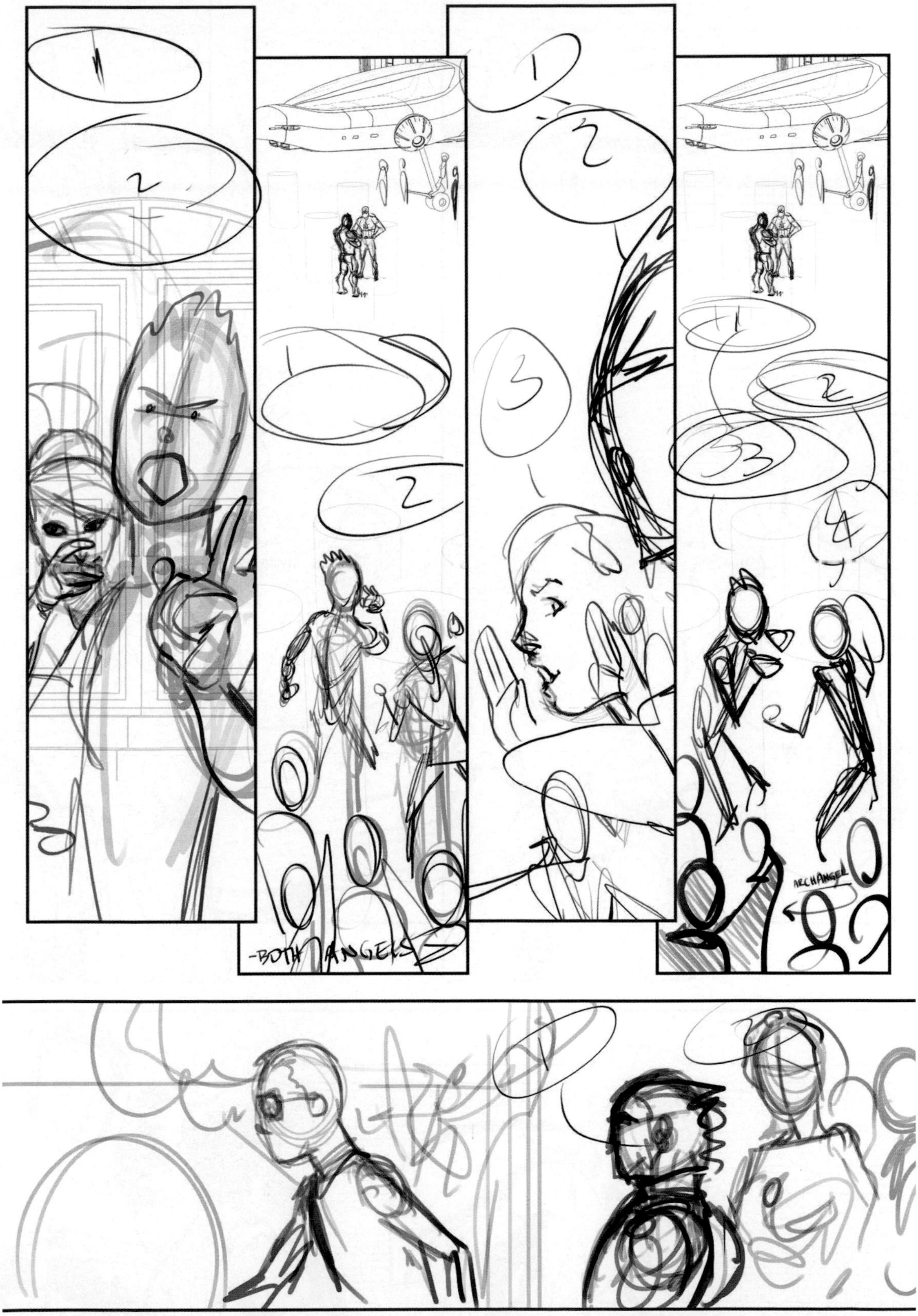

-BOTH ANGELS
ARCHANGEL

FINAL INKS

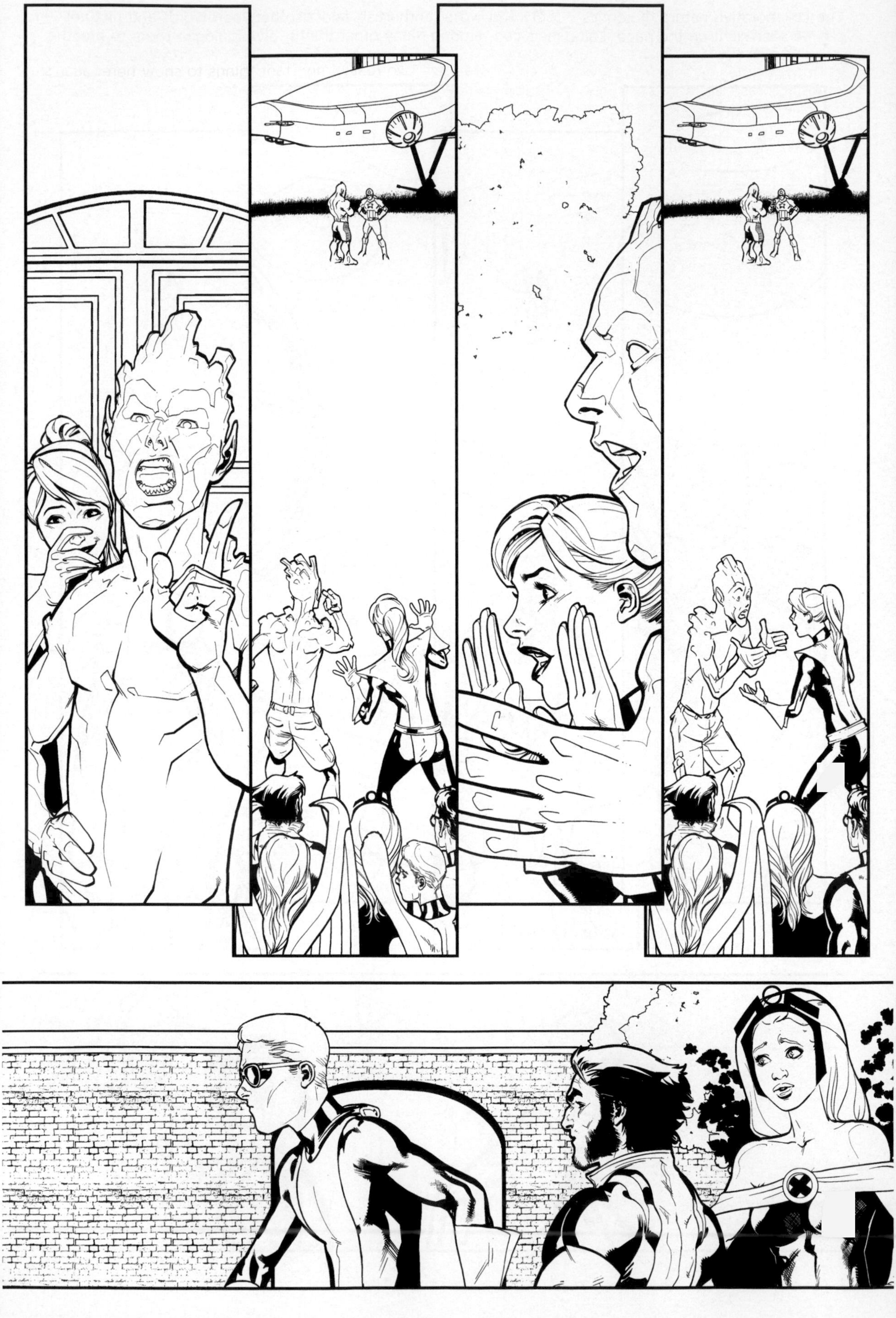

The last page of the issue — and the last page of my three-issue run on *All-New X-Men* — and such a huge moment for Jean. We really needed to get this page right. There was a lot of back-and-forth discussion between Nick, Jordan, Brian and myself about how to sell the moment that Jean takes charge, and possibly begins down a very dark path. There were two really important things to show here: Jean's imposing presence, and the stunned — and horrified — reaction of her teammates.

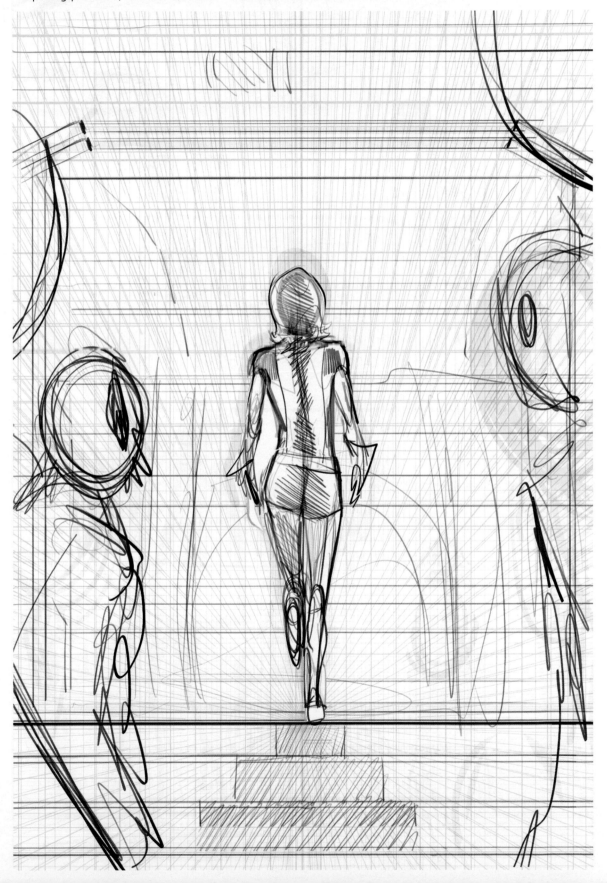

As you can see from all the sketches, most of initial drawings were really focused on Jean, without showing much of the other X-Men.

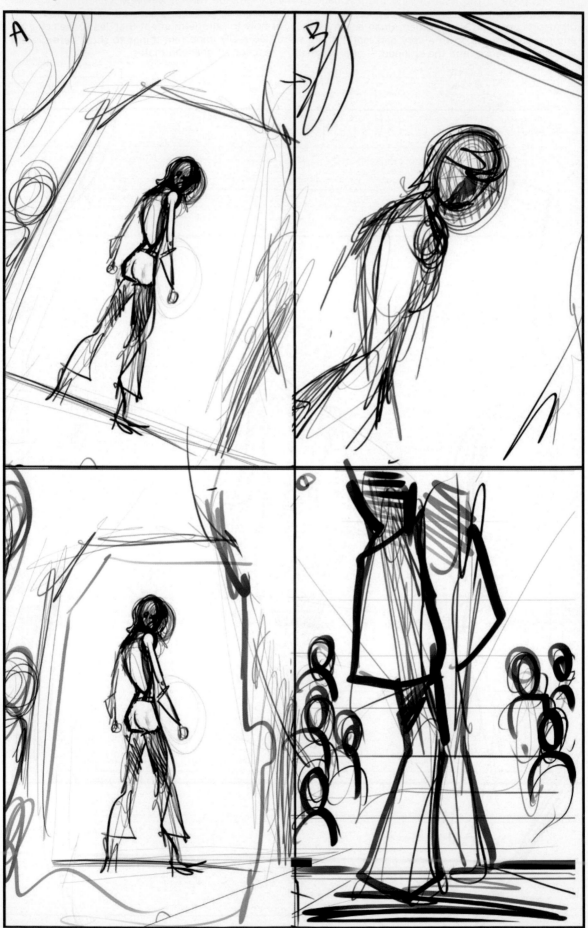

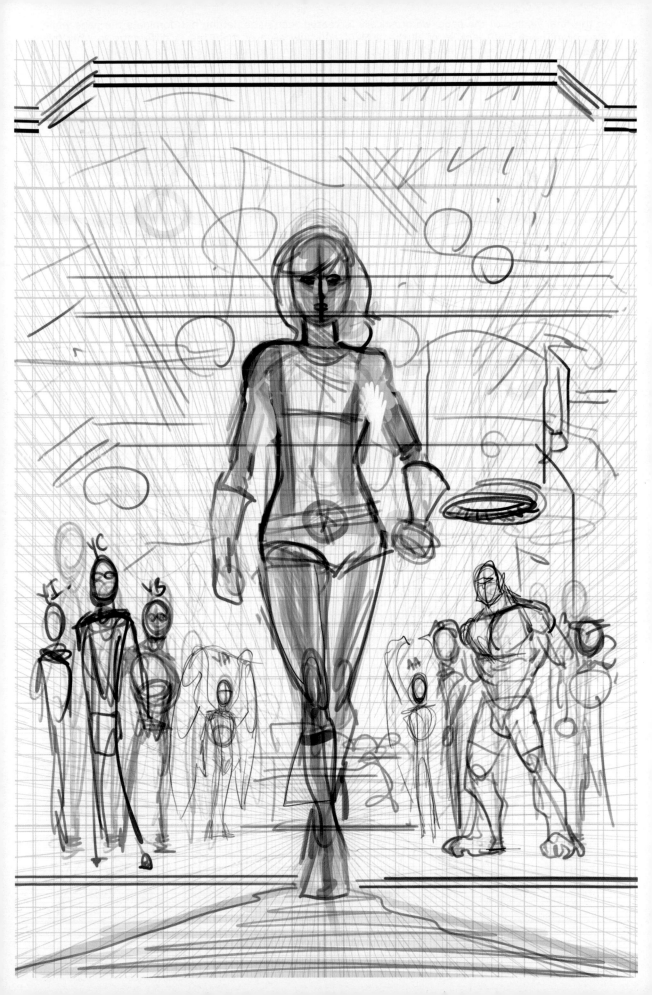

In the final version of the page, we drastically increased Jean's size, letting her dominate the page while also giving us a clear look at of all the X-Men, and how each of them reacts differently to what this person they love so much has said and done, and what it might mean for all of their futures.

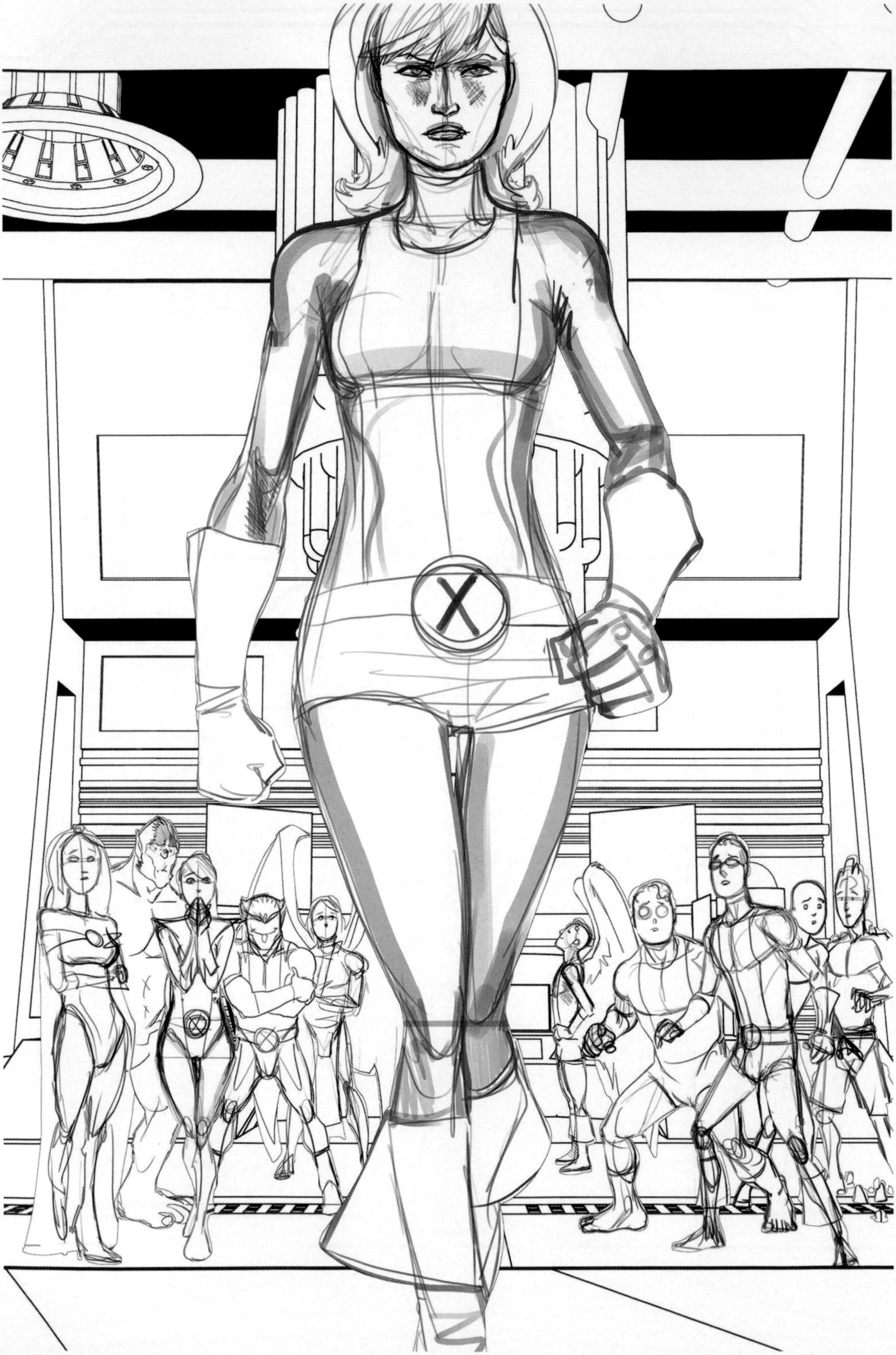

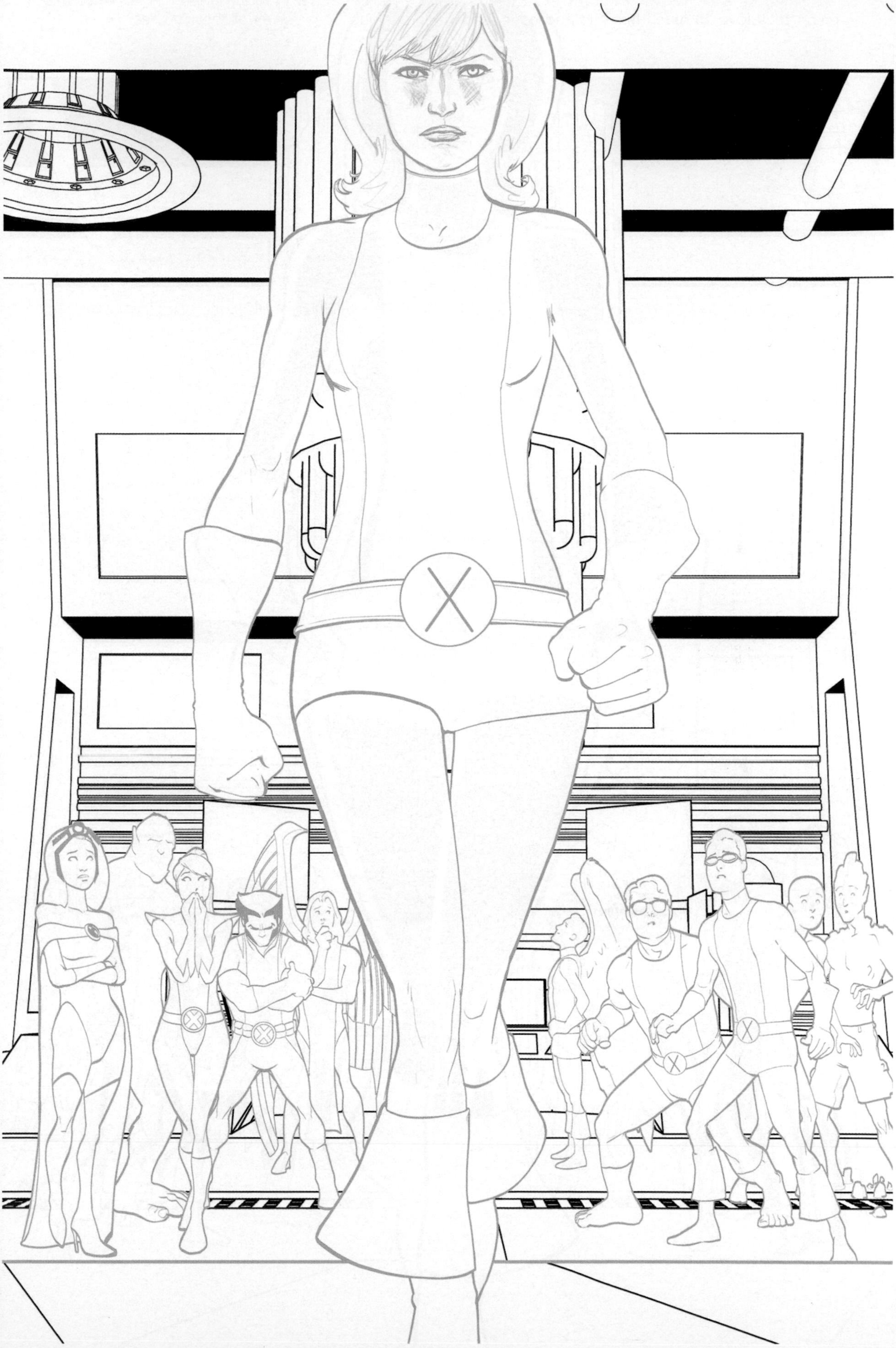

FINAL INKS

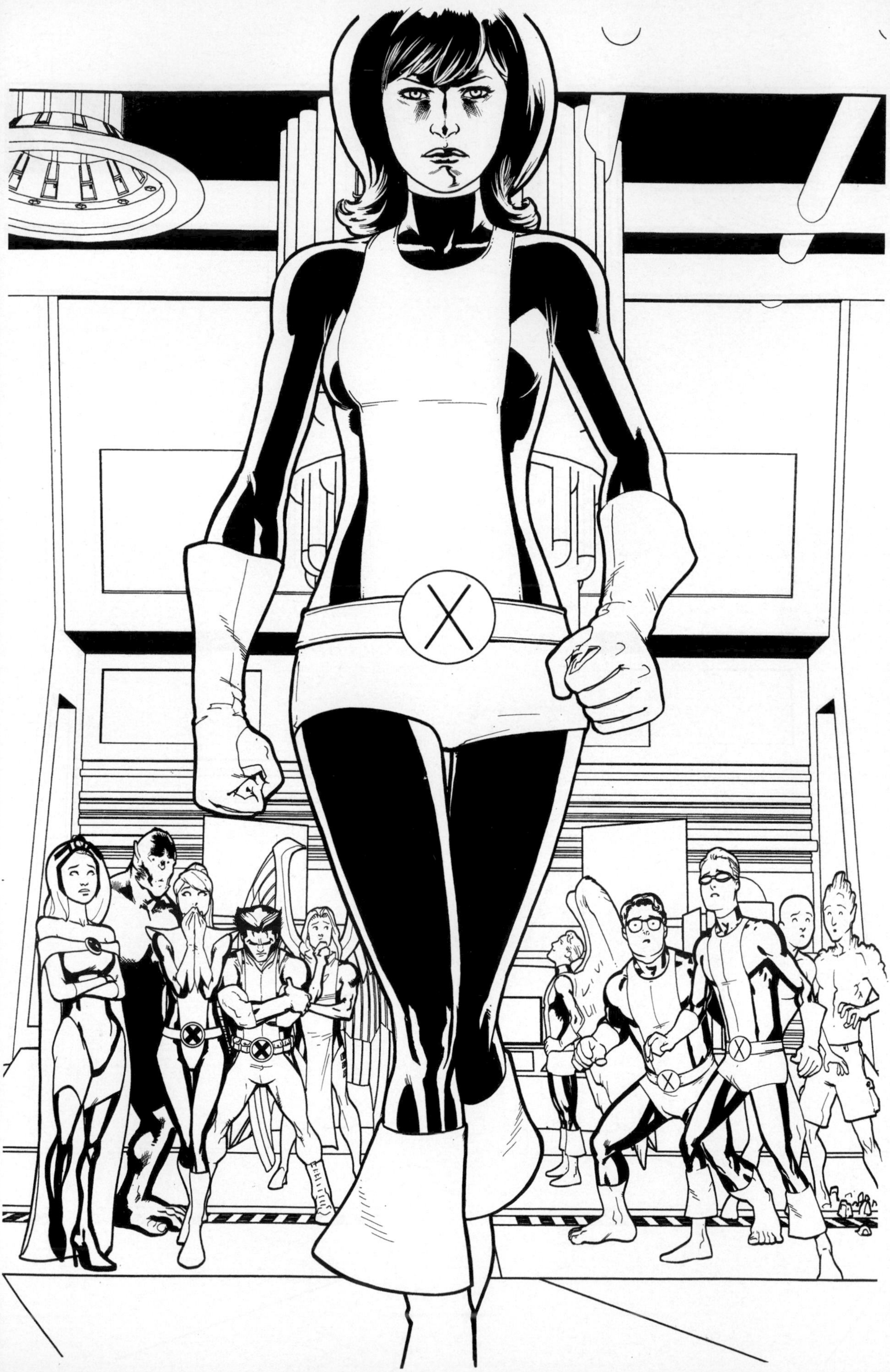